A Chronology of World Christianity

A Chronology of
World Christianity

John Bowden

with Margaret Lydamore and Hugh Bowden

continuum

Continuum
The Tower Building, 11 York Road, London, SE1 7NX
80 Maiden Lane, Suite 704, New York, NY 10038 USA

www.continuumbooks.com

First published 2007

British Library Cataloguing-in-Publication Data
A catalogue record for this book is available from the British Library.

ISBN-13 978 0 8264 9633 1 (hardback)
ISBN-10 0 8264 9633 4 (hardback)

Designed by Benn Linfield
Typeset by Fakenham Photosetting
Printed and bound in Great Britain by Cromwell Press, Trowbridge, Wiltshire

Contents

List of icons

Architecture

Art (painting and sculpture)

Film and television

Important person

Literature

Music

Play

References backwards and forwards in time

Religious leader

Saint

Secular ruler

List of boxes

List of illustrations

List of maps

Appendices

Introduction

In essence, a chronology is a diary. So this *Chronology of World Christianity* may be seen as a diary, a listing of events in Christianity all over the world, year by year, month by month and sometimes even day by day, from the time of Jesus to the present. Its format is simple: under each year are listed relevant events, first those which can be given a precise date, and then those whose dating is less specific. Some chronologies set out events in columns, grouping together those in particular categories, but this is not really a good solution. Because there are so many possible categories, and not all of them are featured in every century, the result is a great deal of blank space. Instead, we have used a system of icons, listed on p.vi, to denote the main categories. Boxes, listed on p.vii, have been inserted into the text to describe some important movements and developments which cannot be assigned a particular date and which extend over a number of years. Each century is prefaced by a brief introduction, which does not attempt the impossible task of summing up the century but draws attention to a selection of interesting developments which characterize it. Maps highlight at particular points the progress of Christianity across the world and a series of appendices describes features extending over centuries, particularly in the arts. A glossary explains terms which some readers may find unfamiliar, and finally the index makes it possible to discover the dates of individuals, events, works of art and so on from their names.

But what is Christianity? There are many answers to this question, and the task of listing key moments in its development, as we aim to do, requires that we try to identify what kind of things can be considered to comprise it. We look at Christianity mainly from three perspectives.

First, it is the activity of those who call themselves Christians. That is to say that Christianity is the religious practices of Christian communities and also the organization of those communities, the creation of places of worship, regional administration in the form of parishes, dioceses, provinces, etc. Here we aim to register the emergence and disappearance of the different branches of Christianity, the spread of Christianity around the world, the splits and, less frequently, the reconciliations between different groups, the appointment of its leaders, the building of its churches and cathedrals, and the relationship of Christians with the rest of the world's population. Here it should be remembered that a chronology cannot deal with the practice of prayer, worship and pastoral care which goes on day by day, week by week, month by month and year by year.

Secondly, Christianity is the set of ideas and beliefs that Christians hold. We note the writing of key texts from the letters of Paul and the Gospels to papal encyclicals, and the lives of major Christian thinkers, from the church fathers to modern theologians.

xi

Thirdly, we look at those areas of culture where Christianity has left an indelible mark. There are many works of art and literature which are not liturgical, but which were produced under the influence of Christianity, or where the content is seen as symbolizing important aspects of Christianity. While not necessarily explicitly created as 'Christian art', these works have to be seen as part of the story of Christianity. Christianity does not exist in isolation from the rest of the world.

We also list events that have shaped the development of Christianity without being themselves Christian, particularly the rise and fall of dynasties and the formation of political structures, and writers and thinkers whose works, often themselves not religious in intent, either offer critiques of Christianity, or have had profound influences on it. From its beginnings, Christianity has also had men and women who have been venerated as saints. These are indicated in the *Chronology*, and after canonization became a formal procedure, the dates of their canonization are also given; this is often an indication of the values associated with sainthood at the time.

The strength of a chronology over a history is that it can set side by side events taking place in different parts of the world without going into extreme detail; the compactness of the presentation makes it possible to view a wide horizon. The mere variety of developments, from wars and political changes in well-established societies to exploration of new regions and the spread of missions, from the building of cathedrals and the establishment of universities to the rise of unusual forms of Christian belief and practice, so immediately juxtaposed, can put familiar information in fascinating new contexts. The chronology of the sixteenth century is a particularly good example of this. Though known as the century of the Reformation, with the immense changes which that brought to the fabric of Europe, it is also the century of the development of the Caribbean and South America and of the exploration of the Far East and the consequent expansion of Christianity. So alongside the Protestant controversies we can see the steady spread of the Roman Catholic Church in establishing and institutionalizing Christianity through the intrepid work of missionaries from the religious orders, particularly the Dominicans and the Franciscans. The further Christianity spreads, the more striking the breadth of scenery becomes.

A work of this sort has to be selective. Inevitably there will be imbalances in what is covered, although the question of how the balance could be improved may be answered differently by every reader. To take two examples, a high proportion of the entries deal with Europe and Europeans, and men are mentioned more often than women. This is in part the result of decisions made by the authors, either consciously, when they take a view on what readers will want to know about, or unconsciously, when they exclude things as a result of ignorance or forgetfulness. In part it reflects the nature of historical evidence: recorded history has tended to focus on the actions of men more than women, and on Europe, and in recent times North America, more than the rest of the world. But it is also a consequence of the nature of Christianity. For most of their history, the

Christian churches have tended to subordinate the role of women, justifying this in a variety of ways, and from the age of Emperor Constantine until relatively recently it has been Europeans who have dominated the direction and development of Christianity.

Of course, chronologies have their limitations. Diaries they may be, but the span covered by the more ambitious of them, such as this one, is so vast that many events are inevitably far removed in time and space, and the very essence of a chronology, the identification of a specific date, is often elusive. A chronology does some things better than others. Not all changes have an identifiable starting point, and in many cases even where they do, we do not have the key information, because no one at the time or later thought it worth recording or preserving. Some dates are fairly well recorded, such as the accessions of monarchs, of Popes, of Patriarchs of Constantinople and Archbishops of Canterbury, and these provide a chronological backbone to this book and a framework against which to set other events. But others are vague and disputed, and cannot be regarded as certain. As time goes on, it becomes comparatively easy to determine on what day a famous figure died, but to discover when he or she was born is far more difficult, first because for many centuries Christians were not particularly interested in birthdays, and secondly, because a famous person (and inevitably it is usually famous persons who are listed here) is more likely to be noted than a baby whose potential has yet to be realized. In a number of cases dates given here are preceded by *c.* (Latin *circa*), to indicate that they are approximations. In other cases, where alternative dates are on offer we have gone for the one which seems to have most support (but that does not necessarily mean that it is the right one).

Dates, then, may be approximate, but we think that approximate dates are better than no dates at all. At least they make it possible to get a sense of what happened before what and who came before whom.

Proper names regularly pose a problem. Should a King of Spain be Charles or Carlos, Ferdinand or Fernando? Should we have Joan of Arc or Jeanne d'Arc? Not least to avoid Englishing the world excessively we have opted mostly to give individuals the names they bear in their own setting, but some names are too well-established or too complicated to change (e.g. the Popes and the Patriarchs of Constantinople), so we have accepted the inevitability of inconsistency.

A certain amount of prior knowledge must inevitably be presupposed – it is impossible to start completely from scratch. However, wherever possible some words of explanation have been added to indicate who a person is or what is the significance of a particular event. At the same time, by means of cross-references we have tried to link events together so that they form 'stories', so that it is possible to trace, say, the progress of the Teutonic knights in the Baltic countries in the thirteenth and fourteenth centuries or the history of Christianity in Ethiopia from the fourteenth to the seventeenth century.

One last point: we have followed the modern practice of dating events BCE and CE

xiii

(Before the Common Era and Common Era) where such an indication is needed. But there are also references to BC and AD in the text, since this Christian system of dating is the basis for the modern practice, and has a history of its own. Over the centuries different calendars were of course used in Christianity, not least the Julian calendar which preceded the present so-called Gregorian calendar. We have indicated some important calendar changes but have kept the modern system throughout.

Chronology

First century

Reliable dates are hard to come by in the first century. The Gospel of Luke seems to provide firm dates for the birth of Jesus (2.1–2) and the beginning of the activity of John the Baptist (3.1–2), but scholars have not succeeded in tying its lists of chronological points of reference to particular years.

The Christian system of dating events *anno Domini* (AD) = 'in the year of the Lord' has Jesus born in the year 1, but it has long been recognized that this cannot be the case. Dionysius Exiguus, the sixth-century monk who invented the system in connection with an attempt to determine the correct date for Easter, clearly got his calculations wrong, since the Gospel of Matthew (2.1) states that Jesus was born in the days of Herod the Great, who by our modern reckoning died in 4 BCE. We just cannot ascertain the year of Jesus' birth.

There are, though, two firm dates that so to speak provide pegs on which to hang a first-century chronology.

First, an inscription found in Delphi mentions Gallio, proconsul of Achaea, who is referred to in Acts 18.12–17 in connection with an attempt to incriminate Paul before the Roman authorities. Reference to the regnal year of Emperor Claudius on the inscription makes it possible to date it within a year, to 51 or 52. Moving from this to dating Paul's journeys and letters is by no means easy and there are varying conjectures, but it is a starting point.

Secondly, there is the capture and destruction of Jerusalem by the Romans in 70 CE after a Jewish revolt that broke out in 66 CE. Remarkably enough there is virtually no reference to this cataclysmic event in the New Testament, except perhaps in the apocalyptic passages of Mark 13, Matthew 24 and Luke 21, though in some ways it was as devastating for Christians as it was for Jews.

The first Christian century was very nearly the first century of the Roman empire, and from the beginning of the century, when Judaea was made a Roman province, to the end, when there seems to have been an organized campaign against Christians under Domitian, Rome is dominant in the Christian story, with Nero blaming Christians for the great fire of Rome in 64 as a central event.

The century sees the birth, activity and death of Jesus and John the Baptist, both of whom have a significant following of disciples, and the spread of a movement after the crucifixion of Jesus among those who believe him to have been raised from the dead. For much of the century these Christians are to all outward appearances very little different from Jews, even worshipping in the Jerusalem temple when it still exists. However, from the start there is tension within the Christian movement in Jerusalem between the Christians who speak Hebrew and the Christians who speak Greek, find themselves persecuted, and soon have a base of their own in Antioch. Paul's extensive missionary activities among non-Jews raise the acute question how far it is necessary for Christians to observe all the precepts of the Jewish law, not least those relating to food; despite attempts to come to some compromise the issue proves intractable and towards the end of the century Jews are ejecting from the synagogues Christians who worship with them.

During this century most of the books of the New Testament are written, along with a few which do not find their way into the New Testament, such as the Didache (Teaching), which among other things gives instructions on how to carry on mission, to baptize and celebrate the eucharist. However, precisely when they are to be dated is no more than conjecture.

This is a century during which the church has a variety of forms of organization and there are as yet no Christian buildings. Much is still in a state of flux.

Before the first century

*c.*6 BCE

The probable date of the birth of Jesus of Nazareth (▶ after 20). The Christian system of dating is not worked out until 525, by the monk Dionysius Exiguus. However, it is generally reckoned that he is several years out in his starting point.

*c.*4 BCE

♛ March/April: Herod the Great, King of Judaea, dies. A Roman client king, who enjoys the favour of Emperor Augustus, he is known for his cruelty towards his family and for his many building projects, notably the great fortress of Masada by the Dead Sea (▶ 74 CE) and the Jerusalem temple, which he restores in splendour (▶ 70 CE).

First century

6

Judaea is made a Roman province after Archelaus, son and successor of Herod (◀ *c.*4 BCE), is banished for making a scandalous marriage.

14

♛ August 19: Augustus, the first Roman emperor, dies, and is succeeded by his adopted son Tiberius (▶ 19, 37).

18

Caiaphas (▶ 37) is appointed high priest, a post he will occupy at the time of the trial of Jesus (▶ *c.*30).

19

Tiberius (◀ 14, ▶ 37) expels Jews from Rome, allegedly for trouble-making and proselytism.

after 20

Jesus (◀ *c.*6 BCE, ▶ *c.*30) becomes a disciple of John the Baptist, a Jewish prophetic teacher and ascetic, in the Judaean wilderness near the Dead Sea.

✠ John is killed by Herod Antipas on the prompting of his daughter Salome; he is subsequently venerated as a saint: feast day June 24.

26

Pontius Pilate (▶ 36) is appointed Roman prefect of Judaea.

*c.*30

Jesus (◀ after 20) is put on trial and crucified in Jerusalem by the Romans, probably on a political charge.

*c.*35

✠ Stephen, one of a group of seven Greek-speaking Jews who have gained prominence in the Jerusalem church, and who are known as the 'Hellenists', is stoned to death by a mob.

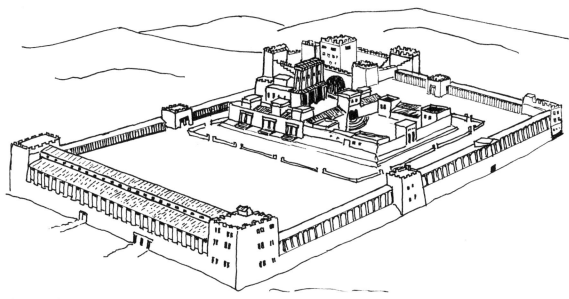

The Jerusalem temple as rebuilt by Herod the Great: a reconstruction, 4 BCE

As a result of his death the Hellenists flee Jerusalem and make their base in Antioch. Stephen is subsequently venerated as a saint: feast day December 26.

36

Pontius Pilate (◀ 26) is recalled to Rome, accused of maladministration, by Vitellius, the governor of Syria, who is the father of the future emperor Vitellius (▶ 69).

*c.***36**

☦ Paul of Tarsus (▶ c.45–58), a zealous Pharisee, is converted to Christianity and establishes links with the Christian community in Antioch. After his death (▶ 64) he is venerated as a saint and his conversion is celebrated as a feast day on January 25 (▶ 1908).

37

♛ March 16: Tiberius (◀ 14) dies and is succeeded as emperor by Gaius Caligula (▶ 41), whose anti-Jewish policy provokes unrest in Judaea.

Caiaphas (◀ 18) is deposed from the high priesthood.

🌱📖 Flavius Josephus is born; through his *Jewish War*, *Jewish Antiquities* and autobiography, this Jewish historian gives a unique picture of Jewish history. Dies 100.

40

Caligula (◀ 37) orders that his statue is to be set up in the temple of Jerusalem but is dissuaded by Herod Agrippa (▶ 41).

The Roman empire (31 BCE–284 CE)

More than any other system of government in history, the Roman empire is focused on the person of the emperor. The imperial regime is created in a series of settlements between Augustus, the first emperor, and the Senate of the city of Rome in the decades after his victory in civil war in 31 BCE. The settlements give Augustus and his successors responsibility for the military administration of the territories Rome has conquered. These include all of continental Europe west of the Rhine and south of the Danube, Asia as far west as the Euphrates, Egypt, and the coast of North Africa as far as the straits of Gibraltar. The emperors are responsible not only for maintaining this territory, but also wherever possible for extending it. In the two centuries following Augustus Roman territory is increased to include Britain as far as the Antonine Wall in southern Scotland (▶ 142), Dacia (roughly modern Romania, ▶ 101–6) and briefly parts of Mesopotamia and northern Arabia (▶ 114–17). The frontiers of the empire are never considered permanent, and they are very porous, and Roman cultural influence spreads into the territories beyond direct imperial control, so that when later 'barbarians' cross in the other direction, they are already to some extent 'romanized'.

As well as military control, emperors are given the authority to make laws, and to direct the administration of Rome and its provinces as they see fit. From the second century onwards imperial judgements, answers to requests and instructions to officials are taken as authoritative in Roman law, and it is from these documents that we learn most about official Roman responses to Christianity.

The emperor is the central figure in the religious life of the Roman empire. Augustus and his successors are members of all the major priestly colleges in Rome, and hold the position of Pontifex Maximus, chief priest (although the duties associated with the post may have been ignored when the emperors became Christian, it is only in the reign of Gratian (▶ 382) that the title is passed from emperor to pope). As a result, the emperor is involved in all the major rituals considered crucial for the continuing fortune of the empire. At the same time the emperor is himself worshipped as a god throughout most of the empire. In Rome and Italy, where the emperor's position is technically that of first citizen rather than all-powerful ruler, such a cult certainly exists, although less emphasis is placed upon it, and here the Senate has a role in establishing whether emperors have been accepted into the Roman pantheon after their deaths.

For as long as Roman rule prospers, the position of the emperor is secure. Then the half century after 235 sees sustained pressure on the northern and eastern frontiers. Emperors in rapid succession are deposed and killed when they prove unable to deal with the military crisis, until stability returns with the accession of Diocletian in 284, by which time the nature of the empire has significantly changed.

41

♛ January 24: Caligula (◀ 37) is assassinated, and is succeeded as emperor by Claudius (▶ 43, *c*.49).

♛ Herod Agrippa I (◀ 40, ▶ 44), who enjoys imperial favour, becomes King of Judaea and Samaria.

43

Claudius (◀ 41, ▶ c.49) invades Britain and captures Colchester, where he establishes a colony of veteran soldiers.

44

Herod Agrippa (◀ 41) turns against the Christians, and James the brother of John, one of Jesus' disciples, is killed. Peter (▶ c.49) is arrested but escapes.

☦ James is subsequently venerated as a saint: feast day July 25.

Herod Agrippa dies. Judaea again becomes a Roman province.

c.45–58

Paul (◀ 36) embarks on a series of missionary journeys with intervals between them. In the first he travels from Antioch to Cyprus and Asia Minor. In the second he crosses over to Europe, visiting places in Greece before returning via Ephesus to Caesarea. In the third, he again visits Greece before returning via the coast of Asia Minor to Jerusalem. The precise dates of these journeys are controversial. His missionary work raises the question of what conditions should be imposed on non-Jews who want to become Christians. He writes letters to Asia Minor, Thessalonica, Philippi, Corinth and Rome from which it is evident that some of the churches there antedate him.

c.49

Peter (◀ 44, ▶ 64), Paul (◀ c.45–58) and James the brother of Jesus (▶ 62), who has become head of the Jerusalem church in a way that is not entirely clear, hold an 'apostolic council' to determine what requirements are to be imposed on Paul's non-Jewish converts. Paul's sphere of mission is recognized.

Claudius (◀ 43, ▶ 54) expels the Jews from Rome for constantly making disturbances. Jewish Christians may be among those expelled, and indeed may have caused the disturbances by their preaching; at this time they are not members of a separate movement distinct from Judaism.

50

The Jewish philosopher Philo dies; his allegorical interpretations of scripture influence Clement of Alexandria (▶ c.150) and Origen (▶ c.185).

The Romans found Londinium, present-day London.

51/52

An inscription of this date discovered in Delphi, which mentions Gallio as proconsul of Achaea, gives a firm chronological point of reference for Paul's (◀ 49, ▶ 56) activities (see Acts 18.12–17).

54

♛ October 13: Claudius (◀ c.49) dies and is succeeded as emperor by Nero (▶ 68).

7

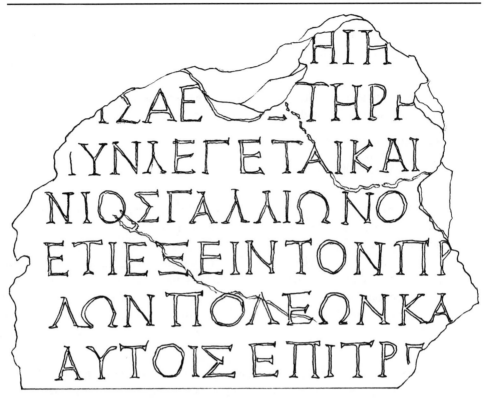

The Gallio inscription at Delphi. The name Gallio appears in the fourth line. This is one of four fragments of a stone which refer to Gallio as proconsul of Achaea; he is mentioned in Acts 18.12, and as the stone is dated it makes it possible to date Paul's visit to Corinth described there to 51/52

c.56

Paul (◀ c.45–48, ▶ c.58) visits Jerusalem to bring an offering from his churches, incurs the hostility of a mob and for his own protection is arrested by the Romans.

c.58

Paul (◀ c.56, ▶ 64) is taken under Roman guard to Rome, where he is placed under house arrest.

62

James the brother of Jesus (◀ c.49) is stoned to death by Jews in Jerusalem during a period of chaos and anarchy.

64

Nero (◀ 54, ▶ 68) blames a great fire in Rome on the Christians and this leads to their persecution.

✠ The tradition is that Peter (◀ c.49, ▶ c.66) was executed at this time (and possibly also Paul, ◀ c.58). He is subsequently venerated as a saint: feast day June 29.

8

66

May: Jewish nationalists rebel against Roman oppression and this leads to a first Jewish War which brings much suffering.

*c.***66**

According to the historian Eusebius (▶ *c.*260), the Christians in Jerusalem flee and settle in Pella, which is across the Jordan and outside Judaea.

✠ According to the earliest lists of Bishops of Rome, Linus (▶ *c.*78) becomes the second Bishop of Rome in succession to Peter (◀ *c.*64), but Linus and most of the early bishops are no more than shadowy figures. Strictly speaking they are not popes (▶ 189), as that office had not yet developed.

67

May 22: Vespasian (▶ 69), a successful general, is appointed commander of the Roman armies in the Jewish War (◀ 66, ▶ 74).

68

♛ June 9: Nero (◀ 54) commits suicide. Galba (▶ 69) is proclaimed emperor.

A settlement in Qumran by the Dead Sea, probably that of members of the Jewish sect of the Essenes, is destroyed. We know of its existence through the Dead Sea Scrolls (▶ 1947).

69

♛ January 2: Vitellius is proclaimed emperor by his troops in Germany.

♛ January 15: Galba (◀ 68) is killed in Rome. Otho is proclaimed emperor by the Praetorian Guard.

♛ April 16: Otho commits suicide.

♛ April 19: Vitellius is proclaimed emperor by soldiers and the Senate of Rome.

♛ July 1–3: Vespasian (◀ 67) is proclaimed emperor by legions in Egypt, Syria and Judaea.

♛ October: Vitellius is killed.

70

September 8: After a siege, Jerusalem is captured and devastated by the Romans under Vespasian's son, Titus (▶ 79), and the temple (◀ *c.*4 BCE) is destroyed.

74

March 31: The Jewish fortress of Masada by the Dead Sea falls, marking the end of the first Jewish War (◀ 67).

*c.***78**

✠ Linus, Bishop of Rome (◀ *c.*66), dies. He is subsequently venerated as a saint: feast day September 23.

9

> **The New Testament**
>
> The New Testament consists of 27 short writings composed in Greek between 50 and 130 CE. They are not originally written as part of a 'New Testament', to succeed the 'Old Testament', the Jewish Bible. The idea of a closed collection of holy scriptures does not develop until around 180 CE, and for a long time after that there is a dispute as to whether some of the writings now in the New Testament (Hebrews, James, 2 Peter, 2 and 3 John, Jude and Revelation) should be included.
>
> There is widespread disagreement among scholars about the dating of the New Testament books. One key issue is whether or not the figures named as their authors actually wrote them, or whether names such as Matthew, James and Peter are in fact pseudonyms. Some of the letters attributed to Paul are certainly authentic, but others (Ephesians, Colossians and later the letters to Timothy and Titus) look as if they were attributed to him by disciples writing in his spirit. Given this disagreement it is impossible to say more than that the indubitably authentic letters were written between c.50 and c.62 and that the rest were written after that.
>
> The New Testament Gospels and the Acts of the Apostles are written between 70 and 100 CE; again, it is hard to determine their precise dates, but Mark is the earliest and the Gospel of John the latest, and they all presuppose the fall of Jerusalem. The letter to the Hebrews is written before 95; 1 Peter and James perhaps a little later and the letters of John some time after the Gospel of John. The letter of Jude is dependent on the letter of James, and 2 Peter, usually reckoned to be the latest book of the New Testament, is dependent on Jude. The book which concludes the New Testament, Revelation, is probably written around c.95 CE, given that it reflects hostility to Christians at the end of the reign of Emperor Domitian.

79

♛ June 24: Vespasian (◀ 69) dies, and is succeeded by his son Titus (◀ 70, ▶ 81) as emperor.

*c.***79**

♁ Anacletus is elected Bishop of Rome (▶ 91).

81

♛ September 13: Titus (◀ 79) dies, and is succeeded as emperor by Domitian (▶ 96), who constructs the *limes*, the fortified line of defence of the Roman empire between the Rhine and the Danube.

84

The Christians are expelled by the Jews from their synagogues, marking the beginning of a parting of the ways for the two faiths.

91

♁ Anacletus, Bishop of Rome (◀ *c.*79), dies.

♁ Clement is elected Bishop of Rome (▶ *c.*100). To him is attributed the First Letter of Clement to the Corinthians (who are engaged in a fierce internal dispute).

96

♛ September 18: Domitian (◀ 81) is assassinated and is succeeded by Nerva (▶ 98) as emperor.

98

♛ January 27/28: Nerva (◀ 96) dies and is succeeded as emperor by Trajan (▶ 101–6, 117).

100

♟ Flavius Josephus (◀ 37) dies.

*c.*100

☦ Clement, Bishop of Rome (◀ 91), dies. He is subsequently venerated as a saint: feast day November 23 in the West, November 24 in the East.

☦ Evaristus is elected Bishop of Rome (▶ *c.*109).

♟ Justin (▶ *c.*135, *c.*155) is born of pagan parents in Shechem, Samaria. He teaches in Ephesus and in Rome, and is executed for his beliefs (▶ *c.*165).

Christianity reaches Edessa (▶ 177), beyond the eastern frontier of the Roman empire, which becomes the most important diocese in Syria.

The apostolic fathers

A body of writings written around the time of the books of the New Testament is known as the apostolic fathers and the period is known as the apostolic age. Special significance is attached to this period, defined as the time between the death and resurrection of Jesus and the death of 'the last apostle', though its end cannot be precisely dated. Although the Apostles' Creed is not now believed to go back to the apostles, it bears witness to the need to derive authority from the apostles, as does the apostolic succession, the belief that bishops today have been ordained in a constant chain of laying on of hands from the apostolic age. The concern to maintain an authoritative list of Bishops of Rome (or Popes) from Peter to the present day is also evidence of this. The works of the apostolic fathers comprise two letters attributed to Clement, Bishop of Rome, seven letters of Ignatius, a letter of Polycarp and an account of his martyrdom, a short work entitled Didache (Teaching), a letter attributed to Barnabas, an anonymous letter to Diognetus, and a long work, the Shepherd of Hermas. It is difficult to give them precise dates.

Second century

The second century is often said to be a 'tunnel period': we are in the dark about much that must have happened during it, and both dates and facts are few and far between. Christianity begins the century as a movement which is only just breaking away from the Judaism in which it originated, and ends it as a quite distinctive religion, with an organized ministry which is to last to the present day. Bishops are in charge of particular areas, known as dioceses, with priests and deacons under them. At the same time what is clearly a mainstream church has dissociated itself from currents that are felt not to be properly Christian. There is marked hostility to these; since with few exceptions, such as the Nag Hammadi Library, works emanating from them have not survived, we know of them only through the attacks of their opponents. Notable among these attacks is a work written by Bishop Irenaeus of Lyons at the end of the century, *Against the Heresies*.

Chief among these deviant groups are the Gnostics, who teach that human beings are imprisoned in matter, which is evil, and have to be redeemed by the knowledge (Greek *gnosis*) that there is a divine spark within them that can be liberated. In the middle of the century Marcion of Pontus, who holds related views and believes that the God of the Old Testament is different from the God of the New, forces Christians to think about what books should be in their Bible by rejecting many that are traditionally accepted.

A second group is made up of the followers of Montanus, a prophet in Asia Minor, who with two women, Priscilla and Maximilla, claims to be inspired by the Holy Spirit, and preaches that the Holy Spirit will soon be poured out on the whole church. Fervent and ascetic, 'Montanism' contrasts with the growing institutionalization of the church. By the end of the century it has been condemned.

There are sporadic attacks on Christians all through the century, but these are local rather than backed by Rome, whose officials prove judicious. Martyrdoms at Lyons and Scilli in North Africa bring a new genre of literature, the martyrology (*Martyrs' Lives*), with a contrast between heroic Christians and gruesome tortures.

Christianity continues to spread and notably becomes established in Edessa in Syria: by the end of the century there are Christians from Spain in the West to (probably) India in the East. The range of regions and traditions in the church begins to raise questions about its unity: one symbol of that is a difficulty in agreeing on a date for celebrating Easter.

After the second Jewish rebellion and destruction of Jerusalem in 135 and sweeping measures against Jews that have their impact on Jewish Christians, Christianity is primarily a Greek-speaking religion. However, with Tertullian, a convert from Carthage, it also finds a Latin voice and, with Pope Victor in the last decade of the century, a Latin-speaking pope.

101–6

Trajan (◀ 98, ▶ 112) extends the Roman empire eastwards, creating a new province of Dacia north of the Danube (▶ 270).

*c.***107**

⊕ Ignatius, Bishop of Antioch, is executed in Rome. En route he stops in Smyrna and is visited by members of neighbouring Christian churches: he is welcomed there by Polycarp (▶ *c.*166) and writes letters to the churches in Ephesus, Magnesia and Tralles. He then goes on to Troas, from where he writes letters to the churches in Philadelphia and Smyrna, and to Polycarp. He is subsequently venerated as a saint: feast day December 20.

*c.***109**

☿ Evaristus, Bishop of Rome (◀ *c.*100), dies.

☿ Alexander I is elected Bishop of Rome (▶ *c.*116).

112

Pliny the Younger enquires by letter of Trajan (◀ 101–6, ▶ 117) how he should treat Christians; he is told not to seek them out actively. In his description of Christians, Pliny describes how they sing hymns 'to Christ as a god'.

114–17

With advances eastwards that lead to the occupation of Parthia, Armenia and Mesopotamia, the Roman empire reaches its greatest extent.

*c.***116**

☿ Alexander I, Bishop of Rome (◀ *c.*109), dies.

117

♛ August 8/9: Trajan (◀ 98) dies, and is succeeded as emperor by Hadrian (▶ 122–28), who consolidates the empire.

*c.***117**

☿ Sixtus I is elected Bishop of Rome (▶ *c.*127).

122–28

Hadrian builds a frontier wall across northern Britain.

*c.***125**

Hadrian writes to Caius Minucius Fundanus, proconsul of Asia, instructing him how to treat Christians. He takes the same line as Trajan with Pliny the Younger (◀ 112): only proper accusations (and not denunciations) are to be acted on.

The earliest extant papyrus fragment of a New Testament book (the Gospel of John, composed *c.*70–100), found in the sands of Egypt, is dated to this time.

*c.***127**

☿ Sixtus I, Bishop of Rome (◀ *c.*117), dies.

☿ Telesphorus (▶ *c.*137) is elected Bishop of Rome.

13

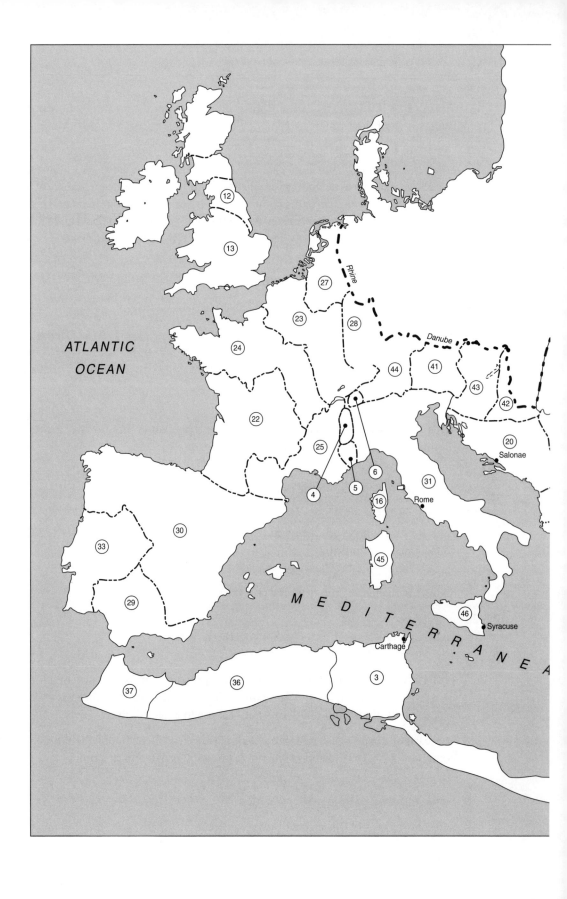

ATLANTIC

OCEAN

MEDITERRANEAN

Rhine

Danube

Salonae

Rome

Carthage

Syracuse

(12)
(13)
(27)
(23)
(28)
(24)
(44)
(41)
(43)
(42)
(20)
(22)
(25)
(4)
(5)
(6)
(16)
(31)
(45)
(46)
(30)
(33)
(29)
(37)
(36)
(3)

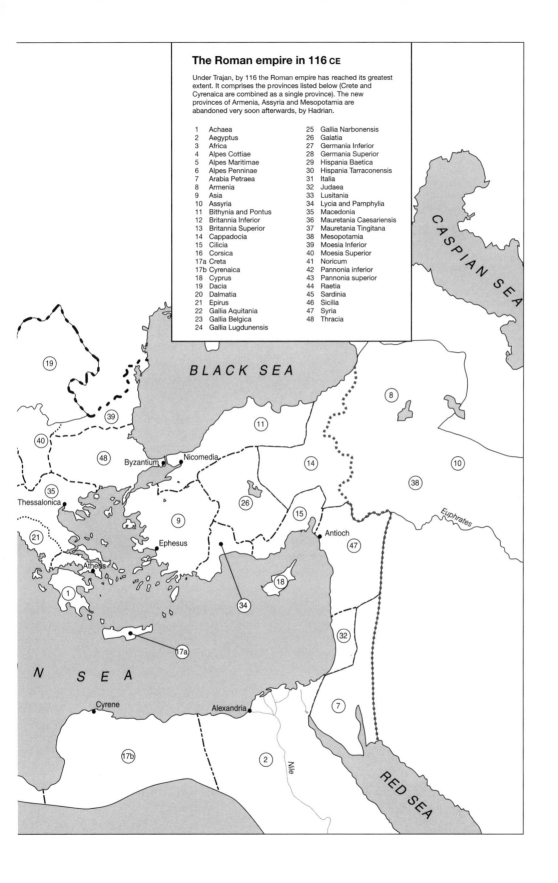

The Roman empire in 116 CE

Under Trajan, by 116 the Roman empire has reached its greatest extent. It comprises the provinces listed below (Crete and Cyrenaica are combined as a single province). The new provinces of Armenia, Assyria and Mesopotamia are abandoned very soon afterwards, by Hadrian.

1	Achaea	25	Gallia Narbonensis
2	Aegyptus	26	Galatia
3	Africa	27	Germania Inferior
4	Alpes Cottiae	28	Germania Superior
5	Alpes Maritimae	29	Hispania Baetica
6	Alpes Penninae	30	Hispania Tarraconensis
7	Arabia Petraea	31	Italia
8	Armenia	32	Judaea
9	Asia	33	Lusitania
10	Assyria	34	Lycia and Pamphylia
11	Bithynia and Pontus	35	Macedonia
12	Britannia Inferior	36	Mauretania Caesariensis
13	Britannia Superior	37	Mauretania Tingitana
14	Cappadocia	38	Mesopotamia
15	Cilicia	39	Moesia Inferior
16	Corsica	40	Moesia Superior
17a	Creta	41	Noricum
17b	Cyrenaica	42	Pannonia inferior
18	Cyprus	43	Pannonia superior
19	Dacia	44	Raetia
20	Dalmatia	45	Sardinia
21	Epirus	46	Sicilia
22	Gallia Aquitania	47	Syria
23	Gallia Belgica	48	Thracia
24	Gallia Lugdunensis		

CASPIAN SEA

BLACK SEA

Byzantium
Nicomedia

Thessalonica

Ephesus

Athens

Antioch

Euphrates

Cyrene

Alexandria

Nile

N SEA

RED SEA

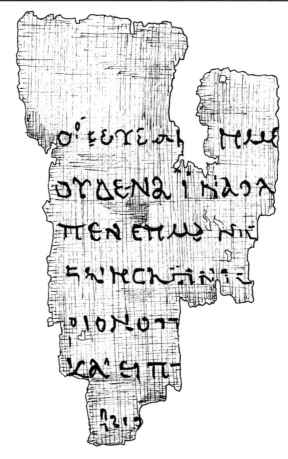

Rylands papyrus fragment P52. It contains lines from John 18.31–33 on the front and John 18.37–38 on the back. It was found in Egypt and is usually dated *c.*125

*c.***130**

Irenaeus is born. He becomes Bishop of Lyons and is the first important theologian of the mainstream church (▶ *c.*180). Dies *c.*200.

Bishop Papias of Hierapolis writes five books of *Interpretation of Sayings of the Lord* (now lost).

132

Simon bar-Kokhba and Rabbi Eleazar spark off a second rebellion by the Jews against the Romans, thus ushering in the Second Jewish War (▶ 135).

135

The Second Jewish War (◀ 132) ends with the destruction of Jerusalem and the defeat of the Jews. Jerusalem is rebuilt as Aelia Capitolina and Judaea is renamed Palaestina. Jewish customs are banned.

Gnosticism

Gnosticism is a term used to describe systems of religion, often within Christianity but sometimes outside it, in which knowledge (Greek *gnosis*) is a key feature in human redemption. The world is seen as evil, created by another god than the supreme God, and human beings are imprisoned in it. But there is a divine spark within them and knowledge of this can liberate them. Key Gnostic teachers during the second century, when Gnosticism begins, are Basilides and Carpocrates in Alexandria, Marcion and Valentinus in Rome and Cerinthus in Asia Minor. Their precise dates are not known, nor have their writings been preserved. There are also groups with names such as Sethites ('people of Seth', the son of Adam) and Ophites ('snake people'). Gnosticism proves to be a major rival to the mainstream church and is opposed by Irenaeus of Lyons (◀ *c.*130), Clement of Alexandria (▶ *c.*150), Origen (▶ *c.*185), Hippolytus of Rome (▶ *c.*170) and Epiphanius of Salamis (▶ *c.*315), who quote Gnostic works, albeit in a hostile context. In 1945 a library of Gnostic texts from the third and fourth centuries is found at Nag Hammadi in Upper Egypt.

*c.*135

📖 Justin (◀ *c.*100, ▶ *c.*155) writes his *Dialogue with the Jew Trypho*, claiming the whole of the Old Testament for Christians.

*c.*137

⚕ Telesphorus, Bishop of Rome (◀ *c.*127), is killed.

⚕ Hyginus is elected Bishop of Rome (▶ *c.*140).

138

👑 July 10: Hadrian (◀ 117) dies and is succeeded as emperor by Antoninus Pius (▶ 142, 161).

*c.*140

⚕ Hyginus, Bishop of Rome (◀ *c.*137), dies.

⚕ Pius I is elected Bishop of Rome (▶ *c.*154).

142

Antoninus Pius builds a wall across Scotland extending the frontier around 100 miles north of Hadrian's wall (◀ 122–28). However, his wall does not prove so durable and is later abandoned.

144

🌑 Marcion of Pontus is excommunicated (▶ 160). A wealthy shipowner, he has formed a separate Christian community; he rejects the Old Testament, whose God he contrasts with the God of Jesus. His radical selection of New Testament books indicates that the church must be more specific about what books it believes to be part of the Bible.

*c.*145

📖 Aristides of Athens writes the earliest surviving *apologia* for (defence of) Christianity, much influenced by Judaism.

c.150

♠☐ Clement of Alexandria (◀ 50, *c.*190) is born. Concerned to relate Christianity to the classical world, he writes three important books: *Stromateis* (Carpets*), Protreptikon* (Exhortation) and *Paidagogos* (The Tutor). He is the earliest Christian writer to discuss what forms of church music are appropriate. Dies *c.*215.

☐ The anonymous *Letter to Diognetus* uses Hellenistic Jewish ideas in its defence of Christianity. It contains a famous passage describing Christians as the soul in the body of the world.

Tatian from Assyria comes to Rome to be a pupil of Justin (◀ *c.*100). He produces a harmony of the four Gospels (Diatessaron).

154

♠ Bardaisan (▶ *c.*179) is born. He holds unorthodox views including a denial of the resurrection. Dies 222.

c.154

⊕ Pius I, Bishop of Rome (◀ 140), dies.

⊕ Anicetus is elected Bishop of Rome (▶ *c.*166).

c.155

☐ In his *First Apology*, Justin (◀ 135, ▶ *c.*165) gives us a full description of the celebration of the eucharist in Rome. He tells us that the president at the eucharist does not use a fixed form of words but prays 'to the best of his ability'.

160

♠ Marcion of Pontus (◀ 144) dies.

c.160

♠ Tertullian is born. He is the first theologian to write in Latin (▶ *c.*200). Dies 220.

161

♛ March 7: Antoninus Pius (◀ 142) dies and is succeeded as emperor by Marcus Aurelius (▶ 180). Despite the persecutions during his reign, which are local in origin, Marcus Aurelius maintains the tolerant position towards Christianity held by Trajan (◀ 112) and Hadrian (◀ 124).

c.165

⊕ Justin (◀ *c.*100) is executed. He is subsequently venerated as a saint: feast day June 1.

c.166

⊕ February 23: Polycarp, Bishop of Smyrna (◀ *c.*107), is executed there; he is a leading Christian in Asia Minor and a fierce opponent of Gnosticism. One of his letters, addressed to the Christians in Philippi, survives, as does a contemporary account of his death. He is subsequently venerated as a saint: feast day February 23.

⊕ Anicetus, Bishop of Rome (◀ *c.*154), dies.

18

✠ Soter is elected Bishop of Rome (▶ c.175); in his time Easter is introduced as an annual festival.

167

Pressure by Germanic groups on the Danube frontier of the Roman empire begins.

c.170

♰ Hippolytus of Rome (▶ c.215) is born. Little is known of him as he becomes an antipope and falls into discredit. Dies 236.

In Phrygia, in reaction to Gnosticism (◀ 132), a prophetic movement led by Montanus (who gives it his name, Montanism) finds a following.

> **Montanism**
>
> Montanism is named after Montanus, a Christian prophet who lives in Phrygia in the second half of the second century CE. Montanus travels round Asia Minor with two women, Prisca and Maximilla, and gains a wide following. 'The Three', as they are called, expect a speedy outpouring of the Holy Spirit on the church; Montanus claims to have received visions and to be the Paraclete mentioned in the Fourth Gospel. Their lifestyle is ascetic and they believe that Christians who fall from grace cannot be redeemed. The theologian Tertullian (▶ c.207) becomes a Montanist, and a letter written by Jerome (▶ c.345) in 385 shows that Montanists are still troubling his correspondent, Marcella, in Rome. Though its influence fades, the movement persists down to the eighth century.

c.175

✠ Soter, Bishop of Rome (◀ c.166), dies.

✠ Eleutherius is elected Bishop of Rome (▶ 189).

Hegesippus is the first Christian to collect historical material about the church; it is used by Eusebius of Caesarea (▶ c.260) in his *Church History*.

177

☩ The Christian community in Lyons is persecuted. We know of this through a contemporary account of the death of a slave girl Blandina, along with that of the local bishop, Pothinus. They are subsequently venerated as saints: feast day June 2.

August 1: In Lyons, Christians are killed in the festival games.

Abgar VIII (▶ c.179) becomes King of Edessa (◀ c.100, ▶ 226) in eastern Syria. He is very favourable towards Christianity.

c.177

📖 Athenagoras of Athens addresses a *Supplication* to Marcus Aurelius (◀ 161) rebutting popular charges made against Christians, especially that they are atheists.

c.179

Bardaisan (◀ c.154, ▶ 227), poet and philosopher at the court of Abgar VIII of Edessa (◀ 177), is converted to Christianity. He becomes an important but unconventional theologian.

19

180

♛ March 17: Marcus Aurelius (◀ 161) dies, and is succeeded by his son Commodus (▶ 192).

✪ July 17: Christians at Scilli, near Carthage, are the earliest to be put to death in North Africa. They defy orders from the proconsul of Africa to forswear Christianity. They are subsequently venerated as saints: feast day July 17.

*c.***180**

📖 Irenaeus (◀ *c.*130, ▶ *c.*190) writes his five books *Against the Heresies*, a classic statement of orthodox Christian doctrine.

*c.***185**

❀ Origen (◀ 50, ▶ *c.*190) is born. A great theologian and a pioneer biblical scholar, who writes many commentaries and homilies, his teachings are later condemned. Dies *c.*254.

189

☯ Eleutherius, Bishop of Rome (◀ *c.*175), dies.

☯ Victor I is elected Bishop of Rome (▶ 198). He is an African and the first Latin-speaking Bishop of Rome, with whom the office begins to gain prominence over other bishops. [From this point onwards, for convenience, Bishops of Rome are referred to as Pope (◀ *c.*66).]

190

Pope Victor I attempts to settle the dispute over the date of Easter: should it be celebrated on 14 Nisan (the date of the Jewish Passover), whatever the day of the week (thus the so-called Quartodecimans), or on the following Sunday (the view which prevails)?

*c.***190**

Pantaenus dies. He is named as the first head of a catechetical school in Alexandria, succeeded by Clement of Alexandria (◀ *c.*150, ▶ *c.*215) and Origen (◀ *c.*185, ▶ *c.*230), and according to tradition he is invited to India to have discussions with Hindu philosophers.

📖 Irenaeus writes his *Proof of the Apostolic Preaching* (*Epideixis*), a short compendium of Christian doctrine.

📖 Melito of Sardis dies. His *Homily on the Passion* (*c.*167) is markedly antisemitic.

192

♛ December 31: Commodus (◀ 180) is killed.

193

♛ January 1: Pertinax is proclaimed emperor by the Praetorian Guard.

♛ March 28: Pertinax is killed and Didius Julianius declared emperor.

♛ June 1: Septimius Severus (▶ 211) is declared emperor by the Senate of Rome and Didius Julianus is executed.

A depiction of the Good Shepherd, discovered in the catacombs of Rome, *c.*200

198

✠ Pope Victor I (◀ 189) dies.

✠ Pope Zephyrinus (▶ 217) is elected.

By now Christian communities extend from Spain in the West to Afghanistan and possibly India in the East.

***c.*200**

✪ Irenaeus (◀ *c.*130) dies. He is subsequently venerated as a saint: feast day August 23 in the East, June 28 in the West.

A Greek epitaph to Abercius Marcellus, Bishop of Hierapolis in Phrygia, mentions travels as far as Rome and indicates that the eucharist is celebrated everywhere.

📖 Tertullian (◀ *c.*160, ▶ *c.*207), *On Baptism*, gives a full description of baptism as practised in North Africa.

▮ Art begins in the catacombs of Rome, vast networks of burial chambers, which have been excavated during the latter part of the century. One of the earliest catacombs is that of Callistus (▶ 222), with its papal crypt, constructed at the beginning of the third century.

21

Third century

To understand the development of Christianity in the third century, we need to understand what is happening to the world in which it exists. The century, and especially the 50 years from 235, sees major transformations to both the Roman empire and its neighbours. The stability that has characterized most of the previous hundred years comes to an end, as Roman emperors find themselves confronting repeated attacks across the frontiers. There are increasing incursions across the Rhine and Danube by Germanic and Gothic tribes, and in the east the Parthians are overthrown by the Sassanian Persians, who are much more active in campaigning along and across the Euphrates. The inability of emperors to deal with these threats leads to their frequent assassination and replacement by successors who in turn find the task too great for them, until under Diocletian some calm is restored. The 'Later Roman empire' that emerges from these trials is different in important ways from the empire of the first two centuries. The empire is now organized to support the army, and the emperor and his court, wherever they are based, have replaced the Roman Senate as the seat of all authority. Rome itself ceases to be a significant administrative centre.

Christians become increasingly caught up in these events. In the first half of the century there are occasional attacks on Christians on a local level, as there have been earlier. But from the middle of the century emperors, most particularly Decius and Valerian, begin to demand religious action from all their subjects, and Christians, when they refuse to sacrifice to the gods, become targets for punishment. The fact that Christianity is increasingly identified as a major challenge to emperors is evidence of its continuing growth throughout the empire. So too is the rise in the number of local councils of bishops called to discuss matters of doctrine and policy.

The aftermaths of periods of persecution cause their own problems. There are differing attitudes to the treatment of those who have lapsed, and especially to those who have paid money to officials to avoid the punishment for not sacrificing. Disputes lead at times to splits within the church, foreshadowing the more significant divisions in the following century. In general, however, heresy is not yet a major concern. Because there is as yet no powerful central Christian authority, bishops have a high degree of autonomy, and there is no one to determine where the line between orthodoxy and heresy should be drawn. However, the century sees the birth of a number of individuals who will, in the following century, fight bitterly over that line.

c.201

♣📖 Plotinus, a Neoplatonist philosopher, is born. His *Enneads* are posthumously published by Porphyry (▶ *c.*232) and influence Christian thought from Augustine (▶ 354) and Dionysius the Areopagite (▶ *c.*500) to the Middle Ages.

🏛 A church building in Edessa (◀ 177) is the first to be mentioned in a public notice.

203

☉📖 Perpetua, a noble lady, and her companions are executed in Carthage. The account of her death, the *Passion of St Perpetua*, is considered to have been written in part by Perpetua herself. It is popular in antiquity and is valued by scholars as one of the earliest works by a Christian woman. Perpetua and her companions are subsequently venerated as saints: feast day March 27.

c.207

Tertullian (◀ *c.*200, ▶ *c.*220) breaks with the majority church and becomes a Montanist (see p.19).

211

♛ February 4: Septimius Severus (◀ 193) dies. His son Caracalla (▶ 217) becomes emperor.

c.213

♣ Gregory Thaumaturgus, Greek theologian and convert of Origen (◀ *c.*185), is born. He is claimed to have had marvellous answers to prayers. Dies 270.

c.215

♣ Clement of Alexandria (◀ *c.*150) dies.

📖 Hippolytus' (◀ *c.*170, ▶ 217) *Apostolic Tradition* gives a full account of Christian prayers and worship at this time. It allows considerable freedom in the choice of words in the liturgy (▶ *c.*339).

216

♣ Mani, the founder of Manichaeism, a religion that sharply contrasts good and evil, light and darkness, is born in Persia. Dies 276.

217

♛ April 8: Caracalla (◀ 211) is killed.

♛ April 11: Macrinus (▶ 218) is declared emperor by his troops.

☉ Pope Zephyrinus (◀ 198) dies. He is subsequently venerated as a saint: feast day August 26.

☿ Pope Callistus I (▶ 222) is elected.

☿ Hippolytus (◀ 215, ▶ 236) sets himself up as antipope.

218

♛ May 15: Elagabalus (▶ 222) is declared emperor. Macrinus (◀ 217) is driven into exile and killed later in the year.

220

♟ Tertullian (◀ c.160) dies.

222

♛ March 11: Elagabalus (◀ 218) is killed. His cousin Severus Alexander (▶ 235) is proclaimed emperor.

☗ Pope Callistus I (◀ 217) dies. He is subsequently venerated as a saint: feast day October 14.

☀ Pope Urban I (▶ 230) is elected.

☀ Bardaisan (◀ 154) dies.

226

♛ Ardashir I (▶ 240) defeats the last Parthian king, Artabanus I, and founds the Sassanian dynasty in Persia. He has himself crowned 'king of kings' and creates a new Persian empire on the eastern frontier of the Roman empire.

The organizational centre of the Persian church moves to Seleucia-Ctesiphon (▶ c.270), the Persian capital, and its theological centre from Edessa (◀ 177) to Nisibis.

230

☗ Pope Urban I (◀ 222) dies. He is subsequently venerated as a saint: feast day August 9.

☀ Pope Pontian (▶ 235) is elected.

c.230

▭ Origen (◀ c.190, ▶ 231) writes *De Principiis* (On First Principles), four books covering the main topics of Christian theology. It survives only in Latin (▶ c.345).

231

Origen begins a polyglot version of the Old Testament, the Hexapla, in six columns containing the Hebrew text, a transliteration and four different Greek translations.

c.232

Porphyry, a Neoplatonist philosopher, is born. He is sceptical about religions, especially Christianity, but his clarifications of the works of Plotinus (◀ c.201), whose *Enneads* he publishes, are widely read by Christians. Dies c.303.

235

♛ March: Severus Alexander (◀ 222) is killed and Maximinus Thrax (▶ 238) becomes emperor.

⚵ Pope Pontian (◀ 230) abdicates on being sentenced to hard labour in the salt mines of Sardinia.

⚵ November 21: Pope Anterus is elected.

236

⚵ January 3: Pope Anterus dies.

⚵ January 10: Pope Fabian (▶ 250) is elected.

⚵ Antipope Hippolytus (*c*.170) dies in the Sardinian salt mines to which he has been condemned.

238

♕ June 24: Maximinus Thrax (◀ 235) is killed.

♕ July 29: Gordian III (▶ 244) is proclaimed emperor.

240

♕ The Persian king Ardashir I (◀ 226) dies and is succeeded by Shapur I (▶ 272).

*c.***240**

🏛◼ The earliest known baptistery in a house church in Dura Europos (▶ 256), Syria, dates from this time. It contains Christian wall-paintings of Christ and the lost sheep and the three Maries going to the tomb.

244

♕ Gordian III (◀ 238) dies on campaign against Shapur I (◀ 240, ▶ 252) on the Euphrates and Philip the Arab (▶ 249) becomes Roman emperor. Philip is seen by later Christian writers as more sympathetic to Christianity than his successors.

248

📖 Origen (◀ 231, ▶ 254), *Contra Celsum* (Against Celsus), is a comprehensive defence of Christianity against a sceptical Jew, Celsus.

A major festival is held in Rome to mark the 1000th anniversary of its foundation.

249

♕ Philip the Arab (◀ 244) is killed in battle against his general, Decius (▶ 251), who becomes Roman emperor.

250

January 3: Decius (◀ 249) decrees a universal sacrifice to the gods of the empire. Those who refuse to take part are to be punished. Christians are the principal victims of this policy, although some escape penalties by buying certificates to indicate that they have sacrificed.

✝ January 20: Pope Fabian (◀ 236) is executed. He is subsequently venerated as a saint: feast day January 20.

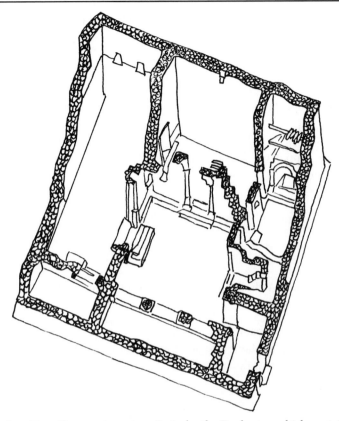

A house church at Dura Europos in eastern Syria, by the Euphrates, which contains a room for assembly and a baptistery, *c.*240

*c.*250

🌲 Arius (▶ *c.*315) is born. He controversially believes that Jesus is not God in the way that God is God, and is subordinate to him. Arius' views are condemned, but he has a wide following long after his death in 336.

🌲📖 Lucius Caecilius Firmianus Lactantius, African Christian apologist, is born. His *The Deaths of the Persecutors* (*c.*318) is an important source for the persecutions of the period. Dies *c.*325.

📖 The poems of Commodian, from Gaza in Palestine, are the earliest Latin poems intended for cultured Christians.

251

⚛ March: Pope Cornelius (▶ 253) is elected.

June: A synod in Carthage urges generous treatment of those who have lapsed as a result of Decius' decree (◀ 250): they should not be denied hope of communion and peace, but must perform long and strict penances. This is the first of several councils there to discuss the issue.

July 1: Decius (◀ 249) is killed in battle against the Goths, who have crossed the Danube. Trebonius Gallus (▶ 253) is proclaimed emperor.

Novatian sets himself up as antipope in a dispute over the treatment of those who lapsed in persecution. He thus initiates a schism that lasts until the fifth century. Those who follow him are known as Novatianists. He is killed in 257/58.

c.251

Antony of Egypt is born. He pioneers solitary monasticism in the desert. Dies 356.

252

Christians in Carthage are threatened by the local magistrate, who requires a general sacrifice to the gods.

The Persian king Shapur I (◀ 244, ▶ 272) launches the first of a series of campaigns against the eastern parts of the Roman empire. In subsequent campaigns Antioch is captured twice (▶ 256, 260) and Armenia is occupied.

253

June: Pope Cornelius (◀ 251) is exiled from Rome and dies soon afterwards. He is subsequently venerated as a saint: feast day September 16.

August: Trebonius Gallus (◀ 251) is killed and Valerian (▶ 260) and his son Gallienus (▶ 268) are proclaimed emperors.

Pope Lucius I is elected, and immediately exiled by Emperor Trebonius Gallus.

Pope Lucius I is recalled from exile.

254

March 5: Pope Lucius I dies.

May 12: Pope Stephen I (▶ 257) is elected. He clashes with Bishop Cyprian of Carthage (▶ 258) over the treatment of those who lapse from Christianity in the persecutions.

c.254

Origen (◀ c.185) dies.

256

Dura Europos (◀ c.240) is captured by the Persians and permanently abandoned.

257

August 2: Pope Stephen I (◀ 254) dies. He is subsequently venerated as a saint: feast day August 2.

August: Pope Sixtus II (▶ 258) is elected.

Valerian (◀ 253, ▶ 258) issues an edict against Christians, exiling their leaders and forbidding services.

258

☉ August 6: Pope Sixtus II (◀ 257) is beheaded. He is subsequently venerated as a saint: feast day August 6.

☉ Cyprian, Bishop of Carthage (◀ 254) and rigorist theologian, is executed. He is subsequently venerated as a saint: feast day September 16.

Under a second edict of Valerian (◀ 257) Christian clergy are recalled from exile, retried, and their property is confiscated.

260

♛ Valerian (◀ 253) is captured on campaign against the Persians and dies in captivity. Gallienus (◀ 253) becomes sole emperor.

⚓ Pope Dionysius (▶ 268) is elected.

Gallienus revokes the edicts of Valerian against the Christians (◀ 257, 258).

*c.***260**

🌢 Eusebius (▶ 324) is born. He becomes Bishop of Caesarea and writes the first church history as well as a chronology of world history. Dies 339.

261

🌢 Paul of Samosata (▶ 268) becomes Bishop of Antioch. He seems to have had a very exalted view of God and believed that Jesus was no more than inspired by God. He is the first bishop we know to have had women in his choir.

268

⚓ December 26: Pope Dionysius (◀ 260) dies.

♛ Gallienus (◀ 253) is killed. Claudius II (▶ 270) becomes emperor. He receives the epithet Gothicus because he inflicts a massive defeat on the Goths in Moesia (present-day Croatia).

Paul of Samosata (◀ 261) is deposed for heresy by a council at Antioch.

269

⚓ January 3: Pope Felix I (▶ 274) is elected.

270

♛ Claudius II Gothicus (◀ 268) dies.

♛ September: Aurelian (▶ 275) becomes emperor. Victories in the East and West enable him to restore the frontiers of the Roman empire at the Rhine and Danube and reunite the empire. In the process he withdraws Roman troops from the old province of Dacia (◀ 101–6). He is suspected by Christian writers of planning persecution of Christians, but does not actually issue any instructions.

☉ Gregory Thaumaturgus (◀ *c.*213) dies. He is subsequently venerated as a saint: feast day November 17.

28

Detail from a Christian sarcophagus showing Jonah and the whale: Jonah's deliverance from the whale was seen as a prefigurement of the resurrection, *c.*270

c.270

The first priest is ordained in Seleucia-Ctesiphon (◀ 226, ▶ *c.*285).

Plotinus (◀ *c.*201) dies.

A sarcophagus in the church of Santa Maria Antiqua, Rome, with a depiction of Jonah as a symbol of the resurrection, is probably the earliest extant Christian example.

272

Denis, Bishop of Paris, and two of his companions are beheaded on a hill outside the city that comes to be known as Montmartre ('the martyrs' mount'). Denis is subsequently venerated as a saint (feast day October 9) and later his tomb becomes a pilgrimage centre (▶ 625).

Shapur I, King of Persia (◀ 240), dies and is succeeded by Bahram I (▶ 276).

Aurelian (◀ 270, ▶ 274), through the coins he issues, advertises the importance of Sol Invictus (the Unconquered Sun) as the chief divine guardian of the Roman emperor and empire. Sol continues to be invoked by Roman emperors up to and including Constantine (▶ 321, 306).

274

December 20: Pope Felix I (◀ 269) dies.

December 25: Aurelian (◀ 272, ▶ 275) dedicates a new temple in Rome to Sol.

29

275

♆ January 4: Pope Eutychianus (▶ 283) is elected.

♛ September/October: Emperor Aurelian (◀ 270) is murdered and succeeded by Tacitus (▶ 276).

276

♛ King Bahram I of Persia (◀ 272) dies and is succeeded by his son as Bahram II (▶ 293), who later loses some provinces to Emperor Carus of Rome (▶ 282).

♟ February: Mani (◀ 216) is flayed alive in Seleucia-Ctesiphon (◀ 226) by order of Bahram II.

♛ June: Emperor Tacitus (◀ 275) dies.

♛ August: Probus (▶ 282) becomes emperor.

> **Manichaeism**
>
> Manichaeism is a religion that originates in the third century CE. It is founded by Mani (◀ 216), who is born near the Persian capital of Seleucia-Ctesiphon and after being exiled to India returns to Persia in 242, later to be executed by the authorities. Most of Mani's writings are lost and the details of accounts of his life are contradictory, so his teaching is difficult to ascertain. However, he certainly teaches an extreme form of Gnostic dualism in which light and darkness are in perpetual conflict. How human beings are saved from imprisonment in darkness is explained at great length in mythical terms; the process of redemption includes strict asceticism.
>
> Manichaeism spreads rapidly and widely and by the sixth century has reached Britain in the west and China in the east. Augustine of Hippo (▶ 354) is a Manichaean for eight or nine years. Manichaeism also seems to have influenced some Christian groups, including Priscillianism (▶ 380) and the Albigensians or Cathars (▶ c.1172) and Bogomils, but 'Manichaean' becomes a blanket term for heresy and details are hard to establish. It lasts at least a thousand years.

282

♛ September/October: Emperor Probus (◀ 276) is killed. Carus (▶ 283) becomes emperor.

283

♛ July/August: Carus (◀ 282) dies. His sons Numerian (▶ 284) and Carinus (▶ 285) become co-emperors.

♆ December 7: Pope Eutychianus (◀ 275) dies.

♆ December 17: Pope Caius (▶ 296) is elected.

284

♛ November 17: Diocletian (▶ 286, 303) is proclaimed Roman emperor. In his reign of over 20 years he restores a degree of stability to the empire.

♛ November: Numerian (◀ 283) dies from illness.

This year, seen by the Coptic Church as the beginning of the era of the martyrs, marks the beginning of the Coptic calendar, which follows the old Egyptian calendar.

285

♛ Carinus (◀ 283) dies in battle.

c.285

Papa bar Aggai is consecrated the first Bishop of Seleucia-Ctesiphon (◀ 270, ▶ 410). He goes on to claim to be the national head of the Persian church (Catholicos).

The Later Roman empire (284–476)

Modern scholars, particularly in the English-speaking world, use the term 'Later Roman empire' to refer to the period starting with the reign of Diocletian. For the Western part of the empire this period ends with the deposition of the last Western emperor in 476. In the East no clear line is drawn between the Later Roman empire and the Byzantine empire. For the inhabitants of the empire, such distinctions do not exist, and they remain 'Romans' until the fall of Constantinople in 1453.

A number of features make the Later Roman empire distinctive. It becomes usual for power to be divided between a number of senior emperors, with the title 'Augustus' – often two but sometimes three – supported by junior emperors, who have the title 'Caesar'. The expectation is that the Caesar will be the successor to his Augustus. The system is flexible, and in the fourth century there are prolonged periods of sole rule under Constantine, Constantius II and Theodosius I. After Theodosius' death in 395, however, no successor ever rules the whole empire again, and a division begins to develop between the two halves of the empire. This division, heightened by language difference between the Greek East and Latin West, is to have a significant effect on the development of Christianity. Other administrative changes include separation of military and civilian administration, and the development of a more complex hierarchy within the imperial court and household. The formal dress of the period survives in some of the vestments of the Christian churches.

The third century sees a separation of the emperor from the city of Rome. Emperors are now permanently on military campaign, and create new imperial cities nearer to the frontiers: these include in the West Milan and Trier, in the East Antioch and, from 327, Constantinople. Large palace-complexes, linked to circuses for chariot-racing, which is largely under imperial patronage, develop at the cities. And just as Rome ceases to be the administrative centre of the empire, so it ceases to be its religious centre. Worship of the emperor continues, even into the reign of Constantine, and so too does the cult of gods closely associated with the emperor, in particular that of Sol Invictus, the Unconquered Sun. From the emperor's point of view, it is not necessarily a major change to adopt the God of the Christians as a patron deity in place of the Sun (or even on the basis that they are the same).

The period sees constant warfare between the Romans and the Sassanian Persians to the east, and pressure on the Rhine-Danube area from Germans and Goths, but the empire maintains its geographical borders, although Britain is abandoned early in the fifth century. However, pressure on the frontier in Europe is eased in part by settling friendly groups within the empire. The Western emperors become increasingly dependent on these 'barbarians' to fight their wars, to the extent that by 476 the role of emperor is itself seen to be redundant, and when Romulus Augustulus is deposed, it is not considered necessary to replace him. So ends the Western Roman empire.

286

♛ Maximian (▶ 303, 305) is made co-emperor with Diocletian (◀ 284, ▶ *c.*299), with responsibility for the Western part of the empire. Diocletian takes on the religious title Jovius (of Jupiter), while Maximian becomes Herculius (of Hercules).

***c.*290**

♟ Pakhom is born. He pioneers communal monasticism in Egypt by founding a monastery at Tabennisi near the Nile where monks follow a simple rule. Dies 346.

293

♛ Constantius I (▶ 305) is appointed Caesar (subordinate ruler) in the West, and Galerius (▶ 303) is appointed Caesar in the East.

King Bahram II of Persia dies (◀ 276) and after the brief reign of his son Bahram III is succeeded by Narseh (▶ 302), son of Shapur I (◀ 272).

296

☉ April 22: Pope Caius (◀ 283) dies.

☉ June 10: Pope Marcellinus (▶ 304) is elected.

***c.*296**

♟📖 Athanasius (▶ 335) is born. As Bishop of Alexandria he becomes a champion of the orthodoxy established at the Council of Nicaea but is not universally accepted and therefore endures many exiles. He writes *On the Incarnation* (*c.*313) and a *Life of Antony* (*c.*356). Dies 373.

297

The Romans defeat Narseh, King of Persia (◀ 293, ▶ 302), who has to cede territories in western Mesopotamia and on the upper Tigris. The treaty signed is to last for 40 years (▶ 337).

***c.*299**

Galerius (◀ 293, ▶ 303) and Diocletian (◀ 286, ▶ 302) purge Christians from the imperial court and the army in the east of the empire.

***c.*300**

David, Bishop of Basra (in present-day Iraq), leaves his diocese for several years to evangelize in India.

Christmas begins to be celebrated by Christians (▶ 352).

Fourth century

This is the most dramatic century of all in the history of Christianity. Its first decade sees the most concerted attempt yet to wipe out the religion; its last decade sees an equally determined campaign to end pagan religious practices. The root of this transformation is generally reckoned to be the conversion of the Emperor Constantine to Christianity, but the situation is a little more complex.

The 'Great Persecution' poses a serious threat to the lives and well-being of thousands of Christians within the Roman empire, but their numbers are already too great for there to be any real possibility of Christianity being totally suppressed. The leaders of the persecution realize this, and it is brought to an end through most of the empire before Constantine becomes involved. Equally, at the other end of the century, the repeated decrees ordering the closing, and later the destruction, of temples and an end to sacrifices, along with the vigorous debate about the Altar of Victory in the Senate House in Rome (357), an important pagan symbol set up by Octavian in 33 BCE to celebrate the defeat of Antony and Cleopatra at Actium, show that pagan religious practices remain popular at both the top and the bottom of the social scale.

What makes the greatest difference to Christianity is that from Constantine onwards, emperors are directing the actions of the church: calling bishops to councils, supporting or rejecting doctrinal formulations. What limits their effectiveness is the fact that emperors take different sides over the most significant dispute of the period, over Arianism, the doctrine that the Son is a created being, not of the same substance as the Father. Arian Christianity spreads outside the frontiers of the empire, and even after the dispute is resolved by Theodosius I, Arian Germans and Goths will move into the lands of the catholic Romans. The church is also split by other conflicts, such as that over Donatism, which takes a divergent view of the treatment of those who have lapsed in persecution.

Once persecution has been abandoned, Christianity becomes much more visible. Major church buildings are constructed in Rome, Jerusalem and across the empire, and a new Christian imperial capital is created at Constantinople. Although there is some resistance, even from Christian emperors, to the destruction of pagan temples in cities, local citizens often take matters into their own hands. The architecture of the cities of the empire is being transformed.

The substance and expression of Christianity begins to change. In Egypt, with Antony (356), Pakhom (320) and Shenoute (c.388) we see the beginnings of monasticism, which is to spread all round the Mediterranean. A cult of saints develops, and associated with it a growing veneration of relics. Helena (326), Constantine's mother, the Bordeaux pilgrim (333) and the devout Egeria (381–84) travel to the Holy Land, marking the start of pilgrimages there and elsewhere. Above all, the large numbers of pagans who convert to Christianity, which has now become the religion to turn to, bring with them imagery and practices that are incorporated into their new faith: it is no coincidence that as worship of the mother goddess Cybele declines, veneration of the Virgin Mary increases.

Although few events are recorded, Christianity is also growing outside the boundaries of the Roman empire, not only among the Germans and the Goths in the 'barbarian' lands beyond the Rhine and Danube, but also to the east in the Persian Sassanian empire and India.

301

⊕ Gregory the Illuminator, a member of the Parthian royal family, who has become a Christian in Cappadocia, converts King Tiridates III of Armenia to the Christian faith. Armenia becomes the first country to adopt Christianity as the state religion and for some time the office of Catholicos (primate) is kept in Gregory's family. After his death he is venerated as a saint: feast day September 30.

302

♛ Narseh, King of Persia (◀ 297), dies and is succeeded by his son Hormizd II (▶ 309).

Emperor Diocletian (◀ 299, ▶ 303) orders the suppression of Manichaeism (◀ 216, 276) in Africa.

303

February 23: Emperor Diocletian and his Caesar Galerius (◀ c.299, ▶ 305) begin the Great Persecution (▶ 311) by issuing an edict ordering the destruction of Christian buildings, the burning of scriptures, the confiscation of church property and the reduction of Christians to the lowest citizen status.

In Italy, Spain and Africa Maximian (◀ 286, ▶ 305) enforces Diocletian's edict. Pope Marcellinus (◀ 296, ▶ 304) hands over the sacred books and offers sacrifice. The Caesar Constantius I (◀ 293, ▶ 305), in Britain and Gaul, is less thorough.

A second edict orders the imprisonment of Christian leaders in the eastern half of the empire: many are forced to sacrifice to the gods and then released.

c.303

Porphyry (◀ c.232) dies.

304

⚓ October 25: Pope Marcellinus (◀ 296) dies.

Diocletian, like Decius (◀ 250) earlier, decrees a universal sacrifice. Enforcement is more thorough in the East than in the West.

305

♛ May 1: Diocletian (◀ 284) abdicates and forces Maximian (◀ 303, ▶ 310) to do the same. Constantius I (◀ 303, ▶ 306) and Galerius (◀ 303, ▶ 306) become emperors (Augusti) while Severus (▶ 306) and Maximinus (▶ 306) are appointed Caesar (subordinate ruler).

Constantius I ends the enforcement of Diocletian's edict (◀ 303) in the Western half of the empire.

306

♛ July 25: Constantius I (◀ 305) dies in battle. His son Constantine (▶ 310) is declared emperor by his troops.

♛ August: Galerius (◀ 305, ▶ 308) promotes Severus (◀ 305, ▶ 307) to the rank of Augustus (emperor) to succeed Constantius I.

35

♛ October 28: Maxentius (▶ 307), son of Maximian (◀ 305), proclaims himself emperor in Rome.

☥ December: Pope Marcellus I (▶ 309) is elected after a three-and-a-half-year vacancy. Shortly before his death he is banished as a troublemaker.

The Caesar Maximinus (◀ 305, ▶ 308) orders a universal sacrifice throughout the territory he controls (Syria, Palestine, Egypt), with consequent persecution of Christians.

Melitius, Bishop of Lycopolis in Egypt, objects to the terms laid down by Peter, Bishop of Alexandria, for the lapsed to return to the church as being too lax. He founds a separate church of his own, causing the so-called Melitian schism.

c.306

♣ Ephrem the Syrian, Syrian church father and poet, is born. He writes many hymns. Dies 373.

A synod in Elvira, in Spain, can be seen as one of the earliest approximations to a general council. It is attended by 19 bishops and 26 presbyters. It firmly marks off the church from the pagan world, Jews and heretics, requires the celibacy of clergy and prohibits figurative paintings in churches.

307

♛ Severus (◀ 306) is killed by Maxentius (◀ 306, ▶ 312).

308

Summer: Maximinus (◀ 306, ▶ 309) suspends persecution of Christians.

♛ November: Licinius (▶ 313) is made Augustus (emperor) by Galerius (◀ 306, ▶ 311), in succession to Severus (◀ 307).

309

☉ January 16: Pope Marcellus I (◀ 306) dies. He is subsequently venerated as a saint: feast day January 16.

Autumn: Maximinus (◀ 308, ▶ 311) renews persecution, ordering the restoration of temples of the gods and a further universal sacrifice.

♛ King Hormizd II of Persia (◀ 302) dies and is succeeded by Shapur II (▶ 379), under whom Persia enjoys a great revival.

310

☥ April 18: Pope Eusebius is elected. He is soon banished.

♛ July: Maximian (◀ 305) declares himself emperor again, but is defeated by Constantine (◀ 306, ▶ 312) and killed.

☥ October 21: Pope Eusebius dies.

c.310

♣ Apollinarius of Laodicea is born. He cannot believe that Christ had a human soul, and is condemned as a heretic. Dies 390.

36

311

April 30: Galerius (◀ 308) issues an edict of toleration in the names of all his colleagues, allowing Christians to meet and build churches, and bringing to an end the Great Persecution (◀ 303).

♛ May: Galerius dies.

☿ July 2: Pope Miltiades (▶ 314) is elected, the first pope to enjoy the favour of the Roman government.

Autumn: The Caesar Maximinus (◀ 309, ▶ 312) renews persecution of Christians in the empire east of the Bosphorus (▶ 313).

A group of North African bishops refuse to accept Caecilian (▶ 314) as Bishop of Carthage because he has been consecrated by someone who had lapsed under Diocletian's persecution. Under a rival bishop Donatus, they separate from the catholic church, claiming that that church is impure, causing the Donatist schism.

*c.***311**

♣ Ulfilas (▶ 341) is born. A missionary to the Goths, he is the first to translate the Bible into Gothic. Because he is an Arian Christian, Arianism (see p.38) becomes the creed of the Ostrogoths, Visigoths and Vandals. Dies 383.

Maximinus (◀ 311, ▶ 313) ends active persecution of Christians, but still forbids them to erect buildings and meet together.

312

April 13: The Roman church celebrates Easter in security for the first time since the persecution.

October 28: Constantine (◀ 306, ▶ 313) wins a decisive victory over Maxentius (◀ 307) at the Milvian Bridge which he later attributes to the vision of a cross-like sign (known as the chi-rho or labarum, see p.62).

Donatism

The Donatists take their name from an African Christian, Donatus Magnus. He and his followers break away from the mainstream church in a dispute over the status of those who recanted their faith during the persecution under Diocletian (◀ 303). They refuse to accept the possibility that such Christians could repent, and do not accept their spiritual authority or sacraments administered by them. Towns in North Africa are divided over the issue, and as the controversy spreads, Emperor Constantine calls a council in Arles (▶ 314). The Donatists refuse to accept its decision against them and Augustine (354–430) has to combat them throughout his time as Bishop of Hippo. The Donatists survive the conquest of North Africa by the Vandals (▶ 429) and its reconquest by the Byzantine general Belisarius (▶ 533) and continue until the Muslim invasion of North Africa (▶ 700).

Arianism

Arianism is a view of the person of Jesus that originates with Arius (◀ c.250), a Christian priest teaching in Alexandria in the early fourth century. He argues that God the Father and God the Son are not both equally eternal; before the incarnation Jesus was a divine being, but had been created by God the Father. As a popular saying had it, 'There was a time when he wasn't,' as opposed to the orthodox 'There never was a was when he wasn't.'

The controversy between Arians and orthodox rages throughout society, and is so vigorous that it threatens to split Christianity. Emperor Constantine, who has made Christianity a legal religion, attempts to resolve it by summoning a council at Nicaea in Turkey in 325, over which he presides. The council drafts a creed that rejects Arianism, but this is not the end of the story. Later Roman emperors, such as Constantine's successor, Constantius II, who sends an Arian missionary, Theophilus, to India (▶ 360), and Valens (▶ 364), promote Arianism, and the Council of Sirmium (▶ 357) approves an Arian creed. But opposition from Athanasius (◀ c.296) and the three Cappadocian fathers (▶ c.335), Basil, Gregory of Nyssa and Gregory of Nazianzus, helps orthodoxy to triumph in the East and it is reasserted at the Council of Constantinople in 381.

Nevertheless, this is still not the end of the story. Ulfilas (◀ c.311) is an Arian missionary to the Goths, and Arianism spreads further when other Germanic tribes which put an end to the Roman empire convert, not to catholicism, the orthodox faith, but to Arianism, and they dominate Western Europe. It is not until the conversion of the Franks to catholicism (▶ 496) that Arianism finally begins to disappear.

313

June 5: Licinius (◀ 308, ▶ 320) issues the Edict of Milan, which tolerates all religious practices including Christianity. Constantine, as co-emperor, signs the edict.

April 30: Licinius (◀ 308) defeats Maximinus (◀ 311) at Adrianople.

♛ August: Maximinus commits suicide. Constantine and Licinius are now the two surviving emperors.

♖ Constantine starts to build a basilica on the site of a palace that used to belong to the Laterani family; this comes to be known as the Lateran Basilica (San Giovanni in Laterano).

♣ Didymus the Blind is born in Alexandria. Teacher of Jerome (▶ c.345) and Rufinus (▶ c.345), he becomes head of the Catechetical School there (◀ c.190). Dies 398.

The Diocese of Cologne is founded.

314

⚲ January 10: Pope Miltiades (◀ 311) dies.

⚲ January 31: Pope Sylvester I (▶ 335) is elected.

♖ The dedication of the cathedral at Tyre is the earliest instance of a church building being dedicated.

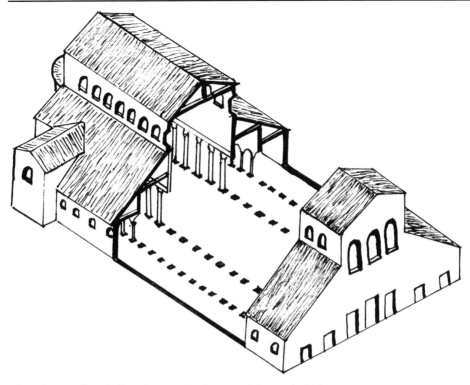

The Salvator Church (San Giovanni in Laterano), begun in 313

A synod in Arles, the first inter-provincial council held in the West under imperial patronage, supports Bishop Caecilian against the Donatists (◀ 311). Three bishops attend from Britain.

A synod in Ancyra seeks to repair the damage to relations in the church caused by persecution.

The Dioceses of Mainz and Trier are founded.

*c.*315

🕯 Cyril, Bishop of Jerusalem (▶ *c.*350), is born. Dies 386.

🕯📖 Epiphanius (▶ 394) is born. He is a defender of orthodoxy and his *Panarion* (Medicine Chest, *c.*374) is a refutation of the heresies. Dies 403.

🕯 Hilary of Poitiers (▶ 356), a vigorous opponent of Arius (◀ *c.*250, ▶ *c.*319), is born. He becomes the leading Latin theologian of his time. Dies 367.

318

Constantine (◀ 313, ▶ 321) allows the church to appoint its bishops, whose jurisdiction is parallel to that of the state.

39

319

Ⅲ Work begins on the building of the basilica church of St Peter's, Rome (▶ 1506).

c.319

Alexander, Bishop of Alexandria, issues an encyclical (circular) letter condemning the views of Arius (◀ c.315, ▶ 325).

320

Licinius (◀ 313, ▶ 324) purges Christians from his palace and army, and restricts Christian activities in the eastern part of the empire.

Pakhom (◀ c.290, ▶ c.321) founds the first cenobitic (communal) monastery at Tabennisi in Egypt and many other monasteries follow.

321

March 8: Constantine (◀ 318, ▶ 324) decrees that divination by traditional means should be permitted to carry on in public, but that all private sacrifices are to be banned (▶ 341).

March: Constantine orders Sunday to be a day of rest in the cities of the Roman empire. This is presented not as a Christian act but as a way of honouring the sun, Sol Invictus (◀ 272).

A law of Constantine authorizes bequests to the church.

c.321

The Rule of Pakhom (◀ 320, ▶ 346) assumes that the Psalms and Gospels are available in Coptic.

324

♛ Constantine defeats Licinius at Adrianople and becomes sole emperor.

Ⅲ A church is built in El Asnam, in present-day Algeria.

▭ Eusebius (◀ c.260, ▶ 339) writes the final edition of his *Church History*, the first such work to be written.

325

May 20: The Council of Nicaea in present-day Turkey is convened by Constantine to resolve the Arian (◀ c.319, ▶ c.327) controversy. It is regarded as the first Ecumenical Council, i.e. a council of the whole church. It produces a definitive creed, later expanded (▶ 381), which contains the key Greek word *homoousios* ('of one substance'): the Son (Jesus) is of the same substance as the Father (God). This proves controversial because it is not scriptural. The council also gives Alexandria a status second only to Rome and above Antioch (▶ 381).

June 19: The Council of Nicaea ends.

♛ Licinius (◀ 324) is executed.

c.325

♠ Lucius Caecilius Firmianus Lactantius (◀ c.250) dies.

40

326

☥ Helena, mother of Constantine, travels to the Holy Land, where she claims to have discovered the 'true cross' of Jesus (▶ 614). She founds basilicas on the Mount of Olives and in Bethlehem (▶ 333). After her death she is venerated as a saint: feast day May 21 in the East and August 18 in the West.

⛪ Work on the Church of the Holy Sepulchre in Jerusalem is begun (▶ c.335).

⛪ The building of St Peter's Cathedral, Trier, is begun, celebrating 20 years of Constantine's reign (▶ 1035).

c.327

✦ Macrina is born. She is the elder sister of Basil of Caesarea (▶ c.330) and Gregory of Nyssa (▶ c.335). Widowed at an early age, she establishes one of the earliest communities of women ascetics. Dies 380.

Arius (◀ 325, ▶ 335) presents a confession of faith to Constantine, which, though falling short of the creed of Nicaea, is accepted.

330

May 11: Constantine dedicates the city of Constantinople, which becomes the centre of his rule from this time on.

King Ezana of Aksum proclaims Christianity the official religion of his country, which extends from Ethiopia on both shores of the Red Sea. Aksum is the first state to use the sign of the cross on its coins.

c.330

✦ Basil of Caesarea is born. In his theology he emphasizes the deity of the Holy Spirit. A liturgy is attributed to him and he promotes the singing of hymns. He describes the hymn 'Hail, gladdening light' as old. Dies 379.

✦ Gregory of Nazianzus is born; he too argues for the deity of the Holy Spirit. Dies c.390.

333

⛪ The Church of the Nativity, Bethlehem, and the Eleona Church on the Mount of Olives, Jerusalem, are built.

The Bordeaux pilgrim, the earliest known pilgrim from Western Europe to Jerusalem, begins his journey. His account of the journey survives. He is in Jerusalem for the founding of the first churches and refers for the first time to many Christian traditions about the holy places.

335

⛪ September 17: The Church of the Holy Sepulchre in Jerusalem (◀ 326) is consecrated.

☥ December 31: Pope Sylvester I (◀ 314) dies. He is subsequently venerated as a saint: feast day December 31 in the East, January 2 in the West.

Constantine includes bishops in the political structure of the Roman empire.

A synod in Tyre condemns and exiles Athanasius, Bishop of Alexandria (◀ c.296), and Marcellus, Bishop of Ancyra, for their opposition to Arianism (◀ c.327, ▶ 336), which despite the Council of Nicaea is still a powerful force. Marcellus teaches that God the Son and God the Spirit are separate entities only for the purposes of creation and redemption. Athanasius goes to Trier (▶ 337).

c.335

✦ Gregory, younger brother of Basil of Caesarea (◀ c.330), is born. He later becomes Bishop of Nyssa. He, Basil and Gregory of Nazianzus (◀ c.330) are known as the Cappadocian fathers; they take over the defence of the Nicene faith (◀ 325) from Athanasius. Dies c.395.

336

☩ January 18: Pope Mark is elected.

☩ October 7: Pope Mark dies.

✦ Arius (◀ c.250) dies.

c.336

✦ Martin, later Bishop of Tours, is born. A former soldier who famously gives his cloak to a beggar, he is active in promoting monasticism (▶ 360). Dies 397.

337

☩ February 6: Pope Julius I (▶ 352) is elected.

Constantine is baptized, on his deathbed.

♕ May 22: Constantine dies. He is succeeded as emperor by his sons Constantine II (▶ 340), who rules Britain, Gaul and Spain; Constans (▶ 350), a vigorous opponent of Arianism and a supporter of Athanasius, who rules Italy, Africa and Illyricum; and Constantius II (▶ 361), who rules over the Eastern provinces and is a supporter of the Arians (◀ 336, ▶ 339).

Athanasius returns to Alexandria from exile on the death of Constantine. Marcellus of Ancyra (◀ 335, ▶ 339) is also restored to office.

✦ Sahak (▶ 360), also known as Isaac of Armenia, is born. He becomes Catholicos, restores churches and monasteries destroyed by the Persians and with Mesrop Mashtots (▶ 360) is said to have invented the Armenian alphabet and translated the Bible. He also writes hymns. Dies 440.

Athanasius introduces a 40-day Lent to the Eastern churches, which he has come to know in the West.

King Shapur II (◀ 309, ▶ 338) of Persia breaks the treaty established with the Romans (◀ 297) and embarks on military conquest. Although he wins a number of victories he makes little progress.

339

✦ May 30: Eusebius of Caesarea (◀ c.260) dies.

☿ Eusebius of Nicomedia, with Arian (◀ 337, ▶ 341) supporters, becomes Patriarch of Constantinople.

Athanasius (◀ 337, ▶ 343) has to flee from Alexandria to Rome, where he has support. Marcellus of Ancyra (◀ 337) is also deposed and comes to Rome. Pope Julius backs Athanasius but not Marcellus.

King Shapur II of Persia (◀ 337, ▶ 353) turns on the Christians there in reaction to the Christianization of the Roman empire by Constantine. He forces them to pay double taxes to finance his war with Rome and goes on to execute church leaders and destroy churches (▶ 409). At the same time he vigorously promotes Zoroastrianism.

c.339

✦📖 Ambrose (▶ 373) is born. He becomes Bishop of Milan, engages in confrontations with the state and writes hymns. In his *On the Sacraments* (c.390) he gives the earliest evidence for the form of the Latin mass in Milan (up to the time of Pope Damasus [▶ 366] the mass is celebrated in Greek in Rome). Dies 397.

Serapion, a disciple of Antony of Egypt (◀ c.251) and friend of Athanasius, becomes Bishop of Thmuis in Egypt. His *Euchologion*, a collection of liturgical prayers, is important evidence for the formalization of Christian worship.

340

♕ Constantine II (◀ 337) invades northern Italy but is defeated by Constans (◀ 337, ▶ 342) and killed.

Optatus of Milevis in Numidia first refers to Circumcellions, violent fanatics who are part of the Donatist (◀ 311) movement.

341

The 'Dedication Synod' in Antioch moves towards abandoning Nicene orthodoxy in favour of an Arian (◀ 339, ▶ 355) approach.

Ulfilas (◀ c.311, ▶ 348) is made bishop and sent to minister among the Goths north of the Danube.

Constantius II (◀ 337, ▶ 342) issues an edict forbidding sacrifice to the gods (◀ 321, ▶ 346).

342

November 1: Constantius II and Constans issue an edict forbidding the destruction of pagan temples outside Rome.

343

The Council of Serdica (present-day Sophia) brings a split between West (for) and East (against) over Athanasius (◀ 339, ▶ 346).

The Diocese of Speyer is founded.

43

345

A colony of Syrians headed by Thomas of Cana (▶ 350), a rich merchant, settles in Malabar, India. Malabar Christians come to be called Syrian Christians.

*c.***345**

✸ Jerome is born. A biblical scholar, he settles in Bethlehem, where he translates the Bible into Latin (the Vulgate, ▶ 383). Dies 420.

✸ Tyrannius Rufinus (▶ 392), Italian monk, historian and translator, is born. He translates many of the works of the Greek fathers, especially of Origen, into Latin (▶ 395). Dies 410.

346

☉ May 9: Pakhom (◀ *c.*290) dies. He is subsequently venerated as a saint: feast day May 15 in the East, May 9 in the West.

December 1: Constantius II and Constans decree the closure of all pagan temples and reiterate the ban on sacrifices (◀ 341, ▶ 356).

Athanasius is again restored as Bishop of Alexandria under pressure from Constans (◀ *c.*343, ▶ *c.*347).

347

✸ John Chrysostom (▶ 381–84) is born. A famous preacher ('golden mouth'), he becomes Patriarch of Constantinople. His writings attest lavish church furnishings, chalices, vestments and veils. A liturgy is attributed to him and he promotes the singing of hymns. Dies 407.

*c.***347**

Frumentius, a Christian freedman who has been tutor to King Ezana of Aksum (◀ 330), requests Athanasius in Alexandria to send a bishop to ordain priests in Ethiopia. Athanasius thereupon consecrates Frumentius, who becomes known as Bishop Salama.

348

Ulfilas (◀ 341, ▶ *c.*350) is expelled by the Goths. He moves to Nicopolis near the Danube (▶ *c.*350).

A synod in Carthage declares against the rebaptism of anyone who has been baptized in the name of the Trinity. This is directed against the Donatists (see p.37).

*c.***348**

✸ Aurelius Prudentius Clemens (Prudentius), Latin poet and hymn writer, is born. Some of his hymns such as 'Of the Father's love begotten' and 'Earth has many a noble city' are still sung today. Dies *c.*410.

350

♛ January 18: Constans (◀ 346) is killed in a revolt.

Thomas of Cana (◀ 345) builds a church in Cranganore.

Aetius, a deacon of Antioch, puts forward the view that the Son is totally different

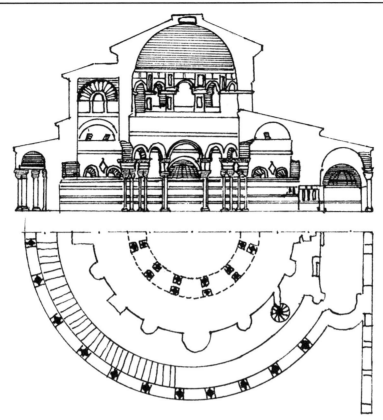

The Mausoleum of Santa Costanza in Rome, built for Constantine's daughter Constantina, *c.*350

(*anomoios*) from the Father, fallible and capable of sin. He has a following (the Anhomoeans).

c.350

The royal house of Georgia is converted through the preaching of the Cappadocian slave girl Nino.

Ulfilas (◀ 348, ▶ 383) translates the Greek New Testament into Gothic.

📖 The *Catechetical Lectures* of Cyril of Jerusalem (◀ *c.*315, ▶ 386) show the beginnings of elaboration in ceremonial and heightened reverence. They are the earliest evidence for the washing of the celebrant's hands at the eucharist and the recitation of the Lord's Prayer after the great eucharistic prayer.

🏛▉ The Mausoleum of Santa Costanza, Rome, built for Constantine's daughter Constantina, contains the earliest extant mosaics in a Christian building. They are on pagan themes.

352

☩ April 12: Pope Julius I (◀ 337) dies.

45

⛪ May 17: Pope Liberius (▶ 366) is elected.

December 25: Christmas is definitely known for the first time to have been celebrated on this date (◀ c.300).

353

Under pressure from Constantius II (◀ 346) a synod at Arles condemns Athanasius (◀ c.347, ▶ 356).

Constantius II signs a peace treaty with King Shapur II of Persia (◀ 339, ▶ 355).

c.353

Paulinus (▶ 400) is born in Aquitaine, of a noble Roman family. He becomes Bishop of Nola in Italy and writes much poetry. Dies 431.

354

🕯 November 13: Augustine (▶ 395) is born. Of a pagan family, he is converted to Christianity and made Bishop of Hippo. A towering theologian, especially on grace and sin, he has dominated the thought of the Western church ever since. Dies 430.

🕯 Theodore, Bishop of Mopsuestia, is born. A biblical scholar, he rejects allegorical interpretation. Dies 427.

A chronograph is produced by Furius Dionysius Philocalus (also known as the Philocalian calendar), listing the consuls of Rome and the death dates of the more famous saints. It also lists the birth of Christ on December 25, indicating the observance of Christmas at this time.

355

👑 November 6: Julian (▶ 361) is appointed Caesar (subordinate ruler) by Constantius II.

⛪ Felix II (▶ 365) is elected Antipope. He holds Arian (◀ 341, ▶ 359) views. A synod in Milan yet again condemns Athanasius (◀ 353, ▶ 356).

356

February 20: Constantius II and Julian ban pagan sacrifice and worship on pain of death (◀ 346, ▶ 381).

☥ Antony of Egypt (◀ c.251) dies. He is subsequently venerated as a saint: feast day June 17.

Athanasius is exiled for the third time by Constantius II, and Pope Liberius (◀ 352) is exiled to Thrace for supporting him (▶ 358).

Hilary of Poitiers (◀ c.315, ▶ 359) is condemned at a synod in Gaul and exiled to Phrygia for four years. He uses his time there to form a picture of Eastern theology.

357

The Blasphemy of Sirmium, an extreme Latin Arian doctrinal formula, is issued by a council there, which also forbids the use of *ousia*, *homoousios* or *homoiousios*.

Constantius II visits Rome. He has the Altar of Victory removed from the Senate House (▶ 362).

358

King Shapur II of Persia (◀ 353, ▶ 364) resumes hostilities, conquering much of northern Mesopotamia.

☧ Pope Liberius (◀ 356, ▶ 366) returns from Thrace.

☧ Antipope Felix II (◀ 355, ▶ 365) is deposed.

359

Emperor Constantius II summons the bishops of West and East to separate synods in Ariminium (Rimini) (the West) and Seleucia (the East) in an attempt to settle the Arian (◀ 355, ▶ 364) dispute. Hilary of Poitiers (◀ 356, ▶ 360) is a leading light at the Synod of Seleucia.

▮ The sarcophagus of Junius Bassus, prefect of Rome, in St Peter's, Rome, is decorated with scenes from the Gospels.

360

⌂ The church of Hagia Sophia in Constantinople (▶ 414) is built by Constantius II.

♣ Mesrop Mashtots is born. An Armenian monk, theologian and linguist, along with Sahak (◀ 337, ▶ 440) he is said to have invented the Armenian alphabet, leading to the preservation of the language and literature of Armenia and later to the translation of the Bible into Armenian (▶ 434). Dies 440.

c.360

♣📖 John Cassian (▶ c.415) is born. He introduces Eastern monasticism to the West and his *Institutes* (c.420) influence the Rule of Benedict (▶ c.480); his view of grace and sin is less harsh than that of Augustine (◀ 334), and is known as Semipelagianism. Dies 435.

With Hilary of Poitiers (◀ c.354, ▶ 367), Martin of Tours (◀ c.336, ▶ 371) founds the Abbey of Ligugé, near Poitiers, the first monastery north of the Alps. It is later put in the shade by Marmoutier (▶ 371).

♣ Pelagius (▶ 410) is born. British, he argues against Augustine that human beings sin through wrong choices and are corrupted by their environment, not through a hereditary fault. His followers are known as Pelagians. Initially he is chaplain for 30 years to the Roman senatorial house of the Anicii and is a friend of Paulinus of Nola (◀ c.353). Dies c.420.

Constantius II sends Theophilus, an Arian Indian, as a missionary to southern Arabia. Theophilus also visits his home on the island of Divus in the Indian Ocean.

361

♛ November 3: Constantius II dies and is succeeded as emperor by Julian (▶ 363), who announces his conversion to paganism. He is consequently known as 'the Apostate'.

47

362

February 21: Athanasius (◀ 356, ▶ 364) returns to Alexandria on the accession of Julian but is exiled again by Julian the same year.

Julian forbids Christians to teach anything involving classical texts.

Julian permits the Altar of Victory to be restored to the Senate House in Rome (◀ 357, ▶ 382).

363

♛ June 26: Julian (◀ 361) is killed in battle against King Shapur II (◀ 358, ▶ 379) during an invasion of Persia; he is succeeded as emperor by Jovian (▶ 364), a Christian, who is taking part in his campaign. Jovian makes peace with the Persians, giving up Nisibis and Roman influence in Parthia.

364

♛ February 17: Jovian (◀ 363) dies.

♛ February 26: The army commanders proclaim Valentinian I, a Christian, emperor at Nicaea.

♛ March 28: Valentinian appoints his brother Valens (▶ 367), a supporter of the Arians (◀ 359, ▶ 381) who persecutes the catholics, ruler of the East while he rules the West.

King Shapur II of Persia (◀ 363) invades Armenia and attempts to introduce Zoroastrianism there. King Arshak II is captured and forced to commit suicide, but with secret support from Rome the nobility successfully resist. Shapur goes on to conquer what is now Afghanistan.

Athanasius (◀ 362, ▶ 365/66) returns once more to Alexandria.

A council in Laodicea attempts to repair the damage done to Christianity during the reign of Julian (◀ 363). It opposes heresy and Judaizing, ruling that there must be no more resting on the Sabbath (Saturday); Christians must limit themselves to honouring Christ on Sundays.

365

☦ November 22: Antipope Felix II (◀ 355, 358) dies.

Valentinian I regains Gaul for Rome.

365/66

Athanasius is forced into a fifth exile.

366

☦ September 24: Pope Liberius (◀ 352) dies.

☦ October 1: Pope Damasus (▶ 384) is elected.

367

♛ August 24: Valentinian I (◀ 364) proclaims his eight-year-old son Gratian (▶ 379) co-emperor.

⊕ November 1: Hilary of Poitiers (◀ c.315) dies. He is subsequently venerated as a saint: feast day January 13.

Valens (◀ 364, ▶ 378) crosses the Danube and devastates the territory of the Visigoths, a Germanic people who have invaded the Balkans. The Visigoths have adopted Arian (◀ c.250) Christianity.

An official ('Festal') letter of Athanasius (◀ 365/66, ▶ 373) gives the earliest known canon (list) of New Testament books as we now have them (▶ 382).

371

♣ July 4: Martin (◀ c.315) is consecrated Bishop of Tours. He founds the Abbey of Marmoutier, near Tours, which soon eclipses Ligugé (◀ c.360).

373

⊕ May 2: Athanasius (◀ c.296, 335, 337) dies. He is subsequently venerated as a saint: feast day May 2.

⊕ December 7: Ephrem the Syrian (◀ c.306) dies. He is subsequently venerated as a saint: feast day June 9.

Ambrose (◀ c.339, ▶ 384) is consecrated Bishop of Milan.

374

The Armenians declare their church independent of the Church of Caesarea, to which it was previously subordinate.

375

♛ November 17: Valentinian I (◀ 364) dies.

♛ Valentinian II (▶ 392) becomes emperor.

378

♛ August 9: Valens (◀ 364) is killed in battle at Adrianople and his army is shattered by the Visigoths (◀ 367, ▶ 401).

379

⊕ January 1: Basil of Caesarea (◀ c.330) dies. He is subsequently venerated as a saint: feast day January 1 in the East, January 2 in the West.

♛ January 19: Emperor Gratian (◀ 367, ▶ 380) proclaims Theodosius I (▶ 380, 395) co-emperor, to rule the East.

♛ King Shapur II of Persia (◀ 309, 364) dies and is succeeded by his brother, Ardashir II (▶ 383), who is also hostile to Christianity.

380

⊕ Macrina (◀ c.327) dies. She is subsequently venerated as a saint: feast day July 19.

February 28: Theodosius, Gratian and Valentinian II issue the edict *Cunctos populos,*

> **The Germanic invasions**
>
> From the fourth century onwards, Roman imperial rule is gradually replaced by the rule of a series of Germanic tribes that in due course establish kingdoms. The invasions begin when the Huns, probably from Central Asia, advance westwards and displace the Visigoths, a tribe that has settled north of the Danube, into the Eastern Roman empire. After a period when they live there in exchange for military service, the Visigoths rebel and defeat a Roman army under Valens at the battle of Adrianople (◀ 378). Valens is killed. Under their king Alaric, the Visigoths advance south and west through Greece and in 410 sack Rome. They then move across Gaul and settle in Aquitaine (▶ 418).
>
> The Burgundians, originally from Scandinavia, cross the Rhine c.406, settling in its valley before moving to the area near Lyons and giving it their name, Burgundy.
>
> Under their king Gaiseric, the Vandals from east of the Danube advance through Gaul to Spain and then invade North Africa, where they establish their base, raiding Sicily and Italy. They pillage Rome in 455 and maintain their kingdom in Africa until well into the next century.
>
> The Huns under their leader Attila also move on the Roman empire and invade Italy and Gaul, but are driven off after a defeat at Chalôns in 451. However, the Ostrogoths from the Balkans, who have often fought with them, are more successful. In 493 they defeat Odoacer, who has proclaimed himself King of Italy, and gain control of Italy.
>
> The Franks, Germanic tribes united under Clovis (▶ c.466), expand from their home on the lower Rhine and conquer Gaul, driving out the Visigoths.
>
> All this means the end of Roman imperial government in the West. Although the Eastern Emperor Justinian wins back much of this territory in campaigns from 527 onwards, driving out the Vandals from Africa and deposing the Ostrogothic king in Italy, his success is not lasting.
>
> In 568 yet another Germanic tribe, the Lombards, conquer the northern plain of Italy.
>
> The success of Arianism among these Germanic peoples means that it proves a competitor for mainstream catholic Christianity for longer than it would otherwise have done.

making the confession of God as Trinity ('as handed down by the apostle Peter to the Romans') binding on all peoples.

A synod held at Saragossa, Spain, condemns ascetical doctrines, including fasting on Sundays, associated with Priscillian, a devout high-ranking layman, though he is not mentioned by name. Despite this, Priscillian becomes Bishop of Avila (▶ 381).

*c.*380

🌿📖 Socrates, church historian, is born. His church history is in seven books, each covering the life of an emperor, and extends from 305 to 439. Dies 450.

381

May: Theodosius I (◀ 380, ▶ 382) convenes a council at Constantinople. It finally resolves the Arian (◀ 364) controversy along the lines of the Council of Nicaea (325) and produces an expanded version of its creed (the 'Nicene Creed' still recited in churches today). It is regarded as the second Ecumenical Council.

The Council of Constantinople also declares that the Bishop of Constantinople shall hold first rank after the Bishop of Rome, thus eclipsing the status of Alexandria (◀ 325). Nectarius, praetor of Constantinople, can be regarded as the first Patriarch of Constantinople (▶ 397).

December 21: Theodosius I issues a decree forbidding divination using pagan sacrifices (◀ 356, ▶ 385).

Priscillian (◀ 380) is exiled; he appeals to Pope Damasus (◀ 366) in Rome and Ambrose (◀ 373) in Milan but is rejected by them. However, the secular authorities reverse the judgement of exile and he returns, to gain a large following (▶ 386).

381–84

The devout Egeria goes on a pilgrimage to the Holy Land. Her account of the biblical sites she visits and the forms of Christian worship she finds there is invaluable. Along with John Chrysostom (◀ 347, ▶ 398) she is the first to mention the use of incense in churches.

382

Emperor Theodosius I concludes a treaty with the Visigoths.

Pope Damasus holds a council and issues a canon (official list) of scriptural books (◀ 367, ▶ 397).

Emperor Gratian (◀ 380, ▶ 383) gives up the title Pontifex Maximus, which had been held by Roman emperors since Augustus (◀ 14). It is adopted by popes from Siricius (▶ 384) onwards.

Gratian removes the Altar of Victory (◀ 362, ▶ 384) from the Senate House in Rome.

383

August 25: Gratian (◀ 367) is assassinated. Theodosius' older son Arcadius (▶ 395) becomes emperor in the East (▶ 408).

King Ardashir II of Persia (◀ 379) dies and is succeeded by Shapur III (▶ 388), son of Shapur II (◀ 379).

Ulfilas (◀ *c*.311) dies.

Spanish troops proclaim a Spaniard, Maximus (▶ 386), emperor in Spain. He takes over the Western provinces (▶ 388).

A certain Dalmatios founds the first monastery in Constantinople.

Jerome (◀ *c*.345, ▶ 386) begins his translation of the Greek Bible into Latin (Vulgate) (▶ *c*.404).

c.383

Melania the Younger is born. She sells her possessions in Rome and with her husband travels to North Africa, Jerusalem and Egypt, finally founding a community of women in Palestine of which she is the head. Dies 439.

51

384

🜨 December 11: Pope Damasus (◀ 366) dies. He is subsequently venerated as a saint: feast day December 11.

⚜ December: Pope Siricius (▶ 399) is elected, the first pope to issue official decrees (decretals).

Pagan senators, who represent a powerful minority, vote for the restoration of the Altar of Victory (◀ 382) to the Senate House in Rome, but are resisted by Ambrose (◀ 381, ▶ 390) and Theodosius I (◀ 382, ▶ 385).

385

May 25: Theodosius I issues a further decree forbidding divination using pagan sacrifices (◀ 381, ▶ 391).

Christians destroy the great pagan temple of Edessa in Upper Mesopotamia.

386

🕆 March 18: Cyril of Jerusalem (◀ c.315) dies.

🕆 Maximus (◀ 383, ▶ 387) puts Priscillian, Bishop of Avila (◀ 381, ▶ 388), on trial for sorcery; he is found guilty and becomes the first Christian to be executed by Christians.

Jerome (◀ 383, ▶ 392) settles in a monastery in Bethlehem.

387

Maximus invades Italy.

King Shapur III of Persia (◀ 383, ▶ 388) signs a peace treaty with Emperor Theodosius I.

388

Theodosius I defeats Maximus. He returns the Western provinces to Valentinian II (◀ 380) but appoints his own man, Arbogast, as adviser. The fall of Maximus helps Priscillianism (◀ 386) to flourish, and it continues down to the sixth century,

👑 King Shapur III of Persia is killed by the nobility which has brought him to power and is succeeded by Bahram IV (▶ 399). Around this time Armenia is divided up between Persia and Rome.

c.388

Shenoute becomes Abbot of the White Monastery, around 50 miles downstream from Nag Hammadi (▶ 1945/46) in Egypt. The community is said to comprise around 4000 monks and nuns and is very strictly ruled.

390

🕆 Simeon Stylites is born. He becomes a hermit and spends his life on top of a pillar. Dies 459.

🕆 Apollinarius of Laodicea (◀ c.310) dies.

Bishop Ambrose of Milan (◀ c.384, ▶ 397) forces Emperor Theodosius I to perform public penance for massacring 7000 rebels in Thessalonica.

c.390

✤ Patrick (▶ 432) is born in Britain; he is captured by pirates at the age of 16 and spends six years in Ireland. He makes his way back to Britain, and after training for the ministry returns to Ireland as bishop for the rest of his life. Dies 460.

☩ Gregory of Nazianzus (◀ c.330) dies. He is subsequently venerated as a saint: feast day January 30 in the East, January 2 in the West.

Bishop Theophilus of Alexandria (▶ 391) compiles tables for calculating the date of Easter.

391

February 24: Theodosius I issues a decree prohibiting sacrifices and visits to temples (◀ 385, ▶ 392).

Monks under the direction of Bishop Theophilus of Alexandria (◀ c.390) destroy the temple of Alexandria and the great library there.

392

♛ May 15: Valentinian II (◀ 375) dies.

♛ August: Arbogast (◀ 388) proclaims Eugenius (▶ 394), a pagan rhetoric teacher, Emperor in the West.

November 8: Theodosius I once again prohibits the worship of pagan gods (◀ 391).

The monk Aterbius of Sceta comes to Jerusalem and accuses Jerome (◀ 386, ▶ c.392) and Rufinus (◀ 345) of disseminating the erroneous teachings of Origen (◀ c.254, ▶ 393), not least excessive allegorization and the final redemption of the whole creation.

c.392

Jerome produces a revised Latin translation of the Psalter based on the Greek, which because of its great popularity in Gaul comes to be called the Gallican Psalter. It becomes the Vulgate Psalter and is the basis of Gregorian chant.

393

♛ January 23: Theodosius I's younger son Honorius is proclaimed co-emperor (▶ 399).

✤ Theodoret of Cyrrhus, theologian and bishop, is born. He is a friend and supporter of Nestorius (▶ 428). Dies 466.

As a result of the accusations of Aterbius of Sceta (◀ 392), Jerome turns violently against the works of Origen, whom he had formerly praised.

394

September 6: Theodosius I defeats the forces supporting Eugenius (◀ 392) at the river Frigidus on the eastern border of Italy.

A synod in Carthage upholds prayers for the dead and purgatory.

In Jerusalem, Epiphanius of Salamis (◀ c.315, ▶ 403) preaches vigorously against supposed errors of Origen (Origenism) (◀ 392, ▶ 400).

395

♛ January 17: Theodosius I (◀ 379) dies. He is the last emperor to rule both halves of the empire. Honorius (◀ 393, ▶ 396) becomes sole ruler of the West.

August 7: Arcadius (◀ 383, ▶ 396) and Honorius reiterate Theodosius I's ban on pagan worship (◀ 392, ▶ 399).

📖 Rufinus translates Eusebius' *Church History* (◀ 324) into Latin.

Augustine (◀ 354, ▶ 397/98) is consecrated Bishop of Hippo.

*c.***395**

✟ Gregory of Nyssa (◀ c.335) dies. He is subsequently venerated as a saint: feast day March 9.

396

December 7: Arcadius and Honorius (◀ 395) abolish existing privileges for pagan priests.

A visit to Britain by Martin of Tours (◀ 371) inspires the British church.

397

✟ April 4: Ambrose (◀ c.339) dies. He is subsequently venerated as a saint: feast day December 7.

August 28: A synod in Carthage issues an official list of the books of the Bible (canon) (◀ 382).

☧ September 27: Nectarius, Patriarch of Constantinople (◀ 381), dies.

✟ November 8: Martin of Tours (◀ c.315) dies. He is subsequently venerated as a saint: feast day November 12 in the East, November 11 in the West.

✟ November 8: Pope Siricius (◀ 384, ▶ 399) sends Ninian, a Cumbrian who has travelled to Rome, to convert the Picts. Ninian establishes a base at Whithorn in Galloway, Scotland, and builds a church there. After his death he is venerated as a saint: feast day August 26.

397/98

📖 Augustine (◀ 393, ▶ 414) writes his *Confessions*.

398

☧ February 26: John Chrysostom (◀ 381–84, ▶ 401) becomes Patriarch of Constantinople.

♟ Didymus the Blind (◀ 313) dies.

▮ The church of Santa Pudenziana in Rome is built, containing the earliest extant mosaics on Christian themes.

399

July 10: Arcadius (◀ 396, ▶ 402) and Honorius (◀ 396, ▶ 405) order the destruction of pagan temples in the countryside (◀ 395, ▶ 407).

⚱ November 26: Pope Siricius (◀ 384) dies.

⚱ November 27: Pope Anastasius I (▶ 401) is elected.

♛ King Bahram IV of Persia (◀ 388) is assassinated and is succeeded by Yazdgird I (▶ 421).

400

Origen's (◀ 394, ▶ 543) works are condemned at a synod called by Pope Anastasius I.

Paulinus of Nola (◀ c.353, ▶ 431) is said to have introduced bells in churches.

♦📖 Sozomen, church historian, is born in Palestine. He writes two histories, one (which is lost) covering the period from the ascension of Jesus to 323, the other the period from 323 to 425. Dies c.450.

Fifth century

The fifth century sees the end of the Roman empire in the West under an onslaught of Germanic tribes from outside its eastern frontier. The Visigoths, the Ostrogoths, the Huns, the Vandals, the Alani and the Burgundians move in and carve out their own territories. In 410 Rome is sacked by the Visigoths and in 455 it is captured by the Vandals. In 476 the last Roman emperor, Romulus Augustulus, is deposed. Ravenna to the north is to become the new seat of government, first for the Romans and then for the Ostrogoths; to the West, towards the end of century, the rise of Clovis, King of the Franks, signals a new (and catholic Christian) power. There are also threats to the East, where Roman emperors continue to rule: in 487 Constantinople comes under siege from the Ostrogoths.

Christianity continues to develop outside the empire. In the West, while the Roman legions withdraw from Britain, opening the way to arrivals of new peoples from Europe, Ireland receives its first bishop and in the East, amid regular persecutions, Christianity thrives in Persia. Here, as in the Roman empire, it is shaped by a combination of theological factors and the personal intervention of the ruler.

In doctrine, the focus moves from the Trinity, where it has been since the Arianism of the previous century, to the person of Jesus Christ: how can he be both fully God and fully man, as salvation requires? By now two different schools have formed: in Antioch, theologians so emphasize the human nature of Jesus alongside his divine nature that the unity of his person is threatened; in Alexandria, there is so much stress on the divinity of Jesus that there is a risk that his human nature will be lost altogether. There is a clash between two church leaders on the issue: Nestorius, Patriarch of Constantinople, who follows the Antiochene school, and Cyril, Bishop of Alexandria, who has greater power at his disposal with which to advocate his position. After much church–political infighting, Cyril seems to gain the upper hand, but once again the intervention of the emperor, in this case Marcian, leads to another council, held at Chalcedon outside Constantinople in 451. Not least thanks to an important contribution by Pope Leo I from the West, the council produces a definition which is presented as the solution to the problem, but it fails to meet with general acceptance and leads to major differences between churches.

The Alexandrian church, followed by the Armenian church and the Syrian-rite church later called 'Jacobite', feels that the Chalcedonian Definition concedes too much to Nestorius and his adherents and moves in the direction of Monophysitism; the Assyrian Church of the East and the Oriental Orthodox churches continue to be Nestorian in their doctrines. The alternation between Monophysitism and Chalcedonian Christianity continues for many years.

Another controversy arises in the West. Here Augustine of Hippo is a towering figure, with his view that individuals are powerless to overcome sin and are dependent upon God's grace alone. His views are opposed by Pelagius, a theologian from Britain, who insists that human beings can play a part in gaining their own salvation. How far Pelagianism represents Pelagius' own views is a matter of dispute, but Pelagianism spreads widely and attracts a considerable following.

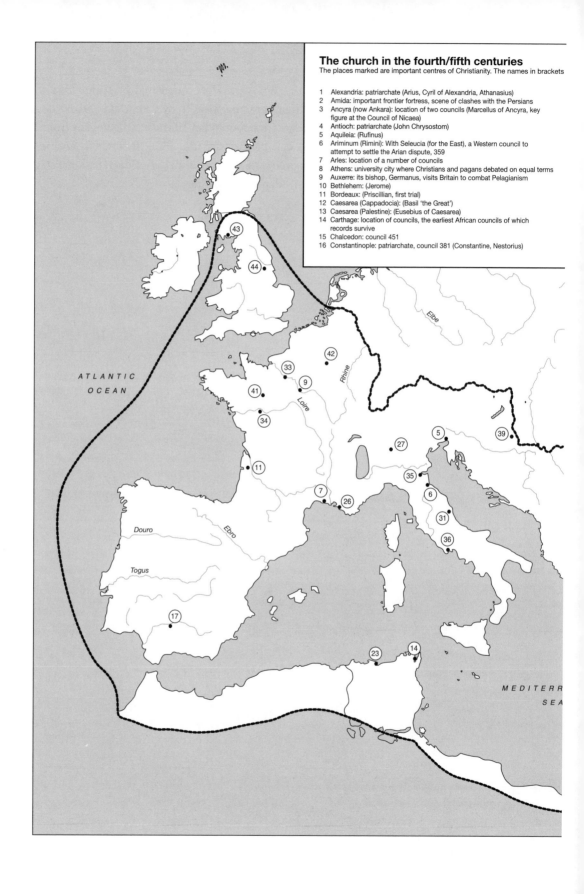

The church in the fourth/fifth centuries

The places marked are important centres of Christianity. The names in brackets

1   Alexandria: patriarchate (Arius, Cyril of Alexandria, Athanasius)
2   Amida: important frontier fortress, scene of clashes with the Persians
3   Ancyra (now Ankara): location of two councils (Marcellus of Ancyra, key
     figure at the Council of Nicaea)
4   Antioch: patriarchate (John Chrysostom)
5   Aquileia: (Rufinus)
6   Ariminum (Rimini): With Seleucia (for the East), a Western council to
     attempt to settle the Arian dispute, 359
7   Arles: location of a number of councils
8   Athens: university city where Christians and pagans debated on equal terms
9   Auxerre: its bishop, Germanus, visits Britain to combat Pelagianism
10 Bethlehem: (Jerome)
11 Bordeaux: (Priscillian, first trial)
12 Caesarea (Cappadocia): (Basil 'the Great')
13 Caesarea (Palestine): (Eusebius of Caesarea)
14 Carthage: location of councils, the earliest African councils of which
     records survive
15 Chalcedon: council 451
16 Constantinople: patriarchate, council 381 (Constantine, Nestorius)

ATLANTIC
OCEAN

Elbe

Rhine

Loire

Ebro

Douro

Togus

MEDITERR
SEA

are of significant figures associated with these places. The black line indicates the frontier of the Roman empire.

17 Cordoba: (Ossius of Cordoba, adviser to Constantine at the Council of Nicaea)
18 Der Mar Antonios (present-day name): Antony of Egypt
19 Edessa: (Ephrem the Syrian)
20 Ephesus: council 341
21 Gangra: council held against excessive asceticism
22 Adrianopolis: scene of the death in battle of Emperor Valens, 378, attempting to crush a revolt by the Goths
23 Hippo Regius: (Augustine of Hippo)
24 Jerusalem: patriarchate (Cyril of Jerusalem)
25 Laodicea: (Apollinarius)
26 Marseilles: (John Cassian)
27 Milan: (Ambrose)
28 Nazianzus: (Gregory of Nazianzus)
29 Neocaesarea: location of council
30 Nicaea: council 325
31 Nursia: (Benedict of Nursia)
32 Nyssa: (Gregory of Nyssa)
33 Paris: episcopal buildings on the Île de la Cité

34 Poitiers: (Hilary of Poitiers)
35 Ravenna: location of the Roman court in the fifth century
36 Rome: patriarchate (Leo the Great)
37 Serdica: council 343 to determine the orthodoxy of Athanasius
38 Seleucia: with Ariminum (for the West), an Eastern council to attempt to settle the Arian dispute
39 Sirmium: important pro-Arian council
40 Tabennisi: (Pachomius)
41 Tours: (Martin of Tours
42 Trier: (Priscillian, second trial)
43 Whithorn: reputedly the earliest church in Scotland (Ninian)
44 York: scene of death of the Emperor Constantius, 306

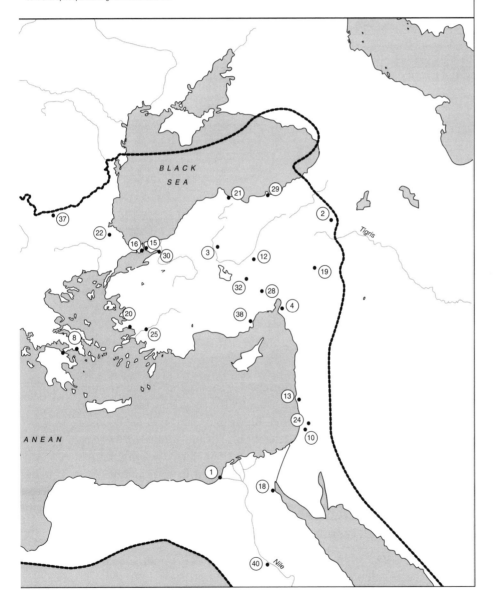

401

⚗ December 19: Pope Anastasius I (◀ 399) dies.

⚗ December 21: Pope Innocent I (▶ 417) is elected. Because he is very active in East and West, not least through letters, he is seen as the first real pope.

The Visigoths (◀ 378) under their king Alaric invade Italy (▶ 410).

As part of a campaign against paganism, Patriarch John Chrysostom (◀ 398, ▶ 403) plunders the remains of the Temple of Artemis at Ephesus, one of the seven wonders of the world.

402

♛ Theodosius II (▶ 407) is made co-emperor with his father Arcadius (◀ 399, ▶ 407).

403

⚗ The Synod of the Oak deposes John Chrysostom (◀ 347) as Patriarch of Constantinople. He has incurred the enmity of the Empress Eudoxia through his attempts at reform.

June 20: John Chrysostom is sent into exile.

June 27: Arsacius, brother of Nectarius (◀ 381), becomes Patriarch of Constantinople (▶ 405).

🌢 Epiphanius (◀ 315) dies.

_c._**404**

Jerome completes the Vulgate (◀ 383).

405

⚗ November 11: Arsacius, Patriarch of Constantinople (◀ 403), dies.

Emperor Honorius (◀ 399) issues an edict commanding the Donatists (see p.37) to return to the catholic church or face the severest penalties.

406

⚗ March: Atticus, a monk born in Armenia, becomes Patriarch of Constantinople (▶ 425).

December: Under pressure from the Huns from present-day Russia, the Vandals (▶ 408), an East Germanic tribe who have adopted Arian Christianity, the Suevi from the Baltic and the Alani, an Iranian nomadic group, cross the frozen Rhine into Gaul. They are opposed by the Romans and the Franks (▶ 481), a confederation of tribes formed in western Germany which after battles with the Romans have become their allies. The Burgundians (▶ 443) also cross the Rhine and settle on the left bank near present-day Strasbourg.

407

☥ September 14: John Chrystostom (◀ 347) dies. He is subsequently venerated as a saint. Feast day November 13 in the East, September 13 in the West.

November 15: Arcadius (◀ 399, ▶ 408), Honorius (◀ 405, ▶ 410) and Theodosius (◀ 402, ▶ 408) order the destruction of pagan statues and altars (◀ 399, ▶ 435).

408

♔ May 1: Emperor Arcadius (◀ 383) dies and Theodosius II (◀ 407, ▶ 414) becomes sole emperor in the East (▶ 450).

The Vandals (◀ 406, ▶ 429) cross the Pyrenees into Spain.

409

King Yazdgird I of Persia (◀ 399, ▶ 421) issues an edict officially ending the attacks on Christians (◀ 339) and allowing them their own organization.

410

August 24: Rome is sacked by the Visigoths under Alaric (◀ 401) and Honorius flees to Ravenna. Pelagius (◀ c.360, ▶ 415) and his disciple Celestius also flee to North Africa, from where Pelagius goes on to Palestine. Their forced departure aids the spread of Pelagianism.

♦ Tyrannius Rufinus (◀ c.345) dies.

The Roman legions are withdrawn from Britain. The way is open for the arrival of Jutes, Angles and Saxons.

The Synod of Isaac, the first council in Persia after the attacks on Christians there, affirms the doctrines of Nicaea and marks the formation of the East Syrian Church. It accepts the primacy of the Bishop of Seleucia-Ctesiphon over the East with the title of Catholicos, on the same footing as the patriarchs of Jerusalem, Antioch, Alexandria and Rome (◀ c.285, ▶ 424).

c.410

♦ Prudentius (◀ c.348) dies.

☉ Honoratus, later Bishop of Arles, founds an abbey on the island of Lérins, off present-day Cannes. It produces many scholars and bishops, notably Vincent (▶ c.450). After his death, Honoratus is venerated as a saint: feast day January 16.

411

At a major council in Carthage, attended by 286 catholic and 279 Donatist (see p.37) bishops, the Roman imperial commissioner Marcellinus rules in favour of the catholics and Donatism is definitively condemned.

Celestius (◀ 410, ▶ 417) arrives in Carthage and applies to Bishop Aurelius for ordination, but is charged with heresy and excommunicated (▶ 417).

Rabbula from Aleppo is appointed Bishop of Edessa. He is a pastor and scholar but also splits the church with his support of Cyril, Bishop of Alexandria (▶ 430).

Episcopal courts are given legal status.

413

Fanatical Christians in Alexandria kill the pagan philosopher Hypatia.

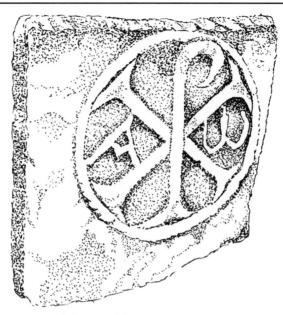

The chi-rho (the first two Greek letters of the name Christ), also known as the labarum, is the sign seen by Constantine in the heavens before his victory at the Milvian Bridge. This later version, from Les Alycamps, Arles, also embraces alpha and omega, the first and last letters of the Greek alphabet, signifying the beginning and the end (Revelation 1.8), *c*.410

414

A fire destroys the church of Hagia Sophia (◀ 360, ▶ 532) in Constantinople. It is rebuilt the next year and dedicated by Emperor Theodosius II (◀ 408, ▶ 431).

Orosius, from Braga in Spain, travels to Africa and is befriended by Augustine of Hippo (◀ 397/98, ▶ 416), who sends him to Jerome (◀ *c*.404) in Palestine to oppose Pelagianism (see p.63).

415

A council held at Diospolis (present-day Lydda) in Palestine acquits Pelagius (◀ 410) of charges of heresy prompted by Jerome and Orosius, who now has to defend himself against such charges.

c.415

John Cassian (◀ *c*.360, ▶ 435) founds two abbeys of St Victor in Marseilles, one for men and one for women.

416

A council in Milevis, attended by Augustine of Hippo (◀ 414, ▶ 422) and prompted by the return of Orosius from Palestine, condemns Pelagianism (see p.63). Because Pelagius has many supporters, the council appeals to Pope Innocent I (◀ 401, ▶ 417).

A letter from Pope Innocent I to the Bishop of Gubbio indicates that the eucharist is not to be celebrated on Good Friday.

417

January: Pope Innocent I accepts the case against Pelagianism.

☯ March 12: Pope Innocent I (◀ 401) dies.

☯ March 18: Pope Zosimus (▶ 418), a Greek, is elected.

September: At an examination in Rome presided over by Pope Zosimus, Celestius (◀ 411) establishes that his faith is satisfactory.

⛨ Constantius (▶ 421), a successful general, marries Emperor Honorius' half-sister Galla Placidia, who gives her name to a beautiful mausoleum in Ravenna (▶ 450).

📖 Orosius (◀ 416) writes a *History against the Pagans* which, like Augustine's *City of God*, rejects the charge that the troubles suffered by Rome stem from its rejection of the ancient gods.

418

April 30: An edict of Emperor Honorius (◀ 410, ▶ 423) banishes the followers of Pelagius from Rome for disturbing the peace.

May 1: A council of 214 bishops is held at Carthage. Pelagius and his teaching are again condemned and Pope Zosimus accepts the verdict.

☯ December 26: Pope Zosimus (◀ 417) dies.

☯ December 28: Pope Boniface I (▶ 422) is elected.

The Visigoths settle in Aquitaine.

420

☦ September 30: Jerome (◀ *c*.345) dies. He is subsequently venerated as a saint: feast day September 30.

A synod under Mar Yaballaha I seeks to mend a schism in the Persian church between those in the east and those in the west, who hold different doctrinal views.

c.**420**

♣ Pelagius (◀ *c*.360) dies.

> **Pelagianism**
> Pelagianism is the belief that human beings can seek to attain salvation by their own efforts without divine grace, and that human nature is not tainted by original sin. It takes its name from Pelagius (◀ *c*.360), but how far he actually holds the whole range of Pelagian views is disputed. Though banished from Rome, Pelagius is not without his supporters (◀ 415) and there is prolonged controversy before he is finally condemned as a heretic (◀ 418). Pelagius then disappears from view but Pelagianism continues, especially in Britain, despite being condemned again at the Council of Ephesus (▶ 431). In Gaul there is a milder form of it, in which human effort and divine grace co-operate, known as Semipelagianism, supported by John Cassian (◀ *c*.360) and Faustus of Riez (▶ *c*.460).

421

February 8: Constantius (◀ 417) is appointed co-emperor in the West as Constantius III.

♛ September 2: Constantius III dies.

♛ King Yazdgird I of Persia (◀ 409) dies and is succeeded by Bahram V (▶ 438). He reverses his predecessor's policy of toleration of Christians and this leads to a war with Rome.

422

☥ September 4: Pope Boniface I (◀ 418) dies.

☥ September 10: Pope Celestine I (▶ 432) is elected.

A peace treaty is signed between King Bahram V (◀ 421, ▶ 438) of Persia and Rome by which both empires respect both Christianity and Zoroastrianism.

📖 Augustine (◀ 416, ▶ 430) finishes *The City of God* (◀ 354).

423

♛ August 15: Emperor Honorius (◀ 393) dies. From this time on the emperors in the West are of minimal importance.

424

The Synod of Adayeshu held at Markabta in Persia declares that the Catholicos (◀ 410) is equal to any patriarch in East or West.

425

☥ October 10: Atticus, Patriarch of Constantinople (◀ 406), dies.

426

☥ February 28: Sisinnius I becomes Patriarch of Constantinople.

427

☥ December 24: Sisinnius I, Patriarch of Constantinople, dies.

428

☥ April 10: Nestorius (▶ 430), a monk from Antioch and a gifted preacher, is appointed Patriarch of Constantinople (▶ 431). He emphasizes the humanity of Christ and criticizes the term *Theotokos* (Mother of God), as used of the Virgin Mary.

🌿 Theodore of Mopsuestia (◀ 354) dies.

429

The Vandals (◀ 406) cross the Straits of Gibraltar into North Africa.

At the request of Palladius, a British deacon, Pope Celestine I (◀ 422, ▶ 432) sends bishops Germanus of Auxerre and Lupus of Troyes to Britain to combat Pelagianism (see p.63). They are both venerated as saints after their deaths: feast days Germanus July 31 and Lupus July 29.

430

⊕ August 28: Augustine (◀ 354) dies during the siege of Hippo in North Africa by the Vandals (◀ 429, ▶ 439). He is later canonized by public acclamation: feast day August 28.

Cyril, Bishop of Alexandria (▶ 433), writes a long letter to Nestorius emphasizing one, divine, nature in Christ.

> **Monophysitism**
> An authoritative definition issued by the Council of Chalcedon (451) states that the incarnate Christ is one person 'in two natures' (Greek *physis*). However, this definition is rejected by many churches in the East, which follow Cyril of Alexandria (◀ 430) in insisting that there is 'one incarnate nature of the Word' (hence their name Monophysites, Greek for 'one nature'). There are different forms of Monophysitism, some more radical than others, within the church, but in due course a widespread and lasting split between Monophysites and catholics develops over the Chalcedonian Definition, which leads to the foundation of separate churches such as the Syriac Orthodox Church and the Armenian Church. A number of Byzantine emperors, and notably Empress Theodora (▶ 537), are Monophysites who promote their faith, and Monophysite missionaries are sent to Nubia (▶ 543, 580) and Ethiopia. Attempts are regularly made to bring about a reconciliation but these are to no avail. The independent Monophysite churches survive to the present day.

431

⊕ June 22: Paulinus of Nola (◀ *c.*353) dies. He is subsequently venerated as a saint: feast day June 22.

June 22: Convened by Emperor Theodosius II (◀ 414, ▶ 439), the Council of Ephesus excommunicates Patriarch Nestorius for his views on the person of Christ and proclaims Mary *Theotokos*. It is regarded as the third Ecumenical Council.

July 11: Nestorius is deposed.

⚜ October 25: Maximian is appointed Patriarch of Constantinople (▶ 434).

⊕ Palladius from Auxerre in France lands in Wicklow and becomes Ireland's first bishop, but his mission is unsuccessful. After his death he is venerated as a saint: feast day July 7.

432

⚜ July 27: Pope Celestine I (◀ 422) dies.

⚜ July 31: Pope Sixtus III (▶ 440) is elected. He builds the earliest recorded monastery in Rome on the Appian Way.

*c.***432**

Patrick (◀ *c.*390, ▶ 445) arrives in Ireland.

■ The church of Santa Maria Maggiore in Rome is restored after a fire and decorated with a cycle of mosaics, including the first depiction of the Virgin Mary, enthroned with her child and martyrs.

65

433

Cyril, Bishop of Alexandria (◀ 430, ▶ 444), and John, Bishop of Antioch, sign a Formula of Reunion expressing agreement on christology.

434

☩ April 12: Maximian, Patriarch of Constantinople (◀ 431), dies. He is succeeded by Proclus (▶ 446), a disciple of John Chrystostom (◀ 407).

The translation of the Bible into Armenian is completed.

435

☉ John Cassian (◀ c.360) dies. He is subsequently venerated as a saint: feast day July 23.

Theodosius (◀ 431, ▶ 449) and Western emperor Valentinian once again forbid pagan worship (◀ 407).

438

♛ King Bahram V of Persia (◀ 421) dies and is succeeded by Yazdgird II (▶ 457). Yazdgird attacks the Eastern Roman empire; suspicious of the loyalty of Christians in the army he expels them and renews hostility to Christianity. He also tries to tie Armenia more closely to his empire by rooting out Christianity and replacing it with Zoroastrianism.

439

October 19: The Vandals (◀ 430, ▶ 442) capture Carthage.

☉ Melania the Younger (◀ c.383) dies. She is later venerated as a saint: feast day June 8.

At the Synod of Riez the term confirmation is recorded for the first time to denote a rite following baptism.

An old Armenian lectionary reconstructed from ancient manuscripts indicates practices in the Jerusalem church beginning with the eight-day celebration of Epiphany between 417 and 439.

440

♦ February 17: Mesrop Mashtots (◀ 360) dies.

☩ August 19: Pope Sixtus III (◀ 432) dies.

☩ August/September: Pope Leo I (▶ 461), sometimes known as 'the Great', is elected.

♦ Sahak (◀ 337) dies.

442

The Romans make a peace treaty giving the Vandals (◀ 439, ▶ 455) Carthage, proconsular Africa and Numidia.

443

The Burgundians (◀ 406, ▶ 493) settle in the region of present-day Lyons, giving it their name, Burgundy.

444

☉ Cyril, Bishop of Alexandria (◀ 430) dies. He is subsequently venerated as a saint: feast day June 9 in the East, June 27 in the West.

445

The first Irish episcopal see is established at Armagh. Patrick (◀ 432, ▶ c.451) builds a stone church there. This is subsequently destroyed and rebuilt 17 times.

446

☾ July 12: Proclus, Patriarch of Constantinople (◀ 434), dies and is succeeded by Flavian (▶ 449).

447

Huns under Attila threaten the Eastern empire (▶ 451).

448

November: A synod at Constantinople condemns Eutyches, head of a large monastery in Constantinople, for teaching that after the incarnation there is only one, divine, nature in Christ (Monophysitism, see p.65).

Pope Leo I (◀ 440, ▶ 452) sends a letter, known as the 'Tome', to Flavian, Patriarch of Constantinople (◀ 446, ◀ 449), expounding the christology of the Latin church. It is formally endorsed at the Council of Chalcedon (▶ 451).

Thousands of Christians are killed in a massacre at Kirkuk in northern Mesopotamia.

449

August 8: A council at Ephesus summoned by Theodosius II (◀ 435, ▶ 450) and dominated by supporters of Monophysitism reverses the decisions of the 448 Constantinople synod. It is known as the 'Robber Synod'.

☾ August 11: Flavian, Patriarch of Constantinople, dies after maltreatment by the council.

November: Anatolius becomes Patriarch of Constantinople (▶ 458).

Hengist and Horsa, joint rulers of the Jutes, settle and form the beginning of the kingdom of Kent.

450

♛ July 28: Emperor Theodosius II (◀ 408) falls from his horse and dies. He is succeeded by Marcian (▶ 457), who is married to Pulcheria, Theodosius' sister. Marcian is an opponent of Monophysitism (▶ 451).

⌂ The Mausoleum of Galla Placidia (◀ 417) in Ravenna is built.

♣ Socrates (◀ c.380) dies.

♣ Sozomen (◀ 400) dies.

c.450

🜨 Vincent of Lérins (◀ *c.*410) dies. In his *Commonitorium* he lays down the famous Vincentian Canon, that catholic Christianity is 'what has been believed everywhere, always and by all'. He is subsequently venerated as a saint: feast day May 24.

451

May 26: At the battle of Avarayr, Armenian rebels under Vartan Mamikonian, a Christian, fight against the Persian army. They are defeated, and Vartan is killed, but this is regarded as a moral victory.

September 20: Attila the Hun (◀ 447, ▶ 452) invades Gaul with an enormous force but is defeated at the battle of Châlons by an army of Romans and Visigoths under the Roman general Aetius.

October 8: Convened by Emperor Marcian, the Council of Chalcedon, regarded as the fourth Ecumenical Council, produces the classic statement on the person of Christ, the Chalcedonian Definition, that Jesus Christ is truly God and truly man, in two natures unconfusedly, unchangeably, indivisibly, inseparably.

✠ Nestorius, former Patriarch of Constantinople (◀ 431), dies.

c.451

🕯 Brigid of Kildare is born. Inspired by the preaching of Patrick (◀ *c.*432, ▶ *c.*460), she becomes a nun and founds several monasteries, notably the Abbey of Kildare, of which she becomes abbess. Dies *c.*525.

452

Near Mantua, Pope Leo I (◀ 448, ▶ 455) personally confronts Attila the Hun, who is ravaging the north of Italy, and persuades him to withdraw.

455

Rome is captured by the Vandals (◀ 442) under Gaiseric (▶ 476), from their base in North Africa. Leo I persuades Gaiseric to refrain from massacre and from burning buildings.

457

♕ January: Emperor Marcian (◀ 450) dies.

♕ February 7: Emperor Leo I (▶ 474) is crowned in a ceremony which is the first known to involve the Patriarch of Constantinople.

♕ King Yazdgird II of Persia (◀ 438) dies and is succeeded by his son Hormizd III (▶ 459).

Victor of Aquitaine produces new tables for calculating the date of Easter, but these are inadequate (▶ 525).

Barsumas, Bishop of Nisibis in Persia, founds an influential Nestorian (◀ 428) theological school.

68

458

☩ July: Anatolius, Patriarch of Constantinople (◀ 449), dies and is succeeded by Gennadius I (▶ 471).

459

☉ September 2: Simeon Stylites (◀ 390) dies. He is subsequently venerated as a saint: feast day September 1 in the East, January 5 in the West.

♛ King Hormizd III of Persia (◀ 457) is killed by his brother, who becomes king as Peroz I (▶ 484). Peroz allows the spread of Nestorian Christianity (◀ 428) but takes measures against other forms of Christianity.

*c.***460**

☉ March 17: Patrick (◀ *c.*390) dies. He is subsequently venerated as a saint: feast day March 17.

Faustus, a former abbot of Lérins (◀ *c.*420), becomes Bishop of Riez in Provence. He is an outspoken opponent of Pelagianism but differs from Augustine (◀ 430) over the need for human effort in overcoming sin. Because of this he is condemned for Semipelagianism (see p.63).

461

☩ November 10: Pope Leo I (◀ 440) dies.

☩ November 19: Pope Hilarus (▶ 468), a Sardinian, is elected.

463

The monastery of Studios, Constantinople, dedicated to John the Baptist, is consecrated. It becomes famous as a centre of Chalcedonian orthodoxy (◀ 451).

466

♣ Theodoret of Cyrrhus (◀ 393) dies.

*c.***466**

♛ Clovis is born (▶ 481). Dies 511.

468

☉ February 29: Pope Hilarus (◀ 461) dies. He is subsequently venerated as a saint: feast day February 18.

☩ March 3: Pope Simplicius (▶ 483) is elected.

471

☩ November 20: Gennadius I, Patriarch of Constantinople (◀ 458), dies.

472

February: Acacius (▶ 488) becomes Patriarch of Constantinople.

69

474

♛ January 18: Emperor Leo I (◀ 457) dies and is succeeded by Zeno (▶ 491), his teenage son-in-law.

476

♛ Gaiseric (◀ 455), King of the Vandals, dies and is succeeded by his son Huneric (▶ 484).

♛ Odoacer, a barbarian rebel, deposes Romulus Augustulus, the last Roman emperor, and sets himself up as King of Italy (▶ 493).

477

In England, a Saxon group, the South Saxe, under Aelle, settles in the area between Kent and present-day Portsmouth and founds the kingdom of Sussex. Its later history is obscure.

480

🏛 Work begins on the building of Ejmiatsin Cathedral, Armenia.

A group of missionary monks fleeing the Byzantine empire because of their opposition to the Chalcedonian Definition (◀ 451) arrive in Ethiopia. They come to be known as the Nine Saints.

***c.*480**

🌱 Benedict of Nursia (▶ 529) is born. He is known as the father of Western monasticism. Dies 547.

🌱📖 Boethius, Roman scholar, philosopher and theologian, is born. His main work, the *Consolation of Philosophy* (523), a defence of providence, is very influential in the Middle Ages. He is executed in 524.

481

Clovis (◀ *c.*466, ▶ 493) becomes King of the Franks (▶ 496) and embarks on a series of conquests. Eventually he rules all Gaul, from the Pyrenees to the Rhine.

482

Emperor Zeno (◀ 474) issues the Henoticon, a text drafted by Patriarch Acacius of Constantinople (◀ 472, ▶ 484), aimed at securing union between the conflicting Christian parties.

483

☸ March 10: Pope Simplicius (◀ 468) dies.

☸ March 13: Pope Felix III (▶ 492) is elected, the first pope to announce his election to the emperor.

The Vandal king Huneric (◀ 476, ▶ 484) convenes a conference in Carthage to argue out the case for catholicism or Arianism.

70

484

February 23: Huneric (◀ 483) closes the conference in Carthage, which is a fiasco, and commands conversion to Arianism by June 1.

♛ December 22: Huneric dies and is succeeded as King of the Vandals by Gunthamund (▶ 496).

♛ King Peroz I (◀ 459) is killed in battle against the White Huns, who invade Persia. He is succeeded by his brother, Balash (▶ 488), who makes concessions to Christians but does nothing to improve the parlous state of the country.

♟ Brendan the navigator, Abbot of Clonfert (▶ 561), is born. Dies 577 or 583.

Pope Felix III excommunicates Acacius, Patriarch of Constantinople (◀ 482, ▶ 488), for supposedly Arian views. This provokes the Acacian schism, the first division between East and West (▶ 519).

The Treaty of Nvarsak, signed by Vahan Mamikonian, brother of Vartan (◀ 451), grants Christian Armenians freedom of religion.

486

The fourth synod of the churches of the Persian empire at Seleucia-Ctesiphon, convened by the Catholicos Acacius (▶ 497), accepts Nestorian christology.

487

Under their king Theodoric, the Ostrogoths, a powerful Germanic people from around the Black Sea who have adopted Arian Christianity, threaten Constantinople. Emperor Zeno (◀ 482, ▶ 491) encourages Theodoric to invade Italy.

488

☦ November 26: Acacius, Patriarch of Constantinople (◀ 471), dies and is succeeded by Fravitta (▶ 489).

Balash, King of Persia (◀ 484), is deposed and blinded; he is succeeded by his nephew, Kavadh I (◀ 531).

489

☦ Fravitta, Patriarch of Constantinople (◀ 488), dies and is succeeded by Euphemius (▶ 496).

490

🏛 The Church of Simeon Stylites, Kiryat Simyan, in northern Syria, is finished.

491

April 9: Emperor Zeno (◀ 474) dies and is succeeded by Anastasius I (▶ 518), who is a committed Monophysite.

492

☦ March 1: Pope Felix III (◀ 483) dies. Pope Gelasius I (▶ 496) is elected.

The Church of Simeon Stylites, Kiryat Simyan, in northern Syria

493

May 13: At a Roman synod Gelasius I is the first pope to be saluted as vicar of Christ.

After a three-year siege Theodoric (◀ 487, ▶ 497) captures Ravenna and murders Odoacer (◀ 476). Ravenna becomes the capital of the Ostrogothic kingdom of Italy.

Clotilde, daughter of the Burgundian (◀ 443) king Chilperic I, and a catholic Christian, is married to Clovis (◀ 481, ▶ 496).

496

☿ Spring: Euphemius, Patriarch of Constantinople (◀ 489), is exiled.

☿ July: Macedonius II (▶ 511) becomes Patriarch of Constantinople.

☿ November 21: Pope Gelasius I (◀ 492) dies.

☿ November 24: Pope Anastasius II (▶ 498) is elected.

Gunthamund (◀ 484), Vandal king, dies and is succeeded by Thrasamund (▶ 523).

⊕ Under the influence of Clotilde (◀ 493, ▶ 545), Clovis (◀ 493, ▶ 507) is baptized by Remigius (Rémy) and the Franks are converted to catholicism. After his death Remigius is venerated as a saint: feast day January 13.

Narsai, a Christian scholar from Kurdistan, establishes a Persian Christian school in Nisibis. It becomes a centre for the spread of Nestorianism in the Persian church.

The Gelasian Missal, a book of prayers, chants, and instructions for mass, appears.

497

Theodoric (◀ 493, ▶ 526) is recognized by Emperor Anastasius I (◀ 491, ▶ 512) as 'King of the Goths and the Romans'.

Catholicos Acacius (◀ 486) dies and is succeeded by Babai, who convenes the fifth synod of the Church of the East. This firmly repudiates Monophysitism.

Nestorian Christians begin a mission among the White Huns.

498

⚕ November 19: Pope Anastasius II (◀ 496) dies.

⚕ November 22: Pope Symmachus (▶ 514), a Sardinian convert from paganism, is elected.

⚕ November 22: Laurentius (▶ 501) is elected antipope.

***c.*500**

♠📖 An author who adopts the name of Dionysius the Areopagite, said to have been converted by Paul in Athens (Acts 17.34), writes a highly influential body of mystical writings. He makes the first reference to the use of incense in Christian worship.

♠ Jacob Baradaeus is born. A Monophysite monk from Constantinople, he is clandestinely consecrated Bishop of Edessa and spends the rest of his life travelling round as a beggar (hence his epithet) and secretly ordaining clergy for a separate hierarchy. The name 'Jacobite', which is sometimes used for the Syriac Orthodox Church, derives from him. Dies 578.

▮ Striking mosaics are made for the church of Hagios Georgios, Thessaloniki; they are among the relatively few preserved after the Iconoclastic Controversy (▶ 726).

Sixth century

During the century Christianity flourishes in the west of the British Isles. After the withdrawal of the Roman legions in 410, Roman influence has diminished, and formative influences come from the direction of the Irish Sea. Following on from the beginnings made in Ireland by Patrick, Palladius and Brigid of Kildare (dies 525), where the monastery rather than the episcopal diocese is the focal point, Irish monks and pilgrims disseminate their forms of Christianity to Scotland, northern England, Wales and Brittany. Columba, who founds a monastery on the island of Iona, and Aidan, who in the next century becomes a bishop on Lindisfarne, are important figures here. David (c.545), Deiniol (514) and Kentigern (c.550) found monasteries in Wales, and important Irish monasteries are founded by Comgall (555) and Brendan the Navigator (561). Brendan takes his title from an extraordinary pilgrimage in which he engages. Pilgrimage, the journey to an unknown destination where one can be alone with God, explains the location of some remote Christian outposts such as Skellig Michael off the coast of County Derry (588).

At this time there is no such entity as England. Rather, in what will become England seven kingdoms are in the making – Northumbria, Mercia, East Anglia, Wessex, Essex, Kent and Sussex – not all of which attain equal status. They used to be called the heptarchy, and sometimes still are. Founded by pagan immigrants from the European continent, Angles, Saxons and Jutes, they become Christian at different times and in different ways, but the Christianity they adopt is largely Roman. It is brought to Kent by Augustine and 40 monks sent by Pope Gregory I; they are welcomed by King Ethelbert, who is married to Bertha, a Christian princess (597). During the next century there will be a clash between Roman practices and those already existing in the British Isles.

Under Emperor Justinian I the Byzantine empire wins back substantial territory in the West, in Italy, Sicily and North Africa, thanks to victorious campaigns by the general Flavius Belisarius. Ravenna is captured from the Ostrogoths and becomes the seat of Byzantine government in Italy. However, a new force, the Lombards, invades Italy towards the end of the century, and Emperor Maurice has to concede northern Italy to them. The Persians launch an attack on Constantinople, but the threat is for the moment countered with the signing of a peace treaty between King Khosroe II and Emperor Maurice.

The Germanic peoples, early sixth century

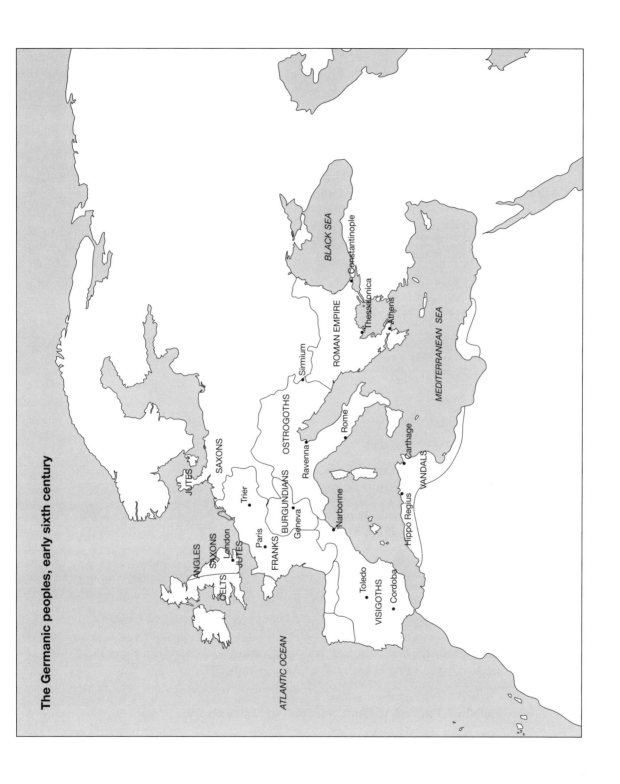

ATLANTIC OCEAN

ANGLES
SAXONS
CELTS
JUTES
London

JUTES
SAXONS

Paris
FRANKS
Trier

Geneva
BURGUNDIANS

Narbonne

Toledo
VISIGOTHS
Cordoba

Hippo Regius
VANDALS
Carthage

Ravenna
OSTROGOTHS
Rome

Sirmium

ROMAN EMPIRE

MEDITERRANEAN SEA

BLACK SEA

Constantinople
Thessalonica
Athens

501 or 506

⊕ Antipope Laurentius (◀ 498) dies.

506

A council in Agde, southern France, presided over by Caesarius of Arles, rules on matters such as clerical celibacy, the appropriate age for ordination and the religious obligations of the faithful. Its rulings shed light on the state of the church at the time.

At the First Council of Dvin (▶ 551) the Armenian Church accepts the Henoticon (◀ 482) and rejects the Chalcedonian Definition (◀ 451).

507

The Franks under Clovis (◀ 496, ▶ 511) defeat the Visigoths at Vouillé, allowing them to control south-west France.

507 or 508

Fulgentius is appointed Bishop of Ruspe in North Africa. Soon afterwards he is banished by Thrasamund (◀ 496), along with 60 other catholic bishops, to Sardinia.

510

Fulgentius (◀ 507 or 508) is recalled to Africa by Thrasamund (◀ 507 or 508, ▶ 523) for doctrinal discussions (▶ 512).

511

⊕ August: Macedonius II, Patriarch of Constantinople (◀ 495), is exiled.

♛ November 27: Clovis (◀ 466) dies.

⊕ Timothy I (▶ 517) becomes Patriarch of Constantinople.

512

Severus (▶ 518), a Monophysite monk, becomes Patriarch of Antioch with the support of Emperor Anastasius I (◀ 497, ▶ 518).

Fulgentius (◀ 510) is banished again (▶ 523).

514

⊕ July 19: Pope Symmachus (◀ 498) dies.

⊕ July 20: Pope Hormisdas, a rich Italian aristocrat, is elected (▶ 523).

⊕ Deiniol, traditionally the first Bishop of Bangor in North Wales, founds an abbey there. He is subsequently venerated as a saint: feast day September 11.

517

⊕ April 5: Timothy I, Patriarch of Constantinople (◀ 511), dies.

⊕ April 17: John II of Cappadocia (▶ 520) becomes Patriarch of Constantinople.

518

♛ July 9: Emperor Anastasius I (◀ 491) dies. He is succeeded by Justin I (▶ 527), a champion of orthodoxy, who deposes Severus as Patriarch of Antioch (◀ 512, ▶ 536). Severus is replaced in Antioch by Patriarch Timothy III and henceforward is regarded as the champion of Monophysitism.

519

The Acacian schism (◀ 484) ends.

♛ A Saxon leader, Cerdic, establishes the kingdom of the West Saexe (Wessex, ▶ 634).

520

☩ January 19: John II of Cappadocia, Patriarch of Constantinople (◀ 517), dies.

☩ February 25: Epiphanius (▶ 535) is appointed Patriarch of Constantinople.

In England the North Folk and the South Folk unite to form the kingdom of the East Engle (East Anglia) (▶ 593).

*c.***521**

♣ Columba is born. From an Irish royal family, he is trained in Irish monasteries and becomes a missionary, founding a community on the island of Iona off the west coast of Scotland (▶ 563). Dies 597.

523

☩ August 6: Pope Hormisdas (◀ 514) dies.

☩ August 13: Pope John I (▶ 526) is elected. He is the first pope to pay a visit to Constantinople.

♛ Thrasamund (◀ 496) dies and is succeeded as King of the Vandals by Hilderic (▶ 530), oldest son of Huneric (◀ 484), who later converts to catholicism.

Fulgentius (◀ 512) returns from exile.

524

♣ Boethius (◀ 480) is executed for treason (▶ 1883).

525

The system of dating by AD is invented by the monk Dionysius Exiguus for his new set of tables for calculating Easter.

The Persian church splits over Monophysitism (◀ 497, ▶ 539).

*c.***525**

✪ Brigid of Kildare (◀ c.451) dies. She is venerated as a saint even during her lifetime. Feast day: February 1.

526

☩ May 18: Pope John I (◀ 523) dies in prison, having been arrested by King Theodoric (▶ 497).

☩ July 12: Pope Felix IV (▶ 530) is elected.

♛ August 30: King Theodoric (◀ 493) dies and is succeeded by Athalric (▶ 534); his monumental mausoleum is built at Ravenna.

526–30

▣ The apse mosaic of Santi Cosma e Damieno in Rome introduces depictions of large figures: alongside Christ are Peter, Paul, Cosmas and Damian and Pope Felix IV.

527

♛ August I: Emperor Justin I (◀ 518) dies and is succeeded by his nephew Justinian (▶ 565), who proclaims his wife Theodora (▶ 543) empress.

⌂ Justinian orders the building of the Monastery of the Transfiguration (St Catherine's Monastery) on Mount Sinai to enclose the Chapel of the Burning Bush, built on the orders of Helena after her visit to the Holy Land (◀ 326).

♛ Aescwine founds the kingdom of Essex (East Saexe or East Saxons), covering a wider territory than the present county (▶ 604).

528

Grod, King of the Huns, is converted to Christianity, but when he melts down pagan images priests kill him.

529

Benedict (◀ *c.*480, ▶ 540) founds Monte Cassino monastery, between Rome and Naples.

A council in Orange condemns Semipelagianism (see p.63).

Justinian closes the Neoplatonic school in Athens.

530

☿ September 22: Pope Felix IV (◀ 526) dies.

☿ September 22: Pope Boniface II (▶ 532) is elected. He is the first Germanic Pope.

☿ September 22: Dioscorus is elected Antipope.

☿ October 22: Antipope Dioscorus dies.

♛ Gelimer, an Arian, supplants Hilderic (◀ 523) as Vandal king because of Hilderic's conversion to catholic Christianity (▶ 533).

Monophysites begin to appoint their own clergy, leading to the existence of two separate churches, Monophysite and Chalcedonian (◀ 451).

c.530

♣ Venantius Fortunatus is born. A Latin Christian poet, educated at Ravenna, he writes such famous hymns as *Pange lingua* ('Sing, my tongue, the glorious battle') and *Vexilla regis* ('The royal banners forward go'). Dies *c.*600.

531

♛ Kavadh I, King of Persia (◀ 488), dies and is succeeded by his son Khosroe I (▶ 579), who initially signs a peace treaty with Rome. He is tolerant of Christianity.

532

☩ October 17: Pope Boniface II (◀ 530) dies.

🏛 The church of Hagia Sophia (◀ 360, 414) in Constantinople is destroyed in riots. It will be rebuilt in great splendour by Emperor Justinian (▶ 537).

533

☩ January 2: Pope John II (▶ 535) is elected.

September 13: After the Battle of Ad Decimum, Flavius Belisarius (▶ 535), Justinian's (◀ 529, ▶ 534) general, recaptures Carthage from the Vandals (◀ 442). Gelimer (◀ 530) flees.

534

♛ King Athalric (◀ 526) dies.

The Byzantine empire

From a point in time over which scholars are not agreed, the East Roman empire comes to be called the Byzantine empire, centred on Byzantium, which began as Constantinople. After the fall of the West Roman empire in 476, this empire varies considerably in extent from period to period. During the reign of Justinian I (◀ 527), the empire wins back substantial parts of the former West Roman empire, including Italy, Sicily and North Africa; it also secures peace on its eastern frontier by a treaty with Persia. However, these gains are forfeited in the next century by hostilities with Persia in which the Sassanian regime advances into Egypt, Syria and Armenia, the Lombards invade northern Italy and the Muslim Arabs begin their inexorable advance. With this constriction of the empire goes reorganization, and the last traces of Roman influence disappear in favour of Greek.

Expansion begins again from the ninth century onwards, when the empire regains control of southern Italy, Greece and the Balkans and expands into Asia. However, from the early eleventh century onwards weak rulers dissipate these gains. The Normans drive the Byzantines from Italy and Sicily and the Seljuk Turks overrun Anatolia, leaving Byzantium with only a strip of land on the Asian coast and Greece and the southern Balkans. In the twelfth century Manuel I Comnenus (▶ 1143) extends Byzantine territory in Asia Minor and the Balkans, makes alliance with the Crusaders and secures some client kingdoms. However, after his death not only is Constantinople sacked by the Crusaders, in 1204, but the Byzantine empire begins an irreversible decline, being almost completely eliminated before the final capture of Constantinople by the Turks in 1453.

It is significant for the history of Christianity that whereas for quite some time Western Europe is characterized by a conflict between the popes, as spiritual rulers, and the secular rulers, in the Byzantine empire there is a 'symphony' between church and state: emperors and patriarchs are closely associated, and, as we have seen, emperors regularly play a part in the affairs of the church.

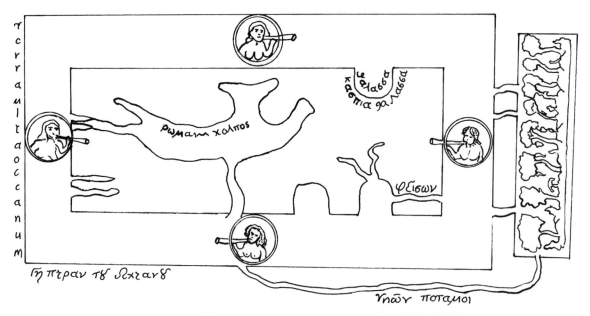

Γῆ πέραντȣ Ω λιανȣ ἀνθ α πρδ τȣ καταχλυσμȣ χατωχουν οἱ ἄνθρωποι

Map of the world by Cosmas Indicopleustes, patterned on the tabernacle in Jerusalem; four rivers of paradise water the earth, c.535

The Law Code of Justinian is promulgated, containing almost 5000 laws and spanning the period from Hadrian (◀ 117) to Justinian.

535

☩ May 8: Pope John II (◀ 533) dies.

☩ May 13: Pope Agapetus I (▶ 536) is elected.

☩ June 5: Epiphanius, Patriarch of Constantinople (◀ 520), dies and is succeeded by Anthimus I, a Monophysite (▶ 536).

August: Catholic Christianity is restored in North Africa.

Belisarius (◀ 533, ▶ 536) invades Italy.

c.535

📖 Cosmas Indicopleustes, Greek sailor turned Nestorian monk and traveller, writes his *Topographica Christiana*. It includes one of the earliest maps of the world, which he claims to be flat.

536

☩ March: Pope Agapetus I (◀ 533) deposes Anthimus I, Patriarch of Constantinople (◀ 535).

80

☯ March 13: Emperor Justinian appoints Menas as Patriarch of Constantinople (▶ 552); Menas is consecrated by Pope Agapetus I. His patriarchate represents the height of Roman influence there.

☯ April 22: Pope Agapetus I (◀ 533) dies.

☯ June 8: Pope Silverius (▶ 537) is elected. He is son of Pope Hormisdas (◀ 514).

August 6: Severus (◀ 518, ▶ 537) is banished from all the cities of the empire.

December 9: Belisarius (◀ 533) enters Rome at the request of the Pope and withstands a long siege from the Ostrogoths.

> **Patriarchs of Constantinople**
> From the sixth century onwards the Patriarch of Constantinople has been known as the Ecumenical Patriarch, i.e. patriarch of the whole inhabited world. In this capacity he is first of all the Orthodox bishops and their primary spokesman, though he has no direct jurisdiction over other patriarchs or independent churches. The patriarchate is traced back to the foundation of Constantinople in 330 CE, and it survives the conquest of Constantinople by the Turks in 1453, lasting down to the present day. The list of Patriarchs of Constantinople from 330 contains 244 names, and it seems important that the succession of Patriarchs of Constantinople should appear in a chronology of Christianity alongside the succession of Popes or Archbishops of Canterbury. However, there are a number of problems here. Because of the close bond between church and state, the patriarchs are often deeply entangled in political situations; some of them resign or are deposed and then reinstated more than once. Under Turkish sovereignty the patriarchate is even awarded to those who paid the largest sum for it. Patriarchs change frequently and often we know no more than the name of a particular patriarch. So while there is a list of all those who have held office, in a number of periods it is hardly significant and tells us little. However, that does not mean that there have been no great patriarchs; one of the greatest of them, Bartholomew I (▶ 1991), has been a key figure for the twentieth-century churches.

537

☯ March: Pope Silverius is deposed by Belisarius.

☯ March: Pope Vigilius (▶ 555) is elected through the work of Belisarius, backed by the Monophysite Empress Theodora.

☯ December 2: Pope Silverius (◀ 536) dies.

🕍 December 27: The Church of Hagia Sophia (◀ 532) in Constantinople is dedicated.

A Nestorian Christian reports many converts and churches on what is now Sri Lanka.

Severus (◀ 536) dies in Egypt, having now authorized the consecration of Monophysite bishops (◀ 530).

538/39

♣ Gregory of Tours (▶ 590), historian of the Franks (◀ 406), is born. Dies 594.

Hagia Sophia, Constantinople, 537

540

Benedict (◀ 529, ▶ 547) composes his Rule, which becomes influential all over Europe.

Khosroe I (◀ 531, ▶ 542) invades Syria and resumes war with the Romans.

Belisarius (◀ 533) captures the Ostrogothic (◀ 493) capital Ravenna, which becomes the seat of Byzantine government in Italy.

542

In a war against Constantinople the Persians under Khosroe I (◀ 540, ▶ 579) sack Antioch and destroy its churches.

543

Emperor Justinian (◀ 536, ▶ 543/44) and Empress Theodora (◀ 527, ▶ 548) send Julian, a Monophysite, to Nubia; he converts the north Nubian state of Nobatia to Christianity.

Justinian publishes a condemnation of Origen (◀ 400, ▶ 553).

543/44

The Three Chapters, an edict of Justinian condemning the supporters of Nestorius, is issued.

544

Mar Aba, Catholicos of the Persian church, holds a synod, the sixth, which reorganizes and reunites the church, extends theological education and founds a new theological school in Seleucia-Ctesiphon.

545

⊕ Clotilde (496), Queen of the Franks, dies. She is subsequently venerated as a saint: feast day June 3.

*c.***545**

The Synod of Brefi is held in Llandewi Brefi in Wales to condemn Pelagianism (see p.63). David, later patron saint of Wales, is said to have attended it.

546

The Ostrogoths under Totila occupy and sack Rome.

547

⊕ March 21: Benedict of Nursia (◀ *c.*480) dies (▶ 1220).

⌂▇ San Vitale, Ravenna, is completed. Some of its mosaics depict the imperial court with Justinian and Theodora.

548

♛ June 28: Empress Theodora (◀ 527) dies.

549

⌂▇ The church of San Apollinare in Classe, Ravenna, with its striking mosaics, is consecrated.

*c.***550**

⊕ Kentigern, a Scottish missionary, founds the monastery of St Asaph in Wales. He is subsequently venerated as a saint: feast day January 13.

Church bells begin to be used in France.

Lent now starts on a Wednesday (Ash Wednesday) rather than on a Sunday.

The crucifix develops as an ornament.

551

At the Second Council of Dvin, Moses, Catholicos of Armenia, corrects the date of Easter in the Armenian calendar. A new cycle begins in 552. The Armenian Church reiterates its rejection of the Chalcedonian Definition (◀ 451).

The Slavs cross the Danube.

552

⚖ August 24: Menas, Patriarch of Constantinople (◀ 536), dies and is succeeded by Eutychius (▶ 582).

The Byzantine general Narses captures Sicily from the Ostrogoths (▶ 831).

553

Emperor Justinian (◀ 543/44, ▶ 565) convenes the Second Council of Constantinople to condemn works favourable to Nestorius (◀ 451) and the writings of Origen (▶ 543). It is regarded as the fifth Ecumenical Council.

554

Cassiodorus, a retired Roman statesman, establishes a monastic community near Naples, Vivarium, where he builds up a large library, commissions the copying of manuscripts and has Greek works translated into Latin.

555

⚓ June 7: Pope Vigilius (◀ 537) dies.

Comgall (▶ 602), a former soldier, founds Bangor Abbey in County Down, Ireland. He is a friend of Brendan the Navigator (◀ 484, ▶ 561).

556

⚓ April 16: Pope Pelagius I (▶ 561) is elected.

560

⚜ Isidore of Seville is born. His textbooks preserve much of ancient learning. Dies 636.

*c.***560**

🏛 A cathedral is consecrated in Angoulême, France (▶ 1017).

561

⚓ March 3: Pope Pelagius I (◀ 556) dies.

⚓ July 17: Pope John III (▶ 574) is elected.

Brendan the Navigator (◀ 484, ▶ 577 or 583) founds a monastery at Clonfert, Ireland.

562

Cassiodorus uses the AD system (◀ 525, ▶ 725) in his *Computus paschalis*, a textbook on how to determine Easter and other dates.

563

Columba (◀ *c.*521) founds a community on the island of Iona off the west coast of Scotland.

The First Council of Braga, in Spain, enacts a number of measures against Priscillianism (◀ 380) and to ensure uniformity of worship. It decrees that at the eucharist the president shall greet the people with 'The Lord be with you' and that they shall reply 'And with thy spirit', a custom brought from the East, and that nothing shall be sung in church but the Psalms and parts of the Old Testament (▶ 572).

A peace treaty is signed between Rome and Persia.

565

✠ January 30: Eutychius, Patriarch of Constantinople (◄ 552, ► 565), is arraigned by Emperor Justinian (◄ 553) and banished.

✠ April 12: John III Scholasticus (► 577) is appointed Patriarch of Constantinople.

♕ November 14: Emperor Justinian (◄ 527) dies and is succeeded by Justin II (► 578).

568

The Lombards, a Germanic tribe from what is now Hungary, under their king Alboin (► 572), invade Italy. Some Lombards are pagans, others are Arians (◄ c.250), leading to a resurgence of Arianism in their territory.

569

The Lombards conquer Milan, the main Roman centre of northern Italy.

The Synod of Victoria is held to reinforce the decrees against Pelagianism issued at the Synod of Brefi (◄ c.545).

*c.***569**

Chaledonian Christians convert Makouria, the central state of Nubia (◄ 543), to Christianity.

*c.***570**

☙ Muhammad, the Prophet and founder of the Muslim community, is born (► c.610). Dies 632.

☙▭ John Climacus is born. A monk on Sinai, his work *The Ladder* (► c.600) presents the achievement of Christian perfection as climbing 30 steps. Dies 649.

571

Emperor Justin II (◄ 565, ► 577) requires all clergy to sign a creed against Monophysitism (◄ 449).

572

♕ Alboin, King of the Lombards (◄ 568), is murdered; he has no immediate successor.

Pavia becomes the capital of the new Lombard kingdom of Italy.

The Second Council of Braga (◄ 563) enacts regulations concerning bishops, forbids the receiving of any fees and rules that any priest celebrating the eucharist without fasting beforehand shall be dismissed (► 675).

573

♕ Leovigild, an Arian, becomes King of the Visigoths and sole ruler of Spain. He establishes Toledo as his capital and builds a basilica there. He appoints Arian bishops.

574

✠ July 13: Pope John III (◄ 561) dies.

575

✠ June 2: Pope Benedict I (► 579) is elected.

85

Islam

The birth of the Prophet Muhammad, recipient of the Qur'an, in Mecca c.570, marks the beginning of the third great monotheistic religion, Islam. In 622, Muhammad and his followers flee to Medina, and this year is taken as the beginning of the Islamic calendar. After Muhammad's death in 632, he is succeeded by four caliphs, Abu Bakr (632–34), 'Umar (634–44), 'Uthman (644–56) and 'Ali (656–61), under whom the Arabs embark on a series of highly successful conquests, extending to the north as far as Asia Minor and to the west right across North Africa, and even across the Straits of Gibraltar into the Iberian peninsula. They capture Cetsiphon, the Persian capital, in 637 and Jerusalem the next year, going on to invade Egypt (641) and large parts of Armenia (645). Under subsequent caliphs of the 'Umayyad dynasty, after seizing Cyprus (649) and Rhodes (654) they move westwards, founding the garrison town of Kairouan (670) near Carthage, and by the end of the seventh century they have virtually eliminated Christianity from North Africa.

In 711 Tariq ibn Zayd leads his troops across the Straits of Gibraltar, and the Moors (as they are called at this stage) conquer the Iberian peninsula, advancing further northwards until their advance is stopped by Charles Martel in 732 at the battle of Tours. They will not be driven back to Africa until 1492, when Granada is finally recaptured by Christians. In the East there are constant clashes with the Byzantine empire, which from the eleventh century is fatally weakened, and Turkish Muslims finally capture Constantinople in 1453, going on to besiege Vienna in 1529 and 1683.

Initially, the many Christians under Muslim rule enjoy friendly relations with Muslims as a 'people of the book' and some come to hold high office; however, as time goes on, Muslim attitudes harden, restrictions are imposed on Christians, and the practice of Christianity becomes more difficult. Islam later spreads south into Africa and to the Far East, where it eventually becomes a vigorous rival of Christianity in the mission field.

577 or 583

Brendan the Navigator (◄ 484) dies. He is subsequently venerated as a saint: feast day May 16.

577

August 31: John III Scholasticus, Patriarch of Constantinople (◄ 565), dies.

October 3: Emperor Justin II (◄ 571, ▶ 578) reinstates Eutychius (◄ 565) as Patriarch of Constantinople (▶ 582).

578

July 30: Jacob Baradaeus (◄ c.500) dies.

October 4: Emperor Justin II (◄ 565) dies and is succeeded by Tiberius II (▶ 582).

Mar Sergis, an East Syrian Christian leader, settles at Lintao in China, the earliest named missionary to that country.

579

July 30: Pope Benedict I (◄ 575) dies.

November 26: Pope Pelagius II (▶ 590) is elected.

King Khosroe I of Persia (◀ 531) dies and is succeeded by Hormizd IV (▶ 590), whose refusal to take measures against Christians earns him many enemies.

580

Longinus, Monophysite Bishop of Philae, south of Aswan, converts the southern Nubian state of Alwa to Monophysite Christianity.

c.580

Maximus Confessor, Greek theologian and ascetic, is born. Dies 662.

582

April 5: Eutychius, Patriarch of Constantinople (◀ 552), dies.

April 11: John IV Nesteutes ('the Faster', ▶ 588) is appointed Patriarch of Constantinople (▶ 595).

August 14: Emperor Tiberius II (◀ 578) dies and is succeeded by Maurice (▶ 602), who has been crowned the previous day. Maurice has some success in reorganizing imperial administration.

584

In an attempt to hold the remaining Byzantine territories in Italy, Maurice groups them in a new administrative structure centred on Ravenna (◀ 540, ▶ 751).

c.585

Columbanus (▶ 615), a monk from Bangor in Ireland (◀ 555), goes to Gaul and with twelve companions establishes a monastery at Luxeuil in the Vosges.

Creoda (▶ 593), the earliest known King of Mercia, in the English Midlands, comes to power.

586

The Rabbula Gospels are produced by the monk Rabbula in Mesopotamia, written in Syriac and illuminated.

587

The Visigoths of Spain convert to catholicism under King Recared (▶ 589).

588

John IV Nesteutes (◀ 582, ▶ 595), Patriarch of Constantinople, is the first to use the title 'Ecumenical Patriarch', which is objected to by the West.

A monastery of stone 'beehive' huts is built at Skellig Michael, a remote island off the coast of present-day County Derry, Ireland.

589

May 4: The conversion of the Visigoths of Spain under King Recared is proclaimed at the Third Council of Toledo. The Council issues decrees against Arians and Jews. It directs that the creed of Constantinople (◀ 381) shall be recited at the eucharist, but with the addition of the word *filioque* ('and from the Son'), which proves to be a lasting bone of contention between the Western and Eastern churches.

Under Theodolinda (▶ 590), the Catholic Christian wife of King Authari, the Lombards convert to Nicene (◀ 325) Christianity.

590

☸ February 7: Pope Pelagius II (◀ 579) dies.

☸ September 3: Pope Gregory I (▶ 604) is elected. Called 'the Great', he is the first monk to be pope.

♛ September 5: Authari, King of the Lombards (◀ 589), dies and is succeeded by Agiluf, who also marries Theodolinda (◀ 589).

♛ King Hormizd IV of Persia (◀ 579) is deposed by the general Bahram Chobin, blinded and later killed. Bahram reigns as King Bahram VI for a brief period (▶ 591).

Gregory of Tours (◀ 538/39, ▶ 594) mentions glass (▶ *c*.628) in church windows.

c.590

Amandus, monk and missionary to Flanders (▶ 628), is born in the Loire valley. Dies *c*.675.

591

♛ Khosroe II (▶ 602), son of Hormizd IV, is made King of Persia by his father's opponents, with the help of Emperor Maurice of Constantinople (◀ 584, ▶ 598), and signs a peace treaty (▶ 628).

593

♛ Creoda, King of Mercia (◀ *c*.585), is succeeded by his son Pybba (▶ 606).

♛ Redwald (▶ *c*.600) becomes King of East Anglia (◀ 520).

594

☥ Gregory of Tours (◀ 538/9) dies. He is subsequently venerated as a saint: feast day November 17.

595

☸ September 2: John IV Nesteutes (◀ 582), Patriarch of Constantinople, dies and is succeeded by Cyriacus (▶ 606), who causes tension with Pope Gregory I by insisting on continuing to use the title Ecumenical Patriarch (◀ 588).

596

Pope Gregory I (◀ 590, ▶ 600) sends Augustine (▶ 597) and 40 monks to convert the Anglo-Saxons.

597

Augustine arrives in Thanet. He sends an envoy to Ethelbert (▶ 604), King of Kent, the most powerful Anglo-Saxon king of his day, married to Bertha, a Christian Frankish princess.

Ethelbert visits Augustine and invites him and his followers to settle in Canterbury, giving him a church which had been a place of worship during the Roman occupation of Britain (present-day St Martin's Church). Canterbury is the first of the English dioceses. Ethelbert is converted to Christianity. This is the first datable event in the history of Kent. After her death Bertha is venerated as a saint.

June 9: Columba (◀ *c.*521) dies. He is subsequently venerated as a saint: feast day June 9.

Autumn: Augustine is consecrated Bishop of the English in Arles.

598

Maurice (◀ 591, ▶ 602) cedes northern Italy to King Agiluf of the Lombards (◀ 590).

*c.***598**

Augustine establishes a monastery east of Canterbury dedicated to St Peter and St Paul. There is to be constant hostility between the monks and the chapter of Canterbury Cathedral (▶ 613).

600

Pope Gregory I (◀ 596, ▶ 601) founds the *Schola Cantorum* in Rome, the predecessor of cathedral choir schools.

*c.***600**

Venantius Fortunatus (◀ *c.*530) dies. He is subsequently venerated as a saint: feast day December 14.

Redwald, King of East Anglia (◀ 593, ▶ 616), becomes a Christian, but has difficulty in persuading his people to follow him.

A manuscript of this date contains the Verona or Leonine Sacramentary (a liturgical book containing those parts of the rites read by the celebrant), the earliest known to us (*c.*750).

Seventh century

This century sees the rise of Islam. The new monotheistic faith, whose Prophet is Muhammad from Mecca, the recipient of the revelations which form the Qur'an, literally dates its origin from 622, when Muhammad and his followers move from Mecca to Medina. After Muhammad's death in 632, the caliphs who succeed him embark on wars of expansion which prove immensely successful. By 638 the Arabs have occupied Syria and captured Jerusalem; in 641 they invade Egypt and in 645 Armenia; they capture Cyprus in 649 and Rhodes in 654 and in 670 found the garrison town of Kairouan, near Carthage in North Africa. By the end of the century they have overrun North Africa, and the thriving Christianity there has been virtually eliminated. However, in the former Byzantine territories of Palestine, Egypt and Syria many Christians welcome Muslim rule as a relief from state oppression and the constant warring between their different theological groupings. Administrators are needed for the new Muslim territories, and former imperial officials are often best suited to the work.

The century begins well for the Byzantine empire, when Emperor Heraclius regains a good deal of lost territory and defeats the Persians in a war which has broken out despite the peace treaty signed in the previous century; however, the empire not only loses its gains in Asia Minor but also suffers further attacks from the Lombards in northern Italy, leaving it with little more than a toehold in the south, along with cities such as Venice and Naples. More territory has to be ceded after an invasion of the Balkans by the Bulgars, and for four years an Arab fleet blockades Constantinople. The empire is fighting for its survival.

Christianity spreads through the kingdoms of England with the conversion of rulers, the establishment of dioceses and the building of churches and cathedrals. Kings Saebert of Essex (604), Edwin of Northumbria (627) and Cynegils of Wessex (635) are among the first to be converted to Christianity. Bishop Mellitus, who came over with Augustine of Canterbury, builds the first St Paul's Cathedral (604) and Justus builds Rochester Cathedral the same year; King Oswald of Northumbria builds a first stone church in York (637) and King Cenwalh dedicates a minster church in Winchester (648). Benedict Biscop founds monasteries at Wearmouth (674) and Jarrow (682), and King Oswy of Northumbria an abbey at Whitby (655), of which Hilda is abbess (657). The Synod of Whitby in 664 is a key event, taking British Christianity close to Roman traditions, not least because of the efforts of Wilfrid, Bishop of York, and in 672 the Council of Hertford reorganizes the church into smaller and more manageable dioceses under the leadership of the Archbishop of Canterbury, Theodore of Tarsus. From England at the end of the century missionaries go out who are instrumental in the conversion of Germany, notably Willibrord and Boniface.

90

601

Pope Gregory I (◀ 590) sends a second group of missionaries including Honorius (▶ 627), Justus (▶ 604), Mellitus (▶ 604) and Paulinus (▶ 619) to strengthen the mission of Augustine (◀ 598, ▶ 602), who is given authority over the bishops in England as archbishop.

*c.***601**

☩ David, Welsh monk, dies. He is responsible for founding the monastery in Pembrokeshire which bears his name, is subsequently venerated as a saint and becomes the patron saint of Wales: feast day March 1.

602

Augustine (◀ 597) meets with the Welsh bishops near Chepstow and accuses them of acting contrary to church teachings, neither baptizing nor keeping Easter according to the Roman rite. They reject his views, and again in 604.

🏛 Augustine begins the construction of a stone-built abbey church at Canterbury, which later becomes a cathedral.

👑 November: Emperor Maurice (◀ 582) is murdered, having been overthrown by Phocas (▶ 610), who as emperor recognizes the primacy of the Pope in matters of religion, but persecutes Monophysites and Jews. King Khosroe II (◀ 591, ▶ 611) takes the opportunity to plunder Syria and Asia Minor.

Comgall (◀ 555) dies (▶ 1951).

603

The Lombards (◀ 568) are converted to catholicism.

604

☩ March 23: Pope Gregory I (◀ 590) dies. He is subsequently canonized by popular acclaim: feast day September 3.

Augustine of Canterbury (◀ 597) consecrates Mellitus (◀ 601, ▶ 616) Bishop of London. Mellitus builds the first St Paul's Cathedral, probably of wood (▶ 675).

☩ May 26: Augustine dies and is succeeded by Laurence (▶ 619), one of the missionaries who came to England with him, and whom Augustine has chosen during his lifetime. Augustine is subsequently canonized by popular acclaim: feast day May 27.

⚖ September 13: Pope Sabinianus (▶ 606) is elected.

The Diocese of Rochester is established with Justus (◀ 601) as its first bishop.

🏛 The building of Rochester Cathedral is begun.

King Ethelfrith of Bernicia, north of the River Tees, conquers Deira (the equivalent of present-day Yorkshire) and unites the two kingdoms as Northumbria (▶ 616).

King Saebert of Essex (◀ 527) is converted to Christianity (▶ 616).

91

Pope Sabinianus is said to have sanctioned the use of church bells (◄ 400), and a church bell is attested in Rome.

606

⚓ September 22: Pope Sabinianus (◄ 604) dies.

⚓ October 29: Cyriacus, Patriarch of Constantinople (◄ 595), dies.

♛ Pybba, King of Mercia (◄ 593), is succeeded by Cearl (► c.626), of the same family.

607

⚓ January 23: Thomas I (► 610) is appointed Patriarch of Constantinople.

⚓ February 19: Pope Boniface III is elected.

⚓ November 12: Pope Boniface III dies.

608

⚓ September 15: Pope Boniface IV (► 615) is elected.

609

May 13: The celebration of a Feast of All Saints is mentioned for the first time.

🏛 The Pantheon in Rome is consecrated as Santa Maria Rotonda.

610

⚓ March 10: Thomas I, Patriarch of Constantinople (◄ 607), dies.

⚓ April 18: Sergius I (► 638) is appointed Patriarch of Constantinople.

♛ October 5: Heraclius (► 641), son of the Roman governor of Africa, has Phocas (◄ 602) executed and becomes emperor.

Pretzels are said to have been invented by an Italian monk as a reward for children who say their prayers. The name comes from the Italian *bracchioli*, the pretzel representing arms folded in prayer.

c.610

The Prophet Muhammad (◄ c.570, ► 613) receives his first revelation.

611

The forces of Emperor Khosroe II of Persia (◄ 591) capture Antioch from the Byzantines and go on to capture Damascus.

613

🏛 The abbey church in Canterbury (◄ 602) is completed and dedicated to St Peter and St Paul.

Sisebar, Arian Visigothic King of Hispania, decrees that Jews must either convert to Christianity or be expelled.

Muhammad (◄ c.610, ► 622) begins his public preaching.

614

The forces of King Khosroe II of Persia (◀ 611, ▶ 627) invade Palestine, looting and plundering; they carry off the 'true cross' (◀ 326, ▶ 629). Only the church of St Helena in Bethlehem is spared.

615

Columbanus (◀ c.585) founds the monastery of Bobbio in Italy.

⚕ May 8: Pope Boniface IV (◀ 608) dies.

⚕ October 19: Pope Adeodatus I (▶ 618) is elected.

☗ November 21: Columbanus dies. He is subsequently venerated as a saint: feast day November 21.

616

☗ February 24: Ethelbert, King of Kent (◀ 597), dies, leaving a written code of laws, the earliest in any Anglo-Saxon kingdom; among other things they give protection to the church. He is subsequently venerated as a saint: feast day February 25 or 26. He is succeeded by his son Eadbald, who initially renounces his baptism and rejects Christianity (▶ c.635). However, Eadbald is reconverted by Archbishop Laurence (◀ 604).

Raedwald, King of East Anglia (▶ c.600, ▶ 625), defeats King Ethelfrith of Northumbria in battle and installs Edwin (▶ 627), a prince of Deira (◀ 604), as king in his place. For the moment East Anglia becomes the most powerful of the English kingdoms.

Sexred, Saeward and Sexbald, the new Kings of Essex, expel the Christian missionaries (◀ 604) and return to paganism.

618

⚕ November 8: Pope Adeodatus (◀ 615) dies.

The Tang dynasty in China begins with Li Yuan, who accedes as Emperor Gaozu. It is to prove favourable for Christianity (▶ 635).

619

☗ February 2: Laurence, Archbishop of Canterbury (◀ 604), dies and is succeeded by Mellitus, Bishop of London (◀ 604, ▶ 624). Laurence is subsequently venerated as a saint: feast day September 13.

⚕ December 23: Pope Boniface V (▶ 625) is elected.

Paulinus (◀ 601, ▶ 625) moves from Canterbury to the court of King Edwin of Northumbria (◀ 616).

622

Easter: Emperor Heraclius I (◀ 610, ▶ 627) leaves Constantinople in a campaign against the Persians, clad as a penitent and bearing an image of the Virgin Mary.

September 20: The Hegirah, the move of Muhammad (◀ c.610, ▶ 628) and his followers

93

from Mecca to Medina, marks the birth of Islam and is the event from which the Muslim calendar is dated.

624

☦ April 24: Mellitus, Archbishop of Canterbury (◀ 619), dies and is succeeded by Justus (◀ 604, ▶ 627). Mellitus is subsequently venerated as a saint: feast day April 24.

Heraclius I has spectacular success in his campaign against the Persians, crossing Asia Minor and Armenia to reach Azerbaijan.

625

☯ October 25: Pope Boniface V (◀ 619) dies.

☯ October 27: Pope Honorius I (▶ 638) is elected. He endorses a letter from Sergius I, Patriarch of Constantinople (◀ 610, ▶ 626), stating that Jesus had only one, divine will and no human will (Monothelitism). He is condemned at the Third Council of Constantinople (▶ 681).

♛ King Raedwald of East Anglia (◀ 616) dies. Thereafter the kingdom of East Anglia declines (▶ 794).

The Diocese of York (▶ 678) is founded by Paulinus (◀ 619).

The Frankish king Dagobert I founds the Abbey of St Denis (◀ 272), near Paris.

626

Constantinople comes under siege from both Slavs and Persians. In the absence of the emperor, Patriarch Sergius I (◀ 625, ▶ 638) plays a major role in the defence and the attacking forces withdraw.

c.626

♛ Cearl, King of Mercia (◀ 606), dies and is succeeded by Penda, who allows Christian missionaries into Mercia (◀ 642).

627

♛ April 12: King Edwin of Northumbria (◀ 616, ▶ 633) is baptized in a wooden church specially built for the occasion in York (traditionally the first York Minster, ▶ 637).

☦ November 10: Justus (◀ 624), Archbishop of Canterbury, dies and is succeeded by Honorius (◀ 601, ▶ 653). Justus is subsequently venerated as a saint: feast day November 10.

Heraclius I (◀ 624, ▶ 629) defeats the Persians at Nineveh and destroys Khosroe II's (◀ 614) palace at Seleucia-Ctesiphon.

628

Amandus (◀ c.590) is consecrated bishop and engages in missionary work in Flanders and Carinthia (▶ 633).

♛ Khosroe II, King of Persia (◀ 590), is murdered. After his death no Persian king rules for long before the empire is conquered by the Arabs (▶ 636).

Muhammad (◀ 622, ▶ 632) rides unopposed back into Mecca.

*c.*628

Benedict Biscop is born (▶ 674). Of a Northumbrian family, he comes with Theodore of Tarsus (▶ 668) to Canterbury as abbot of the monastery there. Dies 690.

629

Having successfully negotiated for the return of the 'true cross' from the Persians (◀ 614), Heraclius I (◀ 610, 624) restores it to Jerusalem.

630

Bishop Felix from Burgundy, of the Roman tradition, establishes his see at Dunwich in East Anglia; Bishop Fursey of the British tradition is also active there.

⊕ After their deaths, Bishop Felix and Bishop Fursey are venerated as saints: feast days Felix March 8, Fursey January 16.

632

♣ June 7: Muhammad (◀ 570) dies. He is succeeded as leader of the Muslims by Caliph Abu Bakr (▶ 634), who brings rebel Arab tribes into line and begins wars of expansion by moving into Persia and Syria.

Emperor Heraclius I forces Jewish communities in North Africa to be baptized.

633

December 5: The Fourth Council of Toledo, presided over by Isidore of Seville (◀ 560, ▶ 636), rules on disciplinary matters, calls for uniformity of liturgy and enacts stringent measures against baptized Jews who lapse. It contains the first unambiguous reference to the crozier as the bishop's staff; it allows poetic texts to be used in hymns and also forbids clergy to consult magicians.

⊕ King Edwin of Northumbria (◀ 627) is killed at the Battle of Hatfield Chase. He is subsequently venerated as a saint: feast day October 12.

Amandus (◀ 628, ▶ *c.*675) founds two monasteries in Ghent.

634

♛ After a confused period of war with Cadwallon, King of Gwynedd, Oswald (▶ 637), son of Ethelfrith (◀ 616), becomes King of Northumbria. He re-establishes Christianity by appointing Aidan (▶ *c.*635), a monk from Iona, to engage in mission.

♣ Wilfrid (▶ 664), a Benedictine and later Bishop of York, is born. He is instrumental in bringing England closer to Rome and replacing prevailing British usages with Roman ones. Dies 709.

Pope Honorius I (◀ 625, ▶ 638) launches a mission to found a church in Wessex without reference to the Archbishop of Canterbury. He sends Birinus, who is consecrated bishop.

Caliph Abu Bakr (◀ 632) dies. He is succeeded by Caliph 'Umar (▶ 644), who presides over a vast expansion of the Islamic empire. Dies 644.

635

Bishop Birinus (◀ 634, ▶ 643) founds an abbey at Dorchester-on-Thames. He baptizes King Cynegils of Wessex there and Wessex is converted to Christianity. This is the first certain event in its history. After his death, Birinus is venerated as a saint: feast day December 3.

The Arabs capture Damascus.

The Nestorian Christian monk Alopen, from Persia, arrives in Xi'an, the Tang capital of China, in a period of religious toleration (◀ 618, ▶ 698). He translates parts of the Bible into Chinese. A number of churches are founded.

c.635

Aidan (◀ 634, ▶ 651) settles on Lindisfarne and is consecrated bishop.

Eabald, King of Kent, builds the first nunnery in England in Folkestone, for his daughter Eanswith and her nuns.

636

April 4: Isidore of Seville (◀ 560) dies (▶ 1598).

August 20: At the Battle of the Yarmuk River the Arabs defeat a Byzantine army led by Heraclius I (◀ 632, ▶ 638).

Churches are built at Glastonbury, St Albans and Winchester.

At the Battle of al-Qadissiyah the Arabs defeat the Persians.

c.636

Cuthbert (▶ 685) is born. He becomes a monk and later Prior at Melrose, Scotland, and is later consecrated Bishop of Lindisfarne. But he spends much of his life as a hermit on a remote Farne Island. Dies 687.

637

King Oswald of Northumbria (◀ 634, ▶ 642) completes a stone church in York to enclose the original wooden church (◀ 627, ▶ 669). After his death, Oswald is venerated as a saint: feast day August 5.

The Arabs capture the Persian capital, Ctesiphon.

638

October 12: Pope Honorius I (◀ 625) dies.

December 9: Sergius I, Patriarch of Constantinople (◀ 610), dies and is succeeded by Pyrrhus I (▶ 641).

Heraclius I (◀ 636, ▶ 641) issues a document, the *Ecthesis*, stating that Jesus has only one divine will (Monothelitism).

The Arabs capture Jerusalem.

639

♦ Aldhelm, later Abbot of Malmesbury and Bishop of Sherborne, is born. He is one of the leading Anglo-Saxon churchmen. Dies 709.

640

♛ January 20: King Eadbald of Kent (◀ 616) dies. He is succeeded by his son Eorcenberth (▶ 664), said to be the first king in England to order the destruction of pagan idols and the observance of Lent (▶ 664).

☉ May 28: Pope Severinus is elected.

☉ August 2: Pope Severinus dies.

☉ December 24: Pope John IV (▶ 642) is elected.

641

♛ February 11: Heraclius I (◀ 610) dies.

♛ September: Constans II Pogonatus (▶ 668) becomes emperor at the age of eleven; the senate of Constantinople acts as regent.

☉ September: Pyrrhus I, Patriarch of Constantinople (◀ 638), is deposed and is succeeded by Paul II (▶ 653).

The Arabs invade Egypt and establish the garrison town of Fustat (near present-day Cairo),

642

☉ October 12: Pope John IV (◀ 640) dies.

☉ November 24: Pope Theodore I (▶ 649), a Greek born in Jerusalem, is elected.

♛ The Mercians under King Penda (◀ c.626, ▶ 655) defeat the Northumbrians at the Battle of Maserfield (present-day Oswestry). King Oswald (◀ 634) is killed. He is succeeded by his brother Oswy (▶ 655).

After a siege the Byzantines hand over Alexandria peacefully to the Arabs, who go on to capture Cyrenaica.

643

November 18: The Arabs capture Tripoli.

♛ King Cynegils of Wessex (◀ 635) dies and is succeeded by Cenwalh (▶ 674), who has been baptized while in East Anglia. He encourages Birinus to build many churches in his kingdom.

644

November 7: Caliph 'Umar (◀ 634) dies. He is succeeded by Caliph 'Uthman (▶ 656), who is responsible for creating the basic authoritative text of the Qur'an.

645

The Arabs conquer large parts of Armenia, though some still remain within Byzantine control.

646

King Cenwalh, son of King Cynegils of Wessex (◀ 635), is baptized in East Anglia.

648

♛ Constans II Pogonatus (◀ 641) issues the *Typos*, which prohibits any discussion of the number of wills in Christ.

⊓ King Cenwalh (◀ 646, ▶ 674) dedicates a minster church in Winchester to St Peter.

649

☦ May 14: Pope Theodore I (◀ 642) dies.

☦ July 5: Pope Martin I (▶ 653, 655) is elected. He holds a synod in the Lateran that condemns Monothelitism (◀ 625) and the *Typos* (◀ 648).

⊓ Catholicos Narses ('the builder') begins to build the Cathedral of St George in Zvartnots, Armenia.

♦ John Climacus (◀ *c*.570) dies.

The Arabs capture Cyprus.

651

☉ Aidan (◀ *c*.635) dies. He is subsequently venerated as a saint: feast day August 31.

Cedd, brother of Chad (▶ 669), is consecrated Bishop of the East Saxons (▶ *c*.654).

653

☦ September 30: Honorius, Archbishop of Canterbury (◀ 627), dies.

Pope Martin I (◀ 649) is carried off to Constantinople, put on trial for condemning the *Typos* (◀ 648), and found guilty of treason.

☦ December: Paul II, Patriarch of Constantinople (◀ 641), dies.

654

March 26: Pope Martin I (◀ 653) is exiled to Crimea.

☦ August 10: Pope Eugenius I (▶ 657) is elected while his predecessor is still alive.

☦ Peter (▶ 666) is appointed Patriarch of Constantinople.

The Arabs capture Rhodes.

98

Church of St Cedd, Bradwell-on-Sea, Essex, *c*.654

c.654

The Benedictine Abbey of Jumièges in Normandy is founded by Philibert and becomes an important missionary centre (▶ 841). After his death Philibert is venerated as a saint: feast day August 20.

Bishop Cedd (◀ 651, ▶ 664) builds a church at Bradwell-on-Sea in Essex with stones from the nearby Roman fort of Othona. Still in regular use for worship, it is known now as the chapel of St Peter-on-the-Wall.

655

September 16: Pope Martin I (◀ 654) dies in exile. He is subsequently venerated as a saint: feast day September 20 in the East, April 13 in the West.

Deusdedit is consecrated Archbishop of Canterbury (▶ 664), the first Saxon archbishop.

Oswy, King of Northumbria (◀ 642, ▶ 657), defeats Mercian forces at the Battle of the Winwaed, kills King Penda of Mercia (◀ 642) and becomes the most powerful ruler in Britain. He founds a monastery at Medehamstede (Peterborough) and an abbey at Whitby (▶ 657). Mercia goes into decline (▶ 716).

The Irish text *De mirabilibus sacrae scripturae* shows that its compilers are familiar with all the church fathers.

*c.***655**

♣📖 John of Damascus, Greek theologian, is born. His *Feast of Wisdom* becomes a textbook in the Orthodox Church. Dies *c.*750.

656

June 17: Caliph 'Uthman (◀ 644) is assassinated by rebellious soliders. He is succeeded by Caliph 'Ali (▶ 661), regarded as the last of the 'rightly-guided' caliphs, but the succession is disputed and civil war breaks out.

Diuma, an Irishman, becomes the first Bishop of Mercia.

📖 The final version of the Qur'an (◀ 644) is completed.

657

☯ June 2: Pope Eugenius I (◀ 654) dies.

☯ July 30: Pope Vitalian (▶ 672) is elected.

King Oswy (◀ 651) appoints Hilda, a Northumbrian princess, Abbess of Whitby Abbey in Yorkshire, a monastery for both men and women (▶ 664, *c.*679).

658

♣ Willibrord (▶ 690), apostle to the Frisians (▶ 695), is born in Northumbria. Dies 739.

*c.***660**

Corbie Abbey is founded by monks from Luxeuil (◀ *c.*585). Its scriptorium becomes an important centre for manuscript illumination.

661

Caliph 'Ali (◀ 656) is assassinated.

662

☩ Maximus Confessor (◀ *c.*580) dies. He is subsequently venerated as a saint: feast day August 13.

The Diocese of Winchester is founded.

664

☯ July 14: Deusdedit, Archbishop of Canterbury (◀ 655), dies.

♛ July 14: Eorcenberth, King of Kent (◀ 640), dies. After his death the kingdom goes into decline.

Largely under the influence of Wilfrid (◀ 634, ▶ 655), the Synod of Whitby approves Roman rather than British practices, including the date for Easter. It is attended, among others, by King Oswy (◀ 657, ▶ 670), who accepts the ruling, Hilda (◀ 657) and Cedd (◀ 651), who acts as interpreter.

☩ October 26: Cedd (◀ 651) dies. After his death he is venerated as a saint: feast day October 26.

St Peter's, York, boys' public school, is founded.

665

Wilfrid is consecrated Bishop of York at Compiègne by Frankish bishops because he refuses to be consecrated by the British church. He remains at his monastery in Ripon.

666

☧ Wighard, a Saxon, is appointed Archbishop of Canterbury but while in Rome is cut off from England by the plague and is never consecrated.

☧ October: Peter, Patriarch of Constantinople (◀ 654), dies.

667

☧ April 17: Thomas II (▶ 669) is appointed Patriarch of Constantinople.

668

☧ March 26: Theodore of Tarsus (▶ 678) is appointed Archbishop of Canterbury (▶ 690) by Pope Vitalian (◀ 657, ▶ 672) to reorganize the English church. He is the first archbishop to be recognized by the whole English church.

♛ September 15: Constans II Pogonatus (◀ 641) is murdered and Constantine IV (▶ 685), son of Constans, becomes emperor.

669

☧ Chad, a disciple of Aidan (◀ c.635) and brother of Cedd (◀ 651), becomes Bishop of Lichfield. He dies the next year and is subsequently venerated as a saint: feast day March 2. His shrine in Lichfield becomes a place of pilgrimage (▶ 699).

☧ November 15: Thomas II, Patriarch of Constantinople (◀ 667), dies and is succeeded by John V (▶ 675).

🏛 Wilfrid (◀ 665, ▶ 678) takes office as Bishop of York. He repairs Oswald's church (◀ 637) which has fallen into disrepair (▶ 741) and builds many churches, including a monastery at Hexham.

670

♛ February 15: King Oswy of Northumbria (◀ 642) dies. He is succeeded by his son Egfrid (▶ 685).

The Arabs found the garrison town of Kairouan, near Carthage.

672

☧ January 27: Pope Vitalian (◀ 657) dies.

☧ April 11: Pope Adeodatus II (▶ 676) is elected.

The Council of Hertford, the first all-England synod, is held to reorganize the English church, breaking up the large dioceses.

673

A community of monks and nuns in what is now Ely is founded by Etheldreda (▶ 679).

c.673

✦ The Venerable Bede (▶ 725) is born. A monk at Jarrow in Northumbria (▶ 682), he writes *An Ecclesiastical History of the English People* (▶ 731). Dies 735.

674

♛ Cenwalh, King of Wessex (◀ 643), dies, and a series of short-reigning rulers follow (▶ 685).

Glass is first used in English church windows (◀ *c.628*).

Benedict Biscop (◀ *c.628*, ▶ 682) founds a monastery at Wearmouth.

An Arab fleet that has entered the Bosphorus to attack Constantinople is met with 'Greek fire', a predecessor of the flamethrower. But the siege lasts for four years.

675

☧ August: John V, Patriarch of Constantinople (◀ 669), dies.

☧ September 2: Constantine I becomes Patriarch of Constantinople (▶ 677).

St Paul's Cathedral, London (◀ 604, ▶ 685), is destroyed by fire.

The Third Council of Braga (◀ 572) rules that milk and grapes may not be offered at the eucharist and that the sacred vessels must not be profaned; it repeats the prohibition against receiving fees.

c.675

✦ Wynfrith (later known as Boniface, ▶ *c.700*), missionary, is born in Wessex. Dies 754.

☉ Amandus (◀ *c.590*) dies. He is subsequently venerated as a saint: feast day February 6.

676

☧ June 17: Pope Adeodatus II (◀ 672) dies.

☧ November 2: Pope Donus (▶ 678) is elected.

The Diocese of Hereford is founded by Putta, Bishop of Rochester, whose diocese has been invaded.

677

☧ August 9: Constantine I, Patriarch of Constantinople (◀ 675), dies and is succeeded by Theodore I (▶ 679).

678

☧ April 11: Pope Donus (◀ 676) dies.

☧ June 27: Pope Agatho (▶ 681) is elected.

Theodore of Tarsus, Archbishop of Canterbury (◀ 668), divides the Diocese of York (◀ 625) into three, at which its bishop, Wilfrid (◀ 669, ▶ 680), leaves in protest for Rome. On the way he preaches in Frisia.

679

☦ June 23: Etheldreda (◀ 673) dies (▶ 695). She is subsequently venerated as a saint: feast day June 23.

☦ November: Theodore I, Patriarch of Constantinople (◀ 677, ▶ 687), is deposed and is succeeded by George I (▶ 686).

Adamnan, from an Irish royal family, becomes Abbot of Iona. He writes a life of Columba (◀ c.521) and is active in promoting Roman observances.

*c.***679**

☦ Hilda of Whitby (◀ 657) dies. She is subsequently venerated as a saint: feast day November 17.

680

The Diocese of Worcester is founded by Theodore of Tarsus, Archbishop of Canterbury (◀ 678, ▶ 690).

681

☦ January 10: Pope Agatho (◀ 678) dies.

Emperor Constantine IV (◀ 668, ▶ 685) convenes the Third Council of Constantinople (the First Trullan Council) to deal with Monothelitism (◀ 625, 649). It is regarded as the sixth Ecumenical Council.

After a Bulgar invasion of the Balkans, a treaty signed between the Bulgar Khan Asparukh and Emperor Constantine IV is regarded as the foundation of the state of Bulgaria (▶ 862).

Gloucester Abbey is founded by Osric, under-king of the Hwicce, an Anglo-Saxon people.

Wilfrid (◀ 678) is reinstated in Rome as Bishop of York, but on his return is imprisoned by King Egfrid (◀ 670). He moves to Sussex where he engages in mission, founding Selsey Abbey (▶ 686).

The Arabs occupy Morocco.

682

☦ August 17: Pope Leo II (▶ 683) is elected.

Benedict Biscop (◀ 674, ▶ 690) founds a monastery at Jarrow.

683

☦ July 3: Pope Leo II (◀ 682) dies.

684

☦ June 26: Pope Benedict II (▶ 685) is elected.

John Maron is elected first patriarch of the Maronite church in Lebanon (▶ 1584), which traces its origin to a Christian hermit, Maron, who is a contemporary and friend of John Chystostom (◀ 347).

685

March 26: Cuthbert (◀ c.636) is consecrated Bishop of Lindisfarne.

⚰ May 8: Pope Benedict II (◀ 684) dies.

May 20: The Picts defeat the Northumbrians at the Battle of Dunnichen. The Northumbrian king Egfrid (◀ 670) is killed. He is succeeded by his half-brother, Aldfrith (▶ 704).

⚰ July 23: Pope John V (▶ 686), a Syrian from Antioch, is elected.

♛ September: Constantine IV (◀ 668) dies and is succeeded by Justinian II (▶ 695), who is only sixteen.

♛ Caedwalla becomes King of Wessex. He conquers Sussex and Kent and also invades the Isle of Wight, a pagan kingdom, where he is wounded in battle (▶ 688).

🏛 St Paul's Cathedral (◀ 675, ▶ 961) is rebuilt by Bishop Erkenwald. After his death
✝ Erkenwald is venerated as a saint: feast day April 30.

686

⚰ January: George I, Patriarch of Constantinople (◀ 679), dies.

⚰ August 2: Pope John V (◀ 685) dies.

♛ August 23: Charles Martel (▶ 723), Mayor of the Palace and Duke of the Franks (◀ 481), is born. He extends the Frankish realm and wins a victory over the Arabs at the battle of Tours (▶ 732). Dies 741.

⚰ October 21: Pope Cono (▶ 687) is elected.

Wilfrid (◀ 681, ▶ 702) is reinstated as Bishop of York.

687

✝ March 20: Cuthbert (◀ c.636, ▶ 995) dies. He is subsequently venerated as a saint: feast day March 20.

⚰ September 21: Pope Cono (◀ 686) dies.

⚰ December 15: Pope Sergius I (▶ 701) is elected. He introduces the *Agnus Dei* into the mass.

⚰ December 28: Theodore I, former Patriarch of Constantinople (◀ 677, 679), dies.

688

⚰ Paul III (▶ 693) is elected Patriarch of Constantinople.

♛ King Caedwalla of Wessex (◀ 685) abdicates and goes on a pilgrimage to Rome. He is succeeded by Ine, of the family of Cynegils (◀ 635).

689

The Arabs control what is now Iraq.

690

✞ September 19: Theodore of Tarsus, Archbishop of Canterbury (◀ 668), dies. He is subsequently venerated as a saint: feast day September 19.

✞ Benedict Biscop (◀ c.628) dies. He is subsequently venerated as a saint: feast day January 12.

Willibrord (◀ 658) goes to West Frisia as a missionary with twelve companions (▶ 695).

692

Justinian II (◀ 685) holds the Second Trullan Council in Constantinople to issue disciplinary decrees arising from the two previous councils (◀ 681).

693

☩ June 29: Bertwald (▶ 702), Abbot of Glastonbury, an Anglo-Saxon, is appointed Archbishop of Canterbury (▶ 731).

☩ August 20: Paul III, Patriarch of Constantinople (◀ 688), dies and is succeeded by Callinicus I (▶ 705).

694

The Arabs overrun Armenia.

695

October 17: The body of Etheldreda (◀ 679) is moved from her monastery into a Saxon church in Ely.

♔ In a revolt against Justinian II (◀ 692), Leontius, one of his generals, is proclaimed emperor (▶ 698). He cuts off Justinian's nose (hence the Greek epithet Rhinotmetos subsequently given to him) and banishes him to Crimea (▶ 705).

Willibrord (◀ 690, ▶ 698) is consecrated Archbishop of the Frisians by Pope Sergius.

698

♔ A German army officer in the Byzantine army named Apsimar captures Constantinople, mutilates and imprisons Leontius (◀ 695), and becomes Emperor Tiberius III (▶ 705).

The Arabs conquer Carthage.

Christians in China suffer under Empress Wu Zetian, whose policies aim to benefit Buddhism (◀ 635, ▶ 712).

Willibrord (◀ 695, ▶ c.700) founds a monastery at Echternach in Luxembourg.

699

✞ Guthlac, of the Mercian royal family, settles in an old burial mound at Crowland in the Fens, where he remains as a hermit until his death. He is subsequently venerated as a saint: feast day April 11.

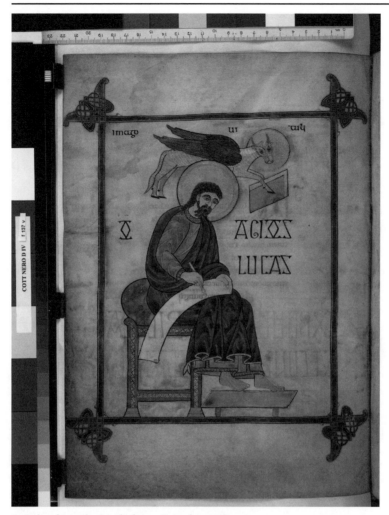

St Luke, from the Lindisfarne Gospels, *c*.700

Bishop Hedda of Lichfield builds a church to house the bones of St Chad (◀ 669).

700

The Arabs control what is now Algeria and virtually eliminate Christianity from North Africa.

c.**700**

Missionary work continues in Germany by Willibrord (◀ 698, ▶ 739) and Wynfrith (◀ *c*.675, ▶ 716).

Eggs are decorated by Christians to celebrate Easter.

▮ The Lindisfarne Gospels, one of the world's greatest illuminated manuscripts, are created.

106

Eighth century

The Arabs continue their triumphant progress, crossing what become known as the Straits of Gibraltar, named in Arabic Jabal (rock of) Tariq after their leader Tariq ibn Zayid, and advancing north through the Iberian peninsula. They capture Barcelona, Narbonne and Bordeaux and sack Poitiers, but their advance is stopped at Tours in 732 by the Frankish leader Charles Martel. They continue to invade the Frankish kingdom until 759, when Charles Martel's son Pepin III recaptures Narbonne and drives them back over the Pyrenees.

The Frankish kingdom flourishes under Pepin III and his son Charlemagne. In 774 Charlemagne defeats the Lombards, who have extended their rule in Italy to include the Duchy of Rome, and becomes their king as well. He also wages a series of long and bloody wars against the Saxons to convert them to Christianity. In 800, at the end of the century, he is crowned emperor: the start of the Holy Roman Empire. In the same year he completes a magnificent chapel in Aachen. During his reign culture flourishes: Alcuin from England develops a programme of education and pioneers a new calligraphy, Einhard writes a notable life of Charlemagne as well as supervising the building of the Aachen chapel and Theodulf makes an important contribution to liturgy and poetry, as well as revising the Vulgate. Missionary work continues in Frisia (present-day the Netherlands) and Germany under Wynfrith, Boniface and Willibrord, extending as far as Bavaria.

The Byzantine Empress Irene attempts a marriage alliance with Charlemagne which, had it succeeded, would have reunited the two halves of the old Roman empire, but quite apart from the obstacle of the difference of cultures, Irene is deposed before anything can come of it. Constantinople, which has lost so much territory, is again besieged by the Arabs during the century, but the century is dominated by a doctrinal matter: in 726, Emperor Leo III proclaims all images and icons to be idolatrous. This marks the beginning of what is known as the Iconoclastic Controversy. Icons, flat pictures of Jesus, the Virgin Mary and the saints, are a prominent element in the prayer and worship of the Eastern churches and are venerated in many ways, so it is not surprising that when the emperor bans them and removes the image of Jesus above the palace gate in Constantinople riots should follow. The controversy rages for more than 50 years, with persecution of those who continue to venerate icons, until in 784 Tarasius, chief secretary to Empress Irene, makes the restoration of icons a condition of his appointment as Patriarch of Constantinople. This is decreed at the Second Council of Nicaea in 787, but is not the end of the story; iconoclasm returns in the next century.

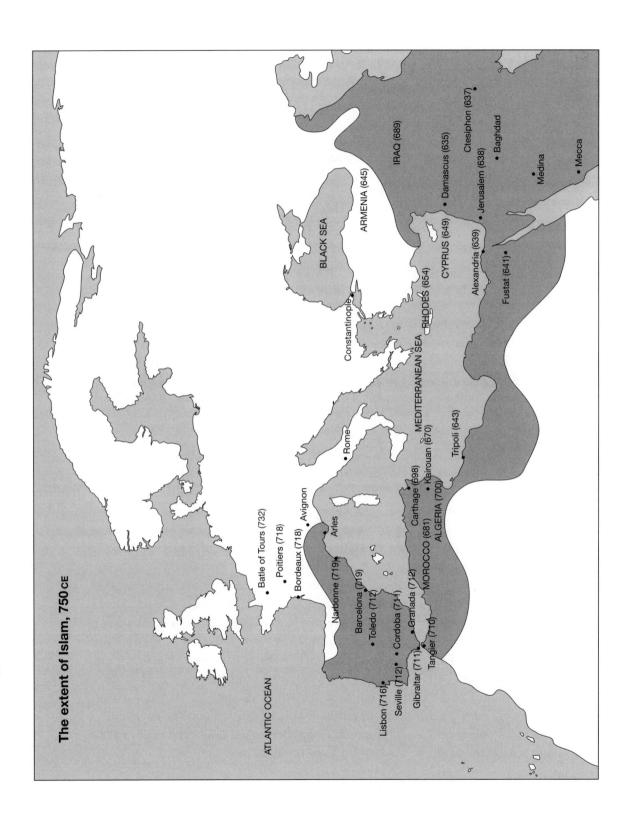

The extent of Islam, 750 CE

ATLANTIC OCEAN

Battle of Tours (732)
Poitiers (718)
Bordeaux (718)
Avignon
Arles
Narbonne (719)
Barcelona (719)
Toledo (712)
Cordoba (711)
Granada (712)
Gibraltar (711)
Seville (712)
Lisbon (716)
Tangier (710)
MOROCCO (681)
ALGERIA (700)
Kairouan (670)
Carthage (698)
Tripoli (643)

Rome

MEDITERRANEAN SEA

BLACK SEA

ARMENIA (645)

Constantinople

RHODES
CYPRUS (649)

IRAQ (689)

Ctesiphon (637)
Baghdad
Damascus (635)
Jerusalem (638)
Alexandria (639)
Fustat (641)

Medina
Mecca

701

✝ September 9: Pope Sergius I (◀ 687) dies.

✝ October 30: Pope John VI (▶ 705), a Greek by birth, is elected.

702

The Council of Easterfield under Bertwald (◀693,▶731) again deposes Wilfrid (◀686,▶709), who again appeals to Rome. He is subsequently made Bishop of Hexham.

704

♛ December 14: Aldfrith, King of Northumbria (◀ 685), dies. From now on the kingdom of Northumbria declines and its rule becomes unstable (▶ 867).

705

✝ January 11: Pope John VI (◀ 701) dies.

✝ March 1: Pope John VII (▶ 707), a Greek by birth, is elected.

✝ Spring: Callinicus I, Patriarch of Constantinople (◀ 693), dies and is succeeded by Cyrus (▶ 712).

♛ Justinian II Rhinotmetos (◀ 695, ▶ 710/11) recaptures Constantinople and again becomes emperor.

✝ Tiberius III (◀ 698) is executed.

The first Wells Cathedral is founded (▶ 1180).

707

✝ October 18: Pope John VII (◀ 705) dies.

708

✝ January 15: Pope Sisinnius, a Syrian by birth, is elected.

✝ February 4: Pope Sisinnius dies.

✝ March 25: Pope Constantine (▶ 715), a Syrian by birth, is elected.

709

♠ Aldhelm (◀ 639) dies (▶ 1606).

✟ Wilfrid (◀ 686) dies. He is subsequently venerated as a saint: feast day October 12.

✟ Mont St Michel is founded in Normandy by Aubert, Bishop of Avranches. Aubert is subsequently venerated as a saint: feast day September 10.

710

The Berber general Tariq ibn Zayid captures Tangier.

710/11

At the request of Emperor Justinian II Rhinotmetos (◀ 705), Pope Constantine (◀ 708) makes a year-long journey to the East, where he receives a royal reception.

109

711

Tariq ibn Zayid leads his troops across the Straits of Gibraltar and lands on the western side of the rock. The rock, in Arabic Jabal (rock of) Tariq, is named after him. He advances to capture Cordoba. From this point the Muslims in Spain are known as Moors (meaning 'dark-skinned').

Justinian II Rhinotmetos sends the patrician Philippicus Bardasanes (▸ 713) to crush a revolt in the Crimea, but Bardasanes joins forces with the rebels, is proclaimed emperor under the name Philippicus, seizes Constantinople and has Justinian and his family killed. He is a Monothelite (◂ 625) and Pope Constantine refuses to recognize him.

712

☮ Cyrus, Patriarch of Constantinople (◂ 705), dies and is succeeded by John VI (▸ 715).

♛ Liutprand (▸ 728) becomes King of the Lombards (◂ 598); he extends Lombard territory to include the duchy of Rome.

The revival of the church in China (◂ 698, ▸ 713) begins under Emperor Xuanzong.

712/13

The Muslim governor of North Africa, Musa ibn Nusayr, and his son capture Toledo, Seville and Granada.

713

♛ June 3: An army coup deposes and blinds Philippicus Bardasanes (◂ 711) and Anastasius II (▸ 715) is chosen as emperor. Anastasius assures Pope Constantine of his orthodoxy.

The Nestorian bishop Zhilie arrives in China (◂ 712, ▸ 744) with an Arab delegation.

715

☮ April 9: Pope Constantine (◂ 708) dies.

☮ May 19: Pope Gregory II (▸ 731) is elected; he proves a resolute opponent of the iconoclasm (▸ 726) enforced in the East.

♛ May: Rebel troops proclaim as emperor, against his will, an obscure tax collector who becomes Theodosius III (▸ 717), and go on to capture Constantinople.

☮ July: Anastasius II (◂ 713) flees and becomes a monk in Thessalonica.

☮ John VI, Patriarch of Constantinople (◂ 712), dies and is succeeded by Germanus I (▸ 730).

716

♛ Ethelbald becomes King of Mercia (◂ 655). He presides over the revival of the kingdom but is reproved by Wynfrith (◂ *c.*700, ▸ 718) for his treatment of the church and its property (▸ 757).

Wynfrith (◀ c.675) makes his first missionary journey to Frisia, but is frustrated by war.

The Moors (◀ 712/13) capture Lisbon.

717

♛ March 25: Theodosius III (◀ 715) abdicates in favour of Leo III the Isaurian (▶ 741) and enters a monastery.

August 15: The Arabs begin a year-long siege of Constantinople.

Cordoba is made the capital of Muslim al-Andalus, Andalucia.

718

Wynfrith (◀ 716, ▶ 725) goes with a group of pilgrims to Rome where Pope Gregory II commissions him to be a missionary east of the Rhine. Pope Gregory changes his name to Boniface.

The Moors capture Bordeaux and pillage Poitiers.

719

The Moors capture Barcelona and Narbonne.

*c.***719**

☉ The monastery of St Gallen in present-day Switzerland is founded on the site of a hermitage occupied by the missionary Gall in the previous century. Gall is subsequently venerated as a saint: feast day October 16.

720

♛ Leo III (◀ 717, ▶ 722) makes his son Constantine (▶ 741) co-emperor.

*c.***720**

🏛 King Ine (▶ 726) of Wessex (◀ 688) builds a stone church at Glastonbury Abbey.

722

Emperor Leo III orders the forcible baptism of Jews and Montanists (◀ c.170).

723

♛ Charles Martel (◀ 686) secures the Frankish kingdom and puts an end to the civil wars that have been waged within it (▶ 732).

725

Boniface (◀ 718, ▶ 739) begins ten years of missionary work in Thuringia. He fells the Oak of Thor at Geismar, a pagan sacred tree, which gains him many converts.

📖 Bede's (◀ c.673, ▶ 731) *De ratione temporum* (On the Reckoning of Time) calculates dates from the birth of Jesus (◀ 525, 562). The AD system is subsequently adopted throughout Western Europe.

The Iconoclastic Controversy
Iconoclasm means the destruction of images and the Iconoclastic Controversy represents a clash over the veneration of icons in the Greek church between 726 and 843. The reasons for the controversy are not easy to assess because we only have the accounts of the victors, the iconodules, those who venerate icons. Contributory factors may have been Monophysitism, which played down the human side of Christ, and the success of Islam, in which images were banned. The course of events is dictated by the leanings of emperors: Leo III (◀ 726) begins the controversy by banning images and removing the image of Jesus above the palace gate in Constantinople. Riots take place leading to the persecution of the iconodules. Veneration of idols is restored at the Second Council of Nicaea in 787 under Empress Irene (▶ 780), but iconoclasm returns in 815 with Leo V the Armenian and his successors. Only under another empress, Theodora, is veneration of idols finally restored in 843.

726

Leo III (◀ 722) declares all images and icons to be idols. This marks the outbreak of the Iconoclastic Controversy. He also promulgates the Ecloga, a revision of Justinian's Code of Civil Law (◀ 534) in a Christian direction.

♛ King Ine of Wessex (◀ c.720) abdicates and goes on a pilgrimage to Rome, where he founds a hospice for English pilgrims. He is succeeded by Ethelheard (▶ 740).

728

Liutprand, King of the Lombards (◀ 712, ▶ 744), meets Pope Gregory II (◀ 718, ▶ 731). In an agreement some hill towns in Latium are given to the papacy.

730

☦ January 17: Germanus I, Patriarch of Constantinople (◀ 715), resigns rather than subscribe to the iconoclastic decree of Leo III (◀ 726, ▶ 731). He is succeeded by Anastasius (▶ 754).

731

☦ January 13: Bertwald, Archbishop of Canterbury (◀ 693), dies.

✛ February 11: Pope Gregory II (◀ 715) dies. He is subsequently venerated as a saint: feast day February 11.

☦ March:18: Pope Gregory III (▶ 741), a Syrian, is elected. He is the last pope to seek a mandate from Byzantium.

☦ June 10: Tatwin, a monk from Mercia, is appointed Archbishop of Canterbury (▶ 734).

November 1: Gregory III holds a synod that rejects iconoclasm and excommunicates anyone who destroys images; by implication this includes Emperor Leo III and the Patriarch of Constantinople.

📖 Bede, *Ecclesiastical History of the English People*, is the first history to date events from the birth of Jesus (◀ 725, ▶ 735).

732

Charles Martel (◀ 723, ▶ 774), leader of the Franks, stops the Moors' advance northwards (◀ 719) at the Battle of Tours in France.

734

☉ July 30: Tatwin, Archbishop of Canterbury (◀ 731), dies. He is subsequently venerated as a saint.

735

☩ Nothelm, Archpriest of St Paul's Cathedral, London, is appointed Archbishop of Canterbury (▶ 739).

The Province of York is created: Egbert is its first archbishop.

♟ Bede (◀ c.673) dies (▶ 1899).

737

The Moors (◀ 732) capture Avignon.

739

☉ October 17: Nothelm, Archbishop of Canterbury (◀ 735), dies. He is subsequently venerated as a saint: feast day October 17.

☉ November 7: Willibrord (◀ 658, 695) dies. He is subsequently venerated as a saint: feast day November 10.

Boniface (◀ 725, ▶ 742) founds the Dioceses of Passau, Regensburg, Freising and Salzburg in Bavaria, paving the way for the incorporation of Bavaria into the Frankish empire.

740

♛ King Ethelheard of Wessex (◀ 726) dies and is succeeded by his relative, Cuthred (▶ 756).

☩ Cuthbert, Bishop of Hereford, is appointed Archbishop of Canterbury (▶ 760).

▦ The oldest extant Western depiction of the crucifixion is placed in Santa Maria Antiqua, Rome.

*c.***740**

♟ Alcuin (▶ 781) is born. Educated in York, he becomes adviser to Charlemagne on religion and education and is the most important figure in the Carolingian Renaissance. Dies 804.

741

♛ June 18: Emperor Leo III (◀ 717) dies and is succeeded by his son Constantine V (◀ 720, ▶ 754), who is also a firm iconoclast. He campaigns successfully against Bulgars and Arabs.

♛ October 22: Charles Martel (◀ 686) dies. He is succeeded by his sons Pepin (▶ c.742) in the West (in Neustria, roughly the present France) and Carloman (▶ 747) in the East (in Austrasia, roughly the present Germany), who become mayors of the palace.

November 28: Pope Gregory III (◀ 731) dies. He is subsequently venerated as a saint: feast day November 28.

December 3: Pope Zacharias (▶ 752), the last Greek pope, is elected.

York Minster (◀ 669) burns down but is rebuilt in splendour.

Work begins on a minster at Erfurt, Germany, on the site of the present cathedral (▶ 1153).

The Diocese of Würzburg is founded.

742

Carloman summons the Concilium Germanicum, the first major synod in the Eastern Frankish kingdom. Boniface (◀ 739, ▶ 754) is appointed head of the Austrasian church.

c.742

Charlemagne (▶ 768), son of Pepin (◀ 741, ▶ 747), is born. As King of the Franks he brings almost all Western Europe together and summons the best minds in the church, chief among them Alcuin (◀ c.740), to be his advisers. Dies 814.

744

Liutprand, King of the Lombards (◀ 712), dies.

Sturm, a disciple of Boniface, founds the Benedictine Abbey of Fulda in Germany for missionary work among the Saxons, on land donated by Carloman.

Bishop Jihe arrives in China (◀ 713, ▶ 781) from Persia with new missionaries.

747

August 15: Carloman (◀ 741) renounces his position and becomes a monk in Rome. He goes on to Monte Cassino (◀ c.480). Pepin (◀ 742, ▶ 751) becomes sole mayor of the palace (▶ 751).

750

Alfonso I, Duke of Cantabria, creates the kingdom of Galicia in the far northwestern corner of Iberia.

c.750

John of Damascus (◀ 655) dies. He is subsequently venerated as a saint: feast day December 4.

Theodulf of Orleans is born. He will make an important contribution to Charlemagne's court over liturgy, poetry and hymns, including the writing of 'All glory, laud and honour'. He also revises the Vulgate (◀ 383). Dies 821.

A manuscript of this date containing the Gelasian Sacramentary (◀ c.600) shows the mix of Roman and Gallican practices characteristic of this period (▶ 786).

751

The Lombards (◀ 568) under King Aistulf (▶ 754) capture Ravenna (◀ 584).

♛ With the support of Pope Zacharias (◀ 752), Pepin III ('the Short', ◀ 747, ▶ 753) is elected King of the Franks and anointed and crowned in Soissons Cathedral.

752

☦ March 15: Pope Zacharias (◀ 741) dies.

☦ March 22: Pope Stephen II is elected.

☦ March 26: Pope Stephen II dies before his consecration. Modern lists do not regard him as a pope and give subsequent Stephens a dual numbering. Only the modern numbering is given after the next entry.

☦ March 26: Pope Stephen II (III) (▶ 757) is elected.

*c.***752**

There is a peal of three bells at St Peter's, Rome.

753

October 14: Pope Stephen II (◀ 752) goes to seek the help of King Pepin III (◀ 751) against the Lombards.

754

☦ January: Anastasius, Patriarch of Constantinople (◀ 730), dies.

April 14: Pepin III (◀ 751, ▶ 754–68) commits himself to defend the Roman church and the papacy and also guarantees as papal possessions the duchy of Rome, Ravenna and its territory, and other areas in northern Italy ('the Donation of Pepin').

☩ June 5: Boniface (◀ *c.*675) is killed in Frisia. He is subsequently venerated as a saint: feast day June 5.

☦ August 8: Constantine II becomes Patriarch of Constantinople (▶ 766).

August: Pepin defeats Aistulf (◀ 751) and makes him promise to hand over the territories promised to the Pope (▶ 756).

A synod at Hieria on the Bosphorus presided over by Constantine V (◀ 741, ▶ 775) endorses the decisions of the iconoclasts.

754–68

Pepin III replaces the Gallican liturgy with the Roman liturgy in Gaul.

755

📖 *On the Triune Nature of God*, an anonymous treatise that is the oldest known Christian work in Arabic, appears.

756

January 1: Aistulf (◀ 754) breaks his promise and besieges Rome.

June: Pepin III invades Italy, defeats Aistulf and secures the papal possessions.

♛ Aistulf dies and is succeeded as King of the Lombards by Desiderius.

115

♛ King Cuthred of Wessex (◀ 740) dies, and after the brief reign of Sigeberth is succeeded by Cynewulf (▶ 786), who loses territory to King Offa of Mercia (▶ 757).

757

⚒ April 26: Pope Stephen II (◀ 752) dies.

⚒ May 29: Pope Paul I (▶ 767) is elected.

♛ King Ethelbald of Mercia (◀ 716) is murdered. After the very brief reign of Beornrad, he is succeeded by Offa, who is the first ruler to be called King of the English and is regarded as one of the strongest Anglo-Saxon kings (▶ 796).

♛ Eadberth, King of Northumbria (◀ 756, ▶ 786), abdicates and enters a monastery in York.

759

♦ Theodore of Studios, Greek monastic reformer, is born. His monastery becomes the centre of monastic life in the East. Dies 826.

King Pepin III (◀ 756, ▶ 768) recaptures Narbonne (◀ 719), ending all Muslim rule north of Iberia.

760

⚒ October 26: Cuthbert, Archbishop of Canterbury (◀ 740), dies.

◼ The Book of Kells, a beautifully illuminated manuscript of the Gospels, is produced.

761

⚒ September 27: Bregwin, a Saxon from the continent of Europe, is appointed Archbishop of Canterbury (▶ 764).

764

⚒ August 24: Bregwin, Archbishop of Canterbury (◀ 761), dies.

765

⚒ February 2: Jaenbert, Abbot of St Augustine's, Canterbury, is appointed Archbishop of Canterbury (▶ 792).

🏛 King Fruela of Asturias builds a basilica dedicated to San Salvador in Oviedo, Spain (▶ 794).

766

⚒ August 30: Constantine II, Patriarch of Constantinople (◀ 754), dies.

⚒ November 16: Nicetas becomes Patriarch of Constantinople (▶ 780).

767

⚒ June 28: Pope Paul I (◀ 757) dies.

⚒ July 5: A nobleman, Duke Toto of Nepi, and his supporters impose Toto's brother Constantine as pope (antipope).

768

✠ July 30: The Lombards invade Rome and seek to impose a pope of their own, Philip, who is immediately rejected.

✠ August 6: Constantine (◀ 767) is deposed, imprisoned in a monastery and blinded.

✠ August 7: Pope Stephen III (▶ 772) is elected.

♛ September 28: Pepin III (◀ 751) dies. The kingdom of the Franks is divided between his sons Charles (later known as Charlemagne, ▶ 771) and Carloman (▶ 771), who receives Austrasia (◀ 741).

769

April 12/13: Constantine (◀ 768) is formally arraigned by Pope Stephen III and sentenced to penance for life in a monastery.

770

♟ Einhard, Frankish historian, is born. He is a member of Charlemagne's palace school at Aachen. Dies 840.

771

♛ Carloman (◀ 768) dies and Charlemagne (◀ 768) becomes sole ruler. He marries Hildegard of Swabia, daughter of Desiderius, King of the Lombards (◀ 756).

772

✠ January 24: Pope Stephen III (◀ 768) dies.

✠ February 1: Pope Hadrian I (▶ 795) is elected.

Charlemagne begins a series of long and bloody wars against the Saxons to the north of his kingdom to convert them to Christianity.

Desiderius (◀ 756) invades Rome; Pope Hadrian I appeals to Charlemagne.

774

April 6: Charlemagne meets with Pope Hadrian I in Rome and formally confirms Pepin's donation of land to the Pope (◀ 754).

June: Charlemagne conquers the Lombard capital Pavia and Desiderius (◀ 756), King of the Lombards, surrenders. Charlemagne makes himself King of the Lombards.

775

♛ September 14: Emperor Constantine V (◀ 741) dies and is succeeded by his son Leo IV (▶ 780). Initially Leo shows moderation to the supporters of icons.

778

Basque forces defeat Charlemagne's army at Roncevalles in the Pyrenees.

780

✠ February 16: Nicetas, Patriarch of Constantinople (◀ 766), dies and is succeeded by Paul IV (▶ 784).

117

♛ September 8: Leo IV (◀ 775) dies and is succeeded by Constantine VI (▶ 797), who is ten years of age, under the guardianship of his mother Irene (▶ 790).

Leo IV (◀ 775) begins a persecution of those who support icons.

781

Charlemagne pays a second visit to Rome and has his three oldest sons crowned kings by Pope Hadrian. He extends the territories granted to the Pope in 774.

Alcuin (◀ c.743) becomes adviser to Charlemagne.

A Nestorian monument is erected in the northern province of Shensi, which records the arrival of Christianity in China (◀ 744, ▶ 842).

782

Charlemagne allegedly executes 4500 Saxons at Verden in Lower Saxony.

784

☩ August 31: Paul IV, Patriarch of Constantinople (◀ 780), dies.

☩ December 25: Tarasius, a layman and chief secretary to Empress Irene (◀ 780), is appointed Patriarch of Constantinople (▶ 806). He makes it a condition of his appointment that icons should be restored.

785

The Saxon leader Widukind is baptized.

Charlemagne issues the Capitulary on Saxony, a document that presents the alternative 'Be baptized or die'.

⌂ The Great Mosque in Cordoba (▶ 1236) is built.

786

August 17: The Second Council of Nicaea is convened to end the Iconoclastic Controversy (◀ 726). It is broken up by mutinous troops. It is regarded in the East as the seventh and last Ecumenical Council; subsequent councils are recognized only by the West (▶ 869).

♛ King Cynewulf of Wessex (◀ 756) is assassinated and replaced with Beorthric (▶ 802), who is supported by Offa, King of Mercia (◀ 757). With Offa, he holds a synod in Chelsea, at which, with the support of Pope Hadrian I (◀ 781, ▶ 795), Lichfield is elevated to an archdiocese to counter the power of Canterbury (▶ 803).

⌂ Charlemagne begins building the Palatine Chapel in Aachen.

The *Sacramentum Hadrianum*, sent by Pope Hadrian I (◀ 772) to Charlemagne, contains liturgical forms to be used in his empire.

787

September: The Second Council of Nicaea (◀ 786) reconvenes. It decrees the restoration of icons and defines what veneration is to be paid to idols.

Charlemagne further expands the papal states (◀ 774).

King Offa of Mercia pays a church tax to papal legates; it comes to be known as Peter's Pence and further payments continue to be made (▶ 1534).

The English missionary Willehad establishes a Christian community in Bremen and is made its bishop. After his death, Willehad is venerated as a saint: feast day November 8.

The Diocese of Bremen is founded (▶ 864).

789

Charlemagne orders the Roman rite to be used throughout his empire and imposes the Benedictine Rule on all monks.

790

The army proclaims Constantine VI sole ruler and has his mother Irene arrested (◀ 780, ▶ 792).

791

Alfonso II becomes King of Asturias; he secures the realm and moves his capital to Oviedo, building churches and a palace there (▶ 794).

792

August 12: Jaenbert, Archbishop of Canterbury (◀ 765), dies.

Constantine VI pardons Irene and accepts her as co-ruler (◀ 790, ▶ 797).

793

June 8: Vikings (who can also be referred to as Danes or Norsemen) sack the monastery of Lindisfarne in a surprise raid, the first of many.

July 21: Ethelhard, Abbot of Louth in Lincolnshire, is consecrated Archbishop of Canterbury (▶ 805) under the influence of King Offa of Mercia.

Alcuin (◀ 781, ▶ 804) becomes Abbot of St Martin of Tours and founds a school of calligraphy.

St Albans Abbey is founded by King Offa of Mercia.

794

May 20: King Offa of Mercia has King Ethelbert of East Anglia killed and takes over the kingdom. Ethelbert's body is buried in a wooden church in Hereford. He is subsequently venerated as a saint: feast day May 20.

The Moors destroy the basilica of San Salvador in Oviedo (◀ 765). It is subsequently restored by King Alfonso II (◀ 791, ▶ 798) and becomes a cathedral (▶ 802).

The Vikings sack Jarrow monastery (◀ 682).

119

795

☨ December 23: Pope Hadrian I (◀ 772) dies.

☨ December 26: Pope Leo III (▶ 816) is elected.

The Vikings sack Iona (▶ 806).

796

♔ July: Offa, King of Mercia (◀ 757) dies. After the brief reign of his son Egfrith, he is succeeded by a kinsman, Coenwulf (▶ 821).

797

♔ August: Irene (◀ 790) has Constantine VI (◀ 780) deposed and blinded for divorcing his wife and marrying his mistress. She then reigns alone as empress.

798

King Alfonso II of Asturias (◀ 794, ▶ 813) captures Lisbon from the Moors.

The Gallarus Oratory, County Kerry, Ireland. Shaped like an upturned boat, this miniature church is on the Dingle Peninsula, c.800

800

December 25: Charlemagne is crowned emperor by Leo III (◂ 795, ▸ 816); this marks the beginning of the Holy Roman Empire.

Charlemagne's chapel at Aachen (◂ 786, ▸ 814) is completed.

Minuscule writing is developed at Charlemagne's court to replace the uncial script which has previously been common.

Propter quam cauſam non con
eoſuocare dicenſ nuntiabo no
meiſ Inmedio eccleſiae laudab

Carolingian minuscule, 800

***c.*800**

The Galarus Oratory, one of the best preserved early Christian churches in Ireland, is built on the Dingle peninsula.

Ninth century

Eastern Europe comes into the picture as a mission field during the century with the evangelization of Moravia by the brothers Cyril and Methodius. Scholars from Constantinople, they are invited by Prince Rastislav to counter the influence of German priests and propagate Christianity in the Slavonic language. To do so they devise the Glagolitic alphabet, a predecessor of Cyrillic, and translate liturgical and biblical texts into Old Church Slavonic. Remarkably, they have the patronage of both the Pope and the Patriarch of Constantinople. The situation is different in Bulgaria, where the conversion of Tsar Boris leads to a competition between Constantinople and Rome for influence. Originally he toys with an alliance with the Franks, but the Byzantines invade Bulgaria and he is forced to sign a peace treaty which stipulates his conversion to Christianity: in 865 he accepts baptism from Photius, Patriarch of Constantinople. When his pagan boyars rebel because of his conversion and he does not find the support from Photius he expects in setting up an independent church, he turns to Pope Nicholas I for help. This move leads to a split between the Pope and the Patriarch of Constantinople which is a prelude to the schism which in the eleventh century will separate the two churches. The Bulgarian church becomes independent after the Fourth Council of Constantinople in 870, but Bulgaria still remains a bone of contention between East and West.

In 845, Viking raiders from Scandinavia destroy Hamburg, forcing the transfer of the comparatively new diocese to Bremen; in 860, Scandinavian Vikings sail down the Bosphorus to Constantinople, plundering monasteries on their way. In England, the Vikings (now referred to as Danes) continue the raids which they began in the previous century. In 850/1 they winter in England for the first time and go on to sack Canterbury Cathedral; they invade East Anglia, capture York and come to control a territory known as the Danelaw, north of a line from London to Chester. They are opposed by King Alfred ('the Great') of Wessex, under whom peace is established between the Danes and the English. King Alfred's great achievement is a legal code reconciling the long-established laws of the Christian kingdoms of Kent, Mercia and Wessex and known as the Book of Dooms. He also promotes church reform and a revival of learning, gathering together a group of scholars from England and Wales and the European continent to translate Latin works into Old English. He does some of the translation himself, including Psalms 1–50 and works by Boethius and Augustine, and founds monastic communities.

801

April 4: Louis the Pious, son of Charlemagne, captures Barcelona from the Moors and makes it the capital of the region.

♠ Anskar is born. A monk of Corbie (◀ c.660) in France, he evangelizes Sweden and Denmark, but the countries revert to paganism after his death. Dies 865.

802

♛ A conspiracy dethrones Empress Irene (◀ 790, ▶ 803) and makes Nicephorus I, her finance minister, emperor (▶ 811).

♛ Beorthric, King of Wessex (◀ 786), dies and is succeeded by Egbert (▶ 825), under whom, after the decline of Mercia under Offa (◀ 796), Wessex becomes the most powerful kingdom in England (▶ 825).

🏛 Oviedo Cathedral in Spain is begun (▶ 1386).

803

♛ August 9: Empress Irene (◀ 780) dies.

October 12: At the Synod of Clofesho the Archdiocese of Lichfield (◀ 787) is reduced to a diocese.

804

♠ May 19: Alcuin (◀ c.740) dies.

Saxony is conquered (◀ 772).

c.804

♠ Gottschalk, monk and heterodox theologian, is born. He puts forward an extreme doctrine of predestination that leaves little for human effort; he is condemned to perpetual imprisonment in 849. Dies c.869.

805

☿ May 12: Ethelhard, Archbishop of Canterbury (◀ 793), dies.

☿ October 18: Wulfred, who has been the first Archdeacon of Canterbury, is appointed Archbishop of Canterbury (▶ 832).

806

☿ February 18: Tarasius, Patriarch of Constantinople (◀ 784), dies.

☿ April 12: Nicephorus is appointed Patriarch of Constantinople (▶ 815).

The Vikings sack the monastery of Iona again (◀ 795).

807

📖 The Book of Armagh, a vellum codex containing texts in Latin relating to Patrick (◀ c.460) together with parts of the New Testament, is written in Ireland by the scribe Ferdomnach.

123

c.810

♣ Johannes Scotus Eriugena is born. An Irish theologian able to read Greek, he is head of the palace school at Laon in France. Dies 877.

811

♛ July 26: Emperor Nicephorus I (◀ 802) is killed in battle with the Bulgars. Michael Rhangabe (▶ 813) becomes emperor. He recognizes Charlemagne's title as Holy Roman Emperor in return for the ceding to Byzantium of Venice and other Adriatic cities.

813

♛ Leo V the Armenian (▶ 820), one of his generals, deposes Michael Rhangabe (◀ 811).

A hermit 'discovers' the grave of St James (Santiago), believed to have brought the gospel to Spain, in Galicia. This leads to the rise of Santiago de Compostela as a great pilgrimage centre. King Alfonso II of Asturias (◀ 798) is said to have been the first pilgrim there (▶ 829).

814

♛ January 28: Charlemagne (◀ 771) dies and is buried in his Palatine Chapel (◀ 800). He is succeeded by his son Louis the Pious (▶ 840), who sees himself as emperor of the Christians and not of a series of ethnic groups.

815

✠ March: Emperor Leo V (◀ 813, ▶ 820) deposes Nicephorus, Patriarch of Constantinople (◀ 806), who is succeeded by Theodotus I Cassiteras (▶ 821).

Leo V convenes a synod which reimposes the decrees of the iconoclast synod of Hieria (◀ 754). This marks the beginning of the Second Iconoclastic Controversy (▶ 843).

c.815

♣ Methodius is born. With his brother Cyril (▶ 826) he is sent to organize the Slav church in Moravia. Dies 885.

816

✠ June 12: Pope Leo III (◀ 795) dies (▶ 1673).

✠ June 22: Pope Stephen IV (▶ 817) is elected.

♛ October: Pope Stephen IV crowns Louis the Pious (◀ 814, ▶ 817) in Reims Cathedral; he also anoints him, the first anointing of an emperor by a pope.

817

✠ January 24: Pope Stephen IV (◀ 816) dies.

✠ January 24: Pope Paschal I (▶ 824) is elected.

♛ Lothair (▶ 823), son of Louis the Pious (◀ 816, ▶ 840), is crowned co-emperor by his father.

818

⌂ The 'old cathedral' in Cologne is completed (▶ 1248).

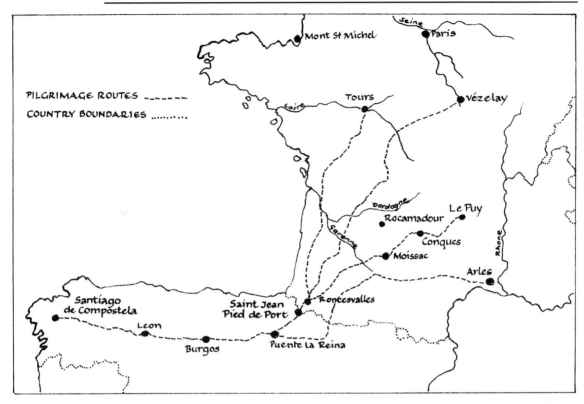

Pilgrimage routes to Santiago de Compostela. The four traditional routes begin in France from Tours, Vézelay, Le Puy and Arles and converge south-west of present-day Pamplona, reaching Santiago de Compostela by the 'Camino Francés'. Other routes came in from various locations in Spain, 813

820

♛ December 25: Emperor Leo V (◀ 813) is assassinated in Hagia Sophia by friends of Michael the Amorian, whom he has just condemned to death. Michael becomes emperor as Michael II (▶ 829). He is a more moderate iconoclast. His son Theophilus (▶ 829) is crowned as co-emperor.

c.820

☩ Photius is born. As Patriarch of Constantinople (▶ 858), he condemns the Roman addition of *filioque* (◀ 589) to the creed and becomes the focal point of a schism. Dies 893.

📖 The *Heliand* epic, an Old Saxon biblical poem that presents Jesus as a liege lord and his disciples as faithful vassals, is written.

821

☩ January: Theodotus I Cassiteras, Patriarch of Constantinople (◀ 815), dies and is succeeded by Antony I (▶ 837).

♛ Coenwulf, King of Mercia (796), dies. Mercia soon afterwards loses its supremacy to Wessex.

♟ Theodulf of Orleans (▶ c.750) dies.

823

♛ On a visit to Rome Lothair (◀ 817, ▶ 824) is recrowned by Pope Paschal I, anointed and presented with a sword as a symbol of temporal power.

824

☩ February 11: Pope Paschal I (◀ 817) dies.

☩ June 5: Pope Eugenius II (▶ 827) is elected.

November 11: With Pope Eugenius' agreement Lothair (◀ 823, ▶ 843) publishes the 'Roman Constitution', which reinforces Frankish control of the papacy: among other things, it grants immunity to all under imperial protection, allows citizens to be judged under Roman, Frankish or Lombard law depending on where they live, and establishes a commission to supervise the papacy and report to the emperor.

At the Battle of Ellandun (in Wiltshire), King Egbert of Wessex (◀ 802) defeats King Beornwulf of Mercia; Kent, Sussex, Essex and East Anglia submit to him (▶ 829).

826

♟ Cyril (▶ 863) is born. With his brother Methodius (◀ c.815) he is sent to organize the Slav church in Moravia. He invents a new alphabet based on Greek minuscules, called Glagolitic. A Slavonic liturgy and Slavonic version of the scriptures is also introduced. Dies 869.

☦ November 11: Theodore of Studios (◀ 759) dies. He is subsequently venerated as a saint: feast day November 11.

827

☩ August 27: Pope Eugenius II (◀ 824) dies.

☩ August: Pope Valentine is elected.

☩ September: Pope Valentine dies.

☩ September: Pope Gregory IV (▶ 844) is elected.

The kingdom of Essex (◀ 527) becomes part of the kingdom of Wessex.

829

♛ October 2: Emperor Michael II (◀ 820) dies and Theophilus (◀ 820, ▶ 842) becomes sole emperor. He has a violently iconoclastic policy and persecutes those who venerate icons.

King Egbert of Wessex (◀ 824, ▶ 839) conquers Mercia and King Eanred of Northumbria accepts him as overlord.

🏛 The first church is built at Santiago de Compostela (◀ 813) on the orders of King Alfonso II of Asturias.

830

Anskar (◀ 801) establishes a church at Birka, near Stockholm.

831

The Diocese of Hamburg is founded, with Anskar (◀ 830, ▶ 847) as its first bishop (▶ 845).

The Arabs capture Palermo in Sicily (◀ 552) and go on to conquer the rest of the island (▶ 902).

831–33

📖 Paschasius Radbertus, *De Corpore et Sanguine Domini* ('On the Body and Blood of the Lord', revised 844), appears, the first doctrinal treatise on the eucharist, stressing the real presence of Christ in the flesh in the eucharist.

832

✠ March 24: Wulfred, Archbishop of Canterbury (◀ 805), dies.

✠ June 9: Feologild, abbot of a monastery in Kent, becomes Archbishop of Canterbury.

✠ August 30: Feologild, Archbishop of Canterbury, dies.

■ The richly illustrated Utrecht Psalter is produced at Reims. Its illustrations include the depiction of an organ.

833

✠ July 27: Ceolnoth, Dean of Canterbury, is appointed Archbishop of Canterbury (▶ 870).

*c.***835**

■ The Vespasian Psalter is produced in southern England. It is written in uncials, beautifully decorated, and contains the book of Psalms, letters of Jerome (◀ *c.*345), hymns and canticles.

837

✠ January: Antony I, Patriarch of Constantinople (◀ 821), dies.

✠ January 21: John VII Grammaticus becomes Patriarch of Constantinople (▶ 843).

839

♛ King Egbert of Wessex (◀ 802) dies and is succeeded by his son Ethelwulf (▶ 855), who is deeply religious.

840

♠ March 14: Einhard (◀ 770) dies.

♛ June 20: Louis the Pious (◀ 814) dies.

841

The Avars, an Eastern European tribe, become Christian after being defeated by the Franks.

127

The Viking leader Thorgist, having conquered Ulster, founds Dublin.

The Abbey of Jumièges (◀ c.654) is destroyed by the Vikings.

842

♛ January 20: Emperor Theophilus (◀ 829) dies and is succeeded by his son Michael III (▶ 867); his widow Theodora becomes regent.

Nestorian monasteries in China (◀ 781, ▶ 907) are closed.

843

✠ March 4: John VII Grammaticus, Patriarch of Constantinople (◀ 836), dies and is succeeded by the monk Methodius (▶ 847).

March 11: On the first Sunday of Lent there is a great celebration of the icons, which are restored to the churches. This is celebrated thereafter as the Feast of Orthodoxy.

♛ In the Treaty of Verdun Charlemagne's three surviving grandsons divide the Holy Roman Empire between them. Lothair (◀ 824, ▶ 850) receives the central portion of the empire, what later becomes the Low Countries, Lorraine, Alsace, Burgundy, Provence and Italy, and is nominally emperor. Louis the German receives much of what later becomes Germany. Charles the Bald (▶ 875) receives much of what later becomes France.

844

✠ January 25: Pope Gregory IV (◀ 827) dies and is succeeded by Pope Sergius II (▶ 847).

845

Viking raiders destroy Hamburg (◀ 831, ▶ 864).

846

Saracen (as the Arabs come to be called in the region) pirates land at the mouth of the Tiber and plunder St Peter's, Rome, which is outside the city walls (▶ 852).

847

✠ January 27: Pope Sergius II (◀ 844) dies.

✠ April 10: Pope Leo IV (▶ 855) is elected.

✠ June 14: Methodius, Patriarch of Constantinople (◀ 843), dies and is succeeded by Ignatius I (▶ 858).

✠ Anskar (◀ 831, ▶ 854) is made Bishop of Bremen.

849

♛ Alfred the Great (▶ 891) is born. He repels the Danes from his kingdom of Wessex and recruits a circle of scholars who translate many Latin Christian works into Old English. He even translates works himself. In his 'Doom Book' he reconciles the laws of the Christian kingdoms of Wessex, Mercia and Kent. Dies 899.

850

♔ Pope Leo IV (◀ 847) crowns Louis II (▶ 855), son of Lothair (◀ 843), Holy Roman Emperor with his father.

*c.***850**

The 'False Decretals' appear, a collection of forged canon law documents defending the rights of bishops against their metropolitans and claiming authority for papal supremacy. They claim to go back to early popes.

The first church is built in Denmark.

850/51

The Vikings (in connection with Britain from now on referred to as Danes) winter for the first time in England.

851

🏛 The Danes sack Canterbury Cathedral (▶ *c.*1020).

852

🏛 June 27: Pope Leo IV dedicates new city walls for Rome, bringing St Peter's within the city.

854

Anskar (◀ 847, ▶ 865) converts Erik, King of Jutland, to Christianity.

855

⚱ July 17: Pope Leo IV (◀ 847) dies.

⚱ September 25: Pope Benedict III (▶ 858) is elected.

♔ September 29: Lothair (◀ 817) dies. Louis II (◀ 850, ▶ 875) is sole emperor. He has to campaign against the Arabs in southern Italy.

King Ethelwulf of Wessex (◀ 839, ▶ 856) goes to Rome where he makes many lavish donations (▶ 858).

♪ The earliest known attempts at polyphonic music appear.

856

♔ King Ethelwulf of Wessex (◀ 855) is forced to abdicate and is succeeded by his oldest son Ethelbald (▶ 860).

858

⚱ April 17: Pope Benedict III (◀ 855) dies.

⚱ April 24: Pope Nicholas I (▶ 867) is elected. He declares that his bishops are not subject to secular rulers.

⚱ October: Emperor Michael III (◀ 842, ▶ 866) deposes Ignatius I, Patriarch of Constantinople (◀ 847, ▶ 863).

129

✠ December 25: Michael III appoints Photius (◀ c.820, ▶ 863), a layman and civil servant, Patriarch of Constantinople.

860

June 18: A fleet of Scandinavian Vikings, who have been active in what is now Russia, sails down the Bosphorus to Constantinople, plundering monasteries on the way.

♔ December 20: King Ethelbald of Wessex (◀ 856) dies and is succeeded by his brother Ethelbert (▶ 866), who is engaged in several battles with the Danes (▶ 871). He is widely regarded as a saint.

862

Boris, King of Bulgaria (◀ 681), seeks support from the Germans against Moravia in exchange for accepting Christianity from the German church (▶ 865).

863

An army from Constantinople invades Bulgaria and Boris capitulates. His loyalties then turn to Constantinople.

Cyril (◀ 826, ▶ 869) and Methodius (◀ 815, ▶ 885) are sent out to Moravia from Constantinople. Later they translate parts of the New Testament into Old Church Slavonic for the court of Prince Rastislav.

Pope Nicholas I, who supports the deposed patriarch Ignatius I (◀ 858, ▶ 867), excommunicates Photius (◀ 858, ▶ 865), leading to a breach between Rome and Constantinople, the Photian Schism.

864

May 31: The Dioceses of Hamburg (◀ 845) and Bremen (◀ 787) are amalgamated.

865

☦ February 3: Anskar (◀ 801) dies. He is canonized by Pope Nicholas I the same year: feast day February 3.

King Boris of Bulgaria (◀ 863, ▶ 866) is baptized by Photius, Patriarch of Constantinople (◀ 859).

The pagan boyars of Bulgaria rebel against King Boris's acceptance of Christianity.

A Danish army invades East Anglia.

866

King Boris puts down the boyar rebellion and turns to the Germans and Pope Nicholas I, who send missionaries to Bulgaria.

♔ Ethelred succeeds Ethelbert (◀ 860) as King of Wessex.

The Danish army (◀ 865) moves north and captures the city of York.

♔ May: Emperor Michael III (◀ 858, ▶ 867) makes his chamberlain Basil the Macedonian (▶ 867) co-emperor.

867

Photius (◀ 865, ▶ 869) denounces the presence of Latin missionaries in Bulgaria as an intrusion on Greek territory. A council in Constantinople excommunicates the Pope.

♛ September 23: Emperor Michael III (◀ 842) is murdered by Basil the Macedonian (◀ 866, ▶ 870), who succeeds him as Basil I.

⚭ September 23: Photius is deposed.

☦ November 13: Pope Nicholas I (◀ 858) dies. He is subsequently venerated as a saint: feast day November 13.

⚭ November 23: Ignatius I (◀ 863, ▶ 877) is reinstated, thus ending the Photian Schism.

⚭ December 14: Pope Hadrian II (▶ 872) is elected.

Northumbria (◀ 704) becomes the northern kingdom of the Danelaw.

869

☦ February 14: Cyril (◀ 826) dies. He is subsequently venerated as a saint in the Orthodox Church: feast day May 11 (▶ 1880).

October 5: The Fourth Council of Constantinople opens. It condemns Patriarch Photius (◀ 867, ▶ 877); it is recognized only by the West as the eighth Ecumenical Council.

*c.***869**

♟ Gottschalk (◀ 804) dies.

870

⚭ February 4: Ceolnoth, Archbishop of Canterbury (◀ 833), dies. He is succeeded by Ethelred, a monk of Canterbury (▶ 888).

March 4: An extraordinary session of the Council of Constantinople is reconvened and decides that the Christianity in Bulgaria (◀ 862) should be from Constantinople.

The Danes destroy Etheldreda's monastery in Ely (◀ 679). They ravage the Fen Country and the population takes refuge in a monastery in Peterborough (◀ 655), but it is destroyed and they are all killed.

☦ November 20: The Danes kill King Edmund of East Anglia and seize his kingdom. He is regarded as a martyr and venerated as a saint, and his shrine at present-day Bury St Edmunds becomes one of the principal places of pilgrimage in England: feast day November 20.

♛ Basil I (◀ 867, ▶ 877) makes his son Leo VI co-emperor (▶ 912).

871

♛ April 23: King Ethelred of Wessex (◀ 866) is killed fighting against the Danes at the Battle of Merton and is succeeded by his brother Alfred (◀ 849, ▶ 886).

131

871/72

Danes capture and occupy London (▶ 886).

872

☦ November: Pope Hadrian II (◀ 867) dies.

☦ December 14: Pope John VIII (▶ 882) is elected.

Alfred buys peace with the Danes (◀ 871). Further battles with varying results take place until 878.

Borivoj I, Duke of Bohemia, and his wife Ludmila, are converted to Christianity.

875

♛ August 12: Louis II (◀ 855) dies.

♛ December 25: Pope John VIII crowns Charles the Bald (◀ 843) Holy Roman Emperor (▶ 877).

877

♛ October 5/6: Holy Roman Emperor Charles the Bald (◀ 875) dies.

☦ October 23: Ignatius, Patriarch of Constantinople (◀ 867), dies and Basil I (◀ 871, ▶ 886) reinstates Photius (◀ 869).

♟ Johannes Scotus Eriugena (◀ 810) dies.

878

At the Peace of Wedmore, England is divided into Wessex in the south and the Danelaw in the north. The Danish leader Guthrum accepts Christianity and is baptized as Ethelstan.

879

♛ Ethelstan (◀ 878) becomes King of East Anglia (▶ c.890).

881

♛ Charles the Fat becomes Holy Roman Emperor as Charles III (▶ 888).

882

☦ December 16: Pope John VIII (◀ 872) dies, the first pope to be assassinated.

☦ December 16: Pope Marinus I (▶ 884) is elected.

884

☦ May 15: Pope Marinus I (◀ 882) dies.

☦ May 17: Pope Hadrian III (▶ 885) is elected.

885

☦ April 6: Methodius (◀ c.815) dies. He is subsequently venerated as a saint in the Orthodox Church: feast day May 11 (▶ 1880).

☦ May 15: Pope Hadrian III (◀ 884) dies.

⚓ September: Pope Stephen V (▶ 891) is elected. He prohibits the Slavonic liturgy and seeks to Germanize the Moravian church.

886

♛ August 29: Basil I (◀ 867) dies and Leo VI (◀ 870, ▶ 907) becomes sole emperor. His Imperial Laws become the law code of the Byzantine empire.

⚓ September 29: Emperor Leo VI deposes Photius, Patriarch of Constantinople (◀ 877, ▶ 893).

⚓ December 18: Stephen I, Leo VI's youngest brother, becomes Patriarch of Constantinople (▶ 893).

Alfred (◀ 871, ▶ 899) recaptures London from the Danes (◀ 871/72) and becomes supreme monarch.

888

♛ January 13: Holy Roman Emperor Charles III (◀ 881) dies and Charlemagne's empire finally disintegrates.

⚓ June 30: Ethelred, Archbishop of Canterbury (◀ 870), dies.

890

⚓ Plegmund, a monk from Mercia, becomes Archbishop of Canterbury (▶ 923).

*c.***890**

♛ Ethelstan (◀ 879) dies.

891

⚓ September 14: Pope Stephen V (◀ 885) dies.

⚓ October 8: Pope Formosus (▶ 896) is elected.

893

⚓ February 6: Photius (◀ 886) dies.

⚓ May 17: Stephen I, Patriarch of Constantinople (◀ 886), dies.

⚓ August: Antony II Kauleas is appointed Patriarch of Constantinople (▶ 901).

896

⚓ April 4: Pope Formosus (◀ 891) dies.

⚓ April: Pope Boniface VI is elected and dies in the same month.

⚓ May: Pope Stephen VI (▶ 897) is elected. He holds a synod in which the exhumed body of Formosus is put on trial, found guilty and thrown in the River Tiber.

897

⚓ August: Pope Stephen VI (◀ 891) is thrown into gaol and strangled.

⚓ August: Pope Romanus is elected.

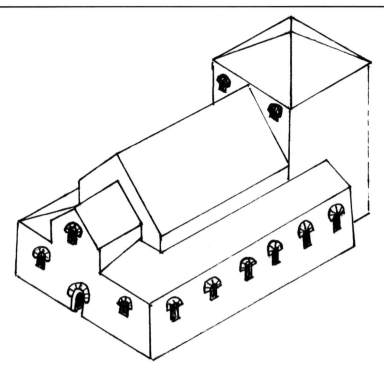

Brixworth church, Northamptonshire, England, in the ninth century

⚓ November: Pope Romanus is deposed. The date of his death is unknown.

⚓ November: Pope Theodore II is elected. He declares the synod with Formosus' corpse (◀ 896) invalid and has the corpse honourably buried.

⚓ November: Pope Theodore II dies.

898

⚓ January: Pope John IX (▶ 900) is elected.

899

♛ October 26: Alfred the Great (◀ 849) dies. He is succeeded by his son Edward the Elder (▶ 924) as King of the English.

🏛 A pre-Romanesque church is built at Santiago de Compostela, leading to its development as a major place of pilgrimage (◀ 829, ▶ 1128).

900

⚓ January: Pope John IX (◀ 898) dies.

⚓ May/June: Pope Benedict IV (▶ 903) is elected.

*c.***900**

♩ From this date, for around six centuries the organ becomes almost exclusively a church instrument.

134

Tenth century

The Abbey of Cluny in Burgundy, founded in 909, is to exercise an enormous influence on the spread of monasticism and the character of the monastic life. Intended to bring a new strictness into life under the Benedictine Rule, it has a series of gifted leaders, notably Odo (927–42) and Odilo (994–1049), who enlarge the original abbey and increase the number of communities under it. An emphasis on the spiritual life, and long, solemn and splendid worship, go with a reduction in the amount of manual labour usually performed by monks. By the end of the century Cluny has become the leading force in Western monasticism, and when its influence peaks, there are as many as 1000 Cluniac priories. In the East, 961 sees the first monastic settlement on Mount Athos in northern Greece, Lavra, founded by the Byzantine monk Athanasius of Trebizond, which is to be the first of 20. Mount Athos becomes an important centre of Greek Orthodox spirituality.

The first moves are made to establish Christianity in north-eastern Europe. Haakon, a Norwegian at the court of King Ethelstan of East Anglia, becomes King of Norway and attempts its conversion (946), as later does King Olaf Tryggvason (995); Harald Bluetooth unifies his kingdom and becomes a Christian (960); the Polish Duke Mieszko is baptized and the Poles convert to Christianity (966). Later in the century the Magyar prince Geza is baptized (985). As an aid to mission the Archdiocese of Hamburg-Bremen, the most important church centre in the area, is extended to cover the Scandinavian countries (948), while Magdeburg on the Elbe becomes an archdiocese in order to further the evangelization of the Slavs (968). At the end of the century Norse colonists take Christianity to Iceland and Greenland. The pagan Wends, between the Elbe and Pomerania, are the greatest threat to mission. They rebel against Emperor Otto II and go on to sack Hamburg. They will later become the object of a special crusade.

In the East, in 957 Olga, Queen of Kiev, is baptized in Constantinople, having been overwhelmed by the glories of worship in Hagia Sophia. She has a church with the same dedication built in Kiev. And in 988 Prince Vladimir of Kiev is baptized prior to his marriage with Anna Porphyrogeneta, daughter of Emperor Romanus II. This is followed by a mass baptism of his subjects in the River Dnieper, an event known as 'the Christianization of Rus'.

901

☦ February 12: Antony II Kauleas, Patriarch of Constantinople (◀ 893), dies.

☦ March 1: Nicholas Mysticus is appointed Patriarch of Constantinople (▶ 925).

A list of dioceses subject to the Patriarch of Constantinople, the *Taxis*, is published, with 455 of them under 56 metropolitans (▶ 1437) and 50 independents directly subject to the patriarchate.

902

With the capture of Taormina, the Arabs complete their conquest of Sicily (◀ 831).

903

☦ August: Pope Benedict IV (◀ 900) dies.

☦ August/September: Pope Leo V is elected.

☦ October: Pope Leo V is deposed, imprisoned and subsequently murdered.

☦ October: Pope Christopher (▶ 904) is elected. He is sometimes considered an antipope.

🏛 St Martin, Tours, is built, featuring the first ambulatory with side chapels.

904

☦ January 29: Pope Christopher (◀ 903) is deposed.

☦ January 29: Pope Sergius III (▶ 911) is elected.

907

☦ February 1: Emperor Leo VI (◀ 886, ▶ 912) deposes Patriarch Nicholas Mysticus (◀ 901) and appoints Euthymius I Syncellus Patriarch of Constantinople (▶ 912).

The Tang dynasty in China ends and with it the Nestorian church in China disappears (◀ 842, ▶ 1275).

909

September 2: The Benedictine Abbey of Cluny (▶ 927), a great centre of monastic reform, is founded by William the Pious, Duke of Aquitaine.

The Diocese of Bath and Wells is founded. Athelm (▶ 923) is its first bishop.

911

☦ April 14: Pope Sergius III (◀ 904) dies.

☦ June: Pope Anastasius III (▶ 913) is elected.

In the treaty of St Clair-sur-Epte, the Frankish king Charles the Simple grants Rollo and his Norse followers land round the mouth of the Seine. This becomes Normandy. Rollo agrees to become a Christian.

912

♛ May 11: Emperor Leo VI (◀ 886) dies.

✠ May 15: Nicholas Mysticus (◀ 913) is reinstated as Patriarch of Constantinople in place of Euthymius I Syncellus (◀ 907).

c.912

♟ Ethelwold, later Bishop of Winchester, is born. He is a leading figure in the tenth-century monastic revival (▶ *c.*970).

913

✠ August: Pope Anastasius III (◀ 911) dies.

✠ August: Pope Lando (▶ 914) is elected.

♛ Constantine VII (▶ 959) becomes emperor. He will write many books on the Byzantine empire and not involve himself in government. Patriarch Nicholas Mysticus (◀912, ▶925) acts as regent.

914

✠ March: Pope Lando (◀ 913) dies.

✠ March/April: Pope John X (▶ 928) is elected.

915

June: Pope John X personally leads an army into battle near the river Garigliano in central Italy and decisively defeats the Saracens, who have been marauding in Italy for 60 years.

919

♛ Heinrich, Duke of Saxony ('the Fowler'), is crowned Heinrich I, to begin a line of Saxon kings of Germany (▶ 936).

♛ Constantine VII (◀913, ▶959) marries the daughter of his admiral Romanus I Lacapenus (▶ 933) and crowns him co-emperor the next year.

923

✞ August 2: Plegmund, Archbishop of Canterbury (◀ 890), dies and is succeeded by Athelm, Bishop of Bath and Wells (◀ 909, ▶ 926). Plegmund is subsequently venerated as a saint: feast day August 2.

924

♛ July 17: Edward the Elder, King of the English (◀ 899), dies. He is succeeded by his son Athelstan (▶ 939).

925

✠ May 15: Nicholas Mysticus, Patriarch of Constantinople (◀ 901), dies.

✠ June 29: Stephen II of Amasea becomes Patriarch of Constantinople (▶ 928).

🏛 Vaclav (Wenceslas) I, Duke of Bohemia (▶ 929), builds a Romanesque rotunda on the site of what is now Prague cathedral (▶ 1060).

Christ in Majesty: Spanish whalebone carving, 925

926

☩ January 8: Athelm, Archbishop of Canterbury (◀ 923), dies and is succeeded by Wulfhelm, Bishop of Bath and Wells (▶ 941).

927

⌂ Cluny Abbey I (◀ 909, ▶ 981) is dedicated. Odo (▶ 942) becomes abbot, and is instrumental in making it famous and influential.

928

☩ May: Pope John X (◀ 914) is deposed.

☩ May: Pope Leo VI is elected.

☩ July 18: Stephen II of Amasea, Patriarch of Constantinople (◀ 925), dies.

☩ December 14: Tryphon becomes Patriarch of Constantinople (▶ 931).

☩ December: Pope Leo VI dies.

☩ December: Pope Stephen VII (▶ 931) is elected.

929

☩ The deposed Pope John X (◀ 928) dies.

138

✪ Vaclav I, Duke of Bohemia (◀ 925), is murdered by his brother Boleslav. Vaclav is subsequently venerated as a saint: feast day September 28.

St George's Cathedral, Zvartnots (◀ 649), is destroyed in an earthquake.

931

✞ February: Pope Stephen VII (◀ 928) dies.

✞ February/March: Pope John XI (▶ 936) is elected.

✞ August: Tryphon, Patriarch of Constantinople (◀ 928), dies.

932

Alberic II, Duke of Spoleto (▶ 954), controls Rome as prince and nominates popes.

933

✞ February: Theophylactus, son of Emperor Romanus I (◀ 919, ▶ 944), is appointed Patriarch of Constantinople (▶ 956).

936

✞ January: Pope John XI (◀ 931) dies.

✞ January 3: Pope Leo VII (▶ 939) is elected.

♛ July 2: Heinrich I of Germany (◀ 919) dies and is succeeded by Otto I, the Great (▶ 973), as King of the Germans.

939

✞ July 13: Pope Leo VII (◀ 936) dies.

✞ July 14: Pope Stephen VIII (▶ 942) is elected.

♛ October 27: Athelstan, King of the English (◀ 924), dies and is succeeded by his half-brother Edmund I (▶ 946).

Madrid is recaptured from the Muslims.

941

✞ February 12: Wulfhelm, Archbishop of Canterbury (◀ 926), dies.

942

✞ October: Pope Stephen VIII (◀ 939) dies.

✞ October 30: Pope Marinus II (▶ 946) is elected.

✞ Oda, a Dane and Bishop of Ramsbury and Sunning, is appointed Archbishop of Canterbury (▶ 958).

✪ Odo, Abbot of Cluny (◀ 927), dies. He is later venerated as a saint.

944

♛ The sons of Romanus I Lacapenus (◀ 933) compel him to become a monk.

946

♁ May: Pope Marinus II (◀ 942) dies.

♁ May 10: Pope Agapetus II (▶ 955) is elected.

♛ May 26: Edmund I, King of the English (◀ 939), is murdered and is succeeded by his brother Edred (▶ 955).

♛ Haakon, a Norwegian fostered by King Ethelstan of East Anglia (◀ 879), becomes King of Norway and makes vain efforts to establish Christianity there.

948

January 2: A papal bull extends the jurisdiction of the Archdiocese of Hamburg-Bremen over Denmark and other Scandinavian countries.

*c.***949**

🕯 Simeon the New Theologian is born. Regarded as the greatest of Byzantine writers, he prepares the way for Hesychasm. Dies *c.*1022.

950

♫ An organ plays for the coronation of the Archbishop of Cologne.

954

♛ Alberic II (◀ 932) dies.

♛ Eric Bloodaxe, King of York, is killed. From now on kings of Wessex rule a single kingdom of England.

955

♛ November 23: Edred, King of the English (◀ 946), dies and is succeeded by Edwy (▶ 959), son of Edmund I (◀ 939).

♁ December: Pope Agapetus II (◀ 946) dies.

♁ December: Pope John XII (▶ 963) is elected, bastard son of Alberic II of Spoleto.

956

♁ February 27: Theophylactus, Patriarch of Constantinople (◀ 933), dies.

♁ April 3: Polyeuctus is appointed Patriarch of Constantinople (▶ 970).

957

Olga, Queen of Kiev, is baptized in Constantinople, overwhelmed by the glories of worship in Hagia Sophia (◀ 537). She has a church with the same dedication built in Kiev (▶ 1037).

958

✠ June 2: Oda, Archbishop of Canterbury (◀ 942), dies and is succeeded by Aelfsige, Bishop of Winchester. However, Aelfsige dies of cold crossing the Alps before reaching Rome to be consecrated. Oda is subsequently venerated as a saint: feast day June 2.

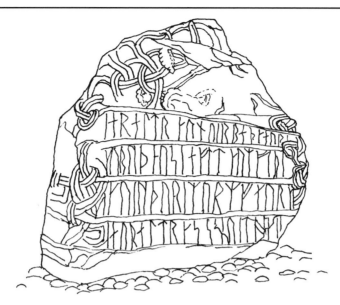

Harald Bluetooth's three-sided stone at Jelling on the Jutland peninsula, once Viking capital of Denmark and now a small village: the inscription commemorates his conversion of Denmark to Christianity; the other faces depict Christ and a lion, 960

959

✵ Berthelm, Bishop of Wells, chief minister of King Edwy (◀ 955), is appointed Archbishop of Canterbury. However, King Edwy dies before Berthelm can be consecrated.

♛ October 1: King Edwy (◀ 955) dies and is succeeded by his brother Edgar (▶ 973), who is the patron of a great monastic revival.

♛ November 9: Constantine VII (◀ 913) dies and is succeeded by his son Romanus II (▶ 963).

960

✵ King Edgar annuls the appointment of Berthelm as Archbishop of Canterbury (◀ 959), and Dunstan (▶ 988), his chief minister and Bishop of London, is consecrated.

Harald Bluetooth, King of Denmark, unifies his kingdom and adopts Christianity, erecting a carved stone at Jelling to commemorate his conversion.

961

March 7: The Byzantine army under Nicephorus Phocas (▶ 962) recaptures Crete from the Arabs and restores Christianity.

The first monastic settlement, Lavra, is founded on Mount Athos by the Byzantine monk Athanasius of Trebizond (▶ 1000).

Danes pillage St Paul's Cathedral (◀ 685). Rebuilding begins the next year.

141

962

♛ February 2: Pope John XII crowns Otto I, King of Germany (◀ 936, ▶ 973), emperor, thus restoring the Holy Roman Empire.

Nicephorus Phocas (◀ 961) regains territory in Cilicia and Syria from the Arabs.

963

♛ March 15: Emperor Romanus II (◀ 959) dies.

♛ August 16: Nicephorus II Phocas (◀ 962, ▶ 969) is crowned emperor.

☉ December 4: Pope John XII (◀ 955, ▶ 964) is deposed by a synod under Otto I of Germany.

☉ Otto I chooses Leo VIII (▶ 964) as pope.

964

☉ February 26: Pope Leo VIII is deposed by Pope John XII (◀ 963) at a synod in St Peter's, Rome.

☉ May 14: Pope John XII dies.

☉ May 22: Pope Benedict V is elected.

☉ June 23: Pope Benedict V is deposed.

☉ June 23: Pope Leo VIII (▶ 965) is reinstated.

965

☉ March 1: Pope Leo VIII (◀ 964) dies.

☉ October 1: Otto I (◀ 963, ▶ 973) chooses John XIII as pope, but John is expelled by the Romans. He flees to the protection of the emperor (▶ 967).

966

April: The Polish Duke Mieszko (▶ 990) is baptized and the Poles are converted to Christianity.

☉ July 4: The deposed Pope Benedict V (◀ 964) dies.

967

♛ December 25: Pope John XIII (◀ 965, ▶ 972) crowns Otto II (▶ 973), son of Otto I (◀ 936), co-emperor with his father in the West.

968

Magdeburg on the Elbe becomes an archdiocese and plays a major role in the colonization of the Slavs. The first archbishop is Adalbert, a former archbishop of the Archdiocese of Hamburg-Bremen and an experienced missionary.

969

♛ December 10/11: Nicephorus II Phocas (◀ 963) is murdered by John Tzimisces, his general and commander of the Byzantine army in the East. John I Tzimisces (▶ 976) becomes emperor.

970

☩ February 5: Polyeuctus, Patriarch of Constantinople (◀ 956), dies and is succeeded by Basil I Skamandrenus (▶ 974).

*c.***970**

☙ In his *Regularis Concordia*, a book of rules and advice for the English Benedictines, Bishop Ethelwold of Winchester (◀ *c.*912, ▶ 983) includes the text of a dialogue between the women at the tomb of Jesus (known as *Quem Quaeritis?*, 'Whom do you seek') which has come to be included in the Mass, and gives directions about how to stage it as a dramatic action. This is thought to mark the beginning of the Easter play.

Bishop Ethelwold also founds a Benedictine monastery (▶ 1083) on the site of Etheldreda's monastery in Ely (◀ 870).

972

☩ September 6: Pope John XIII (◀ 965) dies.

▥ The monastery at Peterborough (◀ 870) is rebuilt as part of a Benedictine abbey (▶ 1116).

♫ An organ plays at the consecration of the Benedictine abbey in Bages, Spain.

973

☩ January 19: Pope Benedict VI (▶ 974) is elected.

♛ May 7: Emperor Otto I (◀ 962) dies and is succeeded by Otto II (◀ 967, ▶ 974) as sole emperor.

♛ Whitsunday: Dunstan (◀ 960, ▶ 988) crowns the West Saxon king Edgar (◀ 960, ▶ 975) as the ruler of all Britain.

974

☩ March: Basil I Skamandrenus, Patriarch of Constantinople (◀ 970), dies and is succeeded by Anthony III Studites (▶ 979).

☩ June: Pope Benedict VI (◀ 973) is murdered.

☩ June: Boniface VII (▶ 985) is elected antipope, supported by the powerful Roman Crescentii family.

☩ July: Antipope Boniface is expelled from Rome by Otto II (◀ 973, ▶ 982).

☩ October: Pope Benedict VII (▶ 983) is elected.

975

♛ Edgar, King of the English (◀ 973), dies and is succeeded by his son Edward 'the Martyr' (▶ 978).

976

♛ January 10: In the East, Emperor John I Tzimisces (◀ 969) dies and is succeeded by Basil II Bulgaroctonus ('Slayer of the Bulgars', ▶ 1014), the son of Romanus II (◀ 959). Basil appoints his brother Constantine VIII co-emperor (▶ 1025).

978

♕ Edward, King of the English (◀ 975, ▶ 1001), is murdered at Corfe Castle, Dorset. He is succeeded by his half-brother Ethelred 'the Unready' (▶ 1016).

979

⊕ March: Anthony III Studites, Patriarch of Constantinople (◀ 974), dies and is succeeded by Nicholas II Chrysoberges (▶ 991).

A series of Danish raids (◀ 850/1) begins which results in the Danish conquest of most of England (▶ 1014).

980

🦶 Avicenna is born; a Muslim physician and philosopher, he is particularly important in mediating Aristotelianism to the Middle Ages. Dies 1037.

🏛 The building of Mainz Cathedral begins (▶ 1009).

981

🏛 Cluny Abbey II is dedicated (◀ 927, ▶ 1080), having been enlarged to house more monks.

982

Otto II (◀ 974, ▶ 983) is defeated by the Arabs at Cap Colonna in Calabria. This triggers off a rebellion of the pagan Wends, who live between the Elbe and Pomerania.

983

⊕ July 10: Pope Benedict VII (◀ 974) dies.

⊕ August 1: Ethelwold, Bishop of Winchester (◀ c.970), dies. He is subsequently venerated as a saint: feast day August 1.

⊕ December: Pope John XIV (▶ 984) is elected.

♕ December 7: Otto II (◀ 973) dies. His son and successor as King of Germany, Otto III (▶ 1002), becomes a ward of his grandmother, the Dowager Empress Adelaide.

The Wends sack Hamburg.

984

⊕ August: Pope John XIV (◀ 983) is deposed by Antipope Boniface VII (◀ 974, ▶ 985). He returns to Rome financed by Byzantium, and dies in prison.

985

⊕ July 20: Antipope Boniface VII (◀ 974) dies.

⊕ August: Pope John XV (▶ 996) is elected.

In Hungary, the Magyar price Geza is baptized into the Roman Catholic Church.

986

Basil II Bulgaroctonus (◀ 976) begins a long war against Bulgaria (▶ 1014).

987

♛ Hugues Capet (▶ 996) becomes King of France. His descendants will occupy the throne until 1792.

A Benedictine abbey is founded at Cerne Abbas.

988

♱ May 19: Dunstan, Archbishop of Canterbury (◀ 960), dies (▶ 1029). He is succeeded by Athelgar, Bishop of Selsey (▶ 990).

☉ June 5: Vladimir, prince of Kiev, is baptized prior to his marriage to Anna Porphyrogeneta, daughter of Emperor Romanus (◀ 963). He is regarded as the ruler who brought Christianity to the Russian people. After his death he is venerated as a saint: feast day July 15.

990

♱ February 12: Athelgar, Archbishop of Canterbury (◀ 988), dies and is succeeded by Sigeric, Bishop of Ramsbury and Sonning (▶ 994).

☉ In the earliest officially recognized canonization Pope John XV declares Ulrich, Bishop of Augsburg, a saint: feast day July 4.

Duke Mieszko (◀ 967) places Poland directly under the protection and authority of the Pope.

c.990

♫ An organ is built in Winchester Cathedral with 4000 pipes which is said to take 70 men to blow.

991

♱ Nicholas II Chrysoberges, Patriarch of Constantinople (◀ 979), dies and there is a vacancy for four years.

♫ Archbishop Gerbert of Reims is said to have put an organ in the cathedral at this time.

994

♱ October 28: Sigeric, Archbishop of Canterbury (◀ 990), dies.

Odilo becomes Abbot of Cluny (▶ 1049). Under him the number of Cluniac houses grows, and their organization is centralized.

995

♱ April 21: Aelfric, Bishop of Ramsbury and Sonning, is appointed Archbishop of Canterbury (▶ 1005).

Monks from Lindisfarne, needing a home for the relics of Cuthbert (◀ 687), settle on a peninsula of the River Wear and build a church: the settlement becomes the city of Durham (▶ 1093). The Diocese of Durham is founded.

King Olaf Tryggvason spreads Christianity in Norway with the help of English missionaries, but does not have lasting success (▶ 1015).

996

☦ March: Pope John XV (◄ 985) dies.

☦ April 12: Sisinnius II is appointed Patriarch of Constantinople (► 998).

☦ May 3: Otto III (◄ 983, ► 1002) arrives in Rome and secures the election of Pope Gregory V (► 999), who is his cousin, as the first German pope.

♛ May 21: Gregory V crowns Otto III Holy Roman Emperor. Otto sees himself as the head of world Christianity.

Hugues Capet, King of France (◄ 987), dies and is succeeded by Robert II (► 1031).

998

☦ August 24: Sisinnius II, Patriarch of Constantinople (◄ 996), dies and there is a vacancy for three years.

November 2: The celebration of All Souls Day is instituted by Abbot Odilo (◄ 994) in the monastery of Cluny (◄ 981).

999

☦ February 18: Pope Gregory V (◄ 996) dies.

☦ April 2: Pope Sylvester II (► 1003) is elected, the first French pope.

1000

☦ Athanasius of Trebizond (◄ 961) is canonized: feast day July 5.

Christianity reaches Iceland and Greenland through Norse colonists.

Eleventh century

From the middle of the century Christendom is no longer formed of one church: tensions between West and East which have been building up for some time finally reach breaking point. The one church has long risked being divided by its existence in two cultures, Latin and Greek, different forms of theology and different practices; in areas between East and West such as the Balkans, there have been clashes over jurisdiction between Rome and Constantinople. It is one such clash which is the immediate occasion for the schism of 1054: Latin customs are forced on the Greek churches in southern Italy and Sicily and in retaliation the Latin churches in Constantinople are closed. What is intended as a meeting to achieve an alliance turns into an exchange of excommunications; the two churches part company in great bitterness and despite subsequent attempts at reunion to the present day lead separate existences as the Roman Catholic Church and the Orthodox Church.

A major factor in the schism is the claim by Pope Leo IX to have primacy over the four Eastern patriarchates, Constantinople, Alexandria, Antioch and Jerusalem, which is unacceptable to them; another papal claim leads to a further controversy in the West, known as the Investiture Controversy. In it Pope Leo IX and his successor Gregory VII reject the lay control of the church represented by the practice of lay rulers bestowing the ring and staff, signs of office, upon new abbots and bishops. Gregory claims that the Pope alone can depose or appoint bishops; he can even depose emperors. This leads to a conflict particularly with King Heinrich IV of Germany, in which Gregory, initially gaining the upper hand, eventually dies in exile. The controversy marks a crucial change in the unified theocratic world-view of Christianity. Whereas such a view has been preserved in Islam, in Christianity there is henceforth a steady separation of the spiritual and the temporal, the secular and the religious, church and state.

A third major development during the century is the rise of the university, with the founding of the oldest existing university in Europe, in Bologna. The university is a Christian creation. It arises out of a type of school called the *studium generale*, open to students from all over Europe and intended to give a better education to clergy and monks than the schools attached to cathedrals and monasteries. Bologna is followed by Paris and Oxford, and universities rapidly spread all over Europe and later into the New World. Along with the rise of the university will come the beginnings of a new kind of theology with the great figures of Anselm (1033) and Abelard (1079). Their thinking seeks to relate different standpoints to one another by asking questions and providing answers, rather than simply gathering together a series of 'authorities', and is a prelude to later Scholasticism.

Architecturally, the century sees a flowering of Romanesque architecture with the building of cathedrals in Angoulême, Bamberg, Basle, Bayeux, Braga, Cahors, Canterbury, Durham, Hereford, Hildesheim, Lichfield, Lincoln, Mainz, Norwich, Old Sarum, Pisa, Rochester, Rouen, Speyer, Strasbourg, Trier, Winchester, Worcester, York, Zurich; in London Westminster Abbey is built. At the end of the century the beginnings of a new development, Gothic architecture, appear at St Germain des Prés. An enormous church is built at the Abbey of Cluny. Important abbeys are founded at Bec and Jumièges in Normandy, along with the Monastery of Montserrat near Barcelona and the Monastery of Caves in Kiev.

1001

✠ July: Sergius II (▶ 1019) becomes Patriarch of Constantinople.

☩ Edward, King of the English (◀ 978), is canonized by Pope Sylvester II: feast day March 18.

*c.***1001**

Christianity reaches Canada from Greenland.

The formal constitution for the church in Hungary is laid down by King István (Stephen) I (▶ 1081).

1002

♛ January 23: Otto III (◀ 996) dies.

♛ June 7: Heinrich II (▶ 1014), cousin of Otto III, becomes King of Germany.

1003

✠ May 16: Pope Sylvester II (◀ 999) dies.

✠ May 16: John Sicco, of whose background nothing is known, is elected as Pope John XVII.

✠ November 6: Pope John XVII dies.

✠ December 25: A Roman cardinal priest of St Peter's, John Fasanus, is elected as Pope John XVIII (▶ 1009).

1005

✠ November 16: Aelfric, Archbishop of Canterbury (◀ 995), dies.

1006

✠ Aelfheah (more popularly Alphege), Bishop of Winchester, is appointed Archbishop of Canterbury (▶ 1012).

1009

✠ June/July: Pope John XVIII (◀ 1003) dies.

✠ July 31: A Roman, Peter, Bishop of Albano, is elected as Pope Sergius IV (▶ 1012).

▥ August 29: Mainz Cathedral (◀ 980) burns down on the day of its consecration (▶ 1037).

October 18: The Church of the Holy Sepulchre, Jerusalem (◀ 335, ▶ 1034), is destroyed by Caliph al-Hakim of Egypt (▶ 1012).

▥ Work begins on Hildesheim Cathedral, south-east of Hanover (▶ 1015).

1010

Bernard of Angers is overawed by the gilded reliquary-statue of Sainte Foy in Conques, France, one of the earliest examples after the classical period of sculpture in the round.

149

Gilded reliquary of Sainte Foy, Conques, 1010

1012

✠ April 19: Alphege (Aelfheah), Archbishop of Canterbury (◀ 1006), is murdered by the Danes in a drunken feast because he will not ransom himself at the expense of poor tenants (▶ 1078).

⌂ May 6: Bamberg Cathedral is consecrated (▶ 1081).

✠ May 12: Pope Sergius IV (◀ 1009) dies.

✠ May 17: Theophylact, a lay nobleman, is elected as Pope Benedict VIII (▶ 1024).

Romuald (▶ 1582) founds the monastic Order of the Camaldolese, a contemplative branch of the Benedictines.

Caliph al-Hakim (◀ 1009) orders the destruction of all Jewish and Christian places of worship.

1013

The Danish king Sweyn Forkbeard (▶ 1014) invades England and conquers all of it but London. King Ethelred (◀ 978, ▶ 1014) goes into exile and Sweyn is accepted as king.

✠ Lyfing, Bishop of Wells, is appointed Archbishop of Canterbury (▶ 1020). He is captured by the Danish army of Sweyn Forkbeard and leaves England.

1014

♛ February 14: Pope Benedict VIII crowns King Heinrich II of Germany (◀ 1002, ▶ 1024) Holy Roman Emperor in Rome, restoring full relations with the German royal house.

Sweyn Forkbeard dies and his younger son Canute, a Christian, is proclaimed king. Ethelred (◀ 1013) returns and drives Canute (▶ 1016) out of England.

Basil II (◀ 986, ▶ 1025) wins a victory over the Bulgars, blinding the survivors of the defeated army. The kingdom is incorporated into the Byzantine empire.

1015

✠ Olaf II Haraldson declares himself King of Norway and gains the acceptance of Christianity throughout the kingdom. After his death he is venerated as a saint: feast day July 29.

⌂ Bishop Werner von Habsburg lays the cornerstone of Strasbourg Cathedral on the foundations of a Carolingian basilica (▶ 1439).

▮ Bishop Bernward commissions bronze doors for Hildesheim Cathedral, Germany, with images from the history of Adam and Christ. They are unprecedented in Christian art.

1016

♛ April 23: King Ethelred of England (◀ 978) dies and is succeeded by his son Edmund II Ironside.

♛ November 30: King Edmund II dies and his territories are handed over to Canute (◀ 1014, ▶ 1018), who is recognized as King of England.

Depiction of Adam and Eve on the Bernwald doors of Hildesheim Cathedral, near Hanover, 1015

1017

🏛 A cathedral is consecrated in Angoulême, France, replacing an earlier one which has been burnt down (◄ 560, ► 1128).

1018

👑 Canute (◄ 1016, ► 1035), King of England, becomes King of Denmark as well.

Buckfast Abbey in Devon is founded; it later becomes a Cistercian house (► 1882).

1019

☩ July: Sergius II, Patriarch of Constantinople (◄ 1001) dies and is succeeded by Eustathius (► 1025).

🏛 October 11: Basle Cathedral (► 1356) is consecrated.

1020

☩ June 12: Lyfing, Archbishop of Canterbury (◄ 1013), dies.

☩ November 13: Ethelnoth, Dean of Canterbury and counsellor to King Canute (◄ 1018), is appointed Archbishop of Canterbury (► 1038). He restores and beautifies the cathedral.

1022

August 1: At the Synod of Pavia under Heinrich II and Pope Benedict VIII (◄ 1014, ► 1024) marriage and concubinage are prohibited for all clergy.

*c.***1022**

🕯 Simeon the New Theologian (◄ *c.*949) dies.

1023

A hospice in Jerusalem, destroyed by Caliph al-Hakim (◄ 1012), is rebuilt and served by Benedictines.

1024

☩ April 9: Pope Benedict VIII (◄ 1012) dies.

☩ April 19: Romanus, younger brother of Pope Benedict VIII, is elected as John XIX (► 1032).

👑 July 13: Heinrich II, Holy Roman Emperor and last of the Ottonian Saxon dynasty, dies (► 1146).

👑 September 8: Conrad II is crowned King of Germany (► 1027).

The monastery of Montserrat near Barcelona, associated with the Castle of the Holy Grail, is founded by Abbot Oliba of Ripoli.

1025

☩ December: Eustathius, Patriarch of Constantinople (◄ 1019), dies.

☩ December 15: Alexius I Studites becomes Patriarch of Constantinople (► 1043).

153

♛ December 15: Emperor Basil II Bulgaroctonus (◀ 976) dies. His brother Constantine VIII (◀ 976, ▶ 1028) becomes sole emperor.

1027

♛ March 26: Pope John XIX (◀ 1024, ▶ 1032) crowns the German king Conrad II (◀ 1024, ▶ 1039) Holy Roman Emperor, the first of the Salian dynasty.

1028

♛ Easter day: Heinrich III, son of Conrad II (◀ 1027), is crowned King of Germany.

♛ November 11: Constantine VIII (◀ 976, 1025) dies. He is succeeded by Romanus III Argyrus, who marries Zoe (▶ 1034), daughter of Constantine VIII. She becomes empress consort.

1029

☦ Dunstan (◀ 988) is canonized by Pope John XIX: feast day May 19.

1030

🏛 Work on Speyer Cathedral in Germany is begun as the last resting-place for Emperor Conrad II (◀ 1027). For 300 years it will be the burial place of the German emperors (▶ 1061).

1031

July 20: Robert II, King of France (◀ 996), dies and is succeeded by Henri I (▶ 1060).

1032

⚓ October 20: Pope John XIX (◀ 1024) dies.

⚓ October 21: Theophylact, nephew of Pope John XIX and Benedict VIII, is elected pope as Benedict IX (▶ 1045, 1047). He is the only pope to hold office for three different periods (▶ 1043).

1033

♟📖 Anselm (▶ 1060) is born in Aosta, Italy. He becomes a monk in Normandy and later Archbishop of Canterbury. He writes three important books: *Soliloquy*, *Discourse* and *Why the God Man*, and develops the ontological argument for the existence of God: God is that than which nothing greater can be conceived. Dies 1109.

1034

♛ April 11: Romanus III Argyrus (◀ 1028) dies and is succeeded by Michael IV the Paphlagonian (▶ 1041), who marries Zoe (◀ 1028, ▶ 1042), Romanus' wife. Michael makes peace with the Egyptian Fatimid caliphate and is allowed to renovate the Church of the Holy Sepulchre in Jerusalem.

1035

♛ November 12: Canute (◀ 1018) dies and is succeeded as co-ruler of England by his son Hardicanute, who also becomes King of Denmark (▶ 1037).

⌂ Constantine's cathedral in Trier (◀ 326), extensively damaged, is rebuilt and enlarged in the Romanesque style.

⌂ The building of Bremen Cathedral begins.

The Christian kingdom of Aragon in north-east Spain is established (▶ 1469).

*c.*1036

The Order of Vallombrosa, following a more austere form of the Rule of Benedict, is founded near Florence by John Gualbert.

1037

❦ June: Avicenna (◀ 980) dies.

♛ Harold Harefoot, brother of Hardicanute (◀ 1035, ▶ 1041), seizes the English throne in Hardicanute's absence (▶ 1040).

The Christian kingdom of Castile-Leon in northern Spain is established.

⌂ The rebuilding of Mainz Cathedral (◀ 1009) is largely complete. It will be the scene of the coronation of many German kings.

⌂ Prince Yaroslav the Wise rebuilds the Church of Holy Wisdom (Hagia Sophia, ◀ 957) in Kiev on a grandiose scale.

1038

✠ October 29: Ethelnoth, Archbishop of Canterbury (◀ 1020), dies and is succeeded by Edsige (▶ 1050), who has been chaplain to King Canute (◀ 1016).

1039

♛ June 4: Emperor Conrad II (◀ 1027) dies and his son King Heinrich III (◀ 1028) of Germany becomes sole ruler (▶ 1046).

The Abbey of Bec in Normandy is founded by Herluin, a Norman knight; it becomes a great centre of eleventh-century intellectual life (▶ 1045).

1040

♛ March: King Harold Harefoot of England (◀ 1037) dies.

June 17: King Hardicanute (◀ 1037, 1041) takes possession of England.

The Benedictine Weihensstephan Abbey in Bavaria establishes the oldest brewery still in operation today.

1041

♛ December 10: Emperor Michael IV the Paphlagonian (◀ 1034) dies and is succeeded by his nephew Michael V Calaphates (▶ 1042).

♛ Edward the Confessor (▶ 1043), in exile in Normandy, returns to England to become co-ruler with King Hardicanute (◀ 1040, ▶ 1042), his half-brother.

1042

♛ June: King Hardicanute (◀ 1035) dies.

♛ August 20: Michael V Calaphates (◀ 1041) is deposed by his enemies, blinded and sent to a monastery, where he dies.

♛ November 15: Empress Zoe (◀ 1034, ▶ 1050) and her sister Theodora (▶ 1055) are proclaimed co-empresses. Zoe then marries Constantine IX Monomachus (▶ 1043), who becomes emperor, and eclipses Theodora. He tries to ally with the papacy against the Normans.

Gottschalk, a Wendish prince at one time of the court of Canute (◀ 1016) and a Christian, takes power in Oldenburg-Mecklenburg (▶ 1066).

1043

☉ February 20: Alexius I Studites, Patriarch of Constantinople (◀ 1025), dies.

☉ March 25: Michael Cerularius becomes Patriarch of Constantinople (▶ 1058, 1059). He thwarts Constantine IX's attempts to ally with the papacy.

♛ April 3: Edward the Confessor, son of Ethelred (◀ 978), is crowned King of England by Edsige, Archbishop of Canterbury (▶ 1066).

1044

September: An insurrection forces Pope Benedict IX (◀ 1032) to leave Rome.

1045

☉ January 20: The Romans elect Bishop John of Sabina as Pope Sylvester III.

☉ March 10: Pope Benedict IX becomes pope for the second time and excommunicates Pope Sylvester III (▶ 1046).

☉ May 1: Pope Benedict IX abdicates in favour of his godfather John Gratian, who is elected as Pope Gregory VI (▶ 1046).

Lanfranc (▶ 1066) becomes Abbot of Bec (◀ 1039) and opens a school in the monastery which gains a great reputation.

1046

☉ December 20: On the orders of King Heinrich III of Germany (◀ 1039, ▶ 1056), Pope Gregory VI calls the Council of Sutri to resolve the confusion over the papacy. The Council sentences Pope Sylvester III to be stripped of his orders and imprisoned in a monastery and deposes Gregory VI (◀ 1045).

☉ December 24: Benedict IX is deposed at an extension of the Council held in Rome.

☉ December 24: Suidger, Bishop of Bamberg, is elected as Pope Clement II (▶ 1047) on the nomination of Emperor Heinrich III.

♛ December 25: Heinrich III, King of Germany, is crowned Holy Roman Emperor (▶ 1056). He is a strong supporter of Cluniac reform and the last emperor who can dominate the papacy.

1047

✠ October 9: Pope Clement II (◀ 1046) dies and Pope Benedict IX (◀ 1046, ▶ 1048) is elected for the third time.

1048

✠ July 16: Pope Benedict IX is dethroned.

✠ July 17: Poppo, Bishop of Brixen in the Tyrol, is elected as Pope Damasus II.

✠ August 9: Pope Damasus II dies.

1049

✠ February 12: Bruno, son of Count Hugh of Egisheim, Alsace, is elected as Pope Leo IX (▶ 1054).

Odilo, Abbot of Cluny (◀ 994), dies (▶ 1063).

1049–53

Pope Leo IX holds reforming synods in Pavia, Reims, Mainz, Rome and other centres.

1050

✠ October 29: Edsige, Archbishop of Canterbury (◀ 1038), dies.

♛ Empress Zoe (◀ 1042) dies.

🏛 Work begins on St Sophia Cathedral, Novgorod, on the site of a previous wooden church. It is the oldest church building in Russia.

In the foundation of the Diocese of Exeter from Crediton, Edward the Confessor (◀ 1043) installs Leofric as bishop and the Minster of St Mary and St Peter becomes Exeter Cathedral.

c.1050

♪ Polyphonic singing replaces Gregorian chant.

1051

✠ March: Edward the Confessor appoints the Norman Robert of Jumièges, Bishop of London, as Archbishop of Canterbury, but there is too much opposition to the appointment and Robert returns to his native France.

Ilarion becomes the first native metropolitan of the Eastern Orthodox Church in Kievan Rus.

c.1051

The Monastery of Caves is founded in Kiev.

1052

✠ September: Stigand, Bishop of Winchester, is appointed Archbishop of Canterbury (▶ 1070) but is not recognized by Rome.

1053–1056

🏛 The building of Westminster Abbey (▶ 1065) begins under Edward the Confessor (◀ 1051, ▶ 1066).

🏛 A cathedral is built on the site of the wooden church in Hereford (◀ 794, ▶ 1056).

The Normans in southern Italy force Greek churches there to conform to Latin usage. In retaliation Michael Cerularius (◀ 1043) forces the Latin churches in his diocese to use the Greek language and liturgy; when they refuse, he closes them.

1053

May: Pope Leo IX makes an unsuccessful attack on the Normans (◀ 1052), who are marauding in the papal states.

June 18: The Normans defeat the papal forces at the Battle of Civitate and Pope Leo IX is taken prisoner.

1054

Pope Leo IX sends a delegation to Constantinople to negotiate an alliance with the emperor, but Michael Cerularius (◀ 1043) again thwarts his attempts.

⦿ April 19: Pope Leo IX (◀ 1049) dies. He is subsequently venerated as a saint: feast day April 19.

July 16: One of the papal delegation, Humbert of Silva Candida, enters Hagia Sophia and excommunicates Michael Cerularius and his clergy. Cerularius summons a synod and excommunicates the delegates. This finalizes the split between Eastern and Western churches (The Great Schism).

1055

♛ January 11: Constantine IX Monomachus dies (◀ 1042) and Theodora (◀ 1042, ▶ 1056) becomes empress.

☿ April 13: Gebhardt of Dollnstein-Hirschberg in Swabia is elected as Pope Victor II (▶ 1057).

1055/56

☿ The former Pope Benedict IX (◀ 1032, 1048) dies.

1056

♛ August: Theodora (◀ 1042, 1055) dies and is succeeded by Michael VI Stratioticus (▶ 1057).

♛ October 5: Holy Roman Emperor Heinrich III (◀ 1046) dies.

♛ Heinrich IV, oldest son of Heinrich III, becomes King of Germany at the age of six (▶ 1105).

The Patarenes, a radical reform movement in Milan, appear, calling for clerical celibacy and demanding an end to simony, the sale of church offices for money.

Hereford Cathedral (◀ 1052) is burned down by Griffin, King of the Welsh; the bishop and many clergy are killed.

The Great Schism

In 1054 the churches of East and West split in a schism which has still not healed today. The immediate cause is to do with church politics at the time, but differences going back over centuries play a major role.

From the fifth century onwards the Eastern church is increasingly estranged from the Western church. The transference of the capital of the Roman empire to Constantinople (◀ 330) has made its patriarchate more and more important after the eclipse of Alexandria and Antioch with the rise of Islam (◀ 642) and it is unwilling to accept papal claims to supremacy over the whole church. Eastern theology is essentially philosophical, whereas Western theology has roots in Roman law. These different approaches make the unilateral insertion of the Latin word *filioque* ('and from the Son') with reference to the origin of the Holy Spirit into the creed of Constantinople (◀ 381) at the Third Council of Toledo (◀ 589) offensive to the East. The East is also alienated by the Roman enforcement of clerical celibacy, the use of unleavened bread in the eucharist and the limitation of the right to confirm Christians to the bishop.

Matters come to a head in the mid-eleventh century. The Normans in control of southern Italy and Sicily compel the Greek churches there to adopt Latin customs (◀ 1052). In retaliation the Patriarch of Constantinople, Michael Cerularius, closes the Latin churches in Constantinople if they refuse to adopt Greek customs. Pope Leo IX (◀ 1049) sends a delegation to Constantinople to negotiate an alliance, but one of its members, Humbert of Silva Candida, enters Hagia Sophia and excommunicates Michael Cerularius; in turn Michael Cerularius excommunicates the delegates.

The schism between the churches is made worse by the sack of Constantinople by Crusaders (▶ 1204), but nevertheless attempts are made to heal it. The Second Council of Lyons (▶ 1274) brings the two sides together but the Eastern clergy are firmly opposed to any reunion; at the Council of Florence (▶ 1369) the Patriarch of Constantinople signs a Decree of Union, but again his clergy refuse to accept it. With the capture of Constantinople by the Turks (▶ 1453), further rapprochement is impossible. However, in 1965 the mutual excommunications of 1054 are withdrawn.

1057

♛ June 8: Army leaders proclaim Isaac I Comnenus emperor (▶ 1059) and he defeats and replaces Michael VI Stratioticus (◀ 1056).

☤ July 28: Pope Victor II (◀ 1055) dies.

☤ August 2: Frederick of Lorraine, Abbot of Monte Cassino, is elected as Pope Stephen IX (▶ 1058).

1058

☤ March 29: Pope Stephen IX (◀ 1057) dies.

☤ April 5: John Mincius, Cardinal Bishop of Velletri, is elected antipope by a group of nobles as Benedict X.

November 2: Emperor Isaac I Comnenus (◀ 1057, ▶ 1059) dethrones and exiles Michael Cerularius, Patriarch of Constantinople (◀ 1054, ▶ 1059).

December 6: Gerard, Bishop of Florence, is elected as Pope Nicholas II (▶ 1061) and Antipope Benedict X is deposed.

Aldred, Bishop of Worcester, is the first English bishop to make a pilgrimage to Jerusalem.

1059

February 2: Michael Cerularius, Patriarch of Constantinople (◀ 1043, 1058), dies and is succeeded by Constantine III Lichoudas (▶ 1063).

April 14: A synod at the Lateran Palace under Nicholas II rules that papal elections are to be conducted by the College of Cardinals to protect them from secular influence. It also calls for the renewal of monastic life. As a result the Augustinian Canons (also known as the Black Canons or Canons Regular) are formed as groups of clerks living communally and within vows of poverty, celibacy and obedience.

December 25: Believing himself to be mortally ill, Isaac I Comnenus abdicates and appoints Constantine X Ducas emperor (▶ 1067). Isaac recovers, but becomes a monk.

1060

May: Normans (◀ 911) under Robert Guiscard and Roger de Hauteville begin an attack on Sicily (◀ 902, ▶ 1091).

August 4: Henri I, King of France (◀ 1031), dies and is succeeded by Philippe I (▶ 1108).

October: A Byzantine army defeats the Normans.

Anselm (◀ 1033) becomes a monk at Bec Abbey (◀ 1039) and is made abbot three years later (▶ 1093).

The Diocese of Prague is founded and a Romanesque basilica is built to replace the rotunda (◀ 925).

1061

July 26: Pope Nicholas II (◀ 1058) dies.

September 30: Anselm, Bishop of Lucca, is elected as Pope Alexander II (▶ 1073).

October: Peter Cadalus, a wealthy German and Bishop of Parma, is nominated by the German court as Antipope Honorius II (▶ 1064).

Lady Richeldis de Favershes, a widow living in Walsingham, Norfolk, experiences an appearance of the Blessed Virgin Mary.

Most of West Frisia (later Holland) is conquered and given to the Bishop of Utrecht.

Speyer Cathedral (◀ 1030) is completed.

1063

August 9: Constantine III Lichoudas, Patriarch of Constantinople (◀ 1059), dies.

⊕ Odilo, Abbot of Cluny (◀ 998), is canonized by Pope Alexander II: feast day January 1 or April 2.

🔲 The present St Mark's, Venice, is begun.

🔲 Pisa Cathedral is begun.

🔲 Rouen Cathedral, the third to stand on the site, is consecrated.

1064

☥ May: Antipope Honorius II (◀ 1061) is deposed.

The Seljuk Turks (▶ 1068) from Central Asia under their sultan Arp Aslan invade Armenia.

☥ John VIII Xiphilinus, a native of Trebizond, is appointed Patriarch of Constantinople (▶ 1075).

1065

🔲 December 28: Westminster Abbey is consecrated (◀ 1052).

⊕ Earl Thorfinn of Orkney dies. After a pilgrimage he has built a church on Birsay, Orkney. He is grandfather of Magnus (▶ 1108). He is subsequently venerated as a saint: feast day January 8.

1066

♛ January 5: Edward the Confessor (◀ 1043) dies (▶ 1161) and Harold son of Godwin, Earl of Essex, becomes King of England.

June 7: The Wends rebel against the Christian rule of Gottschalk (◀ 1042) and kill him.

♛ October 14: Duke William of Normandy, having invaded England, defeats the English army at the Battle of Senlac (Hastings). King Harold is killed.

♛ December 25: Duke William (William the Conqueror) is crowned King of England (▶ 1087) in Westminster Abbey.

Lanfranc, Abbot of Bec (◀ 1045), becomes Abbot of St Stephen's, Caen (▶ 1070).

1067

♛ May 22/23: Constantine X Ducas (◀ 1059) dies.

Jumièges Abbey (◀ c.654) in Normandy is rededicated by William the Conqueror.

1068

♛ January 1: Romanus IV Diogenes, a member of the Cappadocian military aristocracy, becomes emperor (▶ 1072) and marries the widow of Constantine X Ducas (◀ 1067).

The Seljuk Turks (◀ 1064) invade Georgia and the Byzantine emperor Romanus IV Diogenes is provoked into a response.

1069

Benedict founds Selby Abbey in Yorkshire.

1070

✠ April 11: Papal legates lay charges against Stigand, Archbishop of Canterbury (◀ 1052, ▶ 1072); he is condemned and imprisoned.

✠ August 29: Lanfranc (◀ 1045, 1066, ▶ 1089), who came over with William the Conqueror, succeeds Stigand as the first Norman archbishop.

🏛 Lanfranc begins to rebuild Canterbury Cathedral (◀ 1020, ▶ 1503).

🏛 York Minster is rebuilt by Thomas of Bayeux, first Norman Archbishop of York (▶ 1075).

Margaret, Queen of Scotland (▶ 1250), founds Dunfermline Abbey, Fife.

1071

The Seljuk Turks (◀ 1068) inflict a devastating defeat on the Byzantines at the Battle of Manzikert, near Lake Van. Emperor Romanus IV Diogenes (◀ 1068, ▶ 1072) is captured.

1072

👑 October 24: Michael VII Ducas (▶ 1078), son of Constantine VIII (◀ 1025), is proclaimed emperor.

👑 Romanus IV Diogenes (◀ 1071) dies, having been blinded and exiled to the Sea of Marmara on his release.

The Norman Roussel de Bailleul sets up an independent principality in Byzantine Asia Minor. Michael VII Ducas appeals to the Turks for aid, thus facilitating their conquest of Asia Minor.

Stigand (◀ 1070) starves himself to death.

The Diocese of Lincoln is founded.

1073

✠ April 21: Pope Alexander II (◀ 1061) dies.

✠ April 22: Hildebrand, Archdeacon of the Church of Rome, is elected as Pope Gregory VII (▶ 1074).

Hamburg is sacked by the Vikings (◀ 864).

The English church is reorganized. York is subordinated to Canterbury.

1074

Clerical celibacy is made compulsory. Pope Gregory VII (◀ 1073, ▶ 1085) excommunicates married priests.

1075

March: Pope Gregory VII issues his *Dictatus Papae*, 27 points asserting the supremacy of the Pope.

☸ August 2: John VIII Xiphilinus, Patriarch of Constantinople (◀ 1064), dies and is succeeded by Cosmas I (▶ 1081).

Pope Gregory VII forbids lay people to nominate and appoint individuals to positions within the church. King Heinrich IV of Germany (◀ 1056) takes vehement exception to this ruling. The long-running dispute that follows is known as the Investiture Controversy and is an important step towards the separation of sacred and secular authority, church and state, in Western Christianity.

The Diocese of Chichester is founded.

The Danes destroy York Minster.

The Investiture Controversy

The Investiture Controversy is a conflict in the late eleventh and twelfth centuries over whether lay rulers have the authority to bestow on a bishop or abbot the signs of his office. The issue arises particularly in the German states, where a lay person can own a church or monastery ('proprietary church'), and where kings claim by divine right to have rule over the church, but also spreads elsewhere. It begins in the pontificate of Leo IX (◀ 1049) and comes to a head in that of Gregory VII (◀ 1073). Gregory prohibits the investiture of clergy by lay persons and in his *Dictatus papae* (◀ 1075) declares that only the Pope can appoint or depose bishops; he can also depose emperors. The next year he excommunicates and deposes King Heinrich IV of Germany, who is forced to do penance before being reinstated (▶ 1077). However, Heinrich consolidates his power, deposes Pope Gregory, appoints an antipope and sends an army against Rome, driving Gregory into exile, where he dies (▶ 1085).

At about the same time, Pope Gregory has also been in conflict with King Henry I of England. Anselm (◀ 1033), Archbishop of Canterbury, insists on observing the papal decrees against lay investiture, refusing to consecrate bishops whom Henry has invested. A compromise is achieved in the Concord of London (▶ 1107); this is followed by the Concordat of Worms (▶ 1123), with another compromise.

The controversy is a turning point in the history of religious authority and in the relationship between the spiritual and the temporal, the secular and the religious, heralding the modern separation between church and state.

1076

January 24: Heinrich IV convenes a synod of bishops in Worms which votes to depose Pope Gregory VII (◀ 1075, ▶ 1080).

February 22: Gregory VII excommunicates and deposes Heinrich IV for nominating bishops.

1077

January 25–27: Heinrich IV does penance at Canossa and his excommunication is lifted.

Bayeux Cathedral is consecrated: the first bishop is Odo, half-brother of William the Conqueror (◀ 1066).

163

1078

♛ January 7: After there is rioting against Michael VII Ducas (◀ 1072) in Constantinople, Nicephorus III Botaneites (▶ 1080), governor of Anatolia, is proclaimed emperor in Nicaea.

March 31: Nicephorus III Botaneites marches on Constantinople and Emperor Michael VII Ducas (◀ 1072) abdicates.

✪ Alphege (◀ 1012) is canonized by Pope Gregory VII: feast day April 19.

The Diocese of Salisbury is founded.

1079

♠ Peter Abelard (▶ 1140), pioneer theologian, is born. He falls in love with Heloise whom he then marries; enemies later castrate him. Dies 1142.

🏛 The foundations of Winchester Cathedral are laid by Walkelin, the first Norman Bishop of Winchester.

1080

Renewing the Investiture Controversy (see p. 163), Gregory VII again excommunicates Heinrich IV.

⚜ June 25: Heinrich IV (◀ 1056) declares Pope Gregory VII (◀ 1076, ▶ 1084) deposed and elects Guibert (▶ 1084), an Italian nobleman at the German court, antipope.

In a struggle between Emperor Nicephorus III Botaneites (◀ 1078, ▶ 1081) and a usurper, Nicephorus Melissenus, appeals by both sides for Turkish aid result in the loss of most of Asia Minor.

King Alfonso VI of Castile-Leon (◀ 1037, ▶ 1085) replaces the Mozarabic rites in use with the Roman liturgy.

🏛 Work begins on the rebuilding of Hereford Cathedral (◀ 1056).

🏛 York Minster is rebuilt (◀ 1075).

🏛 Work begins on Cluny Abbey III (◀ 981, ▶ c.1088).

1081

♛ April 4: Nicephorus III Botaneites abdicates (◀ 1080) and enters a monastery. Alexius I Comnenus becomes emperor (▶ 1118).

⚜ May 7: Cosmas I, Patriarch of Constantinople (◀ 1075), abdicates and is succeeded by Eustathius Garidas (▶ 1084).

✪ King István I of Hungary (◀ c.1001) is canonized by Pope Gregory VII: feast day August 16.

Bamberg Cathedral (◀ 1012) is partially destroyed by fire (▶ 1111).

1083

⛪ The building of the present nave of Rochester Cathedral (◀ 604) is begun by Bishop Gundulf.

⛪ Abbot Simeon lays the foundations of the present Ely Cathedral (◀ c.970, ▶ 1109).

1084

☉ March 24: Heinrich IV (◀ 1056) enters Rome and enthrones Guibert (◀ 1080) as Antipope Clement III (▶ 1100). Gregory VII (◀ 1081, ▶ 1085) is forced into exile in Salerno.

♛ March 31: Antipope Clement III crowns Heinrich IV Holy Roman Emperor. However, the approach of a Norman army compels Heinrich and Clement to leave Rome, and Clement takes refuge in Ravenna.

☉ July: Eustathius Garidas, Patriarch of Constantinople (◀ 1081), abdicates and is succeeded by Nicholas III Grammaticus (▶ 1111).

☉ The Carthusian Order is founded by Bruno of Cologne at Chartreuse, near Grenoble. After his death he is venerated as a saint: feast day October 6.

⛪ Bishop Wulfstan (▶ 1203), the only Anglo-Saxon bishop remaining after the Norman Conquest, begins the rebuilding of Worcester Cathedral (▶ 1394).

1085

May 6: The Christian reconquest of the Iberian peninsula begins with the capture of the Muslim city of Toledo by Alfonso VI of Castile-Leon (◀ 1080).

☉ May 25: The exiled Pope Gregory VII (◀ 1084) dies in Salerno.

⛪ Work begins on a Norman cathedral in Lichfield to replace Chad's Saxon church (◀ 700, ▶ 1195).

Isleifur Gissurarson becomes the first Bishop of Iceland (◀ 1000).

1086

☉ May 24: Desiderius, Abbot of Monte Cassino, who has good relations with the Normans, is elected as Pope Victor III (▶ 1087), but is forced back to Monte Cassino by rioting in Rome.

1087

☉ May 9: Pope Victor III is consecrated in Rome.

♛ September 9: King William I ('the Conqueror') of England (◀ 1066) dies and is succeeded by his son William, who becomes William II ('Rufus') (▶ 1089, 1100).

☉ September 16: Pope Victor III (◀ 1086) dies.

⛪ St Paul's Cathedral, London, is burnt down in a fire in the city and work on a vast Norman cathedral begins (◀ 961, ▶ 1310). It comes to be known as Old St Paul's.

165

1088

✠ March 12: Odo of Lagery, at one time Abbot of Cluny, is elected as Pope Urban II (▶ 1099).

The University of Bologna is founded, the oldest existing university in Europe.

*c.***1088**

⌂ The building of a new abbey church at Cluny (◀ 1080), known as the Great Church, is begun.

1089

✠ May 28: Lanfranc, Archbishop of Canterbury (◀ 1070), dies. King William II (◀ 1087, ▶ 1095) holds the archbishopric open for four years and appropriates its incomes.

⌂ Braga Cathedral, Portugal, is consecrated; it will not be completed for two centuries.

The expression *Curia Romana* first appears in a papal bull.

1090

♟ Bernard of Clairvaux (▶ 1146) is born. A Cistercian, he founds the Abbey of Clairvaux in France and is a powerful figure in the church politics of his time. Dies 1153.

⌂ Work begins on the building of Zurich Grossmünster.

1091

The Normans take Noto, the last Arab stronghold in Sicily (◀ 1060).

The Synod of Benevento makes universal the ceremony of placing ashes on the forehead as a sign of penitence on Ash Wednesday.

The Diocese of Norwich is founded.

1092

⌂ The cathedral built by Bishop Remigius in Lincoln is consecrated (▶ 1141).

⌂ A cathedral is built at Old Sarum, outside present-day Salisbury, but it burns down five days after it is consecrated (▶ 1190).

1093

✠ December 4: Anselm (◀ 1060, ▶ 1095), Abbot of Bec in Normandy, is appointed Archbishop of Canterbury (▶ 1109).

The monastery of Maria Laach near Koblenz is founded as an offshoot of Cluny (◀ *c.*1088).

⌂ The building of Durham Cathedral (◀ 995) is begun (▶ 1133).

⌂ Winchester Cathedral (◀ 1079) is consecrated.

1095

October 25: Urban II consecrates the high altar of the Great Church at Cluny (◀ *c.*1088).

November 18: A council is convened in Clermont in the Auvergne for the reform of the church.

November 27: At the council, Pope Urban II issues a call to go on the First Crusade to aid Christians in the East and to regain the holy places.

Anselm (◀ 1093, ▶ 1100) goes into exile in Rome after a dispute with King William II (◀ 1089, ▶ 1101) over royal authority in ecclesiastical matters (see p. 163). William seizes his lands (▶ 1100).

The Crusades

In 1095 Pope Urban II calls for a 'war of the cross', a crusade, to liberate Jerusalem from Muslim occupation, to be rewarded with forgiveness of sins and rich plunder. His call meets with an immediate and enthusiastic response and is followed by a series of crusades to the Holy Land. The First Crusade succeeds in capturing Jerusalem in 1099 and establishing Crusader states, but a disorganized People's Crusade comes to grief in Constantinople (1096). Further crusades also fail: the Second Crusade (1145) collapses after a failure to capture Damascus; the Third Crusade (1189) captures Acre and Cyprus but does not get as far as Jerusalem; the Fourth Crusade is diverted to Constantinople, which the Crusaders capture and loot in 1204. The Fifth Crusade (1218) and Sixth Crusade (1227) achieve little, as does a final crusade to the Holy Land launched by King Louis IX of France in 1248.

The ideology of crusading proves so effective that it is extended to other areas, first to the reconquest of the Iberian peninsula, beginning with an unsuccessful invasion of the Balearic islands in 1114. In 1198 Archbishop Hartwig II of Bremen launches a crusade against the Wends in Livonia, in north-east Europe, and in 1209 Pope Innocent III launches a first crusade against the Albigensians or Cathars in southern France; Pope Honorius III proclaims a second crusade against them in 1218. All these crusades have the promise of the same rewards as crusades to the Holy Land. The idea of the crusade is still alive when a crusade is proclaimed against the Hussites in 1420.

---

*c.***1095**

🌳📖 Peter Lombard is born. He is known for his *Sentences*, four volumes of quotations from the church fathers, forming a summary of doctrine. Dies 1169.

1096

A group of Crusaders travelling through the Rhineland massacre Jews in Cologne, Mainz, Worms and Speyer.

August 1: Crusaders led by Peter the Hermit (the 'People's Crusade') reach Constantinople. They are ferried across the Bosphorus and massacred soon afterwards. Peter is safe in Constantinople.

December 23: The main force of Crusaders reaches Constantinople.

🏛 Work begins on the building of Norwich Cathedral.

1097

April 9 and 22: Two more Crusader forces arrive in Constantinople.

1098

June 3: The Crusaders capture Antioch.

♣ ♫ Hildegard of Bingen is born. A German mystic, she is abbess of a community, author of an impressive range of writings, and composer of music. Her major literary work is *Scivias* ('Know the Way', 1151) and her major musical composition *Symphonia harmoniae caelestium revelationum* ('Symphony of the Harmony of Heavenly Revelations', *c*.1155). Dies 1179.

The Abbey of Cîteaux and its Cistercian Order are founded by Robert of Molesme (▶ 1222).

1099

July 15: The Crusaders capture Jerusalem.

✠ July 29: Pope Urban II (◀ 1088) dies.

✠ August 13: Rainerius, a monk and cardinal priest in Rome, is elected as Pope Paschal II (▶ 1118).

1100

♛ August 2: King William II of England (◀ 1087) dies and is succeeded by his brother, who becomes King Henry I (▶ 1135).

✠ September 8: Antipope Clement III (◀ 1084) dies.

♛ December 25: The Crusader Baldwin of Boulogne is crowned the first King of Jerusalem.

King Henry I recalls Anselm to England (◀ 1095, ▶ 1103).

♣ Arnold of Brescia, radical reformer, is born. He is hanged in 1155.

🏛 Gothic architecture appears with St Germain des Prés, France.

***c*.1100**

🏛 The building of Cahors Cathedral, France, with two huge domes, begins (▶ 1119).

Twelfth century

The century is above all a century of crusades: after the First Crusade has come to a successful end with the capture of Jerusalem and the establishment of a Christian king there, there is enthusiasm for further crusades, particularly among those who for some reason have missed the opportunity of crusading. Two further crusades are far less successful, because of the opposition of the skilled Muslim general Saladin; the Fourth Crusade, called for by Pope Innocent III right at the end of the century, has disastrous consequences: the crusaders are diverted to Constantinople, which they capture and plunder, establishing a Latin kingdom there as well. Once the crusades are launched, the idea of the crusade, promoted with a mixture of the promise of spiritual rewards and the threat of divine judgement on those who do not take part, is extended to areas other than the Holy Land. In 1115 an attack on the Muslim-held Balearic Islands is pronounced a crusade; in 1147 Pope Eugenius III authorizes crusading in Spain and beyond the north-eastern frontier of Germany; in 1171 Pope Alexander III equates crusades against the pagan Estonians and Finns with crusades in the Holy Land; in 1179 the Third Lateran Council proclaims a crusade against the Albigensians or Cathars, a sect in the south of France which in the tradition of Manichaeism regards matter as evil, and in 1193 Pope Celestine III proclaims a crusade against the Wends in the Baltic, which is endorsed in 1198 by Hartwig II, Archbishop of Bremen. Subsequently campaigns in the Balkans and war on the Hussites are regarded as crusades.

Religious orders come into being in the Holy Land. In 1113 the Knights of St John (Hospitallers) are founded to care for pilgrims to Jerusalem and create a hospice near the Church of the Holy Sepulchre; in 1118 the Knights Templar are founded to protect pilgrims in the Holy Land, and in 1190 an Order of German Hospitallers is founded during the siege of Acre; this later becomes the Teutonic Order. The Knights Templar and the Teutonic Knights take on a dominant military aspect and fall into disrepute. Around 1154 the ascetic Carmelite Order is founded in Palestine by Berthold of Calabria, who has gone there as a pilgrim. In France in 1120 the Order of Premonstratensian Canons, an austere Augustinian order, is founded by Norbert. Domingo de Guzman (Dominic), who founds the Order of Preachers (Dominicans), and Francis of Assisi, who founds the Order of Friars Minor (Franciscans), are both born in the century: their orders will play a major role in preaching, missionary work, scholarship and the combating of heresy.

Another form of combating heresy appears with the establishment of the episcopal Inquisition by Pope Lucius III in 1184: bishops are to seek out heretics in their dioceses and hand them over to the secular authorities for punishment. This is directed not only against the Albigensians but against the Waldensians, a reform movement founded by Peter Waldo after 1170, characterized by poverty, itinerant preaching and the use of scripture in the vernacular. Both reform movements and the Inquisition are to develop further in coming centuries.

1101

🏛 Work begins on the construction of the Assumption Cathedral in Smolensk (▶ 1674).

1103

April: Anselm (◀ 1100, ▶ 1106) breaks with King Henry I over investiture (◀ see p. 163) and goes to Rome.

The Diocese of Lund in Sweden becomes independent of the German Archdiocese of Hamburg-Bremen (◀ 864) and is made the first archdiocese in Scandinavia.

🏛 Work begins on the construction of Lund Cathedral.

1104

Basil, the leader of a Manichaean-type sect called the Bogomils, centred in Bulgaria but spreading both eastwards and westwards, is burned alive on a pyre in the Hippodrome at Constantinople.

1105

👑 Heinrich V becomes King of Germany (▶ 1111) and forces the abdication of his father, Holy Roman Emperor Heinrich IV (◀ 1084).

1106

Anselm (◀ 1103, ▶ 1109) returns to England.

1107

By the Concord of London Henry I of England (◀ 1100, ▶ 1121) abandons lay investiture (◀ see p. 163) but maintains authority over bishops and abbots in his realm.

🏛 Bishop Urban instigates the building of Llandaff Cathedral, Wales.

1108

Magnus (◀ 1065, ▶ 1115) becomes the first Earl of Orkney.

👑 July 29: Philippe I, King of France (◀ 1060), dies and is succeeded by Louis VI (▶ 1137).

Klosterneuburg Abbey near Vienna is founded (▶ c.1150). It becomes famous for its wines.

William of Champeaux, Archdeacon of Notre Dame, Paris, moves his school to the hermitage of St Victor (▶ 1113) near the city.

The Magdeburg Appeal, a letter to the clergy of Saxony, the Rhineland and Flanders, calls for military support against the Wends (◀ 982).

Chichester Cathedral is consecrated but is badly damaged by fire (▶ 1199).

1109

☥ April 21: Anselm, Archbishop of Canterbury (◀ 1093), dies (▶ 1494). His death is followed by a five-year vacancy.

Ely is made a diocese and the church there (◀ 1083) becomes a cathedral (▶ 1189).

171

1110

The earliest record of a miracle play is of one at Dunstable, Kent.

Robert d'Abrissel founds the Abbey of Fontevrauld near Saumur, France. As well as housing an order of monks and nuns it becomes a burial place for nobility and the English royal family, notably Richard I Lionheart (▶ 1189).

Worms Cathedral is consecrated. The present building is not completed until later (▶ 1181).

Work begins on the building of Porto Cathedral, Portugal.

1111

Heinrich V (◀ 1105, ▶ 1119) becomes Holy Roman Emperor.

May: Nicholas III Grammaticus, Patriarch of Constantinople (◀ 1084), dies.

May 24: John IX Agapetus becomes Patriarch of Constantinople (▶ 1134).

At the Synod of Rath Bresail the Irish church begins to organize itself on diocesan rather than on monastic lines as hitherto with the introduction of the provinces of Armagh and Cashel (▶ 1152).

A new Bamberg Cathedral (◀ 1081), built by Bishop Otto of Bamberg (▶ 1124), is consecrated.

1113

Under Gildwin, successor to William of Champeaux (◀ 1108), St Victor in Paris becomes a richly endowed abbey and centre of learning.

The Knights of St John (Hospitallers) are founded to care for pilgrims to Jerusalem; they create a hospice near the Church of the Holy Sepulchre.

1114

April 26: Ralph d'Escures, Bishop of Rochester and administrator of the vacancy of the Archbishopric of Canterbury (◀ 1109), is appointed Archbishop of Canterbury (▶ 1122).

Exeter Cathedral (◀ 1050) is rebuilt in the Norman style.

1115

April 16: Magnus, Earl of Orkney (◀ 1108), is killed on Egilsay (▶ 1135).

A joint force of Catalans and Pisans invades the Balearic Islands but has little success. This is regarded as a crusade.

The Abbey of Clairvaux is founded. Bernard is its first abbot.

1116

Peterborough Abbey (◀ 972) is destroyed in an accidental fire (▶ 1118).

⬚ Parma Cathedral, one of the most important Romanesque cathedrals in Europe, is consecrated by Pope Paschal II. It is destroyed by an earthquake the next year and has to be rebuilt.

1118

☥ January 21: Pope Paschal II (◀ 1099) dies.

☥ January 24: Giovanni di Gaeta, Roman chancellor, is elected as Pope Gelasius II (▶ 1119).

March 18: Maurice Burdinus, Archbishop of Braga, is proclaimed Pope (Antipope) as Gregory VIII (▶ 1119).

♛ August 15: Emperor Alexius I Comnenus (◀ 1081) dies and is succeeded by his son John II Comnenus (▶ 1143), who campaigns to regain lost Byzantine territories.

The Order of Knights Templar is formed to protect pilgrims in the Holy Land (▶ 1129).

⬚ The rebuilding of Peterborough Abbey (◀ 1116) begins (▶ 1238).

1119

☥ January 29: Pope Gelasius II (◀ 1118) dies.

☥ February 2: Guido, son of Count Guillaume of Burgundy, is elected as Pope Callistus II (▶ 1124).

⬚ September 10: The Cathedral of Cahors, France (◀ c.1100), is consecrated by Pope Callistus II.

October 30: 427 bishops at the Council of Reims excommunicate Emperor Heinrich V (◀ 1111) and Antipope Gregory VIII (◀ 1118, ▶ 1121).

1120

The Order of Premonstratensian Canons, an austere Augustinian order, is founded by Norbert (▶ 1582) at Prémontré near Laon, France.

⬚ Work begins on the building of Autun Cathedral, France.

⬚ Work begins on the building of St Front Cathedral, Perigueux, France, which resembles St Mark's, Venice.

c.1120

♣ Thomas Becket (▶ 1162), English churchman, is born. He becomes Archbishop of Canterbury, but falls out with King Henry II. He is murdered in 1170.

⬚ Tournus Abbey in Burgundy is consecrated.

1121

April: Antipope Gregory VIII (◀ 1119) is made by Pope Callistus II to ride in disgrace backwards on a camel through Rome and is imprisoned for the rest of his life.

Reading Abbey is founded by King Henry I (◀ 1107, ▶ 1135) and becomes one of the major pilgrimage centres of medieval England.

1122

September 23: The Concordat of Worms (▶ 1123) settles the Investiture Controversy (see p. 163) with a compromise over the respective rights of pope and emperor.

✠ October 20: Ralph d'Escures, Archbishop of Canterbury (◀ 1114), dies.

Suger is elected Abbot of St Denis (◀ 625, ▶ 1140).

1123

✠ February 18: William de Corbeil, Prior of the Augustinian priory in St Osyth in Essex, is appointed Archbishop of Canterbury (▶ 1136).

March 11–27: The First Lateran Council meets under Pope Callistus II. It solemnly ratifies the Concordat of Worms (◀ 1122). It is regarded in the West as the ninth Ecumenical Council.

St Bartholomew's Hospital, London, is founded.

1124

✠ December 14: Pope Callistus II (◀ 1119) dies.

✠ December 21: Lamberto Scannabecchi, Cardinal Bishop of Ostia, is elected as Pope Honorius II (▶ 1130).

Otto, Bishop of Bamberg, begins a mission in Pomerania.

1125

A Norwegian, Arnald, is consecrated Bishop of Greenland.

1126

♛ Alfonso VII becomes King of Leon and Castile (▶ 1157). His reign sees the supremacy of the western kingdoms of Spain over the eastern (Navarre and Aragon). He introduces the Cistercians to Spain and captures Almeria from the Moors.

🌷 Averroes is born. An Islamic lawyer and philosopher, he writes commentaries on Aristotle by means of which Aristotle enters the Western world. Dies 1198.

1127

Archbishop Raimondo of Toledo establishes a translation school to translate classical works (from Arabic) (▶ 1269).

Vicellinus, a priest from Hamelin, is commissioned by the Archbishop of Hamburg-Bremen (◀ 864) to engage in missionary work among the Wends (◀ 981).

1128

☩ The Abbey of Holyrood is founded by King David I of Scotland, who after his death is venerated as a saint: feast day May 24.

⌂ A third cathedral in Angoulême, France (◀ 1017), with a line of four stone domes, is consecrated.

⌂ The Cathedral of Santiago de Compostela is consecrated (◀ 899).

1129

The Council of Troyes defines the Rule of the Knights Templar (◀ 1118).

1130

☦ February 13: Pope Honorius II (◀ 1124) dies.

☦ February 14: Gregorio Papareschi, a Roman patrician, is clandestinely elected as Pope Innocent II (▶ 1143) under the influence of the powerful Roman chancellor Aimeric.

☦ February 14: Cardinal Pietro Pierloni is elected as Antipope Anacletus II (▶ 1138) by the majority of cardinals.

September 27: With the support of Antipope Anacletus II, Roger II of Sicily (▶ 1154) is made king and Sicily becomes a kingdom. Roger II thus brings all the Norman conquests in southern Italy under consolidated government. At times he controls Malta and parts of North Africa. The kingdom becomes Roman Catholic, with a Latin culture.

⌂ October 25: The Great Church of Cluny (◀ c.1088) is dedicated by Pope Innocent II. At the time it is the largest in Europe.

*c.***1130**

▮ The sculptor Gislebertus creates the dramatic Last Judgement tympanum on Autun Cathedral, France.

1131

May 9: Walter de Clare, Lord of Chepstow, founds Tintern Abbey, the first Cistercian monastery in Wales.

1132

♣ Joachim of Fiore is born. An Italian mystic, he interprets history in terms of the Trinity: the Old Testament is the age of the Father; the New Testament to his day the age of the Son; the new age of the Spirit is imminent. Dies 1202.

Fountains Abbey in Yorkshire, a Cistercian monastery, is founded.

Rievaulx Abbey in Yorkshire is founded.

1133

⌂ Durham Cathedral is consecrated (◀ 1093).

⌂ The building of Exeter Cathedral (◀ 1050, ▶ 1258, *c.*1400) begins.

The Diocese of Carlisle is founded.

1134

✠ April: John IX Agapetus, Patriarch of Constantinople (◀ 1111), dies and is succeeded by Leo Styppes (▶ 1143).

1135

♟ March 30: Maimonides is born. A Spanish Jewish philosopher, his work on Aristotle influences Albertus Magnus (▶ 1193) and Thomas Aquinas (▶ 1225). Dies 1204.

♛ December 1: King Henry I of England (◀ 1100) dies and is succeeded by King Stephen (▶ 1154), who is the last Norman King of England.

☉ Magnus, Earl of Orkney (◀ 1115), is canonized by Pope Innocent II.

1136

✠ November 21: William de Corbeil, Archbishop of Canterbury (◀ 1123), dies.

Emperor John II Comnenus (◀ 1118, ▶ 1143) founds the Pantocrator Monastery in Constantinople, the largest and best-endowed in the Byzantine period.

1137

♛ August 1: Louis VI, King of France (◀ 1108), dies and is succeeded by Louis VII (▶ 1180).

🏛 The building of Kirkwall Cathedral, Orkney (▶ 1468), begins.

🏛 Duke Henry the Lion (▶ 1147) begins to build Lübeck Cathedral.

1138

✠ January 8: Theobald, Abbot of the Abbey of Bec in Normandy, is consecrated Archbishop of Canterbury (▶ 1161).

January 25: Antipope Anacletus II (◀ 1130) dies.

1139

April 3–19: Pope Innocent II (◀ 1130, ▶ 1143) holds the Second Lateran Council, which is regarded in the West as the tenth Ecumenical Council. It condemns the teachings of Arnold of Brescia (◀ 1100), who attacks the church's wealth and tries to revive the ideal of apostolic poverty.

🏛 Work begins on the building of the Old Cathedral of Coimbra, Portugal.

1140

June: The Council of Sens condemns Abelard (◀ 1079, ▶ 1142) for his revisions of Christian theology.

📖 Gratian, a monk, finishes his 'Decree', a compilation of thousands of texts from the church fathers, councils and popes. He attempts to resolve the contradictions in them.

🏛 Building of the Gothic church of St Denis, Paris, begins under Abbot Suger (◀ 1122). It has the first rose window.

⌂ Crusaders renovate the Church of the Holy Sepulchre in Jerusalem, using French Romanesque cathedral architecture as a model (◀ 1034).

1141

February 11: Hugh of St Victor dies. He is the most distinguished of the Victorines, scholars living at the Abbey of St Victor (◀ 1113).

⌂ Lincoln Cathedral (◀ 1092) is damaged by fire and partly rebuilt (▶ 1185).

1142

April 21: Abelard (◀ 1079) dies.

1143

☥ January: Leo Styppes, Patriarch of Constantinople (◀ 1134), dies and is succeeded by Michael II Kurkuas (▶ 1146).

♛ April 8: John II Comnenus (◀ 1118) dies and is succeeded by his son Manuel I Comnenus (▶ 1180).

☥ September 24: Pope Innocent II (◀ 1130) dies.

☥ September 26: Guido of Città di Castello in Umbria, a pupil of Peter Abelard (◀ 1079), is elected as Pope Celestine II (▶ 1144).

The citizens of Rome riot and set up a commune with its own independent senate (▶ 1145).

Peter the Venerable of Cluny makes a Latin version of the Qur'an.

1144

☥ March 8: Pope Celestine II (◀ 1043) dies.

☥ March 12: Gherardo Caccianemici, Roman chancellor and a friend of Bernard of Clairvaux, is elected as Pope Lucius II (▶ 1145).

Zangi, Governor of Mosul in what is now northern Iraq, captures Edessa from the Christians.

1145

☥ February 15: Pope Lucius II (◀ 1144) is killed in an attack on the senate of the Roman commune (◀ 1143).

☥ July 8: Bernardo Pignatelli is elected as Pope Eugenius III, the first Cistercian pope (▶ 1153).

December 1: In the papal bull *Quantum praedecessores*, Pope Eugenius proclaims the Second Crusade.

📖 In his *Chronicles* the German chronicler Otto of Friesing makes the first mention of Prester (Presbyter) John, a Nestorian priest and king who is said to have defeated the Muslims and to have set out for Jerusalem to bring aid to the Holy Land.

⌂ Building of a cathedral in Chartres, France, begins on the site of an earlier Romanesque cathedral (▶ 1194).

1146

March 31: At Vézélay in France, Bernard of Clairvaux (◀ 1090, ▶ 1153) preaches the need for a second crusade in order to recapture Edessa in Syria and fight against Muslims in Spain.

☉ Heinrich II, King of Germany (◀ 1024), is canonized by Pope Eugenius III: feast day July 17.

☧ Michael II Kurkuas, Patriarch of Constantinople (◀ 1143), dies and is succeeded by Cosmas II Atticus (▶ 1147).

1147

☧ February 26: Cosmas II Atticus, Patriarch of Constantinople (◀ 1146), is deposed.

April 13: In the papal bull *Divina dispensatione*, Pope Eugenius III authorizes crusading in Spain and beyond the north-eastern frontier of Germany.

September: Crusaders on the Second Crusade arrive in Constantinople.

October 25: The Crusaders' army is defeated and massacred by the Muslims at Dorylaeum.

Henry the Lion of Saxony (◀ 1137) and Albert the Bear of Brandenburg launch a campaign against the Wends (◀ 982).

☧ December: Nicholas IV Muzalon becomes Patriarch of Constantinople (▶ 1151).

1148

July 28: Another Crusader force has to retreat from Damascus after a failed siege.

1149

⌂ Rebuilding of the Church of the Holy Sepuchre, Jerusalem (◀ 1140), is completed.

1150

♕ Sancho VI becomes King of Navarre (▶ 1194).

c.1150

♟▣ Nicholas of Verdun, French craftsman, is born. The greatest enamellist and goldsmith of his day, he creates the altarpiece of the abbey church of Klosterneuburg in Austria (*c*.1180) and the Shrine of the Three Kings in Cologne Cathedral (1180). Dies *c*.1210.

⌂ A stave church is built at Urnes in Norway, involving timber posts sunk into the earth.

The University of Paris grows up as a corporation around the Cathedral of Notre Dame.

Recitation of the *Ave Maria* ('Hail, Mary') becomes general.

The stave church at Urnes, Norway, *c.*1150

1151

♨ Nicholas IV Muzalon, Patriarch of Constantinople (◀ 1147), dies and is succeeded by Theodotus II (▶ 1153).

1152

♛ March 4: Friedrich I Barbarossa (▶ 1155) becomes King of Germany (▶ 1190).

Following the Synod of Rath Bresail (◀ 1111), the Synod of Kells extends the diocesan system throughout Ireland with the creation of the provinces of Tuam and Dublin. The primacy of the Irish church moves from Canterbury to Armagh.

⌂ Amiens Cathedral is built in the Romanesque style (▶ 1218).

1153

♨ July 8: Pope Eugenius III (◀ 1145) dies.

♨ July 8: Corrado, Cardinal Bishop of Santa Sabina, is elected as Pope Anastasius IV (▶ 1154).

♣ August 21: Bernard of Clairvaux (◀ 1090) dies (▶ 1190).

♨ October: Theodotus II, Patriarch of Constantinople (◀ 1151), dies and is succeeded by Neophytus I, who is elected but not consecrated.

179

☸ November: Neophytus I dies and is succeeded by Constantine IV Chliarenus (▶ 1156).

ⅲ Erfurt Cathedral (◀ 741) collapses, and work begins on a Romanesque replacement.

1154

♛ February 26: Roger II, King of Sicily (◀ 1130), dies and is succeeded by his son Guglielmo I (▶ 1166).

♛ October 25: King Stephen of England (◀ 1135) dies. He is succeeded by Henry, grandson of King Henry I (◀ 1100), who becomes King Henry II (▶ 1189) and rules over an empire extending from the Scottish border to the Pyrennees.

☸ December: Pope Anastasius IV (◀ 1153) dies.

☸ December 4: Nicholas Breakspear, a successful papal legate in Scandinavia, is elected as Pope Hadrian IV (▶ 1159), the only English pope. The title 'vicar of Christ' (◀ 493) comes to be used regularly from his reign onwards.

Christianity is introduced into Finland by King Erik of Sweden.

c.1154

The ascetic Carmelite Order is founded in Palestine by Berthold of Calabria, who has gone there as a pilgrim.

1155

♛ June 18: Friedrich I Barbarossa, King of Germany (◀ 1152, ▶ 1164), is crowned Holy Roman Emperor.

♠ June: Arnold of Brescia (◀ 1100) is hanged.

1156

☸ May: Constantine IV Chliarenus, Patriarch of Constantinople (◀ 1153), dies and is succeeded by Luke Chrysoberges (▶ 1169).

1157

♛ August 21: King Alfonso VII of Leon and Castile (◀ 1126) dies. On his death the kingdom is divided: in Castile his son reigns as Sancho III only one year (▶ 1158); his son Fernando II becomes King of Leon (▶ 1188).

♛ Valdemar (to be known as Valdemar the Great) becomes King of Norway, ushering in an age of prosperity with the construction of many Romanesque churches.

1158

♛ Alfonso VIII (▶ 1164), grandson of Alfonso VII (◀ 1157), becomes King of Castile at the age of three (▶ 1214). He presides over the reconquest of Spain from the Moors.

ⅲ Work begins on building the Assumption Cathedral, Vladimir, Russia.

1159

☸ September 1: Pope Hadrian IV (◀ 1154) dies.

☮ September 7: Orlando Bandinelli, professor of law in Bologna, is elected as Pope Alexander III (▸ 1181).

☮ September 7: Cardinals who support Emperor Friedrich I Barbarossa (◂ 1152) elect Cardinal Ottaviano of Montecelli Antipope as Victor IV (▸ 1160).

1160

☮ February: The Synod of Pavia pronounces in favour of Victor IV as Pope.

October: A gathering of bishops and heads of monastic orders in the presence of Henry II of England and Louis VII of France supports Pope Alexander III; only Cluny supports Victor IV (▸ 1164).

Building of Laon Cathedral, France (▸ 1225), begins.

1161

☮ April 18: Theobald of Bec, Archbishop of Canterbury (◂ 1139), dies.

King Edward the Confessor (◂ 1066) is canonized by Pope Alexander III: feast day January 5.

1162

☮ June 3: Thomas Becket (◂ *c.*1120, ▸ 1164), Chancellor of England, is appointed Archbishop of Canterbury (▸ 1164). King Henry II has chosen him to curtail the powers of the church, but when appointed he defends them.

1163

Pope Alexander III lays the cornerstone of the new Cathedral of Notre Dame, Paris (▸ 1282).

1164

☮ April 20: Antipope Victor IV (◂ 1160) dies.

☮ April 22: The supporters of Friedrich I Barbarossa (◂ 1155, ▸ 1167) elect Rainald of Dassel, his chancellor, as Antipope Paschal III (▸ 1168).

November 2: Thomas Becket (◂ 1162, ▸ 1170) goes into exile for contempt of court.

♛ Alfonso II becomes King of Aragon (▸ 1196). He allies himself with Alfonso VIII of Castile (◂ 1158) against Navarre and the Moors.

Uppsala becomes an archdiocese: Stefan is consecrated first Archbishop and Primate of Sweden.

1166

♛ May 7: Guglielmo I, King of Sicily (◂ 1154), dies and is succeeded by his son Guglielmo II (▸ 1189), who is only thirteen. He unsuccessfully tries to gain territory from the Muslims and the Byzantines.

1167

Friedrich I Barbarossa (◀ 1164, ▶ 1178) invades Rome.

Narses IV becomes Catholicos of Armenia. As well as being an eminent theologian he writes hymns, chants, lyric poems and a poetic history of Armenia (▶ 1173).

Oxford University begins when King Henry II bans all English students from attending the University of Paris and they congregate in Oxford.

1168

☿ September 20: Antipope Paschal III (◀ 1164) dies. The supporters of Friedrich I Barbarossa (◀ 1167, ▶ 1189) elect Giovanni, Abbot of Struma, as Antipope Callistus III (▶ 1178) to succeed him.

1169

♟ August 21: Peter Lombard (◀ c.1095) dies.

☿ December: Luke Chrysoberges, Patriarch of Constantinople (◀ 1156), dies.

Saladin (▶ 1187), a gifted Muslim general, takes control of Egypt.

1170

☿ January: Michael III of Anchialus becomes Patriarch of Constantinople (▶ 1178).

November 30: Thomas Becket (◀ 1164) returns to England.

♟ December 29: Thomas Becket (◀ c.1120) is murdered in Canterbury Cathedral (▶ 1173).

Pope Alexander III (◀ 1163, ▶ 1171) establishes rules for the canonization of saints.

⌂ Guglielmo II of Sicily (◀ 1166, ▶ 1185) begins the building of Monreale Cathedral, a brilliant example of Romanesque architecture.

1171

In the bull *Non parum animus noster*, Pope Alexander III equates crusades against the pagan Estonians and Finns with crusades in the Holy Land.

*c.***1172**

♟ Domingo de Guzman (Dominic, ▶ 1207) is born. He founds a mendicant religious order, the Dominicans, originally aimed at converting the Albigensians (Cathars), a sect in the south of France which regards matter as evil (▶ 1179). Dies 1221.

1173

March 10: Richard of St Victor dies. He was a scholarly Scotsman who became Abbot of the Abbey of St Victor (◀ 1113) in Paris.

☉ Thomas Becket (◀ 1170) is canonized: feast day December 29.

☉ Narses IV of Armenia (◀ 1166) dies. He is later venerated as a saint.

1174

✠ After a gap of more than two years Richard, Prior of St Martin's, Dover, is consecrated Archbishop of Canterbury (▶ 1184).

1175

♟ Robert Grosseteste is born. Chancellor of Oxford and Bishop of Lincoln, he is a great teacher and reformer. Dies 1253.

♟ Andrew of St Victor dies. A biblical scholar, he studied at the Abbey of St Victor in Paris (◀ 1113).

🏛 Work begins on the building of Spoleto Cathedral, Italy.

c.1175

The placing of candles on the altar is attested for the first time, in connection with the altar of the papal chapel.

▪ The beautifully decorated Winchester Bible is produced, the best example of the century. The great Lambeth Bible is produced at about the same time.

1178

✠ March: Michael III of Anchialus, Patriarch of Constantinople (◀ 1170), dies and is succeeded by Chariton (▶ 1179).

August 29: Antipope Callistus III (◀ 1168) resigns, having lost Emperor Friedrich's (◀ 1167, ▶ 1189) support.

1179

March 5–22: The Third Lateran Council meets. It declares a crusade against the Albigensians (◀ c.1172). It also grants a college of cardinals the sole right to elect the Pope. It is regarded in the West as the eleventh Ecumenical Council.

✠ March: Chariton, Patriarch of Constantinople (◀ 1178), dies and is succeeded by Theodosius I Boradiotes (▶ 1183).

☩ September 17: Hildegard of Bingen (◀ 1098) dies. She is subsequently venerated as a saint: feast day September 17.

Peter Waldo, founder of the Waldensians, attends the Third Lateran Council and is confirmed in his vow of poverty by Pope Alexander III.

Westminster School is founded by the monks of Westminster Abbey.

1180

♛ September 18: Louis VII, King of France (◀ 1137), dies and is succeeded by Philippe II (▶ 1223).

♛ September 24: Emperor Manuel I Comnenus (◀ 1143) dies and is succeeded by his son Alexius II Comnenus (▶ 1183), who is only eleven.

🏛 Work begins on the building of Wells Cathedral.

183

1181

⚓ August 30: Pope Alexander III (◀ 1159) dies.

⚓ September 1: A Cistercian, Ubaldo Allucingoli, Cardinal Bishop of Ostia and Velletri, is elected as Pope Lucius III (▶ 1185).

The first Carthusian monastery in England is founded at Witham.

🏛 Worms Cathedral is completed (◀ 1110).

1182

🏛 June 20: The Romanesque Erfurt Cathedral is consecrated (◀ 1153).

🌱 Francis of Assisi (▶ 1208/9) is born. Converted to a life of total poverty, he founds an order, the Friars Minor (Franciscans), and lives his life as a hermit, finally receiving the stigmata (marks of the crucifixion) on his body. Dies 1226.

🏛 The Cathedral of Notre Dame in Paris is consecrated (◀ 1163).

Philippe II, King of France (◀ 1180, ▶ 1190), banishes Jews from France.

1183

⚓ August: Theodosius I Boradiotes, Patriarch of Constantinople (◀ 1179), dies and is succeeded by Basil II Camaterus (▶ 1186).

👑 October: Andronicus I Comnenus (▶ 1185) is proclaimed co-emperor with Alexius II Comnenus (◀ 1180), whom he subsequently has strangled.

1184

⚓ February 16: Richard of Dover, Archbishop of Canterbury (◀ 1174), dies.

⚓ December 16: Baldwin of Exeter, Bishop of Worcester, is appointed Archbishop of Canterbury (▶ 1190). He obtains land and a manor house at Lambeth in London to establish a secular collegiate church there, but the monks of Christ Church, Canterbury (◀ c.598) oppose this (▶ 1207).

In his bull *Ad abolendam*, Pope Lucius III (◀ 1181, ▶ 1185) establishes the episcopal Inquisition: bishops are to seek out heretics in their dioceses and hand them over to the secular authorities for punishment. This is particularly aimed at the Albigensians (◀ c.1172) and Waldensians (◀ 1179).

1185

September: Sicilian Normans led by King Guglielmo II (◀ 1170, ▶ 1189) capture Thessalonica, the second city of the Byzantine empire. There is rioting in Constantinople and Andronicus I Comnenus (◀ 1183) is killed by a mob. Isaac II Angelus (▶ 1195), his cousin, is proclaimed emperor. His armies drive back the Normans.

⚓ November 25: Pope Lucius III (◀ 1181) dies.

⚓ November 25: Umberto Crivelli, Archbishop of Milan, is elected as Pope Urban III (▶ 1187).

The Inquisition
The Inquisition is a special tribunal concerned to deal with heretics. In fact, over history there have been several different Inquisitions. First is the episcopal Inquisition, which follows the papal bull *Ad abolendam* of 1184 instructing bishops to seek out heresy in their dioceses. Since this is not effective enough, in 1233 Pope Gregory IX appoints Dominicans and Franciscans as full-time Inquisitors. The Spanish Inquisition is set up in 1478 by King Fernando and Queen Isabella to pursue Jews who have only converted nominally to Christianity; it comes to be headed by the notorious Inquisitor General Tomás de Torquemada. It is extended to Peru in 1570 and Mexico in 1571. A Portuguese Inquisition is set up in 1536 and extended to Goa in 1560. Finally, in 1542, Pope Paul III sets up the Congregation of the Holy Office, the Roman Inquisition, to supervise local Inquisitions. Because of its objective to combat heresy the Inquisition has authority only over baptized Christians; those who will not recant are handed over to the local authorities for punishment. In Spain the *auto-da-fé*, a ceremony in which sentence is passed, is a great public occasion. The Portuguese Inquisition is abolished in 1821, the Spanish in 1834. The Holy Office lives on as the Congregation for the Doctrine of Faith.

Lincoln Cathedral (◄ 1092, 1141) is structurally damaged by an earthquake.

The Knights Templar are established in London (the Temple).

1186

The German Meinhard is consecrated Bishop of Uexküll in Livonia (present-day Latvia and Estonia). After his death he is venerated as a saint: feast day October 12.

February: Basil II Camaterus, Patriarch of Constantinople (◄ 1183), dies and is succeeded by Nicetas II Muntanes (► 1189).

1187

Saladin (◄ 1169, ► 1191) proclaims *jihad* (holy war) against the Latin kingdom of Jerusalem for breaking a truce.

July 4: Saladin defeats a Crusader army.

October 2: Saladin captures Jerusalem.

October 19/20: Pope Urban III (◄ 1185) dies.

October 21: Alberto de Morra, Chancellor of the Roman Church, is elected as Pope Gregory VIII.

December 17: Pope Gregory VIII dies.

December 19: Paolo Scolari, Cardinal Bishop of Palestrina, is elected as Pope Clement III (► 1191).

1188

January 22: King Fernando II of Leon (◄ 1157) dies. He is succeeded by his son Alfonso IX (► 1218), cousin of King Alfonso VIII of Castile (◄ 1164).

185

1189

☿ February: Nicetas II Muntanes, Patriarch of Constantinople (◀ 1186), dies and is succeeded by Leontius Theotokites.

May: Emperor Friedrich I Barbarossa (◀ 1167, 1178) sets out on the Third Crusade.

♛ July 6: King Henry II (◀ 1154) of England dies.

♛ September 3: Richard, third son of King Henry II, is crowned King Richard I (▶ 1199). He goes on crusade the next year.

☿ September: Leontius Theotokites, Patriarch of Constantinople, dies and is succeeded by Dositheus of Jerusalem (▶ 1191).

♛ November: King Guglielmo II of Sicily (◀ 1166) dies; in a coup, he is succeeded by Tancred (▶ 1194).

♛ ⍟ Gabriel Mesquel Lalibela becomes ruler of Ethiopia (▶ 1229). He has eleven monolithic churches built in Lalibela, named after him.

⍟ Ely Cathedral (◀ 1109, ▶ 1322) is completed.

1190

February 10: The Order of German Hospitallers is formed during the siege of Acre by the Crusaders. It later becomes the Teutonic Order (▶ 1198).

March 16: Around 150 Jews, men and women, take refuge in Clifford's Tower, York, for protection against a hostile mob. Surrounded, they all commit suicide or are killed.

♛ June 10: Emperor Friedrich I Barbarossa (◀ 1189) dies on crusade in Cilicia.

October 4: King Richard I of England captures Messina, loots and burns it.

King Richard I arrives in Sicily with a large crusading army and is joined by King Philippe II of France (◀ 1182, ▶ 1191) with French crusaders. The people of Messina revolt, demanding the departure of the foreign troops.

☿ Baldwin of Exeter, Archbishop of Canterbury (◀ 1184), dies on crusade in the Holy Land.

♛ Temüjin (the future Genghis Khan) becomes King of the Mongols, an ethnic group from what is now Mongolia, Russia and China (▶ 1206).

☦ Bernard of Clairvaux (◀ 1153) is canonized by Pope Clement III: feast day August 20.

⍟ A second cathedral at Old Sarum (◀ 1092) is completed.

1191

☿ March: Pope Clement III (◀ 1187) dies.

March: After agreeing a treaty with Tancred (◀ 1189, ▶ 1194), the Crusaders leave Sicily.

186

☩ March/April: The aristocrat Cardinal Deacon Giacinto Bodo is elected as Pope Celestine III (▶ 1198).

April: Pope Celestine III crowns Heinrich VI, son of Friedrich I Barbarossa (◀ 1190), Holy Roman Emperor (▶ 1197).

July: Crusaders under Richard I of England and Philippe II of France capture Acre.

September 7: Richard I defeats Saladin (◀ 1187, ▶ 1192) at the Battle of Arsuf.

☩ September: Dositheus, Patriarch of Constantinople (◀ 1189), dies and is succeeded by George II Xiphilinus (▶ 1198).

☩ December 26: Reginald FitzJocelin, Archbishop of Canterbury elect and former Bishop of Wells, dies before he can be consecrated.

c.1191

📖 The French poet Robert de Boron writes the verse romance *Joseph d'Arimathie*, which relates how Joseph of Arimathea collects Christ's blood in the chalice used at the Last Supper and becomes its first guardian: the beginning of the legend of the Holy Grail.

1192

September 2: A peace treaty is signed between Saladin (◀ 1191, ▶ 1193) and the Crusaders, allowing pilgrims access to Jerusalem.

🏛 Bishop Hugh (▶ 1220) begins to rebuild Lincoln Cathedral (◀ 1185) in the Gothic style.

1193

March 3: Saladin (◀ 1192) dies.

Richard I, King of England, is captured in Austria on his way home from the Third Crusade.

☩ December 12: On his return from crusading in the Holy Land with King Richard I, and having helped to raise a ransom for the king's release from captivity, Hubert Walter, Bishop of Salisbury, is appointed Archbishop of Canterbury (▶ 1205).

🕴 Albertus Magnus is born. A German Dominican, he establishes theology as a respectable discipline and writes commentaries on all Aristotle's work. Dies 1280.

Pope Celestine III (◀ 1191, ▶ 1198) calls for a northern crusade against the Baltic pagans.

1194

👑 February 20: Tancred, King of Sicily (◀ 1189), dies.

👑 June 27: King Sancho VI of Navarre (◀ 1150) dies and is succeeded by his son Sancho VII (▶ 1234).

🕴 July 16: Clare of Assisi (▶ 1215) is born. Dies 1253.

187

December 25: Palermo surrenders to Holy Roman Emperor Heinrich VI (◀ 1191, ▶ 1197), thus bringing to an end the Norman kingdom of Sicily.

King Richard I (◀ 1193, ▶ 1199) is recrowned in Winchester Cathedral.

♖ Chartres Cathedral is rebuilt after a great fire destroys all but the west front (▶ 1220).

1195

♛ April 8: Alexius III Angelus, brother of Isaac II Angelus (◀ 1185, ▶ 1203), overthrows him, blinds and imprisons him and becomes emperor.

♟ Anthony of Padua is born. A Portuguese hermit, he becomes a Franciscan and is a fierce opponent of the Albigensians (◀ c.1172). Dies 1231.

♖ Work on the building of Bourges Cathedral, France (▶ 1270), begins.

♖ Work begins on a Gothic cathedral in Lichfield to replace the Norman cathedral (◀ 1085).

1196

♛ King Alfonso II of Aragon (◀ 1164) dies and is succeeded by his son Pedro II (▶ 1213).

1197

September 28: Heinrich VI (◀ 1191), Holy Roman Emperor, dies.

♖ Glasgow Cathedral is consecrated.

1198

☥ January 8: Pope Celestine III (◀ 1191) dies.

☥ January 8: Lotario, Cardinal Deacon of Santi Sergio and Bacco, is elected as Pope Innocent III (▶ 1216).

☥ July 7: George II Xiphilinus, Patriarch of Constantinople (◀ 1190), dies.

☥ August 5: John X Camaterus is appointed Patriarch of Constantinople (▶ 1206).

♟ Averroes (◀ 1126) dies.

The Teutonic Knights (◀ 1190) are re-formed as a military order with the same rule as the Knights Templar (◀ 1185).

Hartwig II, Archbishop of Bremen, proclaims a crusade against the Wends (◀ 982).

Berthold, Abbot of Loccum in Germany, consecrated Bishop of Uexküll in succession to Meinhard (◀ 1186), invades Livonia with an army but is killed.

1199

♛ April 6: King Richard I of England (◀ 1189) dies and is succeeded by his younger brother John (▶ 1216).

♖ Chichester Cathedral is reconsecrated (◀ 1108).

Pérotin, *Alleluia Nativitas, c.*1200

1200

🌺 Beatrice of Nazareth is born. A Belgian spiritual writer, she becomes Prioress of Notre-Dame-de-Nazareth, near Antwerp. Dies 1268.

The Cluniac Order becomes recognized as a distinct form of Cistercian monasticism.

🏛 Work begins on the building of Freiburg Cathedral, modelled on that of Basle (◀ 1019, ▶ 1513).

*c.*1200

🎭 Jehan Bodel, *Le Jeu de St Nicholas*, is the first French miracle play.

🎵 Pérotin, a French composer associated with Notre Dame, Paris, plays a key role in expanding monophony into polyphony, in a style called organum.

189

Thirteenth century

The thirteenth century sees the heyday of Scholasticism. The material which scholars can use for their characteristic way of tackling theological questions by means of bringing together disputed questions and providing answers in the form of systematic theologies (*summas*) has by now grown considerably, as have their linguistic skills. Through the works of the Muslim philosopher Averroes (1126–98) the works of Aristotle have been rediscovered and play an important role, and many other Greek authors, both church fathers and Byzantine thinkers, are translated into Latin. The series of great Scholastics includes Roger Bacon, Bonaventure, Johannes Duns Scotus, William of Ockham and above all Albertus Magnus and Thomas Aquinas. The foundation of universities proceeds apace: Vicenza (1204), Cambridge (1209), Palencia (1211), Salamanca (1218), Montpellier (1220), Padua (1222), Naples (1224), Toulouse (1229), Siena (1246), Piacenza (1248), the Sorbonne in Paris (1257), Coimbra (1290) and Alcala (1293).

The main crusading activity during the century moves to the region of the Baltic Sea. In addition to the Teutonic Knights, the Brothers of the Sword founded by Bishop Albert of Riga in 1202 and the Knights of Dobrin founded by Bishop Christian of Prussia lead campaigns, particularly against pagan Prussia and in Lithuania. Denmark is also active, with a crusade in 1219 led by King Valdemar II, which results in the foundation of Tallinn in Estonia. 1227 sees the conquest of Estonia by Christian forces completed by an army under the papal legate William of Modena. In 1226 Konrad I, Duke of Masovia in central Poland, appeals to the Teutonic Knights to defend his frontiers against the Prussians and in 1231 they cross the Vistula and start building castles there. However, in 1236 the Brothers of the Sword are so heavily defeated by the Lithuanians that the surviving remnant of their order has to merge with the Teutonic Knights. In an advance on Russia the Teutonic Knights in turn are defeated in 1242 by forces led by Aleksandr Nevskiy at Lake Peipus in the Battle of the Ice.

The newly-founded Franciscans are immediately active over a wide area, and in 1219 Francis of Assisi himself visits the Fifth Crusade in Egypt. In 1220 six Franciscans are killed on a mission to Marrakesh, and in 1224 Franciscans arrive in England, where they are to play an important role in intellectual life. In 1233, along with Dominicans, Franciscans are appointed full-time Inquisitors by Pope Gregory IX. In 1246 a papal envoy, the Franciscan Giovanni da Pian del Carpini, arrives at the court of the Mongol Great Khan Kuyuk in Karakoram and invites him to become a Christian. He is followed in 1253 by William of Rubruck, who engages in a debate with Manichaeans, Muslims and Nestorians ordered by the Khan. In 1294 Giovanni da Montecorvino, a Franciscan priest, arrives in Kambalik (Beijing); five years later he builds a church there and goes on to translate the New Testament and the Psalms into Chinese. In 1288 a Franciscan is even elected Pope as Nicholas IV.

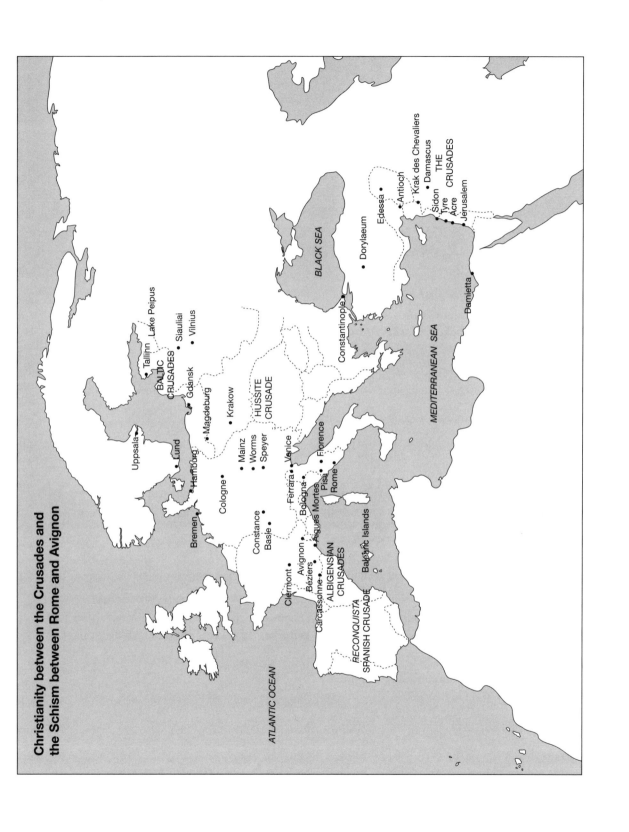

Christianity between the Crusades and the Schism between Rome and Avignon

BALTIC
CRUSADES

Lake Peipus

Siauliai

Vilnius

Tallinn

Gdansk

Magdeburg

Krakow

HUSSITE
CRUSADE

Uppsala

Lund

Hamburg

Cologne

Mainz

Worms

Speyer

Venice

Florence

Bremen

Constance

Basle

Ferrara

Bologna

Aigues Mortes

Pisa

Rome

Clermont

Avignon

Béziers

Carcassonne

ALBIGENSIAN
CRUSADES

Balearic Islands

RECONQUISTA
SPANISH CRUSADE

ATLANTIC OCEAN

BLACK SEA

Dorylaeum

Constantinople

Edessa

Antioch

Krak des Chevaliers

Damascus

THE
CRUSADES

Sidon

Tyre

Acre

Jerusalem

Damietta

MEDITERRANEAN SEA

1201

October 1: Crusaders set sail from Venice on the Fourth Crusade, preached by Pope Innocent III (◀ 1198).

Albert of Buxhoevden founds the city of Riga and becomes its bishop (▶ 1202).

1202

✤ March 30: Joachim of Fiore (◀ 1132) dies.

Bishop Albert of Riga (◀ 1201) founds the Order of the Brothers of the Knighthood of Christ (Livonian Order), known as Brothers of the Sword (▶ 1206), soldier missionaries who spread the gospel in the Eastern Baltic and conquer the tribal kingdoms.

The papal decree (decretal) *Venerabilem* asserts the supremacy of the Pope over worldly rulers.

1203

The Crusaders enter Constantinople and reinstate the deposed Isaac II Angelus as emperor with his son Alexius IV as co-emperor. Alexius III Angelus (◀ 1195) flees to Thrace.

⊕ Wulfstan (◀ 1084) is canonized by Pope Innocent III: feast day January 19.

1204

♛ January 4: Alexius V Ducas leads a revolt against Isaac II Angelus and Alexius IV and is crowned emperor.

♛ February 8: Alexius IV is strangled in prison; Isaac II Angelus dies several days later.

March: Constantinople is sacked by the Crusaders.

April 12: Emperor Alexius V Ducas and Patriarch John X Camaterus (◀ 1198) flee to Thrace.

⌾ May 16: A Latin state is established in Constantinople and one of the Crusaders, Baldwin Count of Flanders and Hainaut (▶ 1205), is crowned emperor in Hagia Sophia. The Byzantine court survives in Nicaea.

♛ November: Alexius V Ducas is captured, condemned to death and executed in Constantinople. There are no Byzantine emperors in Constantinople for 50 years (▶ 1208).

✤ December 13: Maimonides (◀ 1135) dies.

A university is founded in Vicenza, Italy (▶ 1209).

The Cistercian convent of Port-Royal, near Paris (▶ 1625), is founded.

1205

♛ March: Latin Emperor Baldwin engages with an army of Bulgars at Adrianople; he is defeated, taken prisoner and executed.

☧ July 13: Hubert Walter, Archbishop of Canterbury (◀ 1193), dies.

☧ Monks of Christ Church, Canterbury, secretly elect their sub-prior Reginald as Archbishop of Canterbury, but tell him not to reveal this until they have papal approval. Reginald disobeys and the monks withdraw their nomination.

☧ December 11: The monks nominate as Archbishop of Canterbury John de Grey, Bishop of Norwich, favoured by King John (▶ 1206).

♕ Pedro II, King of Aragon (◀ 1196, ▶ 1213), is crowned in Rome by Pope Innocent III. He thus acknowledges the Pope's supremacy.

1206

☧ March 30: Pope Innocent III (◀ 1198) refuses to recognize John de Grey (◀ 1205) as Archbishop of Canterbury.

♕ August: Henry of Hainault, Baldwin's son, becomes Latin Emperor John X .

☧ John X Camaterus, Patriarch of Constantinople (◀ 1198), dies.

The Brothers of the Sword (◀ 1202) defeat the Livonians and move on Latvia.

Temüjin (◀ 1190) unifies all the Mongol and Tatar tribes and is given the title Genghis Khan.

1207

☧ June 17: Pope Innocent III consecrates Cardinal Stephen Langton (◀ 1205, ▶ 1213) from Lincolnshire, who is in Rome, as Archbishop of Canterbury. King John rejects him.

July 15: King John proclaims that anyone who recognizes Stephen Langton as Archbishop of Canterbury is a public enemy, and expels the Canterbury monks who support him.

Dominic (◀ c.1172, ▶ 1221) founds the first Dominican convent for women at Prouille in the south of France.

Lambeth House (as it is called, ◀ 1184) becomes the official residence of the Archbishop of Canterbury (▶ 1685).

c.1207

Bishop Christian of Prussia founds the Brothers of the Knighthood of Christ (also known as the Knights of Dobrin), against the Prussians.

1208

☧ March 20: Michael IV Autoreianus becomes Patriarch of Constantinople (▶ 1213).

March: Pope Innocent III in effect excommunicates the English church.

♕ In Nicaea Theodore I Lascaris (▶ 1221), son-in-law of Alexius III Angelus (◀ 1203), assumes the title of emperor and fights against the Latin emperor John X (◀ 1206, ▶ 1214).

☥ A group of hermits living on Mount Carmel in Palestine is given a Rule written by

193

Albert, Latin Patriarch of Jerusalem. This is the beginning of the Carmelite Order. After his death Albert is venerated as a saint: feast day September 24.

1208/9

Pope Innocent III proclaims a crusade against the Albigensians (◀ c.1172, ▶ 1209).

Francis of Assisi (◀ 1182, ▶ 1219) gives his friars a first Rule.

Franciscans

The Franciscans, the Order of Friars Minor, are founded by Francis of Assisi in 1208/9, when he gives them a first Rule; a later Rule is confirmed by Pope Honorius III (▶ 1223). Not only individuals but the whole Order are to live in poverty, working with their hands or begging. This way of life proves impracticable and a dispute, which lasts for around a century, arises between the 'Spirituals', who insist on the letter of the Rule, and the rest, who are more moderate. The Council of Constance (▶ 1415) officially recognizes the 'Observants' who continue the position of the 'Spirituals', and a century later a General Chapter of the Order declares them the true Franciscan Order (▶ 1517). Soon after this Matteo da Bascio founds the Capuchin Order (▶ 1528), in order to return to the primitive Franciscan simplicity. A Second Order of Franciscans comprises contemplative nuns ('Poor Clares', ▶ 1215) and a Third Order consists of associates who do not take vows and live in the world.

Franciscans become involved in preaching and missionary activities. Franciscans are active in Morocco (▶ 1220) and in China (▶ 1333); they accompany Vasco da Gama on his epic voyage (▶ 1497) and work in the Caribbean (▶ 1503), Mexico (▶ 1524), Argentina (▶ 1539), Guatemala (▶ 1550), the Philippines and Cochin China (▶ 1580) and Canada (▶ 1615), and two Franciscans cross the Sahara desert (▶ 1710). They introduce many popular devotions, including the Christmas crib (▶ 1223), the Angelus (▶ 1269), and the Stations of the Cross (▶ 1342). At an early stage they come to England (▶ 1224) and settle in Oxford, London and Canterbury and from there establish friaries in a large number of places. Franciscan scholars, not least Roger Bacon (▶ 1214), play an important role in the sphere of science. Like the Dominicans, they are also involved in administrating the courts of the Inquisition (see p.185).

1209

♛ October 4: Pope Innocent III crowns Otto V of Brunswick Holy Roman Emperor (▶ 1215).

In the Albigensian Crusade (◀ 1208/9, ▶ 1215), Simon de Montfort and his followers destroy Béziers and Carcassonne.

Cambridge University is founded by scholars leaving Oxford University because of riots and unrest there.

Vicenza University (◀ 1204) is shut down, possibly on suspicion of heresy.

1210

Pope Innocent III sanctions the creation of the Diocese of Turku, Finland.

c.1210

♣ 📖 Mechthild of Magdeburg is born. A Beguine, she writes down her mystical visions in *The Flowing Light of the Godhead*. Dies c.1282.

♣ Nicholas of Verdun (◀ 1150) dies.

The Feast of Corpus Christi commemorating the establishment of the eucharist is founded (▶ 1264).

1211

🏛 The foundation stone of Reims Cathedral (▶ 1311) is laid. It succeeds buildings on the site dating back to the basilica in which Clovis was baptized (◀ 496).

King Alfonso VIII of Castile (◀ 1188, ▶ 1212) founds the University of Palencia.

1212

A coalition of Spanish Christian kingdoms led by Alfonso VIII of Castile defeats the Moors at Las Navas de Tolosa, an important stage in the *Reconquista*, the reconquest of Spain.

1213

January: Pope Innocent III declares that King John (◀ 1207, ▶ 1215) is deposed.

May: King John yields to the Pope and accepts Stephen Langton as Archbishop of Canterbury (◀ 1207).

July: Stephen Langton comes to Canterbury.

☥ August 26: Michael IV Autoreianus, Patriarch of Constantinople (◀ 1208), dies.

♛ September 12: Pedro II, King of Aragon (◀ 1196), is killed in battle against Simon de Montfort and is succeeded by his son Jaume (▶ 1276), who conquers Valencia and the Balearic islands.

☥ September 28: Theodore II Eirenicus is appointed Patriarch of Constantinople (▶ 1215).

In his bull *Quia maior* Pope Innocent III calls for a new crusade. This results in the Fifth Crusade (1217).

1214

♛ October 5: King Alfonso VIII of Castile (◀ 1158) dies (▶ 1217).

♣ Roger Bacon, British philosopher and scientist and Franciscan, is born. He is one of the first to lecture on Aristotle. Dies 1294.

Latin Emperor John X (◀ 1208, ▶ 1216) signs a treaty with Emperor Theodore I Lascaris (◀ 1208, ▶ 1221), defining their respective territories.

1215

☥ January 31: Theodore II Eirenicus, Patriarch of Constantinople (◀ 1213), dies.

195

☥ June 3: Maximus II becomes Patriarch of Constantinople.

June 15: English barons rebel against King John (◀ 1213, ▶ 1216) and compel him to sign a treaty at Runnymede, Magna Carta, containing reforms.

November 20: The Fourth Lateran Council ends the Albigensian Crusade (◀ 1209). It is regarded in the West as the twelfth Ecumenical Council. It requires Christians to go to confession and communion twice a year and takes measures against Jews and heretics (compels Jews to wear yellow badges).

☥ December: Maximus II, Patriarch of Constantinople, dies.

Clare (◀ 1194, ▶ 1253), Abbess at Assisi, founds the Poor Clares, a Franciscan Order for women.

Transubstantiation (i.e. that in the eucharist the whole substance of the bread and wine becomes the whole substance of the body and blood of Christ) becomes the doctrine of the Catholic Church. The term is used for the first time.

♛ Otto V of Brunswick, Holy Roman Emperor (◀ 1209), is deposed.

🏛 Work begins on the building of Siena Cathedral.

1216

☥ January 31: Manuel I Charitopoulos becomes Patriarch of Constantinople (▶ 1222).

♛ June 11: Latin Emperor John X (◀ 1206) dies.

☥ July 16: Pope Innocent III (◀ 1198) dies.

☥ July 18: Cencio Savelli, a Roman aristocrat, is elected as Pope Honorius III (▶ 1227).

♛ October 18/19: King John of England (◀ 1199) dies and is succeeded by his son Henry, aged nine, who becomes King Henry III (▶ 1272).

December 22: Pope Honorius III approves the Order of Friars Preachers (Dominicans).

1217

♛ April 9: Pope Honorius III consecrates Peter of Courtenay Latin Emperor of Constantinople in Rome. Peter leaves for Constantinople by land but never arrives. Yolande, his wife, becomes empress in Constantinople (▶ 1219).

The Fifth Crusade leaves Europe for Egypt.

♛ After the brief reign of the boy king Enrique I, Fernando III becomes King of Castile (▶ 1230, 1252). He presides over the reconquest of Spain and commissions the building of Burgos Cathedral (▶ 1221).

Honorius III approves a simple rule of life for the Franciscans.

1218

The Bergamo Conference brings together the two branches of the Waldensians (◀ 1179).

196

Dominicans

The Dominicans, the Order of Preachers, are founded by Dominic; the Order takes shape at a General Chapter in Bologna in 1220. Like the Franciscans, not only individuals but the whole Order is to live in poverty; however, it possesses its own houses and churches. In addition to the task of preaching stated in its name, it has a strong focus on study, and this comes to be put even before religious observances. Again like the Franciscans, the Dominicans find the ideal of corporate poverty unworkable; but there is less conflict over the issue and their corporate poverty is abolished by Pope Sixtus IV (▶ 1475).

Encounters with the Albigensians (◀ c.1172) have led Dominic to found his Order; he sees it as an instrument for bringing them back to mainstream Christianity. However, this does not happen, and the Dominicans are in the forefront of combating heresy; they are actively involved in the Inquisition (see p.185), and Tomás de Torquemada (▶ 1420), the most famous Inquisitor of the Spanish Inquisition, is a Dominican. They serve the papacy by preaching crusades, and the secular rulers of the time as confessors. They are also very active in mission: in Mozambique (▶ 1506), Cuba (▶ 1512), Mexico (▶ 1526), Siam (▶ 1554), the Philippines (▶ 1611), and China (▶ 1656). Bartolomé de Las Casas (▶ 1474) is a champion of the Indians in South America.

However, it is as scholars and mystics that Dominicans make their greatest mark: Albertus Magnus (◀ 1193) and Thomas Aquinas (▶ 1225) both belong to the Order, as do Johannes ('Meister') Eckhart (▶ c.1260), Johannes Tauler (▶ c.1300) and Heinrich Suso (▶ 1295). Fra Angelico (▶ c.1395) is also a Dominican. The scholarly tradition has continued to the present day with Yves Congar (▶ 1904) and Edward Schillebeeckx (▶ 1914).

In 1207 Dominic has founded a convent for women at Prouille in France and as well as Dominican friars there are also Dominican sisters, most famous of whom is Catherine of Siena (▶ c.1347). Henri Matisse is so moved by the care that he receives from the Dominican sisters that he decorates their Chapel of the Rosary in Vence (▶ 1951).

The Fifth Crusade (◀ 1217, ▶ 1219) arrives in Egypt and lays siege to Damietta.

Pope Honorius III announces a second Albigensian Crusade (▶ 1226).

King Alfonso IX of Leon (◀ 1217, ▶ 1220) founds the University of Salamanca. It attracts many students away from Palencia (◀ 1211).

🏛 Amiens Cathedral (◀ 1152) is destroyed by lightning (▶ 1220).

1219

👑 Empress Yolande (◀ 1217) dies.

A crusade led by King Valdemar II of Denmark and Archbishop Andrew of Lund leads to the foundation of Tallinn in Estonia and the establishment of a diocese there.

The monk Sava (▶ 1253), of royal blood, establishes an autonomous Serbian church.

Francis of Assisi (◀ 1208/9, ▶ 1223) visits the Fifth Crusade in Egypt and presents the gospel to Sultan al-Kamil (▶ 1229) at Damietta.

The Crusaders are massacred by the Sultan's army, and the survivors return home.

1220

January 17: Six Franciscans are killed on a mission to Marrakesh.

April 28: Under Bishop Poore work begins on building a cathedral in Salisbury water meadows to replace that in Old Sarum (◀ 1190). The city of Salisbury rises around it.

August 5: The first Dominicans arrive in England.

November 22: Pope Honorius III crowns Friedrich II Holy Roman Emperor (▶ 1250).

Benedict of Nursia (◀ 547) is canonized by Pope Honorius III: feast day July 11.

Hugh, Bishop of Lincoln (◀ 1192), is canonized by Pope Honorius III: feast day November 17.

Walter de Gray orders the building of a Gothic York Minster (▶ 1470) to compare with Canterbury Cathedral.

The rebuilding of Chartres Cathedral (◀ 1194) is completed (▶ 1260).

The building of the present Amiens Cathedral begins: the date is given by the inscription on a remarkable floor labyrinth. The cathedral is the largest in France (▶ 1401).

The Dominican Order takes its definitive form at a meeting of its governing body in Bologna.

The medical school which forms the basis of the University of Montpellier is founded by Cardinal Conrad von Urach, papal legate of Honorius III.

1221

March 25: Robert of Courtenay, younger son of Peter of Courtenay (◀ 1217), is crowned Latin emperor in Constantinople (▶ 1228).

July 20: Work begins on the building of Burgos Cathedral, Spain.

August 6: Dominic (◀ c.1172) dies (▶ 1232).

November: Theodore I Lascaris (◀ 1208) dies.

c.1221

Bonaventure is born. A scholastic theologian and mystic, he is an important Franciscan and writes a commentary on the *Sentences* of Peter Lombard (◀ c.1095). Dies 1274.

1222

June: Manuel I Charitopoulos, Patriarch of Constantinople (◀ 1216), dies and is succeeded by Germanus II (▶ 1240).

Robert of Molesme (◀ 1098) is canonized by Pope Honorius III: feast day April 29.

John III Ducas Vatatzes (▶ 1225), son-in-law of Theodore I Lascaris (◀ 1208), becomes emperor in Nicaea.

The labyrinth in Amiens Cathedral, 1220

The University of Padua is founded when about a thousand students leave the University of Bologna (◀ 1088).

1223

♕ July 14: Philippe II, King of France (◀ 1180), dies and is succeeded by Louis VIII (▶ 1226).

November 29: Pope Honorius III confirms a revised Rule for the Franciscans (◀ 1208/9).

A Mongol horde defeats a coalition of Russian princes on the Kalka river near present-day Donetsk in the Ukraine.

Francis of Assisi (◀ 1219, ▶ 1226) is said to have made the first Christmas crib at Greccio in Italy.

1224

Conrad of Masovia (Poland) asks the Teutonic Order (◀ 1190) for help against the pagan Prussians; this campaign is regarded as a crusade.

199

The first Franciscans arrive in England. They are to play an important role in intellectual life.

200 Albigensians (◀ 1218, ▶ 1226) are burnt alive on a pyre at Montségur in the south of France.

The University of Naples is founded by Holy Roman Emperor Friedrich II (◀ 1220) to counter the dominant influence of the University of Bologna (◀ 1088), which is controlled by the Pope. He thus creates so to speak the first state university.

1225

🌳📖 Thomas Aquinas is born. The greatest medieval theologian, he produces a system of Christian doctrine, the *Summa Theologiae*, which reconciles it with the philosophy of Aristotle. Dies 1274.

🏛 Laon Cathedral (◀ 1160) is completed.

Emperor John III Ducas Vatatzes (◀ 1222, ▶ *c.*1249) regains control of Asia Minor.

1226

March: In the Golden Bull of Rimini Holy Roman Emperor Friedrich II grants the Teutonic Order (◀ 1190) limitless rights over the territories it conquers.

🌳 October 3: Francis of Assisi (◀ 1182) dies (▶ 1228).

November 8: Louis VIII (◀ 1223) of France dies and is succeeded by Louis IX (▶ 1270).

Konrad I, Duke of Masovia in central Poland, appeals to the Teutonic Knights to defend his frontiers against the Prussians.

🏛 The cornerstone of Toledo Cathedral, Spain, is laid.

Louis VIII of France forces the Languedoc to submit in the Albigensian Crusade (▶ 1229). The first recorded instance of adoration of the Blessed Sacrament is during the celebrations of his victory.

1227

☿ March 11: Pope Honorius III (◀ 1216) dies.

☿ March 19: Ugolino, a nephew of Innocent III (◀ 1198) and a papal legate, is elected as Pope Gregory IX (▶ 1241). He is a friend of Dominic (◀ 1170) and Francis of Assisi (◀ 1182).

An army of the Brothers of the Sword (◀ 1202) under William of Modena completes the conquest of Estonia by Christian forces.

1228

☿ July 9: Stephen Langton, Archbishop of Canterbury (◀ 1207), dies.

☉ July 16: Francis of Assisi (◀ 1226) is canonized by Pope Gregory IX: feast day October 4.

♔ Latin Emperor Robert of Courtenay (◀ 1221) dies and is succeeded by Baldwin II Porphyrogenitus (▶ 1261), son of Yolande (◀ 1217).

The Sixth Crusade, led by Friedrich II (◀ 1220), begins as an attempt to recapture Jerusalem.

1229

☥ January 4: Walter d'Eynsham is appointed Archbishop of Canterbury but is rejected by King Henry III and Pope Gregory IX.

February 18: Sultan al-Kamil (◀ 1219) signs a truce with Friedrich II which gives Friedrich Bethlehem, Nazareth, Sidon, Jaffa and all Jerusalem except the Dome of the Rock in return for military support against al-Kamil's nephew.

March 18: Friedrich II, Holy Roman Emperor, has himself crowned king in Jerusalem.

April 11: The Treaty of Paris ends the Second Albigensian Crusade (◀ 1218).

☥ June 10: Richard le Grant, Chancellor of the Diocese of Lincoln, is appointed Archbishop of Canterbury (▶ 1231).

☉ Gabriel Mesquel Lalibela (◀ 1189) dies. He is subsequently venerated as a saint.

The Synod of Toulouse decrees that lay people may not possess Bibles; it also lays down regulations for inquisition (▶ 1233).

The University of Toulouse is founded by a local earl suspected of being hostile to the crusades to show his piety.

1230

♔ September 23: King Alfonso IX of Leon (◀ 1188) dies and is succeeded by his son Fernando III, who is already King of Castile (◀ 1217, ▶ 1231).

Pope Gregory IX calls for a Prussian crusade.

1231

February: With his bull *Excommunicamus* Pope Gregory IX lays the foundation for the Inquisition.

♠ June 13: Anthony of Padua (◀ 1195) dies (▶ 1232).

August 3: Richard le Grant, Archbishop of Canterbury (◀ 1229), dies.

☥ September 22: Ralph Neville, Lord Chancellor of England, is appointed Archbishop of Canterbury.

☥ December 20: Ralph Neville, Archbishop of Canterbury, dies.

201

♛ King Fernando III of Castile (◀ 1230, ▶ 1236) permanently unites the kingdoms of Castile and Leon.

The Teutonic Knights (◀ 1198) cross the Vistula into Prussia and start building castles.

1232

⚑ March 16: John of Sittingbourne is appointed Archbishop of Canterbury.

⚑ June 12: John of Sittingbourne dies.

⚑ June 26: John Blund is appointed Archbishop of Canterbury (▶ 1233).

♟ Ramon Lull (▶ 1276) is born. A Spanish missionary, he studies Arabic and Christian thought with a view to converting Muslims. Dies 1315.

☉ Dominic (◀ 1221) is canonized by Pope Gregory IX: feast day August 8.

☉ Anthony of Padua (◀ 1231) is canonized by Pope Gregory IX: feast day June 13.

1233

⚑ John Blund, Archbishop of Canterbury (◀ 1232), dies.

Gregory IX appoints full-time Inquisitors, largely from the Dominican and Franciscan Orders, to root out heretics (◀ 1184).

1234

⚑ April 2: Edmund Rich, treasurer of Salisbury Cathedral, is appointed Archbishop of Canterbury (▶ 1240). He is revered as a saint during his lifetime.

♛ King Sancho VII of Navarre (◀ 1194) dies and is succeeded by his nephew Theobald (▶ 1253). Theobald goes on crusade to the Holy Land.

The Diocese of Marrakesh, Morocco, is founded.

1236

♟ Jacopone da Todi is born. He composes a number of hymns known as *Laudi*. The *Stabat Mater* is also attributed to him. Dies 1306.

The Brothers of the Sword (◀ 1202, ▶ 1237) are defeated by the Lithuanians at the Battle of Siauliai and almost exterminated.

Fernando III, King of Castile (◀ 1231, ▶ 1252), conquers Cordoba and consecrates the Great Mosque there (◀ 785) as the city's cathedral (▶ 1523). The Muslim ruler of Granada, Mohammed ibn Alhamar, requests independence under Castile in return for helping Fernando to capture Seville. Fernando agrees.

1237

🏛 The central tower of Lincoln Cathedral (◀ 1192) collapses. A new tower is begun and the cathedral is subsequently enlarged.

The Brothers of the Sword (◀ 1202) become an autonomous branch of the Teutonic Order (◀ 1198).

The Mongols, led by Batu, grandson of Genghis Khan (◀ 1190), invade Russia.

1238

◻ Peterborough Cathedral is consecrated.

1240

November 16: Edmund Rich, Archbishop of Canterbury (◀ 1234), having retired to Pontigny because he has failed to get papal support for his reforms, dies there, and a four-year vacancy follows.

✠ Germanus II, Patriarch of Constantinople (◀ 1222), dies and is succeeded by Methodius II.

✠ Methodius II, Patriarch of Constantinople, dies and a four-year vacancy follows.

◻ The Norman St Paul's Cathedral (◀ 1087) is completed.

The Mongols capture Kiev, the capital of Russia.

c.1240

♟◼ Cimabue, Italian painter, is born. He is the first painter to move away from the flat Byzantine style towards naturalism. He is an influence on Giotto (▶ 1267). Dies 1302.

1241

✠ August 22: Pope Gregory IX (◀ 1227) dies.

✠ October 23: Goffredo da Castiglione, an aristocrat from Milan who is Cardinal Bishop of Sabina, is elected as Pope Celestine IV.

✠ November 10: Pope Celestine IV dies.

The Mongols invade Poland, Hungary and the Balkans, but then retreat from Europe.

1242

In a campaign against Russia the Teutonic Knights (◀ 1198) are defeated by forces under Aleksandr Nevskiy (▶ 1381) at Lake Peipus in Estonia in the Battle of the Ice.

1243

✠ June 25: Sinibaldi Fieschi, canon lawyer and governor of the March of Ancona, is elected as Pope Innocent IV (▶ 1254).

c.1243

Bar Hebraeus, son of a Jewish physician in eastern Turkey, becomes a Jacobite monk. He works to reconcile Nestorian and Jacobite (Monophysite, see p.65) Christians (▶ 1264).

1244

✠ January 15: Boniface, Count of Savoy and Bishop of Belley in Burgundy, is appointed Archbishop of Canterbury. He leaves the next year for the Council of Lyons and does not return to England until 1249. He is uninterested in the spiritual aspect of his office and is disliked by the English because he is demanding, overbearing and a foreigner. Pope Innocent IV orders him to repair Lambeth House (◀ 1207) and he builds the present chapel there (▶ 1270).

Manuel II is appointed Patriarch of Constantinople (▶ 1254).

The Albigensians (◀ c.1172) are finally defeated with the capture of their fortress of Montségur.

1245

June 28–July 17: The First Council of Lyons excommunicates the emperor and preaches a new crusade. It is regarded in the West as the thirteenth Ecumenical Council.

The rebuilding of Westminster Abbey begins (◀ 1065, ▶ 1517).

1246

January 22: A papal envoy, the Franciscan Giovanni da Pian del Carpini, arrives at the court of the Mongol Great Khan Kuyuk in Karakorum (▶ 1253) and invites him to become a Christian. The envoy is told that first the Pope and princes of Europe must come to pay allegiance to the Khan.

Emperor Friedrich II (◀ 1229, ▶ 1249) compels students from Siena to leave Bologna University (◀ 1088). This leads to the foundation of the University of Siena.

1247

The building of Beauvais Cathedral begins.

1248

Cologne 'Old Cathedral' (◀ 818) burns down.

August 15: Work on Cologne Cathedral begins (▶ 1880).

The Sainte-Chapelle in Paris is consecrated to hold the relic of Jesus' crown of thorns.

The University of Piacenza is founded.

King Louis IX of France (◀ 1226, ▶ 1250) sails from his new port of Aigues-Mortes on a Seventh Crusade, against Egypt.

The monk Iyasos-Mo'a founds a monastery and school on an island in Lake Hayq, Ethiopia, marking the start of a new monasticism there.

c.1249

Emperor John III Ducas Vatatzes (◀ 1225, ▶ 1253) promises to become the vassal of Holy Roman Emperor Friedrich II in return for aid in recapturing Constantinople. He also promises to end the schism between East and West if he receives aid from the papacy. Nothing comes of all this.

University College, Oxford, opens, the first Oxford college and for graduates only.

1250

December 13: Friedrich II, Holy Roman Emperor (◀ 1220), dies. A vacancy follows (▶ 1312).

☉ Margaret, Queen of Scotland (◀ 1070), is canonized by Pope Innocent IV: feast day November 16.

King Louis IX (◀ 1248, ▶ 1270) defeats the Egyptians but is captured; he gives up Damietta as a ransom and retreats to Acre.

1251

♪ In *Ars cantus mensurabilis*, Franco of Cologne, papal chaplain and preceptor of the Knights Hospitaller, presents a system in which the shape of a musical note denotes its length, a system still used today.

Grand Duke Mindaugas of Lithuania agrees to be baptized in exchange for which he is to be granted the status of king (▶ 1253).

1252

May 15: The papal bull *Ad extirpanda* authorizes Inquisitors to use torture (◀ 1233).

♛ May 30: King Fernando III of Castile–Leon (◀ 1217) dies (▶ 1671). He is succeeded by his son Alfonso X (▶ 1284), a scholar and astronomer (▶ 1269).

🏛 The Church of St Francis, Assisi, is completed.

1253

After his coronation, King Mindaugas of Lithuania (◀ 1251) transfers lands to the Brothers of the Sword (◀ 1202). He builds a cathedral at Vilnius, but Lithuanians are unprepared to accept Christianity.

♛ July 8: King Theobald I of Navarre (◀ 1234) dies and is succeeded by his son Theobald II (▶ 1270).

♣ August 11: Clare of Assisi (◀ 1194) dies (▶ 1255).

♣ October 9: Robert Grosseteste (◀ 1175) dies.

☉ Sava (◀ 1219) is canonized by the Orthodox Church of Serbia: feast day January 14.

Pope Innocent IV holds reunion discussions with John III Ducas Vatatzes (◀ 1222), but they come to nothing.

The Franciscan William of Rubruck reaches Karakorum (◀ 1246) and engages in a debate with Manichaeans, Muslims and Nestorians ordered by the Khan.

1254

☦ October: Manuel II, Patriarch of Constantinople (◀ 1244), dies and is succeeded by Arsenius Autoreianus (▶ 1259).

November 3: John III Ducas Vatatzes (◀ 1222) dies and is succeeded by his son Theodore II Lascaris (▶ 1258).

☦ December 7: Pope Innocent IV (◀ 1243) dies.

December 12: Rinaldo, Count of Segni, is elected as Pope Alexander IV (▶ 1261).

205

c.1254

The earliest surviving text of the *Dies Irae* attributed to Tommaso de Celano is written. The hymn, which must have been composed around this time, becomes part of the Requiem service until it is removed after the Second Vatican Council (▶ 1965).

1255

September 26: Clare of Assisi (◀ 1253) is canonized by Pope Alexander IV: feast day August 11.

The Diocese of Königsberg is founded.

1256

The Order of Augustinian Hermits is established by Pope Alexander IV.

1257

The Sorbonne is founded by Robert de Sorbon as a theological college of the University of Paris (◀ c.1150).

1258

August 16: Theodore II Lascaris (◀ 1254) dies and is succeeded by his six-year-old son John Lascaris (▶ 1259). Michael VIII Palaeologus is chosen as regent.

September 20: Salisbury Cathedral (◀ 1220) is consecrated (▶ 1330).

Work begins on rebuilding Exeter Cathedral (◀ 1133) in the Gothic style, following the example of Salisbury (▶ c.1400).

1259

Pietro Cavallini is born. An Italian painter and mosaic designer, he is the first to break away completely from the two-dimensional style of Byzantine art towards naturalism. Dies 1330.

Arsenius Autoreianus, Patriarch of Constantinople (◀ 1254, ▶ 1261), is appointed joint guardian of John Lascaris (◀ 1258). His fellow-guardian is murdered by Michael VIII Palaeologus, who seizes the imperial throne in Nicaea after blinding John Lascaris. Arsenius takes refuge in a monastery, refusing to fulfil his duties, and Nicephorus II of Ephesus is appointed Patriarch of Constantinople in his stead (▶ 1261).

The frescoes in Boyana Church, near Sofia, Bulgaria, are painted. They are one of the most complete and well preserved examples of European medieval art. Many depict St Nicholas.

The first recorded instance of flagellants, penitents whipping themselves in public as a demonstration of piety, is recorded in Perugia, Italy.

1260

Chartres Cathedral (◀ 1220) is consecrated.

c.1260

✦ Johannes ('Meister') Eckhart is born. A famous German mystic, towards the end of his life he is suspected of heresy. Dies *c.*1328.

◼ The Rutland Psalter is a fantastic illuminated book decorated with scenes from everyday life, monsters and grotesques.

1261

☾ May 25: Pope Alexander IV (◀ 1254) dies.

July 25: Greek forces under Emperor Michael VIII Palaeologus (◀ 1259, ▶ 1263) recapture Constantinople (◀ 1204) and Latin Emperor Baldwin II Porphyrogenitus (◀ 1228) flees to France.

☾ August 29: Jacques Pantaléon, Patriarch of Jerusalem, is elected as Pope Urban IV (▶ 1264).

☾ August: Arsenius Autoreianus (◀ 1259, ▶ 1265) is reinstated as Patriarch of Constantinople.

Balliol College, Oxford, is founded for graduates.

1263

Michael VIII Palaeologus sends an emissary to Rome with a letter for Pope Urban IV, hinting at the possibility of church unity.

1264

September 8: The papal bull *Transiturus* of Urban IV commands observance of the Feast of Corpus Christi (◀ *c.*1210) by the whole church, though the feast is only celebrated sporadically (▶ 1334).

☾ October 20: Pope Urban IV (◀ 1261) dies.

Merton College, Oxford, is founded for graduates.

Bar Hebraeus (◀ *c.*1243) becomes Maphrion (head of the Asian Monophysite church).

1265

☾ February 5: Guy Foulques, Archbishop of Narbonne, is elected as Pope Clement IV (▶ 1268).

☾ May: Arsenius Autoreianus, Patriarch of Constantinople (◀ 1261), excommunicates Michael VIII Palaeologus for blinding John Lascaris (◀ 1259). Arsenius is then banished.

☾ May 25: Germanus III is appointed Patriarch of Constantinople.

✦ May 29: Dante Alighieri, author of *The Divine Comedy* (▶ *c.*1320), is born. Dies 1321.

August 27: The papal bull *Licet ecclesiarum* reserves to the Holy See the appointment to benefices which fall vacant when the holder is visiting the Curia, a landmark in the centralization of the Western church because it assumes in principle that the Pope appoints to all benefices.

*c.*1266–1271

⚕ September 14: Germanus III, Patriarch of Constantinople, dies.

📖 The *Golden Legend,* a collection of saints' lives and articles on the Christian festivals, is completed.

*c.*1266

♟ Johannes Duns Scotus is born. A Scottish theologian, he becomes a Franciscan and is critical of the theology of Thomas Aquinas. Dies 1308.

1267

⚕ December 28: Joseph I Galesiotes becomes Patriarch of Constantinople (▶ 1275).

♟🖼 Giotto di Bondone, Italian painter, is born. He marks the move away from the Byzantine tradition and is seen as an important herald of the Italian Renaisance. He is famous for his frescoes in Padua (▶ 1305) and Florence (▶ 1320). Dies 1337.

1268

⚕ November 29: Pope Clement IV (◀ 1265) dies.

♟ Beatrice of Nazareth (◀ 1200) dies.

Josephus I Galesiotes, Patriarch of Constantinople, revokes the excommunication of Michael VIII Palaeologus (◀ 1265).

1269

King Alfonso X of Castile–Leon (◀ 1252, ▶ 1284) promotes the translation school of Toledo (◀ 1127) and founds two more, in Seville and Murcia.

At a general chapter of the Franciscans, Bonaventure urges the brothers to propagate the Franciscan custom of reciting three 'Hail, Mary's (◀ *c.*1150) while the evening bell for prayer is ringing. This is a forerunner of the Angelus.

1270

✠ July 18: Boniface of Savoy, Archbishop of Canterbury (◀ 1244), dies. He is later venerated as a saint: feast day July 14.

August 25: The Eighth Crusade sets off under Louis IX of France (◀ 1250). His fleet is destroyed off Sicily and he dies of dysentery in Tunis (▶ 1297). He is succeeded by Philippe III (▶ 1285).

⚕ September 9: The monks of Canterbury (◀ *c.*598) choose Adam Chillenden as Archbishop of Canterbury (▶ 1273).

♛ December: King Theobald II of Navarre (◀ 1253) dies in Sicily returning from the Eighth Crusade. He is succeeded by Henri (▶ 1274), the youngest son of Theobald I (◀ 1253).

🏛 Bourges Cathedral is completed (◀ 1195).

1271

May: Edward (▶ 1272), son of King Henry III of England (◀ 1229, ▶ 1272), arrives in Acre but does little more than help to relieve the siege there. He returns home the next year.

The Crusader fortress of Krak des Chevaliers in Syria, 1271

September 1: After a protracted dispute lasting two years and nine months Tedaldo Visconti, Archdeacon of Liège, is appointed as Pope Gregory X (▶ 1276). He is then on crusade at Acre. To end the dispute the local authorities had kept the cardinals shut in a room until they reached a decision. This seclusion becomes general practice and is known as the conclave.

October: Pope Gregory X invites Emperor Michael VIII Palaeologus (◀ 1268, ▶ 1274) to a council at Lyons to be held in two years time.

The Crusader Castle of Krak des Chevaliers in Syria is captured by the Mamluk sultan Baybars I.

1272

April 13: Pope Gregory X issues invitations to a general council to discuss a new crusade, reunion with the Greek church, and reform of the clergy (▶ 1274).

November 16: King Henry III of England (◀ 1216) dies.

November 16: Edward (◀ 1271), son of King Henry of England, becomes king as Edward I (▶ 1307).

209

1273

☩ February 26: Robert Kilwardby, Provincial Prior of the Dominican Order in England, is appointed Archbishop of Canterbury (▶ 1278), after Adam Chillenden (◀ 1270) has been set aside by Pope Gregory X.

1274

♠ March 7: Thomas Aquinas (◀ 1225) dies (▶ 1323).

May 7–July 17: The Second Council of Lyons receives Greek envoys and a letter from Emperor Michael VIII Palaeologus. However, it forces the Eastern church to capitulate over its differences with the West, including the presence of the term *filioque* ('and the Son') (◀ 589) in the creed. At the Council Pope Gregory X promulgates the law of the conclave, that ten days after the death of a pope the cardinals will meet in one room and remain there until they have chosen a successor (◀ 1271). In the West the Council is regarded as the fourteenth Ecumenical Council

♛ July: King Henri of Navarre dies (◀ 1270), leaving no heir, and the male line becomes extinct. He is succeeded by his daughter Jeanne, aged three (▶ 1284).

♠ July 15: Bonaventure (◀ *c*.1221) dies (▶ 1482).

1275

☩ May: Joseph I Galesiotes, Patriarch of Constantinople (◀ 1267), abdicates over the Council of Lyons and is succeeded by John XI Bekkos (▶ 1282).

The Nestorian Patriarch of Baghdad creates an Archdiocese of Kambalik (Beijing) in China (◀ 907).

1276

☩ January 10: Pope Gregory X (◀ 1271) dies.

January 21: Under the new law of the conclave (◀ 1274), Pierre of Tarentaise is elected as Pope Innocent V, the first Dominican pope.

☩ June 22: Pope Innocent V dies.

☩ July 11: Cardinal Ottobone Fieschi is elected as Pope Hadrian V.

♛ July 27: King Jaume I of Aragon (◀ 1213) dies and is succeeded by Pedro III (▶ 1285).

☩ August 18: Pope Hadrian V dies.

☩ September 8: Cardinal Pedro Julião, a Portuguese, is elected as Pope John XXI (▶ 1277; there is no John XX because a mistake is made in the numbering).

Ramon Lull (◀ 1232, ▶ 1316) opens a training centre to send missionaries to North Africa.

Siger of Brabant, an Averroist philosopher of the University of Paris, is cited for heresy, accused of teaching the 'double truth' that a proposition might be true in philosophy but not in theology.

1277

☨ May 20: Pope John XXI (◀ 1276) is killed when his study ceiling collapses.

☨ November 23: Cardinal Giovanni Gaetano Orsini, a Roman nobleman, is elected as Pope Nicholas III (▶ 1280). He is the first pope to reside in the Vatican.

St George's Cross becomes the national flag of England.

1278

☨ June 5: Robert Kilwardby, Archbishop of Canterbury (◀ 1273), is made a cardinal by Pope Nicholas III and resigns.

☨ July 10: Robert Burnell, Bishop of Bath and Wells, is appointed Archbishop of Canterbury but is rejected by Pope Nicholas III.

***c*.1278**

Rabban Sauma (▶ 1287), a Turk, and his friend Mark (▶ *c*.1281), leave Kambalik (Beijing) to visit the holy places in the West.

1279

☨ February 19: John Pecham, English Provincial of the Friars Minor, is appointed Archbishop of Canterbury (▶ 1292).

1280

☨ August 22: Pope Nicholas III (◀ 1277) dies.

♟ November 15: Albertus Magnus (◀ 1193) dies (▶ 1931).

♟ William of Ockham is born. A scholastic theologian and philosopher, later excommunicated, he devises 'Ockham's razor', the principle that unnecessary information must be removed from an argument. Dies 1348.

***c*.1280**

♟📖 Marsilius of Padua is born. An Italian political philosopher, he writes *Defensor pacis* (▶ 1324), arguing that civil order must be guaranteed by the state. Dies *c*.1343.

1281

☨ February 22: Simon de Brie, Chancellor to King Louis IX of France, is elected as Pope Martin IV (▶ 1285).

***c*.1281**

Mark (◀ *c*.1278) is elected patriarch in Baghdad under the name of Yaballaha III.

1282

♛ December 11: Michael VIII Palaeologus (◀ 1259) dies. The Greek bishops immediately declare the union agreed at the Second Council of Lyons (◀ 1274) invalid. Michael VII Palaeologus is succeeded by his son Andronicus II Palaeologus (▶ 1325, 1328). During his reign the Byzantine empire declines to become a minor state.

☨ December 26: John XI Bekkos, Patriarch of Constantinople (◀ 1275), resigns.

Albi Cathedral, 1282

Albi Cathedral in southern France is built as a fortress against heresy.

*c.*1282

Mechthild of Magdeburg (◀ *c.*1210) dies.

1283

Archbishop Pecham (◀ 1279) gives the Convocation of Canterbury its future form, consisting of bishops and lower clergy (▶ 1583).

1284

March 28: George of Cyprus, the only layman ever to become patriarch without having been in other orders, is appointed Patriarch of Constantinople as Gregory II Cyprius (▶ 1289). He rejects the *filioque* clause imposed at the Council of Lyons (◀ 1274).

April 4: King Alfonso X of Castile–Leon (◀ 1252) dies and is succeeded by his son Sancho IV (▶ 1295).

August 16: Jeanne of Navarre (◀ 1274) marries King Philippe III of France (◀ 1270, ▶ 1285), thus uniting Navarre and France.

By the Statute of Wales, Wales is brought under English rule.

Peterhouse, the oldest Cambridge college, is founded by Hugo de Balsham.

1285

⚱ March 28: Pope Martin IV (◀ 1281) dies.

⚱ April 2: Giacomo Savelli, a grand-nephew of Pope Honorius III (◀ 1227), is elected as Pope Honorius IV (▶ 1287).

♛ October 5: Philippe III, King of France (◀ 1270), dies and is succeeded by Philippe IV (▶ 1314).

♛ November 2: King Pedro III of Aragon (◀ 1276) dies and is succeeded by Alfonso III (▶ 1291).

Osman, a Turkic tribal chieftain, becomes founder of the Ottoman Turks (▶ 1326).

1286

The Dominican John Balbi of Genoa completes the *Catholicon*, a religious Latin dictionary which also aims to interpret the Bible correctly.

1287

⚱ April 3: Pope Honorius IV (◀ 1285) dies.

◼ Work begins on the altar of St James in Pistoia Cathedral, Italy, made of silver and weighing almost a ton. It takes around 200 years to finish.

🏛 Work begins on the building of Uppsala Cathedral.

Rabban Sauma (◀ c.1278) arrives in Rome as part of a delegation sent by Yaballaha III (◀ c.1281). His arrival stimulates interest in the Eastern church.

King Alfonso of Aragon (◀ 1285) commissions Jaume de Montjuich to translate the Bible into Catalan.

1288

February 22: After eleven months of haggling, a Franciscan friar, Girolamo Masci, is elected as Pope Nicholas IV (▶ 1292), the first Franciscan to become pope.

1289

⚱ June: Gregory II Cyprius, Patriarch of Constantinople (◀ 1284), resigns.

⚱ October 14: Athanasius I is appointed Patriarch of Constantinople (▶ 1293).

1290

March 1: The University of Coimbra in Portugal is founded by King Dinis I.

July 18: King Edward I (◀ 1272, ▶ 1307) expels the Jews from England.

🏛 Llandaff Cathedral (◀ 1107) is consecrated.

c.1290

■ The *Mappa Mundi* in Hereford Cathedral, a circular map with Jerusalem at the centre, is finished, the only complete map to have survived from the Middle Ages.

1291

♛ June 18: King Alfonso III of Aragon (◀ 1285) dies and is succeeded by Jaume II (▶ 1327).

♟♫ October 31: Philippe de Vitry, French composer, is born. He writes an important work of music theory, *Ars Nova* (1322), introducing new rhythmic schemes. Dies 1361.

Acre, the last Crusader outpost, falls to the Mamluks, slave soldiers in the service of the Muslim rulers.

1292

☸ April 4: Pope Nicholas IV (◀ 1288) dies.

☸ December 8: John Pecham, Archbishop of Canterbury (◀ 1279), dies.

1293

May 20: King Sancho IV (◀ 1284, ▶ 1295) of Castile founds the *Studium generale* in Alcala, which later becomes the Complutensian University, so called after Complutum, the Latin name for the place (▶ 1499).

☸ October 16: Athanasius I, Patriarch of Constantinople (◀ 1289, ▶ 1303), resigns over opposition from the clergy to his planned reforms.

♟ Jan van Ruysbroeck, a Flemish mystic, is born. His prose helps to shape the Flemish language. Dies 1381.

1294

☸ January 1: John XII becomes Patriarch of Constantinople (▶ 1303).

☸ July 5: After more than two years of dissension among the cardinals, a hermit, Pietro del Morrone, is elected as Pope Celestine V.

August 29: Pietro del Morrone enters L'Aquila in the Abruzzi riding a donkey and is consecrated in his own church there.

☸ September 12: Robert Winchelsey, Archdeacon of Essex, is appointed Archbishop of Canterbury (▶ 1313).

☸ December 13: Pope Celestine V resigns, the only pope ever to do so.

☸ December 24: Cardinal Benedetto Caetani is elected as Pope Boniface VIII (▶ 1303).

♟ Roger Bacon (◀ 1214) dies.

Giovanni da Montecorvino, a Franciscan priest, arrives in Kambalik (Beijing) (▶ 1299). He translates the New Testament and the Psalms into Chinese (◀ 635).

1295

♛ April 25: King Sancho IV of Castile (◀ 1284) dies and is succeeded by Fernando IV (▶ 1312).

♦ Heinrich Suso is born. He is a Swabian mystic and writer. Dies 1366.

1296

🏛 September 9: The first stone is laid of Florence Cathedral, designed to be the largest in the world.

A list of dioceses under the Patriarch of Constantinople drawn up by Emperor Andronicus II Palaeologus (◀ 1282), the *Echthesis*, contains 112 metropolitans, but many of these have one or at most two bishops under them (◀ 901).

c.1296

♦ Gregory Palamas, a leading theologian of Hesychasm, is born. Dies 1359.

1297

◉ King Louis IX of France (◀ 1270) is canonized by Pope Boniface VIII: feast day August 25.

1299

Giovanni da Montecorvino (◀ 1294) builds a church in Kambalik (Beijing) (▶ 1318).

1300

February 22: With the bull *Antiquorum fide relatio*, Pope Boniface VIII inaugurates the first Holy, or Jubilee, Year, giving plenary indulgences for pilgrims visiting the basilicas of St Peter and St Paul in Rome. He declares that in future it will be repeated every 100 years (▶ 1350).

c.1300

♦ Richard Rolle of Hampole, English mystic, is born. Dies 1394.

♦ John Tauler, German mystic, is born. A Dominican, he gains a reputation as a preacher and spiritual director. Dies 1361.

▮ A frontal for the altar of the church of Nes in Norway is a striking example of oil painting anticipating the technique developed in the Netherlands a century later.

♦♫ Guillaume de Machaut, French composer (▶ 1364), is born. Dies 1377.

Fourteenth century

The fourteenth century brings two deadly disasters. Between 1315 and 1317 there is a great famine in Europe because of crop failure and millions die. No amount of prayer can remedy it, and this inevitably casts doubt on the church and its authority. From 1347 onwards the Black Death sweeps across Europe, spreading from Constantinople to Genoa, on to France, Spain and England and from there to Scandinavia and central Europe. It kills a third of the inhabitants of Europe and affects every level of society; again it is a serious problem for the church.

In the West the church has problems of its own. Its supreme ecclesiastical authority, the papacy, is in turmoil. Because of infighting between the Italian families which control the elections of popes, the papal residence is moved to Avignon, where it resembles a royal court. The Avignon popes live like princes in a magnificent palace which is completed in 1364. Clement V (1305–14) and John XXII (1316–34) reorganize and centralize the church's administration so that the papacy now directly controls appointments to church offices, gaining a considerable income; it is enriched by many other forms of payment. When Pope Gregory XI returns to Rome in 1377, the French cardinals elect an antipope, so that for a period there are two popes; at the beginning of the next century there are even three. But great spiritual figures also appear: the French Beguine Marguerite Porete, Johannes ('Meister') Eckhart, Julian of Norwich, Catherine of Siena, Bridget of Sweden, Heinrich Suso, Margery Kempe, Jan van Ruysbroeck and, born at the end of the century, Thomas à Kempis. With John Wyclif and the Lollards in England and later Jan Hus in Bohemia, calls for reform are raised once again.

During the century European culture embarks on a change in what is known as the Renaissance. Classical antiquity is rediscovered; long-neglected authors such as Cicero and Homer, ignored by the Scholastics, are cultivated; ancient Greek is studied alongside Latin; and the Bible is read critically in, and translated from, Greek and Hebrew. The rise of humanism is epitomized in such figures as Dante and Petrarch. Not only does a new literary style develop with them but also, with Giotto, a new style in painting, and with Filippo Brunelleschi a new style in architecture. These changes will lay the foundations for a critical approach to Christianity. With independence of mind, the 'complete man' who potentially can master all areas of art and thought is less under the power and claims of the institutional church and begins to believe that he can master his environment and his nature.

1301

Edward, son of Edward I (◀ 1290), is proclaimed the first English Prince of Wales.

1302

November 18: The papal bull *Unam sanctam* asserts the supremacy of papal power over worldly rulers.

♣▣ Cimabue (◀ *c.*1240) dies.

1303

April 20: By his bull *In supremae*, Pope Boniface VIII founds the University of Rome La Sapienza, to be more under his control than Bologna and Padua.

☥ June 23: Athanasius I (◀ 1289) is reinstated as Patriarch of Constantinople to popular acclaim, displacing John XII (◀ 1294).

A papal bull of Pope Boniface VIII constitutes the University of Avignon from existing schools in the city.

☥ October 11: Pope Boniface VIII (◀ 1294) dies.

☥ October 22: Niccolò Boccasino, Cardinal Bishop of Ostia, is elected as Pope Benedict XI (▶ 1304).

*c.***1303**

♣ Bridget of Sweden is born. She founds a religious order, the Brigittine Sisters. Dies 1373.

1304

☥ July 7: Pope Benedict XI (◀ 1303) dies.

♣ July 20: Petrarch (Francesco Petrarca), Italian poet, scholar and humanist, is born. He is considered the father of the Renaissance. Dies 1374.

> **The Renaissance**
> Renaissance is a term used to describe a set of cultural developments beginning in Italy in the middle of the fourteenth century which introduce new conceptions of human beings and their relationship to the world in which they live. It is marked by a rediscovery of classical antiquity and the rise of humanism, exemplified by Petrarch (◀ 1304), who creates a new literary style centring on the selfhood of the writer, making him the first 'humanist'. In painting, Giotto (◀ 1267) pioneers three-dimensionality, making possible the creation of a separate space within the picture itself containing figures of another time than that of the viewer. The humanistic reference also extends to architecture. With printing, possibilities for the dissemination of knowledge vastly increase, and new techniques are pioneered in art, poetry and architecture. The Renaissance has a great influence on Christianity, not least on the Reformation, through great figures such as Desiderius Erasmus (▶ 1469), and lays the foundations for a critical approach to Christianity.

1305

☉ June 5: Bertrand de Got, Archbishop of Bordeaux, is elected as Pope Clement V (▶ 1314). A Frenchman, he chooses Avignon as his residence, and the papacy remains there until 1377.

▣ Giotto (◀ 1267) paints a notable cycle of frescoes in the Scrovegni Chapel, Padua (▶ c.1320).

1306

January 27: Pope Clement V founds the University of Orleans.

July 22: King Philippe IV of France expels the Jews from France. The decision is reversed in 1315 and imposed again in 1322.

♣ Jacopone da Todi (◀ 1236) dies.

1307

♛ July 7: King Edward I of England (◀ 1272) dies and is succeeded by his fourth son, Edward, who becomes King Edward II (▶ 1327).

1308

September 8: With the bull *Super specula*, Pope Clement V founds the University of Perugia.

♣ November 8: Johannes Duns Scotus (◀ c.1266) dies.

The Teutonic Knights (◀ 1198) capture Gdansk in Poland, massacring its inhabitants and replacing them with German Christian settlers.

c.1308

📖 Dante Alighieri (◀ 1265) begins writing his *Divine Comedy* (▶ c.1320).

1309

☉ September 1: Athanasius I, Patriarch of Constantinople (◀ 1289), dies.

The Teutonic Knights conquer East Pomerania.

1310

☉ May 9: Nephon I becomes Patriarch of Constantinople (▶ 1314).

♣📖 June 1: Marguerite Porete, French Beguine, is burnt at the stake for heresy. Her *The Mirror of Simple Souls* is one of the most important religious documents in Old French.

🏛 Old St Paul's is completed (◀ 1087).

▣ The mosaics in the Church of St Saviour in Chora, Constantinople, are created, one of the finest works of the renaissance under the Palaeologus dynasty.

1311

October 16: The Council of Vienne opens. It is regarded in the West as the fifteenth Ecumenical Council.

🏛 Reims Cathedral (◀ 1211) is consecrated.

Reims Cathedral, 1311

219

1312

March 22: The Council of Vienne dissolves the Knights Templar (◀ 1118).

May 6: Before closing, the Council of Vienne proclaims a new crusade within six years. The Council also condemns the Beguines, but Pope John XXII will permit them to resume their way of life (▶ 1321).

♔ June 29: Heinrich VII is crowned Holy Roman Emperor after a vacancy from the death of Friedrich II (◀ 1250).

♔ September 7: King Fernando IV of Castile–Leon (◀ 1295) dies and is succeeded by his son Alfonso XI (▶ 1350).

1313

� May 11: Robert Winchelsey, Archbishop of Canterbury (◀ 1294), dies.

� May 28: Thomas Cobham, Precentor of York, is appointed Archbishop of Canterbury but his appointment is not confirmed by Pope Clement V.

♔ August 24: Heinrich VII, Holy Roman Emperor (◀ 1312), dies.

� October 1: Walter Reynolds, Bishop of Worcester, Lord Chancellor and Lord Treasurer, is appointed Archbishop of Canterbury (▶ 1327).

In his bull *Pastoralis cura*, Pope Clement V asserts the supremacy of the papacy over the empire.

1314

� April 11: Nephon I, Patriarch of Constantinople (◀ 1310), dies.

� April 20: Pope Clement V (◀ 1305) dies.

♔ November 29: Philippe IV, King of France (◀ 1285), dies and is succeeded by Louis X (▶ 1316).

♔ Amda Siyon becomes ruler of Ethiopia. He conquers large new territories, builds new monasteries and makes possible the spread of Christianity. He dies in 1344.

c.1314

♟ Sergei of Radonezh is born. A Russian hermit, he founds the Monastery of the Holy Trinity and 40 others. The father of Russian monasticism, he also influences the politics of his time. Dies 1392.

1315

� May 12: John XIII Glykys is appointed Patriarch of Constantinople (▶ 1319).

♟ June 29: Ramon Lull (◀ 1232) dies.

1315–17

Europe experiences a great famine as a result of bad weather and crop failure. Millions die.

1316

♛ June 5: Louis X, King of France (◀ 1314), dies and is succeeded by Jean I.

☉ August 7: After two years of disagreement the cardinals elect Jacques Duèse, Bishop of Avignon, as Pope John XXII (▶ 1334).

♛ November 20: Jean I, King of France, dies and is succeeded by Philippe V (▶ 1322).

1317

The Dominicans in Frankfurt commend the saying of the 'Hail, Mary' during the ringing of the bells for evening prayer (◀ 1269).

1318

Pope John XXII creates the Archdiocese of Kambalik (Beijing) with Giovanni da Montecorvino (◀ 1299) as its archbishop. He also establishes the province of Sultanieh, the Persian capital, with six suffragan bishoprics. A Dominican is consecrated as the first archbishop. It embraces all western and central Asia south of the Black Sea, the Caspian Sea and the Himalayas, and eastern North Africa.

Pope John XXII commends the practice of the Angelus, the recitation of the 'Hail, Mary' three times. He orders that all the church bells in Rome shall be rung to remind the people.

1319

☉ May 11: John XIII Glykys, Patriarch of Constantinople (◀ 1315), dies.

1320

☉ Gerasimus I (▶ 1321) is appointed Patriarch of Constantinople.

🏛 King Kazimierz the Great builds Wawel Cathedral, Krakow, Poland.

♪ The first organ with pedals is built.

*c.***1320**

▮ Giotto (◀ 1305, ▶ 1337) paints frescoes for the church of Santa Croce, Florence.

📖 Dante finishes his *Divine Comedy* (◀ 1308).

In Persia, the Dominican Jordan Catalani joins a group of Franciscans going to China. The Franciscans are killed at Thana, near Mumbai, where Catalani remains, becoming a bishop, which costs him his life. He leaves a record of his experiences.

1321

☉ April 20: Gerasimus I, Patriarch of Constantinople (◀ 1320), dies.

♞ September 14: Dante Alighieri (◀ 1265) dies.

Pope John XXII lifts the condemnation of the Beguines (◀ 1312).

1322

January 3: Philippe V, King of France (◀ 1316), dies and is succeeded by Charles IV (▶ 1328).

🕍 The central tower of Ely Cathedral (◀ 1189) collapses and is replaced with an octagonal tower and lantern.

1323

☿ November 11: Jesaias is appointed Patriarch of Constantinople (▶ 1332).

✝ Thomas Aquinas (◀ 1274) is canonized by Pope John XXII: feast day January 28.

Odoric of Pordenone, an Italian Franciscan, missionary and intrepid traveller, visits Sumatra, Java and Borneo.

1324

♫ In his bull *Docta sanctorum patrum*, Pope John XXII warns against counterpoint, which he has forbidden in church music.

📖 In his *Defensor pacis*, Marsilius of Padua (◀ 1280) argues that the church should be ruled by general councils and in turn be completely subordinate to the state.

1325

♛ With the support of the Byzantine nobility, Andronicus III Palaeologus, grandson of Andronicus II (◀ 1282, ▶ 1328), compels his grandfather to appoint him co-emperor (▶ 1341).

♫ The Tournai Mass, the first complete polyphonic mass known, is written by several composers (▶ 1364).

1326

August: Osman (◀ 1285) dies. The Ottoman Turks capture Bursa, an important Byzantine stronghold.

1327

♛ January: A parliament deposes King Edward II of England (◀ 1307) and proclaims his son king as Edward III (▶ 1377). Edward II is later murdered.

♛ November 2: Jaume II, King of Aragon (◀ 1291), dies and is succeeded by his son Alfonso IV (▶ 1335).

☿ November 16: Walter Reynolds, Archbishop of Canterbury (◀ 1313), dies.

1328

♛ January: Ludwig IV of Bavaria is crowned Holy Roman Emperor (▶ 1347).

♛ February 1: Charles IV, King of France (◀ 1322), dies and is succeeded by Philippe VI (▶ 1350).

♛ May: Andronicus III Palaeologus (◀ 1325) makes his grandfather Emperor Andronicus II Palaeologus (◀ 1282) abdicate and enter a monastery. He becomes sole emperor.

☿ June 5: Simon Mepeham, Prebendary of Chichester, is appointed Archbishop of Canterbury (▶ 1333).

♛ Jeanne II, daughter of King Philippe V of France (◀ 1322), becomes Queen of Navarre (◀ 1284) by a treaty with King Philippe VI (▶ 1349).

*c.*1328

♦ Johannes ('Meister') Eckhart (◀ *c.*1260) dies.

♦▣ Pietro Cavallini (◀ 1259) dies.

1330

▥ The spire of Salisbury Cathedral (◀ 1258) is completed.

*c.*1330

♦ John Wyclif is born. An English reformer, on a biblical and patristic basis he distinguishes an ideal church from the actual church, making criticisms which lead to his condemnation. He initiates a translation of the Bible into English. Dies 1384.

1331

The Ottoman Turks (◀ 1326) capture Nicaea.

1332

☦ May 13: Jesaias, Patriarch of Constantinople (◀ 1323), dies.

Pope John XXII founds the University of Cahors in his native city.

1333

☦ October 12: Simon Mepeham, Archbishop of Canterbury (◀ 1328), dies, having been excommunicated after a clash with the Prior of St Augustine's, Canterbury.

☦ November 26: John de Stratford, Bishop of Worcester and Lord Chancellor, becomes Archbishop of Canterbury (▶ 1348).

Pope John XXII sends 27 Franciscan missionaries to China.

1334

☦ February: John XIV Kalekas becomes Patriarch of Constantinople (▶ 1347).

Pope John XXII makes the feasts of Corpus Christi (◀ 1264) and the Holy Trinity feasts of universal usage.

☦ December 4: Pope John XXII (◀ 1316) dies.

☦ December 20: Jacques Fournier, a Cistercian theologian and an Inquisitor, is elected as Pope Benedict XII (▶ 1342).

1335

♛ January 24: Alfonso IV, King of Aragon (◀ 1327), dies and is succeeded by his son Pedro IV (▶ 1387).

Pope Benedict XII orders a papal palace to be built at Avignon (▶ 1364).

1337

♦▣ January 8: Giotto (◀ 1267) dies.

223

May 24: King Philippe VI of France (◀ 1328, ▶ 1350) seizes Aquitaine in France from the English, marking the beginning of the Hundred Years War between France and England.

The Ottoman Turks (◀ 1326) conquer Nicomedia.

Abuna Ya'aqob, metropolitan of Ethiopia, reorganizes the church there into areas based on the monastery of Debra Libanos.

1338

August 6: At the first Diet (imperial council) of Frankfurt the manifesto *Fidem catholicam* states that imperial authority derives directly from God, not from the Pope (and therefore that the electors are competent to choose an emperor).

King Edward III of England (◀ 1327, ▶ 1340) lands in Antwerp to defend his claim to Aquitaine.

1339

July 25: Dauphin Humbert II founds the University of Grenoble.

A massive addition is planned for Siena Cathedral (◀ 1215) but is halted by the Black Death.

The Franciscan Giovanni de' Marignolli, with 32 friars, arrives in Beijing from Avignon (▶ 1347).

1340

♛ February 8: King Edward III of England declares himself King of France in Ghent.

♟ October: Geert de Groote is born. After a life of extravagance he founds the Brethren of the Common Life in the Netherlands to foster personal spirituality. Dies 1384.

♟📖 Geoffrey Chaucer, author of *The Canterbury Tales* (c.1390), is born. Dies 1400.

Sergei of Radonezh (◀ c.1314) founds the Monastery of the Holy Trinity near Moscow (▶ 1452).

1341

♛ June 15: Andronicus III Palaeologus (◀ 1325) dies and is succeeded in Constantinople by his son John V Palaeologus (▶ 1347), who is nine years old. John VI Cantacuzenus, his father's chief minister, designated regent, rebels and has himself crowned emperor in Thrace (▶ 1347).

1342

⚓ April 25: Pope Benedict XII (◀ 1334) dies.

⚓ May 7: Pierre of Rosier d'Egleton, a Benedictine, Archbishop of Rouen and Chancellor of France, is elected as Pope Clement VI (▶ 1352).

The Franciscans take over the care of the sacred sites in Jerusalem. The practice of observing the Stations of the Cross, originally seven points associated with Jesus' journey to his crucifixion, becomes popular there (▶ 1731).

*c.*1342

♣ 📖 Julian of Norwich is born. An English mystic, she is known for her *Revelations of Divine Love*. Dies *c.*1420.

1343

January 27: Clement VI's papal bull *Unigenitus* proclaims a Holy Year (◀ 1300) to be celebrated every fiftieth year, starting in 1350, instead of every hundreth, because of the shortness of the human life span. It also defines the 'treasury of merits' as the basis for the granting of indulgences.

September 3: An edict of Pope Clement VI founds the University of Pisa.

*c.*1343

♣ Marsilius of Padua (◀ *c.*1280) dies.

1344

🏛 November 21: The building of the present Prague Cathedral begins (◀ 925).

1346

July: Edward III lands in Normandy.

August 26: At the battle of Crécy the English under Edward III heavily defeat the French.

1347

☦ February 2: John XIV Kalekas, Patriarch of Constantinople (◀ 1334), is deposed.

☦ May 17: Isidore I becomes Patriarch of Constantinople (▶ 1350).

August 1: The English seize Calais.

♛ October 11: Ludwig IV, Holy Roman Emperor (◀ 1328), dies of a stroke during a bear hunt.

♛ John VI Cantacuzenus (◀ 1341, ▶ 1353) enters Constantinople and becomes co-emperor with John V Palaeologus (◀ 1341, ▶ 1357).

Giovanni de' Marignolli (◀ 1339) leaves China to return to Avignon; on the way back he spends a year in India, where he founds a Latin church in Malabar.

The Black Death is reported in the trading cities of Constantinople and Trebizond and is brought by Italian ships to Genoa, from where it spreads across the Mediterranean.

*c.*1347

♣ Catherine of Siena, Italian mystic, is born. Dies 1380.

225

The Black Death, engraving 1348

1348

April 7: The Charles University of Prague is founded by Charles I of Bohemia.

April 9: William of Ockham (◄ 1280) dies.

August 23: John de Stratford, Archbishop of Canterbury (◄ 1333), dies.

December 14: John de Ufford, Dean of Lincoln and Lord Chancellor, is appointed Archbishop of Canterbury (► 1349).

The Black Death reaches France, Spain and England.

1349

May 20: John de Ufford, Archbishop of Canterbury elect, dies of the Black Death before being consecrated (◄ 1348).

226

⚘ July 19: Thomas Bradwardine, Proctor of Oxford University and Chancellor of St Paul's Cathedral, is consecrated Archbishop of Canterbury by Pope Clement VI in Avignon.

⚘ August 26: Thomas Bradwardine dies of the Black Death soon after his arrival in England.

♛ October 6: Jeanne II, Queen of Navarre (◀ 1328), dies and is succeeded by her son Carlos II (▶ 1387).

⚘ December 20: Simon Islip, Prebendary of St Paul's Cathedral and keeper of the Privy Seal, is appointed Archbishop of Canterbury (▶ 1366).

The Black Death spreads to Scandinavia and Central Europe.

Bridget of Sweden (◀ c.1303) founds the Order of Brigittine Sisters after seeing a vision.

The University of Florence is founded by Lucchino Visconti, ruler of Milan.

1350

♛ March 17: King Alfonso XI of Castile–Leon is the only European monarch to die of the Black Death. He is succeeded by his son Pedro (▶ 1369).

⚘ March: Isidore I, Patriarch of Constantinople (◀ 1347), dies.

⚘ June 10: Callistus I, a proponent of Hesychasm, is appointed Patriarch of Constantinople (▶ 1353).

♛ August 22: Philippe VI, King of France (◀ 1328), dies and is succeeded by Jean II (▶ 1364).

For this Holy Year (◀ 1343, ▶ 1389), San Giovanni in Laterano (◀ 313) is added to the churches to be visited.

1352

⚘ December 6: Pope Clement VI (◀ 1342) dies.

⚘ December 18: Étienne Albert, a distinguished lawyer and former chief judge of Toulouse, is elected as Pope Innocent VI (▶ 1362).

The Ethiopian monk Ewostatewos dies. He leaves a monastic movement in the north led by Filpos, which observes the Sabbath rest (▶ 1400).

1353

⚘ November: Callistus I, Patriarch of Constantinople, refuses to crown Matthew Cantacuzenus (▶ 1357) co-emperor with his father John VI Cantacuzenus (◀ 1347, ▶ 1355) and resigns (▶ 1355). He is replaced by Philotheus Kokkinos (▶ 1355).

1354

The Ottoman Turks (◀ 1326) capture Gallipoli.

1355

January: Co-emperor John VI Cantacuzenus (◀ 1341) abdicates and Callistus I (◀ 1353) is restored as Patriarch of Constantinople in place of Philotheus Kokkinos (▶ 1364).

April 5: Charles IV is crowned Holy Roman Emperor (▶ 1378).

1356

September 19: At the Battle of Poitiers, Edward Prince of Wales (the Black Prince, ▶ 1370) heavily defeats the French and takes King Jean II of France prisoner.

An earthquake and fire destroy Basle Cathedral (◀ 1019). It is rebuilt soon afterwards.

1357

Matthew Cantacuzenus is captured by the rival emperor John V Palaeologus; he is forced to abdicate and retires to write biblical commentaries in a monastery.

1359

March 24: Through a treaty signed in London by the captive King Jean II of France (◀ 1356, ▶ 1364), the English receive much of Aquitaine (◀ 1337).

November 27: Gregory Palamas (◀ c.1296) dies.

1360

Timur (Tamerlane or Tamburlaine, ▶ 1395), a Turk from Transoxania who claims to be a descendant of Genghis Khan, begins a series of barbaric conquests from India and Russia to the Mediterranean.

John Wyclif (◀ c.1330) becomes Master of Balliol College, Oxford.

The first translation of the Bible into Czech is published. It is known as the Dresden Bible.

c.1360

Andrei Rublev (▶ c.1425), icon painter, is born. Dies 1430.

1361

June 9: Philippe de Vitry (◀ 1291) dies.

June 16: John Tauler (◀ c.1300) dies.

An organ is built in Halberstadt Cathedral, the first with a fingering system of twelve notes.

Edward III establishes the principality of Aquitaine, independent of France (▶ 1453).

Emperor Charles IV (◀ 1355, ▶ 1378) officially founds a *studium generale* in Pavia which becomes a university.

Michael Nothburgh, Bishop of London, leaves 1000 marks to found a *mons pietatis*, a charitable institution for lending money on objects pawned. It soon closes as it levies no interest (▶ 1462).

1362

☩ September 12: Pope Innocent VI (◀ 1352) dies.

☩ September 28: Guillaume de Grimoard, Benedictine Abbot of St Victor, Marseilles, is elected as Pope Urban V (▶ 1370).

📖 The earliest extant text of William Langland, *The Vision of Piers Plowman*, a Christian allegorical poem in Middle English, is produced.

1363

☩ August: Callistus I, Patriarch of Constantinople (◀ 1355), dies.

♟ December 14: Jean Gerson, French Catholic theologian, is born. Dies 1429.

1364

♛ April 8: Jean II, King of France (◀ 1350), dies and is succeeded by Charles V (▶ 1380).

☩ October 8: Philotheus Kokkinos (◀ 1353, 1355) again becomes Patriarch of Constantinople (▶ 1376). He opposes Emperor John V Palaeologus's attempts to negotiate with Popes Urban V and Gregory XI.

🏛 The papal palace at Avignon (◀ 1335) is completed.

♪ Guillaume de Machaut (◀ c.1300, ▶ 1377), *Mass of Notre Dame*, is composed for the coronation of Charles V; it is the first known polyphonic setting by a single composer (◀ 1325) and an important example of *Ars Nova*, the introduction of new rhythmic schemes into music (◀ 1291).

The Ottoman Turks (◀ 1326) capture Adrianople, severing the land route westwards from Constantinople.

King Kazimierz of Poland founds the University of Krakow with papal permission.

1365

The University of Vienna is founded by Duke Rudolf IV.

1366

♟ January 25: Heinrich Suso (◀ 1295) dies.

☩ April 26: Simon Islip, Archbishop of Canterbury (◀ 1349), dies.

☩ November 5: Simon Langham, Bishop of Ely, is appointed Archbishop of Canterbury (▶ 1368).

1367

April 30: Pope Urban V and the Curia leave Avignon for Rome. The Pope resides in the Vatican.

1368

☩ November 28: Archbishop Simon Langham (◀ 1366) is made a cardinal and resigns the see.

229

1369

♔ January 15: William Whittlesey, Bishop of Worcester, is appointed Archbishop of Canterbury (▶ 1374).

♛ March 23: Pedro, King of Castile–Leon (◀ 1350), is murdered in a civil war by his half-brother Enrique, who succeeds him as King Enrique II (▶ 1379).

♟ John Hus is born. A Bohemian reformer, he is lured by promises of safe conduct to the Council of Florence, where he is condemned for heresy and burned at the stake (▶ 1415).

1370

August 26: Because of civil unrest in Rome, Pope Urban V returns to Avignon.

♔ December 19: Pope Urban V (◀ 1362) dies.

♔ December 30: Cardinal Pierre Roger de Beaufort, a lawyer, is elected as Pope Gregory XI (▶ 1378), the last French pope.

Edward the Black Prince (◀ 1356, ▶ 1377) massacres the citizens of Limoges after a siege.

c.1370

♟▮ Hubert van Eyck, Dutch painter, is born. Dies 1426.

1371

The Ottoman Turks gain control of much of Macedonia and John V Palaeologus (◀ 1341) is forced to recognize Turkish sovereignty.

1372

Patriarch Gabriel of Alexandria consecrates a Nubian bishop, Qasr Ibrim (▶ 1484).

1373

♟ July 23: Bridget of Sweden (◀ c.1303) dies (▶ 1391).

♛ Manuel II Palaeologus, son of John V Palaeologus (◀ 1341), is crowned co-emperor with him (▶ 1391).

c.1373

♟ Margery Kempe (▶ 1413), English mystic, is born. Dies c.1438.

1374

♔ June 5/6: William Whittlesey, Archbishop of Canterbury (◀ 1369), dies.

♟ July 19: Petrarch (◀ 1304) dies.

1375

♔ June 5: Simon Sudbury, Bishop of London, is appointed Archbishop of Canterbury (▶ 1381).

♙ A mystery play is performed in Chester.

John Wyclif (◄ c.1330) attacks the wealth of the church and the power of the Pope; his followers come to be known as Lollards, meaning idle loafers or babblers.

1376

☉ Philotheus Kokkinos, Patriarch of Constantinople (◄ 1364), dies and is succeeded by Macarius (► 1379).

☺ The earliest reference is made to the York Cycle of mystery plays.

1377

January 17: Gregory XI returns to Rome and resides in the Vatican.

♣♪ April 13: Guillaume de Machaut (◄ c.1300) dies.

♕ June 21: King Edward III of England (◄ 1327) dies and is succeeded by Richard, son of Edward the Black Prince (◄ 1370), as King Richard II (► 1384). He is only ten years old.

♣ Filippo Brunelleschi, Florentine architect, is born. His masterpiece is the dome of Florence Cathedral (► 1420). Dies 1446.

🏛 The nave of Canterbury Cathedral built by Lanfranc (◄ 1070) is demolished and rebuilt as seen today.

1378

☉ March 27: Pope Gregory XI (◄ 1370) dies.

☉ April 8: In Rome, Bartolomeo Prignano, Archbishop of Bari, is elected as Pope Urban VI (► 1389).

August 2: Because of Pope Urban VI's attacks on them, the French cardinals still in Avignon declare the April 8 election invalid.

☉ September 20: The French cardinals in Avignon elect Cardinal Robert of Geneva as Antipope Clement VII (► 1394).

♕ November 29: Charles IV, Holy Roman Emperor (◄ 1355), dies.

c.1378

♣▣ Lorenzo Ghiberti (► 1403), Italian metalworker and sculptor, is born. His bronze doors for the baptistery of Florence Cathedral are considered one of the masterpieces of the century. Dies 1455.

1379

♕ May 29: Enrique II, King of Castile–Leon (◄ 1369), dies and is succeeded by his son Juan I (► 1390).

☉ Macarius, Patriarch of Constantinople (◄ 1376, ► 1390), is replaced by Neilus Kerameus (► 1388).

New College, Oxford, is founded by William of Wykeham for undergraduates as well as graduates.

Stephen of Perm travels north to the White Sea, an inlet of the Barents Sea in Russia, and settles as a missionary among Finno-Ugric tribes.

Antipope Clement VII establishes the University of Erfurt (▶ 1389).

1380

✝ April 29: Catherine of Siena (◀ c.1347) dies (▶ 1461).

♛ September 16: Charles V, King of France (◀ 1364) dies, and is succeeded by Charles VI (▶ 1422).

♫ The organ in Sion Church, Switzerland, is the world's oldest functioning organ.

c.1380

✝ Thomas à Kempis is born. A German monk, he writes *The Imitation of Christ* (▶ 1418). Dies 1471.

1381

☉ June 14: Simon Sudbury, Archbishop of Canterbury (◀ 1375), is beheaded by rebels under Wat Tyler.

☉ October 23: William Courtenay, Bishop of London, who is a vigorous opponent of the Lollards (◀ 1375, ▶ 1401), is appointed Archbishop of Canterbury (▶ 1396).

✝ December 2: Jan van Ruysbroeck (◀ 1293) dies.

☿ Aleksandr Nevskiy (◀ 1242) is canonized by the Russian Orthodox Church but this is not recognized by the papacy: feast day November 23.

1382

Winchester College is founded by William of Wykeham.

John Wyclif is expelled from Oxford.

A translation into English, organized by Wyclif, of the Latin Vulgate Bible, is issued. Like the Lollards (◀ 1375), who read it, it is banned.

1383

The Orthodox Stephen Charp is consecrated bishop of the missionary diocese of Perm, at the foot of the Urals.

1384

🎭 June 18: King Richard II (◀ 1377, ▶ 1397) visits Coventry and attends the Coventry mystery plays.

✝ August 20: Geert de Groote (◀ 1340) dies.

✝ December 31: John Wyclif (◀ c.1330) dies.

1385

August 14: The Union of Krewo provides for the marriage of Queen Jadwiga of Poland

(▶ 1997) to Grand Prince Jogaila of Lithuania and the conversion of the Grand Prince and other leading Lithuanian nobility to Roman Catholicism.

c.1385

♣♫ John Dunstaple (once known as Dunstable) is born. He begins to unify the musical setting of the mass. Dies 1453.

♣♫ Leonel Power is born. He stands alongside John Dunstaple as a composer. His *Missa Alma Redemptoris Mater* is the earliest surviving cyclic *cantus firmus* mass. Dies 1445.

🏛 Work begins on Milan Cathedral, built on the site of churches which date back to the fifth century.

1386

The warlike Rupert I of Wittelsbach founds the University of Heidelberg on the model of the University of Paris. It is the oldest German university.

♣■ Donatello, Florentine artist and sculptor, is born. As well as other sculptures of biblical figures he creates the first nude David since classical times. Dies 1466.

🏛 Work begins on the Gothic Cathedral of Oviedo (◀ 794).

1387

♛ January 1: King Carlos II of Navarre (◀ 1349) dies and is succeeded by his son Carlos III (▶ 1425).

♛ January 5: King Pedro IV of Aragon (◀ 1335) dies and is succeeded by his son Juan I (▶ 1396).

1388

✠ February 1: Neilus Karameus, Patriarch of Constantinople (◀ 1379), dies.

The University of Cologne is founded as a municipal university and becomes a centre of Roman Catholicism.

1389

✠ January 12: Antony IV becomes Patriarch of Constantinople (▶ 1390).

April 8: In the bull *Salvator Noster*, Pope Urban VI announces that 1390 will be a Holy Year (◀ 1300, 1350). Intervals are now intended to be 33 years, Jesus' lifetime on earth, but it had proved impossible to celebrate the Holy Year in 1383. Santa Maria Maggiori is added to the churches to be visited. The number of pilgrims in 1390 is so great that another Holy Year is called for 1400 (▶ 1425).

Pope Urban VI re-establishes the University of Erfurt, as its original charter has been issued by an antipope (◀ 1379).

✠ October 15: Pope Urban VI (◀ 1378) dies.

✠ November 2: Pietro Tomacelli, a Neapolitan aristocrat, is elected as Boniface IX (▶ 1404).

1390

♛ May 29: Juan II, King of Castile–Leon (◀ 1379), dies and is succeeded by his son Enrique III (▶ 1406).

☿ August: Anthony IV, Patriarch of Constantinople (◀ 1389, ▶ 1391), is replaced by Macarius (◀ 1379, ▶ 1391).

📖 The *Theologia Germanica* ('German Theology'), an anonymous mystical treatise, appears.

***c*.1390**

♠▣ Jan van Eyck, Flemish painter, is born. His *Ghent Altarpiece* (▶ 1432) is the masterpiece of medieval art in the Netherlands. Dies 1441.

1391

♛ February 16: John V Palaeologus (◀ 1341) dies. Manuel II Palaeologus (◀ 1373, ▶ 1425) is sole emperor.

March 4: Pope Boniface IX gives permission for the foundation of the University of Ferrara.

☿ March: Macarius, Patriarch of Constantinople (◀ 1390), is replaced by Antony IV (◀ 1390, ▶ 1397).

☉ Queen Bridget of Sweden (◀ 1373) is canonized by Pope Boniface IX: feast day July 23.

A vicious wave of anti-Jewish preaching in Spain results in a massacre of about one third of the Jews in Spain and the conversion of another third.

1392

♠ Sergei of Radonezh (◀ *c*.1314) dies (▶ 1452).

1394

☿ September 16: Antipope Clement VII (◀ 1378) in Avignon dies.

☿ September 28: Pedro de Luna, plenipotentiary legate to France, is elected as Antipope Benedict XIII (▶ 1417).

September 29: Richard Rolle (◀ *c*.1300) dies.

🏛 Work on Worcester Cathedral (◀ 1084) is completed.

1395

Timur (◀ 1360, ▶ 1398) occupies Moscow.

***c*.1395**

♠▣ Fra Angelico, Italian painter, is born. He develops the use of perspective in his frescoes: his masterpiece is the Last Judgement in San Marco, Florence. Dies 1455.

1396

♛ May 19: King Juan I of Aragon (◀ 1387) dies and is succeeded by his brother Martin I (▶ 1410).

⚛ July 31: William Courtenay, Archbishop of Canterbury (◀ 1381), dies.

1397

⚛ January 11: Thomas Arundel, Archbishop of York, is appointed Archbishop of Canterbury.

⚛ May: Antony IV, Patriarch of Constantinople (◀ 1391), dies and is succeeded by Callistus II Xanthopoulos.

⚛ November: Callistus II Xanthopoulos is succeeded by Matthew I (▶ 1410).

⚛ November 30: Thomas Arundel (▶ 1399), Archbishop of Canterbury, is exiled by King Richard II.

♣♫ Guillaume Dufay, composer, is born. His four *cantus firmus* masses are central to the development of fifteenth-century church music. Dies 1474.

1398

⚛ January 21: Roger Walden, Dean of York, is appointed Archbishop of Canterbury (▶ 1399).

December 17: Timur (◀ 1395, ▶ 1401) destroys Delhi.

1399

♛ King Richard II of England is brought before Parliament, where he renounces his throne.

♛ October 13: Henry, grandson of King Edward III (◀ 1327), is crowned as King Henry IV (▶ 1413).

⚛ October 21: Thomas Arundel, Archbishop of Canterbury (◀ 1397, ▶ 1414), is restored to favour by King Henry IV and replaces Roger Walden (◀ 1398).

1400

♣ October 25: Geoffrey Chaucer (◀ 1340) dies.

♣▣ Rogier van der Weyden, Flemish painter, is born. He paints many pictures with religious themes, particularly the removal of Jesus from the cross, an altarpiece *The Seven Sacraments* (c.1445), and *The Last Judgement* (▶ 1451). Dies 1464.

♛ The deposed King Richard II of England (◀ 1399) is murdered in Pontefract Castle.

A royal council is held in Ethiopia by King Dawit to bring the Ewostathians under Filpos (◀ 1352) into line. They are forbidden to continue observing the Sabbath but refuse to obey, and are imprisoned.

c.1400

⛩ Exeter Cathedral (◀ 1258) is completed.

▣ The Sherborne Missal is produced, the largest and most lavishly decorated service book to survive from the Middle Ages.

235

Fifteenth century

In the first half of the century, final attempts are made to heal the two great schisms, the schism between Rome and Avignon with its rival popes and the schism between West and East which began in 1054. The vehicle for this is a council which begins in Constance in 1414, and then moves on to Basle, Ferrara and finally Florence. The council deposes the Roman Antipope John XXIII and the Avignon Pope Benedict XIII and secures the formal resignation of the Roman Pope Gregory XII, who had abdicated at the beginning of the council but not before formally empowering it to elect the new pope, thus ensuring the legitimacy of the Roman line. In their place it elects Pope Martin V, and with this appointment officially brings the schism to an end. In the process the council promulgates an important decree, which because of what has happened sets a general council above the Pope: the council has its power immediately from Christ and everyone of whatever state or dignity, even papal, is bound to obey it in those matters which pertain to the faith. In Ferrara in 1438 the council turns to the question of union with the Eastern church which is represented by 700 delegates including the Byzantine emperor, John VIII Palaeologus, and the Patriarch of Constantinople, Joseph II. A year later agreement is reached and the emperor signs a Decree of Union; however, leaders of the Greek Church subsequently refuse to accept it and hopes for more positive developments change fundamentally in 1453.

In that year Ottoman Turks finally put an end to the Byzantine empire with the capture of Constantinople. They move north to besiege Belgrade, and occupy Bosnia and the Greek peninsula, gaining a foothold in Eastern Europe which they are to maintain for some time. Meanwhile, in the west, with power concentrated in the hands of King Fernando and Queen Isabella, in 1492 the last Muslim bastion there, Granada, falls. How to treat the many Muslims and Jews who have continued to live in Spain becomes an important question: they are confronted with the alternative of being converted or leaving the country. Because there is doubt over the genuineness of some of the conversions, in 1478 Pope Sixtus IV creates the Spanish Inquisition, of which in 1483 Tomás de Torquemada is appointed Inquisitor General. On condemnation, heretics are handed over to the civil authorities and burnt at the stake in what is called an *auto-da-fé*, act of faith.

In 1492 Christopher Columbus sails from Spain in search of the Indies and makes landfall in the Caribbean, and in 1497 Vasco da Gama sets sail for India to pioneer a new sea route and to seek new dominions for Portugal. Spain and Portugal start on their path towards becoming great imperial powers and in the Treaty of Tardesillas divide the New World between them. This is to become a great source of wealth and to have an enormous economic impact on the next century as well as raising grave questions about how its inhabitants are to be treated. Missionaries play an important role here; the first Franciscans land on Hispaniola as early as 1493.

236

1401

March: William Sawtrey, Rector of St Margaret's, King's Lynn (then Bishop's Lynn), is burnt as a Lollard heretic.

♟ Nicholas of Cusa, German philosopher and author of *On Learned Ignorance*, is born. Dies 1464.

⌂ The rebuilding of Amiens Cathedral (◀ 1220) is completed.

De haeretico comburendo, an act of the English Parliament against heresy, is particularly directed against the Lollards (◀ 1375). It is finally repealed in 1559.

Timur (◀ 1398, ▶ 1405) destroys Damascus.

1402

⌂ Work begins on Seville Cathedral, on the site of a mosque.

A university is founded in Würzburg, but it is short-lived.

1403

■ Ghiberti (◀ *c.*1378, ▶ 1455) begins work on the baptistery in Florence.

Emperor Manuel II Palaeologus (◀ 1391, ▶ 1408) negotiates a peace treaty with the Ottoman sultan Mehmed I.

1404

☦ October 1: Pope Boniface IX (◀ 1389) dies.

☦ October 17: Cosimo Gentile de' Migliorati, Archbishop of Bologna, is elected as Pope Innocent VII (▶ 1406).

Dawit, King of Ethiopia, changes his mind and commands that the disciples of Ewostatewos shall observe both the Sabbath and Sunday (◀ 1400).

A Catholic diocese is created at Las Palmas in the Canaries.

1405

February 19: Timur (◀ 1401) dies in an attempt to conquer China.

The University of Turin is founded when lectures in Piacenza (◀ 1248) and Pavia (◀ 1361) are interrupted by war.

1406

☦ November 6: Pope Innocent VII (◀ 1404) dies.

☦ November 30: Angelo Correr, a Venetian aristocrat who is papal secretary, is elected as Pope Gregory XII (▶ 1415).

♛ December 25: Enrique III, King of Castile–Leon (◀ 1390) dies, and is succeeded by his son Juan II (▶ 1454).

♣■ Fra Filippo Lippi, Italian artist, is born. He paints frescoes in Prato and Spoleto cathedrals. Dies 1469.

1408

♛ Emperor Manuel II Palaeologus (◀ 1403, ▶ 1425) crowns his son John VIII Palaeologus (▶ 1425) co-emperor.

1409

January 9: A Lollard (◀ 1375, 1382) revolt led by Sir John Oldcastle is put down.

March 25: The Council of Pisa is convened to end the schism dividing Western Christendom (◀ 1378). It actually makes things worse. Neither Antipope Benedict XIII (◀ 1394, ▶ 1413) nor Pope Gregory XII attends.

☩ May 3: The Council deposes both of them and elects a Greek, Pietro Philargi, a former Archbishop of Milan, as Pope (Antipope) Alexander V (▶ 1410). None of the three is willing to step down. The church now has three 'popes', beginning the 'triple schism'.

December 2: Friedrich I, Elector of Saxony, founds the University of Leipzig when German scholars withdraw from the Charles University, Prague (◀ 1348).

The Suppression of Heresy Act passed by the English Parliament makes heresy an offence against common law.

1410

☩ May 3: Antipope Alexander V (◀ 1409) dies.

☩ May 17: Baldassare Cossa, papal treasurer, is elected as Antipope John XXIII (▶ 1415).

♛ May 31: King Martin I of Aragon (1396) dies and is succeeded by Fernando I, son of King Juan I of Leon and Castile (◀ 1390, ▶ 1416).

☩ August: Matthew I, Patriarch of Constantinople (◀ 1397), dies.

☩ October 25: Euthymius II becomes Patriarch of Constantinople (▶ 1416).

♛ Sigismund is elected Holy Roman Emperor (▶ 1437).

A combined army of Poles and Lithuanians defeats the Teutonic Knights at the Battle of Tannenberg in East Prussia. This marks the beginning of the latter's decline.

*c.*1410

♣♪ Johannes Ockeghem, Netherlands composer, is born. The most important composer between Dufay (◀ 1397) and Josquin Desprez (▶ *c.*1451), he writes 13 surviving masses, including the *Missa Prolationum* and the earliest extant polyphonic requiem mass. Dies 1497.

■ *Les Très Riches Heures du Duc de Berry*, a very richly decorated Book of Hours, which contains prayers to be said at each of the canonical hours, is produced.

1412

♣ January 6: Jeanne d'Arc (▶ 1429) is born at Domrémy in northern France. She is burned at the stake in 1431.

1413

♛ March 20: King Henry IV of England (◀ 1399) dies and is succeeded by his son, who becomes King Henry V (▶ 1422); he has a particular interest in liturgical music and commissions a hymn of praise to be sung after the victory at Agincourt (▶ 1415).

A papal bull of Antipope Benedict XIII confirms the founding of the University of St Andrews, the oldest in Scotland.

Margery Kempe (◀ c.1373, ▶ 1438) goes on pilgrimage to the Holy Land.

1414

☦ February 19: Thomas Arundel, Archbishop of Canterbury (◀ 1397, 1399), dies.

☦ May 30: Henry Chicheley, Bishop of St David's, is appointed Archbishop of Canterbury (▶ 1443). He funds the foundation of All Souls College, Oxford.

November 16: The Council of Constance is convened by Antipope John XXIII at the instigation of Emperor Sigismund to end the schism dividing Western Christianity (◀ 1378, ▶ 1417). The Council continues until 1418. In the West it is regarded as the sixteenth Ecumenical Council.

Jacob of Mies, a follower of Jan Hus (◀ 1369), maintains that the eucharist should be administered as both bread and wine, in both kinds (Latin *sub utraque specie*). Those who hold this view are known as Utraquists.

1415

April 15: The Council of Constance in its decree *Haec sancta* claims even greater authority for general councils than for the Pope himself.

The Council of Constance officially recognizes 'Observant' Franciscans, who follow a stricter rule (▶ 1517).

☦ May 29: Antipope John XXIII (◀ 1410) is deposed.

☦ July 4: Pope Gregory XII (◀ 1406) abdicates.

♣ July 6: Though he has been given free passage to it, Jan Hus (◀ 1369) is condemned by the council and burnt at the stake.

October 25: The English under King Henry V defeat the French at Agincourt.

The Portuguese cross the Straits of Gibraltar and capture Ceuta in North Africa from the Arabs. A first Christian settlement is established there.

1416

☦ March 29: Euthymius II, Patriarch of Constantinople (◀ 1410), dies.

♔ April 2: King Fernando I of Aragon (◄ 1410) dies and is succeeded by his son Alfonso V (► 1458).

☩ May 21: Joseph II becomes Patriarch of Constantinople (► 1439).

1417

☩ November 11: Antipope Benedict XIII (◄ 1394) is deposed. Cardinal Oddo Colonna, an aristocratic lawyer, is elected as Pope Martin V (► 1431).

A diocese is founded in Ceuta (◄ 1415).

1418

April 22: The Council of Constance is dissolved.

December 31: The English capture Rouen after a siege.

📖 Thomas à Kempis' (◄ c.1380, ► 1471) *Imitation of Christ* is first put into circulation anonymously.

1419

In the first Defenestration of Prague (► 1618), Hussites led by Jan Zelivský throw seven council members from the windows of the town hall in protest against the inequality between peasants and the rich Catholic Church. It leads to the Hussite wars.

In the Treaty of Troyes, King Henry V of England is offered Catherine de Valois in marriage and recognized as heir to the French throne.

The University of Rostock on the Baltic is founded by Dukes Johann III and Albrecht V of Mecklenburg.

1420

The Hussites found the town of Tabor in south Bohemia.

March 17: Pope Martin V proclaims a crusade against Hussites, Wycliffites and other heretics in Bohemia.

July: Conservative Hussites, called Utraquists (◄ 1414), present their programme of reform in the Four Articles of Prague.

September 8: Pope Martin V enters Rome.

The Hussites capture the fortress of Vysherad in Prague.

♟ Tomás de Torquemada (► 1483), Spanish Grand Inquisitor, is born. Dies 1498.

🏛 Work begins on the dome of Florence Cathedral (◄ 1377, ► 1436).

c.1420

♟ Julian of Norwich (◄ c.1342) dies.

1422

♛ August 31: King Henry V (◀ 1413) of England dies suddenly of dysentery and is succeeded by his nine-month-old son as King Henry VI (▶ 1461).

♛ October 20: Charles VI, King of France (◀ 1380), dies, and is succeeded by Charles VII (▶ 1461).

1425

Pope Martin V proclaims a Holy Year after only 25 years, and not, as had been formerly set, in 1433 (◀ 1389, ▶ 1450).

♛ September 8: King Carlos III of Navarre (◀ 1387) dies and is succeeded by his daughter Bianca I (▶ 1441).

♛ Emperor Manuel II Palaeologus (◀ 1391) dies. His son John VIII Palaeologus (◀ 1408, ▶ 1448) becomes sole emperor.

Pope Martin V founds the Catholic University of Louvain, the oldest existing Catholic university in the world.

c.1425

▮ Andrei Rublev (◀ c.1360, ▶ 1430) paints his icon of the Holy Trinity, depicting the Trinity in the guise of the three angels who visit Abraham.

1426

♣▮ September 18: Hubert van Eyck (◀ c.1370) dies.

1429

♣ July 12: Jean Gerson (◀ 1363) dies.

Jeanne d'Arc (◀ 1412, ▶ 1430) meets Charles VII of France, who gives her a small army with which she wins back Orleans. This becomes the only part of northern France not occupied by the English.

1430

♣▮ January 29: Andrei Rublev (◀ c.1360) dies.

Jeanne d'Arc (◀ 1429, ▶ 1431) is captured by the English and handed over to the Catholic Church for trial.

The Turks occupy Thessalonica. Mount Athos becomes an autonomous monastic republic.

c.1430

♣▮ Giovanni Bellini, Venetian painter, is born. He develops an individual use of colour and atmosphere. Among his religious pictures he paints many Madonnas and altarpieces. Dies 1516.

1431

☿ February 20: Pope Martin V (◀ 1417) dies.

⚕ March 3: Gabriele Condulmaro, Governor of the March and Bologna, is elected as Pope Eugenius IV (▶ 1437, 1447).

✦ May 30: Jeanne d'Arc (◀ 1429, 1430), having turned the tide of the Hundred Years War in France's favour, is burned at the stake in Rouen for heresy (▶ 1456, 1920).

July 15: The Council of Basle, called by Pope Martin V shortly before his death, meets to continue the work of the Council of Constance (◀ 1414). In the West it is regarded as the seventeenth Ecumenical Council.

December 18: The Council is dissolved on the orders of Pope Eugenius IV but disregards them and continues to meet, reaffirming the decree *Haec sancta* of Constance (◀ 1415) that a general council is superior to a pope.

Pope Eugenius IV founds the University of Poitiers.

1432

■ Jan van Eyck (◀ c.1390, ▶ 1441) completes an altarpiece in Ghent said to have been begun by his brother Hubert (◀ 1426). Among its many features, it depicts an organ.

King Henry VI of England (◀ 1422, ▶ 1440) founds the University of Caen.

1433

✦ October 19: Marsilio Ficino, Italian humanist, is born. Dies 1499.

December 15: By his bull *Dudum sacrum* Pope Eugenius IV recognizes the Council of Constance, which has meanwhile grown considerably and has much support. The Council remains opposed to the Pope and lays down an oath for a pope to take after his election.

✦ Nil Sorsky, Russian monk and mystic, is born. Dies 1508.

1434

May 30: In further warfare, at the Battle of Lipany the Utraquist army crushes the Taborites (◀ 1420).

1435

The Minims, an order of friars devoted to humility, are founded by Francis of Paola.

1436

⌂ March 25: After the completion of its unique octagonal dome, Florence Cathedral, the Basilica di Santa Maria dei Fiore, is consecrated by Pope Eugenius IV.

✦ Francisco Ximenes de Cisñeros, Spanish cardinal, is born. A patron of learning, he founds the University of Alcala and sponsors a multilingual Bible with the Hebrew, Latin and Greek printed in parallel (▶ 1502). Dies 1517.

■ Fra Angelico (◀ c.1395) paints murals at San Marco Monastery in Florence.

The Utraquists (◀ 1414) are granted freedom of religion in the so-called Basle Compacts (▶ 1462).

1436–39

The Bible is translated into Hungarian (Hussite Bible).

1437

September 18: Pope Eugenius IV transfers the Council of Basle (◀ 1431) to Ferrara to consider union with the Greeks. A remnant in Basle deposes Eugenius IV (▶ 1447) as a heretic, appointing Felix V as antipope (▶ 1448).

♕ December 9: Sigismund, Holy Roman Emperor (◀ 1410), dies.

A memorandum by the Patriarch of Constantinople for the Council of Basle lists 67 metropolitans, many of whom have no bishops under them (◀ 901).

1438

January 8: The Council of Ferrara opens in the presence of Emperor John VIII Palaeologus (◀ 1425, ▶ 1439), who has come in search of military aid against the Turks, the Patriarch of Constantinople and a large number of Greek clergy.

July 7: The Pragmatic Sanction of Bourges upholds the right of the French church to administer its property and rejects papal nominations to vacancies.

*c.***1438**

♠ Margery Kempe (◀ *c.*1373) dies.

1439

January 10: The Council of Ferrara is moved to Florence because the papal funds are exhausted and that city will pay the expenses.

☦ June 10: Joseph II, Patriarch of Constantinople (◀ 1416), dies.

July 6: John VIII Palaeologus (◀ 1438, ▶ 1448) signs a Decree of Union, *Laetentur Coeli* (◀ 1437). Leaders of the Greek church subsequently refuse to accept it.

🏛 Strasbourg Cathedral is completed (◀ 1015).

1440

☦ May 4: Metrophanes II becomes Patriarch of Constantinople (▶ 1443).

King Henry VI of England (◀ 1432, ▶ 1441) founds Eton College.

📖 Nicholas of Cusa (◀ 1401, ▶ 1464), *On Learned Ignorance*, argues that knowledge comes through opposites and is relative.

1441

♕ April 3: Queen Bianca I of Navarre dies. She is succeeded by her husband Juan, Prince of Aragon, whom she had married in 1425, as Juan II (▶ 1458, 1479).

♠■ July 9: Jan van Eyck (◀ *c.*1390) dies.

King Henry VI of England founds the University of Bordeaux through a bull of Pope Eugenius IV.

243

King Henry VI of England founds King's College, Cambridge, for boys from Eton College (◀ 1440).

1443

⚉ April 12: Henry Chicheley, Archbishop of Canterbury (◀ 1414), dies.

⚉ June 25: John Stafford, Bishop of Bath and Wells and Lord Chancellor, becomes Archbishop of Canterbury (▶ 1452).

⚉ August 1: Metrophanes II, Patriarch of Constantinople (◀ 1440), dies and is succeeded by Gregory III Mammas (▶ 1450).

1444

♠ 🏛 Donato Bramante, Italian architect, is born. He will be commissioned by Pope Julius II (▶ 1503) to draw up plans for the new St Peter's, Rome (▶ 1506), and this becomes his life's work. Dies 1514.

Pope Eugenius IV establishes the University of Catania.

1445

♠ ♫ June 5: Leonel Power (◀ c.1385) dies.

1446

♠ April 16: Filippo Brunelleschi (◀ 1377) dies.

🏛 William St Clair, Prince of Orkney, builds Rosslyn Chapel outside Edinburgh.

1447

⚉ February 23: Pope Eugenius IV (◀ 1431, 1437) dies.

⚉ March 6: Cardinal Tommaso Parentucelli is elected as Pope Nicholas V (▶ 1455).

♠ Catherine of Genoa, spiritual teacher, is born. Dies 1510.

1448

June: The Council of Basle is forced to move to Lausanne, where the antipope Felix V (◀ 1437) abdicates. It closes itself the next year.

♛ October 31: John VIII Palaeologus (◀ 1425) dies and is succeeded by his brother, Constantine XI Palaeologus (▶ 1453).

Prince Basil II of Russia imprisons Bishop Isidore of Moscow for accepting the Decree of Union (◀ 1439).

The Russian church declares independence from Constantinople and the Council of Bishops appoints Metropolitan Jonas Metropolitan of Moscow and all Russia.

The first Christians are reported in Mauritania.

c.1448

♠ ■ Martin Schongauer is born. He is the most important German printmaker before

Albrecht Dürer (▶ 1471) and paints the magnificent altarpiece of St Martin, Colmar. Dies 1491.

1449

August: Emperor Zara Ya'iqob (Constantine) of Ethiopia holds a council at the monastery of Debra Mitmaq in Shoa, in the central highlands, to reconcile those who observe Saturday as the Sabbath (Saturday) and those who observe Sunday. Henceforth both days are to be observed.

1450

In proclaiming the Holy Year (◀ 1425), Pope Nicholas V decrees that it shall be celebrated every 50 years; in fact in 1470 Pope Paul II will fix the interval at 25 years.

By the bull *Constitutus in speculo*, Pope Nicholas V founds the University of Barcelona.

�})} Gregory III Mammas, Patriarch of Constantinople (◀ 1443), flees to Italy.

*c.***1450**

🌱▣ Hieronymus Bosch, Dutch painter, is born. His pictures, notably *The Garden of Earthly Delights* (*c.*1500), have a unique language, often cruel and fantastic. Dies 1516.

🌱♫ Josquin Desprez (▶ 1502), composer, is born. His music, particularly his motets, has unparalleled expressiveness; he also writes many masses. Dies 1521.

☺ The *Misteri d'Elx*, a sung Spanish mystery play, is first performed.

1451

January 7: The University of Glasgow is founded by William Turnbull, Bishop of Glasgow.

▣ Rogier van der Weyden (◀ 1400, ▶ 1464) paints *The Last Judgement* in the hospital of Beaune, France.

1452

♛ March 19: Pope Nicholas V crowns Friedrich III (▶ 1493), of the house of Habsburg, Holy Roman Emperor in St Peter's, the last such coronation to take place in Rome.

🌱▣ April 15: Leonardo da Vinci (▶ 1498), painter, sculptor, architect and engineer, is born. He is one of the most important figures in Western art. Dies 1519.

�})} May 25: John Stafford, Archbishop of Canterbury (◀ 1443), dies.

June 18: The papal bull *Dum diversos* of Nicholas V authorizes King Alfonso V of Portugal to reduce Saracens and pagans to perpetual slavery.

�})} September 6: John Kemp, Cardinal Archbishop of York, is appointed Archbishop of Canterbury (▶ 1454).

🌱 September 21: Giralomo Savonarola, Italian reformer, is born. He is executed in 1498.

December 12: The Decree of Union (◀ 1439) agreed at the Council of Florence is formally proclaimed in Hagia Sophia, Constantinople.

245

The Fall of Constantinople, 1453

⊕ Sergei of Radonezh (◀ 1392) is canonized: feast day September 25.

1453

May 29: The Ottoman Turks (◀ 1326) under Mehmed II (▶ 1456) capture Constantinople, marking the end of the Eastern Roman empire. The last Byzantine emperor, Constantine XI Palaeologus (◀ 1448), dies in the fighting.

✠ June 1: Gennadius, a monk, is invested with the signs of office of the Patriarch of Constantinople by Sultan Mehmed II, because he has been hostile to attempts at union with the West (▶ 1454).

July 17: The French recapture Aquitaine, ending the Hundred Years War (◀ 1337). The English lose all territories but Calais.

♣♫ December 24: John Dunstaple (◀ c.1385) dies.

The Church of Hagia Sophia in Constantinople (◀ 537) is turned into a mosque.

1454

✠ January 6: Gennadius II is consecrated Patriarch of Constantinople (▶ 1456, 1465).

246

☫ March 22: John Kemp, Archbishop of Canterbury (◀ 1452), dies.

♛ July 20: Juan II, King of Castile–Leon (◀ 1406), dies and is succeeded by his son Enrique IV (▶ 1474).

☫ August 22: Thomas Bourchier, Bishop of Ely, is appointed Archbishop of Canterbury (▶ 1486).

1454–56

Papal grants give Prince Henry the Navigator, son of King John I of Portugal, all lands and power over all missionary bishops south of the Tropic of Cancer.

1455

January 5: The papal bull *Romanus Pontifex* from Pope Nicholas V to King Alfonso V of Portugal extends to the Catholic nations of Europe dominion of lands discovered by them, and encourages slavery.

February 23: Johannes Gutenberg prints a Bible with movable type.

♟ March 18: Fra Angelico (◀ c.1395) dies (▶ 1982).

☫ March 24: Pope Nicholas V (◀ 1447) dies.

☫ April 8: Alfonso de Borgia, a former secretary to King Alfonso V of Spain, is elected as Pope Callistus III (▶ 1458).

♟ December 1: Lorenzo Ghiberti (◀ c.1378) dies.

1456

March 1: Pope Callistus III assembles forces for the recapture of Constantinople.

July 4: Mehmed II (◀ 1453, ▶ 1458–60) besieges Belgrade.

July 7: Pope Callistus III declares Jeanne d'Arc to be innocent of the charges of witchcraft and heresy on which she had been condemned (◀ 1431, ▶ 1920).

July 22: Forces under the Hungarian nobleman John Hunyadi defeat the Turks and raise the siege of Belgrade. To commemorate the victory, Pope Callistus orders the Feast of the Transfiguration to be held on 6 August.

October 17: The University of Greifswald is founded.

☫ Gennadius II (◀ 1454) resigns for the first time as Patriarch of Constantinople (he returns several more times for further periods in office, ▶ 1465). He is succeeded by Isidore II Xanthopoulos.

1457

The *Unitas Fratrum* (Unity of Brethren), the precursor of the Protestant Moravian Church, is formed in Bohemia among followers of Jan Hus (◀ 1369).

The University of Freiburg is founded by Archduke Albrecht of Austria.

1458

♛ June 27: King Alfonso V of Aragon (◀ 1416) dies and is succeeded by his son Juan II (▶ 1479).

☉ August 6: Pope Callistus III (◀ 1455) dies.

☉ August 9: Enea Silvio Piccolomini, a brilliant orator, poet and historian, is elected as Pope Pius II (▶ 1464).

An English pilgrim visiting Jerusalem, William Wey, describes a pilgrimage in Jesus' footsteps from Pilate's house to Calvary. Previously it seems to have been made the other way round.

1458–60

The Ottoman Turks (◀ 1326) under Mehmed II (◀ 1456, ▶ 1462) conquer Athens and almost all the Greek peninsula.

1459

June 1: Pope Pius II convenes a congress in Mantua to launch a crusade against the Turks, but receives no support.

The University of Basle, Switzerland's oldest university, is founded by Pope Pius II.

1460

January 18: In his bull *Execrabilis*, Pope Pius II forbids appeals to a general council against a papal decision.

1461

♛ March 4: King Henry VI of England (◀ 1422, ▶ 1470) is deposed by his cousin Edward of York, who becomes King Edward IV (▶ 1471, 1483).

♛ July 22: Charles VII, King of France (◀ 1422), dies and is succeeded by Louis XI (▶ 1483).

☦ Catherine of Siena (◀ 1380) is canonized by Pope Pius II: feast day April 20.

The Russian church is divided, with Metropolitans at Moscow and Kiev.

1462

Mehmed II (◀ 1458–60) starts to build Topkapi palace in what is now Istanbul. Istanbul is to become capital of the Ottoman empire.

Pope Pius II declares the Basle Compacts (◀ 1436) null and void.

The first successful *mons pietatis* (◀ 1361) is established in Perugia.

1463/64

The Ottoman Turks (◀ 1326) conquer Bosnia; many of its nobility convert to Islam, unlike Serbia, which largely remains Greek Orthodox.

1464

♠■ June 18: Rogier van der Weyden (◀ 1400) dies.

♠ August 11: Nicholas of Cusa (◀ 1401) dies.

☿ August 15: Pope Pius II (◀ 1458) dies.

☿ August 30: Cardinal Pietro Barbo, from a rich merchant family, is elected as Pope Paul II (▶ 1471).

1465

☿ July: Gennadius II (◀ 1454) retires as Patriarch of Constantinople and is succeeded by Joasaph I.

1466

♠■ December 13: Donatello (◀ 1386) dies.

☿ Joasaph I, Patriarch of Constantinople, retires and is succeeded, after the brief tenure of Mark II Xylokaraves, by Symeon I of Trebizond (▶ 1467).

*c.***1466**

♠ John Colet (▶ 1505) is born. A churchman and humanist, he becomes Dean of St Paul's and founds a school there. Dies 1519.

1467

☿ Symeon I of Trebizond (◀ 1466, ▶ 1471) is replaced as Patriarch of Constantinople by Dionysius I (▶ 1471, 1489, 1491).

1468

King James III of Scotland hands over Kirkwall Cathedral, which is now in his kingdom, to the magistrates, council and community of Kirkwall, Orkney (◀ 1137).

The Diocese of Tangier is formed.

1469

♠ February 20: Thomas de Vio Cajetan is born. He is a Dominican, Bishop of Gaeta, and will be a fierce opponent of Martin Luther. Dies 1534.

October 19: Prince Fernando of Aragon marries Isabella, Infanta of Castile (▶ 1474).

♠ October 27: Desiderius Erasmus, Dutch humanist and theologian, is born. He is a friend of Luther, and produces a new Latin version of the New Testament; his best-known work is *In Praise of Folly* (▶ 1509). Dies 1536.

♠ John Fisher is born. He becomes Vice-Chancellor of Cambridge University, to which he attracts many European scholars, and then Bishop of Rochester. His opposition to Henry VIII's divorce from Catherine of Aragon and refusal to sign the Act of Succession lead to his imprisonment in the Tower of London and execution (▶ 1535).

♠■ Fra Filippo Lippi (◀ 1406) dies.

c.1469

♣ Vasco da Gama, Spanish explorer (▶ 1497), is born. He is the first person to sail directly from Europe to India. Dies 1524.

1470

April 19: Pope Paul II issues the bull *Ineffabilis Providentia*, fixing the interval between Holy Years (◀ 1450, ▶ 1475) at 25 years.

♛ October 10: King Henry VI of England (◀ 1461, ▶ 1471) is restored to the throne.

🏰 York Minster (◀ 1220) is completed.

1471

♣▣ May 21: Albrecht Dürer (▶ 1508), German painter, is born. He is an important bridge between south and north European art and is known for many sets of prints including the Apocalypse, and engravings, notably *Praying Hands* (▶ 1508) and *Knight, Death and the Devil* (▶ 1513). Dies 1528.

♛ May 21: King Henry VI (◀ 1470) is murdered in the Tower of London.

♣ July 25: Thomas à Kempis (◀ c.1380) dies.

☯ July 26: Pope Paul II (◀ 1464) dies.

☯ August 9: Francesco della Rovere, General of the Franciscan Order, is elected as Pope Sixtus IV (▶ 1484).

♛ King Edward IV of England regains the throne (◀ 1461, ▶ 1483). He rebuilds St George's Chapel, Windsor.

☯ Dionysius I, Patriarch of Constantinople (◀ 1467), is replaced by Symeon I of Trebizond (◀ 1467), who becomes patriarch for a second term.

The University of Genoa is founded by Pope Sixtus IV.

The Malermi Bible is the first printed translation into Italian.

1472

♣▣ Lucas Cranach the Elder, German painter, is born. His religious paintings come to focus on sin and grace, as in his famous series of depictions of *Adam and Eve*. Dies 1552.

The Duke of Bavaria founds what is now the University of Munich at Ingolstadt, modelling it on the University of Vienna (◀ 1365).

1473

♣ February 19: Nicolas Copernicus is born. A Polish priest and astronomer, he revolutionizes astronomy with his posthumously published book *On the Revolutions of the Heavenly Spheres* (▶ 1543). Dies 1543.

🏰 The Sistine Chapel is built in the Vatican.

1474

♣ August: Bartolomé de Las Casas (▶ 1511) is born. A Spanish missionary and Dominican, he exposes the exploitation of the American Indians and works to improve their lot. Dies 1566.

♣♪ November 27: Guillaume Dufay (◀ 1397) dies.

♛ December 11: Enrique IV, King of Castile (◀ 1454), dies and is succeeded by Isabella (▶ 1469), daughter of King Juan II of Castile–Leon (◀ 1454, ▶ 1504). Her husband, Fernando of Aragon (◀ 1469), becomes King Fernando of Castile (▶ 1479).

1475

☦ January: Raphael I of Constantinople becomes Patriarch of Constantinople (▶ 1476) in place of Symeon I of Trebizond (◀ 1471, ▶ 1481). A Serb, he is the only non-Greek to hold this office.

♣▣ March 6: Michelangelo Buonarotti, Italian sculptor and painter, is born. The religious works for which he is most remembered are the ceiling of the Sistine Chapel (▶ 1535) and his *Pietà*s (▶ 1499, 1555). Dies 1564.

June 1: Pope Sixtus IV grants the Dominican Order (see p. 197) the right to hold property.

June 15: With the bull *Ad decorum militantis ecclesiae*, Pope Sixtus IV gives legal form to the Vatican Library.

The next Holy Year (◀ 1470) is proclaimed by Pope Sixtus IV. From now on, with a few exceptions, they are held at intervals of 25 years.

c.1475

♣▣ Matthias Grünewald, German artist, is born. He brings new life to medieval traditions and paints a great altarpiece in Isenheim (▶ 1511–15), Alsace. Dies 1528.

1476

☦ Raphael I of Constantinople (◀ 1475) is deposed as Patriarch of Constantinople for addiction to alcohol. He is succeeded by Maximus III Manasses (▶ 1481).

1477

Tübingen University is founded by Count Eberhard VI, Duke of Württemberg.

Uppsala University is founded by Sten Sture the Elder and Jakob Ulvsson, Archbishop of Uppsala. It is the first university in Scandinavia.

1478

♣ February 7: Thomas More (▶ 1516) is born. He is appointed Chancellor of England under Henry VIII but opposes the king over his divorce and the Oath of Succession (▶ 1535).

At the request of the Spanish kings, Pope Sixtus IV creates the Spanish Inquisition to root out Jews who have only converted nominally; in the sixteenth century it turns to nominally converted Muslims.

Bonifaci Ferrer produces the first printed Catalan translation of the Bible (◀ 1287).

1479

♛ January 20: King Juan II of Aragon and Navarre (◀ 1458) dies and is succeeded by Fernando II, who is also King Fernando V of Castile (◀ 1474, ▶ 1492). Queen Isabella of Castile (◀ 1474, ▶ 1492) also becomes Queen of Aragon and Navarre. They are thus rulers of a kingdom of Spain.

🕌 The Cathedral of the Dormition in the Kremlin, Moscow, is completed. Here all the Tsars will be crowned.

The University of Copenhagen is founded as a centre of Roman Catholic learning; after the Reformation it becomes a Lutheran seminary.

1480

♟ Francisco de Quiñones, Roman Catholic reformer, is born. He compiles a new breviary which is a great influence on Thomas Cranmer (▶ 1489) in his compilation of the Book of Common Prayer. Dies 1540.

♟ Fernando Magellan, Spanish explorer, is born. He leads the first successful attempt to circumnavigate the earth but dies on the voyage (▶ 1521).

1481

June 21: The papal bull *Aeterni regis* of Pope Sixtus IV grants all further acquisition of lands south of the Canaries to Portugal.

☙ Maximus III Manasses (◀ 1476) is succeeded as Patriarch of Constantinople by Symeon of Trebizond (◀ 1471, 1475, ▶ 1486) for a third term of office.

1482

☧ Bonaventure (◀ 1274) is canonized by Pope Sixtus IV: feast day July 13.

1483

♟■ April 6: Raphael, Florentine painter, is born. He is famous for his Madonnas and altar-pieces. Dies 1572.

♛ April 9: King Edward IV of England (◀ 1471) dies and is succeeded by his twelve-year-old son as King Edward V. His uncle Richard, Duke of Gloucester, escorts Edward V and his brother, Richard, Duke of York, to the Tower of London. They are never seen again.

♛ June 25: Edward V and Richard, Duke of York, are declared illegitimate by Parliament, leaving Richard, Duke of Gloucester, as heir to Edward IV.

♛ July 6: Richard, Duke of Gloucester, is crowned as King Richard III of England (▶ 1485).

August 9: The first mass is celebrated in the Sistine Chapel (◀ 1473) of the Vatican.

♛ August 30: Louis XI, King of France (◀ 1461), dies and is succeeded by Charles VIII (▶ 1498).

October 17: Tomás de Torquemada (◀ 1420, ▶ 1498) is made Inquisitor General of the Spanish Inquisition (◀ 1478). The next year many suspected heretics are publicly burned at the stake (*auto-da-fé*).

November 10: Martin Luther (▶ 1506), German Reformer, is born. Dies 1546.

The Portuguese settle on the unpopulated island of São Tomé and begin to use it as a base for the slave trade.

1484

January 1: Huldrych Zwingli (▶ 1518), Swiss Reformer, is born. Dies 1531.

August 12: Pope Sixtus IV (◀ 1471) dies.

August 29: Cardinal Giovanni Battista Cibò is elected as Pope Innocent VIII (▶ 1492).

December 5: A papal bull, *Summis desiderantes*, condemns witchcraft and leads to one of the worst witch hunts in European history.

Records of a Christian king Joel and a bishop Merki show that the Nubian Christian community has kept itself intact in Muslim surroundings for around a millennium.

1485

August 22: King Richard III of England (◀ 1483) is killed in battle against Henry Tudor, Second Earl of Richmond, who becomes King Henry VII of England (▶ 1509).

Andrea del Sarto, Florentine painter, is born. His paintings include *Madonna of the Harpies* and a fresco of the Last Supper. Dies 1531.

Andreas Karlstadt is born. A radical reformer, he is a prolific writer, second only to Martin Luther. Dies 1541.

c.1485

Hugh Latimer, Reformer and Cambridge University Preacher, is born. Dies 1555.

1486

March 30: Thomas Bourchier, Archbishop of Canterbury (◀ 1454), dies.

December 6: John Morton, Bishop of Ely, is appointed Archbishop of Canterbury (▶ 1500). He is a great builder, pays for the erection of the central tower of Canterbury Cathedral and builds the Gateway Tower of Lambeth House.

Symeon of Trebizond (◀ 1471, 1481) is succeeded as Patriarch of Constantinople by Nephon II (▶ 1489, 1497), who holds several brief periods of office.

Francisco de Vitoria, Spanish theologian, is born. He creates a new school of theology in Salamanca, is a pioneer in international law, and defends the rights of the Indians. Dies 1546.

Malleus maleficarum (Hammer of the evil-doers), by Heinrich Krämer and Jakobus Sprenger, the most infamous of witch-hunt manuals, is published.

The Senegalese chief Behemot is baptized in Lisbon.

*c.*1488

♣ Miles Coverdale (▶ 1535), Bible translator, is born. Dies 1569.

1489

♣ July 2: Thomas Cranmer (▶ 1533) is born. An English Reformer, he becomes Archbishop of Canterbury and is the architect of the Book of Common Prayer. He is burned at the stake as a heretic in 1556.

♣ Thomas Müntzer (▶ 1520), German Anabaptist and radical Reformer, is born. He is executed in 1525.

☩ Dionysius I (◀ 1471) returns as Patriarch of Constantinople (▶ 1491) to replace Nephon II (◀ 1486).

🏛 The Cathedral of the Annunciation in the Kremlin, Moscow, is completed. It will later be extended.

1490

♣🎵 John Taverner, English composer, is born. He writes three large-scale festal masses and represents the flowering of English church music before the Reformation. Dies 1545.

The Nestorian patriarch Simon of Persia sends two bishops, Mar John and Mar Thomas, to India (▶ 1503).

1491

♣ February 2: Martin Schongauer (◀ *c.* 1448) dies.

May 3: King Nzinga a Nkuwu is baptized by Portuguese missionaries at M'banza Kongo, which they call São Salvador. He takes the name João. His son Afonso is baptized a month later (▶ 1506).

♣ November 11: Martin Bucer (▶ 1523), German Reformer, is born. He tries to be a peacemaker between conflicting groups and is an influence on Anglican worship. Dies 1551.

♣ December 24: Ignatius Loyola (▶ 1532), founder of the Jesuits (Society of Jesus), is born. Dies 1556.

☩ Dionysius I (◀ 1489) is succeeded as Patriarch of Constantinople by Maximus IV (▶ 1497), supported by the monks of Mount Athos.

1492

January 2: Muhammad XII, known to the Spaniards as Boabdil, surrenders Granada to them.

March 30: King Fernando II (◀ 1479, ▶ 1501) and Queen Isabella of Spain (◀ 1479, ▶ 1502) issue a decree expelling all Jews from Spain.

☩ July 25: Pope Innocent VIII (◀ 1484) dies.

Columbus reaches the West Indies, woodcut 1493

August 11: Rodrigo Borgia is elected as Pope Alexander VI (▶ 1503).

October 12: Christopher Columbus makes landfall in the Caribbean.

1493

May 4: Pope Alexander VI issues the bull *Inter cetera divina*, dividing the New World between Spain and Portugal.

August 14: Friedrich III, Holy Roman Emperor (◀ 1452), dies and is succeeded by his son Maximilian I (▶ 1519).

The monk Philotheus of Pskov gives Moscow the title 'The Third Rome' in a letter to the Tsar.

Catholic missionaries arrive on Hispaniola.

1494

June 7: In the Treaty of Tardesillas, Spain and Portugal divide the New World between them.

255

○ Anselm (◀ 1109) is canonized by Pope Alexander XI: feast day April 21.

📖 Walter Hilton, *The Ladder of Perfection*, a spiritual guide book, is printed by Wynkyn de Worde.

Bishop Elphinstone of Aberdeen founds the University of Aberdeen.

*c.*1494

🌱 William Tyndale (▶ 1525), English Bible translator and reformer, is born. Dies 1536.

1495

June 1: Friar John Cor records the first known written reference to Scotch whisky.

The University of Santiago de Compostela is founded.

*c.*1496

🌱 Menno Simons (▶ 1536), Dutch Anabaptist leader, is born. The Mennonites are named after him. Dies 1561.

1497

🌱♫ February 6: Johannes Ockeghem (◀ *c.*1410) dies.

🌱 February 15: Philipp Melanchthon (▶ 1530), German Reformer, is born. Dies 1560.

🌱 May 23: Girolamo Savonarola (◀ 1452) is hanged and burned as a heretic. Relics and medals containing his image begin to circulate throughout Europe.

July 18: The Portuguese Vasco da Gama (◀ *c.*1469, ▶ 1498) sets off on his first voyage to India. He is accompanied by two Franciscans.

⚓ Maximus IV, Patriarch of Constantinople (◀ 1491), is succeeded by Nephon II (◀ 1487, ▶ 1498).

1498

👑 April 7: Charles VIII, King of France (◀ 1483), dies and is succeeded by Louis XII (▶ 1515).

May 20: Vasco da Gama (◀ 1487, ▶ 1524) makes landfall in India, opening up the way for a new trade route and the spread of Christianity.

🌱 September 16: Tomás de Torquemada (◀ 1420) dies.

🖼 Leonardo da Vinci (◀ 1452, ▶ 1508) finishes his *Last Supper*.

⚓ Nephon II (◀ 1497) is displaced as Patriarch of Constantinople by Joachim I (▶ 1504), backed by the King of Georgia.

1499

April 30: The University of Valencia is founded.

🌱 October 1: Marsilio Ficino (◀ 1433) dies.

🖼 Michelangelo (◀ 1475, ▶ 1512) completes his *Pietà* in St Peter's, Rome.

Portuguese Augustinian missionaries arrive in Zanzibar.

Francisco Ximenes de Cisñeros, Cardinal Archbishop of Toledo (◀ 1436), converts the *Studium generale* in Alcala into the Complutensian University (◀ 1293).

1500

September 15: John Morton, Archbishop of Canterbury (◀ 1486), dies.

*c.***1500**

Nicholas Ridley, English Reformer and Bishop of London, is born. He is burned at the stake for heresy in 1555.

The spread of Christianity, 1400–1800, and first extended missionary routes

Except where otherwise indicated, the date given is that of the creation of a Roman Catholic diocese; figures

1.	1404	Canaries	15.	1534	São Tomé
2.	(1415)	Ceuta	16.	1537	Cuzco
3.	1511	Puerto Rico	17.	1538	Chiapas
4.	1511	Santo Domingo	18.	1541	Lima
5.	1513	Panama	19.	1547	Asuncion
6.	1514	Funchal	20.	(1549)	Kagoshima
7.	1517	Santiago de Cuba	21.	1551	Bahia
8.	1530	Tlaxcala	22.	1558	La Plata
9.	1531	Nicaragua	23.	1558	Cochin
10.	1531	Caracas	24.	1558	Malacca
11.	1533	Goa	25.	(1560)	Mozambique
12.	1534	Azores	26.	1561	Santiago de Chile
13.	1534	Cape Verde	27.	(1562)	East Timor
14	1534	Cartagena	28.	1564	La Imperial

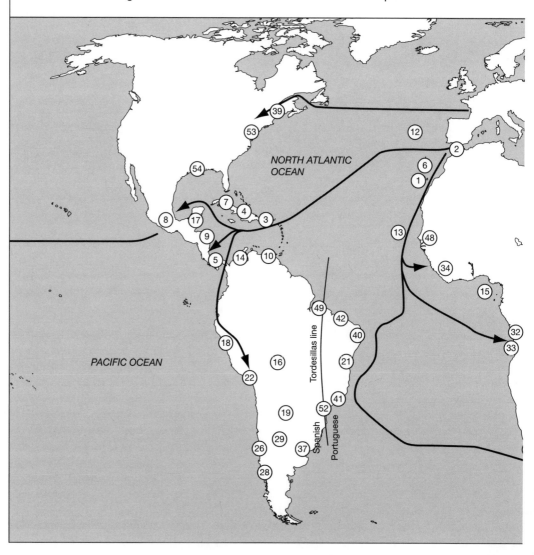

in brackets denote the date of the first Christian settlements. Places in CAPITALS are regions.

29.	1570	Cordoba		43.	1690 (1601)	Beijing
30.	1576	Macao		44.	1690	Nanjing
31.	1579	Manila		45.	(17th century)	Cape (Protestants)
32.	1596 (1491)	São Salvador		46.	(17th century)	MADAGASCAR
33.	1596	Angola e Congo		47.	(1706)	Tranquebar
34.	(1601)	GUINEA				(Protestants)
35.	1606	San Thomé de Meliapur		48.	(1716)	SENEGAL
36.	(1615)	TONGKIN		49	1719	Belem do Para
37.	1620	Buenos Aires		50.	(1720)	Mauritius
38.	(1665)	Reunion		51.	(1724)	Irkutsk (Orthodox)
39.	1674 (1608)	Quebec		52.	1745	São Paulo
40.	1676	Recife		53.	1793	Baltimore
41.	1676	Rio de Janeiro		54.	1793	New Orleans
42.	1677	São Luis da Maranhão				

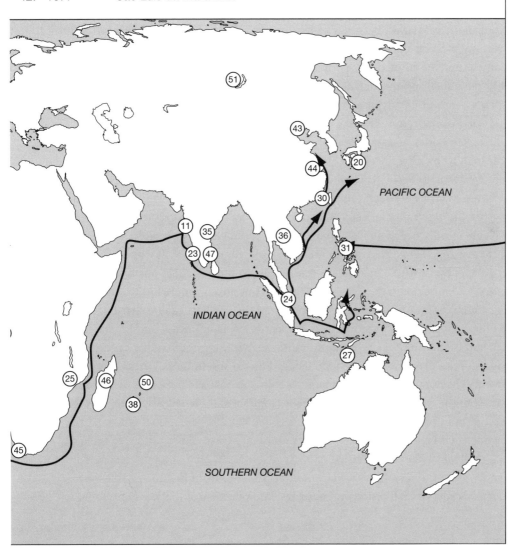

Sixteenth century

The sixteenth century is above all the century of the Reformation, that religious and political upheaval which changes for ever both Christianity and the face of Europe. The protests which lead to reform give some Christians a new name, Protestants. The Reformation begins in Germany with Martin Luther's opposition to the Church of Rome, its beliefs and practices, but soon spreads over continental Europe. In Switzerland Ulrich Zwingli introduces more radical reforms, including the abolition of images, and in Geneva the French Reformer John Calvin establishes a new church order and a new civil constitution. In England developments are rather more complicated because the advance of the Reformation becomes caught up with King Henry VIII's dispute with Pope Clement VII over the divorce that he wants from his queen, Catherine of Aragon. He becomes supreme head of a new church, the Church of England. Catholic influences still remain strong in England, and the Reformation is more moderate than on the continent; indeed its advance is reversed for a while with the accession of Queen Mary I, during whose reign there is a systematic persecution of Protestants. Only with Queen Elizabeth I does it again move forward. In Scotland, on the other hand, with the Reformer John Knox a Presbyterian church is established with greater similarities to the continental pattern. The Reformation also leads to wars of religion in Germany, France and the Low Countries between Catholics and Protestants.

Alongside the story of the Reformation another equally important story runs its course. With the discovery and conquest of the Caribbean islands and Central and South America, together with the exploration of new lands in the Far East by the Spanish and the Portuguese, a whole new area is opened up, in the Americas one of economic exploitation and mission, in the Far East of mission but on a far more limited scale. The spread of Catholic Christianity in the Americas and the Far East can be charted by the activity of missionaries mainly from the religious orders, Dominicans and Franciscans, and later Jesuits, and the steady creation of dioceses. In the middle of the century the first universities in the Americas are founded, in Mexico and in Lima, Peru.

Meanwhile, back in Europe, the Roman Catholic Church sets out on its own course of reform, with the convening of the Council of Trent, which is to shape Catholicism for the next four hundred years. It reforms both dogma and discipline. In dogma it works on those doctrines which are attacked by the Protestants: the use of scripture, the role of tradition, original sin and the doctrine of justification, the sacraments and the doctrine of purgatory. It enacts measures to train the clergy better, including the establishment of seminaries, orders worship, and emphasizes the importance of the role of bishops.

1501

⚜ January 22: Thomas Langton, Bishop of Winchester, is appointed Archbishop of Canterbury. He dies five days later.

⚜ Henry Dean, Bishop of Salisbury, becomes Archbishop of Canterbury (▶ 1503).

Fernando II (◀ 1492, ▶ 1504) declares the kingdom of Granada Christian.

1502

February 12: Queen Isabella (◀ 1492, ▶ 1504) issues a decree giving all remaining Moors in Castile the choice between baptism and expulsion.

October 18: The University of Wittenberg is founded by Frederick the Wise.

♫ Josquin Desprez (◀ *c*.1450, ▶ 1521), *First Book of Masses*, is published in Venice.

Francisco Ximenes de Cisñeros (◀ 1499) begins the composition of the Complutensian Polyglot. It contains the Old Testament with the Hebrew, Latin, Vulgate and Greek Septuagint in parallel columns.

1503

⚜ February 15: Henry Dean, Archbishop of Canterbury (◀ 1501), dies.

⚜ August 18: Pope Alexander VI (◀ 1492) dies.

⚜ September 22: Francesco Todeschini, a nephew of Pope Pius II, is elected as Pope Pius III.

⚜ October 18: Pope Pius III dies.

⚜ November 1: Giuliano della Rovere, who has gained many senior church offices, is elected as Pope Julius II (▶ 1513). He leads his troops to battle in full armour; he is also the patron of Michelangelo (◀ 1499), and plans the new St Peter's in Rome.

🏛 Canterbury Cathedral (◀ 1070) is completed.

The Persian Patriarch Elias V sends a metropolitan, Mar Yarbella, and two bishops, Mar Yakoob and Mar Denaha, to India (◀ 1490).

The first Franciscan college is established on Hispaniola.

1504

⚜ January 24: William Warham, Bishop of London and Keeper of the Great Seal, is appointed Archbishop of Canterbury (▶ 1532). He is a friend of Erasmus (◀ 1469) and for many years Chancellor of Oxford University.

♟ July 18: Johann Heinrich Bullinger (▶ 1536), Swiss Reformer, is born. Dies 1575.

November 15: By the bull *Illius fulciti* Pope Julius II seeks to establish the first ecclesiastical province in the New World on the island of Hispaniola but is opposed by King Fernando II of Spain.

November 26: Queen Isabella of Spain (◀ 1479) dies.

Joachim I, Patriarch of Constantinople (◀ 1498), dies and is succeeded by Pachomius I (▶ 1513).

1505

John Colet (◀ *c.*1466, ▶ 1509) is appointed Dean of St Paul's Cathedral, London.

Portuguese Catholics bring Christianity to Ceylon.

*c.*1505

Thomas Tallis (▶ 1573), English composer, is born. Dies 1585.

1506

April 7: Francis Xavier (▶ 1542), Jesuit missionary to Japan and India, is born. Dies 1552.

April 18: The old basilica of St Peter's, Rome (◀ 319), having been demolished, the foundation stone of the new St Peter's is laid.

Johann Tetzel begins selling indulgences in Germany as part of the fund-raising campaign for the new St Peter's.

Dominican missionaries arrive in Mozambique.

The first Christian hospital is founded in Cochin, India.

1507

Martin Luther (◀ 1483, ▶ 1511) is ordained priest.

1508

Nil Sorsky dies (◀ 1433). After his death he is revered as a saint: feast day May 7.

Albrecht Dürer (◀ 1471, ▶ 1513), *Praying Hands*, is drawn.

Leonardo da Vinci (◀ 1498, ▶ 1591), *Virgin of the Rocks* (second version), is painted.

The Cathedral of the Archangel Michael in the Kremlin is completed.

1509

April 21: King Henry VII of England (◀ 1485) dies and is succeeded by his son as King Henry VIII (▶ 1547).

July 10: Jean Calvin (▶ 1535), French Reformer, is born. Dies 1564.

Erasmus (◀ 1469, ▶ 1516), *In Praise of Folly*, written for his friend Thomas More (◀ 1478), denounces the abuses of his time.

John Colet (◀ 1505, ▶ 1519) founds St Paul's School. Its statutes exclude clerical control.

*c.*1509

King João I of Kongo (◀ 1491) dies and is succeeded by his son Afonso (◀ 1491, ▶ 1543), after opposition from Afonso's half-brother. During the fighting Afonso sees a Christian

1510–1513

vision in the sky; as King of Kongo (present-day Congo and Angola) he introduces Christianity into his kingdom through Portuguese missionaries (▶ 1518).

1510

✿ September 15: Catherine of Genoa (◀ 1447) dies (▶ 1737).

The Portuguese establish a missionary base on Goa, massacring 6000 Muslims in the process.

Benedictines in Normandy create the liqueur named after them.

1511

August 8: By the bull *Pontifex Romanus*, Pope Julius II establishes the Dioceses of Santo Domingo, Concepción de la Vega (in the present-day Dominican Republic) and Puerto Rico.

Martin Luther (◀ 1483) is appointed a teacher at the University of Wittenberg.

The Dominican friar Antonio de Montesinos exhorts the colonists on Santo Domingo to treat their Indians humanely on pain of damnation. He moves the landowner Bartolomé de Las Casas (◀ 1474) to become a Dominican.

The first Catholic priest arrives in Malacca with the Portuguese.

1511–15

■ Matthias Grünewald (◀ *c.*1475, ▶ 1528) creates a striking altarpiece of the crucifixion for the chapel of St Anthony's Hospital in Isenheim, Alsace.

1512

May 3: The Fifth Lateran Council opens. It is concerned mainly with church discipline. It is regarded in the West as the eighteenth Ecumenical Council.

September 26: The Catholic University of Puerto Rico is established.

■ Michelangelo (◀ 1499, ▶ 1535) begins his painting of the Sistine Chapel in the Vatican (▶ 1535).

Dominican missionaries arrive in Cuba.

1513

⚘ February 21: Pope Julius II (◀ 1503) dies.

⚘ March 11: Cardinal Giovanni de' Medici is elected as Pope Leo X (▶ 1521).

⚘ Pachomius I, Patriarch of Constantinople (◀ 1504), is succeeded by Theoleptus I (▶ 1522).

▥ The building of Freiburg Cathedral (◀ 1200) is complete.

■ Albrecht Dürer (◀ 1508, ▶ 1528), *Knight, Death and the Devil*, is drawn.

The Diocese of Santa Maria de la Antigua de Darien is established in Panama.

The Spanish explorer Ponce de Léon discovers Florida.

An Ethiopian psalter is printed in Rome, thanks to the presence of a small community of Ethiopian monks.

1514

♟ March 11: Donato Bramante (◀ 1444) dies.

A diocese is established at Funchal, Madeira, to cover all Portuguese overseas territories.

c.1514

♟ John Knox (▶ 1558), Scottish Reformer, who is responsible for the comparative austerity of the Church of Scotland, is born. Dies 1572.

1515

♛ January 1: Louis XII, King of France (◀ 1498), dies and is succeeded by François I (▶ 1547).

♟ March 28: Teresa of Avila, Spanish mystic, is born. Dies 1582.

♟ July 21: Philip Neri (▶ 1574), founder of the Oratory, a congregation of priests who gather round him in the oratory of the church of San Girolamo, Rome, is born. Dies 1595.

The Lateran Council decree *De impressione librorum* forbids the printing of books without the permission of the authorities.

1516

♛ January 23: King Fernando II of Spain (◀ 1479) dies, having become the most powerful ruler in Europe. He is succeeded by his grandson Carlos I (▶ 1556), born in Flanders, who is also ruler of the Burgundian territories, which he expands in the Low Countries.

♟■ August 9: Hieronymus Bosch (◀ c.1450) dies.

♟ John Foxe, Protestant historian and famous for his *Book of Martyrs* (▶ 1554), is born. Dies 1587.

♟■ Giovanni Bellini (◀ c.1430) dies.

▢ Thomas More (◀ 1478, ▶ 1535), *Utopia*, describes an ideal community living by natural law, reason and religion and attacks contemporary abuses.

An edition of the New Testament is made by Erasmus (◀ 1509, ▶ 1536) in Greek with a new Latin translation which proves both controversial and influential.

The Concordat of Bologna between Pope Leo X and François I of France (ending the Pragmatic Sanction of Bourges, ◀ 1438) gives the French crown the right to nominate certain bishops.

1517

May 31: A general chapter declares that the 'Observant' Franciscans (◀ 1415) are the true Franciscan Order.

October 31: Martin Luther (◀ 1511, ▶ 1518) pins his Ninety-Five Theses to the door of the Castle Church in Wittenberg, Saxony, disputing the power and efficacy of indulgences. This marks the start of the German Reformation.

November 8: Francisco de Cisñeros (◀ 1436) dies.

⌂ The nave of Westminster Abbey (◀ 1245) is completed.

The Diocese of Santiago de Cuba is founded.

1518

October 12: Martin Luther (◀ 1517, ▶ 1519) refuses to withdraw his theses at the Diet of Augsburg.

December 11: Huldrych Zwingli (◀ 1484, ▶ 1523) is elected secular preacher at the Old Minster in Zurich.

The Reformation

The term Reformation describes a series of movements in the sixteenth century which begin with the concern to reform the medieval Roman Catholic Church. Rather than reforming that church, they lead to the formation of a series of alternative forms of Western Christianity, each of which becomes a separate church or confession. Only when these have formed does the Roman Catholic Church reform itself in what is commonly called the Counter-Reformation. The Reformation has major political consequences and leads to a series of wars in Europe.

It begins in Germany with Martin Luther, who, prompted by the sale of indulgences (certificates offering Christians forgiveness of their sins), pins his manifesto to the door of the Castle Church in Wittenberg, Saxony (◀ 1517). This brings him into an ongoing conflict with the Roman Catholic Church, in which, however, he is protected by his prince. At a diet (imperial council) in Speyer (▶ 1529) toleration of Luther's followers is abandoned; because of their protest against this the Lutheran princes become known as 'Protestants'. In the Augsburg Confession (▶ 1530) they state their faith and go on to form a defensive military pact (▶ 1531). Lutheranism spreads north into the Scandinavian countries.

Meanwhile another reform movement has been started in German-speaking Switzerland by Huldrych Zwingli (▶ 1523). He, too, opposes indulgences, presents his manifesto and reforms church faith and practice in Zurich. His views, particularly about the eucharist, are more radical than Luther's; the two clash in a colloquy in Marburg (▶ 1529) and fail to agree. Zwingli's views arouse opposition from other Swiss cantons, and he is killed in battle (▶ 1531).

Jean Calvin heads reforms in Geneva (▶ 1541), which affect not only doctrine and worship but also the life of the city. His *Institutes of the Christian Religion* (▶ 1536, 1559) is the major statement of Reformation doctrine. He emphasizes that salvation depends ultimately on God's election and predestination. His views spread into France.

In England, the clash between King Henry VIII and Pope Clement VII over Henry's divorce from Catherine of Aragon leads to the formation of the Church of England (▶ 1534) and the Reformation takes a more moderate course, being reversed under Queen Mary I (▶ 1553) before being restored under Queen Elizabeth I (▶ 1558). In Scotland the Reformation takes a different course (▶ 1560).

The Reformation also has a radical wing, centred on the Anabaptists (see p.266).

Henrique, son of Afonso I, King of Kongo (◄ c.1509, ► 1543), is the first African to be consecrated bishop.

The first Catholic priests arrive in Colombo, present-day Sri Lanka.

1519

♔ January 12: Maximilian I, Holy Roman Emperor (◄ 1493), dies.

♣▣ May 2: Leonardo da Vinci (◄ 1452) dies.

♔ June 28: King Carlos I of Spain (◄ 1516) becomes Holy Roman Emperor as Carlos V (► 1530).

July 4–17: Johannes Eck, a professor at Ingolstadt in Germany, engages in a 23-day disputation with Luther on the latter's views; although this does not lead to a condemnation by the universities asked to adjudicate, it is instrumental in the issuing of a papal bull condemning Luther (► 1520).

♣ September 16: John Colet (◄ c.1466) dies.

Martin Luther (◄ 1518, ► 1520) writes his Small and Large Catechisms as basic instruction in the Christian faith.

1520

♣▣ April 6: Raphael (◄ 1483) dies.

June 15: The bull *Exsurge Dominus* gives Luther 60 days to recant.

December 10: Luther burns the bull in public.

📖 Martin Luther writes his *Address to the Christian Nobility of the German Nation*, *The Babylonian Captivity of the Church* and *The Freedom of a Christian*.

Thomas Müntzer (◄ 1489, ► 1525) becomes a leader of the Anabaptist movement in Germany.

> **Anabaptists**
>
> 'Anabaptist' comes from the Greek and means 're-baptizer'. It is used to refer to Christians, mainly on the European continent in the sixteenth century, who do not baptize their children and recognize only a baptism of believers. There are several groups of Anabaptists. Those following Thomas Müntzer are involved in the Peasants' War (► 1524–25), after which Müntzer is executed. A group of Anabaptists in Münster create a commune which they call the new Jerusalem; their behaviour proves scandalous and they are massacred. The Swiss Brethren (► 1525) are non-violent. In Moravia, the followers of Jacob Hutter (► 1533) are pacifists who practise a form of communism. The Mennonites (► 1536), followers of Menno Simons in the Netherlands and north-west Germany, have views similar to the Swiss Anabaptists and prove to be the most influential and lasting group; there is a flourishing Mennonite Church today.

1521

January 3: Martin Luther is excommunicated by the papal bull *Decet Romanum Pontificem*.

March 26: Luther defends his doctrines before Holy Roman Emperor Carlos V at the Diet of Worms.

🌰 April 27: Ferdinand Magellan (◀ 1480) dies in a battle with Filipinos.

May 16: Carlos V signs the Edict of Worms, an imperial ban on Luther and his followers. For Luther's own protection he is kept in the castle of the Wartburg, where he translates much of the Bible into German (▶ 1534).

🌰 ♫ August 27: Josquin Desprez (◀ c.1450) dies.

September 13: Hernán Cortés, Spanish explorer, conquers the Aztec city of Tenochtitlán and razes its main temple. The temple stones are used to build a Catholic church.

October 11: Pope Leo X confers the title Defender of the Faith on Henry VIII for attacking Lutheran ideas.

☥ December 1: Pope Leo X (◀ 1513) dies.

The first Catholic priest comes to the Philippines with Magellan.

1522

☥ January 9: Adrian Florensz Dudal, Cardinal of Utrecht, is elected as Pope Hadrian VI (▶ 1523).

☥ December 31: Jeremias I succeeds Theoleptus I (◀1513) as Patriarch of Constantinople and embarks on the longest reign in the history of the patriarchate, 21 years (▶ 1545).

1523

January 2: Huldrych Zwingli (◀ 1518, ▶ 1529) presents 67 theses which among other things argue that the mass is contrary to scripture and that images and pictures ought to be destroyed where there is danger of venerating them.

☥ September 14: Pope Hadrian VI (◀ 1522) dies.

☥ November 19: Giulio de' Medici, Governor of Florence, is elected as Pope Clement VII (▶ 1534).

📖 Zwingli, *A Brief Introduction to Christianity*, explains to the clergy the difference between gospel and law and is the first official Reformation statement of doctrine.

Martin Bucer (◀ 1491, ▶ 1538) settles in Strasbourg.

Lutheranism is introduced into Finland.

267

⌂ The canons of Cordoba with the support of Emperor Carlos V (◀ 1521, ▶ 1527) begin the construction of a Gothic cathedral within the Great Mosque of Cordoba (◀ 1236).

1524

May 3: Thomas de Vio Cajetan (◀ 1469) and Giampetro Carafa (▶ 1555) found the Theatines in Italy, an order aimed at reforming the church.

May: Martin of Valencia, a Franciscan, with eleven other Franciscans, arrives in Mexico. They come to be known as the twelve apostles of Mexico.

✝ December 24: Vasco da Gama (◀ c.1469) dies.

The city council abolishes the Roman Catholic mass in Zurich.

1524–25

In Germany tenant farmers rise against their landlords and are met with force (the 'Peasants' War').

1525

✝ May 27: Thomas Müntzer (◀ 1489) is executed.

The first Anabaptists (see p. 266) appear in the Swiss cantons.

In the Twelve Articles, the farmers in the Peasants' War seek the right to elect their own pastors and have fair living and working conditions.

William Tyndale's (◀ c.1494, ▶ 1530) translation of the New Testament is published in Worms, Germany.

Albert, Grand Master of the Teutonic Order (◀ 1190), becomes a Protestant and converts his realm into a secular state, Prussia.

Spanish Catholic priests come to El Salvador, but because it has no precious metals, Christianization there is slower.

The Diocese of Tlaxcala, Mexico, is founded.

c.1525

✝♫ Giovanni Pierluigi da Palestrina (▶ 1556), Italian composer, a master of counterpoint who writes more than 100 masses, is born. Dies 1594.

✝▣ Pieter Brueghel the Elder is born. As well as peasant scenes which graphically also convey moral lessons, and paintings reminiscent of Hieronymus Bosch (◀ c.1450), he paints many biblical scenes, from the Tower of Babel to the conversion of Paul. Dies 1569.

1526

Roman Catholics and Lutherans at the First Diet of Speyer agree that a council should be held to settle their differences and that meanwhile tolerance should be exercised (▶ 1529).

📖 Martin Cellarius, a friend of Luther and German humanist, defends Unitarian (see p.342) views in his *De Operibus Dei* (On the Works of God).

Dominican missionaries arrive in Mexico.

1527

May 6: Troops of the Holy Roman Emperor Carlos V (◀ 1523, ▶ 1530) who have not been paid occupy Rome and pillage it for more than a month ('the Sack of Rome'). Pope Clement VII takes shelter in Castel Sant'Angelo.

The Swedish Parliament agrees to dissolve the monasteries.

The first Protestant university in Europe is founded at Marburg by Philip of Hesse.

The Diocese of Puebla, Mexico, is founded, with the Franciscan Juan de Zumárraga as its first bishop. He writes a catechism and manual of Christian doctrine and has the Bible translated into local vernaculars.

1528

February 29: The Reformation begins in Scotland, fuelled by the burning at the stake of Patrick Hamilton for advocating Lutheranism.

🌿◼ April 6: Albrecht Dürer (◀ 1471) dies.

🌿◼ August: Matthias Grünewald (◀ *c.*1475) dies.

🌿◼ Paolo Veronese, Venetian painter, is born. His paintings include many biblical scenes such as *The Wedding Feast at Cana*, *Feast in the House of Levi* and *Christ with the Doctors in the Temple*. Dies 1588.

Matteo da Bascio founds the Capuchin Order at Camerino in Italy as an attempt to return to the primitive simplicity of the Franciscan Order (◀ 1182).

1529

March: At the Second Diet of Speyer Roman Catholics reverse the policy agreed on at the First Diet (◀ 1526).

April 25: Six princes and fourteen imperial free cities issue a Letter of Protestation against the Diet of Speyer's rejection of Lutheranism. These protesters (Latin *Protestantes*) are the origin of the name Protestant.

October 1: Luther and Zwingli hold a disputation on the eucharist at Marburg (the Marburg Colloquy).

October 14: Austrian troops defeat the army of the Ottoman empire outside Vienna after a month-long siege. This is the furthest west that the Turks penetrate into central Europe (▶ 1683).

In his *The Return of the Lord*, Melchior Hoffmann prophesies that Christ will come in judgement and bring in a new heaven and earth with Strasbourg as the new Jerusalem. Melchiorites become a group among the Anabaptists (see p. 266).

The Muslim Ahmed Gran (▶ 1543) invades Ethiopia and destroys its army at the Battle of Shimbra Kure. He goes on to ravage churches and monasteries.

1530

June 25: The Lutheran nobility are summoned by Emperor Carlos V to the Diet of Augsburg to account for their Lutheran views; they present him with the Augsburg Confession, written by Philipp Melanchthon (◀ 1497, ▶ 1560).

Tyndale's (◀ 1525, ▶ 1536) Bible is burnt in London as a heretical book.

The first printed French translation of the Bible by Jacques Lefèvre d'Étaples appears in Antwerp.

Michael Weisse, a Franciscan turned Moravian Brother, edits the first Protestant hymn book, *Ein New Geseng Buchlen*.

Denmark adopts a Lutheran creed.

A diocese is founded in Caro, Venezuela (later called Caracas).

1531

October 11: The Swiss Protestant cantons are attacked by the Catholic cantons and Huldrych Zwingli (◀ 1484) is killed in battle.

December 12: Juan Diego has a vision of the Virgin Mary as Our Lady of Guadalupe on the hill of Tepeyac near Mexico City, which becomes a place of pilgrimage.

German Protestant princes and cities form an alliance, the Schmalkaldic League, opposed to Emperor Carlos V.

The Diocese of Nicaragua is founded.

📖 The Spanish theologian Michael Servetus publishes *De Trinitatis Erroribus* ('On the Errors of the Trinity').

The University of Granada is founded by Emperor Carlos V as a university open to different cultures and beliefs.

♣■ Andrea del Sarto (◀ 1485) dies.

1532

May 15: By the Submission of the Clergy Act, King Henry VIII of England makes himself supreme in all ecclesiastical matters (▶ 1533), overriding the authority of Convocation (◀ 1283).

July 14: The monastery of Debra Libanos in Ethiopia is burned to the ground by the forces of Ahmed Gran (◀ 1529). Later they destroy the sixth-century cathedral of Aksum.

July 23: The religious peace of Nuremberg grants German Protestants freedom to practise their faith.

Our Lady of Guadalupe, 1531

✠ December 22: William Warham, Archbishop of Canterbury (◀ 1504), dies.

✝♩ Orlande Lassus, composer, is born. One of the most prolific composers of the sixteenth century, he writes masses, motets and passions. Dies 1594.

Jerome Emiliani founds the Somaschi in Venice to work among the poor and afflicted.

The Franciscan Ferdinand Vaquiero becomes the first Catholic bishop resident in India.

1533

✠ March 30: Thomas Cranmer (◀ 1489, ▶ 1538) is appointed Archbishop of Canterbury (▶ 1553) and declares Henry VIII's marriage with Catharine of Aragon void.

July 11: Henry VIII is excommunicated by Pope Clement VII after marrying Anne Boleyn.

The Act of Restraint of Appeals cuts off the English clergy from Rome and its canon law.

271

Jacob Hutter organizes communities of Anabaptists (see p. 266) in Moravia, the Hutterites; they are characterized by pacifism and Christian communism (▶ 1536).

1534

February 9: A group of Anabaptists under Jan van Leiden create a 'New Jerusalem' in Münster, Germany. The city is besieged and during the siege they practise a form of polygamy and show excessive fanaticism. The movement is put down and the leaders are executed.

✝ August 10: Thomas de Vio Cajetan (◀ 1469) dies.

August 15: Ignatius Loyola (◀ 1491, ▶ 1548) founds the Society of Jesus (Jesuits).

☙ September 25: Pope Clement VII (◀ 1523) dies.

☙ October 13: Alessandro Farnese, Bishop of Parma, is elected as Pope Paul III (▶ 1549).

November 17: The Act of Supremacy makes Henry VIII the 'Only Supreme Head in Earth of the Church of England, called *Anglicana Ecclesia*': the Church of England separates from Rome (◀ 1533, ▶ 1535).

The Act concerning Peter's Pence stops all financial contributions of the church in England to Rome (◀ 787).

The Act for Ecclesiastical Appointments gives the English crown complete control of the church hierarchy.

Luther's German Bible appears. It is not only the first complete German Bible but has a formative effect on the German language.

The Dioceses of the Azores, Cape Verde, São Tomé (including the southern half of West Africa) and Goa are separated from the Diocese of Funchal (◀ 1514).

The Diocese of Cartagena, Colombia, is founded.

The first Portuguese missionary arrives in the Moluccas.

1535

January 15: Henry VIII is proclaimed Supreme Head of the Church of England in the presence of senior members of state.

March 23: Henry VIII requires all public officials to sign the Oath of Succession, which recognizes the right to the throne of Elizabeth (▶ 1558), his daughter by Anne Boleyn (◀ 1533), and implies Henry's supremacy over the church).

June: The Anabaptist movement in Münster is put down by force.

✝ July 6: John Fisher (◀ 1469) and Thomas More (◀ 1478) are beheaded for refusing to sign the Oath of Succession (▶ 1935).

✝ September: Luis de Molina (▶ 1588), Spanish theologian, is born. He teaches that human beings are free to accept or resist grace, a doctrine which becomes known as Molinism. Dies 1600.

c.1535–1536

> **Jesuits**
>
> The Society of Jesus, whose members are known as Jesuits, begins in 1534 when Ignatius Loyola (◄ 1491) and six companions including Francis Xavier (◄ 1506) take a vow of poverty and service, being available to go wherever the Pope may send them. The Order is then approved by Pope Paul III (► 1540). Its first most notable activity is the founding of schools (► 1548) and colleges (► 1553); by the time of Ignatius' death (► 1556) it has 74 colleges on three continents. It also has a marked missionary orientation: Francis Xavier establishes it in India (► 1542) and Japan (► 1549) and Manuel da Nóbrega in Brazil (► 1549). It also does important work in linguistics, particularly in China. There the adoption of compatible Chinese customs leads to a serious controversy ('Chinese rites', ► 1552). And it proves a vigorous opponent of Protestantism. The flexibility of the Order helps it to extend its influence and Jesuits become confessors to kings and princes.
>
> By the middle of the seventeenth century Jesuits have spread throughout the world, at the same time incurring hostility and opposition. On various pretexts, some theological and some political, they come to be expelled from many European countries: Portugal (► 1759), France (► 1764), Spain (► 1767); Pope Clement XIV later suppresses the Order (► 1773).
>
> The Jesuits nevertheless survive, particularly in Russia, Austria, Germany, England and America, and the Society of Jesus is formally restored by Pope Pius VII (► 1814). It flourishes, particularly in the United States, where 22 universities and colleges are founded around this time. The Jesuits are currently the largest religious Order of priests in the Roman Catholic Church, with around 20,000 members in 112 countries.

October: Matthew Coverdale's (► c.1488, ► 1539) Bible appears, the first complete printed Bible in English.

November 25: Angela Merici (► 1807) founds the Ursulines, a teaching order of women, at Brescia.

Jean Calvin (◄ 1509, ► 1536) flees from France to Basle.

Commissioned by Pope Paul III, Michelangelo (◄ 1512, ► 1541) begins to paint the *Last Judgement* in the Sistine Chapel (► 1541).

c.1535

Thomas Cartwright, English Puritan divine and one of the most gifted of the Puritans (► 1549), is born. Dies 1603.

1536

January 8: Pope Paul III established a diocese in Cuzco, Peru, which includes present-day Bolivia.

January 31: Menno Simons (◄ c.1496, ► 1561), a former Roman Catholic priest, becomes an Anabaptist and begins to lead the Anabaptists in the Netherlands; they are known as Mennonites and are constantly persecuted. They spread throughout Europe and later migrate to America and Russia.

February 4: The Act for the Dissolution of Monasteries suppresses all the smaller monasteries in England, claiming that those in them are not living by their vows.

✦ February 25: Jacob Hutter, Moravian Anabaptist leader (◀ 1533), is burnt at the stake for heresy.

February 26: The First Helvetic Confession, drafted by Heinrich Bullinger (◀ 1504), is approved as a confession of faith for all German-speaking Switzerland.

May: Pope Paul III establishes a commission of cardinals to reform the papal court.

July 11: The Ten Articles of Religion are presented to Parliament, the first articles of faith of the Church of England.

✦ July 12: Desiderius Erasmus (◀ 1469) dies.

📖 July: Jean Calvin (◀ 1525, ▶ 1538) settles in Geneva, where the first Latin edition of his *Institutes of the Christian Religion* is published (▶ 1538, 1559). It is regarded as the clearest and most systematic account of Reformation doctrine.

October 1: The Pilgrimage of Grace, a rising against the dissolution of the monasteries, led by Robert Aske, begins.

October 6: William Tyndale (◀ *c*.1494) is burned at the stake for heresy, having been kidnapped from the free city of Antwerp and taken into Catholic Europe.

December 5: The Pilgrimage of Grace is abandoned.

The Evangelisches Stift, a Protestant seminary in the University of Tübingen (◀ 1477), is founded. Its theologians become famous.

King João III of Portugal sets up the Portuguese Inquisition.

The Bharatas, a fishing people on the Coromandel Coast in India, are baptized in return for protection against Muslim raiders.

1537

February 9: Luther issues the Schmalkaldic Articles as a statement of Lutheran doctrine; they are later incorporated into the Book of Concord (▶ 1580).

July 2: In his encyclical *Sublimis deus* Pope Paul III declares the American Indians rational beings who must not be enslaved or robbed.

Matthew's Bible, named after its pseudonymous translator, is issued. A revision of the versions by Tyndale (◀ 1530) and (in part) Coverdale (◀ 1535), it is dedicated to Henry VIII, who licenses it for general reading.

King Christian III decrees that Lutheranism is the religion of Norway and Denmark.

1538

April 14: Pope Paul III establishes a diocese in Chiapas, Mexico.

♟ October 2: Charles Borromeo, Catholic reformer, is born. Dies 1584.

October 28: The Universidad Santo Tomás da Aquino (now the Universidad Autonoma) is founded in Santo Domingo by papal bull.

Martin Bucer (◀ 1523, ▶ 1551) is invited to England by Thomas Cranmer (◀ 1533, ▶ 1553) and becomes Regius Professor of Greek at Cambridge.

📖 Jean Calvin is ordered to leave Geneva and move to Strasbourg. He revises his *Institutes* (◀ 1536, ▶ 1559) and issues a French translation.

1539

The English Parliament passes the Six Articles of Religion, which mark a return towards Catholicism.

Thomas Cromwell orders the Great Bible to be set up in every parish church. It is a version of Matthew's Bible (◀ 1537), revised by Coverdale (◀ 1535).

The first missionaries, Franciscans, arrive in Argentina.

Lutheranism is forcibly introduced into Iceland.

1540

September 27: In his bull *Regimini militantis* Pope Paul III approves the Jesuit Order (◀ 1534).

♟ November 5: Francisco de Quiñones (◀ 1480) dies.

The Icelandic translation of the New Testament is the first book printed in Iceland (▶ 1584).

The Franciscan Vicente de Lagos founds the first seminary for Malabar Syrian Christians in India.

1541

♟ December 24: Andreas Karlstadt (◀ 1485) dies.

♟■ Dominico Theotocopuli (El Greco), Spanish–Greek painter, is born. He combines the Byzantine style with Italian Renaissance painting in a unique way, with elongated figures and exaggerated colours. Dies 1614.

■ Michelangelo completes the *Last Judgement* in the Sistine Chapel (◀ 1535).

Jean Calvin (◀ 1538, ▶ 1559) returns to Geneva. The city approves a church order drawn up by him.

The first Catholic priest arrives in Chile (▶ 1561).

A diocese is established in Lima, Peru (▶ 1547).

A Franciscan friar, Fernando Juan de Padilla, first missionary to the Indians of what is now Kansas, is murdered.

1541/42

After the dissolution of the monasteries (◀ 1536), some of the finest of their churches become cathedrals. The new dioceses are: Chester, Gloucester, Peterborough, Bristol and Oxford.

1542

May 6: Francis Xavier (◀ 1506, ▶ 1549) arrives in Goa on a mission to South-East Asia.

♣ June 24: John of the Cross, Spanish mystic, is born. Dies 1591.

July 21: Pope Paul III establishes the 'Congregation of the Roman Inquisition' (the Holy Office) in Rome to supervise local inquisitions. The most famous case it will deal with is that of Galileo (▶ 1633).

In the 'New Laws' Emperor Carlos V (◀ 1531, ▶ 1556) seeks to protect the rights of the Indians.

The Gustav Vasa translation of the Bible is the first into Swedish.

The Geneva Catechism appears.

1543

February 21: The Ethiopians defeat the army of Ahmed Gran (◀ 1529) at the Battle of Woguera; Gran is killed.

♣ May 24: Nicolas Copernicus (◀ 1473) dies.

📖 Nicolas Copernicus, *De revolutionibus orbium coelestium* ('On the Revolutions of the Heavenly Spheres'), is published.

♣♫ William Byrd (▶ 1592–95), English Catholic composer, a pupil of Thomas Tallis (◀ c.1505), is born. Dies 1623.

The first Portuguese traders arrive in Japan, having been blown off course in a storm (▶ 1639).

The first Protestants are burnt at the stake by the Spanish Inquisition.

👑 Afonso I, King of Kongo (◀ c.1509), dies – still a Christian monarch.

1544

♜ The chapel of King's College, Cambridge (◀ 1441) is completed.

The Lutheran University of Königsberg is founded.

1545

April 16–19: French Catholic forces massacre the Waldensians (◀ 1179) at Merindol in Provence, marking a climax to the persecution of them.

☿ October 18: Jeremias I, Patriarch of Constantinople (◀ 1522) dies.

December 13: The Council of Trent, a major reforming council of the Roman Catholic

Portrait of Luther by Cranach

Church, is summoned. It will last, with intervals, until 1563. It is regarded as the nineteenth Ecumenical Council.

♟♪ John Taverner (◀ 1490) dies.

1546

♟ February 18: Martin Luther (◀ 1483) dies.

☦ April 17: Dionysius II becomes Patriarch of Constantinople (▶ 1554).

♟ August 12: Francisco de Vitoria (◀ 1486) dies.

The Diocese of Quito, Ecuador, is founded.

Six Franciscans under João de Villa do Conde reach Ceylon and build a church in Colombo.

Robert Estienne prints the first scholarly edition of the Greek New Testament (▶ 1557).

1547

♛ January 28: King Henry VIII (◀ 1509) of England dies and is succeeded by his son as King Edward VI (▶ 1553). He is only ten years old and sickly, and the Duke of Somerset acts as regent.

277

March 11: The Council of Trent is moved to Bologna because of an epidemic in Trent, and then suspended (▶ 1551).

♛ July 31: François I, King of France (◀ 1515), dies and is succeeded by Henri II (▶ 1559).

Emperor Carlos V defeats the Lutheran princes of the Schmalkadic League (◀ 1531) at the Battle of Muhlberg. This marks the beginning of the Wars of Religion.

The Six Articles (◀ 1539) are repealed.

November 16: Lima (◀ 1541) becomes an archdiocese, extending along the Pacific coast from Nicaragua to Chile.

A diocese is founded in Asuncion, Paraguay.

1548

May 15: The Augsburg Interim attempts a compromise between Catholics and Protestants.

❦ Giordano Bruno, Italian Renaissance philosopher and one-time Dominican, is born. Dies 1600.

📖 Ignatius Loyola's (◀ 1534, ▶ 1551) *Spiritual Exercises* are published with papal approval.

❦♫ Tomas Luis de Victoria is born. The most famous Spanish composer of the time, he is considered second only to Palestrina (◀ c.1525). He writes a great requiem for Empress Maria, wife of Holy Roman Emperor Maximilian II. Dies 1611.

The first Jesuit (◀ 1540) school is opened in Messina, Sicily.

The Diocese of Guadalajara, California, is formed.

Michael Agricola translates the New Testament into Finnish. He is regarded as the father of Finnish literary language (▶ 1642).

Tasfa Seyon (Petrus Ethiops), a monk from Debra Libanos living in Rome, personally supervises the printing of the Ge'ez New Testament.

1549

January 21: The first English Book of Common Prayer, the First Prayer Book of Edward II, is issued. It is a Protestant–Catholic compromise not widely accepted by either side.

March 29: Manuel da Nóbrega, a Portuguese Jesuit, arrives in Bahia, Brazil, and establishes the first Jesuit mission in the New World.

August 15: Francis Xavier (◀ 1542, ▶ 1552) establishes a Jesuit mission in Japan (▶ 1579). He is accompanied by the exiled Arjiro, from Kagoshima, subsequently baptized Paul of the Holy Faith (Paul of Japan).

� November 10: Pope Paul III (◀ 1534) dies.

The Wars of Religion

From the middle of the sixteenth century, a series of wars are waged in Europe between Catholics and Protestants; only England and the Scandinavian monarchies, Poland, Spain and Italy are untouched by them.

In Germany, after a failed Diet (meeting of the constituent states of the Holy Roman Emperor) at Regensburg (1546), aimed at a peaceful solution of the Catholic–Protestant conflict, Emperor Carlos V attacks the Protestant princes, who have organized themselves into a defensive league, the Schmalkaldic League; he defeats them at the Battle of Muhlberg (◀ 1547). However, he fails to crush the Lutherans, nor does a Diet at Augsburg the next year bring a settlement. The Protestant princes thereupon approach King Henri II of France for support and Carlos V is defeated. Peace is achieved at a further Diet in Augsburg (▶ 1555). The Diet establishes the principle *cuius religio, eius regio*, which stipulates that each part of the empire shall follow the religion of its ruler.

In France, war breaks out between the Calvinists (Huguenots, ▶ c.1560) and the Guises, a powerful Catholic family. Temporary peace is achieved by the Edict of Amboise (▶ 1563) but this proves unacceptable to the Huguenots. A second war follows, ending in the Peace of Longjumeau (▶ 1567), but this leads to a third war, ending in the Peace of St Germain (▶ 1570). A massacre in Paris on St Bartholomew's Day (▶ 1572) heralds a further series of wars, which are brought to an end only by the Edict of Nantes (▶ 1598).

In the Low Countries, Dutch Protestants rebel against the rule of Spain: war breaks out with the Battle of Heiligerlee (▶ 1567). The rebels take possession of many cities but their revolt is suppressed, only to break out again with the capture of Brielle in South Holland (▶ 1571/72). After Spanish troops mutiny and sack Flanders, the Pacification of Ghent (▶ 1576) creates a Protestant alliance against Spain, but the alliance does not last: the southern part of the Netherlands reverts to Roman Catholicism, while the north becomes Protestant. Folllowing a series of border conflicts, a truce lasts from 1609 to 1621, after which the north gradually gains the upper hand, destroying the naval supremacy of Spain at the Battle of the Downs (▶ 1639). These United Provinces gain their independence at the Treaty of Münster (▶ 1648).

Meanwhile, with the outbreak of the Thirty Years War hostilities come to involve many European powers. It is fought between 1618 and 1648, mainly in Germany. It begins with a rebellion of Bohemian Protestants against Emperor Ferdinand II, put down at the Battle of the White Mountain (▶ 1620). Despite the crushing of Protestantism, hostilities continue and prompt Danish intervention, but this is countered by the Catholic general Albrecht von Wallenstein; after two defeats the Danes withdraw, in the Edict of Lübeck (▶ 1629) keeping their territory on condition that they do not interfere in German affairs again. An Edict of Restitution (▶ 1629) promulgated by Emperor Ferdinand II requires Protestants to return all property confiscated from Catholics since the Treaty of Passau (▶ 1552). In 1630 King Gustavus Adolphus of Sweden comes into the war, defeating the Catholics at the Battle of Breitenfeld (▶ 1631), but he is killed the next year. In 1635 France, a Catholic power, declares war on Spain; although this conflict does not end until 1659 with the Treaty of the Pyrenees, the Thirty Years War is ended for the other parties in the conflict with the Peace of Westphalia (▶ 1648). This marks the beginning of a period of religious toleration after all the Wars of Religion.

⌂ A cathedral is built in São Salvador (later M'banza Kongo) in what is now Angola.

Six Jesuits led by Manuel de Nóbrega establish schools and churches in Brazil.

1550

� February 8: Giovanni Maria Ciocchi del Monte, Cardinal Archbishop of Palestrina, is elected as Pope Julius III (▶ 1555).

A great debate is held in Valladolid, Spain, between Bartolomé de Las Casas (◀ 1511, ▶ 1552), champion of the American Indians, and Juan Ginés de Sepúlveda, supporter of the interests of the colonists and the *conquistadores*. Nothing is decided.

Spanish Franciscans arrive in Guatemala.

The Danish Bible appears.

♫ The organ in the Innsbruck Court Chapel is the oldest two-manual organ in the world.

c.1550

♟ Robert Browne (▶ 1580), English Puritan, is born. Dies 1633.

A French Franciscan missionary, Bonferre, goes from Goa to Burma, where he works for three years without success.

1551

February 25: The Diocese of Bahia is founded by Pope Julius III and covers the whole of Brazil, which has previously been part of the Diocese of Funchal (◀ 1514). The first bishop is Fernandes Sardanha.

♟ February 28: Martin Bucer (◀ 1491) dies.

May 1: The Council of Trent (◀ 1547) reopens.

May 12: The Universidad Nacional de San Marcos is established in Lima, Peru, by Dominican friars.

September 21: The Royal and Pontifical University of Mexico is founded by royal decree.

The Council of the Hundred Chapters is held in Russia to reform the clergy.

The Pontifical Gregorian University in Rome is founded as the Roman College by Ignatius Loyola (◀ 1548, ▶ 1552) to be an institute of higher education. It is given its present name in 1576 by Pope Gregory XIII.

1552

April 28: The Council of Trent is suspended (▶ 1562).

July: A treaty concluded at Passau recognizes the right of the Lutheran Church to exist and makes the Augsburg Interim (◀ 1548) irrelevant.

August 31: Prompted by Ignatius Loyola, Pope Julius III founds the German College in Rome for the training of German secular priests.

♣ October 6: Matteo Ricci (▶ 1583), Italian Jesuit and missionary to China, is born. He is prepared to adopt Chinese dress and customs, which causes a controversy ('Chinese Rites', ▶ 1698). Dies 1610.

♣ December: Francis Xavier (◀ 1506) dies (▶ 1623).

♣■ Lucas Cranach the Elder (◀ 1472) dies.

📖 Bartolomé de Las Casas (◀ 1550, ▶ 1566) publishes his account of the oppression of the South American Indians, *A Brief Relation of the Destruction of the Indies*.

A second edition of the Book of Common Prayer, the 'Second Prayer Book of Edward VI', which is more Protestant than the first (◀ 1549), is issued (▶ 1559).

1553

June 19: A royal decree orders Forty-Two Articles of Anglican belief drafted by Thomas Cranmer (◀ 1538, ▶ 1556) to be observed by clergy and academics, but they do not come into force because of Mary's accession to the throne.

♛ July 6: King Edward VI of England (◀ 1547) dies and is succeeded by his half-sister as Queen Mary I (▶ 1558). The country moves back towards Roman Catholicism.

♣ October 27: Michael Servetus (◀ 1531) is tried and burnt as a heretic in Geneva for teaching something akin to Unitarianism (see p.342).

November 13: Thomas Cranmer, Archbishop of Canterbury (◀ 1489), is deposed and put on trial for high treason.

1554

January 25: Jesuit missionaries found a missionary village (*aldeia*) in Brazil which is to develop into the city of São Paulo.

♛ Felipe (Philip) II, King of Naples and Sicily (▶ 1556), marries Queen Mary I of England (◀ 1553, ▶ 1558).

☦ Dionysius II, Patriarch of Constantinople (◀ 1546), is succeeded by Joasaph II (▶ 1565).

A rich Portuguese merchant, Luis d'Almeida, becomes a missionary in Japan. He goes on to found an orphanage, a home for the homeless and a hospital.

The heresy laws are restored in England and trials of Protestants for heresy begin.

📖 John Foxe's (◀ 1516, ▶ 1587) *Acts and Monuments of Matters Happening in the Church* (known as Foxe's *Book of Martyrs*) is published in Strasbourg in Latin (▶ 1563). It gives a vivid account of the executions of Protestants.

Two Dominican priests serving as chaplains to Portuguese soldiers attached to the King of Siam engage in successful missionary work.

c.1554

❦ Richard Hooker is born. Becoming one of the foremost Anglican churchmen, he writes the *Treatise on the Laws of Ecclesiastical Polity* (▶ 1594). Dies 1600.

❦♪ (or 1557) Giovanni Gabriele, Venetian composer, a pupil of Lassus (◀ 1532), is born. Dies 1612.

1555

February 4: John Rogers, a minister and Bible translator, is burnt at the stake in Smithfield, London, as the first Protestant English martyr.

☿ March 23: Pope Julius III (◀ 1550) dies.

☿ April 9: Marcello Cervini, a scholar and reformer, is elected as Pope Marcellus II. He is commemorated by Palestrina (◀ 1525) in his *Missa Papae Marcelli* (▶ 1556).

☿ May 1: Pope Marcellus II dies.

☿ May 23: Giampetro Carafa, Archbishop of Naples and co-founder of the Theatine Order (◀ 1525), is elected as Pope Paul IV (▶ 1559).

August 7: In the constitution *Cum quorundam* Pope Paul IV proclaims the perpetual virginity of the Blessed Virgin Mary before, during and after the birth of Jesus.

September 15: Agreed at the Imperial Diet of Augsburg, the Peace of Augsburg decrees that every land which has been Lutheran before 1552 shall remain so and that it is for the rulers of other lands to decide whether the official religion is to be Catholic or Lutheran.

October 16: Bishops Latimer (◀ c.1485) and Ridley (◀ c.1500) are burnt at the stake in Oxford for heresy.

❦ December 27: Johann Arndt, Lutheran mystical theologian, is born. He is a great influence on Pietism. Dies 1621.

❦ Lancelot Andrewes, English churchman, is born. He is famous for his *Private Prayers*, published posthumously (▶ 1648). Dies 1626.

▪ Michelangelo (◀ 1475) begins work on the *Rondanini Pietà*, which is left unfinished at his death (▶ 1564).

The First Council of Mexico prohibits the ordination of anyone of 'Moorish' race, which includes Indians and those of mixed descent (Mestizos).

The Portuguese catechism, translated into Kikongo by the Jesuit Cornelio Gomes, is the first printed transcription of a Bantu language. No copies survive (▶ 1624).

1556

♛ January 16: Carlos V, Holy Roman Emperor (◀ 1519), abdicates. His son Felipe II (◀ 1554, ▶ 1598) becomes King of Spain, his brother Fernando Holy Roman Emperor (▶ 1564).

✠ March 21: Archbishop Cranmer (◀ 1489) is burnt at the stake in Oxford.

✠ March 22: Reginald Pole is appointed Archbishop of Canterbury (▶ 1558). A cardinal, he does much to remove the schism between England and Rome.

♣ July 21: Ignatius Loyola (◀ 1491) dies (▶ 1623).

July: Pope Paul IV creates a ghetto in Rome into which Jews are forced to move (▶ 1870).

♛ Felipe II (◀ 1554, ▶ 1567) is crowned the first official King of Spain.

♪ Palestrina's (◀ c.1525) *Missa Papae Marcelli* (◀ 1555) is composed.

The ordinary of the mass is printed in Mexico City, the first printed hymn book in America.

1557

The Congregation of the Inquisition under Pope Paul IV issues the first Index of Prohibited Books.

The fourth edition of Robert Estienne's Greek New Testament (◀ 1546) introduces the verse divisions that become the standard way to identify the location of biblical texts.

1558

February 4: The Diocese of Malacca (◀ 1511) is founded under Portuguese patronage, comprising the southern parts of the Malay Peninsula.

♛ November 17: Queen Mary I of England (◀ 1553) dies suddenly and is succeeded by her half-sister Elizabeth as Queen Elizabeth I (◀ 1535, ▶ 1603). Queen Elizabeth immediately attempts to move away from Mary's Catholic policies without going to Protestant extremes.

✠ November 18: Reginald Pole, Archbishop of Canterbury (◀ 1556), dies.

📖 John Knox (◀ c.1514, ▶ 1560), *First Blast of the Trumpet against the Monstrous Regiment of Women*, is an attack on the female monarchs of his day, particularly Mary I of Scotland and Mary I of England.

George Biandrata, an Italian physician from Piedmont, founds a group of Unitarians (see p.342) in Poland. The group is later led by Fausto Sozzini (▶ 1579).

The Diocese of Cochin is created to cover Ceylon and the countries bordering on the Bay of Bengal.

The Diocese of La Plata, Brazil, is founded.

283

1559

April 29: The Act of Uniformity requires uniformity of worship in England. It calls for the use of the second edition of the Book of Common Prayer (◀ 1552) with minor changes to minimize offence to Catholics.

May 25–28: The First National Synod of the French Reformed Church in Paris adopts the Gallican Confession, drafted by Calvin (◀ 1541, ▶ 1564).

August 18: Pope Paul IV (◀ 1555) dies.

December 17: Matthew Parker, Vice-Chancellor of Cambridge University, is consecrated as the first Anglican Archbishop of Canterbury (▶ 1575). He later guides the Church of England skilfully between the supporters of Rome and the Puritans (▶ 1563).

December 25: Giovanni Carlo Medici, Cardinal Archbishop of Ragusa, is elected as Pope Pius IV (▶ 1565).

Henri II, King of France (◀ 1547), dies and is succeeded by François II (▶ 1560).

The final edition of Calvin's *Institutes* (◀ 1536, 1538) appears.

A Jesuit mission, led by Gonçalo da Silveria, is sent from Goa to convert the people of Mutapa (roughly present-day Zimbabwe and Mozambique). Silveria baptizes the king and the king's mother but is subsequently denounced as a sorcerer and killed (▶ 1561).

1560

April 19: Philipp Melanchthon (◀ 1497) dies.

August 17: John Knox (◀ 1558, ▶ 1561) presents the Scots Confession to Parliament. It is ratified, marking the beginning of the Reformed Church in Scotland.

October 10: Jacobus Arminius (Jakob Hermandszoon) is born. A Dutch Protestant theologian, he challenges Calvinistic views on predestination (his followers are called Arminians, ▶ 1616). Dies 1609.

December 5: François II, King of France (◀ 1559), dies and is succeeded by Charles IX (▶ 1574).

The Portuguese Inquisition is established in Goa.

Jesuit missionaries arrive on Mozambique.

The Centuriators of Magdeburg begin to publish a history of the church divided by centuries (hence their name) which is Lutheran and anti-Roman (it continues to appear until 1574).

A Geneva Bible, prepared by Protestant refugees in Geneva, is the first English Bible to introduce the numbering of verses (◀ 1557).

c.1560

The name Huguenot (possibly derived from German *Eidgenossen*, 'confederates') is first applied to French Calvinists.

1561

January 27: The proposals in John Knox, *First Book of Discipline of the Church of Scotland*, are accepted by the Scottish Parliament.

January 28: The Edict of Orleans suspends the persecution of Huguenots.

🝙 January 31: Menno Simons (◀ c.1496) dies.

September 9: At the Colloquy of Poissy, Catherine de Medici, Regent of France, tries to reconcile Protestants and Catholics in France. Later she orders the Huguenots to give back the Catholic churches they have seized.

🏛 St Basil's Cathedral in Moscow is completed.

The first diocese in Chile, Santiago, is founded, subordinate to the Archdiocese of Lima in Peru (◀ 1547).

Gonçalo da Silviera (◀ 1559) is murdered at the court of Mutapa.

The ruler of Timor is converted to Christianity.

1562

January 17: Under the Edict of St Germain Huguenots are allowed to worship publicly out of towns and privately in towns.

January 18: The Council of Trent (◀ 1552) reopens.

March 1: Forces of the powerful Guise family massacre Huguenots at a service in a village in Champagne. This leads to war, in which the Huguenots are supported by the Bourbon family.

May 1: Jean Ribaut of Dieppe and a group of Huguenots establish a colony in Florida.

Catholic missionaries arrive on East Timor.

John Knox, *Book of Common Order*, is approved by the General Assembly of the Church of Scotland.

The Genevan Psalter, a metrical translation of the psalms into French, is published under the direction of Jean Calvin.

The Sternhold and Hopkins Psalter, an English metrical translation of the Psalms, is published.

1563

January 19: The Heidelberg Catechism, a classic Reformed statement of faith seeking to harmonize Lutheran, Calvinist and Zwinglian theologies, is published.

March 19: The Edict of Amboise brings peace between Catholics and Huguenots in France. This is followed by a second war (▶ 1567).

December 4: The Council of Trent ends.

⌂ Work begins on the cathedral in Mexico City (▶ 1667).

📖 Foxe's *Book of Martyrs* (◀ 1554) appears in English.

The Thirty-Nine Articles, a summary of Anglican doctrine, are published.

The term Puritan is first used in England for a group which wants to restore the Church of England to its 'pure' state.

1564

♣ February 15: Galileo Galilei (▶ 1616), astronomer, is born. His support for the views of Copernicus (◀ 1543), brings him into conflict with the Inquisition. Dies 1642.

♣▮ February 18: Michelangelo Buonarotti (◀ 1475) dies.

♣ May 27: Jean Calvin (◀ 1509) dies.

♛ July 25: Fernando I, Holy Roman Emperor (◀ 1556), dies and is succeeded by his son Maximilian II (▶ 1576).

Pope Pius IV creates the Archdiocese of Bogota, Colombia.

The Diocese of La Imperial, Cuba, is founded.

1565

☧ January: Joasaph II, Patriarch of Constantinople (◀ 1554), is deposed and is succeeded by Metrophanes III (▶ 1572), who makes cautious approaches to Rome.

☧ December 9: Pope Pius IV (◀ 1559) dies.

The first Catholic missionary, the Spaniard Andres de Urdaneta, lands on the island of Cebu in the Philippines.

1566

☧ January 7: Michele Ghistri, a Dominican and Inquisitor General, is elected as Pope Pius V (▶ 1572).

May: The Belgic Confession, a classic Reformed statement of faith, drafted by Guido de Bres, is approved at a secret synod in Antwerp.

♣ July 17: Bartolomé de Las Casas (◀ 1474) dies.

The Roman Catechism is issued. Based on the work of the Council of Trent, it is the first official catechism of the Roman Catholic Church.

The Second Helvetic Confession (◀ 1536), also drafted by Heinrich Bullinger (◀ 1536, ▶ 1575) as an extended personal confession of faith, is adopted by the Swiss churches and later by other churches.

1567

March 23: The Peace of Longjumeau ends the second war between Huguenots and Catholics in France (◀ 1563), but a third war follows.

May 15: Claudio Monteverdi, Italian composer, is born. As well as a series of pioneering operas, he writes a famous set of *Vespers* (▶ 1610). Dies 1643.

May 23: The Battle of Heiligerlee, near Groningen in the Netherlands, marks the beginning of the Dutch revolt against Spanish rule, the Eighty Years War.

King Felipe II of Spain (◀ 1556, ▶ 1588) sends an army to put down Protestantism in the Low Countries.

1568

September 29: The English College is founded by Cardinal William Allen at Douai for training Jesuit missionaries to work in England (it lasts until the French Revolution). Work begins on a translation of the Bible by its members, and especially by Gregory Martin (▶ 1578).

The Bishops' Bible is issued, a revision of the Great Bible (◀ 1539), the official version of the Bible before the King James Version.

The revised Roman breviary is issued.

A Congregation for the Conversion of Infidels is set up in Rome.

Jesuits begin successful missions in northern Mexico and Paraguay.

1569

January 20: Miles Coverdale (◀ *c.*1488) dies.

September 9: Pieter Brueghel the Elder (◀ *c.*1525) dies.

December 12: Metropolitan Philip of Moscow is murdered by a minion of Ivan IV Vasilyevich (Ivan the Terrible).

1570

February 25: The papal bull *Regnans in excelsis* excommunicates Elizabeth I and declares that her subjects do not owe her allegiance. It is the last such sentence on a reigning monarch.

August 8: At the Peace of St Germain, which brings to an end the third French War of Religion, Huguenots are allowed complete control of four fortress towns in France as safe havens.

The Roman Missal (Tridentine Missal) is issued by Pius V; it is the foundation for most modern missals.

The first translation of the Bible into Spanish from the Greek and Hebrew is made (Biblia del Osa).

A diocese is founded in Cordoba, Argentina.

A tribunal of the Inquisition is set up in Lima, Peru.

1571

March: Pope Pius V creates the Sacred Congregation of the Index to investigate books denounced as not being free from error (▶ 1917).

♣ ▣ September 29: Michelangelo Caravaggio, Italian painter, is born. He is notable for his naturalism and his contrast between light and shade. His religious paintings include *The Conversion of St Paul*, *The Crucifixion of St Peter* and *The Death of the Virgin*. Dies 1610.

October 7: The Christian league of Venice and Spain decisively defeats the Turks at the Battle of Lepanto. Pope Pius V attributes the victory to the Virgin Mary and declares the day the feast of Our Lady of Victory.

October: The Synod of Emden, held by 23 exiled Dutch Reformed leaders, marks the beginning of the Dutch Reformed Church (▶ 1578).

A tribunal of the Inquisition is set up in Mexico.

1571/72

April 1: The Sea Beggars, a confederacy opposed to Spanish rule of the Low Countries, capture Brielle in southern Holland, marking the beginning of a further revolt.

♣ John Donne, English poet, preacher and Dean of St Paul's Cathedral, is born. Dies 1631.

1572

⊕ May 1: Pope Pius V (◀ 1566) dies (▶ 1712).

⊕ May 4: Metrophanes III, Patriarch of Constantinople (◀ 1565, ▶ 1579), is deposed for going too far along the road towards reunion with Rome. He is succeeded by Jeremias II Tranos (▶ 1579, 1595), who conducts the first important theological exchanges between Orthodox and Lutherans. However, these, too, come to nothing.

⊕ May 14: Ugo Boncampi, an expert in canon law, is elected as Pope Gregory XIII (▶ 1585).

August 24: On St Bartholomew's Day the French Catholic monarchy and council order the massacre of Huguenot leaders gathered in Paris for a royal wedding. The killings spread wider.

♣ November 24: John Knox (◀ *c.*1514) dies.

1573

January 28: The Warsaw Confederation signs articles formalizing religious toleration in the Polish-Lithuanian commonwealth.

♣ October 7: William Laud (▶ 1633), later Archbishop of Canterbury, is born. He attempts to restore some of the pre-Reformation practice of the Church of England and is opposed to the Puritans. He is executed in 1645.

October 7: Pope Gregory XIII renames the Feast of Our Lady of Victory (◀ 1571) the Feast of the Rosary.

♫ Thomas Tallis' (◀ *c.*1505, ▶ 1585) 40-part motet *Spem in alium* is first performed.

1574

February 28: The first *auto-da-fé* in Mexico takes place, when two heretics are burnt at the stake.

May 25: Philip Neri's (◀ 1515, ▶ 1595) Congregation of the Oratory, a community of secular priests and clerics, is formed.

♛ May 30: Charles IX, King of France (◀ 1560), dies and is succeeded by Henri III (▶ 1589).

The Calvinist University of Leiden is established by William the Silent in gratitude for deliverance from a Spanish siege in 1566, in which a third of the population of Leiden was killed.

1575

♦ January 4: Pierre de Bérulle (▶ 1611), French cardinal and reformer, is born. Dies 1629.

♦ April 24: Jakob Boehme, German mystic, is born. Dies 1624.

☩ May 17: Matthew Parker, Archbishop of Canterbury (◀ 1559), dies.

♦ September 17: Johann Heinrich Bullinger (◀ 1504) dies.

The *Book of Bamberg* appears, the first officially published Catholic hymn book.

1576

January 23: A diocese is founded in Macao to serve China.

☩ February 15: Edmund Grindal, Archbishop of York, is appointed Archbishop of Canterbury (▶ 1583).

May 15: Patriarch Jeremias II Tranos of Constantinople (◀ 1572, ▶ 1579) sends a letter to the Lutherans in Tübingen commenting on the articles of the Augsburg Confession, which they have sent to him. An inconclusive correspondence follows, which is published in 1584.

♛ October 12: Maximilian II, Holy Roman Emperor (◀ 1564), dies and is succeeded by his son Rudolf II (▶ 1612), a great patron of the arts.

November 8: After Spanish troops sack Antwerp, the Pacification of Ghent creates a Protestant alliance against Spain.

1577

May 28: The Formula of Concord, the last of the classic Lutheran formulae of faith, is issued.

♦ September: Robert de Nobili (▶ 1605), Italian missionary to India, is born. Dies 1656.

A diocesan synod at Lyons rules that candidates for holy orders must undergo an examination before ordination.

1578

May 31: The catacombs of Rome are discovered.

July 8: The icon of Our Lady of Kazan is discovered.

The first synod of the Dutch Reformed Church on Dutch soil is held at Dordrecht (▶ 1618).

The Second Book of Discipline (◀ 1561), drawn up by Andrew Melville, attempts to restore modified episcopacy in the Church of Scotland.

The English college at Douai (◀ 1568) moves to Reims (until 1582); the translation of the New Testament is published there and becomes known as the Douai-Reims New Testament (▶ 1609–10).

1579

February 6: A diocese is founded in Manila, Philippines, to serve all the Spanish colonies in Asia.

May 1: Pope Gregory XIII founds the English College in Rome for training English (and Welsh) priests.

November 29: Jeremias II Tranos, Patriarch of Constantinople (◀ 1572), is temporarily deposed and replaced by Metrophanes III (◀ 1565), who dies after nine months. Jeremias returns to the throne (▶ 1582).

Fausto Paolo Sozzini, a liberal anti-trinitarian, becomes leader of a group of Unitarians in Poland (◀ 1558). He promotes a moderate form of Unitarianism and his followers are called Socinians.

Francis Drake in his ship the Golden Hind lands near San Francisco in California, which he names Nova Albion and claims for Queen Elizabeth of England. The first service from the Book of Common Prayer on American soil is read out there.

Alessandro Valignano reorganizes the Jesuit mission in Japan (◀ 1549).

The Portuguese Jesuit Joseph Barreira arrives in what is now Angola and engages in successful missionary work.

Jesuits are at the Mughal court in India.

1580

April 24: Vincent de Paul (▶ 1625), French Catholic pastor, is born. He founds charities, especially the Lazarists, who train clergy and carry on missions among country people. Dies 1660.

June 12: The Jesuits Robert Parsons and Edmund Campion (▶ 1581) arrive in England to begin a mission.

290

June 25: The Book of Concord, a collection of documents that form the confessional foundation of Lutheranism, is issued.

Robert Browne (◀ c.1550, ▶ 1633) establishes the first congregation of Independents, a separatist church, in Norwich.

Franciscan missionaries from the Philippines arrive in Cochin China (Vietnam).

1581

July 17: Edmund Campion (◀ 1580) is arrested for treason.

🌳 December 1: Edmund Campion is executed (▶ 1970).

🌳 Jean Divergier de Hauranne, Abbé de Saint-Cyran, who will become leader of the French Jansenists (▶ 1585), is born. Dies 1643.

The Dominican Domingo de Salazar reaches the Philippines as the first Catholic Bishop of Manila.

1582

February 24: In his bull *Inter gravissimas*, Pope Gregory XIII decrees that the Gregorian calendar (named after him) be adopted, so that Easter can be celebrated on the day it was at the time of the Council of Nicaea (◀ 325). Its predecessor, the Julian calendar, is to end on October 4 and the Gregorian calendar to begin the next day, which is to be October 15. The Gregorian calendar is adopted in the papal states, Spain, Portugal and Poland. Other countries are slow to follow.

🌳 October 4: Teresa of Avila (◀ 1515) dies (▶ 1623).

December: The Gregorian calendar is adopted in France and the Netherlands (not in England until 1752).

⊕ Romuald (◀ 1012, feast day June 19) and Norbert (◀ 1120, feast day June 6) are canonized by Pope Gregory XIII.

☥ Jeremias II Tranos, Patriarch of Constantinople (◀ 1579, ▶ 1584), is again deposed.

The Douai-Reims (◀ 1578) New Testament is published (▶ 1609/10).

1583

🌳 March 3: Edward Herbert of Cherbury, English philosopher, is born. Dies 1648.

🌳📖 April 10: Hugo Grotius, Dutch lawyer and theologian, is born. His *On the Law of War and Peace* (1625) dissociates law from theology. Dies 1645.

☥ July 6: Edmund Grindal, Archbishop of Canterbury (◀ 1576), dies.

☥ September 23: John Whitgift, Bishop of Worcester, is appointed Archbishop of Canterbury (▶ 1604). He founds a famous school named after him in Croydon.

🌳🎵 Orlando Gibbons, English composer, is born. Dies 1625.

Michele Ruggieri and Matteo Ricci (◀ 1552, ▶ 1601), Jesuit missionaries, arrive in China and found a mission.

1584

July 5: Pope Gregory XIII establishes a Maronite college in Rome, which helps to preserve the Maronite Church (◀ 684).

August 15–October 18: The Third Council of Lima definitively organizes the church in the Americas. It rules that the native population must be treated as free men and women and that indigenous languages must be used. It also produces a trilingual catechism, establishes seminaries and sets standards for priestly ordination.

✝ November 3: Charles Borromeo (◀ 1538) dies (▶ 1610).

☩ Jeremias II Tranos, Patriarch of Constantinople (◀ 1582, ▶ 1585), returns to office with the support of the Sultan.

The whole Bible is printed in Icelandic (◀ 1540).

The first Slovenian translation of the Bible is printed in Germany and smuggled into Slovenia in barrels so that the Catholic authorities do not discover it.

1585

January 12: The Netherlands adopts the Gregorian calendar.

✝ January 23: Mary Ward is born. An English Catholic who has to work in France, she forms a religious community modelled on the Society of Jesus. Dies 1645.

☩ April 10: Pope Gregory XIII (◀ 1572) dies.

☩ April 24: Felice Peretti, Cardinal and Vicar-General of the Franciscans, is elected as Pope Sixtus V (▶ 1590).

✝♩ September/October: Heinrich Schütz, German composer, is born. He writes about 500 sacred choral works. Dies 1672.

✝ October 28: Cornelius Otto Jansen is born. Bishop of Ypres, he writes *Augustinus*, posthumously published (▶ 1640), about grace and freedom and with pessimistic views of human nature. His followers are known as Jansenists. Dies 1638.

✝♩ November 23: Thomas Tallis (◀ c.1505) dies.

☩ Jeremias II Tranos (◀ 1584, ▶ 1587) temporarily ceases to be Patriarch of Constantinople, being succeeded first by Pachomius II and then by Theoleptus II, because the Ottomans put limits on his tenure and he has to be re-elected.

1586

April 15: The University of Graz, Austria, is founded by Sixtus V. Jesuits are instructed to give public lectures in theology, philosophy and the liberal arts.

December 3: In the constitution *Postquam verus* Pope Sixtus V fixes the maximum number of cardinals at 70. This is not exceeded until the time of Pope John XXIII (▶ 1958).

1587

✝ April 18: John Foxe (◀ 1516) dies.

July 25: Shogun Toyotomi Hideyushi issues an edict expelling all missionaries from Japan. Mission property is confiscated but the edict is not strictly enforced.

☩ Jeremiah II Tranos (◀ 1585, ▶ 1595) again becomes Patriarch of Constantinople.

Jesuits begin missionary work in Argentina, Brazil and Paraguay.

Pope Sixtus V founds the Vatican Press, still responsible for printing papal and curial documents and the Vatican newspaper *L'Osservatore Romano* (▶ 1861).

1588

February 11: In his bull *Immensa dei aeterni* Pope Sixtus V creates 15 congregations of cardinals which function until the Second Vatican Council (1962–65).

✝■ April 19: Paolo Veronese (◀ 1528) dies.

King Felipe II of Spain (◀ 1567, ▶ 1598) sends a fleet, the Spanish Armada, to escort an army to invade Britain and restore it to Catholicism. Much of it is destroyed in a storm. Further unsuccessful armadas are sent in 1596 and 1597.

The Spanish Jesuit Luis de Molina (◀ 1535, ▶ 1600) publishes a work defending free will against predestination.

William Morgan translates the Bible into Welsh.

1589

☩ January 16: Boris Godunov, regent of Russia, persuades Jeremias II Tranos, Patriarch of Constantinople, to establish a Patriarchate of Moscow and all Russia independent from Constantinople. Metropolitan Job of Moscow becomes the first Russian patriarch (▶ 1605).

♛ August 2: Henri III, King of France (◀ 1574), dies and is succeeded by Henri IV (▶ 1610).

The Vatican Library is opened in Rome.

1590

☩ August 27: Pope Sixtus V (◀ 1585) dies.

☩ September 15: Giambattista Castagna, Governor of Bologna, is elected as Pope Urban VII.

☩ September 27: Pope Urban VII dies.

☩ December 5: Cardinal Niccolò Sfondrati, Bishop of Cremona, is elected as Pope Gregory XIV (▶ 1591).

Gáspár Károlyi translates the Bible into Hungarian. This translation is regarded in Hungary as highly as the King James Version in the English-speaking world.

1591

♣ March 15: Alexandre de Rhodes (▶ 1624), Jesuit missionary to Vietnam and Persia, is born. Dies 1660.

♣ July: Anne Hutchinson, dissident Puritan preacher, is born. Dies 1643.

☿ October 16: Pope Gregory XIV (◀ 1590) dies.

☿ October 29: Cardinal Giovanni Antonio Fachinetti, Patriarch of Jerusalem, is elected as Pope Innocent IX.

♣ December 14: John of the Cross (◀ 1542) dies (▶ 1726).

☿ December 30: Pope Innocent IX dies.

1592

☿ January 30: Ippolito Aldobrandini, lawyer and diplomat, is elected as Pope Clement VIII (▶ 1605).

♣ February 22: Nicholas Ferrar (▶ 1626), founder of a commune at Little Gidding, Northampton, England, is born. Dies 1637.

♣ March 28: John Amos Comenius, Bohemian Protestant educational reformer, is born. Dies 1670.

Trinity College, Dublin, is founded by Elizabeth I.

Pope Clement VIII publishes a corrected version of Jerome's Vulgate (◀ c.404) which is the standard text of the Roman Catholic Bible until 1979.

1592–95

♪ William Byrd (◀ 1543, ▶ 1623) writes his masses for three, four and five voices.

1593

♣📖 April 3: George Herbert, English poet, is born. His major collection of poems is entitled *The Temple* (1633). Many of his works are set to music as hymns. Dies 1633.

July 25: Realizing that as a Protestant he has no chance of uniting the kingdom, King Henri IV of France becomes a Catholic: 'Paris is worth a mass.'

December 10: Antonio Bosio makes a descent into the Roman catacombs (▶ 1632).

Sweden adopts the Augsburg Confession (◀ 1530) and becomes officially Lutheran.

The Spanish Jesuit Gregorio de Cespedes is the first Westerner to set foot in Korea (▶ 1784).

The first translation of the Bible into Czech from the original languages (Kralice Bible) is completed.

A Jesuit, Jacob Wujek, produces a classic translation of the Bible into Polish.

1594

♣♫ February 2: Giovanni Perluigi da Palestrina (◀ c.1525) dies.

♣♫ June 14: Orlande Lassus (◀ 1532) dies.

📖 Richard Hooker, *Treatise on the Laws of Ecclesiastical Polity (1–4)*, is published (Book 5 in 1597).

1595

♣ May 26: Philip Neri (◀ 1515) dies (▶ 1623).

August 1: A college which later becomes a university is founded by Jesuits in Cebu City, Philippines.

✇ Jeremias II Tranos, Patriarch of Constantinople (◀ 1572, 1585, 1587), dies.

📖 In *The True Doctrine of the Sabbath*, Nicholas Bound, a Suffolk clergyman, advocates the strict enforcement of the Sabbath on Old Testament lines. This marks the beginning of Sabbatarianism.

The Church of England issues the Lambeth Articles, on predestination, but they are not approved.

1596

✇ February: Matthew II is appointed Patriarch of Constantinople. His tenure is interrupted several times. From this point onwards, election to the patriarchate involves payment of money to the Turkish authorities, and this leads to frequent changes and a chaotic situation. In the century to 1695 there are 61 changes, involving 31 patriarchs. Four are executed for treason (▶ 1695).

♣ March 31: René Descartes (▶ 1637), French philosopher, is born. Dies 1650.

October: The Council of Brest-Litovsk concludes a Union by which the majority of Orthodox in the Ukraine join Rome.

Pope Clement VIII makes Kongo a diocese with its cathedral at São Salvador.

1597

26 Christians are crucified in Nagasaki, Japan.

1598

April 13: King Henri IV of France (◀ 1593, ▶ 1610) proclaims the Edict of Nantes, giving protection to French Protestants.

♛ September 13: King Felipe II of Spain (◀ 1556) dies and is succeeded by his son Felipe III (▶ 1621).

♣■ December 7: Gian Lorenzo Bernini, Roman sculptor and architect, is born. He is put in charge of the architectural work in St Peter's, Rome and designs the papal throne. His sculptures include *The Ecstasy of St Teresa*. Dies 1680.

⊕ Isidore of Seville (◀ 636) is canonized by Pope Clement VIII: feast day April 4.

1599

June 20: The Synod of Diamper in India under the Portuguese Archbishop Alexis de Menezes brings Thomas Christians under Roman Catholic rule and rejects Nestorianism.

1600

❀ February 17: Giordano Bruno (◀ 1548) is burned at the stake in Campo dei Fiori in Rome for speculating on the theological and philosophical implications of Copernicus' theories (◀ 1473).

❀ October 12: Luis de Molina (◀ 1535) dies.

October 21: Tokugawa Ieyasu (▶ 1614) is victorious at the Battle of Sekichara and becomes *de facto* ruler of Japan.

❀ November 2: Richard Hooker (◀ 1554) dies.

❀ William Prynne (▶ 1637) is born. A prominent Puritan, he opposes the policies of Archbishop Laud and denounces morals at court. Dies 1669.

Seventeenth century

The first half of the century is marked by a heightening of the wars between Catholics and Protestants on the European continent. The Thirty Years War, which begins in 1618 with a revolt of Bohemian Protestants against the Catholic Habsburg empire, comes to involve a number of European countries including Sweden, France and Spain, and causes untold suffering until it is brought to an end with a negotiated settlement at the Peace of Westphalia (1648), marking the beginning of religious tolerance and an end to the Wars of Religion. In France the Huguenots continue to be persecuted, and after enduring a siege at La Rochelle in which they are defeated (1627) they lose their political and territorial rights; in 1685 the Edict of Nantes which protected them is revoked.

The wars lead to a wave of emigration to America to avoid the religious persecution that goes with them and to enable the new denominations which are forming to have freedom to express their beliefs. The first Baptist church is founded in 1609 by the English separatist John Smythe, in exile in Amsterdam; three years later the first Baptist church in England is established under the leadership of Thomas Helwys. In 1620 English Congregationalists sail from Plymouth to Massachusetts, where they found another Plymouth; they come to be known as the Pilgrim Fathers. Other Protestants follow, and in 1638 Roger Williams founds a Baptist church at Providence, Rhode Island, while two years later Presbyterians organize a church on Long Island. In 1647 the Society of Friends, the Quakers, is formed by George Fox, and towards the end of the century the Quaker William Penn founds what is to become Pennsylvania, with its capital Philadelphia.

Alongside the literature characteristic of the age of Enlightenment which begins after the Peace of Westphalia, a series of classic works by Protestant writers appears: Lancelot Andrewes, *Private Prayers* (1648); Jeremy Taylor, *Holy Living* (1650) and *Holy Dying* (1651); Richard Baxter, *The Saints' Everlasting Rest* (1650) and *The Reformed Pastor* (1656); Johann Jakob Spener, *Pia Desideria* (1675), the fundamental work of Pietism; and William Law, *A Serious Call to a Devout and Holy Life* (1686). John Milton's *Paradise Lost* is published in 1669 and John Bunyan's *The Pilgrim's Progress* in 1678. Towering over all these, the Authorized/King James Version of the Bible (1611) is published and has a lasting effect on the English language.

If so far missionary activity has largely been by the Franciscans and Dominicans, this is the century of the Jesuits. In 1601 two Japanese Jesuits are ordained priests; in 1603 the Spanish Jesuit Pedro Paez arrives in Ethiopia. In 1607 there is a Jesuit mission in Thailand and in 1610 the first 'reduction', an estate for Indians to live on, is founded by Jesuits in South America. By 1630 there will be 13 of these estates. In 1624 the Jesuit missionary Alexandre de Rhodes arrives in Cochin China, and the next year the French

Jesuit Jean de Brébeuf goes to Canada to live with the Huron natives. In 1626 the Jesuit missionary Antonio del Andrade is the first European visitor to Tibet, where he lays the foundation stone of a Christian church. In 1634 the Jesuit priest Andrew White is one of the first settlers in what is to become the predominantly Catholic American colony of Maryland. In 1644 a German Jesuit, Johann Adam Schall von Bell, is appointed Director of the Chinese Bureau of Astronomy; this leads to the flourishing of Christianity in China. And in 1672 the Jesuit Jacques Marquette begins an exploration of the Mississippi River, ending on Lake Michigan, where he founds a mission on the site of present-day Chicago.

1601

September: Lewis Niabara from Nagasaki and Sebastian Kimura from Hirado, Japanese Jesuits, are ordained Catholic priests.

December 25: In the Indonesian archipelago a small Dutch fleet defeats Portuguese ships sent against it, marking the beginning of the end of Portuguese expansion.

Matteo Ricci (◀ 1583) is allowed to enter the closed city of Beijing, where he spends the rest of his life (▶ 1610).

A visitor to Strasbourg records a Christmas tree decorated with wafers and barley sugar.

1602

The first translation of the New Testament into Irish is printed (▶ 1680).

1603

♛ March 24: Queen Elizabeth I (◀ 1558) dies and is succeeded by King James VI of Scotland, who also becomes King James I of England (▶ 1625). However, he cannot achieve full governmental union (▶ 1707).

April: The Millenary Petition is presented by Puritans to James I on his way from Scotland to London, asking for relief from the burden of Anglican ceremonial. It leads to the Hampton Court Conference (▶ 1604).

April 26: The Spanish Jesuit Pedro Paez arrives in Ethiopia after spending six years as a slave in Yemen. He marks the beginning of Roman Catholic influence in the country (▶ 1622).

♣ December 27: Thomas Cartwright (◀ 1535) dies.

1604

January: A conference at Hampton Court is presided over by King James I to consider Puritan demands for reform in the church.

☦ February 28: John Whitgift, Archbishop of Canterbury (◀ 1583), dies.

♣ March 4: Fausto Paolo Sozzini (◀ 1579) dies.

☦ October 10: Richard Bancroft, Bishop of London, is appointed Archbishop of Canterbury (▶ 1610).

1605

☦ March 5: Pope Clement VIII (◀ 1592) dies.

☦ April 1: Alessandro Ottaviano de' Medici, Cardinal Bishop of Palestrina, is elected as Pope Leo XI.

☦ April 27: Pope Leo XI dies.

☦ May 16: Camillo Borghese, Vicar of Rome and Inquisitor, is elected as Pope Paul V (▶ 1621).

May 20: Robert de Nobili (◀ 1577) arrives in Goa. He pioneers new methods of evangelism, dressing as a Brahmin beggar and adapting Brahmin customs to be compatible with Christianity. The form of Christianity adopted by converts becomes known as Malabar rites.

June 30: Job, Patriarch of Moscow (◀ 1589), is deposed.

November 5: Gunpowder Plot: Robert Catesby and Guy Fawkes attempt to blow up the Houses of Parliament to enable Roman Catholics to seize power.

Balthazar Barreira (◀ 1579) begins work in Sierra Leone, where he opposes the slave trade. He pleads for Sierra Leone to be regarded as the most suitable base for Christianity in Africa.

*c.*1605

Federico Borromeo founds the Ambrosian Library in Milan. It is one of the first large libraries to be open to the general public. Unauthorized removal of books is a sin which only the Pope can forgive.

1606

January 9: The Catholic Diocese of San Thomé de Meliapur, covering Bengal, is founded.

July 15: Rembrandt van Rijn, Dutch painter, is born. His paintings are often on biblical themes, from both Old and New Testaments. Dies 1669.

Hermogenes is appointed Patriarch of Moscow (▶ 1612).

Aldhelm (◀ 709) and Pope Gregory VII (◀ 1085) are canonized by Pope Paul V: feast day May 25.

1607

March 12: Paul Gerhardt, Lutheran poet and hymn writer, is born. His hymns include 'O Haupt voll Blut und Wunden', translated by Robert Bridges as 'O sacred head, sore wounded' (▶ 1899). Dies 1676.

May 14: A small group of English settlers under Captain Christopher Newport found Jamestown and build the first Anglican church in America. At the same time the Plantation of Ulster, the settling of British Protestants in the most Gaelic part of Ireland, is planned (▶ 1641).

The first Jesuit mission in Thailand begins.

Joseph Calasanza (▶ 1767) organizes the Piarist Brotherhood in Rome to educate poor children and young people.

The Carthusians of La Grande Chartreuse (◀ 1084) first produce liqueurs made of green and yellow herbs.

1608

January 6: Antonio Manuel, an ambassador sent by King Alvaro II of Kongo to establish relations with the Vatican, dies on arriving in Rome.

♦ February 6: Antonio Vieira, Portuguese Jesuit diplomat, preacher and missionary, is born. He demands that the Inquisition stops persecuting Jews and new Christians. Dies 1697.

July 3: Samuel de Champlain founds Quebec City, Canada.

♦ September 20: Jean-Jacques Olier is born. He is founder of the seminary of Saint-Sulpice, Paris (the Order of the Sulpicians, ▶ 1642), and writes many books on spirituality. Dies 1657.

♦ December 9: John Milton, English poet, author of *Paradise Lost* (▶ 1667), is born. Dies 1674.

1609

♦ October 19: Jacobus Arminius (◀ 1560) dies.

The first Baptist church is formed by the English separatist John Smythe, in exile in Amsterdam (▶ 1612).

📖 François de Sales (▶ 1610), *Introduction to the Devout Life*, presents a form of devotion meant to be open to anyone.

1609/10

With the completion of the translation of the Old Testament, the Douai-Reims Bible is printed in two volumes: this is the English translation most used by Roman Catholics for the next 300 years (◀ 1578).

1610

January 14: The Remonstrance, a statement of Arminian (◀ 1560, ▶ 1618) beliefs, is formally signed by 46 ministers and presented to the state authorities of Holland and Friesland in July.

♦ May 11: Matteo Ricci (◀ 1552) dies.

♛ May 14: Henri IV, King of France (◀ 1589), dies and is succeeded by Louis XIII (▶ 1643).

June 6: François de Sales (▶ 1665) and Jane Frances de Chantal (▶ 1767) found the Order of Visitandines in Annecy, France, for women who find the older orders too strict.

♦■ July18: Caravaggio (◀ 1571) dies.

♫ July: Claudio Monteverdi's *Vespers* are published.

☗ November 2: Richard Bancroft, Archbishop of Canterbury (◀ 1604), dies.

✪ Charles Borromeo (◀ 1584) is canonized by Pope Paul V: feast day November 4.

The first 'reduction', an estate for Indians to live on, is founded by the Jesuits (◀ 1587) in South America. By 1630 there are 13 and eventually there are more than 30 of them.

1611

� April 9: George Abbot, a former Dean of Winchester and Bishop of London, is appointed Archbishop of Canterbury (▶ 1633). He has Puritan sympathies which become increasingly unfashionable and his career is marred by a hunting incident in which he shoots a gamekeeper. However, he remains in office and in 1625 crowns Charles I king.

♣♫ April 27: Tomás Luis de Victoria (◀ 1548) dies.

November 4: Pierre de Bérulle (◀ 1575, ▶ 1629) founds the French Oratory, modelled on the Oratory of Philip Neri (◀ 1574).

The Authorized/King James Version of the Bible is published.

Dominicans establish the University of St Thomas in the Philippines.

1612

♛ January 20: Rudolf II, Holy Roman Emperor (◀ 1576), dies and is succeeded by his brother Matthias (▶ 1619).

☿ February 17: Hermogenes, Patriarch of Moscow (◀ 1606), is murdered by the Poles who have occupied Moscow.

April 11: Bartholomew Legate of London and Edward Lightman of Burton upon Trent are burnt at the stake in Lichfield for heresy, the last in England to suffer this fate.

♣♫ August 12: Giovanni Gabriele (◀ c.1554) dies.

The first Baptist church in England is established under the leadership of Thomas Helwys (◀ 1609).

1613

♣ August 15: Jeremy Taylor, Anglican devotional writer, is baptized. His best known books are *Holy Living* (▶ 1650) and *Holy Dying*. Dies 1667.

1614

♣▣ April 7: El Greco (◀ 1541) dies.

♣ Margaret Fell (▶ 1660) is born. Her estate of Swarthmoor in Lancashire becomes a centre for Quaker activities. After the death of her first husband she marries George Fox (▶ 1624) and comes to be known as the 'nursing mother' of Quakerism. Dies 1702.

⌂ Carlo Maderno finishes the incomplete façade of St Peter's, Rome (◀ 1506, ▶ 1667).

Tokugawa Ieyasu (◀ 1600), suspicious of Portuguese traders and missionaries, issues an edict expelling Christians from Japan and banning Christianity there. This anti-Christian policy is strengthened by his successors (▶ 1623). Many Japanese Christians move to the Philippines.

The Church of Ireland issues the Irish Articles, 104 articles of faith.

1615

♟📖 November 12: Richard Baxter, English Puritan divine, is born. He writes *The Saints' Everlasting Rest* (1650) and *The Reformed Pastor* (1656). Dies 1691.

Missionaries from the Order of Recollects, a reformed French branch of the Franciscans, begin work in Newfoundland and Quebec.

Mass is celebrated for the first time on the island which is now the site of Montreal.

1616

March 5: Pope Paul V censures Galileo (◀ 1564) for teaching the Copernican theory of the solar system (▶ 1633).

Jesuit missionaries arrive in Tongkin on a mission to Cochin China (present-day South Vietnam).

1618

May 23: In the second Defenestration of Prague (◀ 1419) Bohemian Protestant rebels break up a meeting of Imperial Commissioners and throw three of them out of the window. This leads to a revolt which marks the beginning of the Thirty Years War (▶ 1648).

November 13: The Synod of Dort (Dordrecht) begins; it issues Canons which condemn Arminianism (◀ 1560), representing a victory for strict Calvinism.

The Benedictine Congregation of St-Maur (Maurists) is founded at St Germain des Prés, Paris; it becomes famous for literary and historical work.

King James I issues the *Book of Sports*, which rules on what may or may not be done on a Sunday (◀ 1595). Puritans regard it as too permissive (▶ 1633).

King James I forces through the General Assembly of the Church of Scotland the Five Articles of Perth, intended to bring the church's worship and government in line with that of the Church of England.

1619

👑 March 20: Matthias, Holy Roman Emperor (◀ 1612), dies and is succeeded by Ferdinand II (▶ 1637).

May 9: The Synod of Dort (◀ 1618) ends.

☦ June 2: Philaret is enthroned as Patriarch of Moscow (▶ 1633).

The Dutch establish a base on Java from which they drive the Portuguese out of Indonesia.

1620

September 16: English Congregationalists sail from Plymouth for America in the *Mayflower* and reach Massachusetts, where they found another Plymouth. They come to be called the Pilgrim Fathers.

November 8: At the Battle of the White Mountain in Bohemia the army of the Catholic Duke Maximilian of Bavaria annihilates the Bohemian Protestants, leading to the suppression of Protestantism there.

A diocese is founded in Buenos Aires, Argentina.

1621

January 28: Pope Paul V (◀ 1605) dies.

February 9: Alessandri Ludovisi, Archbishop of Bologna, is elected as Pope Gregory XV, the first Jesuit-trained Pope (▶ 1623).

March 31: Felipe III, King of Spain (◀ 1598), dies and is succeeded by Felipe IV (▶ 1665).

May 11: Johann Arndt (◀ 1555) dies.

1622

March: Influenced by Pedro Paez (◀ 1603), Emperor Susenyos of Ethiopia converts to Roman Catholicism in a public ceremony.

April 17: Henry Vaughan, English spiritual poet, is born. He is deeply influenced by George Herbert (◀ 1593), and produces a collection *Silex Scintillans* (1650). Dies 1695.

May 3: Pedro Paez (◀ 1603) dies.

June 6: Pope Gregory XV creates the Sacred Congregation for the Propaganda of the Faith out of the Congregation for the Conversion of Infidels (◀ 1568).

1623

March 12: Francis Xavier (◀ 1552, feast day December 3), Teresa of Avila (◀ 1582, feast day October 15) and Philip Neri (◀ 1595, feast day May 26) are canonized by Pope Gregory XV.

May 22: Ignatius Loyola (◀ 1556) is canonized by Pope Gregory XV: feast day July 31.

June 19: Blaise Pascal (◀ 1654), French mathematician and theologian, is born. Dies 1662.

July 4: William Byrd (◀ 1543) dies.

July 8: Pope Gregory XV (◀ 1621) dies.

August 6: Maffeo Barberini, prefect of the Signatura, the highest court of appeal in the Roman Catholic Church, is elected as Pope Urban VIII (▶ 1644).

In the 'great martyrdom of Nagasaki' 23 Christians are roasted alive.

The apostolic vicariate is revived. Apostolic vicars are sent on missions as bishops directly responsible to the Pope.

The Benedictines found the University of Salzburg.

1624

January 14: Alfonso Mendez arrives in Ethiopia to succeed Pedro Paez (◀ 1622).

� July: George Fox (▶ 1647), founder of the Religious Society of Friends (Quakers), is born. Dies 1691.

� November 21: Jakob Boehme (◀ 1575) dies.

The Jesuit Alexandre de Rhodes (◀ 1591, ▶ 1627) arrives in Cochin China.

Mateus Cordoso translates the Portuguese Catechism into Kikongo (◀ 1555). It will be the only printed book in the Kongo for centuries.

1625

👑 March 27: King James I of England (◀ 1603) dies and is succeeded by his son as King Charles I (▶ 1633, 1649).

🎵� June 3: Orlando Gibbons (◀ 1583) dies.

June 19: The French Jesuit Jean de Brébeuf lands in Canada and lives with the Huron natives near Lake Huron (▶ 1649).

In France, Vincent de Paul (◀ 1580, ▶ 1633) founds the Congregation of the Mission, also known as Lazarists or Vincentians, to preach the gospel to the poor, especially in the countryside.

A new convent of Port-Royal is founded in Paris, Port-Royal de Paris; the old one (◀ 1204) becomes Port-Royal des Champs.

1626

� January 9: Armand-Jean le Bouthillier de Rancé, monastic reformer, is born. As abbot of the Cistercian monastery of La Trappe in Normandy, he introduces the most stringent regulations. The monks are known as Trappists. Dies 1700.

February: Alfonso Mendez (◀ 1624) as Roman patriarch in Ethiopia suppresses local rites and the Ethiopian calendar, insisting that lay people should be rebaptized and clergy reordained.

April 12: The Jesuit missionary Antonio del Andrade, the first European visitor to Tibet, lays the foundation stone of the first Christian church there.

� September 26: Lancelot Andrewes (◀ 1555) dies.

The Dutch occupy Formosa (▶ 1662).

Nicholas Ferrar (◀ 1592, ▶ 1637) founds Little Gidding, an Anglican community for families.

1627

September 10: Cardinal Richelieu besieges the Huguenot stronghold of La Rochelle (▶ 1628).

September 27: Jacques-Bénigne Bossuet, French Catholic historian and bishop, is born. Dies 1704.

The French astronomer Denis Petau first adds BC to dates (◀ 525).

Alexandre de Rhodes (◀ 1624, ▶ 1660) enters Tongkin (present-day North Vietnam).

1628

June 29: Miguel de Molinos, Spanish priest, is born. He is condemned for teaching Quietism, the view that only contemplation, not action, can lead to perfection. Dies 1696.

October 28: La Rochelle surrenders to the troops of Cardinal Richelieu (◀ 1627); its population has declined from 27,000 to 5000. The Huguenots lose their territorial and political rights, but keep the freedom of religion granted by the Edict of Nantes (◀ 1598).

November 28: John Bunyan is born. An English Baptist minister, he is famous for *The Pilgrim's Progress* (▶ 1678). Dies 1688.

Codex Alexandrinus, a fifth-century Greek text of the Bible, is presented to King Charles I of England by the Patriarch of Constantinople.

1629

June 30: Samuel Skelton is elected first pastor of Salem, Massachusetts. His congregation is the first Congregational church in America.

August 19: Pierre de Bérulle (◀ 1575) dies.

After intervening unsuccessfully in the Thirty Years War, in the Edict of Lübeck King Christian IV of Denmark is allowed to keep his territory, provided that he does not intervene further.

Emperor Ferdinand II (◀ 1619) promulgates an Edict of Restitution which directs Protestants to restore to Catholics all property taken since the treaty of Passau (◀ 1552).

1630

September 17: John Winthrop, an English Puritan, arrives in Shawmut, Massachusetts, with 1000 settlers. He names it Boston after his English home town.

October: John Tillotson, Anglican preacher and Archbishop of Canterbury (▶ 1691), is born. Dies 1694.

1631

March 31: John Donne (◀ 1571/72) dies.

September: King Gustavus Adolphus of Sweden, who has entered the Thirty Years War, defeats the army of the Habsburg Empire at Breitenfeld near Leipzig.

1632

June: A royal charter is posthumously granted to George Calvert, First Baron Baltimore, to establish a province of Maryland to be a haven for persecuted Roman Catholics.

♣ August 29: John Locke (▶ 1689), English philosopher, is born. He helps to lay the foundation for liberal democracy and combines his empiricism with a Christian rationalism. Dies 1704.

♣ 🏛 October 20: Christopher Wren is born. The greatest architect of his day, he is responsible for rebuilding St Paul's Cathedral after the Great Fire of London (▶ 1666) and building 52 London churches, as well as many secular buildings. Dies 1723.

♣ November 24: Benedict de Spinoza (▶ 1670), Dutch Jewish philosopher, is born. His *Tractatus Theologico-Politicus* (▶ 1670) shows him to be a forerunner of biblical criticism. Dies 1677.

After a series of rebellions, Emperor Susenyos (◀ 1622) proclaims freedom of worship in Ethiopia. He then resigns in favour of his son Fasiladas (▶ 1636).

The Presbyterian John Eliot becomes pastor of Roxbury, Massachusetts, and learns the language of the Pequot tribe of the Iroquois (▶ 1651).

📖 Antonio Bosio (◀ 1593), *Roma sotterranea*, marks the beginning of Christian archaeology.

1633

♣ March 1: George Herbert (◀ 1593) dies.

♛ June 18: Charles I (◀ 1625) is crowned King of Scotland.

June 22: Galileo (◀ 1564) is condemned for a second time (◀ 1616) and under threat of torture is forced to recant his views.

✠ August 4: George Abbot, Archbishop of Canterbury (◀ 1611), dies.

✠ September 19: William Laud (◀ 1573), Bishop of London, is appointed Archbishop of Canterbury (▶ 1640) and starts a programme of reform to make the Church of England more catholic, particularly in its ceremonial.

✠ October 1: Philaret, Patriarch of Moscow (◀ 1619), dies.

♣ October: Robert Browne (◀ c.1550) dies.

Cyril Lucaris, Patriarch of Alexandria, publishes a controversial Confession of Faith in Geneva. It appears in both Latin and Greek and surprisingly puts great emphasis on justification by faith alone.

A group of London Separatists in Southwark led by Henry Jacob begin to practise believers' baptism by immersion. They call themselves Particular Baptists and have basically Calvinist views.

Vincent de Paul and Louise de Marillac found the Daughters of Charity in Paris, the first community of non-cloistered sisters, to work among the poor.

King Charles I reissues the *Book of Sports* (◀ 1618); it provokes great protest (▶ 1643).

1634

Pentecost: A Passion Play is given for the first time by the villagers of Oberammergau in Austria in thanksgiving for deliverance from the plague.

Joasaph, Archbishop of Pskov and Velikiye Luki, is appointed Patriarch of Moscow (▶ 1640).

The Jesuit priest Andrew White and two colleagues land on St Clement Island in southern Maryland with a group of Protestant and Catholic settlers.

1635

January 23: Philipp Jakob Spener, German Pietist, is born. His best-known work is *Pia Desideria* (Pious Desires). Dies 1705.

Roger Williams, an English dissenter, founds Providence, Rhode Island (▶ 1638).

1636

Congregationalists found Harvard College.

Emperor Fasiladas of Ethiopia (◀ 1632) makes Gondar a royal city and centre of Orthodoxy, with a palace, a cathedral and many churches.

1637

February 13: Ferdinand II, Holy Roman Emperor (◀ 1619), dies and is succeeded by his son Ferdinand III (▶ 1657).

July 23: The introduction of a new prayer book for the Church of Scotland modelled on the English Book of Common Prayer leads to riots in St Giles' Cathedral, Edinburgh.

July: Thomas Ken is born. An Anglican bishop, he refuses to sign James II's Declaration of Indulgence (▶ 1687) allowing freedom of worship to Non-conformists or an oath of allegiance to William of Orange (▶ 1688), and as a Non-juror is deposed from office. He is the author of the hymn 'Glory to thee, my God, this night'. Dies 1711.

December 4: Nicholas Ferrar (◀ 1592) dies.

December 17: In Japan the Shimabara Rebellion (▶ 1638) begins, opposing the Shogun's suppression of Christianity.

Thomas Traherne, English mystical poet, is born. Dies 1674.

René Descartes (◀ 1596, ▶ 1650), *Discourse on Method*, is published; it contains his famous '*Cogito ergo sum*: I think, therefore I am.'

For his attacks on the court, the Puritan William Prynne (◀ 1600) is sentenced to have his ears cut off and be branded (▶ 1669).

The first Dutch translation of the Bible from Hebrew and Greek, the *Statenvertaling*, appears.

The Diocese of Caracas, Venezuela, is founded.

1638

February 19: King Charles I issues a proclamation enforcing the new Scottish prayer book (◀ 1637). This leads to rebellion against the crown.

February 28: Large numbers of nobles, clergy and others gather at Greyfriars Churchyard, Edinburgh, to sign a National Covenant.

April 15: The Shimabara Rebellion (◀ 1637) ends. Reprisals against rebels are severe, Portuguese traders are expelled from Japan and Christianity is effectively wiped out there (▶ 1873).

✦ May 6: Cornelius Otto Jansen (◀ 1585) dies.

▢ William Chillingworth, *The Religion of Protestants a Safe Way to Salvation*, argues that the Bible is the sole authority in matters of religion and that its interpretation must be left to the individual.

Roger Williams founds a Baptist church at Providence, Rhode Island (◀ 1635, ▶ 1644), the first in America.

1639

March: King Charles I rides north to lead a campaign against the rebel Scots with a largely untrained army (the First Bishops' War).

June 19: Faced with a far more skilled Army of the Covenant, which has seized ports and strongholds against Scotland, King Charles I signs the Pacification of Berwick, agreeing to Scots demands for a free assembly and parliament.

August 30: The National Covenant (◀ 1638) is passed by the Scottish General Assembly: it binds its signatories to maintain that form of church government most in accord with God's will (Presbyterianism).

October 31: At the Battle of the Downs a victory of the Dutch fleet under Maarten Tromp over the Spanish fleet finally brings Spanish naval dominance to an end.

Matthew de Castro arrives in India as the first apostolic vicar (◀ 1623).

1640

August 20: Scottish forces cross the River Tweed to meet an army sent against them and advance as far as Newcastle, which they occupy. A truce is signed in Ripon and King Charles I agrees to hold a new parliament.

William Laud, Archbishop of Canterbury (◀ 1633, ▶ 1645), is arrested for high treason.

☦ Joasaph, Patriarch of Moscow (◀ 1634), dies.

📖 Cornelis Otto Jansen (◀ 1638), *Augustinus*, is published posthumously.

After the banishment or execution of many Ethiopian Catholics, the last surviving Jesuits are executed.

A Presbyterian church is organized at Southampton, Long Island, the first Presbyterian church in the USA.

The Bay Psalm Book, an English metrical translation produced by Congregationalists in Cambridge, Massachusetts, is the first book printed in the English-speaking colonies of North America.

1641

October 23: Gaelic Irish Catholics rebel against the Ulster Plantation (◀ 1607) and massacre many settlers.

November 22: The so-called Long Parliament approves a Grand Remonstrance listing all its grievances against King Charles I and calling for the setting up of an Assembly of Divines to supervise the reform of the church.

1642

♠ January 8: Galileo Galilei (◀ 1564) dies.

July 4: Parliament forms a Committee of Public Safety to prepare for war.

Summer: 10,000 Scottish Covenanter soldiers arrive in Ulster to put down the Irish rebellion. However, the outbreak of the English Civil War prevents this (▶ 1649).

August 22: King Charles I unfurls his standard at Nottingham; this marks the beginning of the English Civil War (▶ 1646).

September: The Synod of Jassy (in Moldavia) is held, the most important Orthodox Church council since the fall of Constantinople in 1453 (▶ 1672). It endorses an authoritative confession of faith, drafted by Peter Moghila, Metropolitan of Kiev.

♠ December 25: Isaac Newton, English mathematician and physicist, is born. Dies 1727.

☩ Joseph is appointed Patriarch of Moscow (▶ 1652).

The Society of Saint-Sulpice (Sulpicians) in Paris is founded by Jean-Jacques Olier (◀ 1608, ▶ 1657).

The first complete translation of the Bible into Finnish is published (◀ 1548).

1643

♛ May 14: Louis XIII, King of France (◀ 1610), dies and is succeeded by Louis XIV (▶ 1714).

♠ August 20: Anne Hutchinson (◀ 1591) dies.

September 25: The Assembly of Westminster, summoned by Parliament, approves a Solemn League and Covenant, an agreement between the English and Scottish

Parliaments, aiming to uphold the Presbyterian Church of Scotland and reform the Church of England.

✿ September 27: Solomon Stoddard, Congregational pastor and theologian, is born. For 60 years he is a revivalist preacher in Northampton, Massachusetts, and he is the first librarian of Harvard College (◀ 1636). Dies 1729.

✿ October 11: Abbé de Saint-Cyran (◀ 1581) dies.

✿ ♪ November 29: Claudio Monteverdi (◀ 1567) dies.

📖 Antoine Arnauld, *On Frequent Communion*, with its rigorist approach, propagates Jansenist (◀ 1585) principles and infuriates the Jesuits.

The first volumes of the *Acta Sanctorum* (Acts of the Saints) are published by the Bollandists, Jesuits led by Jan van Bolland. Their work continues until 1794.

The Book of Sports (◀ 1618, 1633) is burned by the English Parliament.

1644

March 24: Roger Williams is granted an official charter for his Rhode Island colony (◀ 1638).

June: Fulin becomes the first Qing emperor of China when the Manchus capture Beijing, ruling as Shunzhi Emperor (▶ 1661).

☩ July 29: Pope Urban VIII (◀ 1623) dies.

☩ September 15: Cardinal Giambattista Pamfili, a diplomat, is elected as Pope Innocent X (▶ 1655).

✿ October 14: William Penn (▶ 1681), Quaker and founder of Pennsylvania, is born. Dies 1718.

The celebration of Christmas in Britain is forbidden by Act of Parliament.

Johann Adam Schall von Bell, a German Jesuit, is appointed Director of the Chinese Bureau of Astronomy. He becomes a key figure in the growth of the church.

1645

✿ January 10: William Laud, Archbishop of Canterbury (◀ 1633, 1640), is executed for alleged 'popery'. No successor is appointed (▶ 1660).

✿ January 23: Mary Ward (◀ 1585) dies.

February 6: The General Assembly of the Church of Scotland approves the Directory of Public Worship, a Presbyterian replacement for the Book of Common Prayer.

May: Twelve Italian and Spanish Capuchin missionaries arrive in M'banza Soyo, Kongo.

✿ August 29: Hugo Grotius (◀ 1583) dies.

1646

May 5: King Charles I surrenders to the Scots at Southwell, Nottinghamshire.

June 25: Parliamentarian forces capture Oxford. This marks the end of the English Civil War.

July 1: Gottfried Wilhelm von Leibniz, German philosopher, is born. He explains the world in terms of single substances, 'monads', each of which has an infinite substance. His optimistic views are satirized by Voltaire in his book *Candide* (▶ 1759). Dies 1716.

1647

August 27: The Westminster Confession, a Presbyterian statement of doctrine and church order for the British Isles, is ratified.

September 6: A book by John Biddle, master of the free school at Gloucester, entitled 'XII Arguments' (against the Holy Spirit), is burned by the hangman. His followers are known variously as Biddellians, Socinians or Unitarians (see p.342).

Pierre Bayle is born. A French Protestant, he argues that faith cannot be justified by reason and his scepticism influences the Enlightenment. His *Dictionnaire Historique et Critique* (▶ 1695–97) anticipates Diderot's *Encyclopédie* (▶ 1713). Dies 1706.

George Fox (◀ 1624, ▶ 1669) founds the Religious Society of Friends ('Quakers').

1648

January 30: The Treaty of Münster recognizes the independence of the princes of the Netherlands.

February 8: A feast in honour of the Immaculate Heart of Mary is first celebrated in Autun, France.

April 13: Jeanne-Marie Bouvier de la Mothe Guyon ('Madame Guyon'), French mystic and champion of Quietism, is born. Dies 1717.

August 5: Edward Herbert of Cherbury (◀ 1583) dies.

October 24: The Peace of Westphalia ends the Thirty Years War (◀ 1618).

November 12: Sor Juana Inés de la Cruz, nun and scholar, is born. She is barred from studying at the University of Mexico (◀ 1551) but shows her brilliance in a convent and champions women's rights to education. Dies 1695.

December 23: Robert Barclay, Scottish theologian and apologist, is born. Dies 1690.

Lancelot Andrewes (◀ 1555), *Private Prayers,* is published.

1649

January 30: King Charles I of England and Scotland (◀ 1625, 1646) is beheaded. He is subsequently regarded by some as a martyr and between 1662 and 1859 there is a special commemorative service for this day in the Book of Common Prayer.

> **The Enlightenment**
>
> The term Enlightenment is used for a period between 1650 and 1800 when groups of intellectuals emerge who emphasize rationality, freedom of thought and the scientific investigation of nature. Reacting against the conflicts that religion has brought to Europe, in the wake of the Peace of Westphalia (◀ 1648), which puts an end to the Wars of Religion, they advance new ideas about God and human nature, and emphasize progress. In Britain, John Locke (◀ 1632) is a prominent advocate of the toleration which now becomes more widespread, making radical debate possible.
>
> Prominent among British Enlightenment thinkers are the Deists, who believe that while God is the ultimate source of reality he does not intervene in the natural course of events; following Lord Edward Herbert of Cherbury (◀ 1583), leading figures are Matthew Tindal (▶ 1655), John Toland (▶ 1670) and Anthony Collins (▶ 1676). They are criticized by Bishop Joseph Butler (▶ 1692), but his approach is challenged by the scepticism of David Hume (▶ 1711), whose critique of miracles strikes at a cornerstone of Christian apologetic.
>
> In France the champion of toleration is Pierre Bayle (▶ 1647); Voltaire (▶ 1694) is a leading figure, followed by Denis Diderot (▶ 1713) with his *Encyclopédie*, a representative of a group known as the *philosophes*. In Germany Christian Wolff (▶ 1679) and Johann Salomo Semler (▶ 1726) incur the hostility of the Pietists with their rationalist approach. Gotthold Ephraim Lessing (▶ 1729) is responsible for beginning the quest for the historical Jesus with his posthumous publication of works by Hermann Samuel Reimarus (▶ 1694); his play *Nathan the Wise* (▶ 1779) champions religious toleration in the face of the dogmatism of revealed religion.

♦ March 16: Jean de Brébeuf (◀ 1625) is killed when Iroquois Indians destroy his mission station among the Hurons (▶ 1930).

August: Oliver Cromwell (▶ 1653) lands in Ireland to regain control from the Catholics (◀ 1642). He does so with great brutality.

1650

♦ February 11: René Descartes (◀ 1596) dies.

📖 Jeremy Taylor (◀ 1613, ▶ 1667), *Holy Living*, is published. It is a classic devotional manual and is followed the next year by *Holy Dying*.

In his *Annales Veteris et Novi Testamenti* Archbishop James Ussher of Dublin calculates the date of creation as being at nightfall preceding Sunday, October 23, 4004 BC.

1651

♦ August 6: François de Salignac de la Mothe Fénélon, French Catholic mystic and Quietist, is born. Dies 1715.

John Eliot (◀ 1632) baptizes the first Iroquois converts. He founds Natick, Massachusetts, the first of a series of 'praying towns' (▶ 1663).

1652

☦ April 15: Joseph, Patriarch of Moscow (◀ 1642), dies.

May 31: In the bull *Cum occasione*, Pope Innocent X condemns views expressed in Jansen's *Augustinus* (◀ 1640).

August 1: Nikon, a monk from Novgorod, is appointed Patriarch of Moscow (▶ 1658). He goes on to require the Russian Orthodox Church to follow the texts and practices of the Greek Church as they exist in 1652 along with reforms on the Greek model, on the grounds that Russian liturgical books are corrupt. This gives rise to the Old Believers (▶ 1666/67), those who will not accept his reforms; they become quite numerous.

Jan van Riebeeck fortifies a site at the Cape of Good Hope as a station on the way to the East Indies and establishes a farming community.

1653

December 16: Oliver Cromwell (◀ 1649, ▶ 1655) becomes Lord Protector of England (▶ 1658).

James Naylor, a Quaker, is persuaded by his followers that he is a reincarnation of Christ. This leads to a movement called the Fifth Monarchy Men.

Antonio Vieira (◀ 1608, ▶ 1697) returns to Brazil, where he grew up, and works for the welfare of the negro slaves and American Indians there. He encounters much opposition.

1654

Blaise Pascal (◀ 1623, ▶ 1662) is converted to Christianity by a mystical experience.

1655

January 1: Pope Innocent X (◀ 1644) dies.

April 7: Fabio Chigi, papal nuncio in Cologne, is elected as Pope Alexander VII (▶ 1667).

November 24: Oliver Cromwell (◀ 1653, ▶ 1658) prohibits Anglican services in England.

December 18: Oliver Cromwell readmits Jews to England (◀ 1290).

Matthew Tindal, English Deist, is born. His best-known book is *Christianity as Old as the Creation* (1730), which is translated into German and influences German theology. Dies 1733.

The University of Kiel, Germany, is founded to train priests and government officials, the northernmost university in the Holy Roman Empire.

The English Parliament passes the last of three Acts which prohibit any kind of recreation on a Sunday. These are not repealed until the restoration of the monarchy (▶ 1660).

1656

January 16: Robert de Nobili (◀ 1577) dies.

Thomas Bray, founder of the Society for the Promotion of Christian Knowledge (▶ 1698) and the Society for the Propagation of the Gospel in Foreign Parts (▶ 1701), is born. Dies 1730.

The Dominican Luo Wenzao (Gregorio Lopes) is ordained as the first Chinese Catholic priest. He later becomes the only Chinese bishop consecrated in China before the twentieth century.

1657

♛ April 2: Ferdinand III, Holy Roman Emperor (◀ 1637), dies.

♟ April 2: Jean-Jacques Olier (◀ 1608) dies.

♛ July: Leopold I, son of Ferdinand III, becomes Holy Roman Emperor (▶ 1705).

1658

☦ July 19: Nikon, Patriarch of Moscow (◀ 1652), who has lost the support of the Tsar, resigns. Pitirim of Krutitsy (▶ 1672) acts in his place but is not initially elected patriarch (▶ 1667).

♟ September 3: Oliver Cromwell (◀ 1655) dies. He is succeeded as Lord Protector by his third son Richard, who resigns the next year.

The Dutch drive the Portuguese out of Ceylon (▶ 1795).

1660

May 8: The English Parliament proclaims that King Charles II has been the lawful monarch of England and Scotland since the execution of Charles I (◀ 1649).

☦ September 20: William Juxon, Bishop of London, who attended King Charles I on the scaffold (◀ 1649), is appointed Archbishop of Canterbury after a vacancy of 15 years (▶ 1663).

♟ September 27: Vincent de Paul (◀ 1580) dies (▶ 1737).

♟ November 5: Alexandre de Rhodes (◀ 1591) dies.

📖 Margaret Fell (◀ 1614, ▶ 1669) publishes a pamphlet, *Women's Speaking Justified, Proved and Allowed by the Scriptures*.

1661

February 5: Shunzhi Emperor (◀ 1644) dies and is succeeded by his eight-year-old son Xuanye, who rules as Kangxi Emperor (▶ 1698).

April 15–July 24: A conference is held at the Savoy in the Strand, London, consisting of bishops and Presbyterian divines, to review the Book of Common Prayer.

♛ April 23: Charles II, son of King Charles I, is crowned king (▶ 1685).

December 10: The convocations of Canterbury and York approve the new Book of Common Prayer.

♟🏛 Nicholas Hawksmoor, English architect, is born. A pupil of Sir Christopher Wren (◀ 1632), he is particularly known for building six fine London churches. Dies 1736.

1662

May 19: An Act of Uniformity requires all Church of England services to be from the new Book of Common Prayer (◀ 1661).

August 18: Blaise Pascal (◀ 1623, ▶ 1670) dies.

The Chinese drive the Dutch out of Formosa (◀ 1626).

1663

February 12: Cotton Mather, Puritan minister, the most famous of the New English Puritans, is born. Dies 1728.

March 22: August Hermann Francke is born. A friend of Philipp Jakob Spener (◀ 1635), he becomes professor of theology at Halle University (▶ 1694) and contributes towards making it a centre of Pietism. Dies 1727.

June 4: William Juxon, Archbishop of Canterbury (◀ 1660), dies.

August 31: Gilbert Sheldon, Bishop of London, is appointed Archbishop of Canterbury (▶ 1677); he builds the Sheldonian Theatre in Oxford at his own expense.

The Catholic Society of Foreign Missions of Paris is founded for the evangelization of infidel countries and the founding of churches.

John Eliot (◀ 1651) translates the Bible into Algonquin, the first American Bible edition.

1664

May 17: The Conventicles Act, against Non-conformists, forbids meetings of more than five people (except for Church of England worship).

1665

April 19: François de Sales (◀ 1610) is canonized by Pope Alexander VII: feast day January 24.

September 17: Felipe IV, King of Spain (◀ 1621), dies and is succeeded by Carlos II (▶ 1700).

October 30: The army of the Kongo is defeated by the Portuguese in the battle of Mbwila; King António I and many of the Christian ruling class are killed and the kingdom is shattered.

October: The Five Mile Act prevents clergy from living within five miles of a parish from which they have been banned. This means that Non-conformist ministers cannot serve in towns.

Johann van Arkel arrives at the Cape of Good Hope (◀ 1652), the first Dutch Reformed Church minister in South Africa.

Old St Paul's at the beginning of the seventeenth century; it was burned down in the Great Fire of London, 1666

1666

🏛 Old St Paul's Cathedral is destroyed in the Great Fire of London.

The first Armenian Bible is printed.

1666/67

A council endorses Nikon's reforms (◀ 1652) and excommunicates the Old Believers, some of whom are executed.

1667

⚜ May 22: Pope Alexander VII (◀ 1655) dies.

⚜ June 20: Giulio Rospigliosi, secretary of state and cardinal, is elected as Pope Clement IX (▶ 1669).

🌿 August 13: Jeremy Taylor (◀ 1613) dies.

⚜ Joasaph II becomes Patriarch of Moscow (▶ 1672).

🏛 The cathedral in Mexico City is consecrated (◀ 1563).

🏛 The piazza of St Peter's, Rome, is completed.

📖 John Milton (◀ 1608, ▶ 1674), *Paradise Lost*, is published.

1669

🌿🖼 October 4: Rembrandt van Rijn (◀ 1606) dies.

🌿 October 24: William Prynne (◀ 1600) dies.

317

October 27: Margaret Fell (◀ 1660, ▶ 1702) marries George Fox (◀ 1647, ▶ 1691).

✠ December 9: Pope Clement IX (◀ 1667) dies.

1670

✠ April 29: Emilio Altieri, an expert adviser to the papacy, is elected as Pope Clement X (▶ 1676).

♣ November 15: John Amos Comenius (◀ 1592) dies.

♣📖 November 30: John Toland, Deist, is born. His best-known book is *Christianity not Mysterious* (1696). Dies 1722.

📖 Blaise Pascal (◀ 1662), *Pensées,* are published posthumously.

📖 Benedict de Spinoza (◀ 1632, ▶ 1667), *Tractatus Theologico-politicus,* is a pioneering work of biblical criticism.

The feast of the Sacred Heart is celebrated for the first time at the Grand Seminary of Rennes in France.

1671

✪ Fernando III, King of Castile and Leon (◀ 1252), is canonized by Pope Clement X: feast day July 30.

The first edition of the Bible in Arabic is printed in Rome.

Quakers pioneer missionary work in Jamaica.

1672

♣ May 1: Joseph Addison, English politician and writer, is born. His poetry includes hymns such as 'The spacious firmament on high'. Dies 1719.

May 17: The Jesuit Jacques Marquette begins his exploration of the Mississippi River with the trader Louis Joliet. They follow the river almost to the Gulf of Mexico and return to Lake Michigan, where Marquette founds a mission on the site of present-day Chicago.

♣♫ November 6: Heinrich Schütz (◀ 1585) dies.

✠ Joasaph II, Patriarch of Moscow (◀ 1667), dies and is succeeded by Pitirim of Krutitsy (◀ 1658, ▶ 1673).

The Synod of Jerusalem, the most important modern council of the Orthodox Church, is held; it too produces a confession of faith (◀ 1642), drafted by Dositheus, Patriarch of Jerusalem.

1673

March 29: The English Parliament passes the Test Act, excluding Roman Catholics from public office.

✠ Pitirim of Krutitsy, Patriarch of Moscow (◀ 1672), dies.

✝ Pope Leo III (◀ 816) is canonized by Pope Clement X: feast day June 12.

1674

July 13: Smolensk Cathedral (◀ 1101) is demolished because of its decrepit state.

🌱 July 17: Isaac Watts, Non-conformist hymn writer, is born. His hymns include 'When I survey the wondrous cross' and 'O God, our help in ages past'. Dies 1748.

🌱 September 27: Thomas Traherne (◀ 1637) dies.

🌱 November 8: John Milton (◀ 1608) dies.

✪ Joachim becomes Patriarch of Moscow (▶ 1690).

The Diocese of Quebec is founded.

1675

🏛 June 21: The foundation stone of Christopher Wren's new St Paul's Cathedral (◀ 1666) is laid (▶ 1708).

🌱 Jean-Pierre de Caussade, spiritual writer, is born. He is famous for his *Self-Abandonment to Divine Providence* (▶ 1860). Dies 1751.

1676

🌱 June 7: Paul Gerhard (◀ 1607) dies.

🌱📖 June 21: Anthony Collins, English Deist, is born. His *Discourse on Freethinking* (1713) questions the authority of the Bible. Dies 1729.

✪ July 22: Pope Clement X (◀ 1670) dies.

✪ September 21: Benedetto Odescalchi, retired as Bishop of Novara because of ill health, is elected as Pope Innocent XI (▶ 1689).

November 16: The Archdiocese of San Salvador is founded, and dioceses in Recife and Rio de Janeiro.

1677

🌱 February 21: Benedict de Spinoza (◀ 1632) dies.

✪ November 9: Gilbert Sheldon, Archbishop of Canterbury (◀ 1663), dies.

The Diocese of São Luiz da Maranhão, covering north Brazil, is created.

1678

✪ January 27: William Sancroft, Dean of St Paul's, is appointed Archbishop of Canterbury (▶ 1689).

📖 February: John Bunyan (◀ 1628), *The Pilgrim's Progress*, is published.

🌱🎵 March 4: Antonio Vivaldi, Venetian composer, is born. He writes a large number of choral works as well as operas and the concerti for which he is best known. Dies 1741.

Jean-Baptiste De La Salle (▶ 1900) founds the Institute of the Brothers of the Christian Schools (De La Salle Brothers) and becomes a pioneer in education.

📖 Richard Simon, *A Critical History of the Old Testament*, argues that Moses did not write the books of the Bible traditionally attributed to him.

1679

🌱 January 24: Christian Wolff, German philosopher, is born. He becomes a professor at Halle University (▶ 1694), where his emphasis on human reason leads to a clash with the Pietists dominant there and he loses his chair; however, he returns on the accession of his admirer Friedrich II, King of Prussia (Frederick the Great, ▶ 1740). Dies 1754.

1680

🌱◼ November 28: Gian Lorenzo Bernini (◀ 1598) dies.

The first translation of the Old Testament into Irish is printed (◀ 1602).

1681

March 4: King Charles II grants a land charter to the Quaker William Penn (◀ 1644) for the area which now includes Pennsylvania. He intends it to become an ideal commonwealth for all persecuted people.

☿ July 1: Oliver Plunket, Archbishop of Armagh, is executed for treason at Tyburn, in London, the last Catholic to suffer this fate (▶ 1975).

1682

March 19: The Gallican Articles in France list the rights and privileges claimed by the French clergy.

October 27: In Pennsylvania, William Penn (◀ 1681, ▶ 1718) founds Philadelphia, 'the city of brotherly love', laid out on a simple grid plan.

🌱🏛 James Gibbs, British architect, is born. In addition to the Radcliffe Camera in Oxford, his buildings include St Mary-le-Strand and St Martin-in-the-Fields, London. Dies 1753.

1683

July 14: An Ottoman army besieges Vienna (◀ 1529).

September 11/12: An army of the Habsburgs and their allies defeats the Turks and raises the siege.

1684

🌱 March 29: Jean Astruc, French Roman Catholic physician, is born. Seen as one of the founders of modern biblical criticism, he argues that Moses made use of earlier documents in writing Genesis. Dies 1766.

1685

👑 February 6: King Charles II of England and Scotland (◀ 1660) dies and is succeeded by his brother, a Catholic, as King James II (▶ 1688).

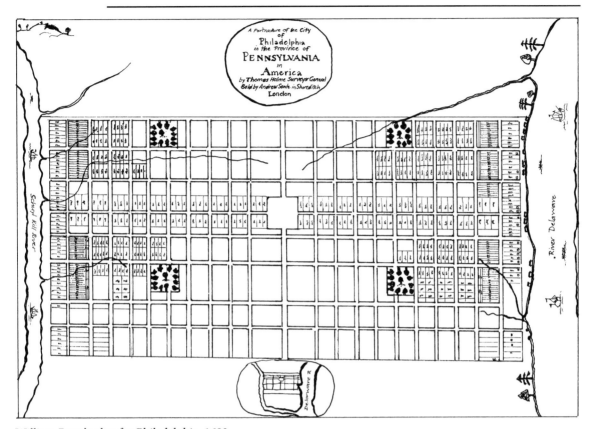

William Penn's plan for Philadelphia, 1682

♦♪ February 23: George Frideric Handel, composer, is born. In addition to *Messiah* (▶ 1742) he writes oratorios centred on many biblical characters and writes much church music. Dies 1759.

♦ March 12: George Berkeley, Irish philosopher, is born. He later becomes Bishop of Cloyne. Dies 1753.

♦♪ March 21: Johann Sebastian Bach, German composer, is born. As well as his best-known works, the *St Matthew Passion* and the *B Minor Mass*, he writes a wealth of organ music, a *St John Passion*, a *Christmas Oratorio*, a *Magnificat* and more than 200 church cantatas. Dies 1750.

October 18: The Edict of Nantes (◀ 1598) is revoked under Louis XIV of France, spurring Protestant migration to America.

Lambeth House (◀ 1207) is renamed Lambeth Palace.

1686

♦ William Law, English mystic, is born. His best known book is *A Serious Call to a Devout and Holy Life* (▶ 1728). Dies 1761.

321

June: King James II disregards the Test Act (◀ 1673) and appoints Roman Catholics to public office.

1687

April 4: King James II issues a Declaration of Indulgence, granting freedom of worship to all.

French Jesuits sent by King Louis XIV arrive in China and work on its geography (◀ 1717).

The Three Hours Devotion on Good Friday is introduced in Lima, Peru, by Fr Alphonsia Messia SJ.

1688

January 29: Emanuel Swedenborg, Swedish philosopher, is born (he is called Svedberg until 1719). He argues the need for a new church as a spiritual brotherhood. The Swedenborgian church is founded after his death in 1772.

June 10: James II has a son, James Francis Edward Stuart (known as the Old Pretender), arousing fears of a Catholic dynasty in Britain.

June 30: Seven Whig (liberal) politicians invite William of Orange, grandson of King Charles I (◀ 1649), to become King of England. He accepts the invitation on September 30.

August 31: John Bunyan (◀ 1628) dies.

November 5: William of Orange lands in England at Brixham.

December 25: King James II (◀ 1685) flees to France.

The Bible is translated into Romanian (the Bible of Bucharest).

The New Testament is translated into Malay (the first Bible translation into a South-East Asian language).

1689

February 12: William of Orange (▶ 1702) and his wife Mary, daughter of James II (▶ 1694), are declared joint monarchs.

August 1: William Sancroft, Archbishop of Canterbury (◀ 1678, ▶ 1690), refuses to recognize William of Orange as king and is suspended from office.

August 12: Pope Innocent XI (◀ 1676) dies.

October: Pietro Ottoboni, Grand Inquisitor and Secretary of the Holy Office, is elected as Pope Alexander VIII (▶ 1691).

The Toleration Act allows Protestant Non-conformists to practise in their own places of worship.

John Locke (◀ 1632, ▶ 1695), *Letters Concerning Toleration* (also 1690, 1692), argues for religious freedom for all except atheists and Roman Catholics.

1690

February 1: William Sancroft, Archbishop of Canterbury (◀ 1678, 1689), is deprived of office.

October 3: Robert Barclay (◀ 1648) dies.

Joachim, Patriarch of Moscow (◀ 1674), dies and is succeeded by Adrian, the last pre-revolutionary patriarch (▶ 1702).

The Diocese of Nanjing, China, is founded.

1691

January 13: George Fox (◀ 1624) dies.

February 1: Pope Alexander VIII (◀ 1689) dies.

May 31: John Tillotson, Dean of St Paul's (◀ 1630), is appointed Archbishop of Canterbury. He is a fierce opponent of the Roman Catholic Church and a famous preacher (▶ 1694).

July 12: Antonio Pignatelli, Archbishop of Naples, is elected as Pope Innocent XII (▶ 1700).

December 8: Richard Baxter (◀ 1615) dies.

1692

May 18: Joseph Butler, bishop and moral philosopher, is born. His best-known book is *The Analogy of Religion, Natural and Revealed* (1736). Dies 1752.

June 2: Witchcraft trials begin to be held in Salem, Massachusetts. 300 men and women are accused, 20 executed.

Emperor Kangxi of China (◀ 1661, ▶ 1698) issues an unlimited edict of toleration of Christianity.

1693

A group led by Joseph Amman break away from the Mennonites (◀ 1536) in Switzerland and South Germany and become known as Amish. They later emigrate to America.

The College of William and Mary is founded in Williamsburg, Virginia, by royal decree.

1694

November 20: Voltaire, French philosopher and writer (▶ 1759), is born. Dies 1778.

November 22: John Tillotson, Archbishop of Canterbury (◀ 1691), dies.

December 22: Hermann Samuel Reimarus, German deist and biblical critic, is born. Writings of his posthumously published by Lessing (▶ 1729) mark the start of the quest of the historical Jesus. Dies 1768.

323

♛ December 28: Queen Mary II of England (◀ 1689) dies.

The University of Halle is founded by Pietists. It plays a major role in sending missionaries to North America.

1695

⚕ January 16: Thomas Tenison, Bishop of Lincoln, is appointed Archbishop of Canterbury (▶ 1715). He plays a major role in the founding of the Society for the Propagation of the Gospel in Foreign Parts (▶ 1701).

♟ April 17: Sor Juana Inés de la Cruz (◀ 1648) dies of the plague.

♟ April 23: Henry Vaughan (◀ 1622) dies.

Between 1695 and 1795 there are 31 Patriarchs of Constantinople involving 23 individuals, a slight improvement on the seventeenth century (◀ 1596), but the financial demands made by the Turkish authorities remain (▶ 1789).

📖 John Locke (◀ 1689, ▶ 1704), *The Reasonableness of Christianity,* maintains that the only firm basis for Christianity is its reasonableness.

1696

♟ September 27: Alphonsus Liguori (▶ 1732), Catholic moral theologian, is born. He founds religious orders for men and women, the Redemptorists and the Redemptorines. Dies 1787.

♟ December 28: Miguel de Molinos (◀ 1628) dies.

Nahum Tate and Nicholas Brady publish the first edition of *A New Version of the Psalms of David.*

1697

♟ July 18: Antonio Vieira (◀ 1608) dies.

The Irish Parliament passes the Banishment Act, banishing all Roman Catholic bishops from Ireland in order to protect the Church of Ireland.

1698

The Society for the Promotion of Christian Knowledge is founded by Thomas Bray (◀ 1656, ▶ 1701).

The Jesuits, supported by Kangxi Emperor (◀ 1692), petition Pope Innocent XII to allow Chinese converts to pay cult to ancestors and celebrate the mass in Chinese ('Chinese Rifes') (▶ 1704).

1700

January 1: Russia adopts the Julian calendar (◀ 1582, ▶ 1918).

February 18: Denmark, Norway and the German Protestant states adopt the Gregorian calendar.

- May 26: Nicholas Ludwig, Count von Zinzendorf, is born. A Moravian Pietist, he founds a Christian community which he calls Herrnhut ('the Lord's Watch'). Dies 1760.

- September 27: Pope Innocent XII (◀ 1691) dies.

- October 27: Armand-Jean le Bouthillier de Rancé (◀ 1626) dies.

- November 1: Carlos II, King of Spain (◀ 1665), dies.

- November 23: Cardinal Giovanni Francesco Albani is elected as Pope Clement XI (▶ 1721).

Eighteenth century

This is a century of evangelical revival. In 1730 the First Great Awakening begins in America in Northampton, Massachusetts, from which it spreads through the American colonies. In 1735 William Tennent founds the Log College, north of Philadelphia, to train pastors who will be active in the revival. The same year John and Charles Wesley go to Georgia to work with English settlers, and in 1739 George Whitefield leaves England for a successful mission there. In 1738, John Wesley has a conversion experience in London; the next year he begins to form societies within the Anglican church whose members come to be called Methodists because of their methodical approach to the Bible, and starts to preach in the open air. In 1744 John and Charles Wesley hold the first Methodist Conference, a form of church government which is to last to the present day. The first Methodist missionaries are sent to America in 1769 and the first Conference is held there in 1773. In 1789 the Methodists open the first church publishing house in America. In 1783 a related society of Calvinist churches known as The Countess of Huntingdon's Connexion is founded by Selina, Countess of Huntingdon. The revival also leads to a wealth of hymn-writing, not least by Charles Wesley. In 1779 John Newton and William Cowper produce a famous set of *Olney Hymns*, which contains the classic 'Amazing Grace'.

It is also a century of two revolutions, the American Revolution or War of Independence (from 1775 to 1783) and the French Revolution (from 1789 to 1795). In addition to their immediate political, social and international consequences, both these revolutions produce documents centred on human rights (the US Declaration of Independence and Bill of Rights and the French Declaration of the Rights of Man and the Citizen) which from then on are to have a worldwide influence. Attention begins to focus on the slave trade, which is such a blatant contradiction of these rights. Granville Sharp works tirelessly for its abolition, as does William Wilberforce, but they are not to see the results of their labours until the next century. Denmark becomes the first country to abolish the slave trade, in 1792.

And it is also again a century of Enlightenment. Prompted by the disastrous Lisbon earthquake of 1755, which raises serious questions about the existence of God, Voltaire combats the optimistic view expressed by Leibniz in the previous century that this is the best of all possible worlds in his satire *Candide* (1759). Gottfried Ephraim Lessing writes his play *Nathan the Wise* (1779) with its message of toleration between the religions, as well as publishing the revolutionary writings about Jesus by Hermann Samuel Reimarus. Immanuel Kant writes his *Critique of Pure Reason* (1781), and in his *A View of the Evidences of Christianity* (1794) William Paley argues for the existence of God from the apparent design of the universe. At the very end of the century, in 1799 in his

Speeches on Religion to its Cultured Despisers Friedrich Schleiermacher defends religion against its Enlightenment critics, arguing that it is a sense of the infinite consisting largely in feeling. There is a wealth of music inspired by Christianity, and some by no means unaffected by the Enlightenment: Bach's *St Matthew Passion* (1727) and *B Minor Mass* (1738), Handel's *Messiah* (1742) and many other operas and oratorios on biblical themes, Mozart's *C Minor Mass* (1783) and *Requiem* (unfinished at his death in 1791), and Haydn's *The Creation* (1798).

1701

♠ January 27: Johann Nikolaus von Hontheim is born. Under the pseudonym Justinus Febronius he writes a book attacking the power of the papacy; it leads to a movement, Febronianism. Dies 1790.

June 16: The Society for the Propagation of the Gospel in Foreign Parts is founded by Thomas Bray (◀ 1698, ▶ 1730).

October 16: The Collegiate School, Yale, is founded by conservative Congregationalists; it later becomes Yale University.

An Act of Settlement bans Catholics and those married to Catholics from ascending the English throne.

1702

January 4: Filofey Leschinsky is consecrated Bishop of Tobolsk, the historic capital of Siberia.

♛ March 8: King William III (◀ 1689) of England dies and is succeeded by Queen Anne, daughter of King James II (◀ 1685, ▶ 1714).

♠ April 23: Margaret Fell (◀ 1614) dies.

☿ Adrian, Patriarch of Moscow (◀ 1690), dies.

The Camisards, fanatical French Protestants, revolt in the Cévennes against the Catholic authorities (▶ 1705).

1703

April 4: Filofei, a Russian Orthodox monk from Kiev, is consecrated Metropolitan of Siberia and Tobolsk and leaves with a group of young monks to engage in mission there. He spends the next 20 years travelling the region.

♠ June 17: John Wesley (▶ 1735), founder of Methodism, is born. Dies 1791.

♠ October 5: Jonathan Edwards, American Calvinist theologian and philosopher, is born. Dies 1758.

The Holy Ghost Fathers or Spiritans are founded in Paris by Claude-François Poullart des Places to work in the French colonies.

1704

♠ April 2: Jacques-Bénigne Bossuet (◀ 1627) dies.

♠ October 28: John Locke (◀ 1632) dies.

November 20: Pope Clement XI rules against missionaries allowing Chinese converts to continue the cult of ancestors (◀ 1698, ▶ 1716). In so doing he supports Franciscans and Dominicans against the Jesuits.

1705

♣ February 5: Philipp Jakob Spener (◀ 1635) dies.

♛ May 5: Leopold I, Holy Roman Emperor (◀ 1658), dies and is succeeded by Joseph I (▶ 1710).

The Camisard revolt (◀ 1702) ends.

Archimandrite Martinia arrives on the Kamchatka peninsula and baptizes a number of converts. He is murdered in 1717.

1706

July 9: The Pietist Lutheran missionaries Bartholomaeus Ziegenbalg (▶ 1711) and Heinrich Plutschau arrive in the Danish south Indian territory of Tranquebar to work among the Tamils.

♣ December 28: Pierre Bayle (◀ 1647) dies.

Francis Makemie organizes the first US presbyterian congregation in Philadelphia; he becomes known as the father of Presbyterianism.

1707

May 1: An Act of Union combines England and Scotland in a single kingdom (◀ 1603), Great Britain (▶ 1801).

♣ August 24: Selina, Countess of Huntingdon, the founder of the Calvinist Methodist Countess of Huntingdon's Connexion (▶ 1783), is born. Dies 1791.

♣ December 18: Charles Wesley (▶ 1735), Anglican/Methodist hymn writer and preacher, is born. Dies 1788.

1708

August: Alexander Mack (▶ 1719) baptizes eight persons in the river Eder near Schwarzenau in Germany, marking the beginning of the Brethren Church, an early Baptist church.

🏛 October 20: The new St Paul's Cathedral, London (◀ 1675), is completed.

December 6: In his bull *Commissi nobis*, Pope Clement XI declares the feast of the Immaculate Conception of the Blessed Virgin Mary (▶ 1854) obligatory for all Catholics.

1709/10

Louis XIV destroys the Benedictine Abbey of Port-Royal (◀ 1625), which has been the centre of Jansenism.

1711

♣ March 19: Thomas Ken (◀ 1637) dies.

♛ April 17: Joseph I, Holy Roman Emperor (◀ 1705), dies and is succeeded by his brother Charles VI (▶ 1740).

♟ April 23: David Hume, Scottish philosopher and historian, is born. His philosophy emphasizes probability and experience. Dies 1776.

♟ September 6: Henry Melchior Mühlenberg, German Lutheran clergyman, is born. He founds the first Lutheran synod in America. Dies 1787.

☉ Pope Pius V (◀ 1572) is canonized by Pope Clement XI: feast day April 30.

Bartholomaeus Ziegenbalg (◀ 1706) completes the translation of the New Testament into Tamil (▶ 1740). It is printed in Tranquebar in 1715.

Two Franciscans, Carlo Maria di Genova and Severino da Silesia, cross the Sahara on a mission but die of sickness on reaching Katsina in what is now northern Nigeria.

1713

April 19: The Pragmatic Sanction, a law designed to ensure that Maria Theresa, daughter of Holy Roman Emperor Charles VI, shall succeed him, is enacted (▶ 1745).

September 8: In his bull *Unigenitus Dei filius*, Pope Clement XI condemns 101 propositions supposed to be Jansenist (◀ 1585), including that 'the reading of Holy Scripture is for all'.

♟ Denis Diderot is born. A French philosopher, from 1751 onwards he produces an *Encyclopédie* in 35 volumes aimed at destroying 'superstitions', especially Catholic dogma, and promoting new knowledge, tolerance and freedom of thought. Dies 1784.

1714

♛ August 1: Queen Anne (◀ 1702) dies and is succeeded by George, Duke of Brunswick-Lüneburg as King George I of Great Britain (▶ 1727), the first monarch of the House of Hanover.

♛ September 1: Louis XIV, King of France (◀ 1643), dies and is succeeded by Louis XV (▶ 1774).

♟ December 27: George Whitefield (▶ 1739), English evangelist, is born. Dies 1770.

1715

♟ January 7: François de Salignac de la Mothe Fénélon (◀ 1651) dies.

♘ December 14: Thomas Tenison, Archbishop of Canterbury (◀ 1695), dies.

1716

♘ January 16: William Wake, Bishop of Lincoln, is appointed Archbishop of Canterbury (▶ 1737). He unsuccessfully engages in negotiations with French Catholics with a view to reunion.

July 28: Mary Hicks and her nine-year-old daughter Elizabeth are hanged for witchcraft in Huntingdon, the last such execution in England.

♟ November 14: Gottfried Wilhelm von Leibniz (◀ 1646) dies.

Christian missionaries are banned from China unless they allow the cult of ancestors to be practised by Chinese converts ('Chinese Rites') (▶ 1742).

1717

✝ June 9: Jeanne-Marie Bouvier de la Mothe Guyon (◀ 1648) dies.

Jesuit missionaries under Jean-Baptiste Régis complete the first accurate map of China.

After numerous interruptions in previous decades the Convocations of the Church of England are finally suspended (▶ 1852).

1718

✝ July 30: William Penn (◀ 1644) dies.

1719

March 4: The Diocese of Belem do Para is founded.

✝ Joseph Addison (◀ 1672) dies.

The Jesuits are expelled from Russia.

Alexander Mack (◀ 1708) and his followers emigrate to Pennsylvania.

1720

The Passionists are founded by Paul of the Cross (▶ 1867) to promote devotion to the passion of Christ, chiefly through missionary work.

1721

☫ March 19: Pope Clement XI (◀ 1700) dies.

☫ May 8: Michelangelo dei Conti, Bishop of Viterbo, is elected as Pope Innocent XIII (▶ 1724).

By the Spiritual Regulation, Peter the Great puts the Russian church under the government-controlled Holy Synod and abolishes the Moscow Patriarchate.

1722

✝ March 11: John Toland (◀ 1670) dies.

♛ December 20: Kangxi Emperor (◀ 1698) dies and is succeeded by his son Yinzhen, who rules as Yongzheng Emperor (▶ 1724).

Count Zinzendorf (◀ 1700) founds the Herrnhut colony.

Hans Egede, a Danish missionary from Copenhagen, arrives in Greenland with his wife and family. He stays until 1736.

Lazarist fathers (◀ 1625) begin the evangelization of Mauritius.

1723

✝ February 25: Christopher Wren (◀ 1632) dies.

331

In the wake of a conflict over Jansenism (◀ 1585) the Chapter of Utrecht, acting independently of Rome, elects Cornelius Steenhoven Archbishop of Utrecht. This marks the beginning of the Old Catholic Church in the Netherlands.

1724

⚒ March 7: Pope Innocent XIII (◀ 1721) dies.

♟ April 22: Immanuel Kant (▶ 1781), German philosopher, is born. Dies 1804.

⚒ May 29: A Dominican, Pietro Francesco Orsini, Archbishop of Benevento, is elected as Pope Benedict XIII (▶ 1730).

♟ July 2: Friedrich Gottlieb Klopstock, German religious poet, is born. He writes a religious epic, *Der Messias* (▶ 1773). Dies 1803.

♟ Tikhon of Zadonsk, later Bishop of Voronezh, is born. Deeply pastoral, he helps those in distress and has a deep mystical spirituality. Dies 1783.

Yongzheng Emperor (◀ 1722, ▶ 1735) orders the expulsion of Christian missionaries from China, claiming that they supported his rivals at the time of his accession.

1725

♟ July 25: John Newton, English evangelical, is born. After adventurous early days at sea, he produces a famous set of *Olney Hymns* (▶ 1779), named after Olney, Buckinghamshire, where he lives, and is influential in the evangelical movement. Dies 1807.

♟ Henry Venn, English evangelical, is born. He is one of the founders of the evangelical Clapham Sect. Dies 1797.

1726

♟ December 18: Johann Salomo Semler is born. Professor of theology at Halle University, he is notable as a critic of biblical documents and church dogmas and comes to be called 'the father of German rationalism'. Dies 1791.

⚒ Callinicus III pays a record 5600 gold pounds to be elected to the patriarchate of Constantinople (◀ 1695). He dies of a heart attack the next day.

⚜ John of the Cross (◀ 1591) is canonized by Pope Benedict XIII: feast day December 14.

1727

♟ March 20: Isaac Newton (◀ 1642) dies.

♫ April 11: First performance of Johann Sebastian Bach's *St Matthew Passion*.

♟ June 8: Hermann Auguste Francke (◀ 1663) dies.

♛ June 11: King George I of Great Britain (◀ 1714) dies and is succeeded by his son as King George II (▶ 1760).

French Ursuline sisters found Catholic Charities in New Orleans. The organization is still active today.

Janet Horne, the last witch to be executed in Scotland, is burned alive in Dornoch.

1728

✤ February 13: Cotton Mather (◄ 1663) dies.

Johann Heinrich Callenberg, Professor of Theology at the University of Halle, founds the Institutum Judaicum as the first Protestant mission centre for evangelizing the Jews.

📖 William Law (◄ 1686, ▶ 1761), *A Serious Call to a Devout and Holy Life*, is almost as influential as John Bunyan's *The Pilgrim's Progress* (◄ 1678) on evangelical spirituality.

1729

✤ January 22: Gotthold Ephraim Lessing (▶ 1779), German philosopher and dramatist, is born. His publication of the writings of Hermann Samuel Reimarus (◄ 1694) will mark the beginning of the quest of the historical Jesus. Dies 1781.

✤ February 11: Solomon Stoddard (◄ 1643) dies.

✤ November 30: Samuel Seabury, American Episcopal Church bishop (▶ 1784), is born, the first American to hold episcopal office. Dies 1796.

✤ December 13: Anthony Collins (◄ 1676) dies.

1730

✤ February 15: Thomas Bray (◄ 1656) dies.

☿ February 21: Pope Benedict XIII (◄ 1724) dies.

☿ July 12: Cardinal Lorenzo Corsini is elected as Pope Clement XII (▶ 1740).

The First Great Awakening begins; it sweeps through the American colonies, peaking in 1740–42.

The Great Awakenings

The Great Awakenings are two waves of religious revivals which sweep across North America, first from around 1730 onwards and then at the beginning of the nineteenth century; they are also paralleled in Europe. Often at camp meetings, large numbers of people are 'converted', in the sense of having a Christian experience which changes their lives. These events are known as 'harvests'. Following the work of Solomon Stoddard (◄ 1643), Jonathan Edwards (◄ 1703) writes the first account of the Awakening in Northampton, Massachusetts, which is read in England by John Wesley (◄ 1703) and influences his preaching. George Whitefield (◄ 1714) travels to America, where he has a successful mission in Savannah, Georgia (1739–41). He is supported by former students of the Log College (▶ 1735).

Whereas in the First Great Awakening the converts are usually already church members, the Second Great Awakening reaches out to those who are not practising Christians. Its beginning is usually seen in a great camp meeting at Cane Ridge, Kentucky (▶ 1801), attracting up to 20,000 people. Such meetings become the means by which churches such as the Baptists and Methodists expand. Prominent figures are Charles Grandison Finney (▶ 1792) and Dwight Lyman Moody (▶ 1837). Billy Graham (▶ 1918) can also be included in the tradition. The Awakenings can be said to mark the start of American evangelicalism.

1731

�_November 26: William Cowper, poet and hymn writer, is born. He collaborates with John Newton (◀ 1725) over the _Olney Hymns_ (▶ 1779). Dies 1800.

Archbishop Firmin of Salzburg expels all Protestants (between 20,000 and 30,000) from his diocese.

Pope Clement XIII fixes the number of Stations of the Cross (◀ 1342) at fourteen (▶ 1742).

1732

🌿♬ March 31/April 1: Joseph Haydn, composer, is born. As well as many symphonies, string quartets and operas he writes 13 settings of the mass, the oratorio _The Creation_ (▶ 1798) and _The Seven Last Words of Our Saviour from the Cross_, originally for orchestra but later arranged for string quartet, piano and then for voices. Dies 1809.

Alphonsus Liguori (◀ 1696, ▶ 1787) founds the Congregation of the Most Holy Redeemer (Redemptorists) at Scala, Italy, for mission work among the poor.

The Moravian (◀ 1457) missionary Christian David arrives in Greenland.

1733

🌿 March 13: Joseph Priestley, English Presbyterian minister and scientist and one of the founders of the Unitarian Society, is born. Dies 1804.

🌿 August 16: Matthew Tindal (◀ 1655) dies.

The Bible is translated into Malay.

1735

🌿 January 8: John Carroll (▶ 1789), Bishop of Baltimore, the first Roman Catholic bishop in America, is born. Dies 1815.

🌿 September 14: Robert Raikes, pioneer of the Sunday School Movement (▶ 1780), is born. Dies 1811.

♛ October 8: Yongzheng Emperor (◀ 1724) dies and is succeeded by his son Hongli, who rules as Qianlong Emperor (▶ 1746).

🌿📖 Granville Sharp is born. Son of an Archbishop of York, he works tirelessly for the abolition of slavery. He writes a treatise _On the Injustice of Tolerating Slavery_ (1769). He is also one of the founders of the British and Foreign Bible Society (▶ 1804). Dies 1813.

William Tennent founds the Log College north of Philadelphia to train pastors. It is the forerunner of the American Protestant seminary.

The Bible is translated into Lithuanian.

John (◀ 1703, ▶ 1738) and Charles Wesley (◀ 1707, ▶ 1739) go to Georgia, North America, to work for three years with the English settlers there. The visit is not a success.

Augustus Gottlieb Spangenberg, a bishop of the Moravian Church (◀ 1457), founds the first Moravian settlements in Georgia. They too are not a success.

1736

♠ February 29: Ann Lee (▶ 1774) is born. The daughter of a Lancashire blacksmith, she joins the 'shaking Quakers' or Shakers, so-called because they shake or tremble to demonstrate sin departing from the body. She has a vision that she is Ann the Word, to whom God's power has been released, and leads a group of followers to New York. Dies 1784.

♠ ⊞ March 25: Nicholas Hawksmoor (◀ 1661) dies.

1737

⚓ January 24: William Wake, Archbishop of Canterbury (◀ 1716), dies.

⚓ February 28: John Potter, Bishop of Oxford, is appointed Archbishop of Canterbury (▶ 1747).

April 23: The Moravian missionary Georg Schmidt settles at Genadendal near Cape Town and works among the Hottentots for seven years (▶ 1792).

📖 November 3: Alexander Cruden presents one of the first copies of his *Concordance of the Holy Scriptures* to Caroline, Queen Consort of Great Britain.

☯ Catherine of Genoa (◀ 1510, feast day April 29) and Vincent de Paul (◀ 1580, feast day September 27) are canonized by Pope Clement XII.

1738

May 24: The heart of John Wesley (◀ 1735), who has returned depressed from America, is 'strangely warmed' at a meeting in Aldersgate, London, marking his conversion.

♫ J. S. Bach completes his *B Minor Mass*.

1739

April 2: John Wesley (▶ 1744) begins to form societies within the Anglican church. They are called Methodists, because of their methodical approach to the Bible. He first begins to preach in the open air.

August: George Whitefield (◀ 1714, ▶ 1770) leaves England for America.

Charles Wesley's *Hymns and Sacred Poems*, his first collection, are published, part of the 5000 hymns he writes.

1740

⚓ February 6: Pope Clement XII (◀ 1730) dies.

⚓ August 17: Prospero Lorenzo Lambertini, Cardinal Archbishop of Bologna, is elected as Pope Benedict XIV (▶ 1758).

♛ October 20: Charles VI, Holy Roman Emperor (◀ 1710), dies and is to be succeeded by his daughter Maria Theresa, who is married to Francis, Duke of Lorraine (▶ 1745). However, the Pragmatic Sanction (◀ 1713) which governs her succession is contested, leading to a war with Friedrich II, King of Prussia (Ferdinand the Great), who has just acceded to the throne.

🕆 Augustus Montague Toplady is born. A Calvinist Anglican, he writes poems and hymns, notably 'Rock of Ages', supposedly inspired by a storm in which he is caught near the Cheddar Gorge, Somerset. Dies 1778.

Johann Philipp Fabricius, a German missionary, arrives in Madras. He produces the first Tamil–English dictionary and grammar and then an improved translation of the Bible into Tamil (◀ 1710).

c.1740

The Doukhobors, 'spirit fighters', a controversial sect, appear in Russia. They believe that Jesus Christ was a normal human being who lived and died in the flesh but whose spirit is in those who act on his teaching.

1741

🕆♫ July 28: Antonio Vivaldi (◀ 1678) dies.

Moravians settle along the LeHigh river in Pennsylvania and found the town of Bethlehem under the guidance of Count von Zinzendorf (◀ 1700).

1742

♫ April 13: Handel's (◀ 1685, ▶ 1759) *Messiah* is first performed, in Dublin.

July 11: The bull *Ex quo singulari* condemns Chinese Rites (◀ 1716).

Pope Benedict XIV urges all churches to have Stations of the Cross (◀ 1731) on their walls (hitherto the observance has been largely out of doors).

Jacobus Capitein, an African from the Gold Coast (now Ghana), is the first African Protestant to be ordained minister.

1743

January 5/6: The first Methodist Association meets near Caerphilly in Wales under the chairmanship of George Whitefield.

🕆 July: William Paley, English scholar, is born. His most famous book is *A View of the Evidences of Christianity* (▶ 1794). Dies 1805.

The Diocese of Guatemala is founded.

In the bull *Omnium sollicitudinem*, Pope Benedict XIV condemns Malabar rites (◀ 1605).

1744

June 25: John and Charles Wesley (◀ 1739) hold the first Methodist Conference at the Old King's Foundry in London.

1745

🕆 February 2: Hannah More, evangelical writer and philanthropist, is born. Dies 1833.

August 20: Francis Asbury is born. He is a key figure in shaping American Methodism. Dies 1816.

September 13: Maria Theresa (◀ 1740) secures the election of her husband Franz I as Holy Roman Emperor. She styles herself Holy Roman Empress, and is the *de facto* ruler (▶ 1765).

December 6: The Diocese of São Paulo is founded.

1746

Qianlong Emperor (◀ 1735, ▶ 1748) orders the expulsion of foreign missionaries from China and orders Chinese converts to recant.

Princeton University is founded by New Light Presbyterians as the College of New Jersey in Elizabeth, New Jersey.

1747

September 9: Thomas Coke, the first American Methodist bishop, is born. Dies 1814.

October 10: John Potter, Archbishop of Canterbury (◀ 1737), dies.

November 24: Thomas Herring, Archbishop of York, is appointed Archbishop of Canterbury (▶ 1757).

December 24: Candles decorated with red ribbons are first distributed to children at a Moravian watchnight service in Marienborn, Germany. These are the forerunners of the Christingles seen today (▶ *c*.1890).

1748

November 25: Isaac Watts (◀ 1674) dies.

A further decree of Qianlong Emperor (◀ 1746, ▶ 1796) bans Christianity in China.

1750

July 28: Johann Sebastian Bach (◀ 1685) dies.

July 30: Christian Friedrich Schwarz, a German Protestant missionary, arrives in Tranquebar. He works in India until his death in 1798.

By a secret treaty, Portugal cedes to Spain the Seven Reductions (◀ 1610) of Paraguay. The Indians, ordered to move out, rebel and cause a war. The Jesuits are said to have had a hand in it.

1751

June 16: Jean-Pierre de Caussade (◀ 1675) dies.

1752

May 14: Timothy Dwight, influential American educator, theologian and poet, is born. He is a grandson of Jonathan Edwards (◀ 1703) and president of Yale for 20 years. Dies 1817.

June 16: Joseph Butler (◀ 1692) dies.

September 14: The Gregorian calendar (◀ 1582) is adopted in Great Britain and Ireland and the British Empire.

Thomas Thompson, the first Anglican missionary to Africa, sent out by the Society for the Propagation of the Gospel, arrives at Cape Coast (in what is now Ghana).

1753

✠ January 14: George Berkeley (◀ 1685) dies.

March 1: Sweden adopts the Gregorian calendar; from now on Easter is celebrated on the same day throughout Western Christianity.

November 17: A group of Moravians move from Bethlehem, Pennsylvania (◀ 1741) to a tract of land purchased by Bishop Spangenberg (◀ 1735) which they call Wachovia. The settlement prospers, and the town of Old Salem is built.

✠ ⊓ James Gibbs (◀ 1682) dies.

1754

✠ April 9: Christian Wolff (◀ 1679) dies.

King George II of Great Britain grants a royal charter for the establishment of King's College, New York. Thirty years later it becomes Columbia University.

1755

November 1: An earthquake in Lisbon causes great loss of life and prompts questions about the goodness of God, notably expressed in Voltaire's (◀ 1694) 'Poem on the Lisbon Disaster'.

1756

✠ ♫ January 27: Wolfgang Amadeus Mozart, composer, is born. Although he writes few religious works (most of his masses at an early stage in his career), the *C Minor Mass* (▶ 1783) and the unfinished *Requiem* (▶ 1791) are among the greatest of their genre. Dies 1791.

1757

☿ March 13: Thomas Herring, Archbishop of Canterbury (◀ 1747), dies.

☿ April 29. Matthew Hutton, Archbishop of York, is appointed Archbishop of Canterbury (▶ 1758).

✠ November 28: William Blake (▶ 1804), English visionary poet and artist, is born. Dies 1827.

1758

☿ March 19: Matthew Hutton, Archbishop of Canterbury (◀ 1757), dies.

✠ March 22: Jonathan Edwards (◀ 1703) dies.

☿ April 21: Thomas Secker, Bishop of Oxford, is appointed Archbishop of Canterbury (▶ 1768).

☿ May 3: Pope Benedict XIV (◀ 1740) dies.

The Lisbon earthquake. A Czech broadsheet, 1755

July 6: Carlo Torre Rezzonico, diplomat and judge, is elected as Pope Clement XIII (▶ 1769).

1759

April 10: George Frideric Handel (◀ 1685) dies.

August 24: William Wilberforce is born. After a Christian conversion experience he enters Parliament and campaigns tirelessly for the abolition of slavery. He also campaigns for other social reforms. Dies 1833.

September 13: The British capture Quebec: free exercise of religion is guaranteed to the Roman Catholics of Canada.

September 24: Charles Simeon (▶ 1782), evangelical Anglican, is born. He helps to found the Church Missionary Society and the British and Foreign Bible Society. Dies 1836.

Following their involvement in the war over the Paraguay reductions (◀ 1750) and allegations of immorality, the Jesuits are suppressed in Portugal.

Voltaire's (◀ 1694, ▶ 1778) *Candide* devastatingly demonstrates the fallacy of Leibniz's (◀ 1646) view of the world.

1760

♣ May 9: Nicholas Ludwig, Count von Zinzendorf (◀ 1700), dies.

♔ October 25: King George II of Great Britain (◀ 1727) dies and his son succeeds him as King George III (▶ 1820).

1761

♣ August 17: William Carey (▶ 1794), Baptist missionary to India, is born. Dies 1834.

♣ William Law (◀ 1686) dies.

1763

🏛 The Church of La Madeleine, Paris, is completed.

1764

February 26: Catherine the Great confiscates church lands in Russia to deprive the clergy of power.

November 26: The Jesuit Order is dissolved in France, following accusations of immorality.

Rhode Island College is founded for students of all religious affiliations. It later becomes Brown University.

1765

February 6: Pope Clement XIII authorizes the mass and devotion of the Sacred Heart.

♔ August 18: Franz I, Holy Roman Emperor (◀ 1745), dies and is succeeded by Joseph II, his oldest son (▶ 1790). Maria Theresa becomes Dowager Empress (▶ 1780).

1766

♣ May 5: Jean Astruc (◀ 1684) dies.

Catherine the Great grants freedom of worship in Russia.

Queen's College is founded by the Dutch Reformed Church in New Brunswick, New Jersey. It later become Rutgers University.

1767

February: 5000 Jesuits are expelled from Spain, prompting military clashes with the Pope.

☩ Joseph Calasanza (◀ 1607, feast day August 25) and Jane Frances de Chantal (◀ 1610, feast day December 12) are canonized by Pope Clement XIII.

1768

♣ March 1: Hermann Samuel Reimarus (◀ 1694) dies.

♆ August 3: Thomas Secker, Archbishop of Canterbury (◀ 1758), dies.

♆ September 30: Frederick Cornwallis, Bishop of Lichfield and Coventry, is appointed Archbishop of Canterbury (▶ 1783).

Friedrich Schleiermacher

🍂 November 21: Friedrich Schleiermacher (▶ 1799), German theologian, is born. Dies 1834.

Andrew Turnbull, British consul in Smyrna and married to a Greek wife, founds New Smyrna, Florida, and populates it with Greek settlers, thus introducing Greek Orthodoxy.

1769

⚓ February 2: Pope Clement XIII (◀ 1758) dies.

⚓ May 10: Cardinal Lorenzo Ganganelli, a Franciscan, is elected as Pope Clement XIV (▶ 1774).

July 16: Father Junipero Serra, a Spanish Franciscan missionary, raises a cross at the site of a mission in San Diego, California, the Mission San Diego de Alcalá. He goes on to found a chain of missions from San Diego to San Francisco.

Dartmouth College, New Hampshire, is founded by Congregationalists 'for the youth of the Indian tribes, English youth and others'.

John Wesley (◀ 1744, ▶ 1784) sends the first Methodist missionaries to America.

341

1770

❦ August 27: Georg Wilhelm Friedrich Hegel, German idealist philosopher, is born. Dies 1831.

❦ September 30: George Whitefield (◀ 1714) dies.

1771

John Jebb, a Cambridge academic, and other divines become Unitarians on the failure of a Parliamentary petition to free clergy from subscription to the Thirty-Nine Articles (◀ 1563).

1772

❦ March 10: Friedrich von Schlegel, German Catholic apologist, is born. Dies 1829.

❦ March 29: Emanuel Swedenborg (◀ 1688) dies.

❦ October 21: Samuel Taylor Coleridge, English romantic poet and philosopher, is born. Dies 1834.

November 28: The Bible in Manx is published.

❦ December 24: Barton Stone (▶ 1832), founder of a renewal movement calling itself the 'Christian' movement, is born. Dies 1844.

🏛 A new cathedral is completed in Smolensk (◀ 1674).

1773

June 14: The first Methodist Conference is held in North America.

August 16: The Jesuits are suppressed by Pope Clement XIV in the bull *Dominus ac redemptor noster*.

📖 Friedrich Gottlieb Klopstock's (◀ 1724, ▶ 1803) great epic poem *Der Messias* is completed.

1774

April: Theophilus Lindsay, who left the Church of England the previous year, opens Essex Chapel in London for Unitarians.

Unitarianism

Unitarianism is a form of Christianity which rejects the doctrines of the Trinity and the divinity of Christ. It has its beginnings in the Reformation with Martin Cellarius (◀ 1526) and Michael Servetus (◀ 1553) and spreads to Poland through George Biandrata (◀ 1558) and Fausto Sozzini (◀ 1579). It first appears in England with John Biddle, a Gloucestershire teacher (◀ 1647), but it is not until 1774 that the first Unitarian chapel is opened in London by Theophilus Lindsey. In eighteenth-century America, Harvard College is markedly Unitarian. James Freeman becomes minister of King's Chapel, Boston, the first Unitarian church in America, but the key figure in Boston is to be William Ellery Channing (▶ 1803) at the Congregational church in Federal Street. The nineteenth century sees the foundation of Unitarian Associations in both Great Britain and the United States (▶ 1825); over the next century the Unitarians link up with the Universalists, with whom in 1961 they form the Unitarian Universalist Association.

♕ May 10: Louis XV, King of France (◀ 1714), dies and is succeeded by Louis XVI (▶ 1792, 1793).

August 6: Ann Lee (◀ 1736, ▶ 1784) arrives in New York City with a band of Shakers and forms a settlement.

♟ August 28: Elizabeth Ann Seton, Catholic convert, is born. She founds the Sisters of Charity, the first American religious community for women, the first American parish school and the first American Catholic orphanage. Dies 1821.

☩ September 22: Pope Clement XIV (◀ 1769) dies.

1775

April 18: The first shots are fired in the American War of Independence (▶ 1783) at Concord, Massachusetts, in a clash between the British Army and revolutionaries. The British are subsequently besieged in Boston.

☩ September 15: Cardinal Giovanni Angelo Braschi, a diplomat, is elected as Pope Pius VI (▶ 1798, 1799).

J. J. Griesbach issues a critical edition of the Greek New Testament in three volumes: the first contains the first three Gospels arranged in parallel columns, the first synopsis.

1776

July 4: The American Declaration of Independence is issued.

♟ August 25: David Hume (◀ 1711) dies.

1777

December: A German prisoner puts up the first Christmas tree in America at Windsor Locks, Connecticut.

1778

♟ May 30: Voltaire (◀ 1694) dies.

♟ August 11: Augustus Montague Toplady (◀ 1740) dies.

Caleb Rich forms the General Society of Universalists in Massachusetts to ordain ministers and issue preaching licenses.

1779

🎭 May: Gottfried Ephraim Lessing (◀ 1729, ▶ 1781), *Nathan the Wise*, a plea for religious tolerance, is published. It is not performed until four years later, after Lessing's death.

John Newton (◀ 1727, ▶ 1807) and William Cowper (◀ 1731, ▶ 1800) publish *Olney Hymns*: Newton's hymns include 'Amazing Grace' and 'Glorious things of thee are spoken'; Cowper's 'God moves in a mysterious way'.

1780

♟ April 7: William Ellery Channing (▶ 1803), Congregationalist minister, is born. He becomes a leading figure in Unitarianism. Dies 1842.

♠ May 21: Elizabeth Fry, Quaker prison reformer, is born. Dies 1845.

♛ November 29: Dowager Empress Maria Theresa (◀ 1765) dies.

Robert Raikes (◀ 1735, ▶ 1811) starts a Sunday school in Gloucester which is to shape a whole Sunday School Movement.

1781

♠ February 15: Gottfried Ephraim Lessing (◀ 1729) dies.

♠ February 18: Henry Martyn (▶ 1805), missionary to India, is born. Dies 1812.

October 13: Holy Roman Emperor Joseph II issues a Patent of Tolerance with limited scope: it excludes atheists and deists. He secularizes church lands and reduces the religious orders. His policy is known as Josephinism.

📖 Immanuel Kant (◀ 1724, ▶ 1804), *Critique of Pure Reason*, is published (second edition 1787).

The Lord's Day Observance Society in England revives Sabbatarianism (◀ 1595), the strict observance of Sunday as a day of rest.

1782

♠ February 15: William Miller, founder of the Millerites (▶ 1831), is born. Dies 1849.

June 17: Anna Göldi is hanged in Glarus, Switzerland; this is the last legal execution of a witch in Europe.

♠ June 19: Hugo Félicité Robert de Lamennais (▶ 1832), French political and social theorist, is born. He accepts the authority of the church in matters of faith but not of practice. He founds an important religious journal, *L'Avenir*, to promote his views. Dies 1854.

November 10: Charles Simeon (◀ 1759, ▶ 1836) begins his evangelical ministry at Holy Trinity Church, Cambridge.

James Freeman is appointed minister of King's Chapel, Boston, which becomes the first Unitarian Church in America.

📖 The *Philokalia* of Macarius Notaras and Nicodemus of the Holy Mountain, a collection of ascetical and mystical writings, is first published in Venice.

1783

☩ March 1: Frederick Cornwallis, Archbishop of Canterbury (◀ 1768), dies.

☩ April 26: John Moore, Bishop of Bangor, is appointed Archbishop of Canterbury (▶ 1805).

♠ August 13: Tikhon of Zadonsk (◀ 1724) dies.

September 3: The Treaty of Paris formally marks the end of the American War of Independence (◀ 1775).

🐦 September 8: Nikolai Fredrik Severin Grundtvig, an influential Danish Lutheran, is born. Dies 1872.

🎵 October 26: First performance of Mozart's (◀ 1756, ▶ 1791) *C Minor Mass*.

Selina, Countess of Huntingdon (◀ 1707, ▶ 1791), founds a small society of Calvinist churches known as The Countess of Huntingdon's Connexion.

1784

🌿 July 31: Denis Diderot (◀ 1713) dies.

🌿 September 8: Ann Lee (◀ 1736) dies.

November 14: Samuel Seabury (◀ 1729, ▶ 1796) is consecrated as first bishop of the Protestant Episcopal Church in the USA in Aberdeen, since this is not possible in England.

December 25: The Methodist Episcopal Church is formed at the Baltimore Christmas Conference.

John Wesley (◀ 1769, ▶ 1791) ordains ministers for England, Scotland and America with power to administer the sacraments.

A Catholic prayer-house is established at Pyongyang in Korea (◀ 1593, ▶ 1786) by a native Korean layman, Yi Seunghun (▶ 1786), who has been baptized while serving as a diplomat in China.

Black settlers from Nova Scotia bring Protestantism to Sierra Leone (▶ 1787).

1785

The first convention of Universalists is held in New England.

The London Society for the Establishment of Sunday Schools is founded.

1786

🌿 May 8: Nathaniel William Taylor, American theologian, is born, the most consistent exponent of New England theology. He becomes the first professor at Yale Divinity School. Dies 1858.

🌿 May 8: Jean-Baptiste-Marie Vianney is born. He is known as the Curé d'Ars, a small village near Lyons in France, to which thousands of penitents come in order to make their confessions to him. Dies 1859.

September 18: The Synod of Pistoia meets to promote reform of the Catholic Church along the lines of Gallicanism (◀ 1682) in France and Josephinism (◀ 1781) in Austria.

Yi Seunghung (▶ 1784, ▶ 1801) creates a group of lay priests in Korea (▶ 1789).

1787

🌿 August 1: Alphonsus Liguori (◀ 1696) dies (▶ 1831).

August 12: Charles Inglis is consecrated Bishop of Nova Scotia, the first colonial bishop.

September 17: The US Constitution separates church and state and provides for full religious freedom.

🌳 October 7: Henry Melchior Mühlenberg (◀ 1711) dies.

November 19: The Edict of Versailles grants religious freedom and legal status to French Protestants.

The African Americans Richard Allen (▶ 1816) and Absalom Jones (▶ 1802) are ejected from St George's Methodist Episcopal Church in Philadelphia; they go on to form churches of their own, Jones the first black episcopal church in the USA.

The British government purchases Sierra Leone from Chief Naimbarna as a settlement for poor black people from London. The first settlement is short-lived (▶ 1793).

1788

🌳 March 29: Charles Wesley (◀ 1707) dies.

🌳 August 9: Adoniram Judson, missionary to Burma, is born. Dies 1850.

🌳 September 12: Alexander Campbell (▶ 1811), founder of the renewal movement the Disciples of Christ, is born. He has a strong expectation of an imminent second coming of Christ. Dies 1866.

English Catholics sign a 'Protestation' denying the temporal authority and infallibility of the Pope.

Richard Johnson, an Anglican chaplain, sails with the first transported convicts to Sydney, Australia. He later builds a small church there.

1789

January 23: John Carroll (◀ 1735) founds Georgetown College, which later becomes Georgetown University, in Washington, DC.

April 1: George Washington becomes the first US President.

⚓ May 1: Neophytus VII becomes Patriarch of Constantinople (▶ 1794, 1798).

July 14: The French Revolution begins: the Bastille is stormed.

🌳◼ July 19: John Martin, English painter, is born. He paints vast canvases, especially on dramatic religious subjects, notably *The Last Judgement*, *The Day of His Wrath* and *The Plains of Heaven*. Dies 1854.

August 27: The National Constituent Assembly issues a Declaration of the Rights of Man and of the Citizen which is to have a permanent influence on the idea of human rights.

October: The Protestant Episcopal Church in the United States (◀ 1784) formally separates from the Church of England so that its clergy are not required to accept the supremacy of the British monarch. At its first General Convention in Philadelphia under

Bishop William White it approves the name Protestant Episcopal Church to distinguish it from the Roman Catholic Church.

November 6: John Carroll (◀ 1735, ▶ 1815) is appointed Bishop of Baltimore, the first US Roman Catholic bishop.

The Vatican rules that the appointment of lay priests in Korea (◀ 1784) is against canon law.

The Methodist Book Concern is formed, the first church publishing house in the US.

1790

♛ February 20: Holy Roman Emperor Joseph II (◀ 1765) dies and is succeeded by Leopold II (▶ 1792).

July 12: The Civil Constitution of the Clergy in France turns the French church into a department of the French government and requires the clergy to take an oath.

♟ September 2: Johann Nikolaus von Hontheim (◀ 1701) dies.

1791

♟ March 2: John Wesley (◀ 1703) dies.

March 13: Pope Pius VI condemns the Civil Constitution (◀ 1790) and suspends all priests who accept it.

♟ March 14: Johann Salomo Semler (◀ 1725) dies.

♟ June 12: Selina, Countess of Huntingdon (◀ 1707), dies.

♟♫ December 5: Wolfgang Amadeus Mozart (◀ 1756) dies, leaving his *Requiem* incomplete.

The Roman Catholic Relief Act removes most of the restrictions on Roman Catholics, provided that they take an oath of loyalty to the Crown.

1792

♛ March 1: Leopold II, Holy Roman Emperor (◀ 1790), dies and is succeeded by Franz II, the last Holy Roman Emperor (▶ 1806).

♟ April 25: John Keble (▶ 1827), English tractarian and poet, is born. Dies 1866.

♟ June 21: Ferdinand Christian Baur, German radical church historian and dogmatician, is born. Dies 1860.

♟ August 4: Edward Irving, Scottish minister, is born. With a blend of Catholicism and Pentecostalism he founds a new church in London, known as the Catholic Apostolic Church; his followers are also known as Irvingites. Dies 1834.

♛ August 10: Louis XVI, King of France (◀ 1774, ▶ 1793), is suspended and arrested.

♟ August 29: Charles Grandison Finney, American revivalist preacher, is born. Dies 1875.

October 2: The Particular Baptist Missionary Society for the Propagation of the Gospel among the Heathen (◀ 1633), later the Baptist Missionary Society, is founded in Kettering, Northamptonshire.

Denmark becomes the first nation to abolish the slave trade.

Three Moravian missionaries successfully revive the work of Georg Schmidt (◀ 1737) near Cape Town.

1793

♛ January 21: Louis XVI (◀ 1774, 1792) is guillotined.

January: 1100 black Christian emigrants set sail from Halifax, Nova Scotia, for Sierra Leone (◀ 1787) and settle in Freetown (▶ 1808).

♣ Henry Francis Lyte is born. An Anglican priest and hymn writer, he writes 'Praise, my soul, the king of heaven' and, two weeks before his death, 'Abide with me'. Dies 1847.

September 15: The National Convention abolishes all universities and colleges throughout France (▶ 1802).

The Catholic Diocese of New Orleans is founded.

1794

☉ Neophytus VII (◀ 1789) is replaced as Patriarch of Constantinople by Gerasimus III (▶ 1797).

William Carey (◀ 1762, ▶ 1834) lands in Bengal to begin his missionary work.

Herman, a lay monk from Sergei Posad, and nine Russian Orthodox missionaries from the Valaamo Monastery in the Karelia region of Russia cross the Bering Strait and bring Christianity to Alaska. The others gradually leave and Herman remains alone until his death there in 1837.

Archimandrite Ioasaf Bolotov lands on the Aleutian Islands on a mission (▶ 1797).

📖 William Paley (◀ 1743, ▶ 1805), *A View of the Evidences of Christianity*, is a classic account of the argument from the design of the universe for the existence of God.

1795

January: A Chinese priest, Zhou Wenmo (James) (▶ 1801), arrives in Seoul, Korea, as a missionary.

The London Missionary Society is founded.

Maynooth College, a Catholic seminary, is founded in Ireland so that priests do not have to travel to the continent in revolutionary times.

The Dutch surrender Ceylon to the British (◀ 1658).

1796

♛ February 9: Qianlong Emperor (◀ 1748) abdicates in favour of his son Yongyan, who rules as Jiaqing Emperor. Qianlong remains the real ruler until his death in 1799.

✤ February 25: Samuel Seabury (◀ 1729) dies.

March: The French General Napoleon Bonaparte invades Italy and goes on to control the Po valley.

Glasgow Missionary Society is founded.

Edinburgh Missionary Society is founded.

1797

February 19: At the Peace of Tolentino Pope Pius VI has to surrender parts of the papal states to Napoleon (◀ 1796).

☩ April 19: Gerasimus III (◀ 1794) is replaced as Patriarch of Constantinople by Gregory, Bishop of Smyrna, who becomes Gregory V (▶ 1798).

✤ June 24: Henry Venn (◀ 1725) dies.

✤ August 26: Ivan Veniaminov (▶ c.1820), who becomes Innocent of Alaska, is born. Dies 1879.

✤ December 27: Charles Hodge, American Calvinist theologian, is born. He is the founder of 'Princeton theology', a conservative Calvinism. Dies 1878.

Archimandrite Ioasaf Bolotov (◀ 1794) is consecrated Bishop in Irkutsk but is drowned on his return journey to the Aleutian Islands. The mission there collapses.

Henry Nott with other London Missionary Society missionaries arrives on Tahiti. He later translates the New Testament into Tahitian (▶ 1819).

c.1797

✤ Sojourner Truth (▶ 1843), African American evangelist and reformer, is born. Dies 1883.

1798

April 15: A French army enters Rome, deposes Pope Pius VI (◀ 1775) and forces him to retire to Tuscany. He never returns.

♩ April 29: Joseph Haydn (◀ 1732, ▶ 1809), *The Creation*, is first performed.

☩ December 18: Gregory V, Patriarch of Constantinople (◀ 1797), is deposed and retires to Mount Athos. Neophytus VII (◀ 1789) again becomes patriarch (▶ 1801).

Napoleon closes the Maronite College in Rome (◀ 1584).

The Netherlands Missionary Society is founded.

1799

✤ February 28: Johann Joseph Ignaz von Döllinger, Bavarian Catholic church historian, is born. He refuses to accept the dogma of papal infallibility (▶ 1870) and becomes an Old Catholic. Dies 1890.

349

March 31: Johannes van der Kemp, a charismatic figure, arrives in Cape Town as a Dutch missionary ordained into the Church of Scotland. He works among the Khoikoi (Hottentots) (▶ 1803).

✠ August 29: Pope Pius VI (◀ 1775, 1798) dies.

The Church Missionary Society is founded in London by evangelical Anglican clergy as the Society for Missions in Africa and the East.

📖 Friedrich Schleiermacher (◀ 1768, ▶ 1821/22), *Speeches on Religion to its Cultured Despisers*, defends religion against its Enlightenment critics, arguing that it is a sense of the infinite consisting largely in feeling.

1800

✠ March 14: Cardinal Luigi Barnabà Chiaramonte, a Benedictine professor of theology, is elected as Pope Pius VII (▶ 1823).

🕯 April 25: William Cowper (◀ 1731) dies.

🕯 August 22: Edward Bouverie Pusey, English theologian, is born. He is associated with John Keble (◀ 1792) and John Henry Newman (▶ 1801) in the Oxford Movement (▶ 1833). Dies 1882.

🕯 October 25: Jacques-Paul Migne, French Catholic priest and publisher, is born. He publishes vast editions of the Latin (220 vols) and Greek (162 vols) church fathers. Dies 1875.

🕯 November 18: John Nelson Darby is born. An Anglican clergyman in Ireland, he leaves the church and is one of a group which founds the Plymouth Brethren. He begins the idea of the 'rapture' in which Christ will unexpectedly snatch believers away from earth and is regarded as the father of dispensationalism (▶ 1843), the view that biblical history consists of a series of successive divine dispensations. Dies 1882.

At a conference in Frederick, Maryland, 13 ministers of largely German-speaking churches in the area adopt the name Church of United Brethren in Christ. They claim to be the first denomination founded in the USA.

Nineteenth century

Under the surface of the political and ecclesiastical events of the century runs, sometimes almost imperceptibly, sometimes more evidently, a current which is to have a great effect on Christianity: an exploration of its origins and its scriptures and, more radically, a critique which raises fundamental questions about the very nature of religious belief.

Archaeologists in the Middle East begin to bring to life the cultures preceding the Bible and the world in which the Bible is set. Hanging precariously in a cradle before a rock face in Persia, in 1837 Henry Creswicke Rawlinson laboriously copies inscriptions which prove a key towards the deciphering of cuneiform, the script used in Mesopotamia. The same year Edward Robinson and Eli Smith, travelling through Palestine, are able to link up biblical names with current Arabic names of towns and abandoned mounds. In 1845 Austen Henry Layard begins excavating the Assyrian city of Nimrud, where he discovers a reference to a king of Israel mentioned in the Bible. In 1865 scholars found the Palestine Exploration Fund and in 1880 the Society of Biblical Literature, just two of many similar associations. As well as illuminating the world of the Bible, these explorations raise a whole range of questions about it: for example, the Epic of Gilgamesh, deciphered in 1872, has a flood story which parallels that in the Bible. Critical issues first raised by scholars such as Richard Simon (1678) and Jean Astruc (1684), who express doubts that the first five books of the Bible were written by Moses, and Hermann Samuel Reimarus, whose work radically questions the Gospel accounts of Jesus, are persistently raised. In his *Life of Jesus* (1835–36), David Friedrich Strauss interprets the Gospel accounts in terms of myth; in South Africa, Bishop Colenso (1814) is excommunicated for persistently pointing to what he regards as absurdities in the Old Testament.

Charles Darwin sets out to use his scientific research to demonstrate the truth of the Bible, but with his doctrine of evolution as presented in *On the Origin of Species by Means of Natural Selection* (1859) comes to pose a devastating challenge to the biblical account of creation and the Christian doctrine based on it. Other critics are a threat from the start. In his *The Essence of Christianity* (1841), Ludwig Feuerbach argues that religion is a human projection; Karl Marx attacks what he regards as the false picture of reality presented by theology; Friedrich Nietzsche sees Christianity leading to degeneration and decadence; Sigmund Freud regards religion as a form of mental illness.

The Roman Catholic Church reacts defensively to these developments, as it does to the Industrial Revolution and its social consequences. Successive popes seek to ward off the advances of modernity by a series of dogmas and prohibitions; disciplinary action is taken against 'Modernists', and a *Syllabus of Errors* (1864) censures a wide range of more liberal views.

351

Nevertheless, this is a century of mission *par excellence*. The Protestant missionary societies founded at the end of the previous century bear fruit. After taking root in Australia, Christianity is brought to India by Henry Martyn (1805), to China by Robert Morrison (1807), to Burma by Adoniram Judson (1813), to New Zealand by Samuel Marsden (1814), to Siam by Karl Gützlaff and Jacob Tomlin (1828), and to Samoa by John Williams (1830). Above all Africa becomes the great mission field. Robert Moffat and his wife arrive in Bechuanaland in 1821 and stay for 50 years; in 1841 they are joined by David Livingstone for a while, before he begins his great explorations. Missionaries from many countries are active in many areas, at great personal cost. After the Berlin Conference of 1884/85, which divides the continent between the European powers, competition multiplies. Such is the enthusiasm for mission that a conference held in 1910, in the spirit of the previous century, adopts as its slogan 'The evangelization of the world in this generation'. Events are to prove different.

1801

January 1: By the Act of Union, the United Kingdom of Great Britain and Ireland (◀ 1707) is created.

✦ February 21: John Henry Newman (▶ 1845), English theologian, is born. Dies 1890.

✦ April 28: Anthony Ashley Cooper, Seventh Earl of Shaftesbury (▶ 1836), a social reformer who takes up the cause of women and children in factories and mines, is born. Dies 1885.

✦ June 1: Brigham Young, second Mormon (▶ 1830) president, is born. In 1847 he leads the Mormons from Nauvoo, Illinois, to Utah, after the death of Joseph Smith (▶ 1805). Dies 1877.

✧ June 17: Neophytus VII (◀ 1798) is succeeded by Callinicus IV (▶ 1806) as Patriarch of Constantinople.

July 16: Napoleon Bonaparte's Concordat with Rome leads to formal restoration of the Roman Catholic Church in France. It remains in force until 1905.

August 6: The Second Great Awakening (◀ 1730) begins at a great camp meeting at Cane Ridge, Kentucky.

On the accession of a new king, Sunjo, the Korean authorities attempt to suppress Christianity in the country (▶ 1866) with the execution of many Korean Christians including Yi Seunghun (◀ 1786) and Zhou Wenmo (◀ 1795).

1802

April 8: In the Organic Articles, Napoleon provides legislation similar to the Concordat (◀ 1801) affecting French Protestants. Pastors are paid by the state and the government has power to veto appointments and doctrinal changes.

✦ April 14: Horace Bushnell, American Congregationalist theologian, is born. He is influenced by Schleiermacher (◀ 1768) and Coleridge (◀ 1772). Dies 1876.

May 1: Napoleon issues a decree establishing a new system of education in France (◀ 1793) which in essentials still exists today.

✦ May 12: Jean-Baptiste Henri Dominique Lacordaire, French Roman Catholic liberal, is born. He later becomes a Dominican. Dies 1861.

September 21: Absalom Jones (◀ 1787) is ordained to the episcopal priesthood, the first African American in the United States to be so.

📖 François Auguste René, Vicomte de Chateaubriand, *The Genius of Christianity*, defends Christianity in terms of its social, cultural and spiritual benefits.

1803

✦ March 14: Friedrich Gottlieb Klopstock (◀ 1724) dies.

✦ May 25: Ralph Waldo Emerson, American transcendentalist, is born. Dies 1882.

353

June 1: William Ellery Channing (◀ 1780, ▶ 1819) becomes minister of Federal Street Congregationalist Church, Boston, where he remains for the rest of his life.

Johannes van der Kemp (◀ 1799, ▶ 1810) settles in Bethelsdorp on the eastern Cape, South Africa.

The first Roman Catholic priests are appointed to Australia.

1804

♣ February 6: Joseph Priestley (◀ 1733) dies.

♣ February 12: Immanuel Kant (◀ 1724) dies.

March 7: The British and Foreign Bible Society is founded.

♣📖 March 28: Ludwig Feuerbach, German philosopher, is born. In his *The Essence of Christianity* (1841), denying transcendence, he sees religion as being the projection of human qualities and hopes on a fictitious God. Dies 1872.

May 18: Napoleon becomes Emperor of the French and King of Italy.

♛ December 2: Pope Pius VII consecrates Napoleon Emperor of France in Paris in a ceremony modelled on the coronation of Charlemagne (◀ 800).

📖 William Blake, 'Jerusalem', is published as part of the preface to a long poem, *Milton*.

1805

⚘ January 18: John Moore, Archbishop of Canterbury (◀ 1783), dies.

⚘ February 21: Charles Manners-Sutton, Bishop of Norwich, is appointed Archbishop of Canterbury (▶ 1828). He promotes the establishment of the Anglican Indian episcopate and presides over the founding of the National Society (▶ 1811).

May 16: Henry Martyn, missionary (◀ 1781, ▶ 1812), arrives in India.

♣ May 25: William Paley (◀ 1743) dies.

♣ July 16: Johann Christoph Blumhardt, Pietist, is born. He founds a healing centre at Bad Boll in Germany. Dies 1880.

♣ August 29: Frederick Denison Maurice, English theologian and socialist (▶ 1853), is born. Dies 1872.

♣ December 23: Joseph Smith, founder of the Mormons (▶ 1830), is born. He is murdered in 1844.

Missionaries from the London Missionary Society (◀ 1795) reach what is now Namibia.

♪ Jeremiah Ingall compiles *The Christian Harmony*, an important collection of hymns and spirituals.

1806

July 12: Napoleon insists that Franz II abandons the title Holy Roman Emperor (◀ 1792); Franz continues to reign as Emperor of Austria (▶ 1835).

✈ September 23: Gregory V (◀ 1798) again becomes Patriarch of Constantinople in succession to Callinicus IV (◀ 1801).

1807

March 25: The Abolition of the Slave Trade Act ends slave trade to the British Colonies.

September 7: Robert Morrison, a Scot with the London Missionary Society, arrives in Guangzhou, China (▶ 1819).

🕯 December 18: Phoebe Worrall Palmer, American evangelist and writer, is born. Her Tuesday Meetings for the Promotion of Holiness are an important part of the Holiness Movement associated with the Great Awakenings (◀ 1730, 1801). Dies 1874.

🕯 December 21: John Newton (◀ 1725) dies.

✪ Angela Merici (◀ 1535) is canonized by Pope Pius VII: feast day January 12.

Jacob Albright, a Lutheran convert to Methodism, becomes the first bishop of the Evangelical Church (▶ 1816).

The Sisters of St Joseph of Cluny work in Réunion, Senegal and Sierra Leone.

1808

January 1: Sierra Leone (◀ 1792) becomes a Crown Colony; its population swells through large numbers of liberated slaves, who dilute the Christian character of the capital, Freetown.

🕯 January 27: David Friedrich Strauss, German theologian and author of a controversial *Life of Jesus* (▶ 1835/36), is born. Dies 1874.

February 2: Napoleon occupies Rome.

✈ September 10: Patriarch Gregory V (◀ 1806) is again deposed and retires to Mount Athos. After a brief further period in office by Callinicus IV (◀ 1801) he is succeeded by Jeremias IV (▶ 1813).

▮ Caspar David Friedrich's *The Cross in the Mountains*, an altarpiece conceived in terms of a romantic Bohemian landscape, arouses controversy.

The Twenty-Five Articles are a Methodist adaptation of the Anglican Thirty-Nine Articles (◀ 1563).

Andover Theological Seminary is founded by orthodox Congregationalists as an alternative to the Unitarianism of Harvard (◀ 1636).

1809

🕯♫ February 3: Felix Mendelssohn is born. An infant prodigy as a composer, he goes on to write two oratorios, *St Paul* (1836) and *Elijah* (▶ 1846), and is instrumental in reviving the music of Johann Sebastian Bach (▶ 1829). Dies 1847.

♣ February 12: Charles Darwin, English scientist, is born. His *On the Origin of Species by Means of Natural Selection* (▶ 1859) with its theory of evolution is to provoke a controversy which is still alive. Dies 1882.

May 17: Napoleon takes over what remains of the papal states (◀ 1797).

July 5: Napoleon arrests Pope Pius VII (▶ 1814).

♣ ♫ Joseph Haydn (◀ 1732) dies.

Settlers build the first Presbyterian church in Ebenezer, near Brisbane, Australia.

*c.*1809

♣ Samuel (Adjai) Crowther is born (▶ 1865). An African sold into slavery, he is rescued by the British and cared for by the Church Missionary Society. He is consecrated Bishop of Western Africa (but not of white clergy). Dies 1891.

1810

December: Johannes van der Kemp (◀ 1803) dies.

The American Board of Commissioners for Foreign Mission is formed.

Edinburgh Theological College is founded, the oldest in the Anglican Communion.

1811

♣ April 5: Robert Raikes (◀ 1735) dies.

♣ ⅏ July 13: George Gilbert Scott, English architect, is born. An evangelical and champion of the Gothic style, he builds churches including St Giles, Camberwell, in London and St George's Minster, Doncaster, and restores countless others. Dies 1878.

October 16: The National Society (for the education of the poor) is founded by Joshua Watson.

The Disciples of Christ (▶ 1832) are founded by Alexander Campbell (◀ 1788).

Salih Abdul Masih, a prominent Muslim, is converted to Christianity and baptized. He works for the Church Missionary Society, but initially receives little support from the Anglican Church (▶ 1825).

The Primitive Methodist Church is founded as a formal movement out of three smaller churches at a camp meeting at Mow Cop, Staffordshire (▶ 1932).

Large numbers of Welsh Protestants leave the Anglican Church in the 'Great Schism'.

1812

♣ October 16: Henry Martyn (◀ 1781) dies.

⅏ December 25: After the last of Napoleon's soldiers leave Moscow, Tsar Alexander announces the building of a Cathedral of Christ the Saviour to express gratitude for divine providence (▶ 1839).

The Congregational Union of Scotland is formed.

The Baptist Union of Great Britain and Ireland is formed.

Princeton Theological Seminary is founded.

1813

⚕ March 4: Jeremias IV, Patriarch of Constantinople (◀ 1808), is succeeded by Cyril VI (▶ 1818).

🕭 March 19: David Livingstone (▶ 1841), Scottish missionary and explorer, is born. He prompts the foundation of the Universities' Mission to Central Africa (▶ 1857). Dies 1873.

🕭 May 5: Søren Kierkegaard, Danish philosopher, is born. Seen as the first existentialist philosopher, he writes on a range of questions relating to faith and institutional religion. Dies 1855.

🕭 June 24: Henry Ward Beecher is born. Brother of Harriet Beecher Stowe (▶ 1852), he becomes one of the most influential Protestants of his time and is a firm opponent of slavery. Dies 1887.

🕭 Granville Sharp (◀ 1735) dies.

October 6: The Wesleyan Missionary Society is formed.

Adoniram Judson (◀ 1788) arrives in Burma.

Joseph Carel Kam, a Dutch missionary, arrives in the Moluccas, where he works for 20 years, adapting Christianity to local patterns.

William Milne of the London Missionary Society arrives in Malacca.

1814

🕭 January 24: John William Colenso, missionary bishop to Africa, is born. His treatment of problems of biblical criticism (▶ 1867) leads to his excommunication. Dies 1883.

March 10: Napoleon releases Pope Pius VII (◀ 1809).

April 11: Napoleon abdicates and is exiled to Elba.

👑 May 2: Louis XVIII, brother of Louis XVI (◀ 1793), proclaims himself King of France (▶ 1824).

🕭 May 3: Thomas Coke (◀ 1747) dies.

May 8: T. F. Middleton is consecrated Bishop of Calcutta, the first Anglican bishop in Asia.

May 18: The American Baptist Missionary Union is founded.

♣ June 28: Frederick William Faber, English hymn writer, is born. Dies 1863.

August 7: In his bull *Sollicitudo omnium ecclesiarum*, Pope Pius VII formally restores the Jesuits (◀ 1773).

♣ ⬚ September 7: William Butterfield, English architect, is born. Inspired by the Oxford Movement (▶ 1833), among other ecclesiastical buildings he designs All Saints, Margaret Street (1859), and St Alban's, Holborn (1863), in London and Keble College, Oxford (1876). Dies 1900.

December 20: Samuel Marsden, an English missionary who has been Anglican chaplain to a penal colony in New South Wales, establishes a mission to Maoris in the Bay of Islands, New Zealand.

1815

June 7: Pope Pius VII (◀ 1814) returns to the Vatican.

♣ August 16: John Bosco (▶ 1859), Italian educational pioneer, is born. He founds the Society of St Francis de Sales (Salesians). Dies 1888.

September 16: The Basle Missionary Society is founded by Pietists (◀ 1635) to be international and interdenominational.

♣ ⬚ November 12: Elizabeth Cady Stanton, American pioneer in women's suffrage and editor of *The Woman's Bible* (1895), is born. Dies 1902.

♣ December 3: John Carroll (◀ 1735) dies.

William O'Bryan founds the Bible Christians in Devon, a breakaway movement from Methodism.

1816

♣ March 31: Francis Asbury (◀ 1745) dies.

April 9: The African Methodist Episcopal Church is founded in Philadelphia by Richard Allen (◀ 1787), a former slave who becomes its first bishop.

June 29: Pope Pius VII condemns the Protestant Bible Societies.

July 23: The Society of Mary (Marists) is founded in Lyons by Jean Claude Marie Colin for mission work.

The American Bible Society is founded by a group of New York philanthropists.

The Evangelical Church (◀ 1807) becomes the Evangelical Association.

1817

♣ January 11: Timothy Dwight (◀ 1752) dies.

January: Robert Moffat and three other Church Missionary Society (◀ 1799) missionaries arrive at the Cape (▶ 1821).

May: General Theological Seminary is founded in New York.

358

September 27: Lutheran and Reformed churches in Prussia form the Evangelical Union.

1818

🌷 January 24: John Mason Neale, English hymn writer, is born. He translates ancient Latin hymns, notably 'Jerusalem the Golden' and 'All glory, laud, and honour', and writes the carol 'Good King Wenceslas'. Dies 1866.

🌷 April: Cecil Frances Alexander is born. A hymn writer, she writes 'All things bright and beautiful', 'There is a green hill far away', and 'Once in royal David's city' to make the catechism come alive for children. Dies 1895.

🌷 May 5: Karl Marx (▶ 1867), German economist, is born. Dies 1883.

☧ December 15: Cyril VI (◀ 1813) is succeeded by Gregory V (◀ 1808, ▶ 1821), who becomes Patriarch of Constantinople for the third time.

♫ Francis Xaver Gruber composes the tune for 'Silent Night'.

London Missionary Society missionaries arrive on Madagascar.

1819

May 5: William Ellery Channing (◀ 1803) preaches a sermon in Baltimore which is regarded as the creed of Unitarianism (see p.342).

May 16: Pomone II, King of Tahiti, is baptized. His power is bolstered by missionaries (◀ 1797). The New Testament is translated into Tahitian.

🌷📖 June 12: Charles Kingsley, English novelist and social reformer, best known for his *The Water Babies* (1863), is born. Dies 1875.

🌷📖 November 22: George Eliot (Mary Ann Cross, née Evans) is born. As well as becoming a novelist famous for *Middlemarch* (1871) and *Daniel Deronda* (1876), she translates radical works of German philosophy and theology by authors such as David Friedrich Strauss (▶ 1835/36) and Ludwig Feuerbach (◀ 1804). Dies 1880.

The Bible is translated into Chinese by Robert Morrison and his companions (◀ 1807).

1820

👑 January 29: King George III (◀ 1760) dies and is succeeded by his son as King George IV of the United Kingdom (▶ 1830).

March 30: American missionaries from New England reach Hawaii.

John Philip arrives at Cape Town as Superintendent of the Church Missionary Society.

The Jesuits are expelled from Russia.

***c*.1820**

The Russian Orthodox priest Ivan Veniaminov (◀ 1797) arrives in Alaska, engages in missionary work and translates the New Testament and liturgical material into the native dialects (▶ 1840).

1821

♣ January 4: Elizabeth Ann Seton (◀ 1774) dies (▶ 1995).

January 4–9: An illuminated star with 110 points is hung in the courtyard of the Moravian school at Niesky, Germany, for Epiphany; it is the precursor of the Advent star.

March 25: The Greek Bishop Germanos of Old Patras proclaims a Greek uprising against the Ottoman empire. The Greeks capture the Peloponnese, but the Turks retaliate with massacres. The struggle is a long one (▶ 1832).

⚓ April 22: Patriarch Gregory V of Constantinople (◀ 1818) is executed by the Turks in reprisals against the Greek uprising. Eugenius II (▶ 1822), who has been imprisoned as a hostage by the Sultan, becomes Patriarch.

♣ July 16: Mary Baker Eddy, founder of Christian Science (▶ 1879), is born. Dies 1910.

🏛 October 29: Governor Lachlan Macquarie lays the foundation stone of St Mary's Roman Catholic Cathedral, Sydney, Australia (▶ 1865).

♣ November 11: Fyodor Dostoevsky, Russian novelist and existentialist, is born. Dies 1881.

The Wesleyan missionary William Walker begins work among the Aborigines of Sydney, with little success (▶ 1838).

Robert Moffat (◀ 1817) and his wife arrive at Kuruman in Bechuanaland, where they stay for 50 years.

The Portuguese Inquisition (◀ 1536) is finally abolished.

1821/22

📖 In his systematic theology *The Christian Faith*, Friedrich Schleiermacher (◀ 1799, ▶ 1834) famously defines religion as the 'feeling of absolute dependence'.

1822

⚓ July 27: Eugenius II, Patriarch of Constantinople (◀ 1821), is succeeded by Anthimus III (▶ 1824).

September 29: Jean François Champollion announces that he can decipher hieroglyphics, thus opening up the whole world of Egyptian history and literature.

♣ December 24: Matthew Arnold, English poet (▶ 1867) and critic, is born. Dies 1888.

In Ireland, Daniel O'Connell founds the Catholic Association to further Catholic emancipation (▶ 1830).

Wesleyan Methodist missionaries open a mission station on North Island, New Zealand.

360

1823

♣▢ February 28: Ernest Renan is born. His *Life of Jesus* (1863), a romanticized account but based on first-hand knowledge of Syria and Palestine, is immensely popular. It rejects the need for institutional religion and therefore brings condemnation from the Roman Catholic Church. Dies 1892.

♫ April 7: Beethoven's *Missa Solemnis* is first performed complete in St Petersburg.

May 3: Pauline Jaricot, a French Catholic lay woman, founds the Society for the Propagation of the Faith, to finance missionary work, in Lyons.

✠ July 20: Pope Pius VII (◀ 1800) dies.

✠ September 28: Annibale Sermattei della Genga, Vicar General of Rome, is elected as Pope Leo XII (▶ 1829).

1824

February 29: The Berlin Missionary Society is founded.

✠ July 9: Anthimus III, Patriarch of Constantinople (◀ 1822), is succeeded by Chrysanthus I (▶ 1826).

♣♫ September 4: Anton Bruckner, Austrian composer, is born. A devout Catholic, as well as nine numbered symphonies he writes many choral works, including seven masses. Dies 1896.

♛ September 16: Louis XVIII, King of France (◀ 1814), dies and is succeeded by his brother as Charles X (▶ 1830).

Liang Fa is ordained by Robert Morrison (◀ 1819) as the first Chinese Protestant evangelist.

Pedro, son of King Garcia V of the Kongo, is ordained priest.

The American Sunday School Union is founded in Philadelphia and becomes a major religious force.

The Quaker John Cadbury opens a chocolate shop in Birmingham which proves immensely successful. Bournville, the factory which he establishes later, is a model for caring employment.

The Glasgow Missionary Society founds the mission station of Lovedale in Cape Province; it is to be an influential missionary centre.

1825

May 25: The American Unitarian Association and the British and Foreign Unitarian Association are formed.

♣ October 31: Charles-Martial-Allemand Lavigerie (▶ 1868), French missionary, is born. He founds the missionary orders of the White Fathers and the White Sisters and is a vigorous campaigner against slavery. Dies 1892.

December 5: Ka'ahumanu, regent of Hawaii (◀ 1820), is baptized. She gives Hawaii a code of laws based on Christian principles but later takes steps to outlaw Roman Catholicism.

Salih Abdul Masih (◀ 1811) becomes the first Indian ordained to the Anglican priesthood. He is a great influence on the mission to Muslims and applies rationalistic methods of Islamic scholarship to biblical interpretation.

1826

September 26: Chrysanthus I, Patriarch of Constantinople (◀ 1824), is succeeded by Agathangelus I (▶ 1830).

University College, London, is founded. It applies no religious tests to its students (▶ 1829).

In Tahiti, the Mamaia movement preaches the imminent return of Christ yet allows erotic dancing, drink and polygamy.

1827

April 2: William Holman Hunt, Pre-Raphaelite painter (▶ 1853), is born. Dies 1910.

August 12: William Blake (◀ 1757) dies.

George Frederick Bodley, an English ecclesiastical architect and designer working in the Gothic revival style, is born. Dies 1907.

John Keble (◀ 1792, ▶ 1833), *The Christian Year*, thoughts for the Sundays and holy days of the year in verse, is published.

1828

April 13: Josephine Butler, social reformer, is born. Dies 1906.

May 9: The Test Act (◀ 1673) is repealed: receiving communion in the Church of England is no longer mandatory for civil and military officers.

July 21: Charles Manners-Sutton, Archbishop of Canterbury (◀ 1805), dies.

August 15: William Howley, Bishop of London, is appointed Archbishop of Canterbury (▶ 1848). He is the last prince archbishop, retaining his own wealth. On his death the Ecclesiastical Commissioners (▶ 1835) control the Archbishop of Canterbury's income.

August 28: Leo Tolstoy, Russian social critic and writer, is born. Dies 1910.

Karl Gützlaff, a German missionary, and Jacob Tomlin of the London Missionary Society arrive in Siam. They translate the Gospels into Siamese.

The Basle Mission starts work on the Gold Coast (now Ghana). The missionaries develop the country's economy by growing cocoa.

1829

January 12: Friedrich von Schlegel (◀ 1772) dies.

✠ February 10: Pope Leo XII (◄ 1823) dies.

♪ March 11: Felix Mendelssohn (◄ 1809, ► 1846) conducts Bach's *St Matthew Passion* in Berlin, the first performance since Bach's death (◄ 1750).

✠ March 31: Francesci Saverio Castiglione, Bishop of Frascati and Grand Penitentiary, is elected as Pope Pius VIII (► 1830).

♟ April 10: William Booth, founder of the Salvation Army (► 1865), is born. Dies 1912.

April 16: In Britain, the Catholic Emancipation Act allows Catholics to vote, stand for Parliament and hold public office.

August 14: King George IV grants King's College, London, a royal charter. It is founded to provide an education on Anglican principles and admits only members of the Church of England.

October 4: The first Provincial Council of US Catholic bishops is held at Baltimore.

1830

April 6: The Mormons (The Church of the Latter-Day Saints) are organized by Joseph Smith (◄ 1805, ► 1844) in Fayette, New York, on the basis of a vision in which an angel comes to him and communicates the text of the Book of Mormon on golden plates.

♛ June 26: King George IV of the United Kingdom (◄ 1820) dies and is succeeded by his brother, the third son of King George III (◄ 1760), as William IV (► 1837).

✠ July 5: Agathangelus I, Patriarch of Constantinople (◄ 1826), is succeeded by Constantius I (► 1834).

July 18: Catherine Labouré, a nun in Paris, experiences a vision of the Virgin Mary in commemoration of which special coins are minted (► 1947).

♛ August 2: Charles X, King of France (◄ 1824), dies and is succeeded by Louis Philippe (► 1848), the last King of France.

✠ November 30: Pope Pius VIII (◄ 1829) dies.

Following a campaign by Daniel O'Connell's Catholic Association (◄ 1822), the Catholic Relief Act repeals the last laws against Roman Catholics and allows them to sit in Parliament.

Alexander Duff establishes a Christian college in Calcutta; his educational work leads to the adoption of English in all Indian government schools.

London Missionary Society missionaries led by John Williams (► 1839) arrive on Samoa.

Two German missionaries, Samuel Gobart and Christian Kugler, arrive at the court of Emperor Sabagadis of Ethiopia, marking the beginning of the modern missionary period there. An initial welcome turns to hostility.

c.1830

In Samoa, the charismatic Siovili founds a movement named after him which offers an indigenous form of Christianity with a focus on the new moon.

1831

☘ February 2: Bartolomeo Alberto Cappellari, Vicar General of the Camaldolese Order (◀ 1012) and Prefect of the Propaganda, is elected as Pope Gregory XVI (▶ 1846). He bans railways in his domain.

♰ August 13: Nikolai Kasatkin (born Ivan Dimitrovich) is born. He introduces the Eastern Orthodox Church into Japan and becomes its archbishop (▶ 1907). Dies 1912.

♰ November 14: Georg Wilhelm Friedrich Hegel (◀ 1770) dies.

☦ Alphonsus Liguori (◀ 1787) is canonized by Pope Gregory XVI: feast day August 1.

William Miller, an American Baptist preacher, forms the Adventists. He begins to preach the end of the world, which he dates first to March 21, 1843, then to October 22, 1844. His followers, the Millerites, survive the disappointment and later become Seventh-day Adventists (▶ 1863).

The first Croatian Bible is published.

Taufaʻahau, a Tongan chief, is baptized under the name of George. He later becomes King George Tupou I of Tonga.

1832

May 11: Greece is recognized as a sovereign state (◀ 1821).

♰ May 21: James Hudson Taylor, missionary, is born. He founds the interdenominational China Inland Mission (▶ 1865). Dies 1905.

May: The Congregational Union of England and Wales is formed.

August 15: The encyclical *Mirari vos* condemns freedom of conscience and the press, and the separation of church and state, associated with F. R. de Lamennais (◀ 1782, ▶ 1854).

December 24: In her journal, the young Princess Victoria of Saxe-Coburg (▶ 1837) marvels at two Christmas trees with lights, sugar ornaments and presents.

The Church of Christ (Disciples) is formed from the Christians led by Barton Stone (◀ 1772, ▶ 1844) and the Disciples of Christ led by Alexander Campbell (◀ 1811, ▶ 1866).

1833

July 14: John Keble (◀ 1827) preaches a sermon in Oxford on national apostasy: this leads to the rise of the Oxford Movement, which aims to restore the Church of England to its Catholic heritage.

♰ July 29: William Wilberforce (◀ 1759) dies.

July: The bishops of liberated Greece (◀ 1832) meet at Nauplion and establish themselves as the synod of a self-governing church.

♦ September 7: Hannah More (◀ 1745) dies.

The Society of Foreign Missions of Paris (◀ 1663) arrives in Lesotho.

1834

♦ February 12: Friedrich Schleiermacher (◀ 1768) dies.

April 23: A Baptist church is formed in Hamburg led by J. L. Oncken; it is the oldest Baptist church in continental Europe.

♦ June 9: William Carey (◀ 1761) dies.

♦ June 19: Charles Haddon Spurgeon, English Baptist preacher, is born. He is so successful that a new church has to be built for him in South London to accommodate the crowds. Dies 1892.

July 15: The Spanish Inquisition (◀ 1478) is formally abolished.

♦ July 23: James Gibbons is born. He becomes Archbishop of Baltimore and a cardinal and brings Catholic practice into the mainstream of American religious life. Dies 1921.

♦ July 25: Samuel Taylor Coleridge (◀ 1772) dies.

August 1: The Slavery Abolition Act abolishes slavery throughout the British empire.

☩ August 18: Constantius I, Patriarch of Constantinople (◀ 1830), is succeeded by Constantius II (▶ 1835).

♦ December 7: Edward Irving (◀ 1792) dies.

1835

March 2: Franz II, Emperor of Austria (◀ 1806), dies.

July 14: Vincent Mary Pallotti founds the Pious Society of Missions, known as the Pallottines (▶ 1963).

☩ September 26: Constantius II, Patriarch of Constantinople (◀ 1834), is succeeded by Gregory VI (▶ 1840).

♦ December 13: Phillips Brooks, preacher and hymn writer, is born. Called the greatest American preacher of the nineteenth century, he is a staunch liberal. He writes 'O little town of Bethlehem'. Dies 1893.

The Ecclesiastical Commissioners are formed to manage the estates and revenues of the Church of England (▶ 1948).

Queen Ranavalona I of Madagascar attempts to eradicate foreign influence in the island by expelling all foreigners, including missionaries, and suppressing Christianity with violence. Her campaign against Madagascan Christians continues until her death in 1861.

365

The first European Protestant missionaries arrive in Korea.

Two Wesleyan Methodist missionaries arrive in Fiji (▶ 1854).

1835/36

📖 David Friedrich Strauss (◀ 1808, ▶ 1874), *The Life of Jesus Critically Examined*, is published. It interprets the life of Jesus in terms of myth.

1836

🌱 November 13: Charles Simeon (◀ 1759) dies.

The Dresden Missionary Society is founded.

The Church Pastoral Aid Society is founded by Lord Shaftesbury to assist the home mission work of the Anglican Church.

William Grant Broughton is consecrated the first (and only) Anglican Bishop of Australia (the country is later divided into smaller dioceses).

After moving into the interior of southern Africa to establish their own homeland in the Great Trek, Dutch-speaking colonists establish the independent republics of Transvaal and Orange Free State.

1837

🌱 February 5: Dwight Lyman Moody, American evangelist, is born. With Ira Sankey (▶ 1873) he has a triumphant mission in England which is the basis for equally eventful missions all over the USA. Dies 1899.

👑 June 20: William IV (◀ 1820), King of the United Kingdom, dies and is succeeded by Victoria, daughter of his brother Edward, the fourth son of King George III (◀ 1760), as Queen Victoria (▶ 1901).

🌱 October 29: Abraham Kuyper (▶ 1880), Dutch Reformed theologian and politician, is born. He founds a Free University of Amsterdam and becomes Dutch Prime Minister in 1901. Dies 1920.

🎵 December 5: Hector Berlioz, *Grande Messe des Morts*, is first performed in the church of St Louis des Invalides, Paris.

Bishop William Grant Broughton (◀ 1836) lays the foundation stone of St Andrew's Cathedral, Sydney.

The Presbyterian Board of Foreign Missions is founded in the USA.

Johann Ludwig Krapf arrives in Ethiopia as a missionary. He has learned Ge'ez and translates some of the New Testament into the language (▶ 1842).

The Bible is first translated into Japanese.

American Presbyterians split into 'Old' and 'New' schools. Accused of theological error, the 'New' school sets out its doctrines in the Auburn Declaration.

Henry Creswicke Rawlinson copies the inscriptions on the cliff face of Behistun in Persia. They prove a key to the deciphering of cuneiform, the script of Mesopotamian inscriptions.

Edward Robinson, an American Old Testament professor, and Eli Smith, a Protestant missionary, set out to explore the Holy Land. They are able to link up biblical names with the current Arabic names of towns and abandoned mounds.

1838

French Marist (◀ 1816) missionaries arrive in New Zealand.

Missionaries from the Dresden Missionary Society arrive in Adelaide to work among the Aborigines (◀ 1821).

1839

The Mormons (◀ 1830) arrive in Nauvoo, Illinois.

The Cambridge Camden Society is founded for the study of ecclesiastical art.

⌂ John Francis Bentley, English architect, is born. A convert to Roman Catholicism, he builds striking churches in the neo-Gothic and Byzantine styles. His masterpiece is Westminster Cathedral (▶ 1903). Dies 1902.

John Williams (◀ 1830) is killed on the island of Vanuatu after working on Rarotonga in the Cook Islands. He is regarded as an inspiration in the region.

⌂ The cornerstone is laid for Christ the Saviour Cathedral, Moscow (◀ 1812, ▶ 1883).

Justin de Jacobis, a Lazarist missionary from Naples, arrives in Ethiopia, giving rise to an Ethiopian Catholic community (▶ 1846).

The Bible is translated into Hawaiian.

1840

✠ February 20: Gregory VI, Patriarch of Constantinople (◀ 1835, ▶ 1867), is succeeded by Anthimus IV (▶ 1841).

May 16: The first issue of *The Tablet*, the British Catholic weekly founded by Frederick Lucas, appears.

December 15: The Orthodox priest Ivan Veniaminov (◀ c.1820) is consecrated Bishop of Kamchatka under the name Innocent (▶ 1850).

December: The first Christmas tree is introduced into France by the Duchess of Orleans.

Francis Liberman, a Jewish convert to Christianity, founds the Missionaries of the Heart of Mary, which is merged with the almost defunct Congregation of the Holy Ghost to become a missionary body focused on Africa.

1841

⚛ May 6: Anthimus IV, Patriarch of Constantinople (◀ 1840, ▶ 1848), is succeeded by Anthimus V (▶ 1842).

July 31: David Livingstone (◀ 1813, ▶ 1847) arrives at the mission station of Robert Moffat in Bechuanaland to begin his missionary work.

October 11: George Ripley, an American Unitarian minister, founds Brook Farm, Massachusetts, which becomes one of the most notable experiments in communal living.

October 17: George Augustus Selwyn is consecrated the first Anglican bishop in New Zealand.

1842

🌱 January 11: William James (▶ 1901), American psychologist and philosopher, is born. Dies 1910.

⚛ June 12: Anthimus V, Patriarch of Constantinople (◀ 1841), is succeeded by Germanus IV (▶ 1845).

August 29: The Treaty of Nanjing provides protection for Protestant missionaries in China.

October 2: William Ellery Channing (◀ 1780) dies.

France takes over rule of Tahiti and the Protestant missionaries (◀ 1819) are replaced by Roman Catholics.

British Wesleyan Methodist missionaries and Anglican Church Missionary Society missionarires come to Nigeria.

Johann Krapf (◀ 1837) is expelled from Ethiopia along with other Western missionaries (▶ 1844).

1843

May 23: Thomas Chalmers leads a withdrawal of 474 clergy from the General Assembly of the Church of Scotland to form the Free Church of Scotland, with himself as moderator. This is known as the Disruption.

🏛 August 15: Honolulu Cathedral is consecrated, the oldest in the United States.

🌱 August 19: Cyrus I. Scofield is born. A lawyer, he is converted to Christianity and becomes a Congregationalist minister, producing the annotated Scofield Reference Bible which interprets the text as a series of divine dispensations. Dies 1921.

October 1: Robert Stephen Hooker, vicar of Morwenstow in Cornwall, introduces the Harvest Festival as commonly celebrated today.

Sojourner Truth (◀ c.1797, ▶ 1883) begins an itinerant ministry.

1844

✝ January 7: Bernadette Soubirous of Lourdes, who is to become famous for her visions of the Virgin Mary (▶ 1858), is born. Dies 1879.

January 7: Johann Krapf, expelled from Ethiopia (◀ 1842), arrives in Zanzibar. He and a colleague translate parts of the Bible into Swahili.

✝ June 27: Joseph Smith (◀ 1805) is killed.

✝ July 28: Gerard Manley Hopkins, Jesuit and English poet, is born. Dies 1889.

✝ October 15: Friedrich Nietzsche, radical German philosopher, is born. Dies 1900.

October 22: The end of the world expected by the Millerites (◀ 1831) does not materialize.

November 9: Barton Stone (◀ 1772) dies.

The Young Men's Christian Association (YMCA) is founded by George Williams.

1845

April 17: Kim Taegon (Andrew Kim) is ordained as the first Korean priest. He is executed the next year (▶ 1984).

☩ April 18: Germanus IV (◀ 1842) is succeeded as Patriarch of Constantinople by Meletius III.

October 9: John Henry Newman (◀ 1801, ▶ 1848) is received into the Roman Catholic Church.

✝ October 12: Elizabeth Fry (◀ 1780) dies.

☩ December 4: Meletius III is succeeded as Patriarch of Constantinople by Anthimus VI (▶ 1848).

The Order of Assumptionists is founded at Nîmes by Emmanuel d'Alzon, dedicated to education and mission work.

Austen Henry Layard begins excavating the Assyrian city of Nimrud, revealing its palaces and monuments and among other things discovering the first link between archaeology and biblical history, a reference to 'Jehu, son of Omri, King of Israel'.

Missionaries from the Baptist Missionary Society arrive in Cambodia.

Southern Baptists begin missionary work in China.

*c.***1845**

Zäkaryas, an influential Muslim teacher, has visions following which he becomes a Christian evangelist in Ethiopia and converts many Muslims.

1846

⛪ May 1: Trinity Church, New York, is consecrated.

May 8–12: The Southern Baptist Convention is formed in Augusta, Georgia, by breakaway Baptists who object to a ruling that slaveholders cannot be missionaries.

June 1: Pope Gregory XVI (◀ 1831) dies.

June 16: Giovanni Maria Mastai-Ferretti, Bishop of Imola, is elected as Pope Pius IX (▶ 1878). He has the longest papal reign in history.

August 10: The interdenominational Evangelical Alliance is founded in London at a conference of over 900 clergy and laity from all over the world.

August 26: Felix Mendelssohn (◀ 1829, ▶ 1847) conducts the first performance of his *Elijah* in Birmingham Town Hall.

September 19: Two shepherd children experience a vision of the Virgin Mary at La Salette, near Grenoble, France.

December 6: Wilhelm Herrmann, German liberal theologian, is born. His *The Communion of the Christian with God* (1886) is seen as a paradigm of liberalism. Dies 1922.

Guglielmo Massaja with a group of Capuchins arrives in Ethiopia. He consecrates Justin de Jacobis (◀ 1839) bishop. This results in a campaign by the authorities against the Catholics (▶ 1860).

1847

April 26: Pastors representing 15 German Lutheran congregations from Saxony found the Evangelical German Lutheran Church Synod of Missouri, Ohio and Other States, which in 1947 becomes the Lutheran Church–Missouri Synod.

July 24: The Mormons under Brigham Young (◀ 1801) found Salt Lake City.

November 4: Felix Mendelssohn (◀ 1809) dies.

November 20: Henry Francis Lyte (◀ 1793) dies.

The United Presbyterian Church in Scotland is formed from the United Secession Church and the Relief Synod, a group which has difficulties with patronage in the Church of Scotland.

David Livingstone settles at Kolobeng, north of Kuruman (◀ 1841, ▶ 1852).

The New Testament is translated into Serbian (▶ 1865).

1848

February 2: John Henry Newman (◀ 1845, ▶ 1849) founds Birmingham Oratory (◀ 1515).

February 11: William Howley, Archbishop of Canterbury (◀ 1828), dies.

February 24: Louis Philippe, King of France (◀ 1830), abdicates.

✠ March 10: John Bird Sumner, Bishop of Chester, and a prominent evangelical, is appointed Archbishop of Canterbury (▶ 1862).

✠ October 14: Anthimus IV (◀ 1841, ▶ 1852) returns for a further period as Patriarch of Constantinople to replace Anthimus VI (◀ 1845, ▶ 1852).

Trappist monks from the Abbey of Melleray in western France found the Abbey of Gethsemani, Kentucky.

John Humphrey Noyes founds the Oneida Community in Vermont which shares property and practises free love (dissolved 1881).

William John Butler, Vicar of Wantage in Oxfordshire, founds the Community of St Mary the Virgin for women who engage in parish work.

John Thomas founds the Christadelphians in America.

1849

December 20: William Miller (◀ 1782) dies.

John Henry Newman (◀ 1848, ▶ 1865) founds Brompton Oratory (◀ 1515).

1850

April 12: Adoniram Judson (◀ 1788) dies.

June 29: The Holy Synod is proclaimed the supreme authority of the self-governed church of Greece.

♫ August 28: First performance at the Weimar Court Theatre of Richard Wagner, *Lohengrin*, the main character in which is a knight of the Holy Grail (◀ c.1191).

September 29: Pope Pius IX re-establishes the Catholic hierarchy in England and Wales.

Bishop Innocent (Ivan Veniaminov, ◀ 1840, ▶ 1868) is consecrated Archbishop of Yakutsk, Alaska (▶ 1868).

Cività Cattolica is founded in Rome as the journal of the Curia and Jesuits.

1851

January: Hong Xiuquan, leader of the Taiping Movement in China, influenced by Christianity and a form of communism, who claims that he is the new Messiah and younger brother of Jesus Christ, starts a revolt which costs millions of lives. The revolt is put down in 1864.

The United Presbyterian Church sets up a mission in Calabar.

An Anglican chaplain is appointed to Tristan da Cunha.

1852

February 4: After much controversy, the Convocation of Canterbury in the Church of England meets and transacts business for the first time since 1717.

April 23: David Livingstone (◀ 1847) sends his wife and children back to England and begins his explorations of Africa (▶ 1856).

May 9: The first Plenary Council of Roman Catholics is held in Baltimore.

♣♫ September 30: Charles Villiers Stanford, Irish composer, is born. His church music will have a central place in Anglicanism. He writes a *Requiem* (1896) and a *Stabat Mater* (1906). Dies 1924.

☩ October 30: Anthimus IV (◀ 1848) is succeeded as Patriarch of Constantinople for a brief period by Germanus IV (◀ 1845) and then again by Anthimus VI (◀ 1845, ▶ 1855).

December 2: Napoleon III, previously President of France, becomes Emperor (▶ 1870).

📖 Harriet Beecher Stowe (◀ 1813), *Uncle Tom's Cabin*, the famous anti-slavery novel, is published.

1853

♣ January 22: Charles Gore (▶ 1889), Anglo-Catholic bishop, is born. He founds the Anglican Community of the Resurrection in Mirfield, Yorkshire (▶ 1892). Dies 1932.

September 15: Antoinette Brown is ordained as first woman minister in the Congregational Church in the USA, but is not recognized by her church (▶ 1863). She later becomes a Unitarian.

October 27: F. D. Maurice (◀ 1805, ▶ 1872) is dismissed from his professorship at King's College, London, for questioning the doctrine of eternal punishment.

■ William Holman Hunt's (◀ 1827, ▶ 1910) painting, *The Light of the World*, is first exhibited.

1854

♣■ February 17: John Martin (◀ 1789) dies.

♣ February 27: Hugo Félicité Robert de Lamennais (◀ 1782) dies.

December 8: The encyclical *Ineffabilis deus* defines the Immaculate Conception of the Blessed Virgin Mary (◀ 1705).

Chief Thakombau of Fiji, along with his people, is converted to Christianity.

1855

☩ September 21: Anthimus VI (◀ 1852, ▶ 1871) is succeeded as Patriarch of Constantinople by Cyril VII (▶ 1860).

♣ November 11: Søren Kierkegaard (◀ 1813) dies.

The Young Women's Christian Association (YWCA) is founded by Emma Robarts.

The Places of Worship Registration Act allows worship in Britain in buildings which are not consecrated.

The Mennonite Community of True Inspiration, immigrants from Germany organized on a strictly communal basis, establishes Amana, a network of seven villages in east central Iowa.

📖 Anthony Trollope, *The Warden*, the first of the Barchester novels, is published. It is followed by *Barchester Towers* (1857) and *The Last Chronicle of Barset* (1867). The trilogy is a classic depiction of Victorian Anglican church life.

1856

♦ May 6: Sigmund Freud (▶ 1927), founder of modern psychoanalysis, is born. Dies 1939.

December 8: The Society of African Missions is founded in Lyons by Bishop Melchior de Marion Brésillac.

December 9: David Livingstone (◀ 1852) arrives back in England after 16 years (▶ 1857).

♦ December 28: Woodrow Wilson is born. A committed Christian and professional academic, he goes into politics and is US President from 1913 to 1921. He tries to establish a new standard for international justice with his Fourteen Points. Dies 1924.

The Nederduits Hervormde Kerk is constituted in the Transvaal as a breakaway church from the Nederduits Gereformeerde Kerk (Cape Synod).

1857

♦📖 February 28: Alfred Loisy, French Catholic Modernist, is born. His radical views on the Bible and Christian origins, especially as expressed in his book *The Gospel and the Church* (1902), lead to his excommunication. Dies 1940.

♦♪ June 2: Edward Elgar, English composer, is born. A Roman Catholic, in addition to symphonies, concerti and occasional music he writes church music and a number of oratorios, most notably *The Dream of Gerontius* (▶ 1900), *The Apostles* (1902/3) and *The Kingdom* (1901–6). Dies 1934.

December: The Universities' Mission to Central Africa is founded in the Senate House, Cambridge, in response to an appeal from David Livingstone (◀ 1856, ▶ 1873).

1858

February 11: In Lourdes in southern France, Bernadette Soubirous (◀ 1844, ▶ 1879) has a vision of the Virgin Mary.

♦ March 10: Nathaniel William Taylor (◀ 1786) dies.

June 18: The Treaties of Tientsin (Tianjin) give foreigners, including missionaries, the right to travel and work within China.

July 26: Lionel de Rothschild takes his seat in the English House of Commons, marking the emancipation of Jews in Britain.

♦ September 15: Charles Eugène de Foucauld, French hermit, is born. He lives for a decade among the Tuareg Muslims until he is assassinated in 1916.

Isaac Hecker founds the first American Catholic order of men, the Paulists.

The first edition of *Crockford's Clerical Directory* is published.

1859

May 12: The English Church Union is founded (as the Church of England Protection Society) to defend the Anglican Catholic tradition.

July: Japanese ports are opened to foreign missionaries.

✦ August 4: Jean-Baptiste-Marie Vianney, the Curé d'Ars (◀ 1786), dies (▶ 1925).

The Society of St Francis de Sales (Salesians) for educating the poor is founded near Turin by John Bosco (◀ 1818, ▶ 1888).

📖 Charles Darwin (◀ 1809, ▶ 1882), *On the Origin of Species by Means of Natural Selection*, sets out the theory of evolution.

The Roman Catholic Catechism of Christian Doctrine ('Penny Catechism') is issued.

1860

✦ March 19: William Jennings Bryan is born. An evangelical Presbyterian, he sees politics as a way of promoting Christian morality. He is three times an unsuccessful US presidential candidate and an opponent of evolution, dying immediately after the Scopes 'monkey trial' (▶ 1925).

☩ October 4: Cyril VII (◀ 1855) is succeeded as Patriarch of Constantinople by Joachim II (▶ 1863).

✦ December 2: Ferdinand Christian Baur (◀ 1792) dies.

✦ Justin de Jacobis (◀ 1839) dies (▶ 1975).

✦ Gaston B. Cashwell is born. A Methodist minister, after his Pentecostal experience at Azuza Street, Los Angeles (▶ 1906), he preaches Pentecost across the southern states. He later returns to Methodism. Dies 1916.

The General Conference Mennonite church is founded.

Dirk Postma founds a conservative Dutch Reformed Church in Burgersdorp, South Africa, known as the Doppers.

📖 Jean-Pierre de Caussade (◀ 1675), *Self-Abandonment to Divine Providence*, is posthumously published.

c.1860

✦ William Wadé Harris, African prophet and evangelist, is born. Dies 1929.

1861

✦📖 February 6: George Tyrrell, Irish Modernist theologian, is born. A Jesuit, he is later excommunicated; his last book, *Christianity at the Crossroads*, published posthumously, explores the possibility of a higher religion beyond Christianity. Dies 1909.

✦ February 25: Rudolf Steiner, Austrian philosopher, is born. He founds the Anthropo-

374

sophical Society, offering a modern spiritual path which values the freedom of each individual. Dies 1925.

April 12: The American Civil War begins with an attack on Fort Sumter, in Charleston Harbour, South Carolina, by Confederate forces (▶ 1865).

July 1: The first issue of *L'Osservatore Romano*, the official Vatican newspaper, appears.

✤ November 21: Jean-Baptiste Henri Dominique Lacordaire (◀ 1802) dies.

Hymns Ancient and Modern is published.

The Convocation of York is revived (◀ 1852).

1862

July 18: Bishop Archibald Campbell Tait of London (▶ 1868) revives the Order of Deaconesses in the Church of England by ordaining Elizabeth Ferard.

☉ September 6: John Bird Sumner, Archbishop of Canterbury (◀ 1848), dies.

✤ November 19: Billy Sunday (▶ 1896), American evangelist, is born. A basketball player, after his conversion he becomes a fire-and-brimstone preacher. Dies 1935.

☉ November 26: Charles Thomas Longley, Archbishop of York, is appointed Archbishop of Canterbury (▶ 1868). He presides over the first Lambeth Conference (▶ 1867).

Dutch missionaries from the Utrecht Missionary Society arrive in New Guinea. They have little success.

1863

January 1: US President Abraham Lincoln's Emancipation Proclamation declares that all slaves in Confederate states are free.

February 7: The first issue of the *Church Times* is published in London.

May 21: The Seventh-day Adventist Church (◀ 1831) is officially organized in the USA.

☉ September 20: Joachim II (◀ 1860, ▶ 1873) is succeeded as Patriarch of Constantinople by Sophronius III (▶ 1867).

✤ September 26: Frederick William Faber (◀ 1814) dies.

Olympia Brown, a Universalist, is the first woman in the United States to be ordained minister and recognized by her church. She later becomes a Unitarian.

Daniel Bliss opens the Syrian Protestant College. It later becomes the American University of Beirut.

The New Testament is translated into Russian (▶ 1875).

1864

✤ ▭ April 21: Karl Emil Maximilian ('Max') Weber, German sociologist, is born. His best-known book is *The Protestant Ethic and the Spirit of Capitalism* (1904–5), which argues

375

that the Protestant ethic broke the hold of tradition and encouraged people to acquire wealth rationally. Dies 1920.

December 8: Pope Pius IX's encyclical *Quanta cura* is issued with the *Syllabus of Errors*, condemning freedom of religion and separation of church and state, as an appendix.

📖 John Henry Newman's (◀ 1849, ▶ 1865) *Apologia pro Vita Sua*, his autobiography, is published.

📖 G. B. de Rossi, *Roma sotteranea Christiana*, begins to appear and demonstrates that Christian archaeology is a modern scientific discipline.

1865

January 31: The 13th Amendment to the Constitution abolishes slavery in the US.

🌲 February 17: Ernst Troeltsch, German philosopher and theologian, is born. He emphasizes the historicity of reality. Dies 1923.

April 9: Confederate soldiers under General Robert E. Lee surrender at Appomattox Courthouse, marking the end of the American Civil War (◀ 1861).

🌲 May 23: John R. Mott (▶ 1888), American churchman, is born. He helps to found the World Student Christian Federation (▶ 1895) and is president of the Edinburgh World Missionary Conference (▶ 1910). Dies 1955.

June 25: James Hudson Taylor (◀ 1832, ▶ 1905) founds the China Inland Mission.

June 29: Sydney Roman Catholic Cathedral (◀ 1821) is destroyed by fire.

August: The Welsh Congregationalist Robert Jermain Thomas is the first Protestant missionary in Korea. He is killed the next year.

The Romanian Orthodox Church becomes self-governing.

William Booth (◀ 1829) founds the Christian Revival Association, which in 1878 becomes the Salvation Army.

The Palestine Exploration Fund is founded by a group of distinguished academics and clergymen.

Samuel Crowther (◀ *c.*1809, ▶ 1891) is the first black Anglican Bishop of Nigeria.

The Old Testament is translated into Serbian (◀ 1847).

📖 John Henry Newman (◀ 1864, ▶ 1890) writes his poem *The Dream of Gerontius* (▶ 1900).

1866

🌲 January 15: Nathan Söderblom, Swedish Lutheran theologian and ecumenist, is born. Dies 1931.

February: A major persecution breaks out in Korea which virtually annihilates the Korean church.

🌳 March 4: Alexander Campbell (◀ 1788) dies.

March 19: Herbert Vaughan founds St Joseph's Society for Foreign Missions (Mill Hill Missionaries) at Mill Hill, London, the first English Roman Catholic missionary society.

🌳 March 29: John Keble (◀ 1792) dies.

🌳 August 6: John Mason Neale (◀ 1818) dies.

🌳 September 8: Charles H. Mason, American evangelist, is born. From 1907 until his death in 1961 he is senior bishop of the Church of God in Christ (▶ 1897), the largest and fastest-growing Pentecostal denomination.

December 27: Richard Benson founds the Society of St John the Evangelist in Oxford (Cowley Fathers).

The Universalist General Convention is founded in the United States (▶ 1942).

The Ku Klux Klan is founded, a terrorist organization which leads resistance against civil rights and the power of newly-freed slaves after the American Civil War. It is disbanded in 1869 (▶ 1915).

1867

February: The *Ausgleich* (Compromise) establishes the monarchy of Austria–Hungary, which is to last until 1918. It guarantees full religious toleration.

🕀 June 29: Paul of the Cross (◀ 1720) is canonized by Pope Pius IX: feast day October 19.

July 17–26: The Holiness Movement has its beginnings at the Holiness Camp Meeting in Vineland, New Jersey.

September 24–28: The First Lambeth Conference, an assembly of the bishops of the Anglican Communion, is called by Archbishop Longley (◀ 1862, ▶ 1868) at the request of the Canadian Anglican Church. Most of the conference is occupied with a discussion of the controversy over the writings of Bishop Colenso (◀ 1814).

☧ Sophronius III (◀ 1863) is succeeded as Patriarch of Constantinople by Gregory VI (◀ 1835, ▶ 1871).

📖 The first volume of Karl Marx (◀ 1818, ▶ 1883), *Das Kapital*, is published (the other two are published posthumously in 1885 and 1895).

The Italian missionary Daniel Comboni founds the Verona Fathers for work in Africa (the Verona Sisters follow in 1872).

Matthew Arnold's (◀ 1822, ▶ 1888) poem 'On Dover Beach', a farewell to the certainties of religious faith, is written.

1868

☧ January 5: Archbishop Innocent of Yakutsk (◀ 1850) becomes Patriarch of Moscow and All Russia (▶ 1879).

February 29: In the decree *Non expedit*, Pope Pius IX forbids Catholics to take part in political life in Italy.

August 6: Paul Claudel, French Catholic poet and dramatist, is born. His masterpiece is *The Satin Slipper* (1929), a drama of the Catholic world of the Renaissance. Dies 1955.

October 28: Charles Thomas Longley, Archbishop of Canterbury (◀ 1862), dies.

December 20: Archibald Campbell Tait, Bishop of London (◀ 1868), is appointed Archbishop of Canterbury (▶ 1882).

The foundation stone is laid for a new Roman Catholic Cathedral in Sydney (◀ 1865).

The White Fathers mission society is founded by Charles-Martial-Allemand Lavigerie (◀ 1825, ▶ 1892) as the Missionaries of Our Lady of Africa of Algeria.

1869

February 18: Johannes Brahms, *A German Requiem*, is first performed complete at the Leipzig Gewandhaus.

December 8: The First Vatican Council is convened by Pope Pius IX to deal with contemporary problems. It is regarded in the West as the twentieth Ecumenical Council. After discussing papal infallibility the fathers are allowed to leave Rome for a few months but before they can return, troops from Piedmont invade Rome.

The Anglican Church in Ireland is disestablished.

1870

July 18: The constitution *Pastor aeternus* defines the doctrine of the primacy and infallibility of the Pope.

July 19: France declares war on Prussia, starting the Franco-Prussian War (▶ 1871).

July 27: Joseph Hilaire Pierre Belloc, Roman Catholic writer and critic, is born. Dies 1953.

September 4: Napoleon III, Emperor of France (◀ 1852), is deposed.

September 20: Italian troops enter Rome and put an end to the last remnant of the papal states (◀ 754). King Victor Emmanuel of Italy demolishes the Jewish ghetto there (◀ 1556).

October 20: The First Vatican Council (◀ 1869) is suspended indefinitely.

December: In Germany the Centre Party is founded to counter the anti-Catholic tendencies in politics (▶ 1933).

Charles Taze Russell founds Jehovah's Witnesses as the Watch Tower Bible and Tract Society of Philadelphia.

The Orthodox Church of Bulgaria becomes self-governing.

A session of the First Vatican Council, 1870

1870–75

The Methodist missionary William Taylor (▶ 1884) founds self-supporting, self-governing and self-propagating churches in South India under the name 'Methodist Episcopal'.

1871

January 18: The German Second Reich is inaugurated at Versailles, uniting Germany under Emperor Wilhelm II and his Chancellor Otto von Bismarck (▶ 1918).

January 28: Paris surrenders to German troops after a long siege, ending the Franco-Prussian war (◀ 1870).

February 12: Charles Freer Andrews, missionary to India, is born. Dies 1940.

May 13: A Law of Guarantees is passed regulating relations between the first government of the kingdom of Italy and the papacy.

May 27: Georges Rouault, French painter, is born. A Catholic, he paints many depictions of Christ and his passion, in a style reminiscent of stained-glass windows. Dies 1958.

September 5: Gregory VI (◀ 1835, 1867) is succeeded as Patriarch of Constantinople by Anthimus VI (◀ 1845, 1852, ▶ 1873), who has a third term of office.

A convention in Munich, led by Johann Josef Ignaz von Döllinger (◀ 1799, ▶ 1890), who has been excommunicated by the Roman Catholic Church, founds the Old Catholic

Church. Its members are Austrian, German and Swiss Catholics who reject the dogma of papal infallibility put forward by the First Vatican Council (◀ 1870). The convention is supported by the Archbishop of Utrecht (◀ 1723).

The *Kulturkampf* begins (until 1887). The German state under Chancellor Otto von Bismarck sets out to diminish the loyalty of Catholics to the Pope. Bismarck abolishes the Catholic Department of the Prussian Ministry of Public Worship.

A missionary from the London Missionary Society enters southern Papua.

1872

🌱 April 1: F. D. Maurice (◀ 1805) dies.

🌱 May 18: Bertrand Russell (▶ 1927), English philosopher, is born. A logical positivist, he is notoriously hostile to Christianity. Dies 1970.

June 25: Otto von Bismarck (◀ 1871) expels the Jesuits from Germany.

🌱 September 2: Nikolai Fredrik Severin Grundtvig (◀ 1783) dies.

🌱 September 13: Ludwig Feuerbach dies (◀ 1804).

🌱♫ October 12: Ralph Vaughan Williams, English composer, is born. His wide-ranging compositions include much music inspired by religious themes; he writes an opera based on *The Pilgrim's Progress* (1951), edits *The English Hymnal* (▶ 1906) and himself writes some famous hymn tunes including Down Ampney ('Come down, O love divine') and Sine nomine ('For all the saints'). Dies 1958.

December 3: George Smith announces the discovery of a flood story similar to that in the Bible in the third millennium BCE Gilgamesh epic, written on cuneiform tablets.

1873

🌱 January 2: Thérèse Martin (Thérèse of Lisieux), Carmelite nun, is born. Dies 1897.

🌱📖 January 7: Charles Péguy, French writer, is born. A nationalist mystic with a love of medieval Catholicism and a deep eucharistic devotion, he writes a play, *The Mystery of the Charity of Joan of Arc* (1910), and a vast religious poem, *Eve* (1913). He is killed by the Germans in 1914.

🌱 May 1: David Livingstone (◀ 1813) dies.

May 10: Father Damien (Joseph de Veuster) arrives at the leper settlement on the Hawaiian island of Molokai. He dies there of leprosy in 1889.

🌱 June 4: Charles Fox Parham, American Pentecostal pioneer, is born. Dies 1929.

♫ June: Dwight Moody (◀ 1837) and Ira Sankey hold revivalist meetings in England. Ira Sankey publishes the first edition of *Sacred Songs and Solos*.

☸ November 23: Anthimus VI (◀ 1845, 1852, 1871) is succeeded as Patriarch of Constantinople by Joachim II (◀ 1860, ▶ 1878).

Dwight L. Moody at the Agricultural Hall rally, 1873

Christianity is legalized in Japan (◀ 1638).

The slave market in Zanzibar is closed and an Anglican cathedral is built on the site.

1874

✤ February 8: David Friedrich Strauss (◀ 1808) dies.

♫ May 22: Verdi's *Requiem* is first performed in Milan Cathedral.

✤ May 29: G. K. Chesterton, Roman Catholic poet and writer, is born. Dies 1936.

✤ August 17: Vednayakam Samuel Azariah (▶ 1912), Indian ecumenical leader, is born. Dies 1945.

✤ October 20: J. H. Oldham is born. He becomes a key figure in the ecumenical movement, being the first full-time secretary of the Student Christian Movement (▶ 1893), secretary to the Edinburgh World Missionary Conference (▶ 1910) and founder of the influential *Christian Newsletter*. Dies 1969.

✤ November 2: Phoebe Worrall Palmer (◀ 1807) dies.

1875

✤ 📖 January 14: Albert Schweitzer (▶ 1913), theologian, physician, musician and missionary to Africa, is born. His *The Quest of the Historical Jesus* (1906) surveys nineteenth-century accounts of the life of Jesus and shows that they are largely the projections of the authors' ideals. Dies 1965.

381

♣ January 23: Charles Kingsley (◀ 1819) dies.

February 5: In the encyclical *Quod numquam* Pope Pius IX condemns the German government policy of abolishing religious orders as part of the *Kulturkampf* (◀ 1871) in Prussia.

June 29: The first Keswick Convention for Evangelicals is held in the English Lake District.

♣ July 26: Carl Gustav Jung, Swiss psychologist, is born. Dies 1961.

♣ August 16: Charles Grandison Finney (◀ 1792) dies.

♣ October 24: Jacques-Paul Migne (◀ 1800) dies.

The World Alliance of Reformed and Presbyterian churches is formed in Geneva.

The Second Lambeth Conference is particularly concerned with union among the churches of the Anglican Communion.

Presbyterians from the Free Church of Scotland (◀ 1843) arrive in Malawi.

The Theosophical Society is founded by Helena Blavatsky in New York.

The Old Testament is translated into Russian (◀ 1863).

1876

♣ February 17: Horace Bushnell (◀ 1802) dies.

♣ November 23: Maude Royden, English preacher and social worker, is born. She is the first woman to be allowed to preach in an Anglican church. Dies 1956.

The Mothers' Union is founded by Mary Sumner.

An evangelical Cambridge Inter-Collegiate Christian Union is formed.

1877

♣ August 29: Brigham Young (◀ 1801) dies.

The first Protestant missionaries arrive in Buganda.

1878

☿ February 7: Pope Pius IX (◀ 1846) dies.

☿ February 20: Gioacchino Vincenzo Pecci, Bishop of Perugia, is elected as Pope Leo XIII (▶ 1903).

♣🏛 March 27: George Gilbert Scott (◀ 1811) dies.

♣ May 24: Harry Emerson Fosdick, American liberal preacher, is born. Dies 1969.

♣ June 4: Frank Buchman (▶ 1938), founder of Moral Rearmament, is born. Dies 1961.

♣ June 18: Charles Hodge (◀ 1797) dies.

☿ October 4: Joachim II (◀ 1860, 1873) is succeeded as Patriarch of Constantinople by Joachim III (▶ 1884).

382

British Baptist missionaries led by Thomas Comber open a mission in São Salvador, Kongo.

1879

🕆 March 31: Archbishop Innocent (Ivan Veniaminov, ◀ 1797) dies (▶ 1977).

🕆 April 16: Bernadette Soubirous of Lourdes (◀ 1844) dies (▶ 1933).

August 21: Women in Knock, Ireland, experience a vision of the Virgin Mary.

🕆 William James Seymour, African American Pentecostal leader, is born. With his followers he initiates the famous Azusa Street revival (▶ 1906). Dies 1922.

The Church of Christ, Scientist, is founded in Boston by Mary Baker Eddy (◀ 1821, ▶ 1910). It is reorganized in 1892.

Anna Howard Shaw is the first woman ordained in the Methodist Protestant Church in America, which later merges with other denominations to form the United Methodist Church.

The first Roman Catholic missionaries (White Fathers) arrive in Buganda.

The Serbian Orthodox Church becomes self-governing.

🏛 St Patrick's Cathedral, New York, is completed.

1880

🕆 February 25: Johann Christian Blumhardt (◀ 1805) dies.

🏛 October 15: Cologne Cathedral (◀ 1248) is consecrated in the presence of Emperor Wilhelm I.

🕆🖼 November 10: Jacob Epstein, controversial sculptor, is born. An American Jew by origin, he produces some notable Christian works including *Lazarus* in New College, Oxford (1947) and *St Michael's Victory over the Devil* in Coventry Cathedral (▶ 1962). Dies 1959.

📖 November 12: General Lew Wallace, *Ben-Hur: A Tale of the Christ*, is published. It is hugely popular, is made into a spectacular stage play in 1899, and is filmed twice (▶ 1925, 1959).

🕆 December 22: George Eliot (◀ 1819) dies.

☧ Cyril (◀ 869) and Methodius (◀ 885) are canonized by the Roman Catholic Church: feast day July 5.

The Free University of Amsterdam is founded as the first Protestant university. Its head is Abraham Kuyper (◀ 1837, ▶ 1920).

The Society of Biblical Literature is founded.

1881

🕆 February 9: Fyodor Dostoevsky (◀ 1821) dies.

♣ ▭ October 15: William Temple (▶ 1941), English theologian and philosopher, is born. He becomes Archbishop of York and Canterbury successively, writes idealist philosophy and a devotional *Readings in St John's Gospel* (1939), but his most influential book is *Christianity and the Social Order* (1942). Dies 1944.

The Church of God (Anderson, Indiana) is formed.

1882

♣ ▣ February 22: Eric Gill, English letterer, sculptor and engraver, is born. Dies 1940.

♣ April 18: Charles Darwin (◀ 1809) dies.

♣ April 27: Ralph Waldo Emerson (◀ 1803) dies.

April 29: John Nelson Darby (◀ 1800) dies.

♫ July 26: First performance at Bayreuth of Richard Wagner, *Parsifal*, his opera centred on the knights of the Holy Grail (◀ 1191).

♣ September 16: Edward Bouverie Pusey (◀ 1800) dies.

⚓ December 1: Archibald Campbell Tait, Archbishop of Canterbury (◀ 1868), dies.

Wilson Carlile, an Anglican priest worried about the church's lack of contact with the working classes, founds the Church Army.

Benedictine monks begin to rebuild Buckfast Abbey in Devon (◀ 1018), in ruins since the dissolution of the monasteries (◀ 1536).

1883

♣ February 4: George Kennedy Allen Bell, Anglican bishop and ecumenist, is born. He is one of the first to recognize the dangers of Nazism and opposes Allied saturation bombing in the Second World War. Dies 1958.

⚓ March 3: Edward White Benson, Bishop of Truro, is appointed Archbishop of Canterbury (▶ 1896).

♣ March 14: Karl Marx (◀ 1818) dies.

▥ May 26: The Cathedral of Christ the Saviour, Moscow (◀ 1839), is consecrated (▶ 1931).

♣ June 20: John William Colenso (◀ 1814) dies.

♣ November 26: Sojourner Truth (◀ *c.*1797) dies.

✠ Boethius (◀ 524) is canonized by Pope Leo XIII as a martyr of the Roman Catholic Church: feast day October 23.

1884

▥ April 16: Brompton Oratory (◀ 1849) is consecrated, the first Roman Catholic church to be built in London since the Reformation.

🌿 August 20: Rudolf Bultmann is born. He becomes famous for his programme of 'demythologizing' the gospel and his radical views on New Testament criticism. Dies 1976.

☦ October 1: Joachim III (◀ 1878, ▶ 1901) is succeeded as Patriarch of Constantinople by Joachim IV (▶ 1887).

October 4: William Alexander Smith founds the Boys' Brigade in Glasgow.

November 5: The Catholic Truth Society is founded under the presidency of Cardinal Vaughan to teach the Catholic faith by the written word.

November 15: The Berlin Conference on Africa (▶ 1885) opens. The European colonial powers scramble to gain control of the interior. The subsequent allocation of territories has a great impact on missionary work.

The journal *Christian Century* is founded in Des Moines, Iowa as *The Christian Oracle*, a Disciples of Christ magazine. It becomes non-denominational in 1916.

William Taylor (◀ 1870–75) founds Methodist Episcopal churches in Liberia, Sierra Leone, Angola, Mozambique and the Belgian Congo.

Nehemiah Tile sets up the Tembu National Church, the first of the Black Churches in Africa.

Horace Allen, a Protestant doctor, is appointed court physician to the Korean royal household and later leader of a Korean legation to the United States. He is able to initiate missionary work.

1885

February 26: The Berlin Conference on Africa (◀ 1884) ends.

February: Seven Cambridge gradutes led by C. T. Studd, who come to be known as 'The Cambridge Seven', leave to join the China Inland Mission after visiting English and Scottish universities for support. Their activity leads to the foundation of the Student Volunteer Movement for Foreign Missions (▶ 1886).

🌿 October 1: Anthony Ashley Cooper, Seventh Earl of Shaftesbury (◀ 1801), dies.

Christians in Buganda, converted by the White Fathers (◀ 1879), are killed in a persecution which lasts until 1887.

The Roman Catholic Baltimore Catechism is published.

1886

🌿 March 25: Aristokles Spyrou, the future Athenagoras I, Ecumenical Patriarch of Constantinople (▶ 1948), is born. Dies 1972.

🌿📖 May 10: Karl Barth (▶ 1934), Reformed Swiss theologian, is born. He writes a revolutionary commentary on Paul's Letter to the Romans (1919); his *magnum opus* is his 13-volume *Church Dogmatics* (1932–69). Dies 1968.

June 3: Mwanga II, ruler of Buganda, burns 35 Christians alive, following a series of earlier executions. They come to be known as the Uganda martyrs (▶ 1964).

August 20: Paul Tillich, German–American philosopher and theologian, is born. His *The Courage to Be* (1952) is widely influential; his *magnum opus* is a three-volume *Systematic Theology* (1951–63). Dies 1965.

September 1: A Roman Catholic hierarchy is established in India.

Robert Wilder, a Princeton student, founds the Student Volunteer Movement for Foreign Missions, and visits many campuses to recruit members.

September 20: Charles Williams, novelist and theological writer, is born. His novels, e.g. *War in Heaven* (1930) and *All Hallows' Eve* (1945), explore the intersection between the spiritual and the physical. He also writes a history of the church, *The Descent of the Dove* (1939). Dies 1945.

The Revised Version of the Bible is published.

The Moody Bible Institute is founded as the Chicago Evangelization Society.

1887

January 22: Joachim IV (◀ 1884) is succeeded as Patriarch of Constantinople by Dionysius V (▶ 1891).

February 24: John Stainer, *The Crucifixion*, is first performed in Marylebone Parish Church, London.

March 8: Henry Ward Beecher (◀ 1813) dies.

May 25: Padre Pio, Capuchin priest, is born. In 1918 he receives the stigmata, the visible wounds of Christ, and becomes famous for his powers of healing. Dies 1968.

August 17: Marcus Garvey, Jamaican crusader for black nationalism, author of the 'back to Africa' movement, and inspiration for the Rastafari movement (▶ *c.*1930), is born. Dies 1940.

The first two organized churches, one Presbyterian and one Methodist, open in Korea.

The Catholic University of America is founded in Washington, DC.

1888

January 31: John Bosco (◀ 1815) dies (▶ 1934).

April 15: Matthew Arnold (◀ 1822) dies.

July 10: Toyohiko Kagawa, Japanese social reformer, is born. He founds the Friends of Jesus, a group of young people living a disciplined life and working with the poor. Dies 1960.

September 26: T. S. Eliot, American/English poet and critic, is born. His play about Thomas Becket, *Murder in the Cathedral* (1935), is widely performed and his *Four Quartets* (1944) plays an important role in theological exploration. Dies 1965.

The St John Ambulance Brigade is founded.

The Third Lambeth Conference approves the Chicago–Lambeth Quadrilateral, four essential principles for a united church: the Bible, the Apostles' Creed, baptism and eucharist, and the historical episcopate.

The Student Volunteer Movement for Foreign Missions is officially organized with John R. Mott (◀ 1865, ▶ 1895) as chairman. Slogan: 'The evangelization of the world in this generation'.

1889

April 26: Ludwig Josef Johann Wittgenstein, Austrian–English philosopher, is born. He makes a lasting impact on discussions of language. Dies 1951.

June 8: Gerard Manley Hopkins (◀ 1844) dies.

September 24: Simon Kimbangu, African church founder, is born. His dramatic healings and Bible teaching start a mass movement, but he spends most of his time in prison as a result. Dies 1951.

September 24: The Declaration of Utrecht, the doctrinal basis of the Old Catholic Church (◀ 1871), is issued.

September 26: Martin Heidegger, German existentialist philosopher, is born. Dies 1976.

The Christian Social Union is founded by Henry Scott Holland and Charles Gore (◀ 1853, ▶ 1892).

Ella Niswanger is the first woman ordained in the Church of United Brethren (◀ 1800).

1890

January 10: Johann Josef Ignaz von Döllinger (◀ 1799) dies.

August 11: John Henry Newman (◀ 1801) dies.

October 9: Aimée Semple Macpherson (▶ 1927), evangelist, is born. She organizes the International Church of the Foursquare Gospel. Dies 1944.

Catholic Pallotine missionaries (◀ 1855) arrive in Cameroon.

The Bible is translated into Swahili.

c.1890

Oranges decorated with a candle and nuts, raisins and sweets, are first used in place of candles at a Moravian watchnight service in Manchester, the first recorded use of Christingles (◀ 1747) in Britain.

387

1891

May 15: The encyclical *Rerum novarum* on capital and labour is issued.

♣ October 12: Edith Stein is born a Jew. She is converted to Roman Catholicism and becomes a Carmelite nun; she is killed in a concentration camp in 1942.

☩ November 8: Dionysius V (◀ 1887) is succeeded as Patriarch of Constantinople by Neophytus VIII (▶ 1895).

♣ December 31: Samuel (Adjai) Crowther (◀ 1809) dies.

1892

♣ January 31: Charles Haddon Spurgeon (◀ 1834) dies.

April 15: Corrie ten Boom (▶ 1971) is born. A Dutch Christian, she helps Jews to escape during the Holocaust and survives Ravensbrück concentration camp. She becomes an influential evangelist. Dies 1983.

♣📖 June 21: Reinhold Niebuhr, American theologian, is born. His *Moral Man and Immoral Society* (1932) and *The Nature and Destiny of Man* (1941) influence a whole generation of American theologians. Dies 1971.

♣ October 12: Ernest Renan (◀ 1823) dies.

♣ November 26: Charles-Martial-Allemand Lavigerie (◀ 1825) dies.

🏛 Work begins on the Episcopal Cathedral of St John the Divine, New York, planned as the world's biggest. It is never completed (▶ 1942, 1999).

The Community of the Resurrection is founded by Charles Gore (◀ 1889, ▶ 1932).

The Free Church Federal Council is founded in London.

Methodist minister Mangeno Mokoni establishes the 'Ethiopian Church' in the Transvaal.

1893

January 1: The Gregorian calendar (◀ 1582) is introduced in Japan.

♣ January 23: Phillips Brooks (◀ 1835) dies.

September 11: The World's Parliament of Religions meets in Chicago, the first formal gathering of representatives of the Eastern and Western spiritual traditions.

November 18: The encyclical *Providentissimus deus* is issued, giving guidelines for biblical study.

🎵 Fauré's *Requiem* is first performed in its final version.

🏛 The Sagrada Familia in Barcelona is begun to the architect Antonio Gaudi's own designs.

H. H. Kelly founds the Society of the Sacred Mission at Kelham, Nottinghamshire.

Holman Bentley completes a translation of the New Testament into Kikongo.

The Federation of University Christian Unions is formed under the name of the Student Christian Movement.

1894

Sultan Abdul Hamid II of Turkey begins a massacre of the Armenians (▶ 1915).

1895

✦ January 19: Neophytus VIII (◀ 1891) is succeeded as Patriarch of Constantinople by Anthimus VII (▶ 1897).

♟ May 8: Fulton J. Sheen (▶ 1940) is born. A Roman Catholic philosopher and bishop, he proves an outstanding speaker on radio and television. Dies 1979.

♟ October 12: Cecil Frances Alexander (◀ 1818) dies.

The First Church of the Nazarene is founded in Los Angeles.

Peter Cameron Scott founds the non-denominational Africa Inland Mission, based in Kenya. He dies of black fever the next year but the mission spreads.

The World Student Christian Federation is founded by John R. Mott (◀ 1888, ▶ 1910).

John Alexander Dowie founds the Christian Catholic Church (later the Christian Catholic and Apostolic Church, ▶ 1904) in Zion, Illinois; it emphasizes faith healing and temperance and expects the second coming of Christ.

1896

September 18: Leo XIII's encyclical *Apostolicae curae* declares Anglican ordinations 'absolutely null and utterly void'.

🏛 September 20: Vladimir Cathedral, Kiev, is consecrated. It has been planned to commemorate the 900th anniversary of the 'baptism of Russia'.

✦ October 11: Edward White Benson, Archbishop of Canterbury (◀ 1883), dies.

♟♫ October 11: Anton Bruckner (◀ 1824) dies.

✦ December 22: Frederick Temple, Bishop of London, becomes Archbishop of Canterbury (▶ 1902).

📖 Henryk Sienkiewicz, *Quo Vadis?*, is published, a best-selling novel depicting the persecution of Christians in first-century Rome but echoing the Polish people's struggle against repression. It is filmed three times (▶ 1912, 1951, 2001).

Billy Sunday (◀ 1862, ▶ 1935) begins preaching.

1897

✦ April 2: Anthimus VII (◀ 1895) is succeeded as Patriarch of Constantinople by Constantine VI (▶ 1901).

🟐 September 30: Thérèse of Lisieux (◀ 1873) dies (▶ 1925).

🟐 November 8: Dorothy Day, American journalist, is born. She founds the *Catholic Worker* (▶ 1933). Dies 1980.

Alfred Tucker becomes the first Anglican bishop of Buganda; he presides over a great growth in Christianity there.

The Fourth Lambeth Conference criticizes excessive praise of the virtues of Buddhism and Hinduism and encourages the evangelization of Jews and 'Mohammedans'.

The Pentecostal Church of God in Christ, largely African American, is founded in the United States.

The Catholic charity *Caritas Internationalis* is founded in Germany by Lorenz Werthmann.

1898

🏛 May: Myeongdong Cathedral, South Korea, is consecrated.

🟐📖 November 29: C. S. Lewis, Anglican writer, author of *The Screwtape Letters* (1942) and the *Chronicles of Narnia* (1950–56), is born. Dies 1963.

The *Scottish Church Hymnary* is published.

The Pentecostal Holiness Church is founded in the United States.

The Roman Catholic Church is established in the Sudan after previous missionary attempts have been exterminated.

1899

🟐 December 22: Dwight Lyman Moody (◀ 1837) dies.

◉ The Venerable Bede (◀ 735) is canonized by Pope Leo XIII: feast day May 25.

An American fleet defeats the Spanish off Manila and the Philippines enter the US sphere.

Gideons International is founded in Boscobel, Wisconsin, as one of the first parachurch evangelical organizations; it places Bibles in hotel bedrooms.

Robert Bridges, *The Yattendon Hymnal*, is published. It forms a bridge between Victorian and modern hymns and contains many of his translations (◀ 1607), including 'All my hope on God is founded'.

1900

🟐🏛 February 23: William Butterfield (◀ 1814) dies.

◉ May 24: Jean-Baptiste De La Salle (◀ 1678) is canonized by Pope Leo XIII: feast day April 7.

🟐 August 25: Friedrich Nietzsche (◀ 1844) dies.

390

♫ October 3: Edward Elgar's (◀ 1857, ▶ 1934) oratorio *The Dream of Gerontius*, based on the poem by John Henry Newman (◀ 1865), is first performed in Birmingham.

Khrisanf, a Russian Orthodox missionary from Kazan in West Siberia, arrives in Korea, travels widely, and establishes a school and mission compound. He has to leave three years later, on the outbreak of the Russo-Japanese war.

The Church Missionary Society opens the first Anglican missionary station in the Sudan.

The United Free Church of Scotland is formed from the United Presbyterian Church (◀ 1847) and the Free Church of Scotland (◀ 1843).

The *Baptist Church Hymnal* is published.

Twentieth century

In October 1917 there is a revolution in Russia in which the Bolsheviks seize power; church and state are separated and for the first time in its history the Russian Orthodox Church has no state support. Thousands of churches and monasteries are taken over by the government and either destroyed or used for secular purposes, from warehouses and recreation centres to museums and concentration camps. Anti-religious propaganda is encouraged, as is the vandalization of churches. Seminaries are closed down, severe restrictions are placed on Orthodox Christians and countless bishops, priests, monks, nuns and lay people are executed. Continuous persecution in the 1930s results in the near-extinction of the church. Over 100,000 are shot during the purges of 1937–38, and by 1939 there are only a few hundred active parishes. The situation improves during the Second World War, as Stalin sees the value of the church as a patriotic organization, and the number of churches grows again. However, in 1959 Nikita Khruschev launches a new campaign against religion and prominent church leaders are imprisoned or forced out of the church; because of their nationalistic character the Ukrainian and Byelorussian churches receive particularly severe treatment over this period.

In Germany, after Adolf Hitler becomes Chancellor in 1933, a series of laws requires Protestant churches to merge into a Protestant Reich Church and support Nazi ideology. The leaders of this Reich Church, the 'German Christians', are markedly antisemitic, introduce pagan elements into Christianity and want to dispense with the Old Testament. They are opposed in 1933 by Martin Niemöller, who founds the Pastors' Emergency League, and in 1934 by a group inspired by Karl Barth, which issues a 'Theological Declaration' in Barmen and forms a 'Confessing Church', of which Dietrich Bonhoeffer is a prominent member. It becomes evident that Adolf Hitler does not see a future for Christianity at all in the Third Reich, but his priority is the elimination of the Jews, against whom a series of measures is taken from 1934 onwards, culminating in ghettoes, concentration camps and death camps and resulting in the deaths of six million.

This genocide committed against the Jews has been preceded by genocide in 1915 in which more than a million Armenians living in Turkey are killed; it is followed in 1958–61 and 1966–69 by genocide in the 'Cultural Revolution' in which more than 30 million Chinese are killed. Such mass killing is also carried out by Kim Il-Sung in North Korea and Pol Pot in Cambodia.

The century is one of fundamentalism in belief, in other religions as well as Christianity. In the face of the many challenges posed by the nineteenth century, large areas of Christianity go on the defensive and Protestantism produces many fundamentalists, who take their name from a series of booklets, *The Fundamentals* (1910–15). The fastest-growing movement of the century, Pentecostalism, has a fundamentalist basis, and a number of fundamentalist organizations come into being, such as Aimée Semple McPherson's International Church of the Foursquare Gospel (1927), Demos Shakarian's Full Gospel Business Men's Fellowship International (1953) and Jerry Falwell's Moral Majority (1979). Fundamentalist views are to split many churches, particularly over issues such as homosexuality.

In 1958, Angelo Giuseppe Roncalli, the 77-year-old Patriarch of Venice, is appointed Pope as John XXIII. To the surprise of many, the next year he announces that a new council of the Roman Catholic Church will be held, the first since the First Vatican Council of 1870/71. The Second Vatican Council, which begins in 1962 and lasts until 1965, is very different from its conservative predecessor, opening up the Catholic Church in an unprecedent way with revised forms of worship, a new theology and widespread use of the vernacular. However, it has its opponents, and towards the end of the century conservative tendencies again grow more dominant.

Countries represented at the Second Vatican Council, 1962–65

The numbers in brackets after each country indicate the number of delegates present:

1 Albania (3)
2 Algeria (6)
3 Angola (7)
4 Arabia (23)
5 Argentina (68)
6 Australia (38)
7 Austria (16)
8 Bahamas (1)
9 Belgium (27)
10 Bermuda (1)
11 Bolivia (22)
12 Botswana (1)
13 Brazil (217)
14 British Honduras (8)
15 Bulgaria (2)
16 Burma (8)
17 Burundi (5)
18 Cambodia (2)
19 Cameroon (11)
20 Canada (100)
21 Cape Verde (1)
22 Central African Republic (5)
23 Ceylon (9)
24 Chad (5)

25 Chile (35)
26 China (67)
27 Colombia (58)
28 Congo (Brazzaville) (4)
29 Congo (Kinshasa) (47)
30 Costa Rica (7)
31 Crete (1)
32 Cuba (6)
33 Czechoslovakia (5)
34 Cyprus (1)
35 Dahomey (5)
36 Dominican Republic (5)
37 Ecuador (25)
38 Egypt (14)
39 El Salvador (8)
40 Ethiopia (7)
41 Falkland Islands (1)
42 Finland (2)
43 France (144)
44 Gabon (3)
45 Gambia (1)
46 Germany (61)
47 Ghana (7)
48 Great Britain (48)

49 Greece (6)
50 Guatemala (11)
51 Guinea (3)
52 Guyanas (3)
53 Haiti (7)
54 Honduras (7)
55 Hungary (12)
56 Iceland (1)
57 India (93)
58 Indonesia (32)
59 Iraq (14)
60 Iran (4)
61 Ireland (31)
62 Israel (3)
63 Italy (451)
64 Ivory Coast (6)
65 Jamaica (1)
66 Japan (16)
67 Jordan (5)
68 Kenya (11)
69 Korea (12)
70 Laos (3)
71 Lebanon (2)
72 Lesotho (3)

73 Liberia (2)
74 Libya (4)
75 Malagasay Republic (19)
76 Malaysia (5)
77 Mali (8)
78 Malta (3)
79 Mauritius (1)
80 Melanesia (6)
81 Mexico (68)
82 Micronesia (3)
83 Morocco (2)
84 Mozambique (8)
85 Netherlands (15)
86 New Guinea (13)
87 New Zealand (6)
88 Nicaragua (8)
89 Niger (1)
90 Nigeria (26)
91 Norway (3)
92 Pakistan (13)
93 Palestine (3)
94 Panama (9)
95 Paraguay (14)
96 Peru (44)

97 Philippines (46)
98 Poland (59)
99 Polynesia (8)
100 Port Guinea (1)
101 Portugal (29)
102 Puerto Rico (6)
103 Reunion (2)
104 Rhodesia (6)
105 Romania (2)
106 Rwanda (4)
107 Senegal (5)
108 Seychelles (1)
109 Sierra Leone (2)
110 Singapore (1)
111 Somalia (1)
112 South Africa (26)
113 South West Africa (2)
114 Spain (87)
115 Spanish Sahara (1)
116 Sudan (5)
117 Swaziland (1)
118 Sweden (1)
119 Switzerland (11)
120 Tanzania (27)

121 Thailand (8)
122 Togo (3)
123 Trinidad and Tobago (6)
124 Tunis (1)
125 Turkey (3)
126 Uganda (11)
127 Ukraine (1)
128 Upper Volta (6)
129 Uruguay (15)
130 USA (247)
131 Venezuela (29)
132 Vietnam (17)
133 West Indies (2)
134 Yugoslavia (28)
135 Zambia (10)

Note: this map is not exhaustive.

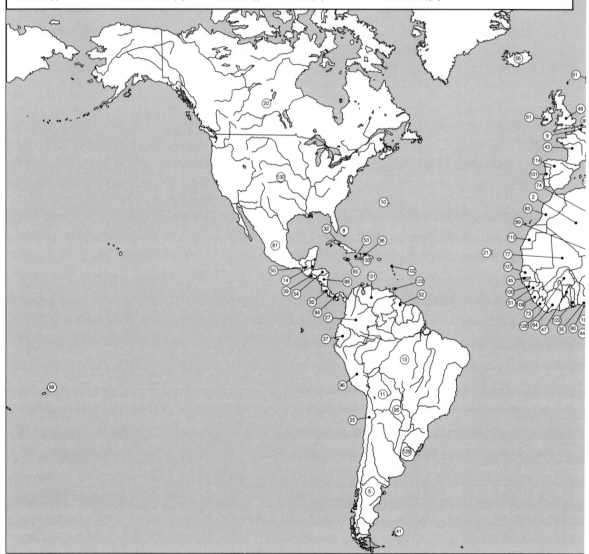

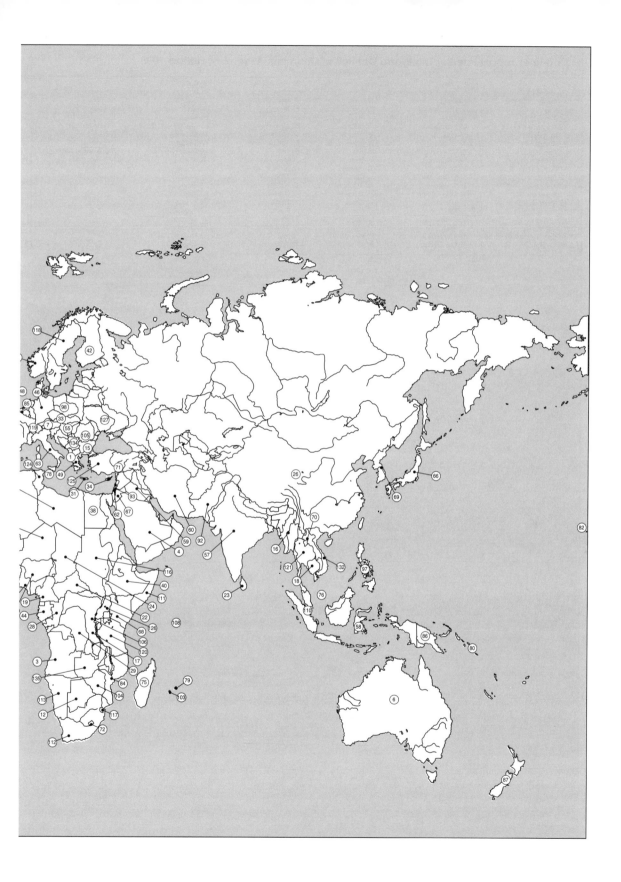

Countries represented at the World Council of Churches Assembly, Harare 1998

The figures in brackets represent the number of churches in the country represented.

1 Albania (1)
2 Algeria (1)
3 American Samoa (1)
4 Angola (4)
5 Antigua (3)
6 Argentina (7)
7 Armenia (1)
8 Australia (3)
9 Austria (3)
10 Bangladesh (2)
11 Belgium (1)
12 Benin (1)
13 Bolivia (2)
14 Botswana (1)
15 Brazil (5)
16 Burundi (2)
17 Cameroon (6)
18 Canada (7)
19 Central African Republic (1)
20 Chile (5)

21 China (2)
22 Congo (Brazzaville) (2)
23 Congo (Democratic Republic) (7)
24 Cook Islands (1)
25 Costa Rica (1)
26 Cuba (1)
27 Curaçao (1)
28 Czech Republic (4)
29 Denmark (2)
30 Egypt (4)
31 El Salvador (2)
32 Equatorial Guinea (1)
33 Estonia (1)
34 Ethiopia (2)
35 Fiji (1)
36 Finland (2)
37 France (4)
38 French Polynesia (1)
39 Gabon (1)

40 Germany (4)
41 Ghana (2)
42 Great Britain (13)
43 Greece (2)
44 Hungary (2)
45 Iceland
46 India (8)
47 Indonesia (27)
48 Iran (1)
49 Ireland (1)
50 Italy (3)
51 Ivory Coast (2)
52 Jamaica (3)
53 Japan (4)
54 Kenya (8)
55 Kiribati (1)
56 Latvia (1)
57 Lebanon (3)
58 Lesotho (1)
59 Liberia (2)

60 Madagascar (3)
61 Malaysia (2)
62 Marshall Islands (1)
63 Mexico (1)
64 Mozambique (1)
65 Myanmar (3)
66 Namibia (2)
67 The Netherlands (7)
68 New Caledonia (1)
69 New Zealand (5)
70 Nicaragua (2)
71 Nigeria (7)
72 North Korea (1)
73 Norway (1)
74 Pakistan (2)
75 Papua New Guinea (2)
76 Peru
77 Philippines (4)
78 Poland (4)
79 Portugal (2)

80 Romania (4)
81 Russian Federation (1)
82 Rwanda (2)
83 Sierra Leone (1)
84 Singapore (1)
85 Slovak Republic (3)
86 Solomon Islands (2)
87 South Africa (11)
88 South Korea (2)
89 Spain (2)
90 Sri Lanka (2)
91 Sudan (2)
92 Suriname (1)
93 Sweden (2)
94 Switzerland (2)
95 Syria (2)
96 Tanzania (3)
97 Taiwan (1)
98 Thailand (1)
99 Togo (2)

100 Tonga (1)
101 Trinidad (1)
102 Turkey (1)
103 Tuvalu (1)
104 Uganda (1)
105 Uruguay (1)
106 USA (25)
107 Vanuatu (1)
108 Western Samoa (2)
109 Yugoslavia (3)
110 Zambia (4)
111 Zimbabwe (4)

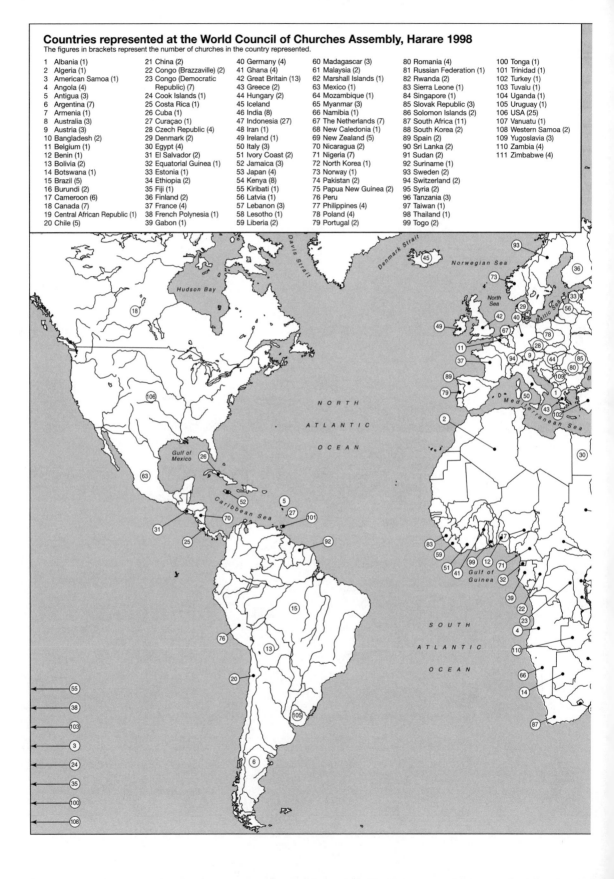

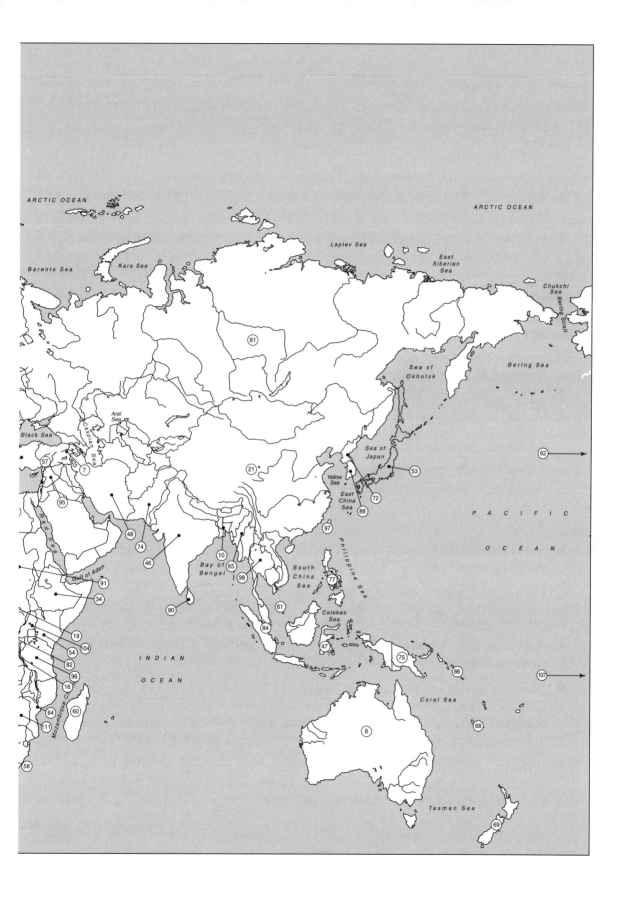

1901

January 1: Agnes Osman speaks with tongues at Bethel Bible College, in Topeka, Kansas; this is seen as the beginning of the Pentecostal movement.

♛ January 22: In Britain, Queen Victoria (◀ 1837) dies and is succeeded by her son Edward VII.

☗ May 26: Constantine VI, Patriarch of Constantinople (◀ 1897, ▶ 1924), is succeeded by Joachim III (◀ 1884, ▶ 1913).

♟ September 27: John Sung (Song Shenjie), influential preacher and evangelist in China, is born. Dies 1944.

📖 William James (◀ 1842, ▶ 1910), *The Varieties of Religious Experience*, applies psychology to the understanding of religion.

1902

♟ February 24: Gladys Aylward, missionary to China, is born. Dies 1970.

March 2: John Francis Bentley (◀ 1839) dies.

♟ October 26: Elizabeth Cady Stanton (◀ 1815) dies.

☗ December 23: Frederick Temple, Archbishop of Canterbury (◀ 1896), dies.

The Filipino priest Fr Gregorio Aglipy becomes the first bishop of the Philippine Independent Church.

The American Standard Version of the Bible, rooted in the Revised Version (◀ 1886), is published.

1903

☗ February 6: Randall Thomas Davidson, Bishop of Winchester, is appointed Archbishop of Canterbury (▶ 1928).

🏛 June 28: Westminster Cathedral (◀ 1839) in London is consecrated.

☗ July 20: Pope Leo XIII (◀ 1878) dies.

☗ August 4: Giuseppe Melchiorre Sarto, Cardinal and Patriarch of Venice, is elected as Pope Pius X (▶ 1914).

♟ November 4: Ni Tuosheng, known as Watchman Nee, is born in China. He becomes a Christian in 1920 and founds an unconventional community, the Little Flock, which has no ordained clergy and does not require baptism. A prolific writer, he is arrested by the Chinese authorities in 1952 and spends the rest of his life in prison. Dies 1972.

♟▮ December 13: John Piper, English artist, is born. His paintings focus on English churches, his stained-glass windows include those for Coventry Cathedral (▶ 1962) and his tapestries are in Chichester Cathedral. Dies 1992.

1904

✦ March 5: Karl Rahner, German Catholic theologian, is born. Dies 1984.

✦ April 8: Yves Congar, French Catholic theologian, is born. Dies 1995.

🏛 July 19: The foundation stone of Liverpool's Anglican Cathedral is laid (▶ 1978).

July: The Vatican breaks off diplomatic relations with France over the French ban on religious education in schools (▶ 1921).

✦ November 24: Arthur Michael Ramsey, English theologian and archbishop (▶ 1961), is born. Dies 1988.

Karl Kumm founds the Sudan United Mission, aimed at creating a chain of mission stations across Africa at points where Islam and Christianity meet.

Missionaries of the Christian Apostolic Church in Zion, sent by John Alexander Dowie (◀ 1895), arrive in South Africa and convert P. L. LeRoux and Daniel Nkonyane. The black churches that result form a network which spreads to Zululand, Swaziland, Basutoland and the Transvaal; they are known as Zionist churches.

Archbishop Davidson (◀ 1903, ▶ 1928) pays the first official visit of an Archbishop of Canterbury to the United States and Canada.

The Methodist Hymn Book is published.

1905

✦ June 3: James Hudson Taylor (◀ 1832) dies.

✦📖 July 29: Dag Hammarskjøld, Swedish economist and statesman, is born. Secretary-General of the United Nations, his spiritual diary *Markings* (1964) is a twentieth-century classic. Dies 1961.

✦ November 29: Marcel Lefebvre (▶ 1974), ultraconservative Roman Catholic bishop, is born. In 1976 he is suspended by Pope Paul VI and in 1988 excommunicated, but he has a growing movement of followers. Dies 1991.

December 9: A law is passed in France separating church and state.

The Baptist World Alliance is founded in London.

1906

✦📖 February 4: Dietrich Bonhoeffer, German Protestant theologian, is born. He is imprisoned by the Nazis and executed in 1945 for his involvement in the plot to kill Adolf Hitler. His *The Cost of Discipleship* (1937) becomes a classic and *Letters and Papers from Prison* (1953) presents radical ideas from his last months.

February 11: In the encyclical *Vehementer nos* Pope Pius X denounces the separation of church and state in France (◀ 1905).

April 9: A gathering in Azusa Street, San Francisco, with speaking in tongues led by William James Seymour (◀ 1879, ▶ 1922), results in the rapid spread of Pentecostalism.

December 17: Bede Griffiths, English mystic, is born. He founds a Christian ashram in India. Dies 1993.

December 24: Reginald Fessenden, a Canadian engineer, beams a radio signal from the coast of Massachusetts to ships at sea. Its content is a Christmas religious service.

December 30: Josephine Butler (◀ 1828) dies.

December: Thomas Ball Barratt, a Norwegian Methodist pastor, conducts the first European Pentecostal services in Oslo.

The Unitarian Unity Temple, designed by Frank Lloyd Wright, is built at Oak Park, Illinois; it is a cubic structure and one of the earliest buildings made with reinforced concrete.

The English Hymnal, edited by Percy Dearmer and Ralph Vaughan Williams (◀ 1872, ▶ 1958), is published.

The Pentecostal Church of God is founded in Cleveland, Tennessee.

Pentecostals

The Pentecostal movement is currently one of the fastest growing within Christianity, with the majority of its members living in the 'Third World'; it is characterized by personal experience of the Holy Spirit, coupled with speaking in tongues.

It is thought to originate in an outbreak of speaking in tongues in Topeka, Kansas (◀ 1901). This influences the African American preacher William J. Seymour, under whose leadership there is a dramatic revival in Azusa Street, San Francisco (◀ 1906). It affects a number of future Pentecostal leaders and has repercussions all over the world. Gaston B. Cashwell (◀ 1860) travels over the southern States preaching Pentecost; Charles H. Mason (◀ 1866) becomes senior bishop of the Church of God in Christ; William H. Durham is instrumental in founding the Assemblies of God (▶ 1914). Thomas Ball Barratt leads Pentecostal services in Oslo (◀ 1906), and travels on to Sweden, England, France and Germany; Pentecostal missionaries establish the Apostolic Faith Mission in South Africa (▶ 1908) from which Pentecostalism spreads over the continent; through the preaching of Willis C. Hoover the Pentecostal revival reaches Chile (▶ 1909) and through Daniel Berg and Gunnar Vingren it reaches Brazil (▶ 1910), in both of which countries it flourishes. The first Pentecostal church in the Soviet Union is founded in 1922 and the flourishing Yoido Full Gospel Church in Korea in 1958; in 1978 Eddie Villaneuva, a political and religious leader, founds the Jesus is Lord Church in the Philippines; in Indonesia in 2001 there are 10,000 Pentecostal churches with a membership of 13 million.

Pentecostal phenomena are experienced in the Roman Catholic Church in the 'charismatic revival' which begins at a retreat at Duquesne University near Pittsburgh and spreads to Notre Dame and the University of Michigan (▶ 1966); it reaches a high point in a conference of around 30,000 charismatics at Notre Dame in 1973. It has spread all over the world and there are also Pentecostal currents in many other churches.

1907

♣ February 21: W. H. Auden, English poet (▸ 1944), is born. Dies 1973.

April 6: Nikolai Kasatkin (◂ 1831, ▸ 1912) is appointed Archbishop of All Japan.

September 8: Pope Pius X issues the encyclical *Pascendi*, against the doctrine of the Modernists, a movement which seeks to bring Catholic tradition more into line with modern thought.

🏛 September 29: The foundation stone of the Anglican Washington National Cathedral is laid (▸ 1990).

♣🏛 October 21: George Frederick Bodley (◂ 1827) dies.

October: The Pentecostal Church of the Nazarene is formed in Chicago from three smaller Holiness churches.

The United Methodist Church of Great Britain is formed from the union of smaller groups.

1908

January 18–25: The Week of Prayer for Christian Unity is founded as the Octave of Christian Unity, to end on the feast of the Conversion of St Paul, January 25 (◂ *c.*36).

July 25–27: The South India United Church is formed in Madras of Presbyterians, Congregationalists and Dutch Reformed Christians, the first interconfessional union in modern times.

♣♫ December 10: Olivier Messiaen, French composer, is born. A devout Catholic, he writes many works with a religious theme: for orchestra (*La transfiguration*, 1969), for smaller ensembles (*Quatuor pour la fin du temps*, 1942), for solo piano (*Vingt regards sur l'enfant Jésus*, 1944), for organ (*La nativité*, 1935; *Le livre du saint sacrement*, 1984) and an opera, *Saint François d'Assise* (1983). Dies 1992.

Pentecostal missionaries establish the Apostolic Faith Mission in Johannesburg, South Africa.

31 denominations form the Federal Council of Churches in the USA. It later becomes the National Council of Churches (▸ 1950).

The Fifth Lambeth Conference is concerned with a decline in the number of candidates for the priesthood and emphasizes the need for Christian education.

1909

♣ February 7: Helder Camara, Brazilian Roman Catholic bishop and champion of the poor, is born. Dies 1999.

April 17: US Jesuits found the journal *America* as a counterpart to *The Tablet* (◂ 1840).

April: John Graham Lake, a former insurance executive, leads a large Pentecostal missionary group to Johannesburg. Two churches are created, the white Apostolic Faith Mission and the black Zion Christian Church.

July 3: The encyclical *Lamentabili sane* condemns the errors of the Modernists (◀ 1907).

July 4: Through the preaching of Willis Hoover in Valparaiso, Pentecostalism spreads throughout Chile.

July 15: George Tyrrell (◀ 1861) dies.

The Church of God (Cleveland, Tennessee) (◀ 1906) begins to ordain women.

1910

May 6: In Britain, King Edward VII (◀ 1901) dies and is succeeded by his son as George V (▶ 1936).

June 14–23: The World Missionary Conference in Edinburgh under the presidency of John R. Mott (◀ 1895, ▶ 1955) envisages the evangelization of the world in a generation.

July: The United Theological College of South India and Ceylon is founded in Bangalore.

August 26: Agnes Goxha Bujaxhiu (Mother Teresa), Albanian missionary and nun, who becomes famous for her work among India's poor, is born. She founds the Order of the Missionaries of Charity (▶ 1950). Dies 1997.

August 26: William James (◀ 1842) dies.

September 1: Pope Pius X imposes an anti-Modernist (◀ 1907) oath on Roman Catholic priests.

September 7: William Holman Hunt (◀ 1827) dies.

October 29: Alfred Jules Ayer, English philosopher, is born. His *Language, Truth and Logic* (1936) popularizes 'logical positivism', the view that metaphysics is nonsense and questions of value are non-existent. Dies 1989.

November 7: Leo Tolstoy (◀ 1828) dies.

December 3: Mary Baker Eddy (◀ 1821) dies.

The Swedes Daniel Berg and Gunnar Vingren arrive in Brazil and form the Brazilian Assemblies of God.

1910–15

The Fundamentals, a series of 12 volumes written by 64 conservative Christians and forming the basis of fundamentalism, are published.

1911

June 29: The Catholic Foreign Mission Society of America ('Maryknoll Missioners') is founded by James Anthony Walsh and Thomas Frederick Price. The Maryknoll sisters are founded the next year.

402

♟ ♫ October 26: Mahalia Jackson, the 'queen' of gospel music, is born in New Orleans. Dies 1972.

1912

♟ February 16: Nikolai Kasatkin (◀ 1831) dies.

♟ August 20: William Booth (◀ 1829) dies.

December 29: V. S. Azariah (◀ 1874, ▶ 1945) is consecrated Bishop of Dornakal in Calcutta Cathedral, the first Indian to be consecrated an Anglican bishop.

🎬 Enrico Guzzoni produces a film version of Henryk Sienkiewicz, *Quo Vadis?* (◀ 1896), the first feature-length film (▶ 1951, 2001).

John Flynn, an Australian Presbyterian minister (▶ 1928), becomes the first superintendent of the Australian Inland Mission.

Ann Allenbach is the first Mennonite woman to be ordained in the First Memorial Church of Philadelphia.

1913

♟ January 13: Werenfried van Straaten, a Catholic who comes to be known as the Bacon Priest, is born. He founds Church Aid to the Church in Need. Dies 2003.

☧ January 28: Joachim III (◀ 1878, 1901) is succeeded as Patriarch of Constantinople by Germanus V (▶ 1918).

March 26: Albert Schweitzer (◀ 1875, ▶ 1965) goes out to Lambaréné in the Congo.

♟ March 29: R. S. Thomas, Welsh priest and poet, is born. Dies 2000.

♟ 📖 June 15: Trevor Huddleston, Anglican bishop and activist against apartheid, is born. His book *Naught for Your Comfort* (1956) is to be widely influential. Dies 1998.

♟ ♫ November 22: Benjamin Britten, English composer, is born. Among his works are many written to be performed in churches or influenced by Christianity, including *A Ceremony of Carols* (1942), *Saint Nicholas* (1948) and *Noye's Fludde* (1958). His *War Requiem* is given its first performance at the dedication of the rebuilt Coventry Cathedral (▶ 1962). Dies 1976.

Bishop Tucker Theological College is founded in Uganda. It later becomes Uganda Christian University.

1914

August 3: The World Alliance for Promoting International Friendship through the Churches is formed in Constance with the help of the Church Peace Union.

August 4: Germany invades Belgium and Britain declares war. The First World War begins (▶ 1918).

☧ August 20: Pope Pius X (◀ 1903) dies (▶ 1954).

August: An English Quaker, Henry Hodgkin, and a German Lutheran, Friedrich

Siegmund-Schulze, resolve in Cologne to found a Fellowship of Reconciliation. It is formed at a conference in Cambridge, England, the next year.

✠ September 3: Giacomo Della Chiesa, Archbishop of Bologna, is elected as Pope Benedict XV (▶ 1922).

♱ September 5: Charles Péguy (◀ 1873) is killed.

♱▢ November 12: Edward Schillebeeckx, Belgian Catholic theologian, is born. His book *Jesus. An Experiment in Christology* (1974) becomes a landmark in twentieth-century Roman Catholic theology.

The Assemblies of God is formed in Hot Springs, Arkansas, under the leadership of William H. Durham.

1915

♱ January 31: Thomas Merton, Trappist monk, mystic and social activist, is born. Dies 1968.

♱♫ May 6: Sydney Carter, poet and and folk singer, is born. He becomes famous for his 'Lord of the Dance', 'When I needed a neighbour were you there?' and the controversial 'Friday morning'. Dies 2004.

♱ May 12: Roger Schutz, Swiss founder of the Taizé community (▶ 1940), is born. He is murdered in 2005.

The Ku Klux Klan (◀ 1866) is refounded by William J. Simmons at Stone Mountain, Georgia, and gains more than four million members in the US; its opponents are extended to Roman Catholics, Jews, Communists and foreigners.

The Turks begin a further massacre of the Armenians (◀ 1894) which goes on until 1918.

1916

♱ December 1: Charles Eugène de Foucauld (◀ 1858) dies.

♱ Gaston B. Cashwell (◀ 1860) dies.

1917

March 25: The Sacred Congregation of the Index (◀ 1571) is abolished.

March: The interdenominational Foreign Missions Association of North America is founded as the accrediting agency for non-denominational faith missions.

May 13: A group of children in Fatima, Portugal, experience a vision of the Virgin Mary.

May 27: A new Roman Catholic code of canon law, *Codex Iuris Canonici*, is issued to simplify the mass of existing material, and remains in force until it is revised in 1983.

October 25: In Russia the Bolsheviks take power and declare the separation of church and state. For the first time in its history the Russian Orthodox Church has no state support. A campaign of persecution follows.

November 5: Tikhon, Metropolitan of Moscow, is elected Patriarch of the Russian Orthodox Church (▶ 1925).

1918

February 5: A Decree of Separation deprives the Russian church of all its property.

February 14: Russia adopts the Gregorian calendar (◀ 1700).

October 12: Germanus V (◀ 1913) ceases to be Patriarch of Constantinople and there is a vacancy for three years.

November 7: Billy Graham (▶ 1954), American revivalist, is born.

November 9: Emperor Wilhelm II of Germany abdicates (◀ 1871).

November 11: The First World War ends (◀ 1914).

December 24: A Festival of Nine Lessons and Carols, devised by the Dean, Eric Milner-White, takes place in King's College, Cambridge (▶ 1928).

A civil war breaks out in Russia between the Bolshevik 'Reds' and the Ukrainian 'Whites'. It lasts until 1921, causes enormous loss of life and further damages the position of the church.

The United Lutheran Church in America is founded.

1919

January: A Sicilian priest, Luigi Sturzo, founds the Italian Popular Party; for the first time, Italian Catholics are allowed to engage in politics.

June 3: Church Assembly is established by the British Parliament. The Enabling Act gives the Church of England power to legislate for itself subject to the control of Parliament.

June 15: John A. T. Robinson, English New Testament scholar and theologian, is born. His questioning *Honest to God* (▶ 1963) is an international sensation, and his *Redating the New Testament* (1976) goes against accepted opinions. Dies 1983.

August 11: By the Weimar Constitution church and state are separated in Germany.

October 16: The Church of Sacré Coeur, Paris, is consecrated.

A Baptist minister, William Bell Riley, founds the World Christian Fundamentals Association in Minneapolis.

1920

March 31: The Welsh dioceses of the Church of England are disestablished and the Church in Wales is formed.

June 14: Max Weber (◀ 1864) dies.

June 30: The Anglican Church Assembly meets for the first time.

405

✤ ♩ October 31: Joseph Gelineau, French Jesuit priest, is born. Influenced by Gregorian chant, he composes many chants for the Taizé community (▶ 1940).

✤ November 8: Abraham Kuyper (◀ 1837) dies.

☉ Jeanne d'Arc (◀ 1456) is canonized by Pope Benedict XV: feast day May 20.

Zäkaryas (◀ *c.*1845) dies.

The Sixth Lambeth Conference rejects all forms of artificial contraception (▶ 1930).

1921

January 2: The first religious radio broadcast, by KDKA, takes place from Pittsburgh's Calvary Episcopal Church.

✤ March 24: James Gibbons (◀ 1834) dies.

May 28: Diplomatic relations between France and the Vatican are resumed (◀ 1904).

✤ July 24: Cyrus I. Scofield (◀ 1843) dies.

November 25: Meletius IV Metaxakis becomes Patriarch of Constantinople (▶ 1923).

December 6: The Anglo-Irish treaty creates a Catholic Irish Free State alongside Protestant Northern Ireland, which remains part of the United Kingdom (◀ 1801).

The International Missionary Council is founded, arising out of the Edinburgh Missionary Conference (◀ 1910) and comprising interdenominational associations of missionary societies.

Originally named The Women of Nazareth, The Grail is founded in the Netherlands by the Jesuit priest Jacques van Ginneken. Its innovative programmes to transform the world by women's leadership have spread all over the world.

1922

✤ January 3: Wilhelm Herrmann (◀ 1846) dies.

✤ January 21: Pope Benedict XV (◀ 1914) dies.

✤ February 6: Ambrogio Damiano Achille Rani, Cardinal Archbishop of Milan, is elected as Pope Pius XI (▶ 1939).

September 11: The British mandate in Palestine begins (▶ 1948).

✤ September 28: William James Seymour (◀ 1879) dies.

The Baptist pastor Ivan Voronaev founds the first Pentecostal Church in the Soviet Union, in Odessa.

Armenia adopts the Gregorian calendar (◀ 551).

1923

✤ February 1: Ernst Troeltsch (◀ 1865) dies.

406

⚱ December 26: Meletius IV Metaxakis (◀ 1921) is succeeded as Patriarch of Constantinople by Gregory VII (▶ 1924).

🎥 Cecil B. de Mille, *The Ten Commandments*, is the first great biblical film epic (▶ 1956).

The Convocation of Canterbury (◀ 1852) formally restores the Order of Deaconesses (◀ 1862); the Convocation of York follows two years later.

Greece adopts the Gregorian calendar (◀ 1582).

1924

January 6: The first religious service is broadcast by the BBC from St Martin-in-the-Fields, London.

♣ February 3: Woodrow Wilson (◀ 1856) dies.

♣♫ March 29: Charles Villiers Stanford (◀ 1852) dies.

November 13: The Polish Orthodox Church is declared autonomous by the Patriarch of Constantinople.

⚱ December 17: Gregory VII (◀ 1923) is succeeded as Patriarch of Constantinople by Constantine VI (◀ 1901, ▶ 1925).

The Finnish Orthodox Church becomes autonomous.

Joseph Cardijn founds Jeunesse Ouvrière Chrétienne (JOC, Jocists), a movement for young factory workers in France.

Michael Williams founds *Commonweal*, the oldest lay Catholic journal in the US.

1925

♣ March 25: Flannery O'Connor, Catholic author and novelist, is born in Georgia. Dies 1964.

March 30: Rudolf Steiner (◀ 1861) dies.

⚱ April 7: Tikhon, Patriarch of the Russian Orthodox Church (◀ 1917), dies. No new Patriarch is appointed until 1943.

☦ May 17: Thérèse of Lisieux (◀ 1897) is canonized by Pope Pius XII: feast day October 1.

☦ May 31: Jean-Baptiste-Marie Vianney (◀ 1859) is canonized by Pope Pius XII: feast day August 4.

June 10: The United Church of Canada is founded through a merger of Methodists, Congregationalists and many Presbyterians.

July 10–25: In the Scopes 'monkey trial', John T. Scopes is tried in Tennessee under state law banning the teaching of evolution, and is convicted.

⚲ July 13: Constantine VI (◄ 1924) is succeeded as Patriarch of Constantinople by Basil III (▶ 1929).

♱ July 26: William Jennings Bryan (◄ 1860) dies.

August 19–30: The Universal Christian Conference on Life and Work in Stockholm gives rise to the Life and Work movement.

December 11: Pope Pius XI's encyclical *Quas primas* institutes the feast of Christ the King.

🎬 December 30: Fred Niblo produces a film of Lew Wallace's novel, *Ben-Hur: a Tale of the Christ* (◄ 1880, ▶ 1959).

Songs of Praise, the first ecumenical hymnbook, is published.

1926

♱ April 8: Jürgen Moltmann, German Protestant theologian and author of a theology of hope, is born.

♱ September 4: Ivan Illich, Catholic educationalist, is born. Dies 2002.

📖 R. H. Tawney, *Religion and the Rise of Capitalism*, attacks Max Weber's (◄ 1864) thesis that the Reformation caused the rise of capitalism and argues that Lutheranism and Calvinism adapted themselves to capitalism.

♫ Leos Janacek, *Glagolitic Mass*, is completed.

The Bible is translated into Esperanto.

1927

March 6: The philosopher Bertrand Russell (◄ 1872, ▶ 1970) delivers his lecture *Why I am not a Christian*.

August: Aimée Semple McPherson (◄ 1890, ▶ 1944) founds the International Church of the Foursquare Gospel.

August 3–12: The First World Conference on Faith and Order meets in Lausanne.

📖 Sigmund Freud (◄ 1856, ▶ 1939), *The Future of an Illusion*, argues that religion is a product of the human mind.

🎬 Cecil B. de Mille, *King of Kings*, is a biblical spectacular about Jesus.

Pius XI consecrates the first Japanese Catholic bishop, Januarius Hayusake, for Nagasaki.

1928

January 6: The encyclical *Mortalium animos* condemns the ecumenical movement.

♱ March 19: Hans Küng, Swiss Catholic theologian, is born. He is to be disciplined by the Vatican for his views on papal infallibility but later makes his name in connection with world religions and the global ethic.

May 17: The Australian 'flying doctor' service, founded by John Flynn (◀ 1912), makes its first call.

June 8: Gustavo Gutiérrez is born. His *Theology of Liberation* (1971) marks the beginning of liberation theology.

October 2: Josemaria Escrivá (▶ 2002) receives a vision which prompts him to found Opus Dei, a controversial Roman Catholic movement aiming at achieving sanctity in personal life.

November 12: Randall Thomas Davidson (◀ 1903) retires as Archbishop of Canterbury, the first to do so.

November 30: Cosmo Gordon Lang, Archbishop of York, is appointed Archbishop of Canterbury (▶ 1942).

December 24: The Festival of Nine Lessons and Carols from King's College, Cambridge (◀ 1918), is broadcast for the first time.

The Fellowship of St Alban and St Sergius is founded.

A Conference of the International Missionary Council (◀ 1921) is held in Jerusalem.

The Inter-Varsity Fellowship comes into being from student evangelical conferences.

The revised Prayer Book approved by the Church of England is rejected by the House of Commons.

1929

January 15: Martin Luther King, Jr (▶ 1963), American civil rights leader, is born. He is assassinated in 1968.

January 29: Charles Fox Parham (◀ 1873) dies.

February 11: The Lateran Treaty between the Vatican and Mussolini establishes Vatican City as a sovereign state.

October 7: Basil III (◀ 1925) is succeeded as Patriarch of Constantinople by Photius II (▶ 1936).

December 31: Pope Pius XI's encyclical *Divini illius magistri* condemns co-education as 'false and harmful'.

William Wadé Harris (◀ c.1860) dies.

Joseph Stalin becomes the effective leader of Russia.

Westminster Theological Seminary is founded by J. Gresham Machen, with campuses in Glenside, Pennsylvania and Dallas, Texas, as a more conservative alternative to Princeton Theological Seminary (◀ 1812).

The United Free Church (◀ 1900) unites with the Church of Scotland. A minority resists and continues as the United Free Church.

The first recorded ordination of a woman to full ministry takes place in the Lutheran church in the Netherlands.

1930

June 29: Jean de Brébeuf (◀ 1649) is canonized by Pope Pius XI: feast day October 19.

July: After allegedly raising a dead body, Joseph Babalola leads a mission which makes Aladura ('the praying people') a mass Christian movement in Nigeria.

December 31: The encyclical *Casti connubii* condemns contraception.

The Anglican Church in India becomes independent as the Church of India, Burma and Ceylon (later also of Pakistan).

The Archbishop of Utrecht and other Old Catholic representatives attend the Seventh Lambeth Conference, presided over by Archbishop Cosmo Gordon Lang (◀ 1928, ▶ 1942). Full communion between the Old Catholics and Anglicans is established two years later. The Conference also approves the use of artificial contraception in limited circumstances.

Emmanuel Milingo is born in Zambia. Later Roman Catholic Bishop of Lusaka, he becomes famous as an exorcist and spiritual healer, as a consequence of which he is asked to resign (▶ 2006).

*c.***1930**

The Rastafari movement emerges in Jamaica among working-class and black people.

1931

May 15: The encyclical *Quadragesimo anno*, on the reconstruction of the social order, appears.

July 12: Nathan Söderblom (◀ 1866) dies.

October 12: Paul Landowki's huge sculpture of Christ the Redeemer on top of Corcovado Mountain, behind Rio de Janeiro, is dedicated.

December 5: The Cathedral of Christ the Saviour, Moscow (◀ 1883), is dynamited by the Soviet authorities (▶ 2000).

Albertus Magnus (◀ 1280) is canonized by Pope Pius XI: feast day November 13.

1932

January 17: Charles Gore (◀ 1853) dies.

The Wesleyan Church and the Primitive Methodist Church (◀ 1811) merge with the United Methodist Church (◀ 1907) to form the Methodist Church of Great Britain.

1933

January 15: Mariette Beco, aged eleven, experiences a vision of the Virgin Mary in Banneux, Belgium.

January 30: Adolf Hitler seizes power in Germany and becomes Chancellor. Under the laws which follow, Protestant churches are forced to merge into a Protestant Reich Church and support Nazi ideology.

May 1: Dorothy Day (◀ 1897, ▶ 1980) hands out the first issues of the *Catholic Worker* in Union Square, New York.

June 5: The foundation stone for Edwin Lutyens' Roman Catholic Cathedral in Liverpool is laid (▶ 1967).

July 5: The Catholic Centre Party (◀ 1870) disbands itself and Germany becomes a one-party state.

July 20: Eugenio Pacelli, Vatican Secretary of State and the future Pius XII (▶ 1939), signs a concordat with Hitler.

August 11: Jerry Falwell, founder of the Moral Majority movement (▶ 1979), is born. Dies 2007.

September 21: Martin Niemöller sets up the Pastors' Emergency League in Germany to combat the Nazification of the church.

Bernadette Soubirous (◀ 1879) is canonized by Pope Pius XI: feast day April 19.

The Bible is translated into Afrikaans.

1934

February 23: Edward Elgar (◀ 1857) dies.

May 29–31: A Synod of the German Evangelical Church meets at Barmen and creates the Confessing Church as opposition to the Nazi 'German Christians'. It issues the landmark Theological Declaration of Barmen, inspired by Karl Barth (◀ 1886).

November 27: Luis Palau, Argentinian evangelist, is born.

John Bosco (◀ 1888) is canonized by Pope Pius XI: feast day January 31.

The Fraternal Council of Negro Churches, the first African–American ecumenical organization, is founded.

The Church of Christ in Thailand is founded.

The Church Union is formed in England out of the English Church Union (◀ 1859) to promote the Catholic faith.

1935

April 17: Sun Myung Moon has a vision of Jesus telling him to complete the mission of saving all humankind (▶ 1954).

411

♣ ♫ September 11: Arvo Pärt, Estonian composer, is born. His works include settings of many of the major Christian liturgical texts.

♣ November 6: Billy Sunday (◀ 1862) dies.

♣ Aleksandr Men, Russian priest, is born. Working in Moscow, he wins the trust of the intelligentsia and brings Aleksandr Solzhenitsyn into the church. He is murdered in 1990.

✪ Thomas More and John Fisher (◀ 1535) are canonized by Pope Pius XI: feast day June 22.

Quakers (◀ 1647), Brethren (◀ 1708) and Mennonites (◀ c.1496) formally structure their work as 'historic peace churches'.

1936

☿ January 18: Photius II (◀ 1929) is succeeded as Patriarch of Constantinople by Benjamin I (▶ 1946).

♛ January 20: In Britain King George V (◀ 1910) dies and is succeeded by his son as Edward VIII.

♣ June 14: G. K. Chesterton (◀ 1874) dies.

♛ December 11: Edward VIII abdicates and is succeeded by his brother as George VI (▶ 1952).

📖 Georges Bernanos, *Diary of a Country Priest*, becomes a classic novel (▶ 1951).

1937

March 19: The encyclical *Divini redemptoris* fiercely attacks Communism.

March 21: The encyclical *Mit Brennender Sorge* denounces breaches of the Concordat with Germany (◀ 1933) and the idea of a German National Church.

The Albanian Orthodox Church becomes self-governing.

1937/38

More than 100,000 priests, monks and nuns are shot in Stalinist purges in the Soviet Union.

1938

♫ June 15: Franz Schmidt, *The Book with Seven Seals*, an oratorio based on the book of Revelation, is first performed in Vienna.

December 12–29: The second International Missionary Council Conference is held at Tambaram.

The Iona Community is founded by George Macleod, a parish minister in Glasgow.

Frank Buchman launches Moral Rearmament.

1939

☩ February 10: Pope Pius XI (◀ 1922) dies.

☩ March 2: Eugenio Maria Giuseppe Giovanni Pacelli (◀ 1933) is elected as Pope Pius XII (▶ 1958).

September 3: The Second World War begins (▶ 1945).

♣ September 23: Sigmund Freud (◀ 1856) dies.

Joseph Kiwanuka is consecrated Bishop of Masaka, Uganda, the first Roman Catholic African diocesan bishop.

1940

📽 March 24 (Easter Day): Protestant Dr Samuel McCrea Cavert and Catholic Bishop Fulton J. Sheen (◀ 1895, ▶ 1979) are the first to preside over televised religious services.

♣ April 5: Charles Freer Andrews (◀ 1871) dies.

♣ June 1: Alfred Loisy (◀ 1857) dies.

♣ June 10: Marcus Garvey (◀ 1887) dies.

November 14: Coventry Cathedral is destroyed in a German air raid (▶ 1962).

♣■ November 17: Eric Gill (◀ 1882) dies.

The Taizé community is founded by Roger Schutz (◀ 1915, ▶ 2005).

The United Methodist Committee on Relief is founded as the humanitarian agency of the United Methodist Church.

1941

January 7–10: Anglicans meet at the Malvern Conference under the presidency of William Temple (◀ 1881, ▶ 1942) to consider in the light of Christianity the crisis facing civilization.

🎭 December 21: The first play in Dorothy L. Sayers' series *The Man Born to be King* is broadcast by the BBC. It proves controversial because of the free way in which she has portrayed Jesus and his followers.

1942

☩ March 31: Cosmo Gordon Lang (◀ 1928) retires as Archbishop of Canterbury.

☩ April 17: William Temple (◀ 1941) is appointed Archbishop of Canterbury (▶ 1944).

♣ August 9/10: Edith Stein (◀ 1891) dies in the gas chambers of Auschwitz (▶ 1998).

📖 Lloyd Douglas, *The Robe*, based on the imagined life of the Roman soldier at Jesus' crucifixion, is published; it sells more than two million copies (▶ 1953).

🏛 The nave of the Episcopal Cathedral of St John the Divine, New York, is opened (◀ 1892, ▶ 1999).

The British Council of Churches (▶ 1990) is created.

The Universalist General Convention (◀ 1866) becomes the Universalist Church of America.

1943

June 29: The encyclical *Mystici corporis* is issued, on the mystical body of Christ.

September 8: A 'concordat' is entered into between the Russian Orthodox Church and Stalin.

September 12: Sergius, Bishop of Nizhny Novgorod, is enthroned as Patriarch of Moscow (▶ 1944).

September 30: The encyclical *Divino afflante spiritu* is issued, on the study of the Bible.

December 7: Chiara Lubich, a school teacher from Trento in northern Italy, has a religious experience which leads her to found the Italian lay movement Focolare, focused on the spirituality of unity.

The Catholic Relief Services is founded by the Catholic bishops of the US to assist the poor and disadvantaged abroad.

1944

January 25: The Anglican Bishop Ronald Hall of Hong Kong ordains Florence Li Tim Oi priest as a pastoral emergency.

January 28: John Tavener, English composer, is born. His works are almost all religious, inspired initially by Catholicism, later by first Russian, then Greek orthodoxy, and most recently by other forms of mysticism.

May 15: Sergius, Patriarch of Moscow (◀ 1943), dies.

August 18: John Sung (◀ 1901) dies.

September 27: Aimée Semple McPherson (◀ 1890) dies.

October 26: William Temple, Archbishop of Canterbury (◀ 1942), dies.

The worker priest movement (▶ 1954) is set up in Paris, led by Fr Henri Perrin.

W. H. Auden (◀ 1907, ▶ 1973) is converted to Christianity by reading Reinhold Niebuhr (◀ 1892) and Kierkegaard (◀ 1813).

1945

January 2: Vedanayakam Samuel Azariah (◀ 1874) dies.

January 27: Soviet troops liberate the Nazi extermination camp of Auschwitz in Poland: Auschwitz becomes a symbol of the evil of the extermination of the Jews which thereafter challenges belief in God to breaking point.

February 2: Geoffrey Fisher, Headmaster of Repton, is appointed Archbishop of

Canterbury (▶ 1961). He shows great interest in reunion, presides over the first meeting of the World Council of Churches (▶ 1948) and travels widely to meet Eastern Orthodox leaders and Pope John XXIII.

February 2: Alexius, Metropolitan of Leningrad, is elected Patriarch of Moscow as Alexius I (▶ 1970).

April 9: Dietrich Bonhoeffer (◀ 1906) is executed by the Nazis in Flossenburg concentration camp.

April 20: Adolf Hitler commits suicide.

May 8: The Second World War (◀ 1939) ends in Europe.

May 15: Charles Williams (◀ 1886) dies.

August 6: The US Army Air Force drops an atomic bomb on Hiroshima, Japan.

August 9: The US Army Air Force drops a second atomic bomb on Nagasaki, Japan.

August 15: Japan capitulates.

September 24: John Rutter, English composer, is born. He writes a large amount of choral music, including a *Gloria* (1974) and a *Requiem* (1985).

October 24: 29 nations ratify the United Nations Charter, bringing the United Nations Organization into being.

Christian Aid is founded as Christian Reconciliation in Europe.

1945/46

The Nag Hammadi Library, more than 40 papyrus codices containing Gnostic works dating from the third to the fifth centuries, is discovered in Egypt.

1946

February 20: Benjamin I (◀ 1936) is succeeded as Patriarch of Constantinople by Maximus V (▶ 1948).

The United Bible Society is formed from European and American Bible Societies.

Church World Service is founded in the US as the relief, development and refugee service of Protestant, Anglican and Orthodox churches.

1947

July 27: Catherine Labouré (◀ 1830) is canonized by Pope Pius XII: feast day November 28.

August 24: Paul Coelho, Brazilian novelist and spiritual writer, is born (▶ 1988).

September 27: The Church of South India is formed by a merger of Anglicans, Methodists and the South India United Church (◀ 1908). It is the first merger of episcopal and non-episcopal churches since the Reformation.

415

December 25: Werenfried van Straaten (◀ 1913) founds Aid to the Church in Need.

The Dead Sea Scrolls are discovered at Qumran by the Dead Sea, containing the library of a sect which ranges from the second-century BCE texts of biblical books to the community's own compositions.

1948

May 14: The State of Israel is proclaimed.

May 15: The British mandate in Palestine (◀ 1922) ends.

July 13: The Ethiopian Church becomes an autonomous patriarchate.

August 23: The World Council of Churches (WCC) is founded at its First General Assembly in Amsterdam; it comes to include almost all churches apart from the Roman Catholic Church and the Unitarian Church (▶ 1961).

September 30: Ronald Knox completes his translation of the Bible, which forms a bridge for Catholics between the Douai-Reims Bible (◀ 1609/10) and the Jerusalem Bible (▶ 1966).

November 1: Maximus V (◀ 1946) is succeeded as Patriarch of Constantinople by Athenagoras I (◀ 1886, ▶ 1972).

December 26: Archbishop Joseph Mindszenty, Primate of Hungary, is arrested and sentenced to life imprisonment. He becomes a symbol for Eastern European Christians.

The Eighth Lambeth Conference is concerned with the Christian doctrine of man, the church and the modern world and the unity of the church.

The Church Commissioners for England are formed, succeeding the Ecclesiastical Commissioners (◀ 1835), to manage the assets of the Church of England.

1949

The National Party in South Africa begins to enact laws to enforce apartheid, racial segregation (▶ 1991).

1950

August 12: The encyclical *Humani generis* attacks 'false doctrines'.

October 26: Mother Teresa (◀ 1910, ▶ 1997) founds the Order of the Missionaries of Charity in Calcutta.

November 1: In the encyclical *Munificentissimus Deus*, Pius XII proclaims the dogma of the Bodily Assumption of Mary to heaven.

World Vision International is established to care for orphans in Asia.

The American National Council of Churches is formed (◀ 1908).

Giovanni Guareschi, *The Little World of Don Camillo*, begins a series of books which pit a village priest against his Communist opponent, Peppone.

416

1951

♣ April 29: Ludwig Josef Johann Wittgenstein (◀ 1889) dies.

▌ June 25: Henri Matisse's Chapel of the Rosary in Vence, France, is consecrated.

♣ October 12: Simon Kimbangu (◀ 1889) dies.

☉ Comgall (◀ 602) is canonized by Pope Pius XII: feast day March 11.

🎬 Another film version of Henryk Sienkiewicz, *Quo Vadis?* (◀ 1896, 1912, ▶ 2001), directed by Mervyn LeRoy, with Robert Taylor, Deborah Kerr and Peter Ustinov, is second only in popularity to *Gone with the Wind*.

🎬 Robert Bresson makes a film version of Georges Bernanos, *Diary of a Country Priest* (◀ 1936).

▌ Salvador Dali paints his *Christ of St John of the Cross*, which depicts the crucified Christ over Port Lligat on the Costa Brava, Spain, Dali's home. It achieves iconic status.

Wu Yaozong (Y. T. Wu), a Cantonese Christian, founds the Three-Self Patriotic Movement in China to remove foreign influence from the churches. The movement promotes self-government, self-support and self-propagation.

The first black church in Britain, the Calvary Church of God, is founded.

1952

♛ February 6: In Britain, King George VI (◀ 1936) dies and his daughter becomes Queen Elizabeth II.

The Revised Standard Version of the Bible (▶ 1989) is published.

1953

🎭 January 22: First performance takes place on Broadway of Arthur Miller, *The Crucible*, dramatizing the Salem witch trials (◀ 1692), inspired by the current anti-Communist witchhunt.

March 5: Joseph Stalin (◀ 1929) dies.

♣ July 16: Hilaire Belloc (◀ 1870) dies.

Demos Shakarian founds the Full Gospel Business Men's Fellowship International.

📖 James Baldwin, *Go Tell It on the Mountain*, a pioneering novel of black awareness set in a Harlem storefront church, is published.

🎬 Lloyd Douglas, *The Robe* (◀ 1942), is the first film in Cinemascope.

1954

March 21: Billy Graham (◀ 1918) launches the Greater London Crusade in Harringay, London.

May 1: Sun Myung Moon (◀ 1935) founds the Unification Church.

August : The Second General Assembly of the WCC (◀ 1948) is held at Evanston on the theme 'Christ the Hope of the World'.

⊕ July 27: Pope Pius X (◀ 1914) is canonized by Pope Pius XII: feast day August 21.

The worker priest movement (◀ 1944) is dissolved by Pius XII.

Alice Lenshina in Northern Rhodesia founds the Lumpa Church, a mass movement rejecting witchcraft, the consumption of alcohol and polygamy (▶ 1964).

The *Bible de Jérusalem* is published (English Jerusalem Bible, ▶ 1966).

1955

♠ January 31: John R. Mott (◀ 1865) dies.

♠ February 23: Paul Claudel (◀ 1868) dies.

December 1: In Montgomery, Alabama, Rosa Parks famously refuses to give up her seat to a white passenger, sparking off a bus boycott the next day. She later becomes an icon of the Civil Rights Movement.

� Le Corbusier, Nôtre Dame du Haut, Ronchamp, France, is completed.

📖 Nikos Kazantzakis' novel *The Last Temptation of Christ* (▶ 1988) is published.

1956

♠ July 30: Maude Royden (◀ 1876) dies.

July 30: Maud K. Jensen is the first woman to receive full clergy rights in the Methodist Church.

📽 Cecil B. de Mille remakes *The Ten Commandments* (◀ 1923) with Charlton Heston and Yul Brynner.

1957

June 25: The United Church of Christ is formed in the USA from the Evangelical and Reformed Church and the Congregational Christian Churches.

September 3: A report by Sir John Wolfenden proposes that homosexual acts between consenting adults in private should no longer be illegal.

The Methodist Church in America begins to ordain women and ends segregation.

1958

♠■ February 13: Georges Rouault (◀ 1871) dies.

February 17: Pope Pius XII designates Clare (◀ 1253) the patron saint of television.

May 15: David Yonggi Chu founds the Pentecostal Yoido Full Gospel Church in Korea.

♠♫ August 28: Ralph Vaughan Williams (◀ 1872) dies.

♠ October 3: George Kennedy Allen Bell (◀ 1883) dies.

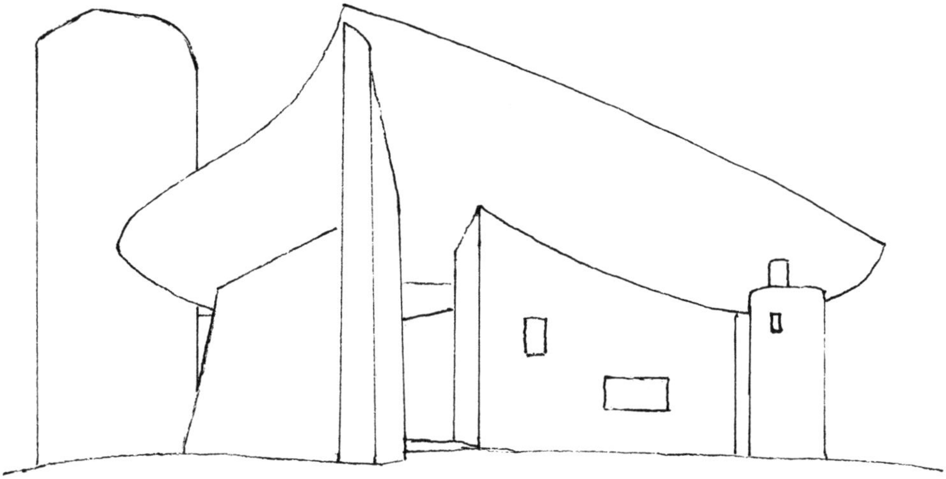

Le Corbusier, Chapel of Notre Dame du Haut at Ronchamp, France, 1955

October 9: Pope Pius XII (◀ 1939) dies.

October 28: Angelo Giuseppe Roncalli, Patriarch of Venice, is elected as Pope John XXIII (▶ 1963).

The Ninth Lambeth Conference rules that family planning and birth control by artificial means are acceptable (◀ 1930).

J. B. Phillips, *The New Testament in Modern English*, is published and becomes a bestseller.

1959

January 25: Pope John XXIII announces that he is going to summon a council of the Roman Catholic Church (▶ 1962).

August 19: Jacob Epstein (◀ 1880) dies.

November 18: William Wyler's *Ben Hur* is released, the second film version of Lew Wallace's novel (◀ 1880, 1925).

Nikita Khruschev launches a new campaign against the church in Russia. Continuous persecution in the 1930s has resulted in its near-extinction and the greater leniency shown by Stalin during the Second World War has had a limited effect.

Dennis Bennett, an Episcopalian priest in California, experiences baptism in the Holy Spirit and speaking in tongues. This prompts a Pentecostal revival.

Geoffrey Fisher becomes the first Archbishop of Canterbury since 1397 to visit the Vatican.

1960

April 23: Toyohiko Kagawa (◀ 1888) dies.

🎭 July 1: The first performance is given in London of *A Man for All Seasons* (▶ 1966), Robert Bolt's play about Sir Thomas More.

🎭 October 17: The first performance is given on Broadway of Jean Anouilh's *Becket or The Honour of God* (▶ 1964).

1961

🎵 January 20: The first performance of Francis Poulenc's *Gloria* is given in Boston, Massachusetts.

☩ May 31: Geoffrey Fisher, Archbishop of Canterbury (◀ 1945), retires.

⚑ June 6: Carl Gustav Jung (◀ 1875) dies.

☩ June 21: Arthur Michael Ramsey (◀ 1904) is appointed Archbishop of Canterbury (▶ 1974).

🎭 June 26: The first performance is given in Nottingham of John Osborne's play *Luther*.

⚑ August 7: Frank Buchman (◀ 1878) dies.

⚑ September 18: Dag Hammarskjøld (◀ 1905) is killed in a plane crash.

🎥 October 1: *Songs of Praise* is first broadcast on BBC television from the Tabernacle Baptist Church in Cardiff.

⚑ November 17: Charles H. Mason (◀ 1866) dies.

November 19–December 5: The Third General Assembly of the WCC (◀ 1948) is held at New Delhi on the theme 'Jesus Christ the Light of the World'. At it the International Missionary Council (◀ 1921) is formally integrated with the WCC and the Russian Orthodox Church joins the WCC.

The New English Bible New Testament is published on the 350th anniversary of the Authorized Version.

🏛 Marcel Breuer, St John's Abbey, Collegeville, Minnesota, is completed.

Unitarians in USA merge with Universalists (◀ 1942) to form the Unitarian Universalist Association.

1962

🏛▮ May 25: The new Coventry Cathedral (◀ 1940) is consecrated on the same day as the new Kaiser Wilhelm Memorial Church in Berlin. The cathedral is notable for its tapestry of *Christ in Glory* designed by Graham Sutherland, its baptistery window by John Piper (◀ 1903) and its sculpture of *St Michael's Victory over the Devil* by Jacob Epstein (◀ 1880).

October 11–December 8: The Second Vatican Council meets (▶ 1965). Its sessions, lasting over four years, will bring major changes to Roman Catholic worship and theology through a series of important documents. It is regarded in the Roman Catholic Church as the twenty-first Ecumenical Council.

The Catholic Association for Overseas Development (CAFOD) is founded in Britain.

1963

☿ January 20: Vincent Mary Pallotti (◀ 1835) is canonized by Pope John XXIII: feast day January 22.

📖 March 19: John A. T. Robinson's (◀ 1919, ▶ 1983) best-selling religious book *Honest to God*, questioning much of traditional Christian belief, is published.

April 11: Pope John XXIII issues the encyclical *Pacem in terris* on establishing universal peace and justice.

☀ June 21: Pope John XXIII (◀ 1958) dies.

☀ August 6: Giovanni Battista Montini, Cardinal Archbishop of Milan, is elected as Pope Paul VI (▶ 1978).

August 28: Martin Luther King (◀ 1929, ▶ 1968) gives his 'I have a dream' speech in Washington, DC.

September 29–December 4: The Second Vatican Council meets again. Among other decisions it gives official approval to vernacular liturgies.

�${} November 22: C. S. Lewis (◀ 1898) dies.

📖 David Wilkerson, *The Cross and the Switchblade*, is published. It sells more than 15 million copies (▶ 1969).

1964

January 5: Pope Paul VI (◀ 1963, ▶ 1966) and Patriarch Athenagoras of Constantinople (◀ 1948, ▶ 1972) meet in Jerusalem, the first meeting between the two heads of churches since the fifteenth century.

August 3: Flannery O'Connor (◀ 1925) dies.

August 3: The Lumpa Church (◀ 1954) is banned by the Zambian govermnent on grounds of national security.

🎬 September 4: Pier Paolo Pasolini, *The Gospel According to St Matthew*, a film influenced by its director's Marxist approach, is released.

September 14–November 21: The Second Vatican Council meets. Its pronouncements include a dogmatic constitution on the church (*Lumen gentium*) and a decree on ecumenism (*Unitatis redintegratio*).

☿ October 18: Pope Paul VI canonizes the Uganda Martyrs (◀ 1886): feast day June 3.

October 28: The first issue of *The National Catholic Reporter* is published in Kansas City.

🎬 The film version of Anouilh's play *Becket* (◀ 1960), directed by Peter Glenville, is released.

421

L'Arche, providing communities for those with learning disabilities, is founded in France by Jean Vanier.

1965

January 1: The Universities' Mission to Central Africa (◀ 1857) and the Society for the Propagation of the Gospel in Foreign Parts (◀ 1701) unite to become the United Society for the Propagation of the Gospel.

✝ January 4: T. S. Eliot (◀ 1888) dies.

January: The first issue of the international theological journal *Concilium* appears in seven languages.

September 3: The encyclical *Mysterium fidei* is issued on the doctrine and worship of the eucharist.

✝ September 4: Albert Schweitzer (◀ 1875) dies.

September 14–December 8: The Second Vatican Council meets for the last time. It issues a declaration on the relation of the church to non-Catholic religions (*Nostra aetate*) and a pastoral constitution on the church in the modern world (*Gaudium et spes*).

✝ October 22: Paul Tillich (◀ 1886) dies.

December 7: The bulls of mutual excommunication issued by the Roman Catholic Church and the Greek Orthodox Church (◀ 1054) are cancelled by Pope Paul VI and Patriarch Athenagoras I.

1966

June 14: The Roman Catholic Church abolishes the Index of Prohibited Books (◀ 1557).

November 23: Michael Ramsey, Archbishop of Canterbury, meets Pope Paul VI in Rome.

🎦 Fred Zinnemann's *A Man for All Seasons*, the film of Robert Bolt's play (◀ 1960), is released.

The Cultural Revolution prevents the expression of Christianity in China (▶ 1979).

A charismatic revival begins in the Roman Catholic Church with Pentecostal experiences at Duquesne University, Notre Dame and the University of Michigan.

The Jerusalem Bible (◀ 1954) is published.

1967

March 26: The encyclical *Populorum progressio* is issued on the development of peoples.

🏛 May 14: Liverpool's Roman Catholic Cathedral (◀ 1933) is consecrated.

The Lutheran Church of Sweden legislates for the ordination of women priests.

1968

✝ April 4: Martin Luther King (◀ 1929) is assassinated.

422

Karl Barth

April 23: The United Brethren and Methodist Churches merge to form the United Methodist Church.

July 4–20: The Fourth General Assembly of the WCC (◀ 1948) is held at Uppsala on the theme 'Behold, I Make All Things New'. It focuses on social and economic issues and Roman Catholic observers are present.

July 25: The encyclical *Humanae vitae* on birth control is issued.

September: The Conference of Latin American Bishops held at Medellín, Colombia, gives official support to 'base ecclesial communities' and liberation theology (▶ 1928).

✤ September 23: Padre Pio (◀ 1887) dies (▶ 2002).

✤ December 9/10: Karl Barth (◀ 1886) dies.

✤ December 10: Thomas Merton (◀ 1915) dies.

The Tenth Lambeth Conference recommends the ordination of women as deacons and finds arguments for their ordination to the priesthood 'inconclusive'.

1969

✤ May 16: J. H. Oldham (◀ 1874) dies.

423

July 25: The National Assembly of the Church of England (◀ 1919), known as Church Assembly, becomes the General Synod.

✦ October 5: Harry Emerson Fosdick (◀ 1878) dies.

🎥 *The Cross and the Switchblade* stars Pat Boone as David Wilkerson (◀ 1963).

1970

✦ January 3: Gladys Aylward (◀ 1902) dies.

✦ February 2: Bertrand Russell (◀ 1872) dies.

March 16: The New English Bible is published (▶ 1989).

✦ April 17: Alexius I, Patriarch of Moscow (◀ 1945), dies.

🏛 May: Oscar Niemeyer's Brasilia Cathedral is consecrated.

☉ July 27: Edward Campion (◀ 1581) is canonized by Pope Paul VI: feast day November 28.

November 22: Elizabeth Platz is the first woman to be ordained into the Lutheran Church in America.

November 29: The Church of North India is formed of the Anglican Church of India, Pakistan, Burma and Ceylon (◀ 1930), the Baptist Church of North India, the Methodist Church and the Disciples of Christ.

🎥 Hal Lindsey, *The Late Great Planet Earth,* interprets biblical imagery in terms of a third world war centred on the Middle East.

The World Alliance of Reformed Churches is created in Kenya.

The Orthodox Patriarchate of Moscow grants the Orthodox Church in America autonomy, i.e. self-governing status.

The Catholic New American Bible is published.

1971

♪ May 17: Stephen Schwartz's musical *Godspell* opens off Broadway (▶ 1973).

✦ June 1: Reinhold Niebuhr (◀ 1892) dies.

♪ September 6: The first performance of Leonard Bernstein, *Mass,* inaugurates the Kennedy Center, New York.

♪ October 12: Andrew Lloyd Webber and Tim Rice, *Jesus Christ Superstar* (▶ 1973), opens on Broadway. It becomes one of the most successful musicals in history.

⚓ Pimen, Metropolitan of Leningrad and Ladoga, is appointed Patriarch of Moscow as Pimen I (▶ 1990).

Joyce Bennett and Jane Hwang in Hong Kong are the first regularly ordained women Anglican priests (◀ 1944).

The New American Standard Version of the Bible is published.

📖 William Per Blatty, *The Exorcist* (▶ 1973), is published.

📖 Corrie ten Boom (◀ 1892, ▶ 1983), *The Hiding Place*, is published.

The ordination of women

From New Testament times onwards there is evidence of women playing important roles in the life of the church, but for the first sixteen centuries of Christianity they feature more prominently as heads of religious communities or as mystics. Names such as Macrina (◀ c.327), Melania the Younger (◀ c.383), Brigid of Kildare (◀ c.451), Hilda of Whitby (◀ 657), Hildegard of Bingen (◀ 1098), Beatrice of Nazareth (◀ 1200), Mechthild of Magdeburg (◀ c.1310), Marguerite Porete (◀ 1310), Julian of Norwich (◀ c.1342), Catherine of Siena (◀ c.1347) and Teresa of Avila (◀ 1515) stand out, but these women do not form part of the ordained ministry of the church.

First moves in this direction come with the Quakers: in 1660 Margaret Fell produces a work entitled *Women's Speaking Justified, Proved and Allowed by the Scriptures*. But only in the nineteenth century are women actually ordained to the ministry, beginning with Antoinette Brown (◀ 1853), a Congregationalist, and Olympia Brown (◀ 1863), a Universalist, both of whom later become Unitarians. The Methodist Protestant Church in America ordains women in 1879, the Church of United Brethren in 1889, the Church of God (Cleveland, Tennessee) in 1909, the Mennonites in 1912. During the First World War Maude Royden (◀ 1876) becomes the first woman to preach in an Anglican church. In 1923 the Church of England formally revives the old Order of Deaconesses, but they never become priests; the Order is abolished again when Anglican women are ordained to the diaconate (▶ 1988). Women are ordained to full ministry in the Lutheran Church in the Netherlands in 1929; the Methodist Church in America ordains women in 1957; the Lutheran Church of Sweden in 1967; the Lutheran Church in America in 1970.

In the Anglican Church, in 1944 Florence Li Tim Oi is ordained priest in Hong Kong as an emergency measure; it is not until 1971 that the first two Anglican women priests are regularly ordained there. The first women priests are ordained in the Anglican Church in Canada in 1976, the Protestant Episcopal Church of the USA and the Anglican Church in New Zealand in 1977. In 1994 the first women priests are ordained in the Church of England. In 1989 women bishops are ordained in the Protestant Episcopal Church of the USA and in the Anglican Church in New Zealand. In 2006 Katharine Jefferts Schori becomes the first woman Presiding Bishop in the Protestant Episcopal Church of the USA.

1972

January 27: Mahalia Jackson (◀ 1911) dies.

May 3: Proposals for Anglican–Methodist reunion in England fail to receive an adequate majority in the Church of England General Synod.

May 30: Watchman Nee (◀ 1903) dies.

✠ July 7: Athenagoras I, Patriarch of Constantinople, dies (◀ 1948) and is succeeded on July 16 by Demetrius I (▶ 1991).

♫ July: David Fanshawe, *African Sanctus*, a work combining a setting of the mass with African music, is first performed at St John's, Smith Square, London.

October: The United Reformed Church is formed from the Presbyterian and Congregationalist churches.

1973

January 2: The US Supreme Court rules that the state cannot restrict a woman's right to abortion during the first three months of pregnancy. This provokes a vigorous 'right to life' movement.

March 16: The Leuenberg Agreement, between Lutheran and Reformed churches in Europe, is adopted.

♠ September 29: W. H. Auden (◀ 1907) dies.

🎬 *Godspell* (◀ 1971), directed by David Greene, opens.

🎬 *Jesus Christ Superstar* (◀ 1971), directed by Norman Jewison, opens.

🎬 *The Exorcist* (◀ 1971), directed by William Fredkin, opens.

1974

☿ November 15: Arthur Michael Ramsey (◀ 1961) retires as Archbishop of Canterbury (▶ 1988).

☿ December 5: Donald Coggan, Archbishop of York, is appointed Archbishop of Canterbury (▶ 1980). A biblical scholar and prolific writer, he strongly supports the ordination of women.

Bread for the World is founded by Arthur Simon, a New York Lutheran minister, to bring justice for the hungry.

Marcel Lefebvre (◀ 1905, ▶ 1991) sets up a seminary in Écone, Switzerland, to train ultra-conservative Roman Catholic clergy.

1975

⊕ September 14: Elizabeth Ann Seton (◀ 1821) is canonized by Pope Paul VI: feast day January 4.

⊕ October 12: Oliver Plunket (◀ 1681) is canonized by Pope Paul VI: feast day July 1.

⊕ October 26: Justin de Jacobis (◀ 1860) is canonized by Pope Paul VI: feast day July 31.

November 23–December 10: The Fifth General Assembly of the WCC (◀ 1948) is held in Nairobi on the theme 'Jesus Christ Frees and Unites'.

The Christian Association of Nigeria is formed to bring together different forms of Christianity.

The Sojourners Community is founded in Washington, DC, to implement the biblical call to social justice.

1976

🌳 May 26: Martin Heidegger (◀ 1889) dies.

🌳 July 30: Rudolf Bultmann (◀ 1884) dies.

October: A new basilica is dedicated to the Virgin of Guadalupe (◀ 1531).

🎵🌳 December 4: Benjamin Britten (◀ 1913) dies.

The Ecumenical Association of Third World Theologians is founded in Dar-es-Salaam, Tanzania.

In a disagreement over synodical government and the interpretation of the Bible 250 more liberal congregations break away from the Lutheran Church–Missouri Synod (◀ 1847) and form the Association of Evangelical Lutheran Churches.

The first women priests are ordained in the Anglican Church in Canada.

The Good News Bible is published.

1977

January 1: Jacqueline Means is the first woman to be ordained priest in the Episcopal Church in the United States of America.

🎬 April 3: Franco Zeffirelli, *Jesus of Nazareth*, is shown as a TV mini series.

June 22: The Australian Uniting Church is formed of the Congregationalist, Methodist and Presbyterian Churches.

📖 July 1: *The Myth of God Incarnate*, a collection of essays edited by John Hick, challenges the doctrine of the incarnation and causes a major controversy.

☦ October 6: The Russian Orthodox Church declares Archbishop Innocent of Alaska (◀ 1879) a saint: feast days March 31 and October 6.

Charles Marnham, a clergyman at Holy Trinity, Brompton, London, devises the Alpha Course, presenting the basic principles of the Christian faith (▶ 1993).

The first women priests are ordained in the Anglican Church in New Zealand.

1978

☯ August 8: Pope Paul VI (◀ 1963) dies.

☯ August 21: Albino Luciani, Patriarch of Venice, is elected as Pope John Paul I.

☯ September 28: Pope John Paul I dies.

☯ October 16: Karol Wojtyla, Archbishop of Krakow, is elected as Pope John Paul II (▶ 2005), the first pope from Poland.

🏛 October 25: A thanksgiving service attended by Queen Elizabeth II marks the completion of Liverpool's Anglican Cathedral (◀ 1904).

The Eleventh Lambeth Conference recognizes the legal right of each Anglican church to make its own decision about the ordination of women to the priesthood.

Eddie Villanueva founds the Jesus is Lord Pentecostal Church in the Philippines.

The New International Version of the Bible is published (▶ 2004).

1979

January 28: The agenda of the Conference of Latin American Bishops held at Puebla, Mexico, seeks to move in a less radical direction than the Medellín Conference (◀ 1968), but this is resisted by the clergy, who call for a 'preferential option for the poor'.

♫ August 20: Bob Dylan, *Slow Train Coming*, is released. This is the first of three overtly evangelical Christian albums from the folk singer who had been associated with the political liberal left in his early career. It shocks many of his fans.

♟ December 9: Fulton J. Sheen (◀ 1895) dies.

🎬 Terry Jones and Terry Gilliam, *Monty Python's Life of Brian,* a satirical film on the life of Jesus, has its premiere.

Jerry Falwell (◀ 1933) founds the Moral Majority, a US conservative Christian group.

Churches in China are reopened for public worship (◀ 1966).

The *Nova Vulgata* is published as the official Roman Catholic Latin text of the Bible, replacing the Clementine Vulgate (◀ 1592).

1980

☥ January 25: Donald Coggan, Archbishop of Canterbury (◀ 1974), retires.

☥ February 25: Robert Runcie is appointed Archbishop of Canterbury (▶ 1991). His time in office sees conflict between the Church of England and the Conservative government, division in the church over homosexuality and the ordination of women deacons (▶ 1988).

♟ March 24: Bishop Oscar Romero of El Salvador is assassinated.

🏛 September 14: The Crystal Cathedral, Garden Grove, CA, is consecrated.

♟ November 29: Dorothy Day (◀ 1897) dies.

November: The Church of England approves the Alternative Service Book, containing revised orders of service to be used alongside the Book of Common Prayer (◀ 1662) for a period of 20 years.

Marjorie Matthews is the first woman bishop to be appointed in the United Methodist Church (◀ 1879).

The China Christian Council is founded.

1981

June: Children in Medjugorje, Bosnia-Herzogovina, experience a vision of the Virgin Mary.

September 14: The encyclical *Laborem exercens* is issued, to celebrate the ninetieth anniversary of *Rerum novarum* (◀ 1891).

1982

January: A Faith and Order paper stating agreed positions on baptism, eucharist and ministry is issued by the WCC Commission on Faith and Order meeting in Peru and known as the Lima document.

September: The South African Belhar Confession against apartheid (◀ 1949, ▶ 1991) is issued.

☉ Fra Angelico (◀ 1455) is canonized by Pope John Paul II: feast day January 4.

📖 Michael Baigent, Richard Leigh and Henry Lincoln, *The Holy Blood and the Holy Grail*, is published. It leads to a whole series of 'conspiracy theory' books about Christianity (▶ 2003).

📖 In Alice Walker, *The Color Purple*, a black woman in the American South writes letters to God about her life.

1983

April 15: Corrie ten Boom (◀ 1892) dies.

June 10: The United Presbyterian Church in the USA merges with the Presbyterian Church in America to form the Presbyterian Church (USA).

July 24–August 10: The Sixth General Assembly of the WCC (◀ 1948) is held in Vancouver on the theme 'Jesus Christ – The Life of the World'.

August 6: The Congregation of the Doctrine of the Faith issues an 'Instruction on Some Aspects of Liberation Theology' which is highly critical of liberation theology.

❦ December 5: John A. T. Robinson (◀ 1919) dies.

1984

February 18: Under a revised Concordat between Italy and the Vatican Roman Catholicism is no longer the state religion of Italy.

❦ March 30: Karl Rahner (◀ 1904) dies.

☉ May 6: Kim Taegon (◀ 1845) is canonized by Pope John Paul II: feast day September 20.

1985

♫ February: Andrew Lloyd Webber's *Requiem* is first performed on Fifth Avenue.

The New Jerusalem Bible (◀ 1966) is published.

1986

☮ September 7: Desmond Tutu is elected as the first black Anglican Archbishop of Cape Town.

429

The Church of England Synod's Deacons (Ordination of Women) Measure allows women to be ordained deacon. The Order of Deaconesses (◀ 1923) is abolished.

1988

February: Archbishop Robert Runcie (◀ 1980, ▶ 1991) ordains the first women deacons in the Church of England in Canterbury Cathedral.

🌿 April 23: Arthur Michael Ramsey (◀ 1904) dies.

🏛 Tadeo Ando, Church on the Water, Hokkaido, Japan, is completed.

🎥 Martin Scorsese's film of Nikos Kazantzakis' novel *The Last Temptation of Christ* (◀ 1955) is released.

📖 Paulo Coelho (◀ 1947), *The Alchemist*, a bestselling novel on the spiritual quest, appears.

The Evangelical Lutheran Church in America is formed.

The Twelfth Lambeth Conference decides that each province should respect the decision of other provinces over the ordination of women to the episcopate.

The Meissen Common Statement pledges unity between the Church of England and the Federation of the Evangelical Churches in the German Democratic Republic and the Evangelical Church in Germany.

1989

February 11: Barbara Harris is consecrated the first woman bishop in the Episcopal Church of the USA as suffragan bishop of Massachusetts. This leads to the formation of a dissenting group, the Episcopal Synod of America.

Penny Jamieson is consecrated as Bishop of Dunedin, New Zealand, the first woman diocesan bishop in the Anglican Communion.

🌿 June 27: Alfred Jules Ayer (◀ 1910) dies.

September 16: Ignazio Ellacuria and five other Jesuit priests are murdered by the security forces on the campus of the University of San Salvador.

🏛 Tadeo Ando, Church of the Light, Osaka, Japan, is completed.

🎥 Denys Arcand's film *Jesus of Montreal* centres on a contemporary restaging of the passion play by a group of underemployed actors and its impact on them.

⬛ Andres Serrano exhibits his controversial photograph *Piss Christ*.

The Revised English Bible is published (◀ 1970).

The New Revised Standard Version is published (◀ 1952).

1990

✠ March 3: Pimen I, Patriarch of Moscow (◀ 1971), dies and is succeeded by Metropolitan Alexius of Tallinn and Estonia as Alexius II.

✝ September 9: Aleksandr Men (◀ 1935) is murdered.

🏛 September 10: Pope John Paul II lays the foundation stone of the Basilica of Our Lady of Peace in Yamoussoukro, Ivory Coast, the largest Christian church in the world.

🏛 September 29: The Anglican Washington National Cathedral is consecrated (◀ 1907).

October 25: A law 'On Freedom of Religious Confessions' is passed in Russia.

December 7: The encyclical *Redemptoris missio* is issued on the church's missionary mandate.

The Council of Churches for Britain and Ireland succeeds the British Council of Churches (◀ 1942).

1991

☸ January 31: Robert Runcie, Archbishop of Canterbury (◀ 1980), retires.

February 7–20: The Seventh General Assembly of the WCC (◀ 1948) is held in Canberra on the theme 'Come Holy Spirit – Renew the Whole Creation'.

✝ March 23: Marcel Lefebvre (◀ 1905) dies.

☸ April 19: George Carey is appointed Archbishop of Canterbury (▶ 2002). An evangelical, he supports the ordination of women and is concerned for inter-faith relations. He is the first Archbishop of Canterbury to publish his memoirs.

☸ October 2: Demetrius I, Patriarch of Constantinople (◀ 1972), dies.

☸ October 22: Bartholomew I becomes Patriarch of Constantinople; he has been active in rebuilding the Orthodox Churches in the former Eastern bloc, in relations with the Roman Catholic Church and in environmental issues.

The pass laws enforcing apartheid in South Africa (◀ 1949) are abolished.

1992

April 4: Maria Jepsen is consecrated Bishop of Hamburg, the first woman bishop in the Evangelical Lutheran Church in Germany.

✝♫ April 27: Olivier Messiaen (◀ 1908) dies.

✝■ June 28: John Piper (◀ 1903) dies.

November 11: The General Synod of the Church of England approves the ordination of women to the priesthood.

The *Catechism of the Catholic Church* is published (English translation 1994).

1993

✝ May 13: Bede Griffiths (◀ 1906) dies.

June 8: The encyclical *Veritatis splendor* is issued on the Roman Catholic Church's moral teaching.

431

June 15: Pope John Paul II consecrates Almudena Cathedral, Madrid.

Nicky Gumbel makes the Alpha Course (◀ 1977) a vehicle for evangelism. It spreads all over the world.

1994

March 12: The first Anglican women priests are ordained in Bristol Cathedral.

November 10: In his apostolic letter *Tertio millennio adveniente*, Pope John Paul II proclaims 2000 as a great Jubilee Year.

The first instalment of *The Vicar of Dibley*, written by Richard Curtis, is broadcast by BBC television, featuring Dawn French as a woman vicar (◀ 1992).

1995

March 25: Pope John Paul II issues the encyclical *Evangelium vitae* on the sanctity of human life.

May 25: Pope John Paul II issues the encyclical *Ut unum sint*, a commitment to ecumenism.

November 5: Yves Congar (◀ 1904) dies.

1996

November 28: In the Porvoo Declaration Nordic and Baltic Lutheran and Anglican Churches formally recognize one another.

Chris Ofili paints *The Holy Virgin Mary*.

1997

June 8: Queen Jadwiga of Poland (◀ 1385) is canonized by Pope John Paul II: feast day July 17.

September 5: Mother Teresa (◀ 1910) dies.

1998

April 20: Trevor Huddleston (◀ 1913) dies.

July 18–August 9: The Thirteenth Lambeth Conference debates homosexuality and under pressure particularly from African bishops condemns it as incompatible with Holy Scripture.

September 14: The encyclical *Fides et ratio* is issued, on the relationship between faith and reason.

October 11: Edith Stein (◀ 1942) is canonized by Pope John Paul II: feast day August 9.

December 3–14: The Eighth General Assembly of the WCC (◀ 1948) meets in Harare, Zimbabwe, on the theme 'Turn to God, Rejoice in Hope'.

1999

August 27: Helder Camara (◀ 1909) dies.

October 31: A Joint Declaration on the Doctrine of Justification is signed by the Roman Catholic and Lutheran Churches.

🏛 It is declared that future work on the Episcopal Cathedral of St John the Divine, New York (◀ 1892, 1942) is abandoned and that the cathedral will be left incomplete.

The Reuilly Common Declaration pledges unity between the Anglican Churches of Great Britain and Ireland and the Reformed and Lutheran Churches of France.

2000

January 1: The Great Jubilee Year (◀ 1994) begins with a World Day for Peace.

Common Praise, the first full revision of *Hymns Ancient and Modern* (◀ 1861), is published.

🏛 August 19: A new Cathedral of Christ the Saviour, Moscow (◀ 1931) is consecrated.

🦋 R. S. Thomas (◀ 1913) dies.

The Church of England Prayer Book *Common Worship* is authorized (◀ 1980).

Twenty-first century

2001

January 6: Pope John Paul II ceremonially ends the Great Jubilee Year.

🎥 A third film version of Henryk Sienkiewicz's novel *Quo Vadis?* (◀ 1896, 1951), directed by Jerzy Kawalerowicz, has its premiere.

2001/2

The Mennonite Church and General Conference Mennonites merge to form the Mennonite Conference USA.

2002

☉ June 16: Padre Pio (◀ 1968) is canonized by Pope John Paul II: feast day September 23.

August 6: Gene Robinson is consecrated as the first openly gay bishop in the Episcopal Church in the United States of America.

☿ October 3: George Carey, Archbishop of Canterbury (◀ 1991), retires.

☉ October 6: Josemaria Escrivá (◀ 1928) is canonized by Pope John Paul II: feast day August 9.

🌿 December 2: Ivan Illich (◀ 1926) dies.

2003

🌿 January 31: Werenfried van Straaten (◀ 1913) dies.

☿ February 27: Rowan Williams is enthroned as Archbishop of Canterbury (▶ 2006). A former Archbishop of Wales and a scholar, he faces a split in the Anglican Communion over homosexuality.

April 17: The encyclical *Ecclesia de eucharistia*, a restatement of eucharistic doctrine, is issued.

📖 Dan Brown, *The Da Vinci Code*, is published. It sells over 70 million copies and revives 'conspiracy theories' (◀ 1982) about Christianity.

2004

February: Today's New International Version of the Bible is published (◀ 1978).

🌿♫ March 17: Sydney Carter (◀ 1915) dies.

🎥 The Mel Gibson film *The Passion of the Christ* has its premiere.

2005

☿ April 2: Pope John Paul II (◀ 1978) dies.

434

left Pope Benedict XVI
right Katharine Jefferts Schori, first woman presiding bishop of the Protestant Episcopal Church of the USA

April 19: Joseph Ratzinger, Prefect of the Congregation for the Doctrine of Faith, is elected as Pope Benedict XVI (▶ 2006).

July 11: The Church of England Synod votes to set in train the process of removing obstacles towards the ordination of women as bishops.

August 16: Roger Schutz (◀ 1915, 1940) is murdered.

2006

January 25: Pope Benedict XVI issues the encyclical *Deus caritas est*, on love.

February 14–23: The Ninth General Assembly of the World Council of Churches meets in Porto Alegre, Brazil, on the theme 'God in Your Grace, Transform the World'.

September 24: Bishop Milingo (◀ 1930) is formally excommunicated for ordaining four married men as bishops without the papal mandate.

November 1: Katharine Jefferts Schori begins a nine-year term as Presiding Bishop of the Episcopal Church in the United States of America, the first woman to achieve the status of Primate.

November 23: Rowan Williams, Archbishop of Canterbury, meets Pope Benedict XVI in Rome on the fortieth anniversary of the historic meeting between Archbishop Michael Ramsey and Pope Paul VI (◀ 1966).

2007

May 15: Jerry Falwell (◀ 1933) dies.

435

Glossary

Abbey
A monastery governed by an abbot or abbess. Abbeys often have priories dependent on them.

Anathema, Anathematize
Complete exclusion from the church; a stronger term than excommunication.

Anglicanism
Relating to a group of churches centred on the Church of England, its beliefs and practices.

Antipope
A rival claimant to the papacy.

Archbishop
A bishop who holds a specially eminent position among other bishops; in the Anglican Church the head of a church province.

Archdeacon
An administrative officer appointed by the bishop to supervise the clergy and administer church property.

Archdiocese
A diocese of which the bishop is an archbishop.

Arminianism
The view, opposed to Calvinism, that God's sovereignty and human free will are compatible and that human dignity requires free will. It takes its name from the Dutch Protestant theologian Jacobus Arminius of the University of Leiden and is expounded in a theological document called the Remonstrance.

Beghards
The male equivalent of Beguines (*see below*).

Beguines
Women living pious lives, but not as members of a religious order; in Germany they live together in quite large groups, in the Low Countries each has her own house within a walled enclosure. They are celibate and live by a rule, working to support themselves and engaging in charitable work as well as prayer and contemplation. They can own private property.

Bull
A general term for a papal letter, indicating that it is authenticated by a leaden seal (Latin *bulla*) and carrying great authority (in more modern times the term used is 'encyclical').

Cardinal
A member of a college nominated by the Pope which meets in secret to elect a new pope. Cardinals hold senior administrative positions in the Roman Catholic Church.

Carolingian Renaissance
An intellectual and cultural revival, in spheres from script to architecture, centred on the reign of Charlemagne.

Cathedral
The bishop's church, so-called because his *cathedra* (throne or seat) is there.

Catholic
The term comes from a Greek word meaning 'universal', but its use is rather more complex. In the first millennium 'catholic' with a small c denotes mainstream Christianity as opposed to deviant forms such as Arian or Monophysite. After the schism of 1054 Catholic (strictly speaking Roman Catholic) Christianity with a capital C in the West is distinguished from Orthodox Christianity in the East.

Catholicos
A title used by the patriarchs of some Eastern churches.

Chapter
The daily assembling of a religious community for discipline and administration, so called because the meeting includes the reading of a chapter from the Rule. The assembly itself comes to be called the chapter and the place where it meets is the chapter house. A general chapter comprises the whole community.

Conclave
The meeting in a closed apartment of the College of Cardinals when they are to elect a new pope. They are shut in until they have arrived at a decision.

Constitution
A law issued by the Pope or a council.

Counter-Reformation
The transformation undergone by the Roman Catholic Church after the Protestant Reformation, chiefly marked by the Council of Trent (1545–63). The fundamental doctrines of the church are reaffirmed, its administration is reformed, new religious orders are founded, seminaries multiply and discipline is reinforced.

Curia
The papal court and its officials, by which the Roman Catholic Church is governed.

Decretal
A papal reply on a particular issue which serves as a precedent for other similar issues.

Deism
A philosophical view which accepts the existence of a supreme God but rejects miracles and super-natural revelation, emphasizing the importance of reason and the natural world. It is a prominent feature of the Enlightenment.

Diet
A meeting of all the rulers of the constituent states of the Holy Roman Empire in Germany.

Diocese
The area governed by a bishop, and centred on his cathedral.

Dyophysites
Those Christians who believe that Jesus Christ has two natures, one human and one divine.

Dyothelites
Those Christians who believe that Jesus Christ has two wills, one human and one divine; these wills never conflict.

Ecumenical
Originally the term means 'worldwide' and is used of councils recognized by the whole church and of the Patriarch of Constantinople. In modern times it is used of the movement which seeks to unite all the churches.

Encyclical
A circular letter sent out to the worldwide church by the Pope.

Excommunication
Exclusion from receiving the sacraments of the church.

filioque
The Latin word for 'and from the Son', inserted unilaterally into the description of the origin of the Holy Spirit (from God the Son as well as from God the Father) by the Western church in 589. It comes to be denounced vigorously by the Eastern church and after being officially sanctioned by Pope Benedict VIII it is one of the factors leading to the great schism between Eastern and Western churches in 1054.

'Great Schism' (*see* **Schism**)

A term confusingly used of two different events: 1. the split between Eastern and Western churches which takes place in 1054; 2. the period between 1378 and 1415 when there are Popes in both Avignon and in Rome.

Hesychasm

Silent inner prayer as practised above all by the monks of Mount Athos. Particular importance is attached to the Jesus Prayer, 'Lord Jesus Christ, have mercy on me, a sinner.' The aim of this is to unite the mind with the heart, and it is believed that in the specially chosen this eventually leads to a vision of the Divine Light.

Icon

A flat picture, usually painted on wood, of Christ, the Virgin Mary or saints, used for prayer and veneration in the Eastern church.

Iconoclasm

Hostility to the use of icons and the suppression and destruction of them.

Indulgence

The remission of temporal punishment due for a sin forgiven.

Jansenism

Named after the Dutch Roman Catholic theologian Cornelius Jansen, who emphasizes the depth of human sin and the irresistible character of grace. His views are not unlike those of Jean Calvin.

Lectionary

A list of biblical readings for each day of the year, for use in public worship.

Mar

Syriac for 'father'; it is used of senior clergy in some Eastern churches, and can also mean 'saint'.

Modernism

A movement within the Roman Catholic Church in the last decade of the nineteenth century and the first decade of the twentieth with a liberal agenda, debating the nature of authority, the role of historical research in theology and the psychology of religious life, running parallel to the same debate in the Protestant churches.

Monophysitism

The view that Jesus has only one, divine, nature rather than a human and a divine nature.

Monothelitism

The view that Jesus has only one, divine, will rather than two wills, one human and one divine, which are always in agreement.

Nestorianism

Named after Nestorius, Patriarch of Constantinople, who emphasizes the humanity of Christ to such a degree that his divinity seems almost to belong to a different person. Nestorius is condemned and deposed, but a number of Eastern ('Nestorian') churches follow in his tradition.

Non-conformist

Not complying with an official church body.

Order

A religious community with a common rule of life.

Orthodox

The Greek term means 'holding the right opinion' and with a small o is used to denote those with the 'right' doctrine as opposed to heretics. After the schism of 1054 Orthodox Christianity with a capital O in the East is distinguished from Catholic (strictly speaking Roman Catholic) Christianity in the West.

Patriarch

A title given to the heads of Eastern churches.

Patristics

The study of the theologians of the early church known as the church fathers.

Pietism

A religious movement within the Lutheran churches of Germany in the seventeenth and eighteenth centuries which emphasizes inner experience and personal commitment in Christian faith. It is also expressed in music, as in the hymns of Paul Gerhardt (1607) and the works of Johann Sebastian Bach (1685).

Priory

A monastery governed by a prior or prioress, which does not have the same status as an abbey, on which it is often dependent.

Protestant

One who holds the views which emerge from the sixteenth-century Reformation.

Province

A group of dioceses adjacent to one another, governed by an archbishop.

Puritans

Members of the Church of England in the sixteenth and seventeenth centuries who feel that the Reformation has not gone far enough or fast enough. They insist on a minimum of ceremony and adornment in worship and emphasize the sovereignty of God in all things and the example of the Bible.

Rector

Originally the priest in charge of a parish entitled to the tithes given by the parish, as opposed to the vicar, the representative of a monastery which controls the tithes. In modern times the distinction has disappeared.

Rule

The body of regulations prescribed for the conduct of members of a religious order.

Sarcophagus

A stone coffin, usually decorated with bas-reliefs, often with a distinctive lid.

Schism

A formal division or break within a religious group.

Scholasticism

A movement marking a revolutionary change in the academic world from expounding texts to asking how to relate different standpoints to one another. It has two forms of literature, *quaestiones*, the questions being asked, and *summas*, systematic works to answer every possible question.

See

From the Latin *sedes*, seat, the centre from which bishops, archbishops or pope administer the area for which they are responsible.

Vicar

From the Latin *vicarius*, representative. The vicar is originally the representative of a monastery controlling a parish; the Pope is called the vicar of Christ.

Appendices

None of the following lists is meant to be exhaustive: each simply brings together in chronological order features of Christianity which extend over part or all of its history and which are mentioned in the *Chronology*.

Art

Christian art or art inspired by Christianity includes paintings, illuminated books, mosaics, sculpture and metalwork.

c.200	Art begins in the catacombs of Rome
c.240	Wall paintings decorate a house church in Dura Europos
c.270	The Jonah sarcophagus in Santa Maria Antiqua, Rome, is an early example of this resurrection motif
c.350	Mosaics are made in the Mausoleum of Santa Costanza, Rome
359	The sarcophagus of Junius Bassus is an important example of the art
398	Mosaics decorate Santa Pudenziana, Rome
c.432	Mosaics decorate Santa Maria Maggiore, Rome
c.500	Mosaics decorate Hagios Georgios, Thessaloniki
526–30	Mosaics decorate Santi Cosma e Damieno, Rome
547	Mosaics decorate San Vitale, Ravenna
549	Mosaics decorate San Apollinare in Classe, Ravenna
c.700	The Lindisfarne Gospels are created
760	The Book of Kells is produced
1010	The gilded reliquary-statue of Sainte Foy, Conques is mentioned for the first time
1015	The bronze doors of Hildesheim Cathedral are commissioned by Bishop Bernwald
c.1130	Gislebertus, Last Judgement tympanum, Autun Cathedral, is carved
c.1175	The Winchester Bible is produced
1180	The Shrine of the Three Kings, Cologne Cathedral, is created
c.1180	The Klosterneuburg altarpiece is created
c.1240	Cimabue is born
1259	Pietro Cavallini is born
1267	Giotto is born
1287	The silver altar of St James in Pistoia Cathedral is begun
c.1290	The *Mappa Mundi*, now in Hereford Cathedral, is finished
c.1300	The altar frontal in Nes church, Norway, is a striking example of oil painting
1305	Giotto paints a notable cycle of frescoes in the Scrovegni Chapel, Padua
1310	Mosaics decorate the Church of St Saviour in Chora, Constantinople
c.1320	Giotto paints frescoes for the church of Santa Croce, Florence
c.1378	Lorenzo Ghiberti makes bronze doors for the baptistery of Florence Cathedral
1386	Donatello is born
c.1395	Fra Angelico is born
c.1400	The Sherborne Missal is produced
1406	Fra Filippo Lippi is born
c.1410	*Les Très Riches Heures du Duc de Berry* is produced
c.1425	Andrei Rublev, *Icon of the Holy Trinity*, is painted
c.1430	Giovanni Bellini is born
1432	Jan van Eyck, *Ghent Altarpiece*, is completed
1436	Fra Angelico paints murals at San Marco Monastery in Florence

441

c.1448 Martin Schongauer is born

1451 Rogier van der Weyden paints *The Last Judgement*

1472 Lucas Cranach the Elder is born

1483 Raphael is born

1485 Andrea del Sarto is born

1498 Leonardo da Vinci paints his *Last Supper*

1499 Michelangelo, *Pietà*, St Peter's, Rome, is completed

c.1500 Hieronymus Bosch paints *The Garden of Earthly Delights*

1508 Albrecht Dürer, *Praying Hands*, is drawn
Leonardo da Vinci paints *Virgin of the Rocks* (second version)

1511–15 Matthias Grünewald produces the *Isenheim Altarpiece*

1513 Albrecht Dürer, *Knight, Death and the Devil*, is drawn

c.1525 Pieter Brueghel the Elder is born

1528 Paulo Veronese is born

1541 Michelangelo, *The Last Judgement,* in the Sistine Chapel is completed
Domenico Theotocopuli (El Greco) is born

1555 Michelangelo's *Rondanini Pietà* is begun

1571 Michelangelo Caravaggio is born

1598 Gian Lorenzo Bernini is born

1606 Rembrandt van Rijn is born

1789 John Martin is born

1808 Caspar David Friedrich, *The Cross in the Mountains*, is painted

1853 William Holman Hunt, *The Light of the World*, is first exhibited

1931 Paul Landowski, *Christ the Redeemer*, Rio de Janeiro, is erected

1947 Jacob Epstein, *Lazarus*, is finished

1951 Henri Matisse decorates the Chapel of the Rosary in Vence
Salvador Dali paints *Christ of St John of the Cross*

1962 Jacob Epstein, *St Michael's Victory over the Devil*, and Graham Sutherland, *Christ in Glory*, are both placed in Coventry Cathedral

1989 Andres Serrano, *Piss Christ*, is exhibited

1996 Chris Ofili, *The Holy Virgin Mary*, is exhibited

Bible translations

As well as simply making the Bible available to those who cannot read Greek, Hebrew or Latin, from the Middle Ages translations of the Bible appear as challenges to Catholic church authority, and as a fundamental part of the Protestant Reformation. From the seventeenth century onwards they are once again made in order to aid the spread of Christianity. In the twentieth century, concerns both about the quality of the texts from which earlier translations have been made, and a desire for translations to be more accessible, lead to a great increase in translations, particularly into English.

c.350	Gothic (New Testament)
383	Latin (Vulgate)
434	Armenian
635	Chinese (parts)
863	Old Church Slavonic (parts of the New Testament)
1287	Catalan
1294	Chinese (New Testament and Psalms)
1360	Czech (Dresden)
1382	English (Wyclif)
1436–39	Hungarian (Hussite)
1471	Italian (Malermi)
1478	Catalan (printed)
1530	English (Tyndale) French
1534	German (Luther)
1535	English (Coverdale)
1537	English (Matthew's)
1539	English (Great)
1540	Icelandic (New Testament)
1542	Swedish
1548	Finnish (New Testament) Ge'ez (New Testament)
1550	Danish
1560	English (Geneva)
1570	Spanish (Biblia del Osa)
1584	Icelandic Slovenian
1588	Welsh
1590	Hungarian (Károlyi)
1593	Polish Czech (from Hebrew and Greek)
1602	Irish (New Testament)
1609/10	English (Douai-Reims)
1611	English (Authorized/King James Version)
1637	Dutch (Statenvertaling)
1642	Finnish
1663	Algonquin
1666	Armenian
1671	Arabic
1680	Irish (Old Testament)
1688	Romanian Malay (New Testament)
1711	Tamil
1733	Malay
1735	Lithuanian
1740	Tamil (improved)
1772	Manx
1819	Chinese Tahitian (New Testament)
c.1820	Aleut (parts of the New Testament)
1831	Croatian
1837	Ge'ez (parts of the New Testament) Japanese
1839	Hawaiian
1847	Serbian (New Testament)
1863	Russian (New Testament)
1865	Serbian (Old Testament)
1875	Russian (Old Testament)
1886	English (Revised Version)
1890	Swahili
1893	Kikongo (New Testament)

443

1902	English (American Standard Version)	1971	English (New American Standard Version)
1926	Esperanto	1976	English (Good News)
1933	Afrikaans	1978	English (New International Version)
1948	English (Ronald Knox)		
1952	English (Revised Standard Version)	1985	English (New Jerusalem)
1954	French (*Bible de Jérusalem*)	1989	English (New Revised Standard Version)
1966	English (Jerusalem)		English (Revised English Bible)
1970	English (New American) English (New English)	2004	English (Today's New International Version)

Cathedrals

The cathedral is the church at the centre of the diocese, where the bishop of the diocese has his seat (*cathedra*). Many cathedrals, particularly those listed here, are of outstanding architectural importance.

314 Tyre (consecrated)
326 Trier I (work begins)
445 Armagh
480 Ejmiatsin, Armenia (work begins)
c.560 Angoulême I (consecrated)
602 Canterbury I (work begins)
604 Rochester I
St Paul's, London I
649 Zvartnots, Armenia (work begins)
669 York I
685 St Paul's, London II
741 Erfurt I
765 Oviedo I
786 Aachen
818 Cologne I (completed)
962 St Paul's, London III (work begins)
980 Mainz I (work begins)
1009 Mainz II (work begins)
Hildesheim (work begins)
1012 Bamberg I (consecrated)
1015 Strasbourg (work begins)
1017 Angoulême II (consecrated)
1019 Basle I (consecrated)
1030 Speyer (work begins)
1035 Trier II
Bremen (work begins)
1050 Novgorod (work begins)
1052 Hereford I
1060 Prague I
1063 Pisa (work begins)
Rouen (consecrated)
1070 Canterbury II (work begins)
York II
1077 Bayeux (consecrated)
1080 Hereford II (work begins)

York III
1083 Rochester II (work begins)
1084 Worcester (work begins)
1085 Lichfield I (work begins)
1087 St Paul's, London IV (work begins)
1089 Braga (consecrated)
1090 Zurich
1092 Lincoln I (consecrated)
Old Sarum I (consecrated)
1093 Durham (work begins)
Winchester (consecrated)
1096 Norwich (work begins)
1101 Smolensk I (work begins)
1103 Lund (work begins)
1107 Llandaff (work begins)
1108 Chichester I (consecrated)
1110 Worms I (consecrated)
Porto (work begins)
1111 Bamberg II (consecrated)
1114 Exeter I (work begins)
1116 Parma I (consecrated), Parma II (work begins)
1119 Cahors (consecrated)
1120 St Front, Perigueux (work begins)
Autun (work begins)
1128 Angoulême III (consecrated)
Santiago de Compostela (consecrated)
1137 Kirkwall (work begins)
Lübeck (work begins)
1139 Coimbra (work begins)
1145 Chartres I (work begins)
1152 Amiens I (work begins)
1158 Vladimir (work begins)
1160 Laon (work begins)
1170 Monreale, Sicily (work begins)

1175 Spoleto (work begins)
1180 Wells (work begins)
1181 Worms II (completed)
1182 Notre Dame, Paris (consecrated)
Erfurt II (consecrated)
1189 Ely (completed)
1190 Old Sarum II (consecrated)
1192 Lincoln II (work begins)
1194 Chartres II (work begins)
1195 Bourges (work begins)
Lichfield II (work begins)
1197 Glasgow (consecrated)
1200 Freiburg (work begins)
1215 Siena (work begins)
1217 Burgos
1220 Salisbury (work begins)
York IV (work begins)
Amiens II (work begins)
1226 Toledo (work begins)
1236 Cordoba I (consecration of former mosque)
1238 Peterborough (consecrated)
1240 St Paul's, London IV (completed)
1247 Beauvais (work begins)
1248 Cologne II (work begins; consecrated 1880)
1258 Exeter II (work begins)
1282 Albi
1287 Uppsala (work begins)
1296 Florence (work begins)
1311 Reims (consecrated)
1320 Krakow
1344 Prague II (work begins)
1356 Basle II (work begins)
1377 Canterbury III (work begins)
c.1385 Milan (work begins)
1386 Oviedo II (work begins)
1402 Seville (work begins)
1479 Cathedral of the Dormition, Moscow (completed)
1489 Cathedral of the Annunciation, Moscow (completed)

1508 Cathedral of the Archangel Michael, Moscow (completed)
1523 Cordoba II (inside former mosque) (work begins)
1549 São Salvador (M'banza Kongo)
1561 St Basil, Moscow (completed)
1563 Mexico City (work begins)
1675 St Paul's, London V (work begins)
1772 Smolensk II (completed)
1821 Sydney Roman Catholic I (work begins)
1837 Sydney Anglican (work begins)
1843 Honolulu (consecrated)
1868 Sydney Roman Catholic II (work begins)
1879 St Patrick's, New York (completed)
1883 Christ the Saviour, Moscow (consecrated)
1892 St John the Divine, New York (work begins; never finished)
1896 Kiev (consecrated)
1898 Myeongdong, South Korea (consecrated)
1903 Westminster Roman Catholic (consecrated)
1904 Liverpool Anglican (completed 1978)
1907 Washington National Anglican (work begins; consecrated 1990)
1933 Liverpool Roman Catholic (work begins; consecrated 1967)
1962 Coventry II (consecrated)
1970 Brasilia (consecrated)
1980 Crystal Cathedral, Garden Grove, CA (consecrated)
1993 Madrid (consecrated)
2000 Christ the Saviour, Moscow II (completed)

Church fathers

The leaders and writers of the early church whose work plays a major part in shaping the church are known as the church fathers. The most important of them are:

c.100–c.165	Justin Martyr
c.130–c.200	Irenaeus of Lyons
c.130	Papias
c.145	Aristides
c.150	Tatian
c.150–c.215	Clement of Alexandria
c.160–220	Tertullian
c.170–236	Hippolytus of Rome
c.185–c.254	Origen
c.213–270	Gregory Thaumaturgus
c.250–c.325	Lactantius
dies 258	Cyprian
c.260–339	Eusebius of Caesarea
c.296–373	Athanasius
c.306–373	Ephrem the Syrian
c.315–367	Hilary of Poitiers
c.315–386	Cyril of Jerusalem
c.330–379	Basil of Caesarea
c.330–c.390	Gregory of Nazianzus
c.335–c.395	Gregory of Nyssa
c.339–397	Ambrose
c.345–410	Rufinus
c.345–420	Jerome
347–407	John Chrysostom
354–430	Augustine of Hippo
c.360–435	John Cassian
c.380–450	Socrates
393–466	Theodoret of Cyrrhus
400–c.450	Sozomen
440–461 (as Pope)	Leo the Great
c.450	Vincent of Lérins
c.580–662	Maximus Confessor
590–604 (as Pope)	Gregory the Great

447

Creeds, confessions and articles of faith

The 'Nicene Creed' and the Chalcedonian Definition are foundation stones in the Christian doctrines of the Trinity and the person of Christ; from Reformation times onwards, confessions and articles of faith are used to define the beliefs of various Protestant churches.

Dioceses

When Christianity becomes established in an area, a first step is to establish an administrative area, the diocese, under a bishop. The establishment of dioceses is an indication of the spread of Christianity. Some of them become archdioceses. It is impossible to date precisely the first dioceses in present-day countries such as Italy, France and Spain and in the Middle East, where Christianity was present from earliest days.

313 Cologne
314 Mainz
    Trier
343 Speyer
597 Canterbury
604 Rochester
    London
625 York
662 Winchester
669 Lichfield
676 Hereford
680 Worcester
739 Regensburg; Passau; Freising;
    Salzburg
741 Würzburg
787 Bremen
831 Hamburg
864 Hamburg and Bremen are
    amalgamated
909 Bath and Wells
948 Hamburg-Bremen is extended to
    cover Denmark
968 Magdeburg
995 Durham
1050 Exeter (originally the Diocese of
     Crediton)
1072 Lincoln
1075 Chichester
1078 Salisbury
1091 Norwich
1103 Lund
1109 Ely
1133 Carlisle
1234 Marrakesh
1275 Kambalik (Beijing) Nestorian
1318 Kambalik (Beijing) Catholic
1404 Las Palmas
1417 Ceuta

1468 Tangier
1511 Santo Domingo; Concepción de
     la Vega; Puerto Rico
1513 Panama
1514 Funchal
1525 Tlaxcala, Mexico
1527 Puebla, Mexico
1530 Caro (later Caracas), Venezuela
1531 Nicaragua
1534 Cape Verde; Azores; São Tomé;
     Goa; Cartagena, Colombia
1536 Cuzco, Peru
1538 Chiapas, Mexico
1541 Lima, Peru
1541/42 Chester; Gloucester;
     Peterborough; Bristol; Oxford
1546 Quito, Ecuador
1547 Asuncion, Paraguay
1548 Guadalajara, California
1551 Bahia, Brazil
1558 Cochin; La Plata, Brazil; Malacca
1561 Santiago, Chile
1564 Bogota, Colombia; La Imperial,
     Cuba
1570 Cordoba, Argentina
1576 Macao
1579 Manila
1606 San Thomé de Meliapur
1620 Buenos Aires, Argentina
1674 Quebec
1676 San Salvador; Recife; Rio de
     Janeiro
1677 São Luiz da Maranhão, Brazil
1690 Nanjing, China
1743 Guatemala
1789 Baltimore
1793 New Orleans

449

Ecumenical councils of the church

Ecumenical councils are intended to be councils of the universal church; initially they are convened by emperors. The first seven councils are held to be ecumenical by both Eastern and Western churches; the Roman Catholic Church recognizes another fourteen councils as having ecumenical authority.

1. 325: Nicaea I
2. 381: Constantinople I
3. 431: Ephesus
4. 451: Chalcedon
5. 553: Constantinople II
6. 681: Constantinople III
7. 786: Nicaea II
8. 869: Constantinople IV
9. 1123: Lateran I
10. 1139: Lateran II
11. 1179: Lateran III
12. 1215: Lateran IV
13. 1245: Lyons I
14. 1274: Lyons II
15. 1311: Vienne
16. 1414–18: Constance
17. 1431–49: Basle
18. 1512–17: Lateran V
19. 1545–63: Trent
20. 1869/70: Vatican I
21. 1962–65: Vatican II

Festivals

Easter and Christmas are the two major festivals of the church, but it is nearly 300 years before Christmas comes to be celebrated. In the first centuries there is a concern to establish the precise date of Easter, so that it can be celebrated universally at the same time.

Easter

*c.*30	Jesus is crucified and his followers believe that he has risen from the dead
*c.*166–*c.*175	Easter is introduced as an annual festival
190	Pope Victor I attempts to settle a dispute about the date on which to celebrate Easter
312	The first celebration of Easter after the end of the Great Persecution takes place
*c.*390	Bishop Theophilus of Alexandria compiles tables for calculating the date of Easter
457	Victor of Aquitaine produces new tables for calculating the date of Easter
525	Dionysius Exiguus publishes a new set of tables for calculating Easter
551	Moses, Catholicos of Armenia, corrects the date of Easter in the Armenian calendar
562	Cassiodorus uses the AD system in his *Computus paschalis*, a textbook on how to determine Easter
602	There is a dispute between Augustine of Canterbury and Welsh bishops over when Easter is to be celebrated
664	The Synod of Whitby settles the date of Easter for the British church
*c.*700	Eggs are decorated by Christians to celebrate Easter
*c.*970	The first beginnings of the Easter play are evident
1582	The Gregorian calendar is introduced by Pope Gregory so that Easter can be celebrated on the day it was at the time of the Council of Nicaea
1753	The Gregorian calendar is introduced in Sweden; from now on Easter is celebrated on the same day throughout Western Christianity
1940	The first televised religious services are held on Easter Day

Christmas

*c.*6 BCE	The probable date of Jesus' birth
*c.*300	Christmas begins to be celebrated
352	Christmas is first definitively known to be celebrated on December 25
354	A chronograph by Furius Dionysius Philocalus (also known as the Philocalian calendar) puts the birth of Christ on December 25, indicating the observance of Christmas at this time
1223	Francis of Assisi constructs a Christmas crib
1601	A decorated Christmas tree is seen in Strasbourg
1644	The celebration of Christmas is forbidden in Britain
1747	Candles decorated with red ribbons are first distributed to children at a Moravian watchnight service in Marienborn, Germany
1777	A German prisoner puts up the first Christmas tree in America
1821	An illuminated star with 110 points is hung in the Moravian school at Niesky, Germany, for Epiphany

451

1832   In her journal, Princess Victoria marvels at Christmas trees

1840   The first Christmas tree is introduced into France

*c.*1890   Christingles are first used at a Moravian watchnight service in Manchester in place of candles

1906   A Christmas service is broadcast to ships at sea

1918   A Festival of Nine Lessons and Carols takes place in King's College, Cambridge, on Christmas Eve

1928   The festival of Nine Lessons and Carols from King's College, Cambridge, is broadcast for the first time

Hymns and psalms

Hymn singing is a part of Christian worship from its very beginning. The words of early Christian hymns are probably drawn from the Bible (especially the Psalms, which have also been sung since earliest times), but from the fourth century, beginning with Basil and Ambrose, new texts are composed. At various times attempts are made to restrict what can be sung in Christian services, but these tend not to last. The Protestant Reformation emphasizes congregational participation in worship and this stimulates hymn writing, though under the influence of Calvin limits are placed on what texts can be used.

112	Pliny describes Christian hymn singing
c.306	Ephrem the Syrian, hymn writer, is born
c.330	Basil of Caesarea is born: he remarks that the hymn 'Hail, Gladdening Light' is already old
337	Sahak of Armenia, hymn writer, is born
c.339	Ambrose is born: the Compline hymn 'Before the ending of the day' is attributed to him
347	John Chrysostom is born. He promotes hymn singing
c.348	Prudentius is born: hymns include 'Of the Father's love begotten' and 'Earth has many a noble city'
c.392	The Gallican Psalter becomes the standard psalter of the Western Catholic Church
c.530	Venantius Fortunatus is born: hymns include 'The royal banners forward go' and 'Sing, my tongue, the glorious battle'
563	The First Council of Braga decrees that all hymns must take their texts from scripture
633	The Fourth Council of Toledo allows poetic texts to be used in hymns
c.750	Theodulf of Orleans is born: hymns include 'All glory, laud and honour'
1236	Jacopone da Todi is born. He composes a number of hymns known as *Laudi* and the *Stabat Mater* is attributed to him
c.1254	The earliest surviving text of the *Dies Irae*, attributed to Tommaso de Celano, dates from this time
1483	Martin Luther is born: hymns include 'A great stronghold our God is still'
1530	Michael Weisse edits the first Protestant hymn book, *Ein New Geseng Buchlen*
1556	The ordinary of the mass is printed in Mexico City, the first printed hymn book in America
1562	The Sternhold and Hopkins Psalter, an English metrical translation of the psalms, is published The Genevan Psalter, a metrical translation of the psalms into French, is published under Calvin's direction
1575	The *Book of Bamberg* appears, the first officially published Catholic hymn book
1593	George Herbert is born: hymns include 'Let all the world in every corner sing' and 'Teach me, my God and King'

453

1607 Paul Gerhardt is born: hymns include 'O sacred head, sore wounded'

1628 John Bunyan is born: hymns include 'He who would valiant be'

1637 Thomas Ken is born: hymns include 'Glory to thee, my God, this night'

1640 The Bay Psalm Book, an English metrical translation, is printed in North America

1672 Joseph Addison is born: hymns include 'The spacious firmament on high'

1674 Isaac Watts is born: hymns include 'When I survey the wondrous cross' and 'O God, our help in ages past'

1696 Nahum Tate and Nicholas Brady publish the first edition of *A New Version of the Psalms of David*

1739 Charles Wesley's *Hymns and Sacred Poems*, his first collection, are published: hymns include 'Hail the day that sees him rise' and 'Hark, the herald angels sing'

1740 Augustus Montague Toplady is born: he writes 'Rock of ages'

1779 John Newton and William Cowper publish *Olney Hymns* (Newton's hymns include 'Amazing grace' and 'Glorious things of thee are spoken' and Cowper's 'God moves in a mysterious way')

1793 Henry Francis Lyte is born: hymns include 'Praise, my soul, the king of heaven' and 'Abide with me'

1804 William Blake's 'Jerusalem' is published

1805 Jeremiah Ingall compiles *The Christian Harmony*

1814 Frederick W. Faber is born: hymns include 'Sweet Saviour, bless us ere we go'

1818 John Mason Neale is born: hymns and carols include a translation of 'All glory, laud and honour' and 'Good King Wenceslas'
      Francis Xaver Gruber composes the tune for 'Silent Night'
      Cecil Frances Alexander is born: hymns include 'There is a green hill far away' and 'Once in royal David's city'

1835 Phillips Brooks is born: hymns include 'O little town of Bethlehem'

1861 *Hymns Ancient and Modern* is published

1872 Ralph Vaughan Williams is born: hymn tunes include Down Ampney ('Come down, O love divine') and Sine nomine ('For all the saints')

1873 Ira Sankey publishes the first edition of *Sacred Songs and Solos*

1898 The *Scottish Church Hymnary* is published

1899 Robert Bridges, *The Yattendon Hymnal*, is published: it includes his translation 'All my hope on God is founded'

1900 *The Baptist Church Hymnal* is published

1904 *The Methodist Hymn Book* is published

1906 *The English Hymnal*, edited by Percy Dearmer and Ralph Vaughan Williams, is published

1915 Sydney Carter is born: songs include 'Lord of the Dance' and 'When I needed a neighbour'

1920 Joseph Gelineau is born: influenced by Gregorian chant, he composes many chants for the Taizé community

1925 *Songs of Praise*, the first ecumenical hymn book, is published

2000 *Common Praise*, the first full revision of *Hymns Ancient and Modern*, is published

Literature

455

457

Bertrand Russell, *Why I am Not a Christian*
1930 Charles Williams, *War in Heaven*
1932 Reinhold Niebuhr, *Moral Man and Immoral Society*
1932–69 Karl Barth, *Church Dogmatics*
1936 Georges Bernanos, *Diary of a Country Priest*
1937 Dietrich Bonhoeffer, *The Cost of Discipleship*
1939 William Temple, *Readings in St John's Gospel*
Charles Williams, *The Descent of the Dove*
1941 Reinhold Niebuhr, *The Nature and Destiny of Man*
1942 William Temple, *Christianity and the Social Order*
C. S. Lewis, *The Screwtape Letters*
Lloyd Douglas, *The Robe*
1944 T. S. Eliot, *Four Quartets*
1945 Charles Williams, *All Hallows' Eve*
1950 Giovanni Guareschi, *The Little World of Don Camillo*
1950–56 C. S. Lewis, *Chronicles of Narnia*
1951–63 Paul Tillich, *Systematic Theology*
1952 Paul Tillich, *The Courage to Be*
1953 Dietrich Bonhoeffer, *Letters and Papers from Prison*
James Baldwin, *Go, Tell It on the Mountain*
1955 Nikos Kazantzakis, *The Last Temptation of Christ*
1956 Trevor Huddleston, *Naught for Your Comfort*
1963 John A. T. Robinson, *Honest to God*
David Wilkerson, *The Cross and the Switchblade*
1964 Dag Hammarskjøld, *Markings*
1970 Hal Lindsey, *The Late Great Planet Earth*
1971 Gustavo Gutiérrez, *Theology of Liberation*
William Per Blatty, *The Exorcist*
Corrie ten Boom, *The Hiding Place*
1974 Edward Schillebeeckx, *Jesus. An Experiment in Christology*
1977 John Hick (ed.), *The Myth of God Incarnate*
1982 Alice Walker, *The Color Purple*
Michael Baigent, Richard Leigh and Henry Lincoln, *The Holy Blood and the Holy Grail*
1988 Paul Coelho, *The Alchemist*
2003 Dan Brown, *The Da Vinci Code*

Music

855 The earliest known attempts at polyphonic music appear

*c.*900 From this date for around six centuries the organ is exclusively a church instrument

950 An organ plays for the coronation of the Archbishop of Cologne

972 An organ plays at the consecration of the Benedictine Abbey in Bages, Spain

*c.*990 An organ is built in Winchester Cathedral with 4000 pipes which is said to take 70 men to blow

991 Archbishop Gerbert of Reims is said to have put an organ in the cathedral at this time

*c.*1050 Polyphonic singing replaces Gregorian chant

*c.*1155 Hildegard of Bingen composes her *Symphonia harmoniae caelestium revelationum*

*c.*1200 Pérotin expands monophony into polyphony in a style called organum

1251 In *Ars cantus mensurabilis*, Franco of Cologne presents a system in which the shape of a musical note denotes its length

1320 An organ with pedals is built

1322 Philip de Vitry, *Ars Nova*, introduces new rhythmic schemes

1324 Pope John XXII forbids the use of counterpoint in church music

1325 The Tournai Mass, the first complete polyphonic mass known, is written by several composers

1361 An organ is constructed in Halberstadt, the first with a fingering system of twelve notes

1364 Guillaume de Machaut, *Mass of Notre Dame*, is the first known polyphonic setting by a single composer and an important example of *Ars Nova*

1380 The organ in Sion Church, Switzerland, is the world's oldest functioning organ

*c.*1385 John Dunstaple is born. He begins to unify the musical setting of the mass
Leonel Power is born. His *Missa Alma Redemptoris Mater* is the earliest surviving cyclic *cantus firmus* mass

1397 Guillaume Dufay is born. His four *cantus firmus* masses are central to the development of fifteenth-century church music

*c.*1410 Johannes Ockeghem is born. His thirteen surviving masses include the *Missa Prolationum* and the earliest extant polyphonic requiem mass

1432 Jan van Eyck, *Ghent Altarpiece*, contains the depiction of a church organ

1490 John Taverner is born

1502 Josquin Desprez, *First Book of Masses*, is published

1532 Orlande Lassus is born

1548 Tomas Luis de Victoria is born

1550 The Innsbruck Court Chapel organ is the oldest authentic two-manual organ

*c.*1554 Giovanni Gabrieli is born

1556 Palestrina, *Missa Papae Marcelli*, is written

1573 Thomas Tallis' forty-part motet *Spem in alium* is written

1583 Orlando Gibbons is born

1585 Heinrich Schütz is born

1592–95 William Byrd, masses for three, four and five voices, are written

459

1610   Claudio Monteverdi's *Vespers* are published

1678   Antonio Vivaldi is born. He writes a large number of sacred choral works as well as the operas and the concerti for which he is best known

1685   George Frideric Handel is born. As well as *Messiah* he writes a number of operas and oratorios on biblical themes

Johann Sebastian Bach is born. As well as the *St Matthew Passion* and *B Minor Mass* he writes a *St John Passion*, a *Christmas Oratorio*, a *Magnificat* and more than 200 church cantatas

1727   Bach's *St Matthew Passion* is first performed

1732   Joseph Haydn is born. As well as many symphonies and string quartets he writes *The Creation* and *The Seven Last Words of our Saviour from the Cross*

1738   Bach completes the *B Minor Mass*

1742   Handel's *Messiah* is first performed, in Dublin

1756   Wolfgang Amadeus Mozart, composer, is born. Dies 1791

1783   Mozart's *C Minor Mass* is first performed

1791   Mozart dies and his *Requiem* is left incomplete

1798   Haydn's *The Creation* is first performed

1823   Ludwig van Beethoven, *Missa Solemnis*, is first performed complete in St Petersburg

1824   Anton Bruckner is born. As well as his symphonies he writes sacred choral works including 7 masses

1829   Felix Mendelssohn conducts Bach's *St Matthew Passion* in Berlin, the first performance since Bach's death

1837   Hector Berlioz, *Grande Messe des Morts*, is first performed

1846   Felix Mendelssohn conducts the first performance of his *Elijah*

1850   Richard Wagner, *Lohengrin*, is first performed

1852   Charles Villiers Stanford is born. As well as much liturgical church music he writes a *Stabat Mater* and a *Requiem*

1857   Edward Elgar is born. As well as the *Dream of Gerontius* (1900) he writes *The Apostles* (1902/3) and *The Kingdom* (1901–06) and much church music

1869   Johannes Brahms, *A German Requiem*, is first performed complete

1874   Giuseppe Verdi, *Requiem*, is first performed

1882   Richard Wagner, *Parsifal*, is first performed at Bayreuth

1887   John Stainer, *The Crucifixion*, is first performed

1893   Gabriel Fauré, *Requiem*, is first performed in its final version

1900   Elgar's oratorio *The Dream of Gerontius* is first performed

1908   Olivier Messiaen is born. A devout Catholic, he writes many works for orchestra, for smaller ensembles and for solo piano and organ which he claims have a religious message

1911   Mahalia Jackson is born in New Orleans, the 'queen' of gospel music

1913   Benjamin Britten is born. Many of his works are written to be performed in churches or are influenced by Christianity

1926   Leos Janacek, *Glagolitic Mass,* is completed.

1935 Arvo Pärt is born. His works include settings of many of the major Christian liturgical texts

1938 Franz Schmidt, *The Book with Seven Seals*, an oratorio based on the book of Revelation, is first performed in Vienna

1942 Britten's *A Ceremony of Carols* is first performed

1944 John Tavener is born. His works are almost all religious, inspired initially by Catholicism, later by Russian and Greek Orthodoxy and other forms of mysticism

1945 John Rutter is born. He writes much church music including a *Gloria* and a *Requiem*

1948 Britten's *Saint Nicholas* is first performed

1958 Britten's *Noye's Fludde* is first performed

1961 Francis Poulenc, *Gloria*, is first performed

1962 Britten's *War Requiem* is first performed

1971 Leonard Bernstein, *Mass*, is first performed

1972 David Fanshawe, *African Sanctus*, a work combining a setting of the mass with African music, is first performed

1979 Bob Dylan, *Slow Train Coming*, is the first of three overtly evangelical Christian albums from the folk singer associated with the political liberal left

1985 Andrew Lloyd Webber, *Requiem*, is first performed

Religious Orders

529	Benedictine Order, founded by Benedict of Nursia
1012	Camaldolese Order, founded by Romuald
c.1036	Order of Vallombrosa, founded by John Gualbert
1059	Augustinian Canons founded
1084	Carthusian Order, founded by Bruno of Cologne
1098	Cistercian Order, founded by Robert of Molesme
1118	Order of Knights Templar
1120	Order of Premonstratensian Canons, founded by Norbert
c.1154	Carmelite Order, founded by Berthold of Calabria
1190	Order of German Hospitallers (the Teutonic Order)
1200	Cluniac Order, recognized as a distinct form of the Cistercian Order
1202	Order of the Brothers of the Knighthood of Christ (Livonian Order), known as the Brothers of the Sword, founded by Bishop Albert of Riga
1208/9	Order of Friars Minor (Franciscans), founded by Francis of Assisi
1215	Poor Clares, Franscican Order for women, founded by Clare of Assisi
1220	Order of Preachers (Dominicans), founded by Domingo de Guzman
1256	Order of Augustinian Hermits, established by Pope Alexander IV
1349	Brigittine Sisters, founded by Bridget of Sweden
1435	Order of Minims, founded by Francis of Paola
1524	Order of Theatines, founded by Cajetan and Giampetro Carafa
1528	Capuchin Order, founded by Matteo da Bascio
1534	Society of Jesus (Jesuits), founded by Ignatius Loyola
1535	Order of Ursulines, founded by Angela Merici
1607	Piarist Brotherhood, founded by Joseph Calasanza
1610	Order of Visitandines, founded by François de Sales and Jane Frances de Chantal
1625	Congregation of the Mission, also known as Lazarists or Vincentians, founded by Vincent de Paul
1626	The Order of Trappists, founded by Armand-Jean le Bouthillier de Rancé
1633	Daughters of Charity, founded by Vincent de Paul and Louise de Marillac
1642	Society of Saint-Sulpice (Sulpicians), founded by Jean-Jacques Olier
1703	Holy Ghost Fathers or Spiritans, founded by Claude-François Poullart des Places
1720	Passionists, founded by Paul of the Cross
1732	Congregation of the Most Holy Redeemer (Redemptorists), founded by Alphonsus di Liguori
1774	Sisters of Charity, founded by Elizabeth Ann Seton
1816	Society of Mary (Marists), founded by Jean Claude Marie Colin
1835	Pious Society of Missions (Pallottines), founded by Vincent Mary Pallotti
1845	Order of Assumptionists, founded by Emmanuel d'Alzon
1856	Society of African Missions, founded by Melchior de Marion Brésillac
1858	Paulists, founded by Isaac Hecker
1859	Society of St Francis de Sales (Salesians), founded by John Bosco

1866 St Joseph's Society for Foreign Missions (Mill Hill Missionaries), founded by Herbert Vaughan
      Society of St John the Evangelist (Cowley Fathers), founded by Richard Benson (Anglican)
1868 White Fathers, founded by Charles-Martial-Allemand Lavigerie as the Missionaries of Our Lady of Africa
1892 Community of the Resurrection, Mirfield, founded by Charles Gore (Anglican)
1893 Society of the Sacred Mission, Kelham, founded by H. H. Kelly (Anglican)
1911 Catholic Foreign Mission Society of America ('Maryknoll Missioners'), founded by James Anthony Walsh and Thomas Frederick Price
1950 Order of the Missionaries of Charity, founded by Mother Teresa

Theatre, film, radio and television

c.970 The exchange between the angel and the women at Jesus' tomb (Mark 16.6–7) is performed in dramatic form in many churches; this marks the beginning of the Easter play

1110 The earliest recorded miracle play is performed at Dunstable, Kent

c.1200 Jehan Bodel, *Le Jeu de St Nicholas*, the first French miracle play, is performed

1375 A mystery play is performed in Chester

1376 The earliest reference is made to the York Cycle of mystery plays

1384 King Richard II visits Coventry and attends the Coventry mystery plays

1634 A passion play is given for the first time by the villagers of Oberammergau in Austria in thanksgiving for deliverance from the plague

1783 Gottfried Ephraim Lessing, *Nathan the Wise*, is first performed

1912 A first film version is made of Henryk Sienkiewicz's novel *Quo Vadis?*

1918 A Festival of Nine Lessons and Carols is held in King's College, Cambridge on Christmas Eve

1921 The first religious radio broadcast takes place from a Pittsburgh church

1923 Cecil B. de Mille, *The Ten Commandments*, is the first great biblical film epic

1925 A first film version is made of Lew Wallace's novel *Ben Hur*

1927 Cecil B. de Mille, *King of Kings*, is a major film about Jesus

1928 The festival of Nine Lessons and Carols from King's College, Cambridge, is broadcast for the first time

1929 Paul Claudel, *The Satin Slipper*, is first performed

1935 T. S. Eliot, *Murder in the Cathedral*, is first performed

1941 Dorothy L.Sayers, *The Man Born to be King*, is first broadcast by the BBC

1951 Ralph Vaughan Williams, *The Pilgrim's Progress*, is first performed at the Royal Opera House, Covent Garden
A second film version is made of Henryk Sienkiewicz's novel *Quo Vadis?*
A film version is made of Georges Bernanos' novel, *Diary of a Country Priest*

1953 Arthur Miller, *The Crucible*, is first performed

1953 A film version is made of Lloyd Douglas' novel, *The Robe*

1956 A second film version is made by Cecil B. de Mille of *The Ten Commandments*

1959 A second film version is made by William Wyler of Lew Wallace's novel *Ben Hur*

1960 Robert Bolt's play *A Man for All Seasons* is first performed
Jean Anouilh's play *Becket or the Honour of God* is first performed

1961 John Osborne's play *Luther* is first performed
Songs of Praise is first broadcast on BBC television

1964 Pier Paolo Pasolini's film *The Gospel According to St Matthew* is released
A film version is made of Jean Anouilh's play *Becket or the Honour of God*

1966 A film version is made of Robert Bolt's play *A Man for All Seasons*

1969 A film version is made of David Wilkerson's book *The Cross and the Switchblade*

1971 Stephen Schwartz's musical *Godspell* is first performed
Andrew Lloyd Webber and Tim Rice's musical *Jesus Christ Superstar* is first performed

464

1973 A film version is made of *Godspell*

A film version is made of *Jesus Christ, Superstar*

A film version is made of William Per Blatty's novel *The Exorcist*

1977 Franco Zeffirelli's television series *Jesus of Nazareth* is shown

1979 Terry Jones and Terry Gilliam's film *Monty Python's Life of Brian* is released

1988 Martin Scorsese's film of Kazantzakis' novel *The Last Temptation of Christ* is released

1989 Denys Arcand's film *Jesus of Montreal* is released

1994 The first instalment of *The Vicar of Dibley* is broadcast on BBC television

2001 A third film version is made of Henryk Sienkiewicz's novel *Quo Vadis?*

2004 Mel Gibson's film *The Passion of the Christ* is released

465

Universities

The university is an invention of the church in the Middle Ages, intended to give a better education to monks and clergy than they could expect from schools attached to cathedrals and monasteries. With the Reformation, Protestant rulers and groups begin to establish their own universities. Subsequently universities gradually undergo a process of secularization. Those listed here can claim Christian origins.

1088	Bologna	1413	St Andrews
c.1150	Paris	1419	Rostock
1167	Oxford (from Paris)	1425	Louvain
1204	Vicenza	1431	Poitiers
1209	Cambridge (from Oxford)	1432	Caen
1211	Palencia	1441	Bordeaux
1218	Salamanca	1444	Catania
1220	Montpellier	1450	Barcelona
1222	Padua (from Bologna)	1451	Glasgow
1224	Naples	1456	Greifswald
1229	Toulouse	1457	Freiburg
1246	Siena (from Bologna)	1459	Basle
1248	Piacenza	1471	Genoa
1257	Paris (Sorbonne)	1472	Munich
1290	Coimbra	1477	Tübingen
1293	Alcala (Studium Generale)		Uppsala
1303	Rome La Sapienza	1479	Copenhagen
	Avignon	1494	Aberdeen
1306	Orleans	1495	Santiago de Compostela
1308	Perugia	1499	Alcala: Complutensian
1332	Cahors		University
1339	Grenoble		Valencia
1343	Pisa	1502	Wittenberg
1348	Prague (Charles University)	1512	Puerto Rico
1349	Florence	1527	Marburg
1361	Pavia	1531	Granada
1364	Krakow	1538	Santo Domingo
1365	Vienna	1544	Königsberg
1379	Erfurt	1551	Rome (Pontifical Gregorian
1386	Heidelberg		University)
1388	Cologne		Lima
1391	Ferrara		Mexico
1402	Würzburg	1574	Leiden (Calvinist)
1405	Turin (from Piacenza and Pavia)	1586	Graz
1409	Leipzig (from Prague)	1592	Dublin, Trinity College

1595 Cebu City, Philippines
1611 Manila, Philippines
1636 Harvard College
1655 Kiel
1693 Williamsburg, College of
       William and Mary
1694 Halle
1701 Collegiate School, Yale
1746 College of New Jersey
       (Princeton)

1754 King's College, New York
       (Columbia)
1764 Rhode Island College (Brown)
1766 Queen's College (Rutgers)
1769 Dartmouth College
1789 Georgetown
1829 London, King's College
1880 Amsterdam, Free University
1887 Catholic University of America,
       Washington, DC

The Virgin Mary

Veneration of

431   The Council of Ephesus gives Mary the title *Theotokos* (Mother of God)

*c.*432   The first extant depiction of the Virgin Mary is in Santa Maria Maggiore, Rome

*c.*1150   Recitation of the *Ave Maria* ('Hail, Mary') becomes general

1318   Pope John XXII commends the recitation of the Angelus three times a day

1555   Pope Paul VI proclaims the perpetual virginity of Mary

1571   The feast of Our Lady of Victory is introduced

1578   The icon of Our Lady of Kazan is discovered

1648   A feast in honour of the Immaculate Heart of Mary is first celebrated in Autun, France (February 8)

1708   The feast of the Immaculate Conception of Mary is declared obligatory for all Catholics

1854   The Immaculate Conception of Mary is defined

1950   The dogma of the Bodily Assumption of Mary to heaven is proclaimed

Visions of

1061   Walsingham, by Lady Richeldis de Favershes

1531   Guadelupe, by Juan Diego

1830   Paris, by Catherine Labouré

1846   La Salette, by two shepherd children

1858   Lourdes, by Bernadette Soubirous

1879   Knock, by a group of women

1917   Fatima, by a group of children

1933   Banneux, by Mariette Beco

1981   Medjugorjge, by a group of children

Index

(unless otherwise indicated, the figure after each entry refers to the relevant year)

Albert the Bear, 1147
Albert of Buxhoevden, Bishop, 1201
Albert of Riga, Bishop, 1202
Albert, Grand Master of the Teutonic Order, 1525
Albert, Latin Patriarch of Jerusalem, 1208
Albertus Magnus, 1135, 1193, 1280, 1931
Albi Cathedral, 1282
Albigensians, c.1172, 1179, 1184, 1195, 1224, 1244
    Crusade, 1208/9, 1215, 1218, 1226, 1229
Alboin, 568, 572
Albright, Jacob, 1807
Alcala, 1502
    Studium Generale, 1293
    University, 1436, 1499
Alcuin, c.740, c.742, 781, 793, 804
Aldersgate, 1738
Aldhelm, Bishop of Sherborne, 639, 709, 1606
Aldred, Bishop of Worcester, 1058
Aldfrith, King of Northumbria, 685, 704
Aleutian Islands, 1794
Alexander, Bishop of Alexandria, c.319
Alexander I, Bishop of Rome, c.109, c.116
Alexander II, Pope, 1061, 1073
Alexander III, Pope, 1159, 1160, 1161, 1163, 1170,
    1171, 1179, 1181
Alexander IV, Pope, 1255, 1256, 1261
Alexander V, Antipope, 1409, 1410
Alexander VI, Pope, 1492, 1493, 1503
Alexander VII, Pope, 1655, 1665, 1667
Alexander VIII, Pope, 1689, 1691
Alexander, Tsar, 1812
Alexander, Cecil Frances, 1818, 1895
Alexandria, 325, 413, 642
    catechetical school of, c.190, 313
    library of, 391
    temple of, 391
Alexius I Comnenus, Byzantine emperor, 1081, 1118
Alexius II Comnenus, Byzantine emperor, 1180, 1183
Alexius III Angelus, Byzantine emperor, 1195, 1203,
    1208
Alexius IV, Byzantine emperor, 1203, 1204
Alexius V Ducas, Byzantine emperor, 1204
Alexius I Studites, Patriarch of Constantinople, 1025,
    1043
Alexius I, Patriarch of Moscow, 1945, 1970
Alexius II, Patriarch of Moscow, 1990
Alfonso, Duke of Cantabria, 750

Alfonso II, King of Aragon, 1164, 1196
Alfonso III, King of Aragon, 1285, 1287, 1291
Alfonso IV, King of Aragon, 1327, 1335
Alfonso V, King of Aragon, 1416, 1458
Alfonso II, King of Asturias, 791, 798, 813, 829
Alfonso VI, King of Castile-Leon, 1080, 1085
Alfonso VII, King of Castile-Leon, 1126, 1157, 1158,
    1211, 1212, 1214
Alfonso VIII, King of Castile-Leon, 1158, 1164, 1188
Alfonso IX, King of Leon, 1188, 1218, 1230
Alfonso X, King of Castile-Leon, 1252, 1269, 1284
Alfonso XI, King of Castile-Leon, 1312, 1350
Alfonso V, King of Portugal, 1452, 1455
Alfred the Great, 849, 871, 872, 886, 899
    Doom Book, 849
al-Hakim, Caliph, 1009, 1012, 1023
'Ali, caliph, 656, 661
al-Kamil, Sultan, 1229
All Saints, Feast of, 609
All Saints, Margaret Street, 1814
All Souls College, Oxford, 1414
All Souls Day, 998
Allen, Horace, 1884
Allen, Richard, 1787, 1816
Allen, William, Cardinal, 1568
Allenbach, Ann, 1912
Almeria, 1126
Alopen, Nestorian monk, 635
Alpha Course, 1977, 1993
Alphege, Archbishop of Canterbury, 1006, 1012, 1078
Alphonsus Liguori, 1696, 1732, 1787, 1831
al-Qadissiyah, Battle of, 636
Altar of Victory, 357, 362, 382, 384
Alternative Service Book, 1980
Alvaro II, King of Kongo, 1608
Alwa, 580
Amana, 1855
Amandus, c.590, 628, 633, c.675
Amboise, Edict of, 1563
Ambrose, Bishop of Milan, c.339, 373, 381, 384, 390,
    397
    On the Sacraments, c.339
Ambrosian Library, Milan, c.1605
Amda Siyon, 1314
America, 1909
American Bible Society, 1816
American Civil War, 1861, 1865

American National Council of Churches, 1908, 1950
American Sunday School Union, 1824
American Unitarian Association, 1825
American University of Beirut, 1863
American War of Independence, 1775, 1783
Amiens Cathedral, 1152, 1218, 1220, 1401
Amish, 1693
Amman, Joseph, 1693
Anabaptists, 1489, 1496, 1520, 1525, 1529, 1533, 1534, 1535, 1536, p.266
Anacletus, Bishop of Rome, *c*.79, 91
Anacletus II, Antipope, 1130, 1138
Anastasius I, Roman emperor, 491, 497, 512, 518
Anastasius II, Byzantine emperor, 713, 715
Anastasius, Patriarch of Constantinople, 730, 754
Anastasius I, Pope, 399, 400, 401
Anastasius II, Pope, 496, 498
Anastasius III, Pope, 911, 913
Anastasius IV, Pope, 1153, 1154
Anatolius, Patriarch of Constantinople, 449, 458
Ancyra, Synod of, 314
Ando, Tadeo, 1988, 1989
Andover Theological Seminary, 1808
Andrade, Antonio del, 1626
Andrea del Sarto, 1485, 1531
Andrew, Archbishop of Lund, 1219
Andrew of St Victor, 1175
Andrewes, Lancelot, 1555, 1626
    Private Prayers, 1555, 1648
Andrews, Charles Freer, 1871, 1940
Andronicus I Comnenus, Byzantine emperor, 1183, 1185
Andronicus II Palaeologus, Byzantine emperor, 1282, 1296, 1325, 1328
Andronicus III Palaeologus, Byzantine emperor, 1325, 1328, 1341
Angela Merici, 1535
Angelico, Fra, 1395, 1455, 1982
Angelus, 1269, 1317
Angles, 410
Anglican Communion, 1867
Anglican–Methodist reunion, 1972
Angola, 1579, 1884
Angoulême Cathedral, *c*.560, 1017, 1128
Anhomoeans, 350
Anicetus, Bishop of Rome, *c*.154, *c*.166
Anne, Queen of England, 1702, 1714

anomoios, 350
Anouilh, Jean, 1960, 1964
    Becket or the Honour of God, 1960, 1964
Anselm, Archbishop of Canterbury, 1033, 1060, 1093, 1095, 1100, 1103, 1106, 1109, 1494
    Discourse, 1033
    Soliloquy, 1033
    Why the God Man, 1033
Anskar, 801, 830, 831, 854, 865
Anterus, Pope, 235, 236
Anthimus I, Patriarch of Constantinople, 535, 536
Anthimus III, Patriarch of Constantinople, 1822, 1824
Anthimus IV, Patriarch of Constantinople, 1840, 1841, 1848, 1852
Anthimus V, Patriarch of Constantinople, 1841, 1842
Anthimus VI, Patriarch of Constantinople, 1845, 1848, 1852, 1855, 1871, 1873
Anthimus VII, Patriarch of Constantinople, 1895, 1897
Anthony of Padua, 1195, 1231, 1232
Anthroposophical Society, 1861
Anti-Modernist oath, 1910
Antioch, *c*.35, *c*.36, *c*.45–58, 107, 252, 325, 350, 542, 601, 1098
    Dedication Synod of, 341
Antiquorum fide relatio, bull, 1300
Antoninus Pius, 138, 142, 161
António I, King of Kongo, 1665
Antony of Egypt, *c*.251, *c*.339, 356
Antony I, Patriarch of Constantinople, 821, 837
Antony II Kauleas, Patriarch of Constantinople, 893, 901
Antony III Studites, Patriarch of Constantinople, 974, 979
Antony IV, Patriarch of Constantinople, 1389, 1390, 1391, 1397
Apartheid, 1949, 1982, 1991
Apollinarius of Laodicea, *c*.310, 390
Apostolic
    fathers, p.11
    Faith Mission, 1908
    vicariate, 1623, 1639
Apostolicae curae, encyclical, 1896
Apsimar, 698
Aquitaine, 418, 1337, 1338, 1359
Arabia, *c*.360
Aragon, 1035, 1126, 1469

472

Baptist church, 1708
  in Amsterdam, 1609
  in England, 1612
  in Hamburg, 1834
  in Providence, Rhode Island, 1638
Baptist Church Hymnal, 1900
Baptist
  Missionary Society, 1845, 1878
  Missionary Union, 1814
  Union of Great Britain, 1812
  World Alliance, 1905
Baradaeus, Jacob, Bishop of Edessa, *c.*500, 578
Bar Aggai, Papa, *c.*285
Barcelona, 719, 801, 1024
  University, 1450
Barclay, Robert, 1648, 1690
Bardaisan, 154, *c.*179, 222
Bardasanes, Philippicus, 711, 713
Bar Hebraeus, *c.*1243, 1264
Bar-Kokhba, Simon, 132
Barmen, 1934
  Synod of, 1934
  Theological Declaration of, 1934
Barratt, Thomas Ball, 1906
Barreira, Balthazar, 1605
Barreira, Joseph, 1579
Barsumas, Bishop of Nisibis, 457
Barth, Karl, 1886, 1934, 1968
  Church Dogmatics, 1886
  Commentary on Romans, 1886
Bartholomew I, Patriarch of Constantinople, 1991
Basil the Bogomil, 1104
Basil of Caesarea, *c.*327, *c.*330, *c.*335, 379
Basil I Macedonian, Byzantine emperor, 866, 867, 870,
  877, 886
Basil II Bulgaroctonus, Byzantine emperor, 976, 986,
  1014, 1025
Basil I Skamandrenus, Patriarch of Constantinople, 970,
  974
Basil II Camaterus, Patriarch of Constantinople, 1183,
  1186
Basil III, Patriarch of Constantinople, 1925, 1929
Basil II, Prince of Russia, 1448
Basle Cathedral, 1019, 1200, 1356
Basle Compacts, 1436, 1462
Basle Council of, 1431, 1437, 1448
Basle Missionary Society, 1815, 1828

Basle University, 1459
Basra, *c.*300
Bath and Wells, Diocese, 909
Batu, Mongol leader, 1237
Baur, Ferdinand Christian, 1792, 1860
Bavaria, 739
Baxter, Richard, 1615, 1692
  The Reformed Pastor, 1615
  The Saints' Everlasting Rest, 1615
Bay of Islands, New Zealand, 1814
Bay Psalm Book, 1640
Bayeux Cathedral, 1077
Bayle, Pierre, 1647, 1706
  Dictionnaire Historique et Critique, 1647
BBC
  first broadcast of King's College Carol Service, 1928
  first religious broadcast, 1924
  The Man Born to be King, 1941
Beatrice of Nazareth, 1200, 1268
Beaune hospital, 1451
Beauvais Cathedral, 1247
Bec, Abbey, 1039, 1045, 1060, 1066
Bechuanaland, 1821
Becket, Thomas, Archbishop of Canterbury, *c.*1120,
  1162, 1164, 1170, 1173
Beco, Mariette, 1933
Bede, Venerable, *c.*673, 725, 731, 735, 1899
  De ratione temporum, 725
  Ecclesiastical History of the English People, *c.*673, 731
Beecher, Henry Ward, 1813, 1887
Beethoven, Ludwig van, 1823
  Missa Solemnis, 1823
Beguines, *c.*1210, 1310, 1312, 1321
Behemot, Senegalese chief, 1486
Behistun, 1837
Beijing, *c.*1278, 1294, 1299, 1318, 1339, 1601, 1644 (*see
  also* Kambalik)
  Nestorian Archdiocese, 1275
Beirut, American University of, 1863
Belgian Congo, 1884, 1913
Belgic Confession, 1566
Belgrade, Siege of, 1456
Belhar Confession, 1982
Belisarius, Flavius, 533, 535, 536, 537, 540
Bell, George Kennedy Allen, 1883, 1958
Bellini, Giovanni, *c.*1430, 1516
Belloc, Joseph Hilaire Pierre, 1870, 1953

Bells, church, 400, *c.*550, 604, *c.*752
Ben Hur, 1880, 1925, 1959
Benedict I, Pope, 575, 579
Benedict II, Pope, 684, 685
Benedict III, Pope, 855, 858
Benedict IV, Pope, 900, 903
Benedict V, 964, 966
Benedict VI, 973, 974
Benedict VII, Pope, 974, 983
Benedict VIII, Pope, 1012, 1014, 1022, 1024, 1032
Benedict IX, Pope, 1032, 1044, 1045, 1046, 1047, 1048, 1055/56
Benedict X, Antipope, 1058
Benedict XI, Pope, 1303, 1304
Benedict XII, Pope, 1334, 1335, 1342
Benedict XIII, Antipope, 1394, 1409, 1413, 1417
Benedict XIII, Pope, 1724, 1726, 1730
Benedict XIV, Pope, 1740, 1742, 1743, 1758
Benedict XV, Pope, 1914, 1922
Benedict XVI, Pope, 2005, 2006
Benedict Biscop, *c.*628, 674, 682, 689
Benedict of Nursia, *c.*480, 529, 547, 1220
 Rule of, *c.*360, *c.*480, 540, 789, *c.*1036
Benedictine(s), 1012, 1510, 1623, 1882
 liqueur, 1510
Benevento, Synod of, 1091
Bengal, 1606, 1794
Benjamin I, Patriarch of Constantinople, 1936, 1946
Bennett, Dennis, 1959
Bennett, Joyce, 1971
Benson, Edward White, Archbishop of Canterbury, 1883, 1896
Benson, Richard, 1866
Bentley, Holman, 1893
Bentley, John Francis, 1839, 1902
Beornrad, King of Mercia, 757
Beornwulf, King of Mercia, 824
Beorthric, King of Wessex, 786, 802
Bergamo Conference, 1218
Berg, Daniel, 1910
Berkeley, George, 1685, 1753
Berlin Conference on Africa, 1884, 1885
Berlin Missionary Society, 1824
Berlioz, Hector, 1837
 Grande Messe des Morts, 1837
Bernanos, Georges, 1936, 1951
 Diary of a Country Priest, 1936, 1951

Bernard of Angers, 1010
Bernard of Clairvaux, 1090, 1115, 1146, 1153, 1190
Bernini, Gian Lorenzo, 1598, 1680
Bernstein, Leonard, 1971
 Mass, 1971
Bernward, Bishop, 1015
Bertha, Queen of Kent, 597
Berthelm, Archbishop of Canterbury, 959, 960
Berthold of Calabria, *c.*1154
Berthold, Bishop of Uexküll, 1198
Bertwald, Archbishop of Canterbury, 693, 702, 731
Bérulle, Pierre de, 1575, 1611, 1629
Berwick, Pacification of, 1639
Bethel Bible College, Topeka, Kansas, 1901
Bethelsdorp, 1803
Bethlehem
 Church of the Nativity, 326, 333
 Church of St Helena, 614
Bethlehem, Pennsylvania, 1741, 1753
Béziers, 1209
Bharatas, 1536
Bianca I, Queen of Navarre, 1425, 1441
Biandrata, George, 1558
Bible
 Afrikaans, 1933
 Algonquin, 1663
 American Standard Version, 1902
 Arabic, 1671
 Armenian, 360, 434, 1666
 Authorized Version, 1611
 Bishops', 1568
 Catalan, 1287, 1478
 Chinese, 635, 1819
 Coverdale, 1535
 Croatian, 1831
 Czech, 1360, 1593
 Danish, 1550
 Douai, 1568
 Douai-Reims, 1609/10
 Dresden, 1360
 Dutch, 1637
 Esperanto, 1926
 Finnish, 1642
 French, 1530
 German, 1534
 Good News, 1976
 Gothic, *c.*311

of the Knighthood of Christ, 1202
of the Knighthood of Christ against the Prussians, 1207
of the Sword (Livonian Order), 1202, *c.*1227, 1236, 1237, 1253
Broughton, William Grant, 1836, 1837
Brown, Antoinette, 1853
Brown, Dan, 2003
 The Da Vinci Code, 2003
Brown, Olympia, 1863
Brown University, 1764
Browne, Robert, *c.*1550, 1580, 1633
Bruckner, Anton, 1824, 1896
Brueghel, Peter, the Elder, *c.*1525, 1569
Brunelleschi, Filippo, 1377, 1446
Bruno of Cologne, 1084
Bruno, Giordano, 1548, 1600
Bryan, William Jennings, 1860, 1925
Bucer, Martin, 1491, 1523, 1538, 1551
Buchman, Frank, 1878, 1938, 1961
Buckfast Abbey, 1018, 1883
Buenos Aires, 1620
Buganda, 1877, 1879, 1885, 1897
Bujaxhiu, Agnes Goxha, 1910 (*see also* Teresa, Mother)
Bulgaria, 681, 863, 865, 866, 870, 986
 Orthodox Church of, 1870
Bulgars, 811, 1014, 1205
Bullinger, Johann Heinrich, 1504, 1536, 1566, 1575
Bultmann, Rudolf, 1884, 1976
Bunyan, John, 1628, 1678, 1688
 The Pilgrim's Progress, 1628, 1678, 1728, 1872
Burgersdorp, 1860
Burgos Cathedral, 1217, 1221
Burgundians, 406, 443, 493
Burma, *c.*1550, 1813
Burnell, Robert, Archbishop of Canterbury elect, 1278
Bury St Edmunds, 870
Bushnell, Horace, 1802, 1876
Butler, Joseph, 1692, 1752
 Analogy of Religion, 1692
Butler, Josephine, 1828, 1906
Butler, William John, 1848
Butterfield, William, 1814, 1900
Byrd, William, 1543, 1592–95, 1623
Byzantine empire, p.79

Cadbury, John, 1824
Cadwallon, King of Gwynedd, 634

Caecilian, Bishop of Carthage, 311, 314
Caedwalla, King of Wessex, 685, 688
Caen, University of, 1432
Caesarea, *c.*45–58, *c.*260
 Church of, 374
Caesarius of Arles, 506
Cahors
 Cathedral, *c.*1100, 1119
 University, 1332
Caiaphas, 18, 37
Caius, Pope, 283, 296
Cajetan, Thomas de Vio, 1469, 1524, 1534
Calabar, 1851
Calais, 1347, 1453
Calasanza, Joseph, 1607, 1767
Calcutta Christian College, 1830
Calendar
 Gregorian, 1582, 1585, 1700, 1752, 1893, 1918, 1922, 1923
 Julian, 1582, 1700
California, 1579
Caligula (Gaius), Roman emperor, 37, 40, 41
Caliph al-Hakim, 1009, 1012, 1023
Callenberg, Johann Heinrich, 1728
Callinicus I, Patriarch of Constantinople, 693, 705
Callinicus III, Patriarch of Constantinople, 1726
Callinicus IV, Patriarch of Constantinople, 1801, 1806, 1808
Callistus I, Patriarch of Constantinople, 1353, 1355, 1363
Callistus II Xanthopoulos, Patriarch of Constantinople, 1397
Callistus I, Pope, *c.*200, 217, 222
 Catacomb of, *c.*200
Callistus II, Pope, 1119, 1121, 1123, 1124
Callistus III, Antipope, 1168, 1178
Callistus III, Pope, 1455, 1456, 1458
Calvary Church of God, 1951
Calvary Episcopal Church, Pittsburgh, 1921
Calvert, George, First Baron Baltimore, 1632
Calvin, Jean, 1509, 1535, 1536, 1538, 1541, 1559, 1564
 Institutes of the Christian Religion, 1536, 1538, 1559
Camaldolese, 1012, 1831
Camara, Helder, 1909, 1999
Cambodia, 1845
Cambridge Camden Society, 1839
Cambridge Inter-Collegiate Christian Union, 1876

Cambridge Seven, 1885
Cambridge University, 1209
Cameroon, 1890
Camisards, 1702, 1705
Campbell, Alexander, 1788, 1811, 1832, 1866
Campion, Edmund, 1580, 1581, 1970
Canada, c.1001, 1608, 1625, 1787
Cane Ridge, Kentucky, 1801
Canon, New Testament, 367, 382
Canossa, 1077
Canterbury, 597, 619
    Cathedral, c.598, 602, 613, 851, 1020, 1070, 1220,
        1377, 1486, 1503
    Diocese, 597
    Province, 1073, 1152
    St Martin's Church, 597
'Cantus firmus', c.1385, 1397
Canute, King, 1014, 1016, 1018, 1020, 1035, 1038,
    1042
Cap Colonna, Defeat of, 982
Cape Coast, 1752
Cape of Good Hope, 1652, 1665, 1817
Cape Province, 1824
Cape Synod, 1856
Cape Town, 1737, 1792, 1799, 1820
Cape Verde, Diocese, 1534
Capitein, Jacobus, 1742
Capitulary on Saxony, 785
Cappadocia, 301
Cappadocian fathers, c.335
Capuchins, 1528, 1645
Caracalla, Roman emperor, 211, 217
Caracas, Venezuela, Diocese, 1637
Carafa, Giampetro, 1524, 1555
Caravaggio, 1571, 1610
Carcassonne, 1209
Cardijn, Joseph, 1924
Cardinals
    College of, 1059, 1179, 1271, 1586
    Congregations of, 1588
Carey, George, Archbishop of Canterbury, 1991, 2002
Carey, William, 1761, 1794, 1834
Caribbean, 1492
Carinus, Roman emperor, 283, 285
Carinthia, 628
Caritas Internationalis, 1897
Carlile, Wilson, 1882

Carlisle, Diocese, 1133
Carloman, Frankish king, 741, 742, 768, 771
Carlos V, Holy Roman Emperor, 1519, 1521, 1523,
    1527, 1542, 1556
Carlos II, King of Navarre, 1349, 1387
Carlos III, King of Navarre, 1387, 1425
Carlos I, King of Spain, 1516, 1519
Carlos II, King of Spain, 1665, 1700
Carmel, Mount, 1208
Carmelite Order, c.1154, 1208
Caro, Venezuela, Diocese, 1530
Caroline, Queen Consort, 1737
Carolingian Renaissance, c.740
Carroll, John, 1735, 1789, 1815
Cartagena, Diocese, 1534
Carter, Sydney, 1915, 2004
    'Friday morning', 1915
    'Lord of the Dance', 1915
    'When I needed a neighbour', 1915
Carthage, 203, 252, 439, 533, 698
    Synod of, 251, 348, 394, 397, 411, 418, 483, 484
Carthusian Order, 1084, 1181, 1607 (*see also*
    Chartreuse, La Grande)
Cartwright, Thomas, c.1535, 1603
Carus, Roman emperor, 276, 282, 283
Cashel, Province, 1111
Cashwell, Gaston B., 1860, 1916
Cassian, John, c.360, c.415, 435
    Institutes, c.360
Cassiodorus, 554, 562
    Computus paschalis, 562
Casti connubii, encyclical, 1930
Castile–Leon, Kingdom of, 1037
Castro, Matthew de, 1639
Catacombs, c.200, 1578
    of Callistus, c.200
Catalani, Jordan, c.1320
Catania, University of, 1444
Catechism of the Catholic Church, 1992
Catechism of Christian Doctrine ('Penny'), 1859
Catesby, Robert, 1605
Cathars, c.1172
Catharine of Aragon, 1533
Catherine of Genoa, 1447, 1510, 1737
Catherine the Great, 1764, 1766
Catherine de Medici, 1561
Catherine of Siena, c.1347, 1380

Catherine de Valois, 1419
Catholic Apostolic Church, 1792
Catholic Association, 1822, 1830
Catholic Association for Overseas Development
    (CAFOD), 1962
Catholic Charities, 1727
Catholic Emancipation Act, 1829
Catholic Foreign Mission Society of America, 1911
Catholic Relief Act, 1830
Catholic Relief Services, 1943
Catholic Truth Society, 1884
Catholic University, Washington DC, 1887
Catholic Worker, 1897, 1933
Catholicon, 1286
Caussade, Jean-Pierre de, 1675, 1751
    Self-Abandonment to Divine Providence, 1675, 1860
Cavallini, Pietro, 1259, *c.*1328
Cavert, Samuel McCrea, 1940
Cearl, King of Mercia, 606, 626
Cebu, 1565
    University, 1595
Cedd, 651, *c.*654, 664, 669
    Church of, *c.*654
Celano, Tommaso de, *c.*1254
Celestine I, Pope, 422, 429, 432
Celestine II, Pope, 1143, 1144
Celestine III, Pope, 1191, 1193, 1198
Celestine IV, Pope, 1241
Celestine V, Pope, 1294
Celestius, 410, 411, 417
Cellarius, Martin, 1526
    De operibus Dei, 1526
Celsus, 248
Centre Party, 1933
Cenwalh, King of Wessex, 643, 646, 648, 674
Ceolnoth, Archbishop of Canterbury, 833, 870
Cerdic, Saxon leader, 519
Cerne Abbas, 987
Cespedes, Gregorio de, 1593
Ceuta, 1415, 1417
Ceylon, 1505, 1546, 1658, 1795 (*see also* Sri Lanka)
Chad, Bishop of Lichfield, 651, 669, 699, 1085
Chalcedon, Council of, 448, 451
Chalcedonian Definition, 451, 480, 506, 551
Chalmers, Thomas, 1843
Châlons, Battle of, 451
Champollion, Jean François, 1822

Channing, William Ellery, 1780, 1803, 1819, 1842
Chant, Gregorian, *c.*1050
Chantal, Jane Frances de, 1610, 1767
Chariton, Patriarch of Constantinople, 1178, 1179
Charlemagne, *c.*740, *c.* 742, 768, 770, 771, 772, 773, 778,
    781, 782, 785, 786, 787, 789, 800, 801, 814, 843,
    888, 1804
Charles the Bald, 843, 875, 877
Charles Martel, 686, 723, 732, 741
Charles the Simple, Frankish king, 911
Charles III (the Fat), Holy Roman Emperor, 881, 888
Charles IV, Holy Roman Emperor, 1355, 1361, 1378
Charles VI, Holy Roman Emperor, 1710, 1713, 1740
Charles I, King of Bohemia, 1348
Charles I, King of England, 1625, 1628, 1633, 1638,
    1639, 1640, 1641, 1642, 1646, 1649, 1660, 1661
Charles II, King of England, 1660, 1661, 1681, 1685
Charles IV, King of France, 1322, 1328
Charles V, King of France, 1364, 1380
Charles VI, King of France, 1380, 1422
Charles VII, King of France, 1422, 1429, 1461
Charles VIII, King of France, 1483, 1498
Charles IX, King of France, 1560, 1574
Charles X, King of France, 1824, 1830
Charp, Stefan, 1383
Chateaubriand, François Auguste René, Vicomte de,
    1802
    The Genius of Christianity, 1802
Chartres Cathedral, 1145, 1194, 1220, 1260
Chartreuse, La Grande, 1084, 1607
    liqueur, 1607
Chaucer, Geoffrey, 1340, 1400
    The Canterbury Tales, 1340
Chelsea, Synod of, 786
Chepstow, 602
Chester
    Diocese, 1541/42
    miracle play, 1375
Chesterton, G. K., 1874, 1936
Chiapas, Diocese, 1538
Chicago Evangelization Society, 1886
Chicago–Lambeth Quadrilateral, 1888
Chicheley, Henry, Archbishop of Canterbury, 1414, 1443
Chichester
    Cathedral, 1108, 1199
    Diocese, 1075
Chile, 1541, 1561, 1909

481

482

Congar, Yves, 1904, 1995
Congregation
    for the Conversion of Infidels, 1568, 1622
    for the Doctrine of the Faith, 1983
    of the Holy Ghost, 1840
    of the Mission, 1625
    of the Most Holy Redeemer, 1732
    of the Oratory, 1574
    of the Roman Inquisition, 1542, 1557
Congregational
    Church in the USA, 1853
    Union of England and Wales, 1832
    Union of Scotland, 1812
Congregationalists, 1620, 1629, 1636, 1643, 1701, 1769, 1808, 1865
Congregations of Cardinals, 1588
Cono, Pope, 686, 687
Conques, 1010
    Sainte Foy, 1010
Conrad II, King of Germany, 1024, 1027, 1028, 1030, 1039
Conrad of Masovia, 1224
Constance, Council of, 1414, 1415, 1418, 1431, 1433
Constans, Roman emperor, 337, 340, 342, 346, 350
Constans II Pogonatus, Byzantine emperor, 641, 648, 668
Constantina, c. 350
Constantine, Roman emperor, 306, 310, 312, 313, 318, 321, 322, 324, 325, 326, 330, 335, 337
Constantine II, Roman emperor, 337, 340
Constantine IV, Byzantine emperor, 668, 681, 685
Constantine V, Byzantine emperor, 720, 741, 754, 775
Constantine VI, Byzantine emperor, 780, 790, 792, 797
Constantine VII, Byzantine emperor, 913, 919, 959
Constantine VIII, Byzantine emperor, 976, 1025, 1028, 1072
Constantine IX Monomachus, Byzantine emperor, 1042, 1043, 1055
Constantine X Ducas, Byzantine emperor, 1059, 1067, 1068
Constantine XI Palaeologus, Byzantine emperor, 1448, 1453
Constantine I, Patriarch of Constantinople, 675, 677
Constantine II, Patriarch of Constantinople, 754, 766
Constantine III Lichoudas, Patriarch of Constantinople, 1059, 1063
Constantine IV Chliarenus, Patriarch of Constantinople, 1153, 1156

Constantine VI, Patriarch of Constantinople, 1897, 1901, 1924, 1925
Constantine, Antipope, 767, 768, 769
Constantine, Pope, 708, 710–11, 713, 715
Constantinople, 330, 674, 705, 715, 717, 863, 870, 957
    capture of by Turks, 1453
    Council of, 381
    Second Council of, 553
    Third Council of, 625, 681
    Fourth Council of, 869
    Patriarchs of, 1596, 1695
    sack of by Crusaders, 1203, 1204
    siege of, 626
Constantius I, Roman emperor, 293, 303, 305, 306
Constantius II, Roman emperor, 337, 341, 342, 346, 353, 355, 356, 357, 359, 361
Constantius III, Roman emperor, 417, 421
Constantius I, Patriarch of Constantinople, 1830, 1834
Constantius II, Patriarch of Constantinople, 1834, 1835
Constitutus in speculo, bull, 1450
Conventicles Act, 1664
Convocation
    of Canterbury, 1283, 1532, 1661, 1852, 1923
    of York, 1661, 1861, 1923
Cook Islands, 1839
Cooper, Anthony Ashley, Lord Shaftesbury, 1801, 1885
Copenhagen University, 1479
Copernicus, Nicolas, 1473, 1543, 1564, 1600, 1616
    On the Revolutions of the Heavenly Orbs, 1473, 1543
Cor, Friar John, 1495
Corbie, Abbey, c.660, 801
Cordoba, 711, 717, 1523
    Cathedral, 1523
    Great Mosque, 785, 1236
Cordoba, Argentina, Diocese, 1570
Cordoso, Mateus, 1624
Corinth, c.45–58
Cornelius, Pope, 251, 253
Cornwallis, Frederick, Archbishop of Canterbury, 1768, 1783
Coromandel, 1536
Coronation, 751
Corpus Christi, c.1210, 1264, 1334
Cortés, Hernán, 1521
Cosmas I, Patriarch of Constantinople, 1075, 1081
Cosmas II Atticus, Patriarch of Constantinople, 1146, 1147

484

Darby, John, 1800, 1882
Dartmouth College, 1769
Darwin, Charles, 1809, 1859, 1882
 On the Origin of Species by Means of Natural Selection, 1809, 1859
Da Silesia, Severino, 1710
Daughters of Charity, 1633
David, Bishop of Basra, *c.*300
David, patron saint of Wales, *c.*545, *c.*601
David I, King of Scotland, 1128
David, Christian, 1732
Davidson, Randall Thomas, Archbishop of Canterbury, 1903, 1904, 1928
Da Vinci, Leonardo, 1452, 1498, 1519
 Last Supper, The, 1498
 Virgin of the Rocks, 1508
Dawit, King of Ethiopia, 1400, 1404
Day, Dorothy, 1897, 1933, 1980
Deaconesses, Order of, 1862, 1923, 1986
Deacons (Ordination of Women) Measure, 1986
Dead Sea, *c.*4 BCE, after 20, 68, 74
Dead Sea Scrolls, 68, 1947
Dean, Henry, Archbishop of Canterbury, 1501, 1503
Dearmer, Percy, 1906
Debra Libanos, 1337, 1532, 1548
Debra Mitmaq, Council of, 1449
Decet Romanum Pontificem, bull, 1521
De Champlain, Samuel, 1608
Decius, Roman emperor, 249, 250, 251, 304
Declaration
 of Independence, American, 1776
 of Indulgence, 1637, 1687
 of the Rights of Man, 1789
Decree
 of Separation, 1918
 of Union, 1439, 1448, 1452
De Foucauld, Charles Eugène, 1858, 1916
De Groote, Gert, 1340, 1384
De haeretico comburendo, Act of Parliament, 1401
De impressione librorum, 1515
Deiniol, Bishop of Bangor, 514
Deira, 604
Deists, 1655, 1670
De La Salle, Jean-Baptiste, 1678, 1900
Delphi, 51/52
Demetrius I, Patriarch of Constantinople, 1972, 1991
De mirabilibus sacrae scripturae, 655

Denaha, Mar, 1503
Denis, Bishop of Paris, 272
Denmark, *c.*850, 1530, 1792
De Nobili, Robert, 1577, 1605, 1656
Descartes, René, 1596, 1637, 1650
 Discourse on Method, 1637
Desiderius, King of the Lombards, 756, 771, 774
D'Étaples, Jacques Lefèvre, 1530
Deus caritas est, encyclical, 2006
Deusdedit, Archbishop of Canterbury, 655, 664
Diamper, Synod of, 1599
Dictatus Papae, 1075
Diderot, Denis, 1647, 1713, 1784
 Encyclopédie, 1647, 1713
Didius Julianus, Roman emperor, 193
Didymus the Blind, 313, 398
Diego, Juan, 1531
Dies irae, *c.*1254
Dinis I, King of Portugal, 1290
Diocletian, Roman emperor, 284, 286, *c.*299, 302, 303, 304, 305
Diognetus, Letter to, *c.*150
Dionysius I, Patriarch of Constantinople, 1467, 1471, 1489, 1491
Dionysius II, Patriarch of Constantinople, 1546, 1554
Dionysius V, Patriarch of Constantinople, 1887, 1891
Dionysius, Pope, 260, 268
Dionysius the Areopagite, *c.*500
Dionysius Exiguus, *c.*6 BCE, 525
Dioscorus, Antipope, 530
Diospolis, 415
Directory of Public Worship, 1645
Disciples of Christ, 1788, 1811, 1832
Disruption, The, 1843
Dissolution Act, 1536
Diuma, Bishop of Mercia, 656
Divina dispensatione, papal bull, 1147
Divination, 381, 385
Divine Comedy, The, 1265, 1308, 1320
Divini illius magistri, encyclical, 1929
Divini redemptoris, encyclical, 1937
Divino afflante spiritu, encyclical, 1943
Docta sanctorum patrum, bull, 1324
Döllinger, Johann Joseph Ignaz von, 1799, 1871, 1890
Dominic, *c.*1172, 1207, 1221, 1227, 1232
Dominican(s), *c.*1172, 1220, 1233, 1317, p.197

missions, 1506, 1511, 1512, 1526, 1551, 1554, 1581, 1611, 1656, 1704

Dominus ac redemptor noster, bull, 1773

Domitian, Roman emperor, 81, 96

Donatello, 1386, 1466

Donatist(s), 311, 314, 348, 405, 411, p. 37
  schism, 311

Donatus, 311

Donne, John, 1571, 1631

Donus, Pope, 676, 678

Doppers, 1860

Dorchester Abbey, 635

Dort (Dordrecht),
  First Synod of, 1578
  Synod of, 1618, 1619

Dorylaeum, Battle of, 1147

Dositheus, Patriarch of Constantinople, 1189, 1191

Dositheus, Patriarch of Jerusalem, 1672

Dostoevsky, Fyodor, 1821, 1881

Douai, 1568, 1578

Douglas, Lloyd, 1942, 1953
  The Robe, 1942, 1953

Doukhobors, *c.*1740

Dowie, John Alexander, 1895, 1904

Downs, Battle of the, 1639

Drake, Sir Francis, 1579

Dresden Missionary Society, 1836, 1838

Dublin, 841
  Province, 1152

Dudum sacrum, bull, 1433

Dufay, Guillaume, 1397, *c.*1410, 1474

Duff, Alexander, 1830

Dum diversos, bull, 1452

Dunfermline Abbey, 1070

Dunnichen, Battle of, 685

Duns Scotus, Johannes, *c.*1266, 1308

Dunstan, Archbishop of Canterbury, 960, 973, 988

Dunstaple, John, *c.*1385, 1453

Dura Europos, *c.*240, 256

Dürer, Albrecht, 1471, 1528
  Knight, Death and the Devil, 1513
  Praying Hands, 1508

Durham Cathedral, 995, 1093, 1133

Durham, William H., 1914

Dutch Reformed Church, 1571, 1578, 1665, 1766, 1860

Dvin
  First Council of, 506

Second Council of, 551

Dwight, Timothy, 1752, 1817

Dylan, Bob, 1979
  Slow Train Coming, 1979

Eadbald, King of Kent, 616, *c.*635, 640

Eadberth, King of Northumbria, 757

Eanred, King of Northumbria, 829

Eanswith, *c.*635

East Anglia, 520, 593, *c.*600, 616, 625, 825, 865, 870, 879

East Engle, 520

East Saexe, 527

East Saxons, 527, 651

East Timor, 1562

Easter, *c.*166, 602
  date of, 190, *c.*390, 457, 525, 562, 1582, 1753
  eggs, *c.*700
  play, *c.*970

Easterfield, Council of, 702

Ecclesia de eucharistia, encyclical, 2003

Ecclesiastical Commissioners, 1835, 1948

Eck, Johannes, 1519

Eckhart, Joannes ('Meister'), *c.*1260, *c.*1328

Ecloga, 726

Echternach monastery, 698

Ecthesis, 638, 1296

Ecumenical Association of Third World Theologians (EATWOT), 1976

Eddy, Mary Baker, 1821, 1879, 1910

Edessa, *c.*100, 177, *c.*179, 226, 385, 1144, 1146
  pagan temple, 385

Edgar, King of the English, 959, 960, 973, 975

Edict of Milan, 313

Edict of Restitution, 1629

Edinburgh Missionary Society, 1796

Edinburgh Theological College, 1810

Edinburgh World Missionary Conference, 1865, 1874, 1910, 1921

Edmund, King of East Anglia, 870

Edmund I, King of the English, 939, 946, 955

Edmund II Ironside, King of the English, 1016

Edred, King of the English, 946, 955

Edsige, Archbishop of Canterbury, 1038, 1043, 1050

Edward the Elder, King of the English, 899, 924

Edward the Martyr, King of England, 975, 978, 1001

Edward the Confessor, King of England, 1041, 1043, 1050, 1051, 1052, 1066, 1161

Edward I, King of England, 1271, 1272, 1290, 1301, 1307

Edward II, King of England, 1307, 1327

Edward III, King of England, 1327, 1338, 1340, 1377, 1399

Edward IV, King of England, 1461, 1471, 1483

Edward V, King of England, 1483

Edward VI, King of England, 1547, 1553

Edward VII, King of England, 1901, 1910

Edward VIII, King of England, 1936

Edward, First Prince of Wales, 1301

Edward, Prince of Wales (the Black Prince), 1356, 1370, 1377

Edwards, Jonathan, 1703, 1752, 1758

Edwin, King of Northumbria, 616, 619, 627, 633

Edwy, King of the English, 955, 959

Egbert, Archbishop of York, 735

Egbert, King of Wessex, 802, 824, 829, 839

Egede, Hans, 1722

Egeria, 381–84

Egfrid, King of Northumbria, 670

Egfrith, King of Mercia, 796

Egilsay, 1115

Egypt, c.125

Einhard, 770, 840

Ejmiatsin Cathedral, 480

Elagabalus, Roman emperor, 218, 222

El Asnam church, 324

Eleazar, Rabbi, 132

Eleona church, Mount of Olives, 326, 333

Elgar, Edward, 1857, 1934
 The Apostles, 1857
 The Dream of Gerontius, 1857, 1900
 The Kingdom, 1857

El Greco, 1541, 1614

Eleutherius, Bishop of Rome, c.175, 189

Elias V, Patriarch of Persia, 1503

Eliot, George, 1819, 1880
 Daniel Deronda, 1819
 Middlemarch, 1819

Eliot, John, 1632, 1651, 1663

Eliot, T. S., 1888, 1965
 Four Quartets, 1888, 1944
 Murder in the Cathedral, 1888, 1935

Elizabeth I, Queen of England, 1535, 1558, 1570, 1592, 1603

Elizabeth II, Queen of England, 1952

Ellacuria, Ignazio, 1989

Ellandun, Battle of, 824

El Salvador, 1525

Elvira, Synod of, c.306

Ely, 673, 695, 870, c.970
 Cathedral, 1083, 1109, 1189, 1322

Emden, Synod of, 1571

Emerson, Ralph Waldo, 1803, 1882

Emiliani, Jerome, 1532

Enabling Act, 1919

English Church Union, 1859, 1934

English Civil War, 1642, 1646

English College
 Douai, 1568, 1578
 Rome, 1579

English Hymnal, The, 1872, 1906

Enlightenment, p.313

Enrique I, King of Castile, 1217

Enrique II, King of Castile–Leon, 1330, 1369, 1379

Enrique III, King of Castile–Leon, 1390, 1406

Enrique IV, King of Castile–Leon, 1454, 1474

Eorcenberth, 640, 664

Ephesus, c.45–58, c.107
 Council of, 431, 449
 Temple of Artemis, 401

Ephrem the Syrian, c.306, 373

Epiphanius of Salamis, c.315, 394, 403
 Panarion, c.315

Epiphanius, Patriarch of Constantinople, 520, 535

Episcopal
 Cathedral of St John the Divine, New York, 1892, 1942, 1999
 Synod of America, 1989

Epstein, Jacob, 1880, 1959, 1962
 St Michael's Victory over the Devil, 1962

Erasmus, Desiderius, 1469, 1504, 1509, 1536
 Greek New Testament, 1516
 In Praise of Folly, 1469, 1509

Erfurt
 Cathedral, 741, 1153, 1182
 University, 1379, 1389

Eric Bloodaxe, King of York, 945

Erik, King of Jutland, 854

Erik, King of Sweden, 1154

Erkenwald, Bishop of London, 685

Escrivá, Josemaria, 1928, 2002

Essenes, 68

missionaries, 1220, 1333, 1524, 1539, 1550, 1580, 1615, 1704

    Observants, 1415, 1517

Francke, Hermann Auguste, 1663, 1727

Franco-Prussian War, 1870, 1871

Franco of Cologne, 1251

    Ars cantus mensurabilis, 1251

François I, King of France, 1515, 1516, 1547

François II, King of France, 1559, 1560

François de Sales, 1609, 1610, 1665

    Introduction to the Devout Life, 1609

Frankfurt, Diet of, 1338

Franks, 406, *c*.466, 481, 496, 507, 538/39, 751, 841

Franz I, Holy Roman Emperor, 1745, 1765

Franz II, Holy Roman Emperor, 1792, 1806, 1835

Fraternal Council of Negro Churches, 1934

Fravitta, Patriarch of Constantinople, 488, 489

Frederick the Great *see* Friedrich II, King of Prussia

Fredkin, William, 1973

Free Church Federal Council, 1892

Free Church of Scotland, 1843, 1875

Freeman, James, 1782

Freetown, Sierra Leone, 1793, 1808

Free University of Amsterdam, 1837, 1880

Freiburg

    Cathedral, 1200, 1513

    University, 1457

Freising, Diocese, 739

French, Dawn, 1994

French

    Oratory, 1611

    Reformed Church, 1559

    Revolution, 1789

Friedrich, Caspar David, 1808

    The Cross in the Mountains, 1808

Freud, Sigmund, 1856, 1927, 1939

    The Future of an Illusion, 1927

Friedrich the Wise, 1502

Friedrich I, Elector of Saxony, 1409

Friedrich I Barbarossa, Holy Roman Emperor, 1152, 1155, 1159, 1164, 1167, 1168, 1178, 1189, 1190

Friedrich II, Holy Roman Emperor, 1220, 1224, 1226, 1228, 1229, 1246, *c*.1249, 1250, 1312

Friedrich III, Holy Roman Emperor, 1452, 1493

Friedrich II, King of Prussia, 1679, 1740

Friends of Jesus, 1888

Frisia, 678, 695

West, 690, 1061

Fruela, King of Asturias, 765

Frumentius, *c*.347

Fry, Elizabeth, 1780, 1845

Fulda Abbey, 744

Fulgentius of Ruspe, 507 or 508, 510, 512, 523

Fulin, Emperor of China, 1644

Full Gospel Business Men's Fellowship International, 1953

Funchal, Diocese, 1514, 1534

Fundamentalism, 1910–15

Fundamentals, The, 1910–1915

Fundanus, Caius Minucius, *c*.125

Fursey, Bishop, 630

Fustat, 641

Gabriel, Patriarch of Alexandria, 1372

Gabriele, Giovanni, *c*.1554, 1612

Gaiseric, 455, 476

Gaius (Caligula), 37

Galarus Oratory, *c*.800

Galba, Roman emperor, 68, 69

Galerius, Caesar, 293, 299, 303, 305, 306, 308, 311

Galicia, 750, 813

Galileo Galilei, 1542, 1564, 1616, 1633, 1642

Gall, *c*.719

Galla Placidia, 417

    Mausoleum of, 450

Gallican

    Articles, 1682

    Confession, 1559

    liturgy, 754–68

    Psalter, *c*.392

Gallicanism, 1786

Gallienus, Roman emperor, 253, 260, 268

Gallio, 51/52

Gaozu, Chinese emperor, 618

Garcia V, King of the Kongo, 1824

Garvey, Marcus, 1887, 1940

Gaudi, Antonio, 1893

Gdansk, 1308

Geismar, 725

Gelasian Missal, 496

Gelasian Sacramentary, *c*.750

Gelasius I, Pope, 492, 493, 496

Gelasius II, Pope, 1118, 1119

Gelimer, 530, 533

Gelineau, Joseph, 1920
Genadendal, 1737
General Conference Mennonite Church, 1860, 2001/2
General Society of Universalists, 1778
General Theological Seminary, New York, 1817
Geneva, 1536, 1538, 1541
   Bible, 1560
   Catechism, 1542
   Psalter, 1562
Genghis Khan, 1190, 1206, 1237
Gennadius I, Patriarch of Constantinople, 458, 471
Gennadius II, Patriarch of Constantinople, 1453, 1454, 1456, 1465
Genoa University, 1471
Genova, Carlo Maria di, 1710
George of Cyprus, 1284
George I, King of England, 1714, 1727
George II, King of England, 1727, 1754, 1760
George III, King of England, 1760, 1820, 1830
George IV, King of England, 1820, 1829, 1830
George V, King of England, 1910, 1936
George VI, King of England, 1936, 1952
George I Tupou, King of Tonga, 1831
George I, Patriarch of Constantinople, 679, 686
George II Xiphilinus, Patriarch of Constantinople, 1191, 1198
Georgetown University, 1789
Georgia
   Russia, c.350, 1068
   USA, 1735
Gerasimus I, Patriarch of Constantinople, 1320, 1321
Gerasimus III, Patriarch of Constantinople, 1794, 1797
Gerbert, Archbishop of Reims, 991
Gerhardt, Paul, 1607, 1676
German Christians, 1934
German College, 1552
German Hospitallers, Order of, 1190
Germanic invasions, p.50
  tribes, 167
Germanos of Old Patras, 1821
Germanus I, Patriarch of Constantinople, 715, 730
Germanus II, Patriarch of Constantinople, 1222, 1240
Germanus III, Patriarch of Constantinople, 1265
Germanus IV, Patriarch of Constantinople, 1842, 1845, 1852
Germanus V, Patriarch of Constantinople, 1913, 1918

Germanus of Auxerre, 429
Gerson, Jean, 1363, 1429
Gethsemani Abbey, Kentucky, 1848
Geza, Magyar prince, 985
Ghent, 633
   Pacification of, 1576
Ghettto, Roman, 1556, 1870
Ghiberti, c.1378, 1403, 1455
Gibbons, James, 1834, 1921
Gibbons, Orlando, 1583, 1625
Gibbs, James, 1682, 1753
Gibraltar, 711
Gibson, Mel, 2004
   The Passion of the Christ, 2004
Gideons International, 1899
Gildwin of St Victor, 1113
Gill, Eric, 1882, 1940
Gilliam, Terry, 1979
Ginneken, Jacques van, 1921
Giotto, c.1240, 1267, 1305, c.1320, 1337
Giovanni da Montecorvino, 1294, 1299, 1318
Giovanni de' Marignolli, 1339, 1347
Gislebertus, c.1130
Glagolitic, 826
Glasgow Cathedral, 1197
Glasgow Missionary Society, 1796, 1824
Glasgow University, 1451
Glass windows, 590, c.628
Glastonbury, 636, c.720
Glenville, Peter, 1964
Gloucester
   Abbey, 681, c.720
   Diocese, 1541/42
Gnosticism, c.166, c.170, p. 17
Goa, 1510, 1542, c.1550, 1559, 1560, 1605
   Diocese, 1534
Gobart, Samuel, 1830
Godunov, Boris, 1589
Godspell, 1971,1973
Gold Coast, 1828
Golden Legend, 1265
Göldi, Anna, 1782
Gomes, Cornelio, 1555
Gondar, 1636
Gordian III, Roman emperor, 238, 244
Gore, Charles, 1853, 1889, 1892, 1932
Gospel of John, c.125

Gunthamund, 484, 496
Gustavus Adolphus, King of Sweden, 1631
Guthlac, 699
Guthrum, 878
Gutiérréz, Gustavo, 1928
    A Theology of Liberation, 1928
Gützlaff, Karl, 1828
Guyon, Madame, 1648, 1717
Guzzoni, Enrico, 1912

Haakon, King of Norway, 946
Habsburg, House of, 1452, 1683
Hadrian, emperor, 117, 122–28, *c.*125, 138
Hadrian I, Pope, 772, 774, 786, 795
Hadrian II, Pope, 867, 872
Hadrian III, Pope, 884, 885
Hadrian IV, Pope, 1154, 1159
Hadrian V, Pope, 1276
Hadrian VI, Pope, 1522, 1523
Haec sancta, 1415, 1431
Hagia Sophia
    Constantinople, 360, 414, 532, 537, 957, 1054, 1204,
        1452, 1453
    Kiev, 957, 1037
Hagios Georgios Church, Thessaloniki, *c.*500
Hall, Bishop Ronald, 1944
Halle, University of, 1663, 1679, 1694, 1728
Hamburg, 1073, 1834
    Diocese, 831
Hamburg-Bremen, Archdiocese, 864, 948, 968, 1103,
    1127
Hamilton, Patrick, 1528
Hammarskjøld, Dag, 1905, 1961
    Markings, 1905
Hampton Court Conference, 1603, 1604
Handel, George Frideric, 1685, 1759
    Messiah, 1685, 1742
Harald Bluetooth, King of Denmark, 960
Hardicanute, King of Denmark, 1035, 1037, 1040, 1041,
    1042
Harold, King of England, 1066
Harold Harefoot, 1035, 1037, 1040
Harris, Barbara, 1989
Harris, William Wadé, *c.*1860, 1929
Hartwig II, Archbishop of Bremen, 1198
Harvard College, 1636, 1643, 1808
Harvest Festival, 1843

Hatfield Chase, Battle of, 633
Hauranne, Jean Divergier de, 1581
Hawaii, 1820, 1825, 1873
Hawksmoor, Nicholas, 1661, 1736
Hayusake, Januaris, Bishop of Nagasaki, 1927
Haydn, Joseph, 1732, 1798, 1809
    The Creation, 1732, 1798
    The Seven Last Words of Our Saviour from the Cross,
        1732
Hecker, Isaac, 1858
Hedda, Bishop of Lichfield, 699
Hegel, Georg Wilhelm Friedrich, 1770, 1831
Hegesippus, *c.*175
Hegirah, 622
Heidegger, Martin, 1889, 1976
Heidelberg
    Catechism, 1563
    University, 1386
Heiligerlee, Battle of, 1567
Heinrich I, Saxon king (Henry the Fowler), 919, 936
Heinrich II, King of Germany, 1002, 1014, 1022, 1024,
    1146
Heinrich III, King of Germany, 1028, 1039, 1046, 1056
Heinrich IV, King of Germany, 1056, 1075, 1076, 1077,
    1084, 1105
Heinrich V, King of Germany, 1105, 1111, 1119
Heinrich VI, Holy Roman Emperor, 1191, 1194, 1197
Heinrich VII, Holy Roman Emperor, 1312, 1313
Helena, mother of Constantine, 326, 527
Heliand, *c.*820
Hellenists, *c.*35
Heloise, 1079
Helvetic Confession
    First, 1536
    Second, 1566
Helwys, Thomas, 1612
Hengist, 449
Henoticon, 482, 506
Henri I, King of France, 1031, 1060
Henri II, King of France, 1547, 1559
Henri III, King of France, 1574, 1589
Henri IV, King of France, 1589, 1593, 1598, 1610
Henri I, King of Navarre, 1270, 1274
Henrique, first Bishop of Kongo, 1518
Henry I, King of England, 1100, 1107, 1121, 1135, 1154
Henry II, King of England, *c.*1120, 1154, 1162, 1167,
    1189

493

Henry III, King of England, 1216, 1271, 1272
Henry IV, King of England, 1399, 1413
Henry V, King of England, 1413, 1415, 1422
Henry VI, King of England, 1422, 1432, 1440, 1441, 1461, 1470, 1471
Henry VII, King of England, 1485, 1509
Henry VIII, King of England, 1478, 1509, 1521, 1532, 1533, 1534, 1535, 1537, 1547
Henry of Hainault *see* John X, Latin emperor of Constantinople
Henry the Lion, 1137, 1147
Henry the Navigator, 1454–56
Heraclius I, Byzantine emperor, 610, 622, 624, 627, 629, 632, 636, 638, 641
Herbert of Cherbury, Lord, 1583, 1648
Herbert, George, 1593, 1633
   The Temple, 1593
Hereford
   Cathedral, *c*.792, 1052, 1056, 1080, *c*.1290
   Diocese, 676
Herluin, Norman knight, 1039
Herman, Russian Orthodox monk, 1794
Hermogenes, Patriarch of Moscow, 1606, 1612
Herod Agrippa, 40, 41, 44
Herod the Great, *c*.4 BCE
Herring, Thomas, Archbishop of Canterbury, 1747, 1757
Herrmann, Wilhelm, 1846, 1922
   The Communion of the Christian with God, 1846
Herrnhut, 1700, 1722
Hertford, Council of, 672
Hesychasm, *c*.949, *c*.1296, 1350
Hexham, 669, 702
Hick, John, 1977
Hicks, Mary, 1716
Hideyushi, Shogun Toyotomi, 1587
Hierapolis, *c*.200
Hieria, Synod of, 754, 815
Hieroglyphics, 1822
Hilarus, Pope, 461, 468
Hilary of Poitiers, *c*.315, 356, 359, *c*.360, 367
Hilda of Whitby, Abbess, 657, *c*.679
Hildebrand, 1073
Hildegard of Bingen, 1098, 1179
   Scivias, 1098
   Symphonia harmoniae caelestium revelationum, 1098
Hildegard of Swabia, 771

Hilderic, 523
Hildesheim Cathedral, 1009, 1015
Hilton, Walter, 1494
   The Ladder of Perfection, 1494
Hippolytus of Rome, *c*.170, *c*.215, 217, 236
   Apostolic Tradition, *c*.215
Hiroshima, 1945
Hispaniola, 1493, 1503, 1504
Hitler, Adolf, 1933, 1945
Hodge, Charles, 1797, 1878
Hodgkin, Henry, 1914
Hoffmann, Melchior, 1529
   The Return of the Lord, 1529
Holiness
   Camp Meeting, 1867
   Church, 1898
   Movement, 1807, 1867
Holland, Henry Scott, 1889
Holy Blood and the Holy Grail, The, 1982
Holy Ghost Fathers, 1703
Holy Office, 1542
Holy Sepulchre, Jerusalem, Church of, 326, 335, 1009, 1034, 1113, 1140, 1149
Holy Synod
   Greek, 1850
   Russian, 1721
Holy Trinity, Brompton, 1977
Holy Year, 1300, 1343, 1350, 1389, 1425, 1450, 1475 (*see also* Jubilee Year)
Holyrood Abbey, 1128
homoiousios, 357
homoousios, 325, 357
Homosexuality, 1957, 1980, 1998, 2003
Honest to God, 1963
Hong Kong, 1944, 1971
Hong Xiuquan, 1851
Honolulu Cathedral, 1843
Honoratus, Bishop of Arles, *c*.410
Honorius, Archbishop of Canterbury, 601, 627, 653
Honorius, Roman emperor, 393, 395, 396, 399, 407, 410, 418, 423
Honorius I, Pope, 625, 634, 638
Honorius II, Antipope, 1061, 1064
Honorius II, Pope, 1124, 1130
Honorius III, Pope, 1216, 1217, 1218, 1220, 1223, 1227, 1285
Honorius IV, Pope, 1285, 1287

Hontheim, Johann Nikolaus von, 1701, 1790
Hooker, Richard, c.1554, 1600
    Treatise on the Laws of Ecclesiastical Polity, c.1554, 1594
Hooker, Robert Stephen, 1843
Hoover, Willis, 1909
Hopkins, Gerard Manley, 1844, 1889
Hormisdas, Pope, 514, 523
Hormizd II, King of Persia, 302, 390
Hormizd III, King of Persia, 457, 459
Hormizd IV, King of Persia, 579, 590
Horne, Janet, 1727
Horsa, 449
Hottentots, 1737, 1799
Howley, William, Archbishop of Canterbury, 1828, 1848
Huddleston, Trevor, 1913, 1998
    Naught for Your Comfort, 1913
Hugh, Bishop of Lincoln, 1192, 1220
Hugh of St Victor, 1141
Huguenots, c.1560, 1561, 1562, 1563, 1567, 1570, 1572, 1627, 1628
Hugues Capet, French king, 987, 996
Humanae vitae, encyclical, 1968
Humani generis, encyclical, 1950
Humbert II, Dauphin, 1339
Humbert of Silva Candida, 1054
Hume, David, 1711, 1776
Hundred Chapters, Council of, 1551
Hundred Years War, 1337, 1431, 1453
Huneric, 476, 483, 523
Hungary, 568, 985, c.1001
Huns, 406, 447, 528
Hunt, William Holman, 1827, 1910
    The Light of the World, 1853
Hunyadi, Jan, 1456
Hurons, 1625
Hus, Jan, 1369, 1414, 1415
Hussite(s),1419, 1420, 1434
    Crusade, 1420
    Wars, 1419, 1436
Hutchinson, Anne, 1591, 1643
Hutter, Jacob, 1533, 1536
Hutterites, 1533
Hutton, Matthew, Archbishop of Canterbury, 1757, 1758
Hwang, Jane, 1971

Hwicce, 681
Hyginus, Bishop of Rome, c.137, c.140
Hymns, 112, c.306, c.330, 337, c.339, 347, c.348, c.530, 563, 633, c.750, 1166, 1236, 1593, 1607, 1637, 1672, 1674, 1740, 1793, 1814, 1818, 1835, 1872
Hymn books, 1530, 1556, 1575, 1739, 1779, 1861, 1898, 1899, 1900, 1904, 1904, 1925, 2000
Hymns Ancient and Modern, 1861
Hypatia, 413

Ice, Battle of the, 1242
Iceland, 1000, 1085, 1539
Iconoclasm, 715, 731, 741, 754, 820, 829
Iconoclastic Controversy, p.112
    First, c.500, 726, 786
    Second, 815
Ignatius, Bishop of Antioch, c.107
Ignatius I, Patriarch of Constantinople, 847, 858, 863, 867, 877
Ignatius Loyola, 1491, 1534, 1548, 1551, 1552, 1556, 1623
    Spiritual Exercises, 1548
Ilarion, 1051
Illich, Ivan, 1926, 2002
Illius fulciti, bull, 1504
Immaculate Conception of the Blessed Virgin Mary, 1708, 1854
Immaculate Heart of Mary, feast of, 1648
Immensa dei, bull, 1588
Imperial, La, Diocese, 1564
In supremae, papal bull, 1303
Incense, 381–4
Independents, 1580
Index of Prohibited Books, 1557, 1571, 1966
India, c.190, 198, c.300, c.360, 1497, 1498, 1503, 1532, 1540, 1577, 1579, 1639, 1886
Indonesia, 1601, 1619
Ine, King of Wessex, 688, c.720, 726
Ineffabilis Deus, encyclical, 1854
Ineffabilis Providentia, bull, 1470
Inés de la Cruz, Sor, 1648, 1695
Ingall, Jeremiah, 1805
    The Christian Harmony, 1805
Inglis, Charles, 1787
Ingolstadt, 1472, 1519
Innocent I, Pope, 401, 416, 417
Innocent II, Pope, 1130, 1139, 1143

Jarrow monastery, *c.* 628, 682, 794

Jassy, Synod of, 1642

Jaume I, King of Aragon, 1213, 1276

Jaume II, King of Aragon, 1291, 1327

Jaume de Montjuich, 1287

Java, 1323, 1619

Jean I, King of France, 1316

Jean II, King of France, 1350, 1356, 1359, 1364

Jeanne d'Arc, 1412, 1429, 1430, 1431, 1456, 1920

Jeanne of Navarre, 1274, 1284

Jeanne II, Queen of Navarre, 1328

Jebb, John, 1771

Jehovah's Witnesses, 1870

Jelling Stone, 960

Jensen, Maud K., 1956

Jepsen, Maria, 1992

Jeremias I, Patriarch of Constantinople, 1522, 1545

Jeremias II Tranos, Patriarch of Constantinople, 1572, 1576, 1579, 1582, 1584, 1585, 1595

Jeremias IV, Patriarch of Constantinople, 1808, 1813

Jerome, *c.*345, 383, 386, 392, 393, *c.*404, 414, 415, 420, 1592

Jerusalem, *c.*30, *c.*35, *c.*56, 62, *c.*66, 70, 638, 1187
   Crusader capture of, 1099
   destruction of, 70, 135
   kingdom of, 1187
   Synod of, 1672
   temple of, *c.*4 BCE, 40, 70

Jesaias, Patriarch of Constantinople, 1323, 1332

Jesuits, 1491, 1534, 1586, 1643, 1687, 1750, 1851, 1909, p. 275
   expulsion of, 1719, 1764, 1767, 1820, 1872
   mission, 1549, 1554, 1560, 1568, 1579, 1583, 1610, 1616, 1634, 1640, 1687, 1698, 1717
   restoration of, 1814
   suppression of, 1759, 1764, 1773

Jesus of Nazareth, *c.* 6 BCE, after 20, *c.*30

Jeunesse Ouvrière Chrétienne (JOC, Jocistes), 1924

Jewish War
   First, 66, 67, 74
   Second, 132, 135

Jewison, Norman, 1973

Jews, 19, *c.*49, 70, 132, 135, 589, 602, 613, 632, 633, 722, 1096, 1182, 1190, 1215, 1290, 1306, 1391, 1478, 1492, 1556, 1608, 1655, 1858, 1870, 1945

Jiaqing Emperor, 1796

Jihe, Bishop, 744

Joachim of Fiore, 1132, 1202

Joachim I, Patriarch of Constantinople, 1498, 1504

Joachim II, Patriarch of Constantinople, 1860, 1863, 1873, 1878

Joachim III, Patriarch of Constantinople, 1878, 1884, 1901, 1913

Joachim IV, Patriarch of Constantinople, 1884, 1887

Joachim, Patriarch of Moscow, 1674, 1690

Joannicus I, Patriarch of Constantinople, 1546

João I, King of Kongo, 1491, *c.*1509

João III, King of Portugal, 1536

João de Villa do Conde, 1546

Joasaph I, Patriarch of Constantinople, 1465, 1466

Joasaph II, Patriarch of Constantinople, 1554, 1565

Joasaph I, Patriarch of Moscow, 1634, 1640

Joasaph II, Patriarch of Moscow, 1667, 1672

Job, Patriarch of Moscow, 1589, 1605

Joel, King of Nubia, 1484

Jogaila, Grand Prince of Lithuania, 1385

Johannes Scotus Eriugena, *c.*810, 877

John the Baptist, after 20

John, Bishop of Antioch, 433

John, Gospel fragment, *c.*125

John, Mar, 1490

John, King of England, 1199, 1207, 1215, 1216

John I, King of Portugal, 1454–56

John I Tzimisces, Byzantine emperor, 969, 976

John II Comnenus, Byzantine emperor, 1118, 1136, 1143

John III Ducas Vatatzes, Byzantine emperor, 1222, 1225, *c.*1249, 1253, 1254

John V Palaeologus, Byzantine emperor, 1341, 1347, 1357, 1364, 1371, 1373, 1391

John VI Cantacuzenus, Byzantine emperor, 1341, 1347, 1353, 1355

John VIII Palaeologus, Byzantine emperor, 1408, 1425, 1438, 1439, 1448

John Lascaris, Byzantine emperor, 1258, 1259

John X, Latin emperor of Constantinople, 1206, 1208, 1214, 1216

John Chrysostom, Patriarch of Constantinople, 347, 398, 401, 403, 407

John II of Cappadocia, Patriarch of Constantinople, 517, 520

John III Scholasticus, Patriarch of Constantinople, 565, 577

John IV Nesteutes, Patriarch of Constantinople, 582, 588, 595

Lateran Palace, 1059
Lateran Treaty, 1929
Latimer, Hugh, *c.*1485, 1555
Latvia, 1206
Laud, William, Archbishop of Canterbury, 1573, 1633, 1640, 1645
Laurence, Archbishop of Canterbury, 604, 616, 619
Laurentius, Antipope, 498, 501
Lausanne, 1448
Lavigerie, Charles-Martial-Allemand, 1825, 1868, 1892
Lavra, monastery, 961
Law, William, 1686, 1761
   A Serious Call to a Devout and Holy Life, 1686, 1728
Law on Freedom of Religious Confessions, 1990
Law of Guarantees, 1871
Layard, Henry, 1845
Lazarists, 1580, 1625, 1722, 1839
Le Corbusier, Notre Dame du Haut, Ronchamp, 1955
Lee, Ann, 1736, 1774, 1784
Lefebvre, Marcel, 1905, 1974, 1991
Legate, Bartholomew, 1612
Leibniz, Gottfried Wilhelm von, 1646, 1716, 1759
Leiden University, 1574
Leigh, Richard, 1982
Leipzig University, 1409
Lenshina, Alice, 1954
Lent, 337, *c.*550, 640
Leo I, Roman emperor, 457, 474
Leo III, Byzantine emperor, 717, 720, 722, 726, 730, 741
Leo IV, Byzantine emperor, 775, 780
Leo V, Byzantine emperor, 813, 815
Leo VI, Byzantine emperor, 870, 886, 907, 912
   Imperial Laws of, 886
Leo Styppes, Patriarch of Constantinople, 1134, 1143
Leo I, Pope, 440, 448, 452, 455, 461
   Tome of, 448
Leo II, Pope, 682, 683
Leo III, Pope, 795, 800, 816, 1673
Leo IV, Pope, 847, 850, 852, 855
Leo V, Pope, 903
Leo VI, Pope, 928
Leo VII, Pope, 936, 939
Leo VIII, Pope, 963, 964, 965
Leo IX, Pope, 1049,1049–53, 1053, 1054
Leo X, Pope, 1513, 1516, 1521
Leo XI, Pope, 1605

Leo XII, Pope, 1823, 1829
Leo XIII, Pope, 1878, 1896, 1900, 1903
Leofric, Bishop of Exeter, 1050
Leonine Sacramentary, *c.*600
Leontius, Roman emperor, 695, 698
Leontius Theotokites, Patriarch of Constantinople, 1189
Leopold I, Holy Roman Emperor, 1657, 1705
Leopold II, Holy Roman Emperor, 1790, 1792
Leovigild, King of the Visigoths, 573
Lepanto, Battle of, 1571
Lérins, *c.*410, 450, 460
Le Roux, P., 1904
Le Roy, Mervyn, 1951
Leschinsky, Filofey, 1702
Lesotho, 1833
Lessing, Gotthold Ephraim, 1694, 1729, 1779, 1780
   Nathan the Wise, 1779
Leuenberg Agreement, 1973
Lewis, C. S., 1898, 1942, 1963
   Chronicles of Narnia, 1898
   Screwtape Letters, 1898
Liang Fa, 1824
Liberation theology, 1928, 1968, 1983
Liberia, 1884
Liberius, Pope, 352, 356, 358, 366
Liberman, Francis, 1840
Licet ecclesiarum, bull, 1265
Lichfield, 1612
   (Arch)diocese, 669, 786, 803
   Cathedral, 1085, 1195
Licinius, Roman emperor, 308, 313, 320, 324, 325
Life and Work, 1925
   Conference, Stockholm, 1925
Lightman, Edward, 1612
Ligugé, Abbey, *c.*360, 371
Lima, 1570, 1687
   (Arch)diocese, 1541, 1547, 1561
   Document, 1982
   Third Council of, 1584
   University, 1551
Limes, 81
Lincoln
   Cathedral, 1092, 1141, 1185, 1192, 1237
   Diocese, 1072
Lincoln, Abraham, 1863
   Emancipation Proclamation, 1863
Lincoln, Henry, 1982

Marist Fathers, 1816, 1838

Mark, Pope, 336

Mark Xylokaraves, Patriarch of Constantinople, 1466

Marmoutier Abbey, c.360, 371

Marnham, Charles, 1977

Maron, 684

Maronite
  Church, 684, 1784
  College, 1584, 1798

Marquette, Jacques, 1672

Marrakesh, 1234
  Diocese, 1220

Marsden, Samuel, 1814

Marseilles, c.415

Marsilius of Padua, c.1280, 1324, c.1343
  Defensor pacis, 1324

Martin, Bishop of Tours, c.336, c.360, 371, 396, 397

Martin I, King of Aragon, 1396, 1410

Martin I, Pope, 649, 653, 654, 655

Martin IV, Pope, 1281, 1285

Martin V, Pope, 1417, 1420, 1425, 1431

Martin, Gregory, 1568

Martin, John, 1789, 1854
  The Day of His Wrath, 1789
  The Last Judgement, 1789
  The Plains of Heaven, 1789

Martin, Thérèse, 1873, 1897 (*see also* Thérèse of Lisieux)

Martinia, Archimandrite, 1705

Martyn, Henry, 1781, 1805, 1812

Marx, Karl, 1818, 1867, 1883
  Das Kapital, 1867

Mary I, Queen of England, 1553, 1554, 1558

Mary II, Queen of England, 1689, 1692

Mary I, Queen of Scotland, 1558

Maryknoll Missioners, 1911

Maryland, 1634
  St Clement Island, 1634

Masada, c.4 BCE, 74

Maserfield, Battle of, 642

Masih, Salib Abdul, 1811, 1825

Mason, Charles H., 1866, 1961

Massaja, Guglielmo, 1846

Mather, Cotton, 1663, 1728

Matthew Cantacuzenus, Byzantine emperor, 1353, 1357

Matthew I, Patriarch of Constantinople, 1397, 1410

Matthew II, Patriarch of Constantinople, 1596

Matthew's Bible, 1537, 1539

Matthews, Marjorie, 1980

Matthias, Holy Roman Emperor, 1612, 1619

Matisse, Henri, 1951
  Chapel of the Rosary, Vence, 1951

Maurice, Roman emperor, 582, 584, 591, 598, 602

Maurice, Frederick Denison, 1805, 1853, 1872

Maurists, 1618

Mauritania, 1448

Mauritius, 1722

Maxentius, 306, 307, 312

Maximian, Patriarch of Constantinople, 431, 434

Maximian, Roman emperor, 286, 303, 305, 306, 310

Maximilian I, Holy Roman Emperor, 1493, 1519

Maximilian II, Holy Roman Emperor, 1548, 1564, 1576

Maximilian, Duke of Bavaria, 1620

Maximinus, Caesar, 305, 306, 308, 309, 311, 313

Maximinus Thrax, Roman emperor, 235, 238

Maximus, Roman emperor, 383, 386, 387, 388

Maximus Confessor, c.580, 662

Maximus II, Patriarch of Constantinople, 1215

Maximus III Manasses, Patriarch of Constantinople, 1476, 1481

Maximus IV, Patriarch of Constantinople, 1491, 1497

Maximus V, Patriarch of Constantinople, 1946, 1948

Maynooth College, 1795

M'banza Kongo, 1491, 1549

M'banza Soyo, Kongo, 1645

Mbwila, Battle of, 1665

Means, Jacqueline, 1977

Mecca, 622, 628

Mechthild of Magdeburg, c.1210, c.1282
  The Flowing Light of the Godhead, c.1210

Mecklenburg, 1042

Medehamstede, 655 (*see also* Peterborough)

Medellin Conference of Latin American Bishops, 1968, 1979

Medina, 622

Medjugorje, 1981

Mehmed I, sultan, 1403

Mehmed II, sultan, 1453, 1456, 1458–60, 1462

Meinhard, Bishop of Uexküll, 1186, 1198

Meissen Common Statement, 1988

Melanchthon, Philipp, 1497, 1530, 1560

Melania the Younger, c.383, 439

Melchiorites, 1529

Meletius III, Patriarch of Constantinople, 1845

Meletius IV Metaxakis, Patriarch of Constantinople, 1921, 1923
Melitian schism, 306
Melitius, Bishop of Lycopolis, 306
Melito of Sardis, *c.*190
   *Homily on the Passion, c.*190
Melleray Abbey, 1848
Mellitus, Archbishop of Canterbury, 601, 604, 619, 624
Melrose, *c.*636
Melville, Andrew, 1578
Men, Aleksandr, 1935, 1990
Menas, Patriarch of Constantinople, 536, 552
Mendelssohn, Felix, 1809, 1829, 1846, 1847
   Elijah, 1846
   St Paul, 1809
Mendez, Alfonso, 1624, 1626
Menezes, Alexis de, 1599
Mennonite Church, 2001/2
Mennonite Conference USA, 2001/2
Mennonites, *c.*1496, 1536, 1693, 1855, 1860, 1912, 1935
Mepeham, Simon, Archbishop of Canterbury, 1328, 1333
Mercia, *c.*585, 655, 656, 757, 821
Merindol, Massacre of, 1545
Merki, Nubian bishop, 1484
Merton, Battle of, 871
Merton College, Oxford, 1264
Merton, Thomas, 1915, 1968
Mesopotamia, 114–17, 297, 358, 385, 448
Mesrop Mashtots, 337, 360, 440
Messia, Fr Alphonsia, 1687
Messiaen, Olivier, 1908, 1992
Methodism, 1815
Methodist(s), 1739, 1745, 1956
   Book Concern, 1789
   Church in America, 1957
   Church of Great Britain, 1932
   Conference, 1744, 1773
   Episcopal Church, 1784, 1870–5
   Protestant Church, 1879
Methodist Hymn Book, 1904
Methodius, *c.*815, 826, 863, 885
Methodius, Patriarch of Constantinople, 843, 847
Methodius II, Patriarch of Constantinople, 1240
Metrophanes II, Patriarch of Constantinople, 1440, 1443
Metrophanes III, Patriarch of Constantinople, 1565, 1572, 1579

Mexico, 1524, 1526, 1568, 1571, 1574
   City, 1531, 1556
   City Cathedral, 1563, 1667
   First Council of, 1555
   Twelve apostles of, 1524
   University, 1551, 1648
Michael I Rhangabe, Byzantine emperor, 811
Michael II, Byzantine emperor, 820, 829
Michael III, Byzantine emperor, 842, 858, 866, 867
Michael IV the Paphlagonian, Byzantine emperor, 1034, 1041
Michael V Calaphates, Byzantine emperor, 1041, 1042
Michael VI Stratioticus, Byzantine emperor, 1056, 1057
Michael VII, Ducas, Byzantine emperor, 1072, 1078
Michael VIII Palaeologus, Byzantine emperor, 1258, 1259, 1261, 1263, 1271, 1274, 1282
Michael Cerularius, Patriarch of Constantinople, 1043, 1052, 1054, 1058, 1059
Michael II Kurkuas, Patriarch of Constantinople, 1143, 1146
Michael III of Anchialus, Patriarch of Constantinople, 1170, 1178
Michael IV Autoreianus, Patriarch of Constantinople, 1208, 1213
Michelangelo Buonarotti, 1475, 1499, 1503, 1512, 1535, 1541, 1564
   Last Judgement, 1535, 1541
   Rondanini Pietà, 1555
   St Peter's Pietà, 1499
Michigan, Lake, 1672
Middleton, T. F., 1814
Mies, Jacob of, 1414
Mieszko, Polish duke, 966, 990
Migne, Jacques-Paul, 1800, 1875
Milan, 569
   Cathedral, *c.*1385
   Edict of, 313
   Synod of, 355
Milevis, Council of, 416
Milingo, Emmanuel, 1930, 2006
Mill Hill Missionaries, 1866
Millenary Petition, 1603
Mille, Cecil B. de, 1923, 1927, 1956
   King of Kings, 1927
   The Ten Commandments, 1923, 1956
Miller, Arthur, 1953
   The Crucible, 1953

Miller, William, 1782, 1831, 1849
Millerites, 1782, 1831, 1844
Milne, William, 1813
Milner-White, Eric, 1918
Miltiades, Pope, 311, 314
Milvian Bridge, 312
Milton, John, 1608, 1667, 1674
   Paradise Lost, 1667
Mindaugas, King of Lithuania, 1251, 1253
Mindszenty, Archbishop Joseph, 1948
Minims, 1435
Minuscule script, 800
Miracle play, 1110, *c.*1200
Mirari vos, encyclical, 1832
Mirfield, 1853
Missal, Roman, 1570
Mission de Paris, 1833
Missionaries
   of Charity, 1910, 1950
   of the Heart of Mary, 1840
   of Our Lady of Africa, 1868
Mississippi River, 1672
Misteri d'Elx, *c.*1450
Mit brennender Sorge, encyclical, 1937
Modernism, 1861, 1907, 1909, 1910
Moffat, Robert, 1817, 1821
Mohammad ibn Alhamar, 1236
Mokoni, Mangeno, 1892
Molina, Louis de, 1535, 1588, 1600
Molinism, 1535
Molinos, Miguel de, 1628, 1696
Molokai, 1873
Moltmann, Jürgen, 1926
Moluccas, 1534, 1813
Monastery of Caves, *c.*1051
Mongols, 1190, 1206, 1223, 1237, 1240, 1241
'Monkey trial', 1860, 1925
Monophysitism, 449, 450, 497, *c.*500, 518, 525, 530,
   535, 571, 580, 602, 1243, 1264, p.65
Monothelitism, 625, 638, 649, 681, 711
Monreale Cathedral, 1170
Mons pietatis, 1361, 1462
Montanism, *c.*170, *c.*207, 722, p.19
Montanus, *c.*170
Monte Cassino, *c.*480, 529, 747, 1086
Montesinos, Antonio de, 1511
Monteverdi, Claudio, 1567, 1610, 1643

Vespers, 1610
Montmartre, 272
Montpellier University, 1220
Montreal, 1615
Mont St Michel, 709
Montségur, 1224, 1244
Montserrat, monastery, 1024
Monty Python's Life of Brian, 1979
Moody, Dwight Lyman, 1837, 1873, 1899
Moody Bible Institute, 1886
Moon, Sun Myung, 1935, 1954
Moore, John, Archbishop of Canterbury, 1783, 1805
Moors, 711
Moral Majority, 1933, 1979, 2007
Moral Rearmament, 1938
Moravia, *c.*815, 826, 862, 863, 1533
Moravian
   Brothers, 1732, 1792
   Church, *c.*815, 826, 885
   Protestant Church, 1457, 1735, 1737, 1741, 1747,
      1753, 1821, *c.*1890
More, Hannah, 1745, 1833
More, Thomas, 1478, 1509, 1516, 1535, 1935, 1960
   Utopia, 1516
Morgan, William, 1588
Mormon, Book of, 1830
Mormons, 1801, 1805, 1830, 1839, 1847
Morocco, 681
Morrison, Robert, 1807, 1819, 1824
Mortalium animos, encyclical, 1928
Morton, John, Archbishop of Canterbury, 1486, 1500
Morwenstow, 1843
Moscow, 1395, 1812
   Cathedral of the Annunciation, 1489
   Cathedral of the Archangel Michael, 1508
   Cathedral of the Dormition, 1479
   Metropolitan of, 1461
   Patriarchate of, 1589, 1721
   as the Third Rome, 1493
Moses, Catholicos of Armenia, 551
Mothers' Union, 1876
Mott, John R., 1865, 1888, 1895, 1910, 1955
Mow Cop, 1811
Mozarabic rite, 1080
Mozambique, 1506, 1560, 1884
Mozart, Wolfgang Amadeus, 1756, 1791
   C Minor Mass, 1756, 1783

Ostrogoths, *c.*311, 487, 493, 536, 540, 546, 552
Oswald, King of Northumbria, 634, 637, 642, 669
Oswy, King of Northumbria, 642, 655, 657, 664, 670
Otho, emperor, 69
Othona, *c.*654
Otto, Bishop of Bamberg, 1111, 1124
Otto I, Holy Roman Emperor, 936, 962, 963, 965, 967, 973
Otto II, Holy Roman Emperor, 967, 973, 982, 983
Otto III, Holy Roman Emperor, 983, 996, 1002
Otto V, Holy Roman Emperor, 1209, 1215
Otto of Freising, 1145
Ottoman Turks, 1285, 1326, 1331, 1337, 1354, 1364, 1371, 1430, 1438, 1453, 1456, 1458–60, 1463/64
Our Lady of Victory, Feast of, 1571, 1573
Oviedo, 791
    Cathedral, 765, 794, 802, 1386
Oxford
    Diocese, 1541/42
    Movement, 1800, 1833
    University, 1167, 1209

Pacelli, Eugenio, 1933, 1939
Pacem in terris, encyclical, 1963
Pachomius I, Patriarch of Constantinople, 1504, 1513
Pachomius II, Patriarch of Constantinople, 1585
Padilla, Fernando Juan de, 1541
Padua University, 1222, 1303
Paez, Pedro, 1603, 1622
Pakhom, *c.*290, 320, 346
    Rule of, *c.*321
Palaestina, 135
Palau, Luis, 1934
Palencia University, 1211, 1218
Palermo, 831, 1194
Palestine, 614
    British mandate in, 1922, 1948
    Exploration Fund, 1865
Palestrina, Giovanni Pierluigi da, *c.*1525, 1548, 1555, 1556, 1594
    Missa Papae Marcelli, 1556
Paley, William, 1743, 1805
    A View of the Evidences of Christianity, 1743, 1794
Palladius, 431
Pallotti, Vincent Mary, 1835, 1963
Pallottines, 1835, 1890
Palmer, Phoebe Worrall, 1807, 1874

Panama, 1513
Pantaenus, *c.*190
Pantheon, 609
Pantocrator Monastery, Constantinople, 1136
Papa bar Aggai, *c.*285
Papal states, 774, 787, 1053, 1797, 1809, 1870
Papias, Bishop of Hierapolis, *c.*130
    Interpretation of the Sayings of the Lord, *c.*130
Papua New Guinea, 1871
Paraguay, 1568, 1587, 1750, 1759
Parham, Charles Fox, 1873, 1929
Paris
    Treaty of, 1229, 1783
    University of, *c.*1150, 1167, 1257, 1386
Parker, Matthew, Archbishop of Canterbury, 1559, 1575
Parks, Rosa, 1955
Parma Cathedral, 1116
Parsons, Robert, 1580
Pärt, Arvo, 1935
Parthia, 114–17, 226, 301, 363
Particular Baptists, 1633
    Missionary Society, 1792
Pascal, Blaise, 1623, 1654, 1662, 1670
    Pensées, 1670
Pascendi, encyclical, 1907
Paschal I, Pope, 817, 823, 824
Paschal II, Pope, 1099, 1116, 1118
Paschal III, Antipope, 1164, 1168
Paschasius Radbertus, 831–33
    De Corpore et Sanguine Domini, 831–33
Pasolini, Pier Paolo, 1964
    The Gospel According to St Matthew, 1964
Passau
    Diocese, 739
    Treaty of, 1552, 1629
Passionists, 1720
Pastor aeternus, constitution, 1870
Pastoralis cura, bull, 1313
Pastors' Emergency League, 1933
Patarenes, 1056
Patent of Tolerance, 1781
Patriarchs of Constantinople, p. 81
Patrick, *c.*390, *c.*432, 445, *c.*451, *c.*460, 807
Paul of the Cross, 1720, 1867
Paul of Samosata, 261, 268
Paul of Tarsus, *c.*36, *c.*45–58, *c.*49, 51/52, *c.*56, *c.*58, 64
Paul II, Patriarch of Constantinople, 641, 653

Paul III, Patriarch of Constantinople, 688, 693

Paul IV, Patriarch of Constantinople, 780, 784

Paul I, Pope, 757, 767

Paul II, Pope, 1450, 1464, 1470, 1471

Paul III, Pope, 1534, 1535, 1536, 1537, 1538, 1540, 1542, 1549

Paul IV, Pope, 1555, 1556, 1559

Paul V, Pope, 1605, 1610, 1616, 1621

Paul VI, Pope, 1905, 1963, 1964, 1966, 1970, 1975, 1978

Paul of the Holy Faith (Paul of Japan), 1549

Paulinus of Nola, *c.*353, *c.*360, 400, 431

Paulinus, Bishop of York, 601, 619

Paulists, 1858

Pavia, 572, 774
  Synod of, 1022, 1160, 1405
  University of, 1361, 1405

Peasants' War, 1524–25

Pecham, John, Archbishop of Canterbury, 1279, 1283, 1292

Pedro II, King of Aragon, 1196, 1205, 1213

Pedro III, King of Aragon, 1276, 1285

Pedro IV, King of Aragon, 1335, 1387

Pedro, King of Leon-Castile, 1350, 1369

Pedro, Prince of the Kongo, 1824

Péguy, Charles, 1873, 1914
  Eve, 1873
  The Mystery of the Charity of Joan of Arc, 1873

Peipus, Battle of Lake, 1242

Pelagianism, *c.*360, 410, 414, 416, 417, 429, *c.*460, *c.*545, 569, p.63

Pelagius, *c.*360, 410, 415, 416, 418, *c.*420

Pelagius I, Pope, 556, 561

Pelagius II, Pope, 579, 590

Pella, *c.*66

Penda, King of Mercia, *c.*626, 642, 655

Penn, William, 1644, 1681, 1682, 1718

Pennsylvania, 1681, 1682, 1719, 1741

Penny Catechism, 1859

Pentecostals, 1860, 1866, 1873, 1879, 1897, 1898, 1901, 1906, 1907, 1909, 1910, 1922, 1958, 1959, 1966, 1978, p.400

Pepin III, King of the Franks, 741, 747, 751, 753, 754, 756, 757, 759, 768
  Donation of, 754, 759, 774

Perigueux Cathedral, 1120

Perm, 1379

Pérotin, *c.*1200

Peroz I, King of Persia, 459, 484

Perpetua, 203

Perrin, Henri, 1944

Persecution, 177, *c.*250, 306, 309, 339, 1835, 1885, 1917, 1937/38, 1959
  The 'Great', 303, 311

Persia, 216

Perth, Five Articles of, 1618

Pertinax, Roman emperor, 193

Perugia University, 1308

Petau, Denis, 1627

Peter, 44, *c.*49, 64, *c.*66

Peter, Bishop of Alexandria, 306

Peter of Courtenay, Latin emperor of Constantinople, 1217, 1221

Peter, Patriarch of Constantinople, 654, 666

Peter the Great, 1721

Peter the Hermit, 1096

Peter Lombard, *c.*1095, 1169, *c.*1221
  Sentences, *c.*1095, *c.*1221

Peter the Venerable, 1143

Peterborough
  Abbey, 655, 870, 972, 1116, 1118
  Cathedral, 1238
  Diocese, 1541/42

Peterhouse, Cambridge, 1284

Peter's Pence, 787, 1534

Petrarch, 1304, 1374

Philadelphia, Asia Minor, *c.*107

Philadelphia, USA, 1682

Philaret, Patriarch of Moscow, 1619, 1633

Philibert, *c.*654

Philip the Arab, Roman emperor, 244, 249

Philip, Metropolitan of Moscow, 1569

Philip Neri, 1515, 1574, 1595, 1611, 1623

Philip, John, 1820

Philippe I, King of France, 1060, 1108

Philippe II, King of France, 1180, 1182, 1190, 1191, 1222

Philippe III, King of France, 1270, 1285

Philippe IV, King of France, 1285, 1306, 1314

Philippe V, King of France, 1316, 1322

Philippe VI, King of France, 1328, 1337, 1350

Philippi, *c.*45–58, *c.*166

Philippicus Bardasanes, 711, 713

Philippine Independent Church, 1902

Philippines, 1521, 1565, 1581, 1595, 1614

Raedwald, King of East Anglia, 616, 625
Rahner, Karl, 1904, 1984
Raikes, Robert, 1735, 1780, 1811
Raimondo, Archbishop of Toledo, 1127
Ralph d'Escurses, Archbishop of Canterbury, 1114, 1122
Ramsey, Arthur Michael, Archbishop of Canterbury, 1904, 1961, 1974, 1988
Ranavalona I, Queen of Madagascar, 1835
Rancé, Amand-Jean le Bouthillier de, 1626, 1700
Raphael, 1483, 1520
Raphael I, Patriarch of Constantinople, 1475, 1476
Rarotonga, 1839
Rastafarians, 1887, c.1930
Rastislav, Prince of Moravia, 863
Rath Bresail, Synod of, 1111, 1152
Ravenna, 410, 417, 450, 493, 526, c.530, 540, 584, 751, 754
Rawlinson, Henry Creswicke, 1837
Reading Abbey, 1121
Recared, King of the Spanish Visigoths, 587, 589
Recife, Diocese, 1676
Recollects, 1615
Reconquista, 1212
Redemptorines, 1696, 1732
Redemptoris missio, encyclical, 1990
Redemptorists, 1696, 1732
Reductions, 1610
    Seven reductions of Paraguay, 1750, 1759
Redwald, King of East Anglia, 593, c.600
Reformation, 1517, 1523, 1528, p.265
Regensburg, Diocese, 739
Regimini militantis, bull, 1540
Reginald, Sub-prior of Christ Church, Canterbury, 1205
Régis, Jean Baptiste, 1717
Regnans in excelsis, bull, 1570
Reimarus, Hermann Samuel, 1694, 1729, 1768
Reims, 1578
    Cathedral, 816, 1211, 1311
    Council of, 1119
Relief Synod of Scotland, 1847
Religious broadcast, first, 1921
Religious Society of Friends, 1624, 1647 (*see also* Quakers)
Rembrandt van Rijn, 1606, 1669
Remigius, Bishop of Lincoln, 1092

Remigius (Rémy), 496
Remonstrance, 1610
Renaissance, p.217
Renan, Ernest, 1823, 1892
Requiem mass, c.1254, c.1410
Rerum novarum, encyclical, 1891, 1981
Reuilly Declaration, 1999
Réunion, 1807
Reynolds, Walter, Archbishop of Canterbury, 1313, 1327
Rhine, 81, 270, 406, 718
Rhode Island, 1638, 1644
    College, 1764
Rhodes, 654, 1635
Rhodes, Alexandre de, 1591, 1624, 1627, 1660
Ribaut, Jean, 1562
Rice, Tim, 1971
Ricci, Matteo, 1552, 1583, 1601, 1610
Rich, Caleb, 1778
Rich, Edmund, Archbishop of Canterbury, 1234, 1240
Richard of Dover, Archbishop of Canterbury, 1174, 1184
Richard le Grant, Archbishop of Canterbury, 1229, 1231
Richard I, King of England, 1110, 1189, 1191, 1193, 1194, 1199
Richard II, King of England, 1377, 1384, 1397, 1399, 1400
Richard III, King of England, 1483, 1485
Richard of St Victor, 1173
Richard, Duke of York, 1483
Richeldis de Favershes, Lady, 1061
Richelieu, Cardinal, 1627, 1628
Ridley, Nicholas, Bishop of London, c.1500, 1555
Riebeeck, Jan van, 1652
Rievaulx Abbey, 1132
Riez, Synod of, 439
Riga, 1201
Riley, William Bell, 1919
Rimini, Golden Bull of, 1226
Rio de Janeiro, Diocese, 1676
Ripley, George, 1841
Robarts, Emma, 1855
Robber Synod of Ephesus, 449
Robert II, King of France, 996, 1031
Robert d'Abrissel, 1110
Robert of Courtenay, Latin emperor of Constantinople, 1221, 1228

515

Society of Biblical Literature, 1880
Society of Foreign Missions of Paris, 1663
Society of Jesus *see* Jesuits
Society of Mary (Marists), 1816
Society for Missions in Africa and the East, 1799 (*see also* Church Missionary Society)
Society for the Promotion of Christian Knowledge (SPCK), 1656, 1698
Society for the Propagation of the Faith, 1823
Society for the Propagation of the Gospel (SPG), 1656, 1695, 1701, 1752, 1965
Society of the Sacred Mission, 1893
Society of St Francis de Sales (Salesians), 1815, 1859
Society of St John the Evangelist (Cowley Fathers), 1866
Society of Saint-Suplice (Sulpicians), 1642
Socinians, 1647
Socrates, church historian, *c.*380, 450
Söderblom, Nathan, 1866, 1931
Soissons Cathedral, 751
Sojourner Truth, *c.*1797, 1843, 1883
Sojourners Community, 1975
Sol Invictus, 272, 274, 321
Solemn League and Covenant, 1643
Sollicitudo omnium ecclesiarum, bull, 1814
Solzhenitsyn, Aleksandr, 1935
Somaschi, 1532
Songs of Praise, hymn book, 1925
    television programme, 1961
Sophronius III, Patriarch of Constantinople, 1863, 1867
Sorbon, Robert de, 1257
Sorbonne, 1257
Sorsky, Nil, 1433, 1508
Soter, Bishop of Rome, *c.*166, *c.*175
Soubirous, Bernadette, 1844, 1858, 1879, 1933
South Africa, 1665
    National Party, 1949
South Folk, 520
South India, 1870–75
    Church of, 1947
    United Church, 1908
South Korea, 1898
South Saxe, 477
Southampton, Long Island, 1640
Southern Baptist Convention, 1846
Southern Baptists, 1845
Sozomen, 400, 450
Sozzini, Fausto Paolo, 1558, 1579, 1604

Spangenberg, August Gottlieb, Bishop, 1735, 1753
Spener, Philipp Jakob, 1635, 1663, 1705
    Pia Desideria, 1635
Speyer
    Cathedral, 1030, 1061
    Diet of, First, 1526, 1529
    Diet of, Second, 1529
    Diocese, 343
    massacre of Jews in, 1096
Spinoza, Benedict de, 1632, 1670, 1677
    Tractatus Theologico-Politicus, 1632, 1670
Spiritans (Holy Ghost Fathers), 1703
Spiritual Regulation, 1721
Spoleto Cathedral, 1175
Sprenger, Jacobus, 1486
Spurgeon, Charles Haddon, 1834, 1892
Sri Lanka, 537, 1518 (*see also* Ceylon)
Stabat Mater, 1236
Stafford, John, Archbishop of Canterbury, 1443, 1452
Stainer, John, 1887
    The Crucifixion, 1887
Stalin, Joseph, 1929, 1953
Stanford, Charles Villiers, 1852, 1924
    Requiem, 1852
    Stabat Mater, 1852
Stanton, Elizabeth Cady, 1815, 1902
Stations of the Cross, 1342, 1731, 1742
Steenhoven, Cornelis, 1723
Stefan, Archbishop of Uppsala, 1164
Stein, Edith, 1891, 1942, 1998
Steiner, Rudolf, 1861, 1925
Stephen, *c.*35
Stephen, King of England, 1135, 1154
Stephen I, Patriarch of Constantinople, 886, 893
Stephen II of Amasea, Patriarch of Constantinople, 925, 928
Stephen I, Pope, 254, 257
Stephen II, Pope, 752
Stephen II (III), Pope, 752, 753, 757
Stephen III (IV), Pope, 768, 769, 772
Stephen IV (V), Pope, 816, 817
Stephen V (VI), Pope, 885, 891
Stephen VI (VII), Pope, 896, 897
Stephen VII (VIII), Pope, 928, 931
Stephen VIII (IX) Pope, 939, 942
Stephen IX (X), Pope, 1057, 1058
Stephen of Perm, 1379

Taufa'ahau, Tongan chief, 1831
Tauler, John, c.1300, 1361
Tavener, John, 1944
Taverner, John, 1490, 1545
Tawney, R. H., 1926
    Religion and the Rise of Capitalism, 1926
Taxis, 901
Taylor, James Hudson, 1832, 1865, 1905
Taylor, Jeremy, 1613, 1667
    Holy Living, 1613, 1650
    Holy Dying, 1613, 1650
Taylor, Nathanael William, 1786, 1858
Taylor, William, 1870–75, 1884
Telesphorus, Bishop of Rome, c.127, c.137
Television
    first televised services, 1940
Tembu National Church, 1884
Temple, Frederick, Archbishop of Canterbury, 1896,
    1902
Temple, William, Archbishop of Canterbury, 1881,
    1941, 1942, 1944
    Christianity and the Social Order, 1881
    Readings in St John's Gospel, 1881
Temügin, 1190, 1206 (*see also* Genghis Khan)
Ten Articles of Religion, 1536
ten Boom, Corrie, 1892, 1971, 1983
Tenison, Thomas, Archbishop of Canterbury, 1695,
    1715
Tennent, William, 1735
Tenochtitlán, 1521
Tepeyac, 1531
Teresa, Mother, 1910, 1950, 1997 (*see also* Bujaxhiu,
    Agnes Goxha)
Teresa of Avila, 1515, 1582, 1623
Tertio millennio adveniente, apostolic letter,1994
Tertullian, c.160, c.200, c.207, 220
Test Act, 1673, 1686, 1828
Tetzel, Johann, 1506
Teutonic Order, 1190, 1198, 1224, 1226, 1231, 1237,
    1242, 1308, 1309, 1410, 1525
Thailand, Church of Christ in, 1934
Thakombau, Chief of Fiji, 1854
Thanet, 597
Theatines, 1524, 1555
Theobald, Archbishop of Canterbury, 1138, 1161
Theobald I, King of Navarre, 1234, 1253, 1270
Theobald II, King of Navarre, 1253, 1270

Theodolinda, Queen of the Lombards, 589, 590
Theodora, Byzantine empress, 527, 537, 543, 547, 548
Theodora, Byzantine empress, 842
Theodora, empress, 1042, 1055, 1056
Theodore, Bishop of Mopsuestia, 354, 428
Theodore I Lascaris, Byzantine emperor, 1208, 1214,
    1221, 1222
Theodore II Lascaris, Byzantine emperor, 1254, 1258
Theodore I, Patriarch of Constantinople, 677, 679,
    687
Theodore II Eirenicus, Patriarch of Constantinople,
    1212, 1215
Theodore I, Pope, 642, 649
Theodore II, Pope, 897
Theodore of Studios, 759, 826
Theodore of Tarsus, Archbishop of Canterbury, c.628,
    668, 678, 690
Theodoret of Cyrrhus, 393, 466
Theodoric, 487, 493, 497, 526
Theodosius I, Roman emperor, 379, 380, 381, 382, 384,
    385, 387, 388, 390, 391, 392, 393, 394, 395
Theodosius II, Roman emperor, 402, 407, 408, 414, 431,
    435, 449, 450
Theodosius III, Byzantine emperor, 715, 717
Theodosius I Boradiotes, Patriarch of Constantinople,
    1179, 1183
Theodotus I Cassiteras, Patriarch of Constantinople,
    815, 821
Theodotus II, Patriarch of Constantinople, 1151, 1153
Theodulf of Orleans, c.750, 821
Theoleptus I, Patriarch of Constantinople, 1513, 1522
Theoleptus II, Patriarch of Constantinople, 1585
Theologia Germanica, 1390
Theophilus, Arian, c.360
Theophilus, Bishop of Alexandria, c.390, 391
Theophilus I, Byzantine emperor, 820, 829, 842
Theophylactus, Patriarch of Constantinople, 933, 956
Theosophical Society, 1875
Theotokos, 428, 431
Thérèse of Lisieux, 1873, 1897, 1925
Thessalonica, c.45–58, 390, 1185, 1430
Thirty Years War, 1618, 1629, 1631, 1648
Thirty-Nine Articles, 1563, 1771, 1808
Thomas à Kempis, c.1380, 1418, 1471
    Imitation of Christ, c.1380, 1418
Thomas Aquinas, 1135, 1225, 1274, 1323
    Summa Theologiae, 1225

'True cross', 326, 614, 629
Trullan Council
    First, 681
    Second, 692
Tryphon, Patriarch of Constantinople, 928, 931
Tuam, Province, 1152
Tübingen,
    Evangelisches Stift, 1536
    University, 1477
Tucker, Bishop Alfred, 1897
Tuesday Meetings for the Promotion of Holiness, 1807
Turin University, 1405
Turku Diocese, 1210
Turnbull, Andrew, 1768
Turnbull, William, Bishop of Glasgow, 1451
Tutu, Desmond, 1986
Twelve apostles of Mexico, 1524
Twenty-Five Articles, 1808
Tyler, Wat, 1381
Tyndale, William, *c.*1494, 1536
    Bible, 1530, 1537
    New Testament, 1525
Typos, 648, 649, 653
Tyre
    Cathedral, 314
    Synod of, 335
Tyrrell, George, 1861, 1909
    Christianity at the Crossroads, 1861

Ufford, John de, Archbishop of Canterbury elect, 1348, 1349
Uganda
    Christian University, 1913
    Martyrs, 1886, 1964
Ulfilas, *c.*311, 341, 348, *c.*350, 383
Ulrich, Bishop of Augsburg, 990
Ulster, 841, 1607, 1641
'Umar, Caliph, 634, 644
Unam sanctam, bull, 1302
Unification Church, 1954
Unigenitus, bull, 1343
Unigenitus Dei filius, bull, 1713
Unitarian Society, 1733
Unitarian Universalist Association, 1961
Unitarianism, 1526, 1553, 1558, 1579, 1771, 1774, 1780, 1782, 1808, 1819, 1825, 1841, 1853, 1863, 1906, 1961, p.342

Unitas Fratrum, 1457
United Bible Society, 1946
United Brethren, 1889, 1968
United Church of Canada, 1925
United Church of Christ, 1957
United Free Church, 1843
United Free Church of Scotland, 1900, 1929
United Lutheran Church in America, 1918
United Methodist Church, 1879, 1932, 1940, 1968
United Methodist Church in America, 1879, 1940
United Methodist Church of Great Britain, 1932
United Methodist Committee on Relief, 1940
United Nations Organization, 1945
United Presbyterian Church of Scotland, 1847, 1851, 1900
United Presbyterian Church in the USA, 1983
United Reformed Church, 1972
United Secession Church, 1847
United Society for the Propagation of the Gospel, 1965
United Theological College, Bangalore, 1910
Unity Temple, Oak Park, Illinois, 1906
Universal Christian Conference on Life and Work, 1925
Universalist(s), 1785, 1863, 1961
    Church of America, 1942
    General Convention, 1866
Universities' Mission to Central Africa (UMCA), 1813, 1857, 1965
University College
    London, 1826
    Oxford, *c.*1249
Uppsala
    Archdiocese, 1164
    Cathedral, 1287
    University, 1477
Urban, Welsh bishop, 1107
Urban I, Pope, 222, 230
Urban II, Pope, 1088, 1095, 1099
Urban III, Pope, 1185, 1187
Urban IV, Pope, 1261, 1263, 1264
Urban V, Pope, 1362, 1364, 1367, 1370
Urban VI, Pope, 1378, 1389
Urban VII, Pope, 1590
Urban VIII, Pope, 1623, 1644
Urdaneta, Andres de, 1565
Urnes, stave church, *c.*1150
Ursulines, 1535, 1639, 1727
US Constitution, 1787

527

Picture credits

The line drawings on pages 5, 8, 16, 21, 26, 29, 39, 45, 62, 80, 120, 121, 125, 134, 138, 141, 179, 189, 199, 255, 317, 321, 339, 419 are by Rachel Bowden; the photographs on pages 72 and 209 are by John Bowden and on pages 99, 150 and 219 by Margaret Lydamore.

The authors and publishers wish to thank the following who have kindly given permission to reproduce illustrations on the pages indicated: AKG, pp. 152, 277, 341, 423; Alamy, p. 212; The Art Archive, p. 271; The Art Archive/Moldovita Monastery Romania, p. 246; Bridgman Art Library, p. 226; The British Library, p. 106; CIRIC, p. 435; Islington Library, p. 379; istock, p. 82; Mary Evans Picture Library, p. 381; Episcopal Church in the USA, p. 435.

529